CARL STREHLOW'S 1909 COMPARATIVE HERITAGE DICTIONARY

AN ARANDA, GERMAN, LORITJA
AND DIERI TO ENGLISH DICTIONARY
WITH INTRODUCTORY ESSAYS

CARL STREHLOW'S 1909 COMPARATIVE HERITAGE DICTIONARY

AN ARANDA, GERMAN, LORITJA AND DIERI TO ENGLISH DICTIONARY WITH INTRODUCTORY ESSAYS

Transcribed and translated from the German by Anna Kenny

Translated from Aranda and Loritja to English by the Inkamala families and members of the Western Aranda community

MONOGRAPHS IN ANTHROPOLOGY SERIES

Australian National University

PRESS

ANU PRESS

Published by ANU Press
The Australian National University
Acton ACT 2601, Australia
Email: anupress@anu.edu.au

Available to download for free at press.anu.edu.au

ISBN (print): 9781760462062
ISBN (online): 9781760462079

WorldCat (print): 1047957658
WorldCat (online): 1047957556

DOI: 10.22459/CSCHD.08.2018

Cover design and layout by ANU Press

CENTRAL LAND COUNCIL

MUSEUM AND ART GALLERY NORTHERN TERRITORY

MUSEUM OF CENTRAL AUSTRALIA & STREHLOW RESEARCH CENTRE

Contents

Disclaimer

This dictionary is a listing of words that the old people of the former Hermannsburg mission put down on paper at the turn of the twentieth century. For cultural reasons, the descendants of these old Aranda and Loritja [Luritja] people have taken out culturally sensitive words so that any Aboriginal people can read it. The handwritten manuscript of this dictionary is held at the Strehlow Research Centre in Alice Springs. Researchers who would like to access it for research purposes can make an application to the Strehlow Research Centre.

While every effort has been made to transcribe the handwritten dictionary manuscript accurately, some errors may have occurred, because in some instances the handwriting in German *Kurrentschrift* and in *Stolze* stenography is not clear enough to be completely certain about the transcription. In these instances, the note [unclear] has been added. Another obstacle to the editing of this resource was Carl Strehlow's spelling, because it did not always provide an accurate pronunciation and made some words unrecognisable. Thus, there is a small possibility that a very few sensitive terms have been included by accident.

Abbreviations

CS	Carl Strehlow
FRM	Finke River Mission
IAD	Institute for Aboriginal Development
IPA	International Phonetic Alphabet
LAA	Lutheran Archives in Adelaide
SRC	Strehlow Research Centre

Foreword

Nicolas Peterson

An excellent heritage dictionary is a cultural foundation stone for any people. This translation of Lutheran missionary Carl Strehlow's previously unpublished comparative Aranda–Luritja dictionary from German into English is one such dictionary. Building on the work of A.H. Kempe, his predecessor at the Hermannsburg mission, Carl Strehlow had over 7,600 entries at the time of his death in 1922, making it by far the largest dictionary for any Aboriginal language up until the present. It was a comparative dictionary because he wanted to show that Aranda and Luritja were two distinct languages, although the people were neighbours.

The enormously painstaking work of transcribing the original manuscript handwritten in four languages, Aranda, Luritja, German and some Dieri, as well as sections in an old form of German shorthand, has been carried out by Dr Anna Kenny. As a native German speaker, she has also translated Carl Strehlow's German glosses into English, checking many of the translations in close collaboration with people whose mother tongue is Aranda and/or Luritja, in particular Rhonda Inkamala and her parents the late Davie Inkamala and Trudy Inkamala.

To introduce the dictionary, Anna Kenny has included six preliminary chapters. She provides an introductory background to the dictionary, and a separate detailed account of the manuscript's complex history. Rhonda Inkamala writes about working on the dictionary and Mark Inkamala provides short biographical sketches of the men who helped Carl Strehlow with learning the language and about Aranda culture. Two further chapters by Dr John Henderson and David Moore, both linguists, spell out in an accessible way many of the complexities involved in any dictionary making, as illustrated by this dictionary. John Henderson shows what important grammatical and other information can be provided by analysing the organisation of the dictionary, the placement of words, and the many choices that Carl Strehlow made in compiling it, while David Moore sets out the fascinating challenges involved in settling on an orthography to represent the sounds in the Aranda language.

Dictionaries are consulted, not read. One reason for consulting this dictionary is as a baseline against which language and linguistic change can be explored. Because it is available electronically, as well as in hard copy, it opens the way to easy comparison with present day Aranda and Luritja as well as other kinds of work. An ideal heritage dictionary, such as the Oxford English Dictionary, is one based on historical principles—that is, besides showing the spelling and meaning of words, it provides their history or biography. Uniquely, this dictionary opens the way for such a historical Aranda–Luritja dictionary. Carl Strehlow collected many and lengthy texts, which when combined with those collected by his son, T.G.H. Strehlow, make it possible for a future Aranda and/or Luritja scholar to quarry this corpus and expand this heritage dictionary to provide exemplary sentences that illustrate usage at known periods in time. It may be many years before this happens but I have no doubt it will.

When this dictionary is added to the seven volumes of Carl Strehlow's ethnography, the work of Sir Baldwin Spencer and Frank Gillen, of T.G.H. Strehlow, of Olive Pink, of Diane Austin-Broos, of John Morton, and other work by Anna Kenny, not to mention the fund of historical information from the mission post-1877, Aranda people have a uniquely rich written record of aspects of their cultural heritage for future generations.

Preface and acknowledgements

I came to the idea of transcribing, translating and publishing Carl Strehlow's handwritten Aranda, Loritja [Luritja], German and Dieri dictionary manuscript into English during my PhD research. But having started on what I thought was a straightforward task I realised that some of my translations from German to English required the original Aranda and Loritja to German translation to be checked by Aranda and Luritja speakers and so I approached members of the Aranda/Luritja community to work at points where there appeared to be some doubt about the original translation into German.

Without the enthusiastic support of Western Aranda people, the publication of this unique document would not have been possible. I thank the members of the Inkamala, Malbunka, Rontji, Katakarinja, Williams, Kenny, Lechleitner, Kantawarra, Ratara, Armstrong, Raggett, Ebatarinja, Pareroultja, Impu, Rubuntja, Renkeraka, Wheeler, Ungwanaka, Mack, McCormack, Pepperill, Kentilja, Moketarintja and Abbott families for their involvement in this project over the years.

Davie Inkamala (1 January 1935 – 11 September 2013) was one of the main contributors to the discussion about my translations of the German glosses into English. He, his wife Trudi Inkamala and his daughters Rhonda and Jennifer Inkamala, who live at Kwale Kwale on the Iwupataka Land Trust in central Australia, have always believed that it is of paramount importance for Aranda and Luritja people to maintain their languages, and to keep their cultures strong, and have dedicated much of their time to doing so.

Figure 1: Davie Inkamala, Trudy Inkamala, Rhonda Inkamala and Anna Kenny at Kwale Kwale, 2013.

Source: Shane Mulcahy.

The research supporting the translation of this dictionary and checking it with Aranda and Luritja speakers has been funded by Australian Research Council Linkage grant (LP110200803) 'Rescuing Carl Strehlow's Indigenous cultural heritage legacy: The neglected German tradition of Arandic ethnography'. This grant was a collaborative project between the Central Land Council and the Strehlow Research Centre, both in Alice Springs, and the providers of generous industry partner funding, the University of Western Australia and The Australian National University. The project had several aims. The principal aim was to transcribe, translate and publish the 7,600 word Aranda and Luritja dictionary compiled between 1894 and 1922 by Lutheran missionary Carl Strehlow at Hermannsburg Mission west of Alice Springs. The grant provided a postdoctoral fellowship for me to work on transcribing and translating the 7,600-word dictionary from the original handwritten manuscript, which is in three Aboriginal languages, Aranda, Luritja and Dieri, as well as German, of which only sections have been available in the past. I received careful guidance and advice on dictionary construction from Dr John Henderson of the University of Western Australia, who has also contributed in two chapters of this publication on the linguistic aspects of the dictionary, and also formatted the dictionary. A further chapter on the complexities surrounding the Mission Orthography has been provided by David Moore.

A second objective was to make better known the unpublished seven-volume ethnography on the Aranda by Carl Strehlow that has not been published in English because of the amount of restricted information it contains. This has been achieved by the publication of *The Aranda's Pepa: An Introduction to Carl Strehlow's masterpiece* Die Aranda- und Loritja-Stämme in Zentral-Australien *(1907–1920)* (Kenny 2013) which discusses the distinctive and interesting findings of Carl Strehlow. Part of this investigation of his ethnography has involved Mr Michael Cawthorn, formerly the director of the Strehlow Research Centre, and Ms Helen Wilmot of the Central Land Council working on T.G.H. Strehlow's genealogical material. The third aim was to bring together scholars to explore the significance of German ethnography in Australia, particularly, but not only, in relation to native title claims. A volume called *German Ethnography in Australia* (2017), edited by Nicolas Peterson and Anna Kenny, has been published, based on a conference held on this theme in June 2015.

The Central Land Council under Director David Ross has been enormously supportive of the project, and without Brian Connelly's day-to-day support, and the help received from him and Helen Wilmot in working through issues of orthography, the project could not have been realised. Thanks go also to Marieke Kijne and Sue Ellison for organising meetings in April 2017 and Hugh Round at the Central Land Council for mapping Carl Strehlow's sites. Michael Cawthorn initiated the involvement of the Strehlow Research Centre, and Adam Macfie, Felicity Green and Graham Shaughnessy continued their support at the Strehlow Research Centre by facilitating access to archival materials, sourcing and dating historical photographs and organising meetings with Aranda people at the Strehlow Research Centre. Thanks to Shane Mulcahy for supplying photographs and manipulations of images and to Roisin Mulcahy for her assistance with the initial transcription. I am also very grateful to Geoff Hunt who meticulously checked the scientific names of flora and fauna, which has allowed an update of some of the Latin names of important plants and animals of central Australia. At the Finke River Mission, thanks are due to Garry Stoll who years ago expressed the need for the dictionary's publication, and Robert Borgas who provided source materials. I thank Anthony Bell and Edward Rontji at the Hermannsburg Office of the Department of the Prime Minister and Cabinet for facilitating meeting with the Wurla Nyinta Local Reference Group; Frau Rosemarie Hänsel of the Stenographic Collection in Dresden and Frau Kathrin Schmiedel of the Nationalbibliothek in Leipzig for providing access to rare and unique manuscripts. I also thank Gavan Breen, John Morton, Margaret Carew, David Price, Jenny Green and Myfany Turpin for their ongoing support of this project, as well as the anonymous reviewers of the draft manuscript of this publication.

I thank the Wurla Nyinta Local Reference Group and Craig DeRossignol and the Tjuwanpa Rangers at Hermannsburg for their assistance in organising meetings.

Figure 2: Western Aranda people who attended discussions about the dictionary at Hermannsburg on Thursday 6 April 2017.

Back row: Wayne Armstrong, Voight Ratara, Trudy Raggett, Beth Inkamala, Hayley Coulthard and Lewis Campbell. Front row: Noel Pareroultja, Ivy Pareroultja, June Campbell, Anita Ratara, Galvin Raggett, Hubert Pareroultja, Graham Ebatarinja and Mark Inkamala.

Source: Anna Kenny, Alice Springs.

Special thanks go to the Aranda people who attended and discussed the dictionary and accompanying map at the many Hermannsburg and Alice Springs community meetings between 2012 and 2017. Thanks to Baydon Kantjira, Edward Rontji, Conrad Ratara, Nicholas Williams, Lionel Inkamala, Sonya Braybon, Graham Ebatarinja, Patrick Oliver, Mervin Raggett, Renita Kantawarra, Que Kenny, Helen Stuart, Marion Swift, Pastor Markus Wheeler, Betty Wheeler, Craig Ebatarinja, Trudi Inkamala, Rhonda Inkamala, Jennifer Inkamala, Brenda Inkamala, Anita Ratara, Mark Inkamala, Mildred Inkamala, Carl Inkamala, Edward Rontji, Lily Roennfeldt, Kim Malbunka, Mona Kantawarra, Rex Pareroultja, Chistobelle Swan, Auriel Swan, Beth Inkamala, Regina Inkamala, Clara

Inkamala, Noreen Hudson, Lenie Namatjira, Vanessa Inkamala, Kathleen Inkamala, Hetti Meneri, Gloria McCormack, Elfrieda Ungwanaka, Fabian Raggett, Christopher Ungwanaka, August Ebatarinja, Daryl Kantawarra (junior), Henry Impu, Ellis Malbunka, Benice Meneri, Bronwyn Lankin, Tanya Malbunka, Diane Ebatarinja, Mervin Raggatt, Malcolm Kenny, Ada Lechleitner, Mavis Malbunka, Serena Williams, Mark Malbunka, Bronwyn Lankin, Tania Malbunka, Dianne Ebatarinja, Augustine Malbunka, Malcolm Kenny, Jean Mack, June Campbell, Rosa Pareroultja, Trudy Raggett, Ivy Pareroultja, Drusilla Pareroultja, Rosa Moketarinja, Hubert Pareroultja, Wayne Armstrong, Hayley Coulthard, Noel Pareroultja and Raymond Ebatarinja.

Anna Kenny
27 July 2018

Contributors

Dr John Henderson is a researcher in Linguistics at the University of Western Australia. His research focuses on Australian Indigenous languages, and in addition to the present project he has conducted research on Eastern and Central Arrernte, Pertame (Southern Arrernte), dialects of the Western Desert language, Ngatju and Mirning, Noongar, and Pilbara languages. He has a special interest in lexicography, and is a co-compiler (with Veronica Dobson) of the *Eastern and Central Arrernte to English Dictionary* (1994). He also has interests in Indigenous language education, interpreting and translation, and language in native title.

Mark Inkamala is a senior Western Aranda man. He grew up on Western Aranda country where he still lives and is active with cultural heritage projects. He has a real passion for preserving the language as well as traditions and customs of his people. He has worked as a research officer at the Strehlow Research Centre and is often employed as a cultural adviser to the Central Land Council and other organisations in central Australia.

Rhonda Inkamala is a senior Western Aranda woman. She is a speaker of Western Aranda, Luritja and Pitjantjatjara and understands other Arandic and Western Desert dialects. She also reads and writes in these languages and is proficient in the Institute for Aboriginal Development and Finke River Mission orthographies as well as familiar with the orthographies of the Strehlows. She was a teacher and the cultural principal at the Yipirinya School in Alice Springs for many years and is regularly employed as a cultural adviser to Parks and Wildlife and the Central Land Council. Currently, she is working as a freelance translator, Aranda teacher and cultural facilitator and guide.

Dr Anna Kenny is a consultant anthropologist who has been based in Alice Springs for over 24 years and was between 2012 and 2016 an Australian Research Council postdoctoral fellow in the School of Archaeology and

Anthropology at The Australian National University. She has conducted field research with Indigenous people in the Northern Territory since 1991 as well as in Queensland and Western Australia. She has written 12 Connection Reports for Native Title claims and is the author of a book on Carl Strehlow's ethnography, titled *The Aranda's Pepa: An Introduction to Carl Strehlow's Masterpiece* Die Aranda-und Loritja-Stämme in Zentral-Australien *(1907–1920)* (2013) and the coeditor of *German Ethnography in Australia* (2017). Currently she is working on a book about T.G.H. Strehlow and Arandic ethnography called *Shadows of a Father*.

David Moore supports the teaching of Arrernte and translation studies as the linguist at the Alice Springs Language Centre of the Northern Territory Education Department. He is an interpreter in the Alyawarr language and a Bible translator. As a doctoral candidate in linguistics at the University of Western Australia in Perth, he is currently researching the linguistic work and translation practice of the Hermannsburg Mission between 1890 and 1910.

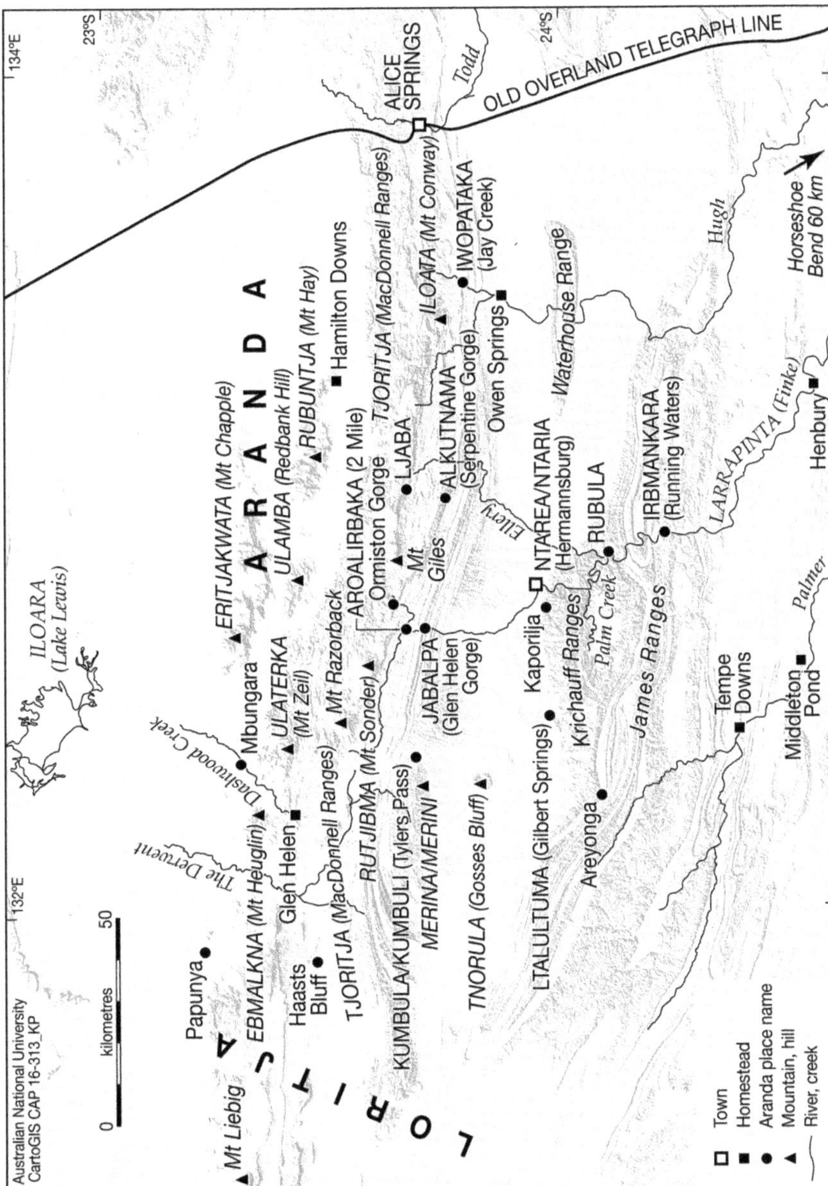

Figure 3: Carl Strehlow's study area in central Australia showing some place names in his spelling system.

Source: ANU CartogGIS CAP, 2017.

1

A heritage dictionary

Anna Kenny

Carl Strehlow's comparative dictionary manuscript is a unique item of Australian cultural heritage: it is a large collection of circa 7,600 Aranda, 6,800 Loritja [Luritja][1] and 1,200 Dieri to German entries compiled at the beginning of the twentieth century at the Hermannsburg mission in central Australia. It is an integral part of Strehlow's ethnographic work on Aboriginal cultures that his editor Baron Moritz von Leonhardi, a German armchair anthropologist, published as *Die Aranda- und Loritja-Stämme in Zentral-Australien* (Strehlow 1907–20) in Frankfurt. Strehlow and his editor had planned to publish a language study that consisted of a comparative dictionary and grammar of the languages, both for their linguistic significance and to facilitate more sophisticated readings of the many Aranda and Loritja texts they had published.

1 'Loritja' is Carl Strehlow's rendering of this language name and 'Luritja' is the preferred contemporary spelling. The spelling 'Loritja' is used in the context of Strehlow's heritage dictionary and 'Luritja' when referring to this Western Desert language in a contemporary context.

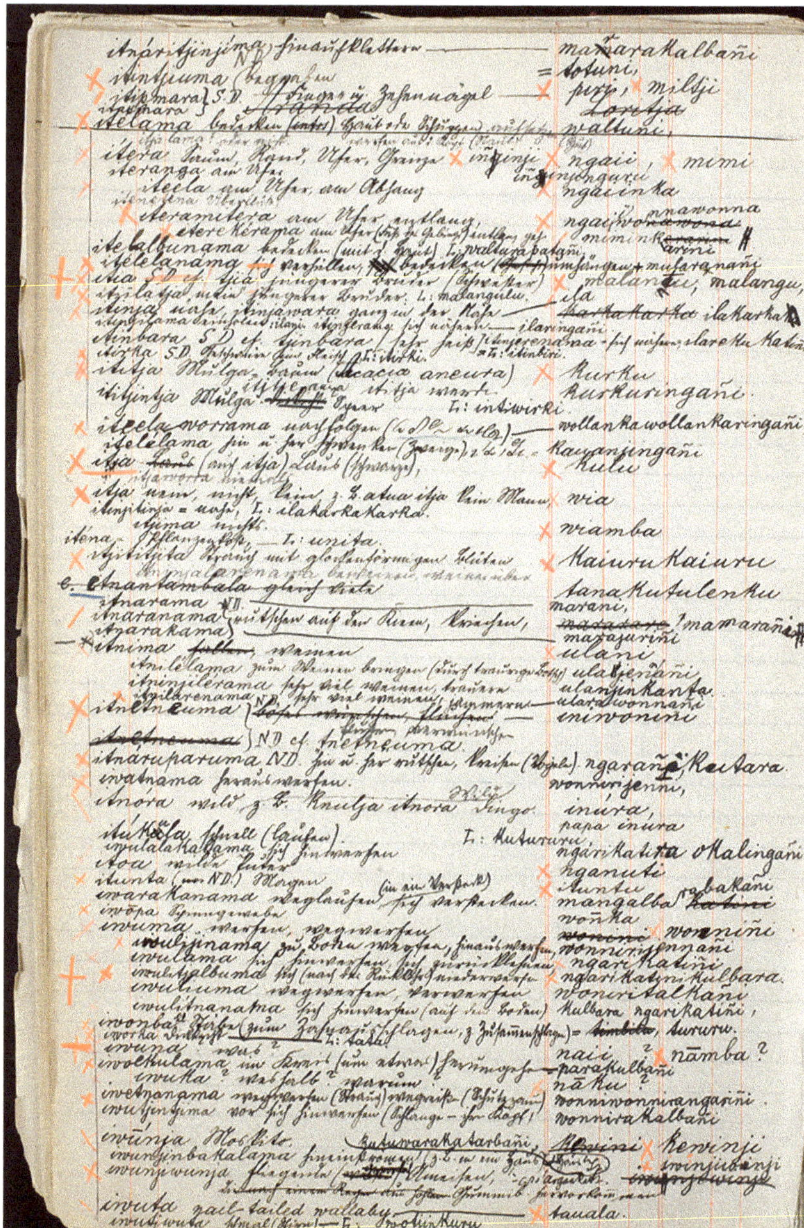

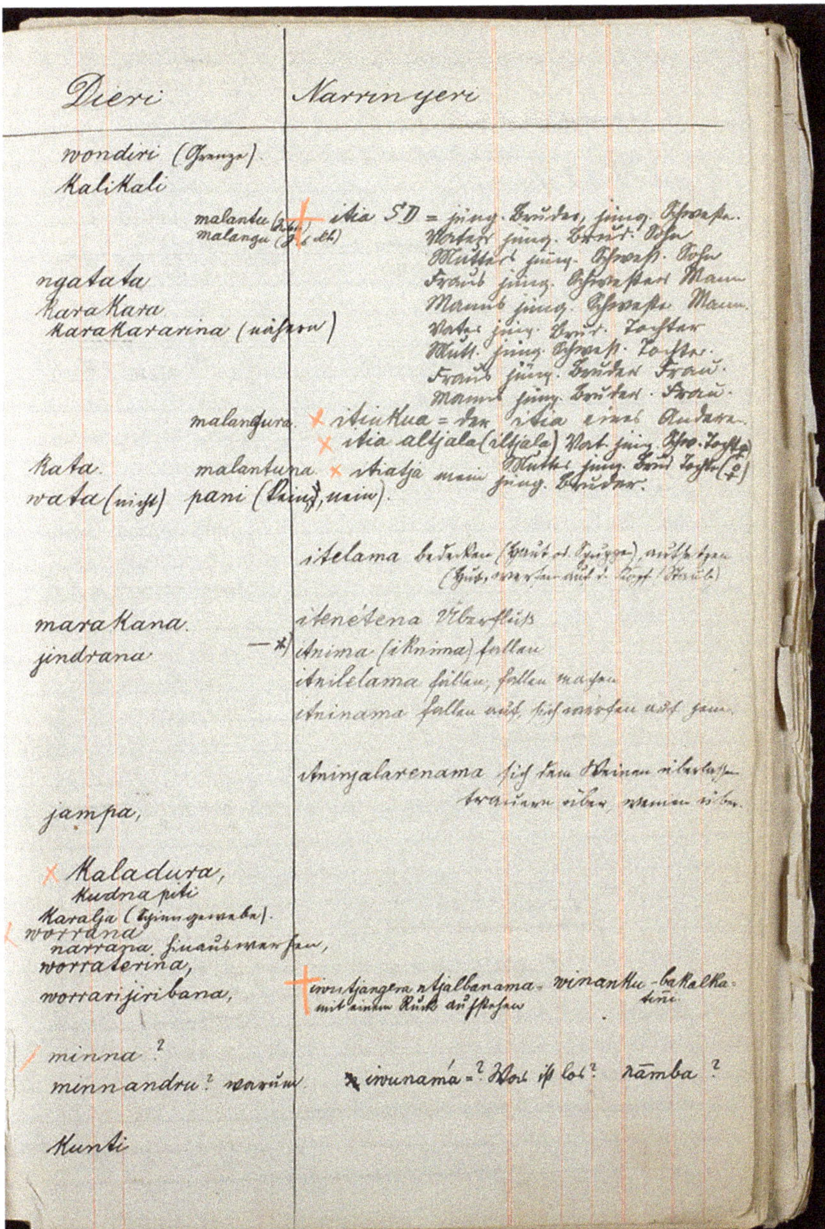

Figure 4: Page 71 of Carl Strehlow's handwritten Aranda, German, Loritja and Dieri Dictionary, 1906–09.

Source: Strehlow Research Centre, Alice Springs.

At the turn of the twentieth century it was common for German scholars who were interested in philology, such as Carl Strehlow and his editor, to collect original texts and compile grammars and dictionaries for the comprehensive documentation and description of languages. Strehlow's comparative Aranda, Loritja and Dieri to German dictionary is the only vocabulary among many attributed to him that has a clearly identifiable purpose. Its primary functions were to describe the Aranda and Loritja languages and to interpret the Indigenous textual materials he had elicited from his Aboriginal informants.

Its comparative component was to illustrate theoretical points made by the emerging *Kulturkreislehre* (culture circle theory), and to demonstrate that Aranda and Luritja were two different languages and as complex as any other languages in the world (see Chapter 4).

The Aranda and Luritja terms and derivatives relate to mythology, flora and fauna, kinship, ceremonial proceedings, material culture and social life. Although Aranda was the core language, the body of Luritja terms reaches circa 90 per cent coverage of the Aranda terms, while the circa 1,200 Dieri words seem simply to have been added on, because he knew the Dieri language from his previous posting at Lake Killalpaninna in South Australia. The dictionary contains a substantial amount of vocabulary, but it does not encompass all the words collected by Carl Strehlow. Not included are hundreds of place names, personal names and some specialist ceremonial terms that he recorded in his ethnography, held at the Strehlow Research Centre in Alice Springs, and, it appears, some terms that he recorded after the completion of the dictionary manuscript.[2]

Strehlow's linguistic work is of great significance for the conservation of language as well as historically and anthropologically, because it probably represents the largest and most comprehensive wordlist compiled in Australia during the early stages of contact. It is a unique documentary record and an important primary source for Luritja and Aranda speakers of whom there are several thousand today. Both languages are spoken in homes and taught in schools in central Australia, but they are nevertheless quite vulnerable.

2 Carl Strehlow's materials are held at the Strehlow Research Centre in Alice Springs, as well as in the Lutheran Archives and Barr Smith Library in Adelaide.

The reasons for presenting this work as a heritage dictionary—that is, as an exact transcription of the original form of the handwritten manuscript—are to follow the Western Aranda people's wishes and to maintain its historical authenticity (Kenny 2017b: 278). There is a history of reworking parts of this dictionary, extracting from it and updating its orthography without indicating who made these changes and why. Some of these versions, in particular the attempts by P.A. Scherer (1940s or 1950s) and G.O. Liebchen[3] (1980s), have fed into contemporary work without being referenced. To clarify these previous uses and make this early work available as a reliable resource that can be reworked transparently, the original form is likely to prove indispensable for future projects.

Thus, this transcription has been kept as close as is possible to the original handwritten manuscript—no amendments have been made to spellings, stresses or diacritics, even if they seemed inconsistent. The only additions to this dictionary are English glosses for the Aranda, Loritja and Dieri entries. Most words in Kempe's first collection of Aranda words with circa 1,750 words (Kempe 1891a), the *Western Arrarnta Analytical Dictionary* with circa 2,000 entries (Oberscheidt 1991), the *Introductory Dictionary of Western Arrernte* (Breen et al. 2000)[4] with circa 2,000 words and the *Western Arrarnta Picture Dictionary* (Roennfeldt 2006)[5] with circa 580 words have been crosschecked with Carl Strehlow's information, because the words in these dictionaries are in the public domain and have been confirmed and illustrated by contemporary speakers. This process of crosschecking also contributed to making sure that restricted words have been excluded.

However, the most important factor to be able to bring this work into the present was the detailed collaboration with senior Aranda and Luritja people, to both inform them about their heritage and to include

3 G.O. Liebchen was a prisoner of the H.M. Prison in Brisbane. He grew up in Germany and offered to translate Carl Strehlow's work, because he was a German speaker and had gone to a 'Gymnasium' (a demanding German secondary school). He wrote to T.G.H. Strehlow that he had been a 'proprietor of an Artefact Shop in Surfers Paradise Qld., dealing in aboriginal and Papua New Guinean artefacts. On the 26. Sept. 1977 I was sentenced to 4 ½ years imprisonment for burglary which gives me the time necessary to undertake the translation' (Letter from G.O. Liebchen to T.G.H. Strehlow, 26 November 1977). After T.G.H. Strehlow's death, his widow took the offer up.

4 Among Breen's main informants were Pastor Eli Rubuntja (now deceased) and Gregory Armstrong Senior as well as Sylvester Renkeraka (now deceased); Breen generally worked with senior Western Arrernte people from the Iwupataka Aboriginal Land Trust and Alice Springs town camps.

5 Roennfeldt worked with members of the communities of Ntaria, Ipolera, Gilbert Springs, Kulpitarra, Undarana, Red Sand Hill, Old Station and other outstations.

their knowledge to at least some degree. After I had transcribed and to some degree translated most of the German glosses in the handwritten manuscript, I worked with a small group of speakers who are fluent in both Aranda and Luritja on the translation into English. We worked through the list discussing approximations for the meanings of both the Aranda and Luritja terms that they recognised. People working with me on Carl Strehlow's unpublished dictionary manuscript (1909) call its content *ankatja*[6] *inguia* 'old language',[7] *ankatja ekarlta* 'strong language' that has 'heavy' words and *ankatja ekarlta* 'hard language'—meaning the language of the 'old people', their ancestors. This 'real old language' is distinguished from 'church language' and 'modern language', which is sometimes called *angkatja lyartinya* 'today's language'.

It was often difficult to find an English gloss, because some words were not known, others seemed familiar or similar to known words but the specific form of the word was unclear or the spelling did not provide an accurate pronunciation guide due to under- or over-differentiation of sounds that made words unrecognisable. Although Strehlow tried to systematically and consistently employ an orthography that he called 'continental'[8] (Kenny 2013: 98), unsurprisingly, he was unable to capture all sound distinctions adequately. It takes quite some work to interpret this resource, as Rhonda Inkamala remarks, but at the same time the very process of working through this type of material can enrich people's understanding of their culture and heritage.

On those occasions when no meaning could be worked out, I was asked what the German gloss meant; often it was decided to use the direct translation from the German as the English gloss or it was slightly altered. The German glosses provide sometimes only part of the semantic range of a word that may be specific and/or metaphorical in the context it is used in Strehlow's publications (Strehlow 1907–20). Some of the English glosses are therefore also incomplete, while others are more extensive than the German glosses. It is a difficult task to find a one-to-one translation from one language to the other, and even more so when the underlying cultures are very different, such as are Arandic and English cultures. During the

6 See in this dictionary *ankatja* (Wort [word], Sprache [language]; auch 'Märchen, Fabel, Mythe' [fairytale, fable, myth]).

7 *Ngketye* (language, word, speech), *ingkweye* (old), *ikerlte* (strong, hard) in common Arandic Institute for Aboriginal Development (IAD) orthography (Breen et al. 2000).

8 Carl Strehlow to von Leonhardi, 13 December 1906 (SH-SP-7-1).

search for English glosses, the risk of publishing words that might have been gender restricted and what the old people might have meant were often discussed, and consequently some words have been taken out.

The orthography of Western Aranda was discussed at length, indeed it was more often discussed than aspects of meaning during group consultations. The spelling system of Western Aranda has undergone more changes than any other Arandic language variety and is highly politicised (see Kenny 2017b). This is, for example, reflected in the many spellings of the name of this Arandic dialect that became known as Aranda and more specifically today as 'Western Aranda' or 'Tjoritja Aranda'. Over the past 130 years of the Western Aranda's contact history the spelling systems of their Arandic dialect that were developed by the Lutheran missionaries and T.G.H. Strehlow have been taught in at least seven different variations due to frequent revisions and additionally by the Institute for Aboriginal Development (IAD) in a phonemic system called the common Arandic orthography. In the contact history of the Aranda, the Lutheran missionaries played a significant role. Their colonial involvement included, among other changes, a Lutheran inscription on the Aranda language that they achieved by (i) codifying this language in multiple orthographies, (ii) semantic changes to key terms (e.g. altjira, kutungulu) and (iii) the reduction of vocabulary (also partly the result of the sedentarisation at the mission due to the pastoral encroachment) by discouraging and limiting many cultural practices. For example, while Strehlow recorded over 40 terms for different types of spirits, nearly all of them are not used and instead these spirits are referred to with the general term *pmara kutata*,[9] meaning spirit of the land (Kenny 2004a, 2004b).

The early Lutheran missionaries at Hermannsburg A.H. Kempe (between 1879 and 1891) and then Carl Strehlow (between 1894 and 1922) used a fairly uniform orthography and interpreted the sound system of the Aranda language, which resulted in some spelling inconsistencies caused by over- and under-differentiations of sounds; also, later orthographies for this Arandic language variety tried to capture these sounds accurately. Despite its limitations, Carl Strehlow's orthography was used into the 1970s, as is evidenced in letters and postcards written by Aranda people that have survived. They are read by Aranda speakers today although some older words are not recognised, but these can be looked up in this dictionary.

9 This term may also be spelled *tmara kutata* or *pmere kwetethe*.

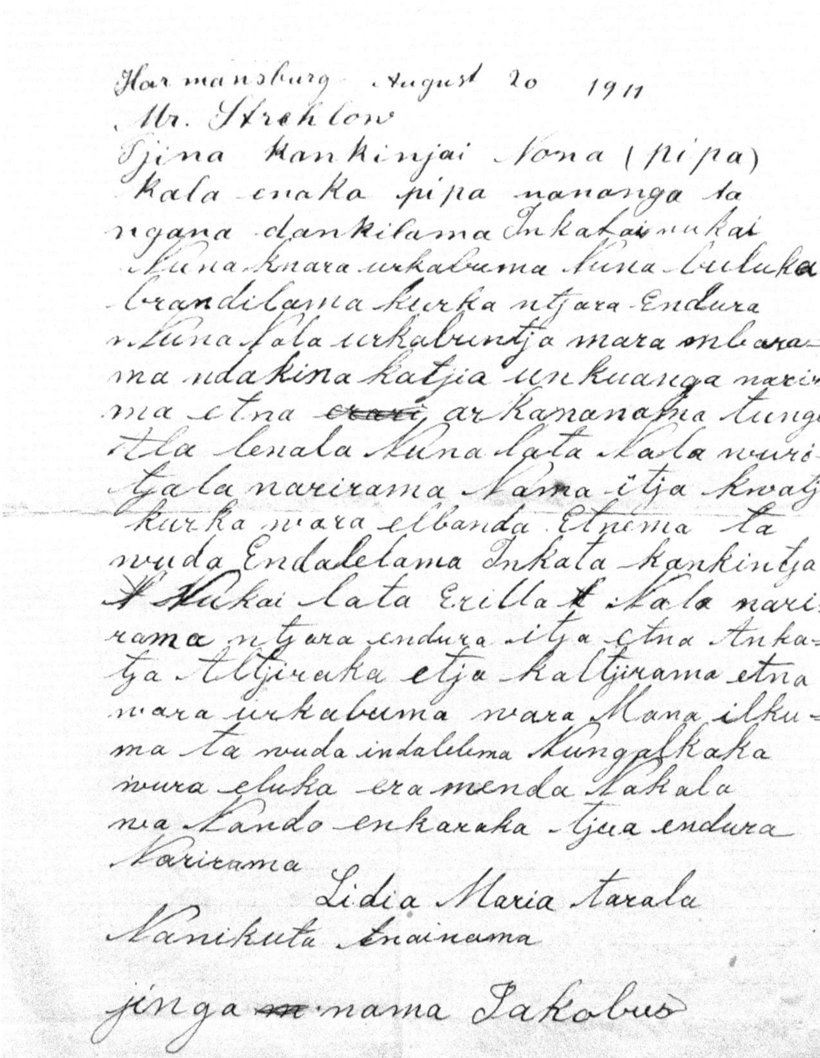

Harmansburg August 20 1911
Mr. Strehlow
Tjina Kankinjai Nona (nipa)
Kala enaka pipa nananga ta
ngana dankilama Inkatainukai
Luna knara urkabuma Luna buluka
brandilama kurka ntjara Endura
n Luna lala urkabuntja mara unbarana
ma ndakina katjia unkuanga narira
ma etna ~~erari~~ arkananaka tunga
tla lenala Luna lata Lala nwuri-
tjala narirama Lama itja kwatja
kurka nwara elbanda Etnema ta
nwuda Endalelama Inkata kankintja
Nukai lata Erilla Lala narirama ntjara endura itja etna Ankatja Altjiraka etja kaltjirama etna
nwara urkabuma nwara Mana ilkuma ta nwuda indalelima Kungalkaka
nwura eluka eramenda Lakala
nua Lando enkaraka tjua endura
Narirama
Lidia Maria Larala
Nanikuta Inainama
jinga ~~na~~ nama Jakobus

Figure 5: Letter written by Jakobus to Carl Strehlow using the phonetic Mission Orthography for the Aranda language, 20 August 1911.

Source: ARA 1911-21-1, Strehlow Research Centre, Alice Springs.

There are a number of Arandic orthographies in use currently. The development of the orthography of Western Aranda is atypical within those of other Australian languages, because it is the result of its unique historical circumstances. Most languages that were documented in the early contact period are not spoken or written anymore, and most of those that are spoken and written today were codified when modern phonemic systems had become the standard. The Western Aranda people, unlike many other groups, have continued to speak and write their language since contact and have been exposed to three quite different orthographies within this short time period that are associated with different ideologies.

Figure 6: Aranda children and Carl Strehlow at the Hermannsburg mission school, circa 1902/03.

Source: SRC 07791, Strehlow Research Centre, Alice Springs.

Initially it was proposed to include two of the commonly used modern phonemic orthographies in this dictionary. The use of modern Arandic orthographies by some young Western Aranda who were and are taught the common Arandic orthography at the Yipirinya School in Alice Springs and others who are exposed to Roennfeldt's recent version of the Finke River Mission Orthography at Hermannsburg suggested an inclusive approach. Such an approach would have allowed people who are familiar with one of the modern phonemic orthographies to move between the different spelling systems. However, after many discussions since 2012 with the Western Aranda, they decided that they wanted a heritage dictionary with only Carl Strehlow's spellings that reflects their history and identity, rather than converting to or adding spellings in the modern orthographies. This avoids the issues that communities face when having to devise modern spellings for the many words of Aranda and Luritja in the dictionary that are not recognised today, and the exact pronunciation of which cannot be accurately determined from Strehlow's spelling. It also avoids having to tackle the fraught politics of orthography, which are mainly the result of the colonial involvement of the Lutheran mission at Hermannsburg and that cause some conflict in the community.

The present volume is both a valuable heritage item and a linguistic resource for the Aboriginal community as well as for those involved with teaching and developing dictionary projects. Comprehensive dictionaries for Western Aranda and some Luritja language-varieties are yet to be produced—and this document can be of great assistance in their development. At the same time, it is of considerable interest to linguists, particularly those interested in language change. Strehlow often makes remarks about words in footnotes of his published work indicating that already in his time his informants considered some terms as 'old'. Often when words were not recognised during consultations and the German translation was considered, I was offered alternative ways of how people express that particular concept. Some words are still used, but in different contexts or have made semantic shifts (Austin-Broos 2010; Green 2012; Kenny 2013). There are also further sets of vocabularies (e.g. Kempe 1891a; T.G.H. Strehlow n.d.) that were collected before and after Strehlow senior's time that can be compared with this collection of words and allow the development of an extensive Western Aranda dictionary.

To assist communities, and other readers, in the ongoing task of interpreting the document, this volume includes a brief guide to finding pronunciations from Strehlow's spelling and a more extensive discussion in David Moore's chapter. Following the essays that contextualise this comparative work ethnohistorically and linguistically are the user guides to the pronunciation of the Arandic and Luritja words in Carl Strehlow's orthography and the dictionary entries. In Chapters 2 and 3, Rhonda Inkamala and Mark Inkamala write about the contemporary significance of this dictionary for Western Aranda people. In Chapter 4, I outline the contact history of the Aranda and Luritja, Carl Strehlow's life in central Australia, and the content of his ethnographic manuscripts, their philosophical and theoretical setting and some of their linguistic aspects.

John Henderson's linguistic analysis in Chapter 5 shows the linguistic work and thought that went into this comparative dictionary and what potential it offers for the study of these languages today, including more wide-ranging historical dictionaries for both Arandic and Western Desert languages. He discusses the lexicographical achievement in Strehlow's work outlining the coverage, the balance of detail, the morphology (i.e. derivation, compounding, inflection) and semantics of this compilation, and discusses some of the limitations of Strehlow's dictionary.

David Moore addresses in Chapter 6 the difficulties of developing writing systems for Arandic languages and Carl Strehlow's use of what he has coined the 'Mission Orthography' that was first used by A.H. Kempe. Moore explores how the early Lutheran missionaries at Hermannsburg mission interpreted the sound systems of the Indigenous languages and produced a practical orthography for community use. He shows that the missionaries took a considered approach, which was informed by the best practices of that time, but which by modern standards resulted in spelling inconsistencies. Finally, he shows how the modern orthographies of these languages emerged to capture sounds in a more sophisticated way and discusses the phoneme in detail. A phoneme expresses the sound differences in a given language that are significant because they differentiate the words of the language, abstracting away from minor sound differences that do not. In an ideal phonemic orthography, there would be a one-to-one correspondence between the graphemes and phonemes.

The dictionary manuscript has remained unpublished until now due to a number of complicated historical and personal circumstances of the main characters involved with the dictionary.

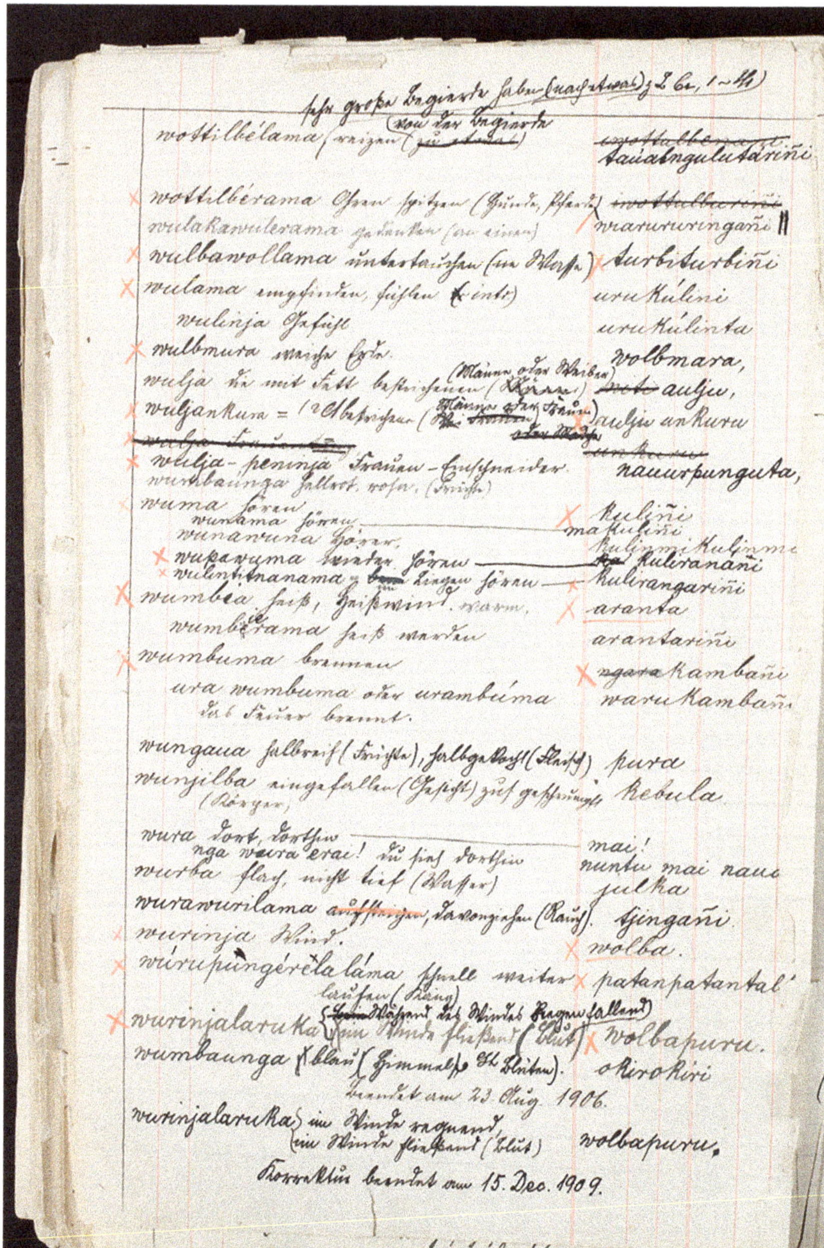

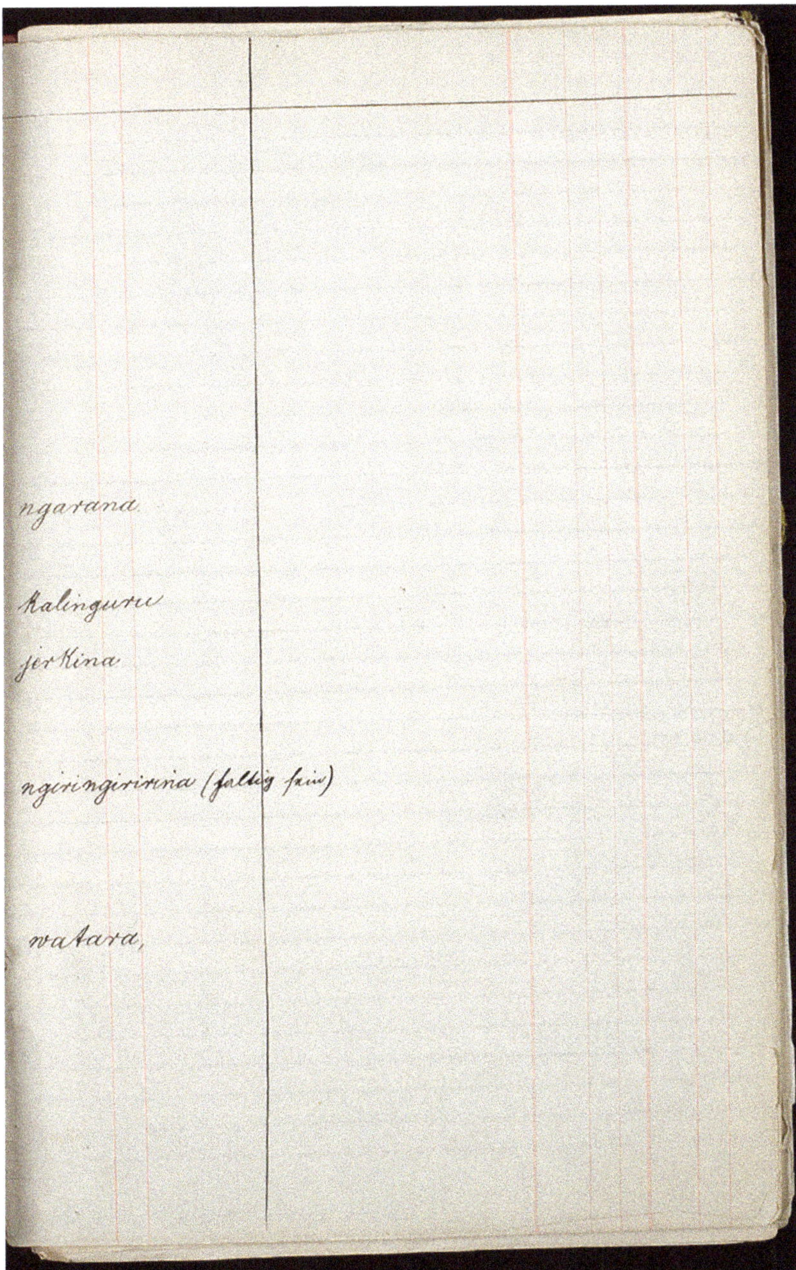

Figure 7: Last page of handwritten dictionary manuscript, 'Beendet am 23. Aug. 1906' (Completed on 23 August 1906) and 'Korrectur beendet am 15. Dec. 1909' (Corrections completed on 15 December 1909).

Source: Strehlow Research Centre, Alice Springs.

2

Working on the dictionary

Rhonda Inkamala

Aranda[1]

Imanka kngarriparta ntjarra purta urrkapumala ngkitja Aranda nurnaka kngartiwuka pa intalhilaka. Ngkitja intalhilakala nhanha nama marra, rilha ntjarrala, artwala, arrkutjala, kitjia itna kaltjirramala ngkitja nurnakanha ritamilatjika, intalhilatjika, kitjia ntjarranha ikarltala kuta kaltjanthitjika. Kuka yatinya ntjarraka pmara ntilatjika, ngkitja Arandala pmara rritnya ilatjika, marna pa tnuntha rilhakanha ingkarraka ntyarra nthitjika. Kaltjala ntama ngkitja nurnakanha ikarlta kuta tnyinatjinanga.

Pipa Dictionary nhanhala ngkitja nurnakanha Luritja pa Aranda lhangkarama, nthakanha intalhilatja, ritamilatjika ngkitja nurnakanha ikarlta kuta tnyinatjika.

Kwaiya kngarra nuka 'Nangalanha' Clara Ngala Inkamala ira imangka urrkaputjarta CAAMA[2] Radio Imparja Television—*Nganampa Anwernekenhe* Language and Culture Programme. Nhanha ntama ngkitja kuka irala ngkama: 'Ngkitja nurnakanha ilkarlta kuta tnyinatjika'.

1 I choose to use this spelling of our language, because it is phonetic and reflects our history.

2 Central Australian Aboriginal Media Association.

Figure 8: Rhonda Inkamala working at the Strehlow Research Centre, 2017.

Source: Adam Macfie, Strehlow Research Centre, Alice Springs.

Luritja

Irriṯi A<u>n</u>angu nganampa tjuṯa tjungungkuya wangka Luritja kampa kutjupa nguru walkatjunu. Wangka nganampa kwarri palya ngaranyi, uwankarrangku ritamilanytjaku walkatjunkunytjaku.

Nganampa waltja tjuṯaya irriṯi ngurra nyanga tjanala nyinapayi, Ungkungka-la wilurarra, Warumpi-la, ulparirra Meerinee-la, alinytjara Kularata-la. A<u>n</u>angu winkingku wangka nyangatja kantilya wangkapayi.

Kwarri A<u>n</u>angu ma<u>n</u>kurrpa wangka Luritja nyangatja wangkanyi, ka Dictionary nyangatja wiru ngaranyi A<u>n</u>angungku, watingku, minymangku, tjitjingku nyakula ritamilanytjaku, walkatjunkunytjaku.

Ngayuku kangkuṟu pu<u>l</u>ka Lorna Wilsonalu paluṟu wangkangu: 'Wangka nganampa kantilya kutu kanyintyjaku'.

English

Many of my people and I were involved in the translation of this dictionary into English from Aranda and Luritja. Some of the men, including my father, have taken out the old, restricted words so that I and other Aboriginal people can read it without any problems. It was an enriching experience to work on this dictionary because our language is our culture. Before I say more about working on this dictionary, I will introduce myself. It will help you understand what language and culture means to us.

I am an Aboriginal Australian woman of central Australia. I am multilingual and so a fluent speaker of Western Aranda, Luritja and Pitjantjatjara. I also read and write in these languages and understand other Arandic and Western Desert dialects. My language connections are through my parents and grandparents.

My *mia* (mother) speaks Western Aranda and Luritja. My *mia kanha pmara nama* (mother's country), *tjamia kanha pmara nama* (mother's father's country) and my *lyurra kanha pmara nama* (mother's mother's country) are on Tjoritja (also known as West MacDonnell National Park).

My *karta* (father) spoke Western Aranda and Pitjantjatjara. My *mamaku ngurra* (father's country) and *tjamuku ngurra* (father's father's country) lies on Pitjantjatjara territory in the south-west Petermann Ranges. My father spoke Western Aranda because he was adopted by the Inkamalas who grew him up as an Aranda and as their own.

There are many central Australian Aboriginal languages that consist of a variation of dialects. Arandic dialects may have some common words such as *kwatja* (water) in Western Aranda and *kwatye* (water) in Central/Eastern Arrernte; *marra* (good) in Western Aranda and *mwerre* (good) in Central/Eastern Arrernte. Western Desert dialects also have some common words, *kapi* (water), *ma<u>l</u>u* (kangaroo) or *palya* (good) in Luritja and Pitjantjatjara. At the same time all these dialects of a language are also very different from each other.

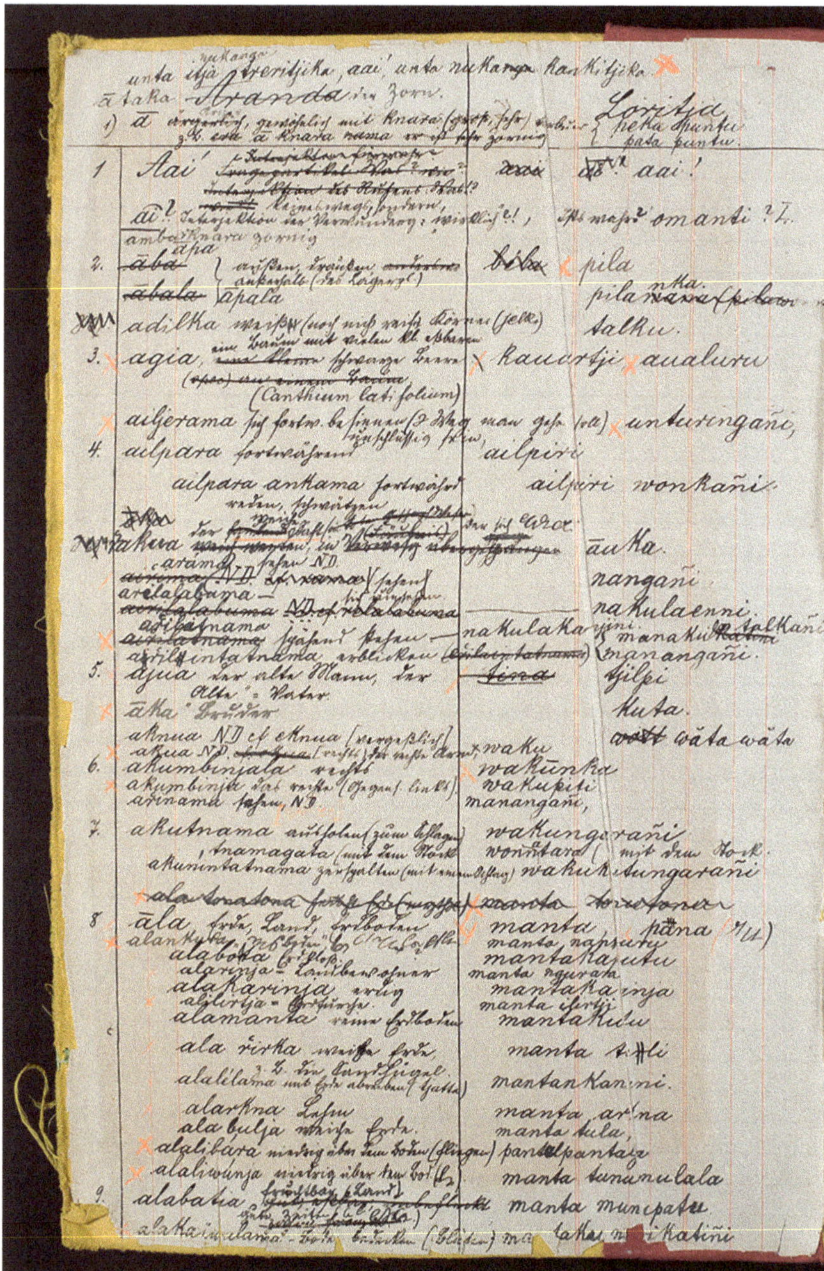
unta itja tteritjika, aai, unta nukanga kankitjika
ātaka Aranda in Zorn. Loritja
1) ā ärgerlich, gereizt pika spantu
1 Aai aai!
ai? omanti?
2. āba / āpa — außen, draußen — pila
ābala — āpala — pilankara
adilka — talku
3. agia — kauartji — aualuru
(Canthium latifolium)
aiļerama — unturinganī
4. ailpara fortwährend — ailpiri
ailpara antama — ailpiri wonkanī
akua — āuka
aramba — nanganī
aralalabuma — nakulaenni
arilatnama — nakulaka — manakulkatalkanī
arilintatnama — nananganī
5. ajua der alte Mann, der Alte = Vater — tjilpi
āka Bruder — kuta
aknua — wātawāta
akua — waku
6. akumbinjala — wakūnka
akumbinja — wakupiti
akinama — manangani
7. akutnama — wakungaranī
tnamagata — wonntara
akunintatnama — wakukutungaranī
8 āla Erde, Land, Erdboden — manta — pāna
alankurka — manta napparu
alabotta — mantakaputu
alarinja — manta ngurara
alakarinja — mantakarinja
aljirtja — manta itirtji
alamanta — mantakutu
ala ṙirka weiße Erde — manta tjilli
alalilama — mantankanni
alarkna — manta arina
ala bulja — manta tula
alalibara — pantalpantara
alaliwunja — manta tunanulala
9. alabatia — manta muncpatu
alakaia — ma lakai nikatiñi

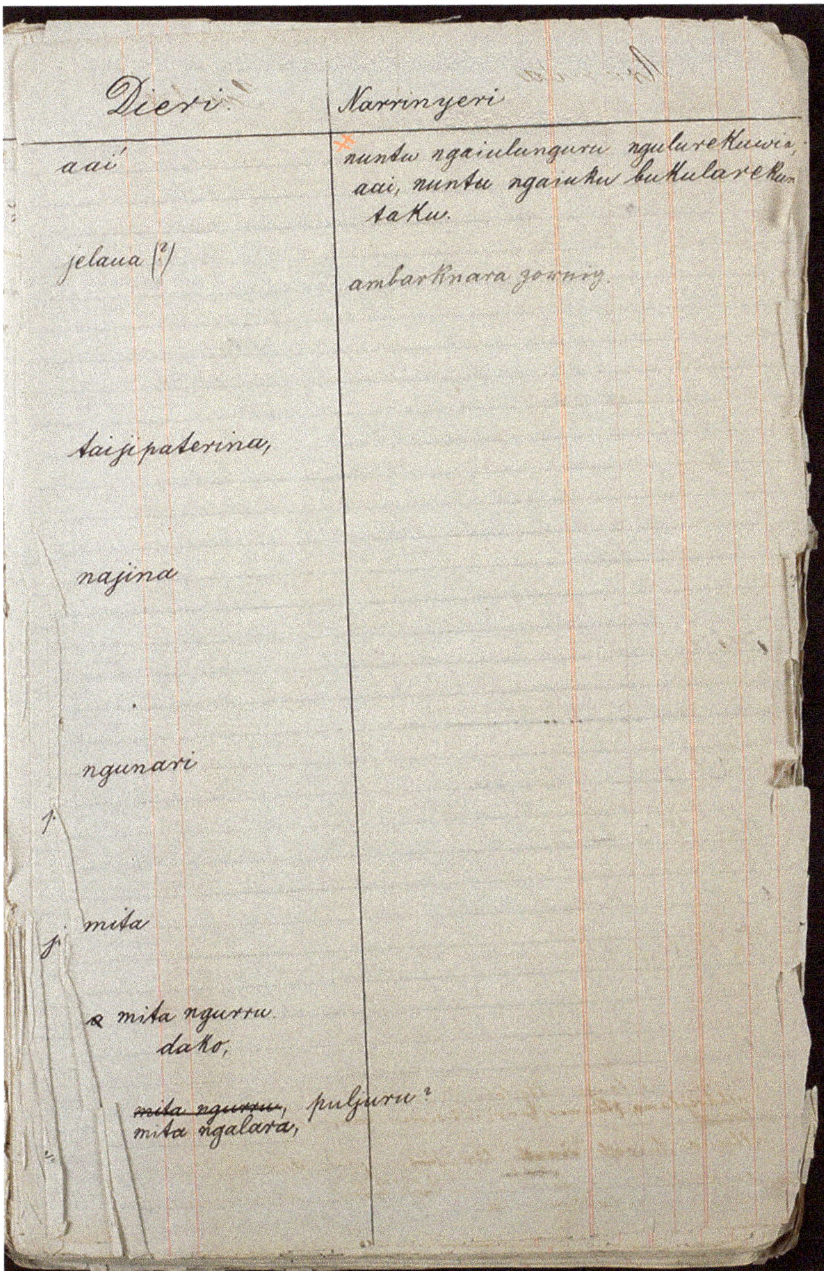

Figure 9: Page 1 of Carl Strehlow's unpublished dictionary manuscript.
Source: Strehlow Research Centre, Alice Springs.

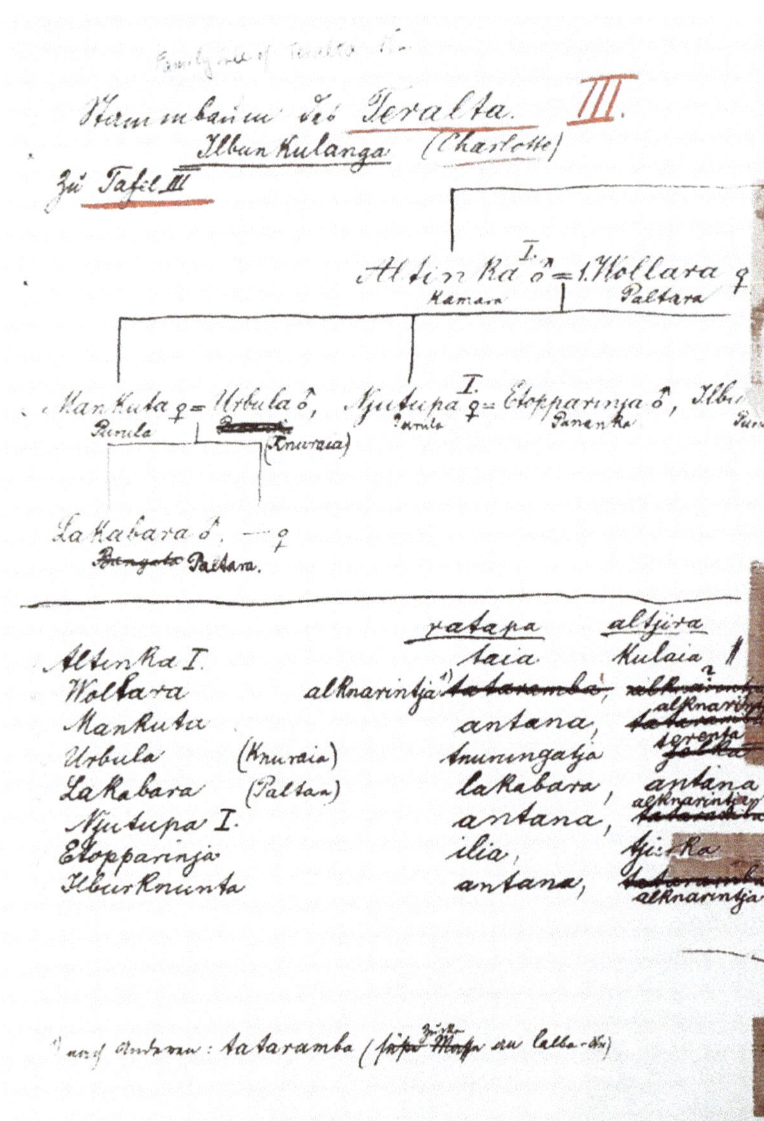
Family tree of Teralta
Stammbaum der Teralta. III.
Ilbunkulanga (Charlotte)
Zu Tafel III
Altinka I. ♂ = 1. Wollara ♀
Kamara
Paltara
Mankuta ♀ = Urbula ♂, Njutupa I. ♀ = Etopparinja ♂, Ilbu
Purula
(Knuraia)
Purula
Pananka
Lakabara ♂. — ♀
Paltara.
ratapa
altjira
Altinka I.
taia
Kulaia
Woltara
alknarintja
alknarintja
Mankuta
antana,
Urbula
(Knuraia)
tnuningatja
Lakabara
(Paltara)
lakabara,
antana
Njutupa I.
antana,
alknarintja
Etopparinja
ilia,
Ilburknunta
antana,
alknarintja
tataramba

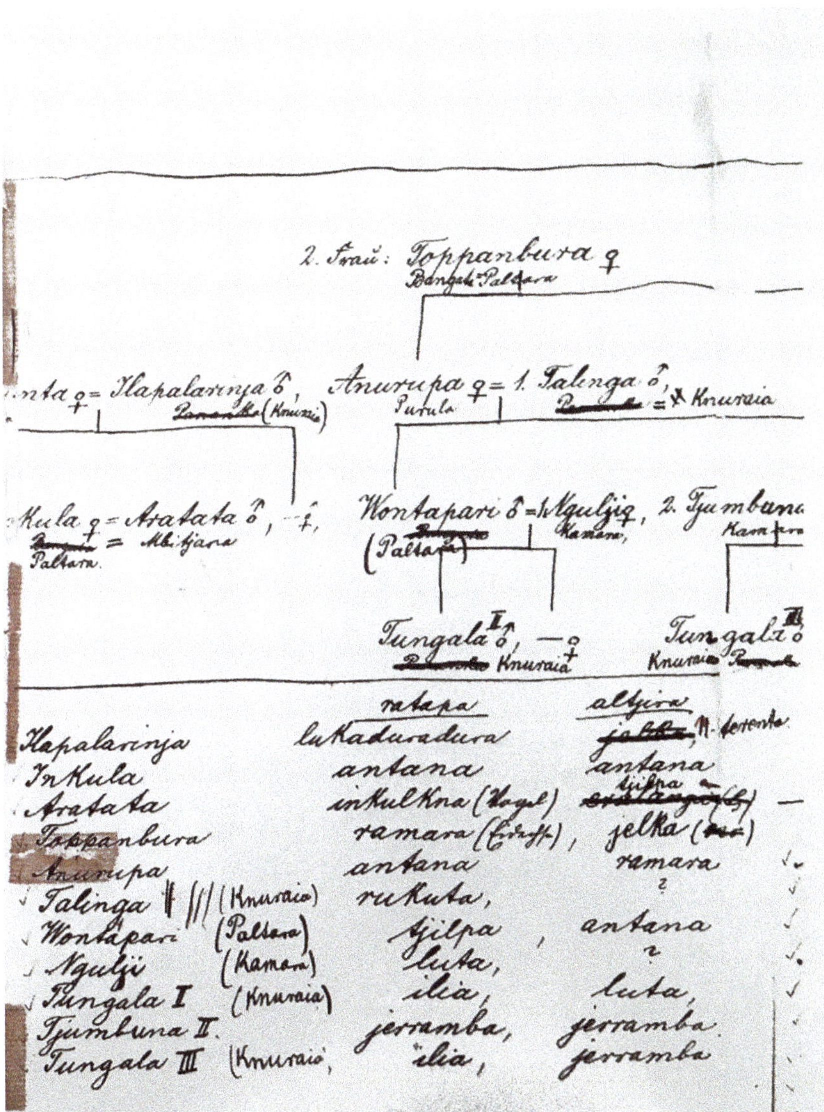

Figure 10: Family tree of Rhonda Inkamala's mother's mother's father Altingka collated by Carl Strehlow circa 1906.

Source: Strehlow Research Centre, Alice Springs.

Languages are an important part of our cultural heritage. A language is a complex of cultural knowledge, identity and spiritual connection through dreamings of our land and ancestors as well as our flora and fauna. Language is empowering, it enables speakers such as myself to communicate with others by expressing thoughts and ideas about subjects such as significant cultural sites and land marks on country.

As a vernacular teacher and cultural principal at the Yipirinya School, I believe teaching and learning our languages is a study of cultural knowledge and their systematic structure and orthographies, which utilise selected letters of the Latin alphabet. Translating the words of the dictionary that my ancestors and Carl Strehlow put down was very difficult as the Aranda words were written down in an old spelling system. Working very closely with both my parents, my mother Trudy Inkamala and my father the late Ingkarta (Pastor) Davie Inkamala, was tremendously helpful as the words were old Aranda words that were used by our great ancestors, and I learnt a lot and gained so much new vocabulary and understanding.

3

Rella nunaka inguia[1] — our old people

Mark Inkamala[2]

It is important to remember the old people (rella nunaka inguia, erilknabata), our ancestors, who taught Carl Strehlow our languages and provided the information to him for this dictionary. Among his main informants were people such as senior Aranda men Loatjira, Pmala (Tmala), Moses Tjalkabota, Hezekiel Malbunka, Nathanael Rauwiraka, Abel Renkeraka and Luritja man Talku. He had many more informants. He practised Aranda every day with our ancestors who helped him to learn it properly.

Loatjira (circa 1849–1924)

Loatjira was a very important Western Aranda man from Mbultjigata and the chief of Ntarea, the waterhole that gives the contemporary community of Hermannsburg its name. We call Hermannsburg Ntaria now. Loatjira was born about 1849, he belonged to the rameia (yellow goanna) dreaming. He was a great *inkata* (ceremonial chief) and *nankara* (healer, doctor). Most of the time he did not live at the mission.

1 I use here the spellings of Carl Strehlow, because this is the spelling system that our ancestors used.

2 With contributions by Anna Kenny and Adam Macfie.

Carl Strehlow's son T.G.H. Strehlow wrote that his father and Loatjira respected each other and were friends, but later their relationship cooled. In his book *Journey to Horseshoe Bend* T.G.H. Strehlow says:

> Loatjira had always been greeted like a loved ruler returning from exile by everyone at Hermannsburg whenever he had come back on his infrequent visits. Strehlow and Loatjira had always met on such occasions. (Strehlow 1969)

Loatjira chose to live outside of Hermannsburg near the Ellery Creek and only came to live at the mission after Strehlow's death. Loatjira was nevertheless Carl Strehlow's main informant about Aranda culture, as he kept Aranda Law strong. He rarely came to Hermannsburg after Strehlow had finished his work on sacred stories and the dictionary. Loatjira was baptised when he was very old. On 4 November 1923, he was christened Abraham. He died not long after his conversion, on 4 October 1924 from the Spanish influenza. Loatjira was baptised because he wanted to be buried on his country—his father's and father's father's country.

On Sunday 10 April 1932, T.G.H. Strehlow wrote into his first field diary:[3]

> After Aranda service today Moses, Jacobus, Able, Josef, and Martin came to the veranda and revived some reminisces of olden times. ... This was interesting to me, ... The four natives in the picture ... are Loatjira, Silas, Lartjinaka, and Moses. Lo[atjira] was, perhaps, the last of the old *nankara* or witchdoctors of the Western Aranda, and a man of first importance in the tribe. He steadfastly used all his influence in the interests of the vanishing beliefs of the knaribata or old men til the death of my father. Furthermore, he was before then not a station native, but preferred to live the old ways of tradition. (Strehlow 1932: 1–2)

3 T.G.H. Strehlow, Field Diary I, 1932, Strehlow Research Centre, Alice Springs.

Figure 11: Loatjira, Pmala (Tmala), Moses Tjalkabota and Luritja man Talku at Hermannsburg, 1906.

Source: SRC 06196, Strehlow Research Centre, Alice Springs.

Silas Tmala Ulakararinja Mbitjana (circa 1860–1923)

Silas was a Western Aranda man from Ndata, not far north-west of Jabulpa (Glen Helen Gorge) and belonged to aranga (euro) dreaming. He was born in about 1860 (Strehlow 1971: xxi, 599, 760) and married Annie Toa in 1890 (see Carl Strehlow 1913: Stammbaum 4; T.G.H. Strehlow family tree FT I. 28, p. 8).

Silas was baptised on 16 April 1900 by Carl Strehlow (T.G.H. Strehlow 1969–70: 157) and was one of the main informants about Aranda stories and language. He appears on Carl Strehlow's genealogy as Ulakararinja (Carl Strehlow 1913). He was later known as Silas (Mbitjana). Although he been blind from youth (T.G.H. Strehlow 1969–70: 211), he often chopped firewood for the Strehlow home, and normally brought down on his head the large bread-setting dish with the fat and innards from the killing pen (T.G.H. Strehlow 1969–70: 125).

He died on 24 June 1923 suddenly of heart failure.

Moses Tjalkabota (circa 1870–1954)

Moses Tjalkabota was the son of Tjita and Aranaljika. He was born around 1870 at Laburapuntja on the Ellery Creek and baptised on 26 December 1890 by A.H. Kempe, one of the first Lutheran missionaries on Aranda country. The children were taught Bible stories, reading and writing as well as some arithmetic. Moses also worked in the mission garden and as a shepherd. Not long after his baptism, his parents told him to leave the mission. He was told:

> Boy, if you continue here, your head will implode, and you will dry up. Then the wind will blow you away to the sand hills like a dried-up cicada, and we will be unable to find you.

However, Moses did not return with his parents to Laburapuntja, he stayed at the mission, where he married Sofia Inkamala on 25 January 1903.

Between 1905 and 1910 Tjalkabota made major contributions to Carl Strehlow's work about traditional stories, family trees and the dictionary. He was blind. Moses also helped Carl Strehlow with the translation of the Bible into Western Aranda between 1913 and 1919, and in the 1950s he helped T.G.H. Strehlow retranslate the Bible.

Figure 12: T.G.H. Strehlow (Carl Strehlow's youngest son), Conrad Raberaba and Moses, Zacharia, Nathanael and Jakobus.

Source: SRC 06050, Strehlow Research Centre, Alice Springs.

After Carl Strehlow's death, Moses Tjalkabota became a Lutheran Evangelist preaching at Deep Well, Horseshoe Bend, Idracowra, Jay Creek, Alice Springs, Undoolya, Arltunga and other places. He travelled by donkey, camel, buggy, on foot and on trucks. Moses died on 6 July 1954 at Hermannsburg.[4]

4 For more detail on Moses see T.G.H. Strehlow (1971: 357, 416, 627), P.G.E. Albrecht (2002: 237–300), P. Latz (2014).

Talku (circa 1867–1941)

Talku was Carl Strehlow's main Luritja informant, but Strehlow was not able to finish Talku's family tree and said (Strehlow 1913: 85, and note 2):

> Unfortunately, I could not gather sufficient data to complete [the family tree], for my informant, Talku, who supplied most of the Loritja myths and songs. He has left our station again, and his tribal companions residing here have married local women and have been included in the family trees of the Aranda.
>
> The man sitting at the end of the row on the right is Talku [see Figure 11]. It was his mission in life to spear the cattle belonging to the whites. During an attempt to escape arrest he was shot through the abdomen. He was subsequently brought to the Mission station and remained here until he left one day to enjoy his golden freedom.

Talku was also an important informant for T.G.H. Strehlow (1970: 137; 1971: xxi, 768). Strehlow wrote that Wapiti was Talku's name in old age. 'Wapiti' means yam in Kukatja-Luritja. He too made some biographical notes on Talku, aka Wapiti:

> Talku, like Loatjira, was not a resident of Hermannsburg. He was the ceremonial chief of the Kukatja yam centre of Merini. Born about 1867, he organised raids upon cattle belonging to Tempe Downs Station at the beginning of the century. A police party surprised these raiders one day south of Ltalatuma, and fired upon them when they sought to evade capture. Talku was hit by a bullet from a police tracker's rifle which passed through his body and emerged again without apparently injuring any vital organs. His upper thigh bone was, however, shattered. He was carried on the backs of his friends across the ranges to Hermannsburg, a distance of some twenty-five miles. His tough constitution and unconquerable courage carried him through this ordeal. After being nursed back to health at Hermannsburg, he showed his gratitude to my father by providing him with detailed information on Loritja totemic rites, sacred songs, and social organization. And then he disappeared again one day into the free wild life of his own country. (Strehlow 1971: xxi)

Talku must have left the station at the very latest in 1909. By 1929 he was back at the mission. On his research trip to Hermannsburg, Norman Tindale made a data card of Wapiti. He died on 14 January 1941.

Hezekiel Malbunka (1889–1965)

Hezekiel Malbunka Knuraia was the son of Petrus Paltara and Rebecka. He was born in the vicinity of Hermannsburg on 28 March 1889 at Ellery Creek (Cawthorn and Malbunka 2005: 71) and baptised nearly one year later on 23 March 1890. He married in 1908 (Strehlow 1969: 129, 153).

Although Hezekiel's family was early on connected to the mission, he and others of their father's and father's father's country that was centred on the tjilpa dreaming of Ltalatuma, Gilbert Springs, learnt the tjilpa's songs which have been transmitted to his descendants and are still known.

Hezekiel was a friend of Carl Strehlow. When Carl got sick in 1922, Hezekiel took a telegram to the Alice Springs telegraph station in a record time and returned even faster. The telegram contained a plea to the Finke River mission board in Adelaide to send help. It was a remarkable feat, according to Carl's son, T.G.H. Strehlow, who wrote that to walk the 130 kilometres distance to Alice Springs in one and a half days was faster than any of their horses would have been capable of. The return trip on foot was even faster once Hezekiel had the reply from the south. It took him one day. In 1960, he told Carl's son:

> I got the paper and I went right through. I didn't sleep somewhere in the middle. I travelled right back to Ntaria [Hermannsburg]. … I didn't camp on the way. … I drank water at Untukuntuka. Then I had another drink of water at Ntjuikarra. … From that soakage. Having drunk there, I headed back home. In the afternoon, around 5 o'clock, I arrived at the Mission. I didn't sleep on the way. (Cawthorn and Malbunka 2005: 73)

Abel (1888–1950)

Abel was also an informant of Carl Strehlow. He was documented on one of Carl's family trees (Strehlow 1913: Stammbaum 4) as well as on one of his son's, T.G.H. Strehlow (family tree I, 22, p. 6). Abel Mbitjana was born on 20 June 1888 at Hermannsburg, his conception site was Nguamina associated with ereakura dreaming. In 1906, he married Ruby Raggatt later called Rosa.

Nathanael Rauwiraka (circa 1871–1950s)

Nathanael Rauwiraka was often mentioned by Carl Strehlow in connection with the bible translation and he also mentions him in his letters. Rauwiraka was another important man like Loatjira, he was Kantjara's grandson, and the main man for Ellery Creek country that is in walking distance (about 20 to 30 km) from the Hermannsburg mission; it lies adjacent to Ntaria country.

Nathanael Rauwiraka documented with T.G.H. Strehlow in his own words (to be found in T.G.H.'s unpublished diaries) how he acquired his conception site and dreaming in Anmatyerr country, his initiation in Luritja country, his traditional marriage arrangements and how he became a *nankara*, a healer with powers. Although he was baptised and 'Christian', he was a traditional man. Like many Aranda 'Christians' he also kept his Aranda beliefs.

He was a true friend and mate of Carl Strehlow, they were the same age. He wrote letters in Aranda to Carl Strehlow when he was on holiday in South Australia and Germany (many have survived at the Strehlow Research Centre). These letters are generally about what is happening at the mission, that is, how he and his wife are going, men building their own shelters, births and deaths, and that they are missing him.

On another day, he sent Carl Strehlow a card written in Aranda that was stamped at Charlotte Waters on 28 August 1911:

> Tjina nuka kankinjai Nona lata pipa kalainaka unkwangana pipa nanakata ngana dankilama wa nuna Nala narirama ltarkna mara etata tota jinga tota lata mara ltarkna nana Nuna etja endura knuerama unkwa ngebera ta kuta etalerama ngana unta pipa nunaka lata lantamanga nuna lata argana narirama jinga tjina unkwanga Nathanael[5]

Nathanael spoke German, although it was not taught at the mission, apart from German hymns, otherwise Aranda and English was taught. Nathanael must have spent much time with the Strehlow family, which would have been the only place to learn German. He spoke Anmatyerr, Luritja and English beside his own language, Aranda.

5 Free translation: My dear friend. Today we received your letter and thank you. We are well, and I am well. We will not forget you and I always think of you. Your letter made us happy today. Your friend, Nathanael.

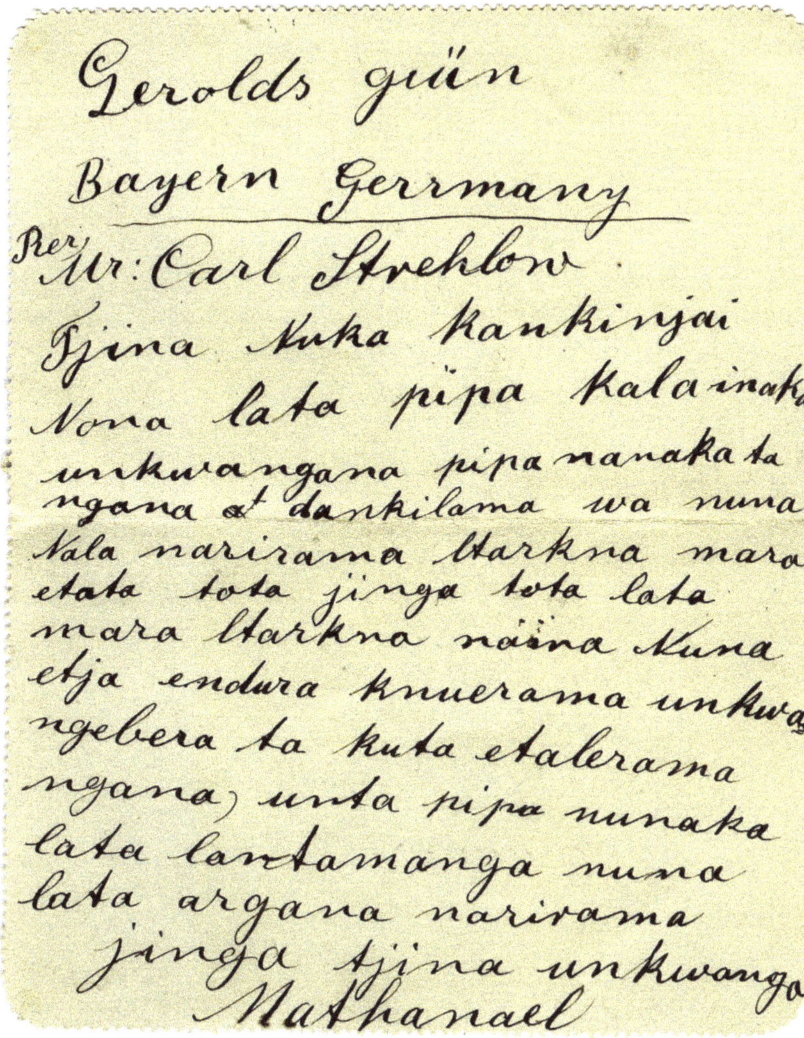
Gerolds grün
Bayern Gerrmany
Rev. Mr: Carl Strehlow.
Tjina Nuka Kankinjai
Nona lata pipa kalainaka
unkwangana pipa nanaka ta
ngana at dankilama wa nuna
Nala narirama Ltarkna mara
etata tota jinga tota lata
mara Ltarkna naina Kuna
etja endura knuerama unkwa
ngebera ta kuta etalerama
ngana, unta pipa nunaka
lata lantamanga nuna
lata argana narirama
jinga tjina unkwanga
Nathanael

Figure 13: Letter written by Nathanael Rauwiraka to Carl Strehlow in Germany, 1911.

Source: ARA-1911-22-1, Strehlow Research Centre, Alice Springs.

Nathanael taught Carl Strehlow alongside Moses the Aranda language when he arrived in 1894. He helped collating traditional stories, teaching children to write Aranda, worked on the cattle run and participated in the bible translation into Aranda.

Nathanael's father was Lutiaka Penangka whose country was the Ellery Creek region, where also Loatjira, the main chief of Ntarea, was living. His mother was Nungalka. Nathanael spent his time between the Ellery Creek and Hermannsburg, but after Carl Strehlow had left the mission, he stayed most of the time outside of the mission supervising the shepherds.

Nathanael Rauwiraka Pengarta was the ceremonial chief of Ellery Creek from his father's father's side. His conception site was in the Iloara (Lake Lewis) area on Anmatyerr country, north of his Ellery Creek country and the Western MacDonnell Ranges. He married his promised wife Maria in traditional ceremony that had been arranged many years earlier. They had one daughter Sara Penangka. She wrote, at the age of 10, to Carl Strehlow when he was on holiday in South Australia in 1903:

> Mr: Strelow
>
> Tjina nukai ennkatanukai jurgo knarra etnika jinga nal nama unta eamaga airama la junga Sara[6]

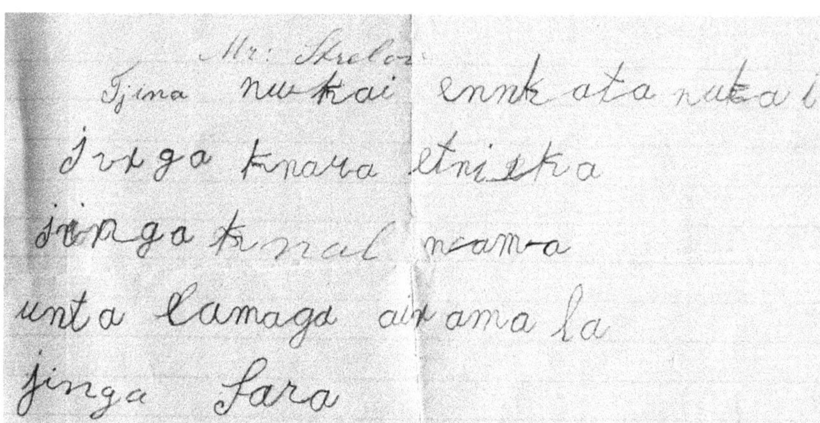

Figure 14: Note written in circa 1903/04 by Sara, Nathanael Rauwiraka's 10-year-old daughter.

Source: ARA-c1903-2-1, Strehlow Research Centre, Alice Springs.

6 Free translation: Mr Strehlow, My friend, I cried very much when I saw you leaving, Sara.

Figure 15: Nathanael Rauwiraka, his wife Maria and daughter Sara at Hermannsburg, circa 1903.

Source: SRC 05810, Strehlow Research Centre, Alice Springs.

In 1932 T.G.H. Strehlow (1932: 132) commented on Nathanael whom he had not seen for 10 years:

> Nathanael is the chief overseer over the shepherds, and is also camped permanently at Long Water Hole [Thata] or on the No 4 Block. He is the only 'gentleman' amongst the natives at the Mission, a good-natured, jovial, open-hearted fellow, who, one feels, is superior by birth: one almost feels in him a sort of class-mate and school mate of my father's—indeed, his handshake and his hearty 'Guten Tag' …

These are only a few short biographies of our ancestors, there are many more. I found some of the information at the Strehlow Research Centre, where all papers of father and son are held, but I also know many details about my people that were handed down to me from my ancestors. We do not want to forget them and I hope that we will be able to write in time all of their stories down.

Figure 16: Mark Inkamala working with T.G.H. Strehlow's materials out on his country, 2014.

Source: Trevor Frost.

4

The unpublished manuscript

Anna Kenny

Carl Strehlow's comparative dictionary and language description work probably began taking shape in 1905, although he had already been collecting vocabularies for over 10 years mainly for teaching and theological purposes.[1] The impetus for the compilation of the dictionary came from his editor, Baron Moritz von Leonhardi, who played an important role in the formation of Strehlow's ethnolinguistic work. On 9 September 1905, von Leonhardi wrote to Strehlow:

> Myths in the Aranda language with interlinear translations would be of great value; and a dictionary and a grammar would provide the key to them. A dictionary outlining the meaning of words as well as short explanations of the meaning of individual objects, characters in the myths etc., is highly valued in science.[2]

This request indicates that the 'key' he had in mind would go beyond being only an assistance to translating texts, but would also contribute to an understanding of Aranda culture and an analysis and description of their language. He made similar statements about the importance of documenting the Loritja language and provided continuous

1 Carl Strehlow wrote, for instance, a 'Deutsch–Aranda Wörterbuch' (German–Aranda dictionary), which was possibly compiled when he arrived in 1894 at Hermannsburg. The Strehlow Research Centre also holds a manuscript of a Dieri wordlist (circa 1893/94) as well as other wordlists that are likely to have been compiled for theological purposes between 1913 and 1919.

2 Von Leonhardi to Carl Strehlow, 9 September 1905. All German to English translations of letters by the author.

encouragement for collecting mythological texts in both languages. Together this data would make it possible to ascertain whether Loritja and Aranda were distinct languages.[3] Alongside the comparative dictionary, Strehlow also compiled a comparative Aranda and Loritja grammar that he had completed by 18 April 1910.[4] The interests behind this linguistic work were of practical, philological, theoretical and philosophical nature. Such interest was in this German anthropological context not unusual. It at once described the Aranda and Loritja languages, illustrated theoretical points made by the emerging *Kulturkreislehre* or culture circle theory (see Kenny 2013) and demonstrated that Aranda and Loritja were two different languages and as complex as any other languages in the world.

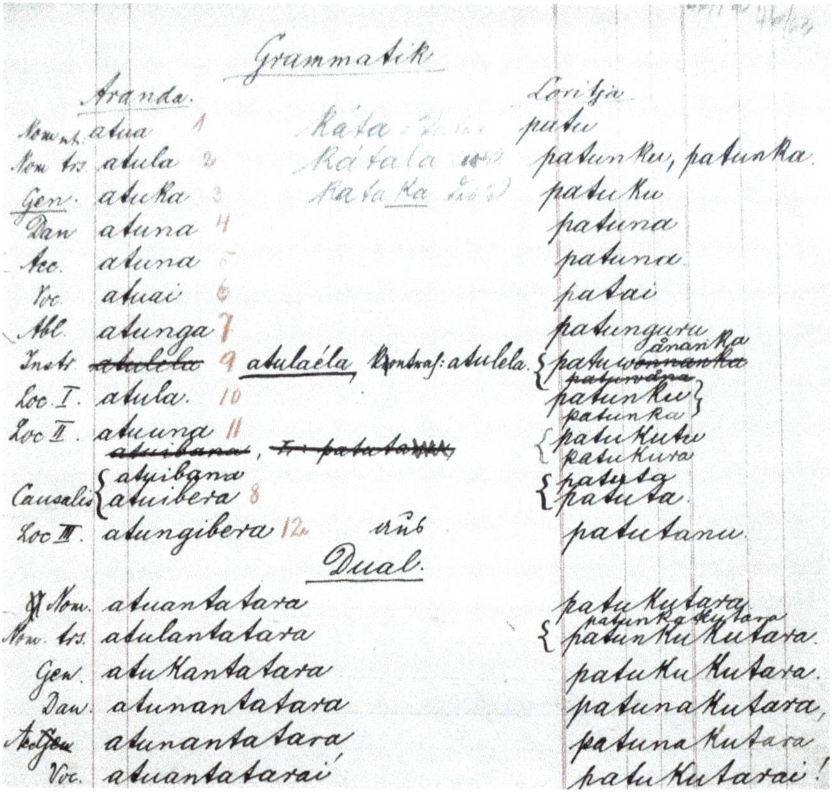
Grammatik

	Aranda.	Loritja.
Nom. abs.	atua 1	patu
Nom. trs.	atula 2	patunku, patunka.
Gen.	atuka 3	patuku
Dat.	atuna 4	patuna
Acc.	atuna 5	patuna.
Voc.	atuai 6	patai
Abl.	atunga 7	patunguru
Instr.	~~atulela~~ 9 atulaéla Kontrakt: atulela.	{patu ånanka ~~wonnanka~~
Loc. I.	atula. 10	{patunku patunka}
Loc. II.	atuunga 11	{patukutu patukura
Causalis	{atuibana atuibera 8	{patuta patuta.
Loc. III.	atungibera 12	patutanu.

Dual.

	Aranda.	Loritja.
Nom.	atuantatara	patukutara
Nom. trs.	atulantatara	{patunkukutara patunkakutara
Gen.	atukantatara	patukukutara.
Dat.	atunantatara	patunakutara,
Acc.	atunantatara	patunakutara
Voc.	atuantatarai	patukutarai!

Figure 17: First page of Carl Strehlow's unpublished comparative Aranda and Loritja grammar, 1910.

Source: SH-SP-48-47, Strehlow Research Centre, Alice Springs.

3 Von Leonhardi to Carl Strehlow, 3 April 1909.

4 Held at the Strehlow Research Centre: Call number SP-46-47.

Prior to his collaboration with von Leonhardi, Strehlow's interests were predominantly theological, with the goal of producing translations of Christian texts. This focus took second place to the ethnographic and linguistic work during Strehlow's five-year period of close collaboration with von Leonhardi between 1904 and 1909. Once he had completed his ethnographic work, Strehlow's interests returned to translation for his missionary work. The focus on the comparative study of language was certainly reminiscent of von Humboldt's paradigm, as well as of Max Mueller's philology, that original texts along with a grammar and dictionary was the way forward in comprehensively documenting a people's language. Due to the nature of this emerging modern comparative and linguistic approach to the documentation of the complexity and richness of central Australian languages and cultures, Strehlow's work now provides an opportunity to chart change and continuity across a century.

Von Leonhardi repeatedly emphasised the importance of a publication of a comparative grammar and dictionary as an essential part of their ethnographic publications on the Aranda and Loritja cultures. Indeed, he thought that the language study would be the culmination of Strehlow's ethnolinguistic work and remarked to him:

> To complete your work you must finally write a language study [Sprachlehre] of Aranda and Loritja—that will be its zenith.[5]

As things turned out, the death of Baron von Leonhardi[6] in 1910 meant that neither the dictionary nor the comparative grammar were ever published.

Aranda and Loritja

Strehlow's study area (see his 1910 map, Figure 18) lies in a transitional zone where Aranda and Loritja speakers meet. Many people who belong to this border area are still fluent speakers of Aranda and Luritja and may switch seamlessly from one language into the other. A.H. Kempe, the first language worker (to borrow a modern term) in this region, had observed that the local language had incorporated words and phrases from the neighbouring language (i.e. Luritja) to the immediate west (Kempe 1891a: 1). This region is not only linguistically complex, but also

5 Von Leonhardi to Carl Strehlow, 23 December 1908.

6 For more details on Baron von Leonhardi see Völker (2001).

culturally, as different Arandic subgroups as well as Western Desert people meet here. In this area the section and subsection systems converged, for example, and two land tenure systems met (Strehlow 1965; Kenny 2010).

The Arandic language variety or dialect documented by Carl Strehlow belongs to the upper Finke River, mainly from the north-western and Hermannsburg areas of the Western Aranda people and the western portion of the MacDonnell Ranges (see T.G.H. Strehlow 1971: xx), though it also includes words that belong to surrounding Arandic varieties. Carl Strehlow often distinguished between the Western, North-Western, Eastern and Southern Aranda in his writings, but without defining exactly where their territories lie. On his map of 1910 he placed the Western Arandic dialect, Aranda Ulbma, on the upper Finke River, roughly between the MacDonnell and James Ranges (including Hermannsburg mission), the Aranda Roara as the dialect for the area between the eastern part of the MacDonnell Ranges and James Ranges including Alice Springs, the Aranda Lada from approximately Henbury along the Finke River and the Aranda Tanka between Charlotte Waters and Oodnadatta along the lower Finke River (see Figure 18). It is impossible to judge what these names and 'language' regions really indicate. Generally, language boundaries are diffuse and may even fluctuate with the movements of their speakers; it also may depend from whose point of view a language variety is described.

The Arandic group Carl Strehlow identified as Aranda Ulbma today identifies as Western Aranda, referring to their dialect as Western or Tjoritja (the name of the West MacDonnell Ranges) Aranda.[7] Strehlow's Aranda informants lived in an area bounded roughly in the north by the West MacDonnell Ranges (Strehlow 1907: 32, 42; T.G.H. Strehlow 1971: 670, note 19) that separates them from the Anmatyerr and Northern Arrernte peoples. In the south, their country stretches along the Finke River past the James Range, to the countries of Southern Arrernte or Pertame and Matuntara (Luritja) peoples. To the west, it extends to The Derwent, the western Aranda–Luritja language border area, and to the east it abuts the territory of today's Central Arrernte people (see also T.G.H. Strehlow 1947: 59).

7 According to Kempe (1891a: 1–2), 'The vocabulary is that of the tribe inhabiting the River Finke, and is also, with only slight variations in the dialect, that of the tribes in the MacDonnell Ranges eastward to Alice Springs, but not far westward of the River Finke, and extending southward to the Peake.' Breen (2001: 64–65) speculates that the dialect now known as Western Arrernte (Western Aranda) arose from mixing of a West MacDonnell Ranges dialect he calls Tyurretye Arrernte ([Tjoritja Aranda) with Southern Arrernte (Pertame) at the Hermannsburg mission in the early contact period. My edits in brackets.

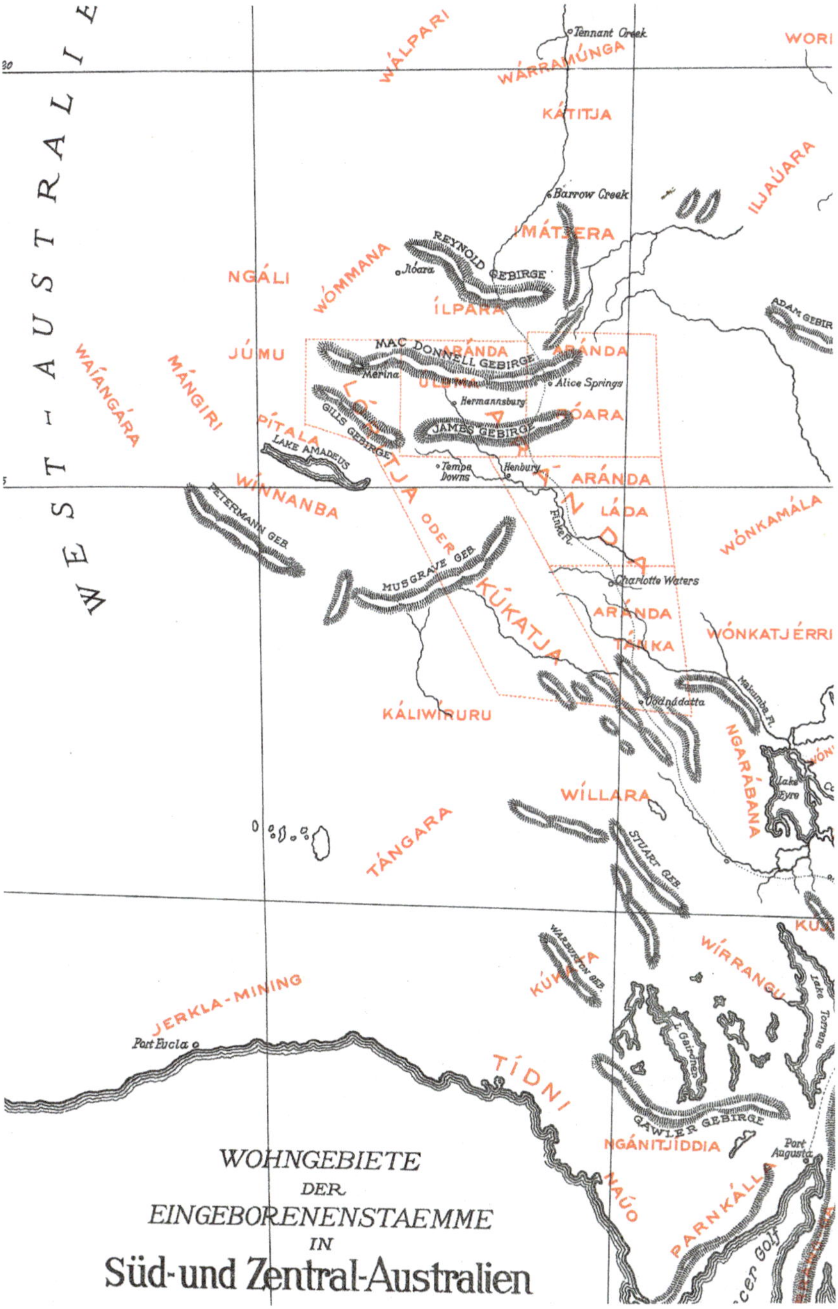

Figure 18: Map of schematic language distribution in the first decade of the twentieth century according to Carl Strehlow (1910b).

Source: Strehlow Research Centre, Alice Springs.

The Western Aranda's first sustained contact with non-Aboriginal people occurred in the 1870s when the Lutheran missionaries arrived in central Australia. Among them were A.H. Kempe (1844–1928) and L.G. Schulze (1851–1924) who began the documentation of the language at a *ratapa* (twin) dreaming[8] place on the upper Finke River where they set up a Lutheran mission, which they named Hermannsburg after the seminary that had trained them. Life on the frontier was incredibly harsh, the missionaries nevertheless pursued their language work, which included the development of a first Arandic orthography and teaching literacy, to spread the gospel in Aranda. By 1891 the mission was abandoned; the missionaries had succumbed to the hardship and challenges of the desert. Three years later, in 1894, Carl Strehlow (1871–1922) arrived to re-establish the mission, and immediately took up the study of Aranda, as would mission staff after his death in 1922. In the contact history of the Aranda, the Lutheran missionaries played an important role. Their colonial involvement included, among other changes, a Lutheran inscription on the Aranda language that they achieved by a) codifying this language in multiple orthographies, b) semantic changes to key terms (e.g. altjira, kutungulu and even tjurunga) and c) the reduction of vocabulary (which was also partly the result of the sedentarisation at the mission from a hunter-and-gatherer lifestyle) by discouraging and limiting many cultural practices.[9]

Luritja is a dialect of the Western Desert language and is not closely related to Aranda. It is not exactly clear when Luritja people encountered the first missionaries. However, by the turn of the century some of the people living to the immediate west of the Western Aranda, who called themselves Kukatja, had moved into the Hermannsburg mission. Carl Strehlow remarked that the people whom the Aranda called 'Loritja', referred to themselves as 'Kukatja' (Strehlow 1907: 57, Anmerkung 9). According to T.G.H. Strehlow, the word Luritja was the Aranda name applied to speech groups west of Aranda territory (1947: 177–78). Today the Western Desert group in the area call themselves Luritja or Kukatja-Luritja when referring to their ancestry and history. The country of the Kukatja-Luritja lies to the west of the Derwent River, which marks broadly the Aranda–Luritja language border. This language boundary

8 See Carl Strehlow (1907: 80–81; 1908: 72 f.3; 1911: 122–24) and T.G.H. Strehlow (1971: 758).

9 For more details on the mission history see Morton (1992), Austin-Broos (2009, 2010) and Kenny (2017a).

zone sometimes determines how people perceive their country. People in the area often describe the border area as 'mix-up' country, referring to the fact that a number of places have both Luritja and Aranda names and that there is no clear boundary between them.

Figure 19: Hermannsburg mission in central Australia, circa 1910s.
Source: SRC 07107, Strehlow Research Centre, Alice Springs.

Carl Strehlow's linguistic and ethnographic investigations built on Kempe[10] and Schulze's work that included an Aranda grammar and vocabulary of circa 1,750 words.[11] His work on language would last nearly three decades. During the intense period of recording Aranda and Luritja myth, song, social life, family trees and vocabulary between circa 1904 and 1909, Strehlow's principal collaborators were Loatjira (c.1846–1924),[12] Moses Tjalkabota (c.1873–1950), Pmala (c.1860–1923), Nathaneal Rauwiraka (c.1871–1950s) and the Luritja man Talku (c.1867–1941) (see Chapter 3).

10 The Strehlow Research Centre and Lutheran Archives in Adelaide (LAA) hold unpublished material by Kempe produced between 1877 and 1891.
11 Carl Strehlow's letters to Kaibel (1899–1909) held at the LAA.
12 According to T.G.H. Strehlow (1971: 753).

Carl Strehlow

Carl Friedrich Theodor Strehlow was born on 23 December 1871 in a little village in northern Germany, as the seventh child of the village schoolteacher. The village pastor Carl Seidel recognised the outstanding potential of the child and sparked his interest in myth and song. With great dedication, Seidel prepared his protégé for entry into a seminary and was able to place him in the Neuendettelsau mission seminary in southern Germany.

Carl graduated with a high distinction ('gut plus') and in April 1892 was sent to his first posting (Liebermeister 1998: 19), Bethesda mission at Lake Eyre in remote and arid Australia. There he joined J.G. Reuther (1861–1914), who had left the Neuendettelsau seminary four years earlier. From the moment he arrived, he studied the language of the local people, and within six months, it is said, he spoke the local language (Schild 2004: 55), and by 1894, in collaboration with Reuther, he had translated the New Testament called *Testamenta marra,* into Dieri, which was published in 1897.

Figure 20: Carl Strehlow, Reuther and Dieri people at Bethesda mission, 1893/94.[13]

Source: SRC 06171, Strehlow Research Centre, Alice Springs.

13 Letter of 15 May 1894 from Carl Strehlow to his fiancée Frieda identifies all people on this photograph.

In late 1894, at the age of 22, he was transferred to the Hermannsburg mission, now called Ntaria after a sacred site in its vicinity, where he stayed for nearly three decades. He ran it as a mission and a cattle and sheep station, providing pastoral care for more than 100 Aboriginal people who became Christians, as well as a large number of their relatives who lived on the fringes of the mission. As soon as the Lutheran mission staff of the Hermannsburg mission managed to acquire a moderate proficiency in the vernacular, they used the Indigenous languages in church services and in school (Moore 2003: 24). Within months of Strehlow's arrival he became fluent in Aranda and preached in the vernacular (Eylmann 1908; Kenny 2013).

Figure 21: Aranda people at the Hermannsburg mission, circa 1906.
Source: SRC 05474, Strehlow Research Centre, Alice Springs.

Despite the desolate condition at the mission, Carl started rebuilding it with great enthusiasm, not least motivated by the prospect that his young fiancée Friedericke [Frieda] Johanna Henriette Keysser would be arriving within the year. Travelling from Germany, Frieda, 19 years of age, joined Carl in 1895. Despite the inconveniences, Frieda embraced her role as a missionary's wife. She started to learn Aranda, to teach the women household skills intended to improve health and living standards. She had six children at the Hermannsburg mission. Her first child Friedrich was born in 1897, her only daughter Martha in 1899, Rudolf in 1900, Karl in 1902, Heinrich in 1905 and her youngest son Theodor in 1908.

Figure 22: The Strehlow children (Friedrich, Karl, Martha with baby Ted, Rudolf and Hermann) at Hermannsburg, 1908.

Source: SRC 05832, Strehlow Research Centre, Alice Springs.

In 1901 Baron Moritz von Leonhardi, a wealthy German armchair anthropologist, wrote to Strehlow asking him for some information about the people of the Hermannsburg mission. A real friendship developed between these men that resulted in a fruitful intellectual exchange between 1901 and 1910 and produced a masterpiece. Von Leonhardi became Carl Strehlow's editor and organised the publication of Strehlow's magnum opus *Die Aranda- und Loritja-Stämme in Zentral-Australien* (1907–20) through the Ethnological Museum of Frankfurt.

In mid-1910, just after Strehlow had completed his ethnographic work, he departed with his family for Germany. The trip was intended as a break for Carl and Frieda, and to secure an education for his children. In his luggage Strehlow took many items with him that his editor had requested, including the dictionary manuscript. Without doubt the publication of the comparative grammar and dictionary of Aranda and Loritja would have followed had it not been for von Leonhardi's premature death. He died from a stroke late in October 1910, only days before he was to meet Carl Strehlow.

After an extended stay in Germany and placing his five eldest children with relatives and friends, he returned in 1912 to central Australia, with his wife Frieda and their youngest son Theodor (1908–1978), who would later become one of the most controversial figures in Australian anthropology. In 1913, not long after his return to the Hermannsburg mission, Carl began the translation of the New Testament into Aranda with Moses Tjalkabota, Nathanael Rauwiraka and Jacobus. They completed it in 1919. Parts of it were published after his death as *Ewangelia Lukaka* (1925) and *Ewangelia Taramatara* (1928), without mentioning the role of the translators. In this period Carl Strehlow extracted data from his original dictionary manuscript and produced a second extensive wordlist, which is likely to have been for the translation of theological texts.[14]

When World War I broke out the Strehlows suffered greatly for leaving their children in Europe, and at the war's end they decided to leave for Germany to see them. However, 30 years of mission effort had taken their toll on Carl. In mid-1922, as he waited for his replacement, he fell sick. All attempts to treat him locally failed and he died on 20 October 1922 at Horseshoe Bend after an agonising journey south on his way to medical help.

On that final journey, he was accompanied by his wife Frieda and his son Theo, who 47 years later wrote a highly acclaimed, award-winning autobiographical novel based on this trip, called *Journey to Horseshoe Bend*. Mother and son travelled on to Adelaide and the dictionary manuscript as well as the original handwritten manuscripts of the publication *Die Aranda- und Loritja-Stämme in Zentral-Australien* journeyed with them.

The manuscripts

Carl Strehlow's published work *Die Aranda- und Loritja-Stämme in Zentral-Australien* was based on three handwritten manuscripts called *Sagen*, *Cultus* and *Leben*. *Sagen* (myths/legends) contains the Aranda and Luritja myth collections, *Cultus* (cults) songs that were sung during ceremonies and *Leben* (life) describes aspects of social life. They were published in seven instalments between 1907 and 1920 and are the richest and densest ethnographic text written on Western Aranda and Luritja cultures of central Australia at the beginning of the twentieth century. The original handwritten manuscripts survived in Australia; Strehlow had sent only copies to Germany in segments for comment and publication (Kenny 2013: 37). Those copies were destroyed in World War II during the bombing of the Ethnological Museum of Frankfurt.

14 Held at the Lutheran Archives in Adelaide.

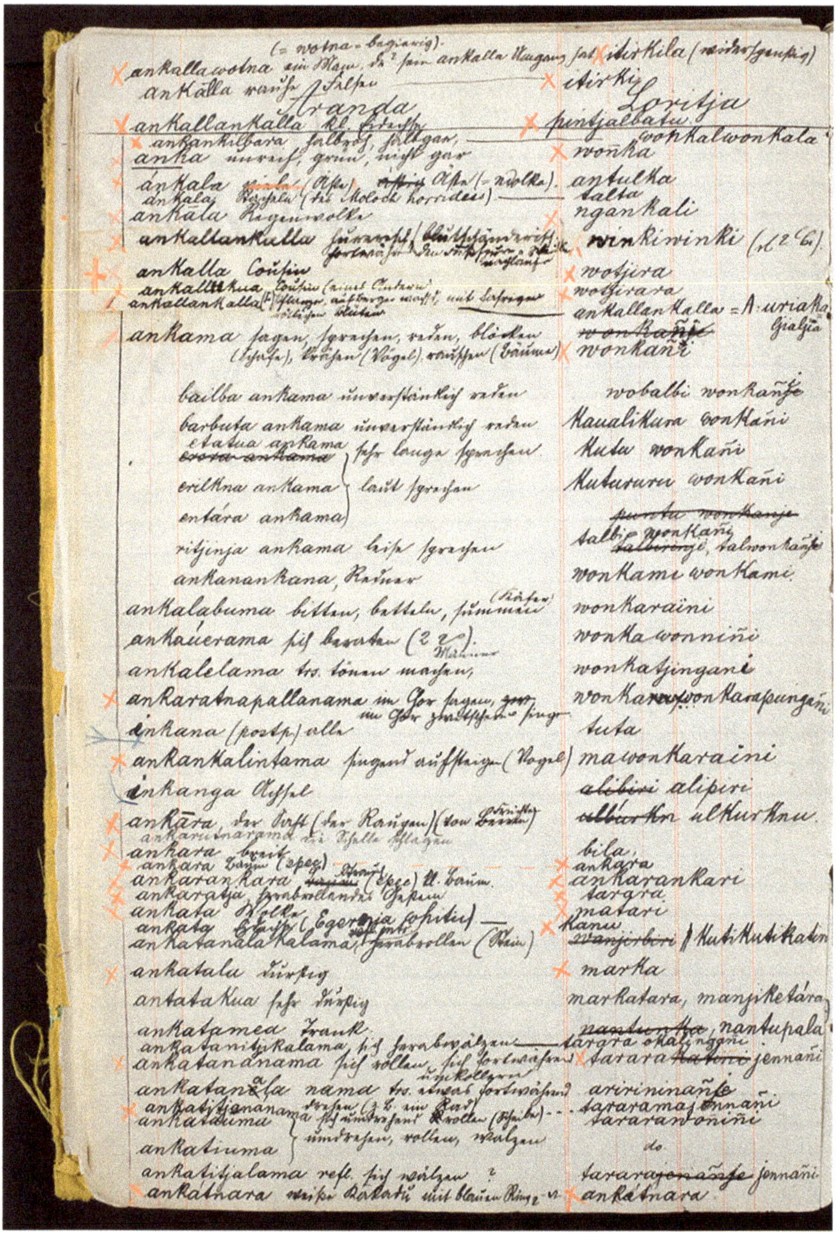

Aranda | Loritja

ankallawotna [illegible] | itirkila
ankalla [illegible] | itirkij
ankallankalla kl. [illegible] | pintjalbatu
ankankilbara [illegible] | wonkalwonkala
anka unreif, grün, nicht gar | wonka
ankala [illegible] | antulka
ankala [illegible] (die Moloch horridus) | talta
ankala Regenwolke | ngankali
ankallankulla [illegible] | winkiwinki
ankalla Cousin | wotjira
ankallakua [illegible] | wotjirara
ankallankalla [illegible] | ankallankalla = A. uriakka
ankama sagen, sprechen, reden, [illegible] | wonkanji

bailba ankama unverständlich reden | wobalbi wonkanje
barbuta ankama unverständlich reden | kaualikura wonkani
etatua ankama sehr lange sprechen | kuta wonkani
erilkna ankama laut sprechen | kutururu wonkani
entára ankama | talbi wonkani, talwonkanje
ritjinja ankama leise sprechen | wonkami wonkami
ankanankana, [illegible] | wonkaraini
ankalabuma bitten, betteln, [illegible] | wonkawonnini
ankauerama [illegible] | wonkatjingani
ankalelama [illegible] | wonkarawonkarapungani
ankaratnapallanama [illegible] | tuta
ankana (postp.) [illegible] | mawonkaraini
ankankalintama [illegible] (Vogel) | alipiri
ankanga [illegible] | ulkurknu
ankara [illegible] | bila
ankara [illegible] | ankara
ankarankara [illegible] Baum | ankarankari
ankaratja [illegible] | targra
ankata Wolke, Egeria [illegible] | matari
ankata [illegible] | kanu
ankatanalakalama [illegible] | kutikutikaten
ankatala durstig | marka
antatakua sehr durstig | markatara, manjiketara
ankatamea krank | nantupala
ankatanitjikalama [illegible] | targra okalingani
ankatanánama [illegible] | tarara jennani
ankatanála nama [illegible] | aririninanje
ankatjanama [illegible] | tararamajennani
ankatiuma [illegible] | tararawonini
ankatijalama [illegible] | tararajennani
ankatnara [illegible] | ankatnara

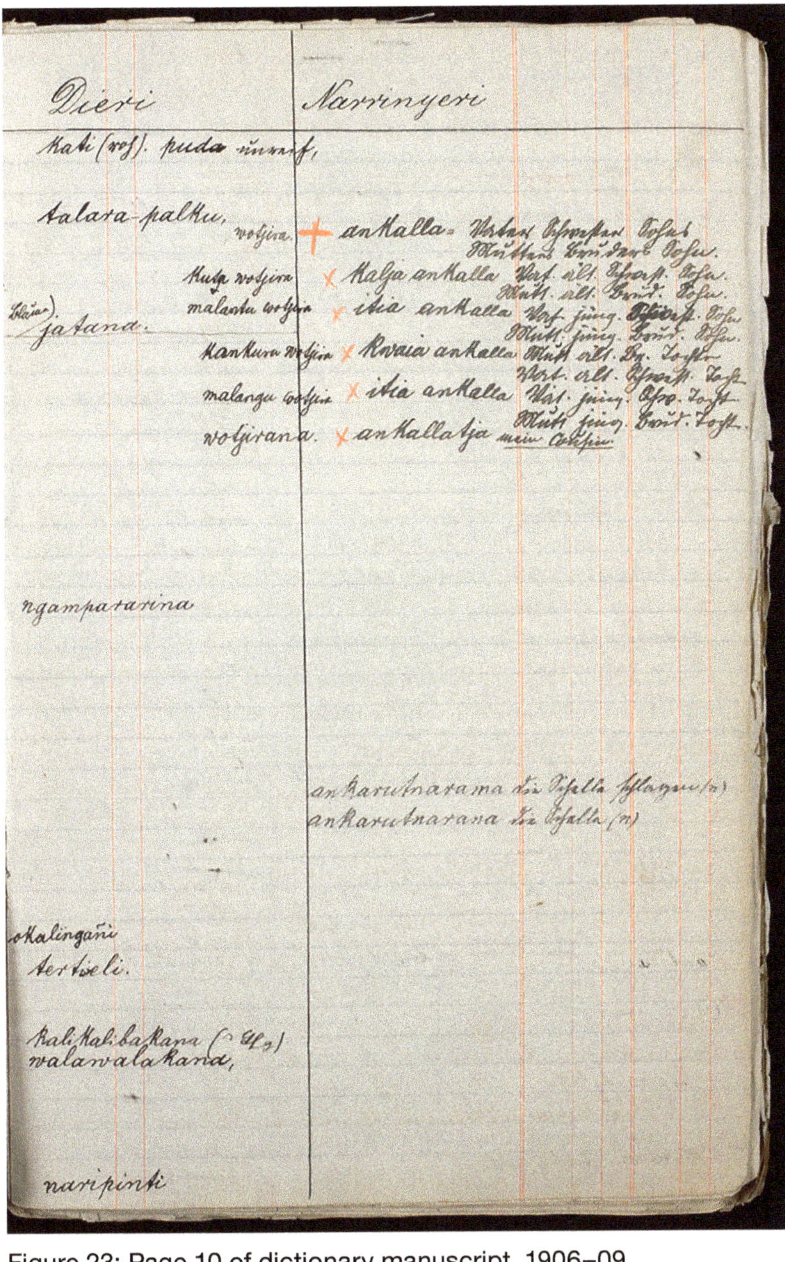

Figure 23: Page 10 of dictionary manuscript, 1906–09.

Source: Strehlow Research Centre, Alice Springs.

The comparative dictionary is the fourth handwritten manuscript and has remained unpublished. It contains thousands of Aranda, Loritja and Dieri to German glosses. It probably represents the largest and most comprehensive collation of Indigenous words of Australian languages compiled around the turn of the twentieth century, closely matched only by Reuther's linguistic and ethnographic work on the Aboriginal cultures of the Lake Eyre Basin (Lucas and Fergie 2017).

Dates within the pages in the dictionary manuscript indicate that Carl Strehlow compiled it around the turn of the twentieth century. He noted on the last page 'Beendet am 23. Aug. 1906' (Completed on 23 August 1906) and 'Korrectur beendet am 15. Dec. 1909' (Corrections completed on 15 December 1909). This original dictionary manuscript and the original volume manuscripts *Sagen*, *Cultus* and *Leben* are now held at the Strehlow Research Centre in Alice Springs. Notes deposited with these manuscripts and letters at the Strehlow Research Centre and the Special Collection of the Barr Smith library suggest that T.G.H. Strehlow had them in his possession from the 1930s until his death in 1978. Although the dictionary manuscript is a unique documentary record in Australia, and despite it being in his scholar son's possession, and then his widow's possession, it has remained nearly unknown for over 100 years. Efforts to publish the dictionary after completion were thwarted not only by the untimely death of von Leonhardi, but also by T.G.H. Strehlow's constant use of it.

The manuscripts travelled back from Germany with Carl Strehlow in 1912 and the dictionary manuscript was used to create a typed wordlist version for Aranda bible translation between 1913 and 1919.[15] All manuscripts were taken in the luggage on his excruciating journey to Horseshoe Bend in 1922, packed by his 14-year-old son in the previous fortnight before leaving the Hermannsburg mission permanently (T.G.H. Strehlow 1969: 9).

After Carl Strehlow's traumatic death, and despite her ambivalence towards her husband's work on the Aranda and Luritja cultures, Frieda gave the manuscripts to her youngest son T.G.H. Strehlow when he started his language studies in the early 1930s. The dictionary manuscript seems to

15 It is a wordlist of simple glosses of Aranda, German and Loritja with an Appendix of additional words. This item is also in the FitzHerbert-Strehlow Papers: Item 2 called '21 typescript pages of Aranda words'. Page 1 is headed 'Anhang zum Woerterbuch von Missionar Strehlow, genannt Neue Woerter' with circa 1,536 words.

have been a lifelong companion of T.G.H. Strehlow. He annotated it in some places by hand and it becomes clear these manuscripts were not only professionally but also emotionally of unimaginable value to him. He took it with him when he returned in 1932 to central Australia (Kenny 2013: 153)[16] and when he died in 1978 it was found on his desk at the University of Adelaide. The manuscripts disappeared for some time but surfaced again in the 1990s. They were among the items[17] confiscated at the house of T.G.H. Strehlow's widow that were at the centre of a dispute over their ownership. They are now deposited at the Strehlow Research Centre in Alice Springs.

Figure 24: T.G.H. Strehlow at the Hermannsburg mission, circa 1920.
Source: SRC 06002 Strehlow Research Centre, Alice Springs.

The dictionary manuscript's form

The dictionary manuscript is a complex document that not only contains four different languages, but also a number of different scripts as well as shorthand that say something about the time period in which it was produced and Carl Strehlow's education and scholarship.

16 T.G.H. Strehlow's Diary I (1932: 2), Strehlow Research Centre.

17 Schedule B of a draft of the *Strehlow Research Centre Act*, held at the Strehlow Research Centre.

The manuscript is organised into four columns with the following languages: Aranda (an Arandic language), German, Loritja (a Western Desert language) and Dieri (a Karnic language). The Aranda column contains circa 7,600 entries, the German column circa 7,600, the Loritja/Kukatja column circa 6,800, and Dieri column circa 1,200 entries. His Loritja was sometimes labelled Kukatja (see Figure 23). This seems to indicate that (i) one of his main informants might have been Kukatja or identified clearly as a Kukatja speaker, rather than being possibly a multilingual Arandic informant, (ii) he changed informant(s) part-way through the research project, or (iii) the language labels were both in use, but he changed his mind on which to use.

He was initially attempting to compare four Indigenous languages. An additional column was set up for Narrinyeri words, but there are no entries in it. He may have run out of time, not have had enough data on Narrinyeri, or the task to include it may have been simply too enormous and work-intense.

A look at an excerpt of a page of his dictionary manuscript illustrates the difficult task of transcribing it. The Aranda, Loritja/Kukatja and Dieri words in the first, third and fourth columns are written in Latin script. Strehlow knew Latin script as it was used in all European countries outside of Germany and by educated Germans who engaged with people outside of their own country.

The words in the second column are German and written in a German script. Carl Strehlow and his son T.G.H. Strehlow used a German script that was called *Kurrentschrift* when writing in German (not *Sütterlin* which was developed much later and was only used in the 1930s). At the turn of the century there were many versions of these scripts used in different parts of Germany. At this time, there were endless public discussions in newspapers and academic publications about the pros and cons of the use of Latin script versus a German script.

In the middle column there is occasionally some shorthand. In the example in Figure 25 from page 40 of the manuscript, someone who knew shorthand added its transcription, that is 'die Abteilung der Gruppe, der ich nicht angehöre' (the group I do not belong to) and 'von einander' (of each other). It appears to be T.G.H. Strehlow's handwriting. However, the shorthand is not always annotated in this way. Carl Strehlow used a shorthand called *Stolze*, which was the preferred system in northern

Germany. There were many competing stenographic systems in Germany at that time. An extensive literature discusses the arguments about which system is best and how to improve it. In the 1930s the National Socialists implemented a common system and prohibited all others.[18]

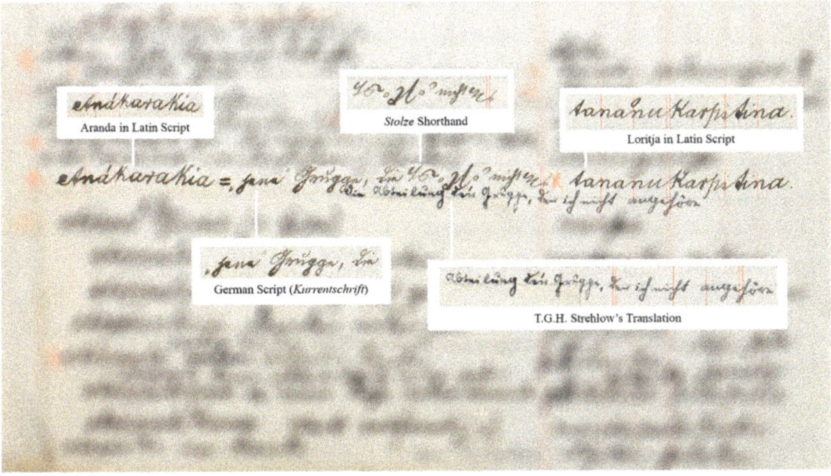

Figure 25: Excerpt of page 40 showing Aranda and Loritja in Latin script (left and far right), German in *Kurrentschrift* (following Aranda) and *Stolze* shorthand (immediately following German *Kurrentschrift*).

Source: Strehlow Research Centre, Alice Springs. Image manipulation: Shane Mulcahy.

Most German scholars knew shorthand; it was one of the distinguishing features of education as well as an efficient technique used by scientists to record information. One could jot down in real time a speaker's narrative and it used very little paper, which was a valuable and scarce resource at the remote Hermannsburg mission in central Australia. It is possible that Carl Strehlow learnt shorthand at school. If he had not acquired this skill before he was trained as a missionary, he would have learnt it from his early mentor Otto Seidel or at the Neuendettelsau seminary.

18 I am thankful for the assistance provided at the stenographic collection in Dresden to help identify the version of shorthand used by Carl Strehlow.

The dictionary content

Carl Strehlow's dictionary contains vocabulary that relates to mythology (in which the flora and fauna play an important role), kinship and ceremonial activities, as well as social life in general and material culture, because these were the focus of Carl's ethnographic work. Although the transcriptions of Indigenous myths and songs in Aranda and Luritja are accompanied by German interlinear and free translations in Strehlow's published work, an Aranda–German–Luritja dictionary is required to understand the full richness of this early ethnography.

The type of mythological text material and its vocabulary that Carl Strehlow collected describes the core of an Arandic belief system that today is referred to in English as the Dreaming or The Law. The myths and songs about the earth-dwelling ancestral beings, called at the turn of the twentieth century in Aranda the *altjirangamitjina* and in Luritja *tukutita*, explain how the world was created and reflect many aspects of traditional Aboriginal life. Strehlow remarked that these narratives represented the Indigenous understanding of the world and their perception of how their laws and social systems came into being. The narratives of the exploits of the *altjirangamitjina*, both in prose and poetics, often transform into a description of the totemic or dreaming animals and plants (Strehlow 1910b: 5). The vocabulary includes names of ancestral beings and spirits, verb forms and adjectives that are used in these myths and descriptions of flora and fauna.

The large number of words for different plants, animals, reptiles and insects—including those that appear in the mythology of the Aranda and Luritja—not only reflected their ontology but also, in Carl's view, their daily engagement with the environment and an Indigenous natural history, 'as the totems of the Aranda' usually belonged to the animal and plant world, reflecting their knowledge of the natural world[19] (Strehlow 1910b: 5). Strehlow published a list of Aranda and Luritja totems containing 442 totems or dreamings, of which 411 were animals and plants (Strehlow 1908: 61–74). Of these, 312 were used as food or as stimulants. There are many other plants and animals listed in his dictionary.

19 Carl Strehlow to N.W. Thomas, mid to end of 1906 (SH-SP-6-1, Strehlow Research Centre).

The dictionary also abounds in useful and important data on social classification, in particular a large number of kinship terms that are mostly still in use in central Australia. The kinship system encompasses the whole population, with the ability to describe the closeness of different relationships. In his work about social life he showed how the two different section systems connected with each other (see Strehlow 1913: 62–89). For example, his account of the 'marriage order' starts with the basic division that organises Aranda people into two groups (exogamous moieties)[20] called *Nákarakia* ('our people') and *Etnákarakia* ('those people') or *Maljanuka* ('the ones belonging to the other group'). These terms are not names for one or the other moiety but were reciprocally used by both groups (Strehlow 1913: 62). Today Arandic people still refer to such groupings and use the section and subsection systems called 'skin' by Aboriginal people in central Australia. The Aranda system is compatible with others in the broader region. The skin or section/subsection systems cross-cut linguistic and social boundaries and facilitate group interaction, ceremonial gatherings and marriage. Strehlow charted the Aranda system in the following way:

Gruppe: A.		B.		C.
Purula	m. +	Pananka	w.:	Kamara.
Kamara	m. +	Paltara	w.:	Purula.
Ngala	m. +	Knuraia	w.:	Mbitjana.
Mbitjana	m. +	Bangata	w.:	Ngala.
Gruppe B.		A.		C.
Pananka	m. +	Purula	w.:	Bangata.
Paltara	m. +	Kamara	w.:	Knuraia.
Knuraia	m. +	Ngala	w.:	Paltara.
Bangata	m. +	Mbitjana	w.:	Pananka.

Figure 26: Arandic subsection or skin chart (Strehlow 1913: 63).

Source: Strehlow Research Centre, Alice Springs.

20 Moieties (halves) divide the social world of a people into two groups that are sociocentric. The same people are always grouped together regardless from whose perspective one is considering people. The division into moieties is evident in a number of social behaviours, ceremonial proceedings and in relationships to land.

Knowledge of the kin terminology and subsection system are indispensable for the understanding of all social institutions and ceremonial proceedings in central Australia, which includes a vast array of public as well as restricted rituals belonging to both men and women. These involve songs connected to myths and ceremonies. Strehlow (1910b, 1911) documented 59 Aranda ceremonies and their associated songs and 21 Loritja ceremonies. Many of these ceremonies were performed individually in public as well as in restricted ceremonial forums or as part of the initiation process that, according to Strehlow, had seven stages at the turn of the twentieth century (Strehlow 1913). The last ceremony[21] was the largest and most prestigious ceremonial gathering, drawing men, women and children together from far places to witness the conclusion of the rites that brought young men into adulthood. According to Carl Strehlow's research, in his time all types of ceremonies and performances had either the purpose of *intitjiuma* meaning 'to initiate into something, to show how something is done' or *mbatjalkatiuma* meaning 'to bring about, make fertile, improve conditions of' (Strehlow 1910b: 1–2) and had public aspects that were witnessed by women, children and the uninitiated. At many stages of initiation, for example, women played a role, performing dances called *ntaperama*[22] (Strehlow 1913: 19) or smoking ceremonies called *ulbuntakelama*[23] (Strehlow 1913: 36). The general public was usually never far off from the privileged procedures offering practical, ceremonial and emotional support.

Strehlow's myth and song texts are accompanied by drawings, descriptions of who performs what at which places in the central Australian landscape, how it is performed, what ceremonial artefacts are used and their purposes. Descriptions and interpretations of material culture are interspersed throughout Strehlow's work to illustrate and enhance the text. His collection included well over 1,000 objects and mundane artefacts that he had sent to Germany.[24] He sent carrying dishes, boomerangs,[25] spears, spear throwers, sacred objects,[26] clubs, shields, hair strings, stone knives and axes, digging sticks, chains made of native beans, and many other

21 Spencer and Gillen's *engwura* and Strehlow's *inkura*.

22 This is a verb meaning 'do the dance *ntapa*'; the dance is called *ntapa*.

23 This is a verb meaning 'put into smoke'; smoke is called *ulbunta*.

24 F.C.A. Sarg (1911) and Vatter (1925) used his collection for their publications.

25 F.C.A. Sarg described in *Die Australischen Bumerangs im Städtischen Völkermuseum* (1911) some of Strehlow's boomerangs.

26 Carl Strehlow to von Leonhardi, probably 10 December 1907 (SH-SP-15-1, Strehlow Research Centre).

items that he lists in this dictionary and the last volume of his work (Strehlow 1920: 8–14) to his editor in Germany. The items mentioned in the dictionary were for most part produced by Aranda and Luritja people, though there are terms for some pieces that were not manufactured in the region and were not recognised by the people I worked with.

The intellectual context of the dictionary

The comparative dictionary and grammar that von Leonhardi had hoped would be an integral part of Carl Strehlow's publications was to provide the key for the interpretation of the extensive collections of the Aranda and Luritja text materials. It was to contribute to the understanding of Aranda and Luritja people's worldviews and show that their languages as well as cultures were distinct. The richness of the linguistic data was also to show that Aboriginal languages were no different to any others in the world and could express the full range of human cognition. Thus, the broader purpose of such a language study or ethnolinguistic project around 1900 had not only empirical dimensions, but was as much theoretical and philosophical in orientation.

The German language tradition that was a hallmark of nineteenth-century German anthropology was in some ways related to Lutheran language theory and practice that reached back to Martin Luther's reformation. It had been a crucial part of Luther's treatises to spread the gospel in German rather than in Latin or even a German rendition of the Vulgate. Luther preached that the word of God was to be taught in vernacular and translated into a people's mother tongue (Wendt 2001: 8; Moore 2015: 39). As a consequence, in the nineteenth century it was characteristic of German Protestant mission theology and practice to pay special attention to a people's language and its implications for idiom and other dimensions of culture (Schild 2004: 54). These studies of Indigenous languages often resulted in the production of grammars and dictionaries as well as collections of myth texts and other aspects of cultures.

German missionaries in Australia brought this linguistic tradition with them. Among the missionaries, it went without saying that they had to learn the language of the people they were sent to serve. This tradition dovetailed with linguistic views of the emerging German discipline of anthropology about the importance of language. One of the main principles of German anthropological thought emanating from Herderian and Humboldtian philosophy, which were expressed by Bastian, Virchow and their anthropological circle in Germany, and by Boas in North America, was the focus on language as the main tool of its empiricism. The meticulous and diligent study and collection of linguistic material (grammar, vocabulary and original text) became central, and was the most important feature of nineteenth-century German anthropology and ethnology.

Probably the main reason for the emphasis on language was that it was seen as the embodiment of a people's culture or spirit, its *Geist*. Literally *Geist* means 'spirit' or 'ghost', however, in this context it means 'the essence of a people' or 'the spirit (mind/intellect/genius) of a people'. This view has its roots in German eighteenth-century philosophy that emphasised the ideas of particularism opposing progressivism and deduction. It became part of mainstream German intellectual life and absorbed into anthropological thought (Marchand 1982: 20).

Thinkers who influenced the development of this sort of anthropological thinking were Johann Gottfried Herder (1744–1803), Georg Foster (1754–1794), the von Humboldt bothers, Wilhelm (1767–1835) and Alexander (1769–1859) as well as Immanuel Kant (1724–1804) to some degree, although Herder was critical of race theory (Mühlmann 1968: 62) and in particular of Kant's. Herder, the founder of German historical particularism, was influential on anthropological thinking, because he was interested in the differences in cultures over time, and from one people to another (Adams 1998: 271).

Herder rejected the concept of race as well as the French dogma of the uniform development of civilisation. He believed that there were many unique sets of values transmitted through history and that civilisations had to be viewed from within—that is, in terms of their own development and purpose (Berlin 1976: 174). Humanity was made up of a great diversity, language being a crucial manifestation that expressed a people's particularity. The *Geist* of a people, he believed, was embodied in their language, which included oral literature and song texts of Indigenous peoples. Therefore language became critical in German anthropological research and a precondition of authoritative ethnography. To achieve their Herderian goal, (i.e. to document the various manifestations of cultures as completely as possible), German anthropologists were committed to inductive science and an empirical methodology. They stressed the need to gather as much information as possible before attempting to generate theories about human difference (Penny and Bunzl 2003: 15).

True to the paradigms of nineteenth-century German anthropology, Strehlow's editor believed that thorough empirical research had to be conducted before universal laws pertaining to humankind and ideas of their origin could be developed. Language was the main tool for such an empirical study of cultures. His editor stated that it 'is simply impossible to penetrate the heart of the beliefs of the Australian Aborigines without thorough knowledge of their language'.[27] He perceived language as the embodiment of a people's mind and spirit that was both Herderian and Humboldtian in character. Wilhelm von Humboldt maintained that there were two steps in language research, which needed to be undertaken to be able to make statements about a people's culture and language. The first step was to describe the structure of the language (grammar and dictionary) and the next its use (*Gebrauch*) (Humboldt [1820] 1994: 16), by which he meant oral literary text (Foertsch 2001: 113).

Thus, in Strehlow and von Leonhardi's central Australian project language was method and phenomenon and could not be separated from culture. Through language, phenomena like myths and social institutions as well as material culture that seemed similar, related or identical, could be established as specific within their own cultural and linguistic context. Language was not only a research tool, it also had a philosophical dimension, showing how other people thought. Von Leonhardi in particular understood the particularity of a culture and saw language and its literature as a reflection of this specificity. The exact description and recording of language and transcription of original Australian Indigenous text, he believed would give insight into people's 'Anschauungen' (views) and their 'Geist' (spirit).[28]

Kulturkreislehre

Another reason for the emphasis on language in Carl Strehlow's research was that in the period in which the material for *Die Aranda- und Loritja-Stämme in Zentral-Australien* was collected—1904 to 1909—a

27 Von Leonhardi to Carl Strehlow, 17 March 1906.

28 Von Leonhardi to Carl Strehlow, 2 June 1906.

new method and theory in German anthropology was emerging. It was called the *kulturhistorische Methode* (culture-historical method) and *Kulturkreislehre* (culture circle theory). The aim of this diffusionist theory was to chart historical movements of peoples as well as to identify traits of 'culture circles'. One of the obvious traits of a culture circle was language or a language group, which presumably helped to distinguish one circle from the other or suggested overlay and mixing of cultures. Through language comparison, which looked at dialect variations and the possible travel of words, myth and song, along with comparative studies of material culture and social systems, it was believed possible to discover migration patterns and how the distribution of peoples over long periods of time across the globe had occurred. Von Leonhardi may have hoped to clarify with Strehlow's linguistic data what happened at the edges or in transitional zones of culture circles, as Carl Strehlow's mission was located in such a linguistic and cultural transitional region.

Prominent German representatives of diffusionist theory were P.W. Schmidt, Fritz Graebner, Bernhard Ankermann and later also Leo Frobenius. In the first decade of the twentieth century most theorising on the *Kulturkreise* and *-schichten* was undertaken in letters between these men and other scholars (Penny 2002) and most of the anthropologists who would publish on this subject were still developing their methods and theories or out in the field collecting ethnographic and linguistic data as well as material culture to bolster their hypothesis. Only occasionally were short pieces published in German anthropological journals such as *Globus*, *Petermann's Mitteilungen* or *Zeitschrift für Ethnologie*. The first major work on the *Kulturkreislehre* was Graebner's *Methode der Ethnologie* published in 1911 followed by Pater Schmidt's *Die Gliederung der Australischen Sprachen*[29] published between 1912 and 1918 in his journal *Anthropos*.

Strehlow's editor, Moritz von Leonhardi, participated in the early phase of the development of the *Kulturkreislehre* and explored the use of comprehensive descriptions of languages to explain hypotheses of the emerging theory. His understanding of language in the context of the

29 P.W. Schmidt, Die Gliederung der Australischen Sprachen und ihre Beziehungen zu der Gliederung der soziologischen Verhältnisse der australischen Stämme. In: *Anthropos* 7 (1912): 230–51, 463–97, 1014–48; 8 (1913): 526–54; 9 (1914): 980–1018; 12/13 (1917/1918): 437–93, 747–817.

Kulturkreislehre was informed by close reading of the limited amount of existing material in the century's first decade and his correspondence with P.W. Schmidt.

Work on the culture circles and their distribution concentrated initially on material culture and social organisation. The first, very brief linguistic contribution on Australian language in the context of the *Kulturkreislehre* was written by Pater W. Schmidt in 1908. The comparison and classification of language was believed to give insight into ethnic origins, migrations and prehistory. Based on some linguistic evidence extracted from the very limited literature, Schmidt (1908) declared that his findings suggested with certainty that the Aranda were not 'primitive', not an earliest form of inferior culture, as social Darwinism wanted to see them.

Schmidt, as well as Graebner, Foy and Thomas in England, saw the population of Australia not as homogeneous, but consisting of a number of layers of peoples and cultures that at different times in prehistory migrated and partially amalgamated. The oldest layer was believed to have spread from Tasmania and thought to have occupied all of Australia at some stage, surviving in the south-east of the continent. On the Tasmanian layer it was believed that at least two further layers had introduced new cultural elements like totemism, the boomerang and the spear thrower.[30] Schmidt (1908: 869) suggested that a fourth layer originating in New Guinea had swamped the Australian continent from the north and reached its southern extent with the Aranda which, he believed, was evident in his linguistic investigations.

For von Leonhardi it was important to try to establish the links or their absence between the languages and cultures of central and south coast Australia. He speculated that very ancient elements of culture may have been preserved on the southern coasts of Australia where apparently no boomerangs, shields, marriage classes or totemism existed and it:

> would be the very oldest population of Australia, probably the Tasmanian one, which may have been pushed by migration waves with a slightly higher culture and differing language to the south and south east and possibly to the south west coast where they seem to have survived.

'However', he concluded in 1909, 'that is all still very problematic.'[31]

30 Von Leonhardi to Carl Strehlow, 2 March 1909.

31 Von Leonhardi to Carl Strehlow, 12 February 1909.

The theory of culture circles and layers was still very hypothetical and most details unclear at the end of the first decade of the twentieth century. Where the two layers and waves of migrations overlaying the original Tasmanian stratum, for instance, had come from, was still a mystery.[32] It was not even clear what traits needed to be present in a culture circle, to define it as such (Kluckhohn 1936: 138–9), and this problem would never be solved—and thus by mid-century the *Kulturkreislehre* had substantially faded into insignificance. Despite its limitations, the ethnolinguistic data that was amassed in its heyday remain an immensely valuable body of work.

Concluding remark

Carl Strehlow's comparative dictionary and his ethnography *Die Aranda- und Loritja-Stämme in Zentral-Australien* were products of a German nineteenth-century style that was language-based and strictly descriptive. A century after their production, they remain invaluable resources for Aranda and Luritja people. Language was not only method for Strehlow, but proof that the Aranda were part of the universal plurality of humanity. His last public remark on language in *The Register* on 7 December 1921, after 27 years of studies in central Australia, makes this clear. Rejecting evolutionary theory explicitly he wrote that 'the wonderfully structured language of the aborigines, and their religious beliefs'[33] show that their languages and cultures are as sophisticated as any others in the world.

32 Von Leonhardi to Carl Strehlow, 2 March 1909.

33 *The Register*, Adelaide, 7 December 1921.

Figure 27: Carl and Frieda Strehlow in central Australia, 1898.
Source: SRC 07767, Strehlow Research Centre, Alice Springs.

5

Assessing Carl Strehlow's dictionary as linguistic description: Present value and future potential

John Henderson

Introduction

The extent and quality of Carl Strehlow's comparative dictionary makes it an extraordinary work for its time, and in some ways it remains so by current standards. The sheer number of entries—around 7,600—is impressive, and for its time it demonstrates a reasonably sophisticated attempt to characterise meanings. This chapter primarily considers the dictionary as a work of language description—in terms of the analytical concepts of linguistics and the methods of modern lexicography. Understanding the value and limitations of Strehlow's dictionary in these ways provides an appreciation of his achievements in the dictionary, its place in relation to other current Aranda[1] and Luritja language resources, and perhaps most importantly its potential contribution to new resources for these languages.

1 Strehlow's spelling 'Aranda' is used in this chapter, except where it is necessary to distinguish the two modern orthographies of Western Aranda in recent published works.

The first section gives a brief overview of the nature of the dictionary. It considers the context from which the dictionary arose, its contribution to more recent work, and the languages that are represented in it. The next section looks at the basic organisation of information into entries in the dictionary. The following sections then focus in detail on the important grammatical information in different types of entries, and the strategies for characterising meaning. The representation of Aranda sounds in the dictionary is discussed here only as it relates to lexicographical and grammatical matters. The accompanying chapter on the Mission Orthography provides a fuller discussion. The analytical concepts of linguistics used in this chapter are introduced for a broader readership at the relevant points.

Overview

The dictionary is examined here as a work in its own right although it is just one component of Strehlow's overall descriptive work. He also collected and documented numerous traditional texts from Aranda and Luritja people, and wrote an analysis of the grammar and other materials (which include an account of Aranda sign language). The collection of texts is particularly significant because texts can provide a wide range of words and expressions used in a range of contexts—necessary information for a high-quality dictionary. His intellectual work in translating texts from Aranda and Luritja, and in translating Christian materials into these languages, must also have contributed to a sophisticated analysis of the grammar and lexicon of both languages. His dictionary can be evaluated for the accuracy, range and depth of its description of the lexicon, and like any other work of language description those things should be evaluated in terms of the author's goals and methods, and the goals of its audience, and in terms of the principles and practices in language description. For modern readers of the dictionary, it is important to understand the nature of the work in order to interpret the individual entries. It is presented in this volume in a publication format like other modern dictionaries, but the content is not a final version ready for publication. It is a handwritten draft which has many inconsistencies and limitations, and interpreting entries is not always straightforward.

As a historical work the dictionary is a record of the language at an earlier point in time. It both documents the local community's language heritage and offers an understanding of the paths of language change over a period of enormous social change. It is clear that today's Aranda and Luritja are fundamentally the same as the languages of Strehlow's time, but as speakers today get the chance to work through this dictionary it will become clearer how much of the 'old language' has changed or been lost. Some words in the dictionary have not been recognised by those Aranda speakers who have had a chance so far to make their own evaluation, though not all these cases necessarily indicate change or loss in the languages. Strehlow's spelling of the Aranda and Luritja words is in many ways not specific enough to indicate which of the sounds of these languages actually occurs in a given word. His definitions vary widely in detail but are mostly only simple glosses in German, and as useful as they may be, we can see from comparison with modern dictionaries that producing a fuller account of the meaning of a word requires a more developed approach. So in some cases, even very knowledgeable speakers might not recognise Strehlow's entry for a word they actually know. In the cases where speakers actually do not already know the word, it is not straightforward to work out how that word was pronounced and what its precise meaning was.

Strehlow's description of the Western Aranda language was preceded by the impressive work of Hermann Kempe, his missionary predecessor at Hermannsburg 1876–91 and a founder of the mission. Kempe's grammatical description and vocabulary was published in 1891. It seems reasonable to assume that Strehlow was influenced by and benefited from Kempe's work, though it is clear from the much greater size of Strehlow's dictionary that he was seeking a much fuller and more detailed coverage of the vocabulary, and must have developed a deep knowledge of the language. Modern experience in producing dictionaries means we can be confident that Strehlow's dictionary was at enormous expense in terms of time and effort. For one thing, it is significant that it is a large handwritten list that is mostly alphabetically ordered, because this must have been preceded by a method of collecting individual words over time before they could be collated into an ordered list. It may be that he used a common method of starting off with a paper slip for each entry as the word was recorded, and inserting it into the stack of slips at the right place in the alphabetical order. By any method though, the task was enormous in a pre-computer age. Given that the practical aspects of his everyday life in the early mission were very demanding (Lohe 1977), his linguistic and cultural description is an even greater achievement.

This volume describes Strehlow's work as a heritage dictionary. This term recognises not just that it has value as part of Aranda and Luritja history, it recognises that the dictionary is a work of its time and context. People looking for a dictionary of the languages today have a range of modern resources available in the current orthographies. The *Western Arrarnta Picture Dictionary* (Roennfeldt et al. 2006) is a school language resource, in the modern orthography used in school programs and some other contexts in the Hermannsburg area. The *Introductory Dictionary of Western Arrernte* (Breen et al. 2000) is in the alternative modern orthography that was used for some years at Yipirinya School in Alice Springs.[2] The *Pintupi/Luritja Dictionary* (Hansen and Hansen 1992) is an extensive dictionary of the Western Dialects adjacent to the Western Aranda area.

Although Strehlow's dictionary is being published for the first time now, it has had a major influence on the modern dictionaries produced in the last few decades, as well as on the unpublished dictionary (and other work) produced by his son T.G.H. Strehlow. Carl Strehlow's dictionary played an important role in the initial stages of the Arandic languages dictionaries program at the Institute for Aboriginal Development (IAD) in Alice Springs. It was the largest source used in developing a starter list for collecting information on words in different Arandic languages (together with work by Ken Hale, Gavan Breen and other researchers). The words in the starter list were used as prompts for speakers to provide information on their own language, and their information is what the modern dictionaries are based on. The series of major dictionaries published by IAD includes the *Eastern and Central Arrernte to English Dictionary* (Henderson and Dobson 1994), the *Introductory Dictionary of Western Arrernte* (Breen et al. 2000), the *Central & Eastern Anmatyerr to English Dictionary* (Green 2010), the *Kaytetye to English Dictionary* (Turpin and Ross 2012) and the *Alyawarr to English Dictionary* (Green 1992; second edition by Blackman et al., forthcoming). In relation to Western Desert languages, the IAD program also produced the *Pitjantjatjara/Yankunytjatjara Dictionary* (Goddard 1996), and has contributed directly and indirectly to other works, including Glass and Hackett's (2003) *Ngaanyatjarra & Ngaatjatjarra to English Dictionary*. The dictionaries program has also contributed in various ways to some of the *Picture Dictionary* volumes published by IAD Press.

2 See Chapter 6 in this volume for a detailed discussion of the differences between the various orthographies.

With these major dictionaries published, and with smaller works and other research, it is now feasible to plan a combined dictionary of the Arandic languages, probably as a digital resource. Such a dictionary should include historical content, especially from Strehlow's dictionary but also from other early sources. Together with the entries from the various individual modern dictionaries, it would document the connectedness, difference and change within the Arandic languages. It would be a major ongoing resource for the Arandic communities and for Australian Indigenous studies more generally.

The languages

This is a comparative multilingual dictionary in that it includes Aranda, Luritja, German and some Dieri (now also written as Diyari).[3] It is not an etymological dictionary: it does not attempt to relate the words of these Australian languages to each other as descendants of common ancestral languages. It also does not identify historical borrowings from one language to another, though it is reasonably clear that the neighbouring Aranda and Luritja languages have borrowed words from each other over a long period of time. A full analysis of this borrowing remains to be done, and no doubt this dictionary, along with others, will be key sources for that analysis.

Since Strehlow's spelling of Aranda and Luritja does not accurately and consistently represent the sounds of those languages, in this chapter his spelling of an Aranda word will generally be followed by its spelling in the two current orthographies for Western Aranda. The two alternative spellings are separated by a double-slash '//', so for example *tanalama {tarnalhama//ternelheme}* 'stretch yourself out'. The first alternative is in the Finke River Mission (FRM) orthography following the model in Roennfeldt et al.'s *Western Arrarnta Picture Dictionary*, and the second is in the IAD orthography following the model in Breen et al.'s (2000) *Introductory Dictionary of Western Arrernte*. For Strehlow's spelling of Luritja words, a modern spelling is provided following the model of Hansen and Hansen's (1992) *Pintupi/Luritja Dictionary*.

3 Interestingly, the names 'Luritja' and 'Aranda'—in any spelling—do not appear in Kempe (1891a), and in fact he gives no names for any varieties. However, the name of the Arandic language at Charlotte Waters was recorded in 1875 by Giles as 'Arrinda' (Taplin 1879).

Strehlow's dictionary is in some ways basically two dictionaries: an Aranda to German dictionary, and an Aranda to Luritja dictionary. Aranda is clearly the primary language in this work overall. The most obvious evidence is that the list is alphabetically ordered—to the extent that it is—according to the Aranda words. Also, while almost 10 per cent of the 7,500-plus entries give an Aranda word with no equivalent in Luritja, there is only a handful of entries where a Luritja word is given without an equivalent in Aranda.

A multilingual dictionary like this may suggest to some readers that Aranda and Luritja are fundamentally equivalent in the meanings of words, that each word in one of these languages has a single corresponding word with the same meaning in the other language. This is generally not true of any two languages (though it might be true of very close dialects of the same language). It is not true of Aranda and Luritja. Certainly, there are many cases where there are corresponding words with the same meaning—or close to it—but there are many cases where there are not.

Firstly, there are cases where Strehlow gives the same Luritja word for two different Aranda words, for example:

Aranda	**Luritja**	
tākama	*alani*	ein Loch in einen hohlen Baum hauen (mit dem Beil). {chop a hole in a hollow tree (with an axe), smash, break}
altjurilama	*alani*	ein Loch machen, öffnen (Tür) {make a hole, open (door)}

In modern dictionaries, we see that Aranda *altjurilama* {*altjurelama*//*altywerileme*} and Luritja *alani* {*alaṉi*} both have at least two senses, (i) to make a hole or opening in something, and (ii) to open a door, hatch etc. However, Aranda *tākama* {*taakama*//*takeme*} has a different meaning: 'smash in, break through, make something collapse (like a house) or cave in (like a burrow)' (Breen et al. 2000). Luritja *alaṉi* and Aranda *taakama*//*takeme* can be both applicable to some particular situations, depending on the physical nature of the situation, but there are also other situations where *alaṉi* is applicable but *taakama*//*takeme* is not. For example, *alaṉi* is used to refer to the normal way of cutting open the belly of a kangaroo to gut it, but Aranda *taakama*//*takeme* is not.

Conversely, in cases such as the following, there are multiple entries for the same Aranda word, with each entry apparently picking out the meaning in different contexts, and for each of these there is a different Luritja equivalent. In this particular case, the entries are consecutive, and it may be that Strehlow has specifically used separate entries to show the relationship between the Aranda and corresponding Luritja expressions.

Aranda	Luritja	
jurankama	*kurangañi* (Rausch, Wind)	sausen (Wind), heulen (Sturm) whistle (wind), howl (storm)
jurankama	*lulumanañi*	rauschen (Meer) sough (sea)[4]
jurankama	*wilijiri wonkani*	fauchen (Schlange) hiss (snake)

Finally, in many other cases, such as the following example, a number of Luritja words are given in the same entry. This should not be taken to mean that these words are necessarily all equivalent in Luritja.

Aranda	Luritja	
nilkna	*ngurtu, kanka, mulata*	heimlich {secretly}

On the basis of the modern dictionaries of related dialects, Aranda *nilkna* {*nyilkngal/nyelknge*} here is roughly 'secretly, stealing; theft' while the Luritja words would appear to have different meanings to each other, although related:

Strehlow	Current spelling	
ngurtu	*ngurrtju*	'selfishly, greedily, without sharing' (Pitjantjatjara/Yankunytjatjara, Goddard 1996)

4 This gloss may seem surprising since these languages are spoken so far from any ocean, but there is also *laia* {laiya//laye} 'sea', 'lake'. It is not clear what local phenomena this might have referred to, but very large bodies of water may have been known about second-hand through a chain of cultural contact between language groups.

mulata	*mulyaṯa*	'illegally, without permission, against a prohibition' (Ngaanyatjarra/Ngaatjatjarra, Glass and Hackett 2003)
kanka	*kaaṉka*	'crow' and metaphorically, 'light-fingered {man/woman}, someone who hangs around suspiciously' (Pitjantjatjara/Yankunytjatjara, Goddard 1996)

Dialects

The Aranda words in the dictionary are said to be from the 'dialect of the Upper Finke area', and today the dictionary is often identified as the Western Aranda dialect, which is strongly associated with Ntaria (Hermannsburg) and neighbouring communities. However, the situation is more complex than this. Firstly, there are close to 300 words annotated by Strehlow as Northern (156 words), Southern (123) and Eastern varieties (8). Most of these are consistent with currently known dialect differences. In about a quarter of these instances, the entry also indicates what the corresponding Western Aranda form is. Secondly, there is evidence of words that are recognised today as other dialects, but are not annotated as such in the dictionary. For example, Strehlow's *matja* 'fire' does not occur in the modern Western Aranda dictionaries, but is found in the southern dialect Pertame (as *metye*). It may be that this type of situation reflects a more mixed population at Hermannsburg in Strehlow's time, with some speakers of dialects from other areas. Dialect divisions are not by nature clear-cut, so it may also be that in some cases the local dialects simply had more than one word with the same meaning—synonyms—and one or more of these synonyms just happened to be shared with another dialect, as so many words are. Finally, it is likely that there were originally smaller dialect distinctions—with perhaps just a few differences—within the 'Upper Finke area'.

The Western Desert language is both traditionally and currently spoken over an enormous area with many local dialects, shading from one into another. Strehlow identifies the Western Desert dialect in the dictionary as 'Loritja' for the first third of the notebook and as Kukatja for the remainder. Speakers of the dialect today usually label their language as Luritja. The naming of varieties of the Western Desert language is traditionally multilayered and somewhat variable depending on context and purpose, but it seems clear that Strehlow's Kukatja and Luritja both refer to basically the same variety.[5] Strehlow reports that Kukatja was the name speakers used for themselves, and Luritja is the name originally used for them by Aranda speakers. In the dictionary, Strehlow identifies only a handful of words as belonging to other specific Western Desert dialects outside of the immediate area. All of these involve more southern or western dialects.

In some of the entries where more than one word is given for Luritja or Aranda, they are at least related in meaning, but may not all be from exactly the same dialect. For Western Desert dialects like Luritja, there is often a number of synonyms for a given meaning (Hansen 1984). The individual synonyms in a dialect are often also found in other dialects—but not necessarily all synonyms in every dialect. For example, in the following case Strehlow presents both Luritja *itára* and *ngápiri* as equivalent to Aranda *para*. Each of these words also occurs in other Western Desert dialects, but as Goddard (1996) shows, there are dialects where only one of these two occurs. Note also the small local differences in meaning in this example.[6]

Aranda	**Luritja**	
para	*itára, ngápiri*	Gummibaum (*Eucalyptus rostrata*) {gumtree}

Strehlow	**Current**	**Dialect**	
ngápiri	*ngapiri*	Pitjantjatjara (not Yankunytjatjara)	'river red gum (*Eucalyptus camaldulensis*)'
itára	*itara*	'some areas only'	'river red gum (*Eucalyptus camaldulensis*)'
		Pitjantjatjara & Yankunytjatjara	'bloodwood (*Eucalyptus opaca*)' (Goddard 1996)

5 The term *Kukatja* is also used for a more remote variety of the Western Desert language spoken at Balgo in Western Australia and, traditionally, it appears to have been used to refer to other Western Desert varieties which distinctively use the word *kuka* for 'meat'.

6 The river red gum is now generally classified as *Eucalyptus camaldulensis* rather than Strehlow's *Eucalyptus rostrata*. The bloodwood was reclassified as *Corymbia opaca* in the 1990s.

This is part of a complex pattern of synonyms in and across Western Desert dialects. Hansen (1984) describes each dialect as having many cases where there is a number of synonyms for a given meaning, though in the individual cases in a given dialect some synonyms are used more than others at a particular point in time. One factor is that if a particular synonym is placed under taboo following the death of a person with a similar-sounding name, other synonyms can be used instead. Speakers are also typically familiar with synonyms that they attribute to dialects other than their own.

Entries, words and expressions

One way to understand the basic organisation of information in a dictionary, and therefore to compare dictionaries, is to ask the question: *What kind of list is this dictionary?* In this section, we will try to answer this question for Strehlow's dictionary.

Basic entry structure and ordering

The basic structural considerations for a dictionary entry are (i) the basis for what constitutes a distinct entry, and (ii) what type and level of information is provided in each entry. There is of course a wide range of possibilities for a given dictionary depending on the information that is available to the compilers, the resources and time that is applied to the work, and the compiler's goals for the use of the dictionary. For example, on the first point here some dictionaries, such as Goddard's (1996) dictionary of Pitjantjatjara and Yankunytjatjara, have entries for individual grammatical suffixes, whereas others such as Hansen and Hansen's (1992) Pintupi/Luritja dictionary do not. In general, Strehlow does not have separate entries for suffixes, but he does annotate around 50 items as postpositions, a group which includes postpositional particles or clitics, and the odd suffix.

In order to get a broad overview of the structure of entries in Strehlow's dictionary we can compare here a single entry, focusing on Luritja, with corresponding entries from a range of dictionaries[7] of Western Desert language dialects that are closely related to Luritja. Note that *nangañi/nyanganyi* and *nyangu* are different tense forms of the same verb.

Strehlow Dictionary (1901–09)

răma sehen nangañi {see, look, …}

Martutjarra Luritja (Cook 1982)

nyangu (wa) Vt see, look at

Pintupi/Luritja (Hansen and Hansen 1992)

nyangu (wa) v. looked; saw; the norm is for limited eye contact in conversations and addressing large gatherings; prolonged eye contact which is the European norm can be offensive, implying that you don't trust or recognise the person; prolonged eye contact with the opposite sex can be interpreted as a sexual advance; see ngurrtju<u>n</u>u, nyirrkingu, warinyangu, nyirrkinyirrkinpa, pinkurrwarra<u>n</u>u, tjarangka<u>n</u>u, taarrnyinangu, pinkulutingu, yinawarra<u>n</u>u, rupungu, mira<u>n</u>u.

Pitjantjatjara/Yankunytjatjara (Goddard 1996)

nyanganyi *transitive verb (ng)*

1. see, watch, look at, notice: Ankulala nyakuku? Shall we go have a look? / *Wanyuli arka<u>r</u>a nyawa!* Let's have a look! / *Wampa. Ngayulu nyakunytja wiya.* Search me. I haven't seen (him). / *Ngayulu pu<u>l</u>ka<u>r</u>a puku<u>l</u>aripai mamangku kuka katinyangka nyakula.* I used to be so happy when I saw (my) father bringing meat. / *Tjitji tju<u>t</u>a pakuringkupai mungangka tipi nyakunytjatjanu.* The kids get tired (during the day) after watching TV at night. / *Wanyuli ma<u>l</u>aku ara nyakunytjikitja.* Let's just go back and check. / *Munul ankula ankula mitu<u>n</u>u ka<u>l</u>aya tjina, pu<u>l</u>ka alatji<u>t</u>u. Munul mawa<u>n</u>a<u>r</u>a nyangu ma<u>n</u>ngungka pupanyangka.* After a while she came upon some emu tracks, really big ones. And she followed and saw (an emu) hunched over its nest.

7 Cook's (1982) entry is from a relatively short vocabulary within an undergraduate Honours thesis, rather than a stand-alone dictionary, but it does represent a useful comparison as a dictionary entry structure intermediate between Strehlow's and the more extensive modern dictionaries.

2. find: *Cassette panya nyuntu nyangu?* Have you found your cassette player? / *Kaya minyma tjuṯangku ankula ankula mina puṯu nyangu.* The women went off but couldn't find (any) water.

3. (with purposive object ending -ku/-mpa) look for.

4. (of telegram, letter, etc.) get, receive: *Telegram-ṉa iyaṉu, paluṟu nyangu. Munu yaaltji-yaaltji mitingi pitjanytja wiya.* I sent (him) a telegram, and he got it. So how come he didn't come (to) the meeting.

nyangu saw (past); nyangangi was watching, would see (past continuous); nyangama could see, keep watching (imperative continuous); nyakuku might see (future); nyakula having seen, on seeing (serial form); nyakunytja (nominal form); nyakupai used to see/watch (characteristic); nyawa look out! (imperative).

anganyanganyi look around to see whether it's safe, be on the lookout for danger (anga- 'block').

nguḻu nyangama keep watch on, keep an eye on (nguḻu 'wary'): *Nyuntunku pika palatja uti nguḻu nyangama.* You should mind that injury of yours.

nyakula waṉaṉi follow (wan_an_i) with the eyes, watch something as it moves along.

nyakula wantinyi ignore, leave alone: *Kuwarimpayal nyakulalta wantinyi palu nganaṉa ngalkupai tjulpu tjuṯa.* These days they (kids) leave them alone but we used to eat birds (when we were kids).

para-nyanganyi look around.

nyakukatinyi transitive verb (Ø)

1. look for while going along: *Maḻu kutjupala nyakukatima.* We should keep a look out for another kangaroo as we go along.

2. watch over an extended period of time.

nyakulinanyi transitive verb (n)

look for something while going along / *Ma-pitjala nganan_a put_u nyakulinangi, mingkuḻpaku.* As we went along we were looking around in vain for native tobacco.

In terms of the types of information, Strehlow's entry clearly has the simplest structure here, with a single Luritja word and a one-word German gloss, 'sehen' {look, see, …}. Cook (1982) adds grammatical information on each verb's conjugation—identified by the label '(wa)'—and its transitivity—'Vt' to indicate a transitive verb. Strehlow explicitly indicates grammatical information such as transitivity only sporadically. It is clear though from his 1910 grammatical notes that he was well aware of the details of Aranda and Luritja grammar. Hansen and Hansen's (1992) entry further adds cultural information that is presented as relevant to this particular word, on eye contact in this case.

The Pintupi/Luritja entry also lists a range of cross-references to other words with related meanings in that dictionary. For example, the first cross-reference *ngurrtjunu* is defined in its entry as 'examined, tested, inspected; to inspect articles with a view to choosing the best one; to look over an object carefully'. Such cross-references have two functions. Firstly, they indirectly add to the definition of *nyangu* by identifying the area(s) of meaning that the word falls in, and point to the aspects of meaning which these related words share with *nyangu*. Secondly, the cross-references indirectly point to the aspects of meaning which distinguish the words from each other. For the language learner, the cross-references can identify the choices to be made in selecting an appropriate word. This type of information can also come from the Finder section of the Pintupi/Luritja dictionary where the entries invite the user to consider what the most appropriate word might be, for example:

> **saw**: rupungu, tjarangkanu, miranu, nyuulykunu, yinawarranu, nyangu.

Goddard (1996) does not provide any cross-references to related words in the particular Pitjantjatjara/Yankunytjatjara (P/Y) entry above, though this dictionary does indicate synonyms in many other entries. The semantic analysis is more sophisticated in distinguishing four specific senses within the range of meaning of the word, and the explication of the meanings of these senses is enriched by providing examples of use in different situations, and translations of these examples. The entry also provides additional grammatical information, a list of the different tense forms: 'nyangu saw (past); nyangangi…'. This is not routinely provided in verb entries in this dictionary because there is a regular pattern of such inflectional forms for each verb conjugation. Without explicitly stating so, the inflectional forms are listed in the *nyanganyi* entry because some of them are irregular (i.e. different from what would be expected for a standard NG-class verb).

Another obvious aspect of the P/Y dictionary is that it groups together as subentries in one complex entry a set of expressions that are based on *nyanganyi*. Strehlow's dictionary also provides such a set of expressions, but they are all independent entries. See the sample below (leaving out the Aranda equivalents). This set is more extensive than in the P/Y dictionary *nyanganyi* entry, primarily because Strehlow is providing these Luritja expressions with the intent of matching each of the Aranda expressions he lists.

sich umsehen	*nakulaenni* *{nyakulayini (?)}*[8]	'to look around (refl.)'
spähend stehen	*nakulakanjini* *{nyakula kanyini}*	'stand looking'
übersehen, nicht sehen	*nakula kanjini* *{nyakula kanyini}*	'overlook, not see'
übersehen, nicht sehen	*ninkiltunkulá nangañi* *{<?> nyanganyi}*	'overlook, not see'
mit eigenen Augen sehen	*kurunka nangañi* *{kurungka nyanganyi}*	'see with own eyes'
mit dem Auge zwinkern	*kuruterbaterbara nangañi* *{kuru-<?> nyanganyi}*	'wink with the eye'
(Gott sehen), träumen	*tukura nangañi* *{tjukurra nyanganyi}*	'(see God), to dream'
sieh! Seht!	*nauai!* *{nyawayi!}*	'see! Look!'
wiedersehen (v. Freunden)	*ngaparku nangañi* *{ngaparrku nyanganyi}* *nakula pungañi* *{nyakula punganyi}*	'see again (friends)'

8 The forms in modern Luritja spelling are the author's interpretation based on the form and meaning given by Strehlow and the available descriptions of neighbouring Western Desert dialects. Interpretation by knowledgeable speakers of Luritja may remove the uncertainties here.

(viele) einander sehen, wieder sehen	*nakunakulapungañi* *{nyakunyakula punganyi}*	'see again'
(herankommen) sehen	*ngalanangañi* *{ngalya-nyanganyi}*	'see (approaching)'
sehen	*nangañi* *{nyanganyi}*	'see'
mit eigenen Augen sehen	*kurultu nangañi* *{kurultu(?) nyanganyi}*	'see with one's own eyes'
zur Seite sehen	*talbanku nangañi* *{tjalpangku(?) nyanganyi}*	'look to the side'
schielen	*kuru niltunku nangañi* *{kuru ngil̲tungka(?) nyanganyi}*	'be cross-eyed'
übersehen	*ninkiltunkula nangañi* *{<?> nyanganyi}*	'overlook'
bei der Rückkehr sehen	*ngalanakulakulbañi* *{ngalya-nyakula kulpanyi}*	'see on the return'
(liegen) sehen	*manangañi* *{ma-nyanganyi}*	'see (lying)'
vor sich liegen sehen	*manakukatiñi* *{ma-nyakukatinyi}*	'see it lying in front of oneself'
auf der Wanderung erblicken	*nangañi jenkula* *{nyanganyi yankula}*	'see on the walk'

These separate entries above are not all actually consecutive in Strehlow's dictionary.

Unlike the P/Y dictionary, Strehlow's is not organised specifically so that separate but related Luritja expressions are grouped together, though this does result coincidentally in some cases. Mostly there is not even an indication of the relationship between expressions like the above (except for a few cross-references). Aranda related expressions are often grouped together simply because of the alphabetical ordering. This happens because of the particular facts of derived word forms in Aranda, and also in some cases because of the way Strehlow's spelling under-differentiates the sounds in words. There are a few cases, though, where Strehlow ignores alphabetical order in order to group related expressions together. These mostly involve multi-word expressions, as we can see in the set of consecutive entries below where none of the indented lines would be in that position if ordered strictly alphabetically. The indenting itself explicitly represents these as subentries of *ankama {ngkama//ngkeme}*. The choice of which expressions are presented as subentries can be inconsistent: we can see more words below related to *ngkama// ngkeme* that are distinct entries, with unrelated words occurring in between in some cases. There is no indenting in most such cases in the dictionary.

ankama	...	say, speak, talk, bleat (sheep), crow (birds), rustle (trees)
bailba ankama	...	talk/speak unintelligible
barbuta ankama	...	talk/speak unintelligible
etatua ankama	...	talk for a very long time
erilkna ankama, entára ankama	...	speak loud
ritjinja ankama	...	speak softly
ankanankana	...	speaker
ankalabuma	...	ask for, beg for, hum (beetle)
ankaúerama	...	discuss with (men)
ankalelama	...	trs. produce sounds
ankaratnapallanama	...	say in chorus, twit and sing in the choir
inkana	...	all
ankankalintama	...	ascend singing (bird)
inkanga	...	armpit
ankāra	...	the juice (of caterpillars, of fruit), type of tree

We can also see another aspect of entry ordering here that relates to the handwritten nature of the original and its status as a draft. The words *inkana* and *inkanga* above, which are well out of alphabetical order, were originally written as *ankana* and *ankanga* respectively and then overwritten with the initial 'i'. The correct forms also occur later in roughly their expected place in alphabetical ordering.

Now that the dictionary has been transcribed into a digital form, there are clear opportunities here to re-present the information to both make expressions easier to find and to indicate the relationships between them. The Aranda expressions in the entries could be sorted into consistent alphabetical order, and a reversal could also list the Luritja expressions in alphabetical order. While this would improve usability for some purposes, we should be aware that each of Strehlow's entries was written in the context of its neighbouring entries, and the original ordering may therefore be necessary to help interpret an entry. In a digital version of the dictionary, normal searching would make it simpler to find words even when they are in quite distant entries. In a more sophisticated digital version, entries could be linked to explicitly show the relationships between them, and though this would be a fairly large task it would make it possible to present to the user a set of related expressions for comparison.

Single and multi-word expressions

In nearly 90 per cent of entries there is a single Aranda headword, as illustrated in the example of *răma* 'see' above. Most of the remainder have multi-word expressions, two or more synonyms, or in just a few cases an example sentence. There are various types of multi-word expressions, including classifier constructions such as *manna inkua* below where the classifier nominal *manna {marna//merne}* PLANT FOOD combines with the nominal *inkua* to focus on this plant as a source of food.

inkua, manna inkua {ingkwa//ingkwe, marna ingkwa// merne ingkwe}	Schilf, dessen Wurzeln gegessen werden	reed, its roots are eaten {bulrush}
untjala ngama {untjala kngama// untyele kngeme}	auf der Schulter tragen (kleine Kinder)	carry on shoulder (small children)

The distinction between single headword and multi-word expressions is not always as straightforward as it might seem. To an extent, it is a matter of writing conventions whether some expressions are written as a single word or as two or more words. There may also be variation between the possibilities. This is a common situation in various languages, including English, where some compounds can be written in different ways, for example *car park*, *car-park* and *carpark* are all in common use. Similarly, among the Luritja forms above related to *nyanganyi* 'see, look, …', Strehlow clearly gives a two-word version *nakula kanjini* and a one-word version *nakulakanjini* for the same expression (*nyakula kanyini*) in different places. In a handful of cases, Strehlow even presents a short sentence as a single word:

Strehlow's spelling:	*ngamilai!*	
Modern spelling:	*ngaama* *ng-ame*	*ilai* il-Ø-aye
Analysis:	2ndPersonSingularSubject-Contrast	say-Imperative-Emphasis
Strehlow's translation:	*Du selbst sagen* {Say it yourself!}	

Citation forms

Dictionary entries are, of course, based on a headword or expression. The headword is typically a conventional citation form which actually represents a whole set of inflected words. For example, most English dictionaries do not have separate entries for *walk*, *walks*, *walking* and *walked*. They have a single entry which expresses the idea that while this is a set of distinct words in one sense, they also together constitute a single word in another sense. In the second sense here, the overall set of these words constitutes the lexeme WALK. The specific words *walk*, *walks*, *walking* and *walked* are the inflectional forms of the lexeme WALK. In a dictionary, one of the inflectional forms (e.g. *walk*) is typically selected as the citation form that represents the lexeme. Citation forms like this are typically chosen by some general principle in a dictionary, rather than on a case-by-case basis. The citation form of verbs in English can be described in grammatical terms as the base form (because it does not include a suffix: *walk* in contrast to *walk-s*, *walk-ing* and *walk-ed*), or as the infinitive form (which is the form that occurs when tense is not represented, especially in the infinitive construction with the preposition *to*, e.g. '*to walk*' or '*to be*'). For English, the citation forms for nouns and verbs are a very well-established tradition going back at least as far as the early dictionaries of the sixteenth century.

When there is no earlier tradition of dictionaries to follow in a language, the citation form is selected by lexicographers on the basis of factors such as whether speakers have a sense that one inflectional form is basic in each lexeme, or even on the basis of common translation practices in the community. It may also take into account the target audience and the ways they are expected to use the dictionary. Sometimes a citation form is chosen because the form itself indicates important grammatical information about the lexeme.

In both Aranda and Luritja, most vocabulary items have a number of distinct inflectional forms: nominals (nouns, adjectives etc.) have different case forms and verbs have different forms according to tense etc., as we see in the following tables (which show only some of the inflectional categories for each).

		Aranda	Luritja
child (intransitive subject)	Nominative	*katjia//ketyeye*	*pipirri(nya)*
child (transitive subject)	Ergative	*katjiala// ketyeyele*	*pipirringku*
for a/the child	Purposive	*katjiaka// ketyeyeke*	*pipirriku*
to(wards) a/the child	Allative	*katjiurna// ketyeyewerne*	*pipirrikutu*
from a/the child	Ablative	*katjianga// ketyenge*	*pipirringuru*
…	…	…	…

For nouns in both Aranda and Luritja, it is a typically a straightforward matter of selecting the form without a suffix. In the above table, this is the Nominative case form, and this is the inflectional form that Strehlow chose. For verbs, the choice of a citation form is more complicated. For one thing, in Luritja there is no regular base form which has no suffixes. For example, in the case below, there is no word *patja* corresponding to the English base form 'bite': every inflectional form of this Luritja lexeme has one suffix or another.

		Aranda	Luritja
bites, is biting	PRESENT	*utnhuma*// *uthneme*	*patjani*
will bite	FUTURE	*utnhitjanha*// *utnhetyenhe*	*patjalku*
bite! (an order)	IMPERATIVE	*utnha!*//*utnhe!*	*patjala!*
bit	PAST	*utnhuka*// *utnheke*	*patjanu*
…	…	…	…

In order to assess Strehlow's choice of Present tense as the citation form for verbs, it is necessary to consider the grammatical structure of words in these languages.

Grammatical information

As the comparison with modern central Australian dictionaries above shows, a lexical description typically requires information on the grammar of individual words, both the internal composition of words and relationships between them, and the properties which determine how they form phrases and clauses together, such as transitivity. Strehlow provides explicit information of this kind only sporadically in the dictionary, but some clues can be found in the citation forms, the grouping of entries, and the definitions. In this section, we examine some key aspects of grammatical information relating primarily to verbs.

Verb inflections and verb classes

Strehlow and Arandic lexicographers since him follow Kempe (1891a) in selecting the Present tense form of the Aranda verb as the citation form, for example *ngama* 'carry' {*kngama*//*kngeme*}.[9] Indeed present tense and similar verbal categories are commonly used as citation forms in

9 The earliest known published list of vocabulary in an Arandic language, Christopher Giles's 1875 vocabulary from Charlotte Waters in northern South Australia (published in Taplin 1879), also gives Aranda verbs in the Present form, but the corresponding English verbs are given in the *–ing* participle form, for example 'dying'.

dictionaries of Australian languages. It is the citation form in the modern *Western Arrarnta Picture Dictionary* (Roennfeldt et al. 2006) and the *Introductory Dictionary of Western Arrernte* (Breen et al. 2000). Present tense seems to be a natural citation form for most verbs for Aranda speakers today. It is the form that is typically given in responses to researchers' and learners' questions such as 'How do you say *eat*?' or 'What's the word for *fall*?' However, the Aranda Present is not the only possible answer to such questions: occasionally older speakers especially may give the Aranda Imperative (order) form, presumably because they interpret the English base form as a request for a translation of the English Imperative, for example 'eat!'.

The Aranda Present citation forms are matched in Strehlow's German translations with the infinitive forms of German verbs, which is the standard citation form in German dictionaries. For example, Aranda *răma* {*rama*//*reme*} and Luritja *nangañi* {*nyanganyi*} are glossed as *sehen* (translated into English as 'see, look, …'). Kempe's (1891a) wordlist gives the base/infinitive form of English verbs. Kempe's choice of the Aranda Present as the citation form in his dictionary may actually have been an attempt to match the English, and perhaps German, Infinitive forms. In a rather unclear statement in his grammatical description, he says that the Aranda Present form 'also represents the Infinitive of the verb, there being no other form to indicate it, so that the meaning is, "I do beat," or "I beat."' (1891: 14). Other Aranda forms also correspond to the English and German Infinitive forms in various functions. The distinct Aranda Imperative form would match the English base/infinitive form in its imperative function, for example 'Look!'. The Aranda Purposive form, for example *ritjaka*//*retyeke* 'see-PURP', matches the English '(to) see' and German 'sehen' Infinitive forms in uses such as 'go to see …'.

With just a couple of exceptions, Strehlow cites Luritja verbs in a similar way to the Aranda, that is, in the corresponding Present tense form, e.g. *nangañi* {*nyanganyi*} 'see, look, …'. The recent *Luritja Picture Dictionary* (Hansen et al. 2011) also uses the Present as the citation form, but some other modern dictionaries of Western Desert dialects have chosen differently. Hansen's Pintupi/Luritja dictionary uses the Past Perfective form, as shown in the comparison of entries above: *nyangu* 'saw'. Glass and Hackett's (2003) *Ngaanyatjarra & Ngaatjatjarra to English Dictionary* uses the Future form: *nyaku* 'will see'. The choice of the citation form in these cases does not necessarily determine the English citation form in definitions. For the Pintupi/Luritja dictionary's Past tense citation form, the definition is a direct translation, that is, with the Past tense form of the English verb, e.g. *nyangu* 'saw'. Cook's wordlist also has the Luritja Past tense as the citation form but gives the English base/infinitive form in the definition, e.g. *nyangu* 'see, look at'. Similarly, the Future tense citation form for Ngaanyatjarra/Ngaatjatjarra words is matched by the English base/infinitive citation form, e.g. *nyaku* 'see, …' rather than 'will see, …'.

Unlike Aranda, in Luritja and other dialects of the Western Desert language there are four basic classes of verbs (also called conjugations). These classes are defined by the overall pattern of the inflectional forms of each verb in the different tenses etc., as demonstrated by an example verb from each class.

Verb class label	Ø	LA	WA	RRA
ALTERNATIVE LABEL	Ø	L	NG	N
	'sit'	'seek'	'hit'	'go'
PERFECTIVE IMPERATIVE[10]	*nyina!*	*ngurrila!*	*puwa!*	*yarra!*
IMPERFECTIVE IMPERATIVE	*nyinama!*	*ngurrinma!*	*pungama!*	*yanama!*
PRESENT	*nyinanyi*	*ngurriṉi*	*punganyi*	*yananyi*
FUTURE	*nyinaku*	*ngurrilku*	*pungkuku*	*yankuku*
PAST PERFECTIVE	*nyinangu*	*ngurriṉu*	*pungu*	*yanu*
PAST IMPERFECTIVE	*nyinangi*	*ngurriṉingi*	*pungangi*	*yanangi*
PARTICIPLE	*nyinarra*	*ngurrira*	*pungkula*	*yankula*
…	…	…	…	…

The verb classes are labelled here in the standard ways used for Western Desert dialects. The top set of labels are based on the form of the Perfective Imperative: LA class verbs mark the Perfective Imperative by adding the suffix *–la* to the verb stem, *ngurri-* above, and similarly with the suffixes *–wa* and *–rra* respectively for WA and RRA class verbs, added to the stems

10 The meanings of the inflectional categories in this language do not precisely match the inflectional categories of English. But, as a rough indication: Perfective Imperative ≈ 'Do it!'; Imperfective Imperative ≈ 'Be doing it!'; Present ≈ 'is doing it'; Future ≈ 'will do it'; Past Perfective ≈ 'did it'; Past Imperfective ≈ 'was doing it'; Participle ≈ '(while/and) doing'.

pu- and *ya-* above. For Ø class verbs, no suffix is added, which means that the word that consists of just the stem—with no suffix—has the specific Perfective Imperative meaning (rather than being a type of neutral form of the verb). The alternative verb class labels reflect the consonant, if any, that immediately precedes the *ku(ku)* part of the Future forms, for example L class verbs have /l/, as in *ngurri.l.ku* above, and N class verbs have /n/, as in *ya.n.kuku* above. In Ø class verbs no consonant occurs in this position, as in *nyina.ku* above.

As noted above, Strehlow did not indicate the verb class in a verb entry, though he was clearly aware of the different inflectional patterns illustrated in the preceding table. Given the inflectional patterns of the four conjugations, Strehlow's choice of the Luritja Present as the citation form does not provide enough information from the form itself to identify the verb class in all cases. The ending of the Present form *ngurrini* in the table above, for example, is sufficient to identify it as a LA class verb since no other verb class has the same ending *…ni* for Present. Once the class of the verb is known, all the inflectional forms follow from that: *ngurrilku* 'will seek' etc. However, with the Present forms *nyinanyi* 'sit', *punganyi* 'hit', and *yananyi* 'go', their respective verb classes cannot be determined because the Ø, WA and RRA classes all end with *…nyi* in the Present form. A reader would need to know that the composition of these verbs is *nyina-nyi, pu-nganyi* and *ya-nanyi* respectively before they could identify the verb class of each. The only clues in the dictionary to the class of such verbs is that in a few cases the verbs also occur in a different inflectional form within another entry, as part of a larger expression or compound word, or in an example sentence. But the other entry has to provide enough information to recognise the verb. For example, in Strehlow's entry for *nintini* 'tell, teach, instruct, show', the example sentence contains the Perfective Imperative form *yarra* plus an emphatic ending *-yi* (his *jerrai!*) but the rather free translation he gives does not make this clear.

Strehlow's spelling:	*kapi*	*nintintaku*	*ngalajerrai!*
Modern spelling:	*kapi*	*nintintjaku*	*ngalya-yarra-yi!*
Analysis:	water:Object	show-Purposive	this.way-go-Emphasis

Strehlow's translation: *Zeig mir das Wasser. (Show me the water!)*

Literal translation: *Water to show (me) come!*

Unfortunately, Strehlow's spelling further reduces the limited ability to distinguish a verb as LA class ending in …*n̲i* versus Ø, WA and RRA classes ending in …*nyi.* He does not reliably represent the important distinction between an alveolar nasal /n/ (as also occurs in English), a retroflex /n̲/ and a laminal /ny/. So from just the spelling of his verb entry *bakani,* it is not strictly possible to know whether it is pronounced *pakan̲i* or *pakanyi,* and it is therefore not possible to deduce which verb class his *bakani* is in, and therefore what the other inflectional forms of this verb are. There is a hint in the fact that when an /i/ vowel follows in the verb endings, he tends to represent /ny/ as <ñ> and /n̲/ as <n>, which would suggest that his *bakani* is probably *pakan̲i* rather than *pakanyi.* But he does not represent these sounds consistently. The uncertainty in this case would be compounded because he also gives the verb as *bakañi* in some other entries such as *wontira bakañi* 'leave one behind', which suggests *pakanyi* instead of *pakan̲i.* A Luritja speaker of course knows the verb *pakan̲i* 'rise, set off, …' and can easily recognise this in Strehlow's spellings *bakani* and *bakañi,* but an accurate representation of the sounds is required for a description of the language.

If the goal of Strehlow's wordlist was just to allow Luritja speakers to find out the German or English equivalents of Luritja words they already know, then there would be no real need to indicate which class a particular verb is in or to list all the different forms of each verb in the dictionary. The speakers of the language already know what the forms of a given verb lexeme are (without even having to know that there are different verb classes). However, in a dictionary like Strehlow's, there are other users and uses. For an old verb that Luritja speakers today do not recognise, or for learners or researchers of Luritja, the requirement is an explicit description of the vocabulary of Luritja in which the class and/or inflectional forms of each verb should be indicated in some way. Most modern Western Desert dictionaries do this by explicitly indicating the appropriate verb class label in the entry, such as 'Ø', as we might do for an entry for *wangkanyi* 'speak, talk, …'. This then tells us all the inflectional forms, for example the Past Perfective *wangkangu* 'spoke, talked, …'. It is also possible to list all the different inflectional forms of a verb in an entry, but printed dictionaries tend not to do this for reasons of space, and perhaps readability of entries. As indicated in the discussion above of the P/Y dictionary entry for *nyanganyi,* the inflectional forms are only listed because this is one of a handful of irregular verbs. Its inflectional forms do not completely follow the pattern of WA class verbs. For example, the Future form is *nyaku,* and not **nyangku* which would be expected by the regular pattern.

Word formation

The standard set of inflectional forms that each lexeme has in Aranda and Luritja can generally be analysed in terms of a specific suffix to represent each inflectional category. In the simplest cases, the inflectional suffix attaches to a single morpheme which constitutes the root of the word, for example, Luritja *patjalku* 'will bite' consists of the Future suffix *-lku* attached to the root morpheme *patja-*. The inflectional suffix may also attach to a combination of morphemes. These structures fall into two general types, derivation and compounding.

Arandic languages have complex verb structures, and for each basic verb there are usually distinct derived lexemes each with a specific variation of meaning. For example, Strehlow lists the following:

CS* Aranda	Translation	Modern spelling
mankama	grow	*maangkama//mangkeme*
mankerama	grow up, grow again (rising generation)	*maangkerrama// mangkirreme*
mankalelama	bring up (children)	*maangkalhelama// mangkelhileme*
mankinja	full-grown (trees), grown up (humans)	*maangkintja// mangkentye*
mankitjintjama	grow up	*maangkatjintyama// mangketyintyeme*
mankalelarama	help to grow big	*maangkalhelarrama// mangkelhilerreme*
mankarankarerama	increase, grow on (clouds)	*maangkarraangkarrerrama// mangkerrangkerrirreme*
mankalankala	grown up, fledged (birds)	*maangkalhaangkalha// mangkelhangkelhe*

* Carl Strehlow

These are not random variations on the basic verb: they all consist of a number of individual distinct parts which each contribute their own meaning to the overall word. The verb root is followed by one or more derivational formatives, and then an inflectional suffix which provides the information about tense and related meanings. For example, in the following words, *maangk-//mangk-* 'grow' is the verb root and the final inflection is the PRESENT tense suffix. The derivational element *-alhel-//-elhil-* contributes a distinct causal meaning, hence 'cause to grow'.

maangk-ama//	*maangk-alhel-ama//*	*maangk-atjintj-ama//*
mangk-eme	*mangk-elhil-eme*	*mangk-ety+inty-eme*
grow-PRESENT	grow-CAUSE-PRESENT	grow-DOUPWARDS-PRESENT
	literally: cause to grow CS: 'bring up (children)'	CS: 'grow up'

Derivational formatives like Causative *-alhel-//-elhil-* play a very important role in expressing meaning in Aranda—they build a large proportion of the lexemes in the language (just as English derivation builds a large number of lexemes in English, and similarly for many other languages). Strehlow's dictionary entries do not identify the specific derivational formative or its individual meaning; however, it can often be inferred from the related words in the dictionary, especially if the particular derivational formative leaves the words together in the alphabetical ordering. Further, the meanings he gives for a derived lexeme do not always directly reflect the meaning of the root. For example, the gloss 'bring up (children)' might not automatically suggest a derivational relationship with a distinct lexeme that means 'grow up' (although in this case the relationship would be more obvious if the meaning was expressed with the local Aboriginal English expression 'to grow someone up'). In general, where Strehlow's definitions do not transparently relate derived and basic forms, there are a couple of reasons. In some cases, he is giving just one use of the derived word in a particular context. Even if this is a common use, there are often other uses of the word. A more developed dictionary of the language will need to not only identify different uses of a derived word but also identify the meaning of the specific derivational element that underlies those different uses. Secondly, in some cases, the meaning of the derived word may subtly go beyond what would be expected from the general meaning of the derivational element.

A full discussion of the different derivational formatives belongs in a grammatical description, but we can at least see the significance here of the different derivational formatives in Aranda by surveying some of the more common ones.

In grammatical terms, the Causative formative *-alhel-//elhil-* above derives a transitive verb stem from certain intransitive verb stems, as in the following examples. The most common result is, as in the preceding case, to cause someone or something to do the action of the intransitive verb stem. Thus, 'to drop something' is expressed as 'to cause something to fall'. This element also derives transitive verbs from certain nominals (nouns, adjectives etc.), such as *gata*{*katha*//*kethe*} below.

ankama[11] {*angkama*// *angkeme*}	say, speak, talk, bleat (sheep), crow (birds), rustle (trees)	*ankalelama* {*angkalhelama*// *angkelhileme*}	(transitive) produce sounds {i.e. cause something to make a sound}
itnima {*tnyima*// *tnyeme*}	fall	*itnilelama* {*tnyilhelama*// *tnyelhileme*}	fell, make fall {to drop something}
gata {*katha*// *kethe*}	place, spot, locality, position, end; outside, visible, flat, public; light {exposed}	*gatalelama* {*kathalhelama*// *kethelhileme*}	(transitive) uncover {expose}

There are also a number of other formatives which derive a transitive verb stem. The *-el-//-il-* formative is related to *alhel-//elhil-*, and also derives transitive verbs from certain nominals, either as an alternative to *alhel-//elhil-*, or in addition to it.

antaka {*antaka*// *anteke*}	wide, broad	*antakilama* {*antakelama*// *antekileme*}	make (something) wider

11 The modern Western Arrarnta pronunciation of these two words is without the initial /a/, and accordingly the standard modern spellings are *ngkama//ngkeme* and *ngkalhelama//ngkelhileme*. Initial <a> is used here in the modern orthographic forms of *ankama* and *ankalelama* to represent the sounds that Strehlow appears to have identified in these words at that earlier time. See Chapter 6 for further discussion of initial <a>.

altjura {*altjura*// *altywere*}	hole (in ground, in wood, in clothes); open	*altjurilama* {*altjurelama*// *altywerileme*}	make a hole, open (a door)
botta {*purta*// *purte*}	lump, ball, tuft of grass	*bottilama* {*purtelama*// *purtileme*}	make (something) into a ball

The Inchoative formative, *-err//-irr* in the examples below, derives an intransitive verb stem from a nominal (noun/adjective), often with a meaning 'to become a certain way', although that may not always be transparent in English translations:

borka {*purrka*// *purrke*}	tired, exhausted, stiff	*borkerama* {*purrkerrama*// *purrkirreme*}	become tired, stiffen
karra {*kaarre*// *karre*}	awake	*karrerama* {*kaarrerrama*// *karrirreme*}	wake up
altjura {*altjura*// *altywere*}	hole (in ground, in wood, in clothes); open	*altjurerama* {*altjurerrama*// *altywerirreme*}	{(something) opens (up)}

The Reflexive formative, *-lh//-elh* in the examples below, derives an intransitive verb stem from a transitive verb stem. The most common meaning is 'do the action of the intransitive verb stem to oneself'. In other cases, it has the effect of de-emphasising either the actor or the affected object, which both serve to focus on the action itself.

ilknama {*ilkngama*// *irlkngeme*}	(transitive) wash {something}, clean {something} (stroke)	*ilknalama* {*ilkngilhima*// *irlkngelheme*}	(reflexive) wash {yourself}
banama {*parnama*// *perneme*}	(transitive) paint on, rub in, build (house); decorate {i.e. put paint, ointment etc. on something}	*banalama* {*parnalhama*// *pernelheme*}	(reflexive) paint on, rub on {i.e. put paint, ointment etc. on yourself}

ilama {*ilama*// *ileme*}	say {something}, tell {about something}	*ilalama* {*ilalhama*// *ilelheme*}	announce (a decision) {more generally: say something about yourself}
ljima {*lyima*// *lyeme*}	mumble (magic words, spells) {sing an object to enact its mystical properties}	*ljélama* {*lyilhama*// *lyelheme*}	sing {i.e. focusing on the action rather than on an object}

The Reciprocal, *-rr//-err* in the examples below, also derives an intransitive verb stem from a transitive one, but in this case, the meaning is 'do the action of the intransitive verb stem to each other'.

erkuma {*irrkuma*// *irrkweme*}	catch, seize, capture, hold tight	*erkurama* {*irrkurrama*// *irrkwerreme*}	embrace {i.e. hold each other}
tuma {*tuma*// *tweme*}	strike {something}, kill	*turuma* {*turrama*// *twerreme*}	fight {each other}, battle

A number of nominalising formatives derive a nominal from a verb stem, for example:

ljélama {*lyilhama*// *lyelheme*	sing {i.e. focusing on the action rather than on an object}	*ljelinja* {*lyilhinja*/// *lyelhentye*}	{a} song {or act of singing}
ankama {*ngkama*// *ngkeme*}	say, speak, talk, bleat (sheep), crow (birds), rustle (trees)	*ankanankana* {*ngkanhangkanha*// *ngkenhengkenhe*}	speaker {i.e. one who speaks}

The example of *ngkanhangkanha*//*ngkenhengkenhe* also illustrates one of the many types of derivation in Aranda which involve reduplication: the suffix *-anh*//*-enh* is attached to the root morpheme *ngk-*, and the whole resulting unit is then doubled.

There is a wide range of formatives which add information about motion that is associated with the verb action. The particular type in the following examples all involve compounding with a motion verb, here *lhama*//*lheme* 'go', and *alpuma*//*alpeme* 'return'.

imbuma {*impuma*// *impeme*}	let, let be, pass by {leave (alone)...}	*imbalalama*[12] {*imparlalhama*// *imperlalheme*}	leave behind, abandon {i.e. leave behind and go}
indama {*intama*// *inteme*}	lie ...	*inditjalbuma* {*intitjalpuma*// *intetyalpeme*}	lie down on return {i.e. return and then lie (down)}
inama {*inama*// *ineme*}	take, fetch, gather, catch	*inilalbuma* {*inarlalpuma*// *inerlalpeme*}	take with you (when returning home) {take and return}

Finally, the various types of derivation shown above are not mutually exclusive, in that a single verb may contain more than one derivational formative. This sometimes results in quite complex verbs.

arrarnama//	*arrarnalhama*//	*arrarnalhitjalhama*//
arrern-eme	*arrern-elh-eme*	*arrern-elh-ety.alh-eme*
put/place-PRESENT	put/place-REFL-PRESENT	put/place-REFL-GO&DO-PRESENT
CS: '(transitive) put, lay, lay down'	literally: place self down CS: '(reflexive) sit down'	literally: go and place self down CS: 'settle down, sit down'

The list of derivational types above is far from exhaustive, but illustrates their enormous role in expressing meaning. In a general sense, the different types of derivation can apply to any basic lexeme, potentially creating a large set of derived lexemes for each basic one. In practice though, only some of the potential lexemes appear to be used with any frequency, and

12 There are actually three distinct entries for this word in different places in the dictionary, each with a slightly different gloss.

this makes it all the more valuable that Strehlow was able to draw on his extensive collection of texts and on everyday speech to identify which derived lexemes occurred in the Aranda of that time.

For a few of the derived lexemes, Strehlow presents an analysis of the word structure in the dictionary. The more common patterns of word structure are described in his separate grammatical descriptions, and in Kempe (1891a). There is, however, a need for further grammatical analysis, in that some words appear to involve word structures that have not yet been described. Many of these cases will require quite careful analysis, and interpretation by speakers, especially where Strehlow's spelling does not clearly represent the actual sounds. For example, Strehlow's *ankankalintama* suggests at least two analyses. The most plausible analysis, shown in the gloss below, interprets his spelling 'int' as the Southern Arrernte (Pertame) verb root *irnt-* 'climb, go up, …'.

ankankalintama

{angk-angk-erl.irnt-eme}

speak/sing-REDUPLICATED-DO.RISING-PRESENT

CS: 'singend aufsteigen (Vogel)' {ascend singing (bird)}

Alternatively, his 'int' may represent the verb root *int-* 'lie', even though its meaning does not appear consistent with the overall meaning of the word above. Such a compound construction is not known in the modern language; however, there is a parallel in the Alyawarr dialect where the corresponding root *aynt-* 'lie' occurs in a compound construction indicating action in an upwards direction. Of course, it may also be that 'int' in this word represents a completely distinct element. Further analysis of the many complex verbs in the dictionary may assist.

Meaning

Strehlow's sensitivity to meaning can be related to his broader focus on describing Aranda culture and documenting traditional texts, as well as the breadth of his knowledge of the language, and the demanding intellectual work of translating Christian materials into Aranda. Words are notoriously difficult to define with any precision, and perhaps more so for definition in a cross-language dictionary. His definitions appear to generally have a relatively high degree of accuracy, especially when compared to other works of his time. It should be remembered that his definitions are in German, and that the English glosses in the dictionary in this volume are a result of translation from Aranda by the speakers who have contributed to this publication project together with the compiler's translation from the German.

The comparison above of Strehlow's *nangañi* 'see' entry with the corresponding entry in some more recent dictionaries illustrates the general point that in a cross-language dictionary the meanings can be expressed in varying detail. Strehlow's German translations are generally relatively compact, although there are some entries where it is extensive. We can observe a number of different patterns of definition, starting from the simple cases where the Aranda or Luritja is translated by a single German word or expression, presumably because there is a close enough match—at least in Strehlow's understanding.

lĕltja {liltye}	Feind	enemy
treranáma {*trerranhama*// *terirrenheme*}	furchtsam aus dem Wege gehen	get out of the way frightened

In some cases, he has a range of German expressions which possibly only differ in style or register, for example:

kekatalama {*kikartalhama*// *kikertelheme*}	tadeln, Vorwürfe machen	reprove, reproach
ekaltilama {*ekarltelama*// *ikerltileme*}	stärken, befestigen	strengthen, fortify

In other cases, he lists a range of expressions with quite different meanings in German but which together sketch out the meaning of the Aranda or Luritja expression. He also often includes information on situations which the expression can refer to, often indicating aspects of the context in brackets. This definitional strategy essentially triangulates the underlying meaning without explicitly stating it as a single expression. While this may not always be optimal for language description, it provides a language learner with some fairly concrete situations for use.

rurkuma[13] {*rwerrkeme*, *rurrkeme*}	Klappern, poltern, knarren, knirren, plätschern (Regen), das mit den Füßen hervorgebrachte Geräusch, knirschen (Klappernd herabfallen (Stein))	Rattle, rumble, creak, splash, patter (rain), noise produced by the feet {walking}, crunch (Clattering down (stone))

Sometimes Strehlow makes attempts to characterise an underlying meaning that cannot be expressed in German with a single word, and often without providing contextual instances that might assist a learner. For example, the following entry might be enhanced by relating this to the behaviour of kangaroos—as did one of the Aranda speakers involved in the project to bring this dictionary to publication.

> *tnanopanama ({compound of} tnama + nopanama)* continually stop and stand for a while after going some distance; after one has been going along, stop, then go on, then stop, etc., continually after one has {gone some distance} {…}, stop and stand for while, stop and stand again and again.

This is a case where the quality of Strehlow's definition helps to clarify how the verb is pronounced. He offers an analysis of this word as a compound consisting of a form of *itnaama//irtname* 'stand' and *napanama//nepaneme* which he glosses as 'always be, have, belong, stay, remain seated'. However, from its meaning and spelling, *tnanopanama* suggests that it might be the equivalent of Eastern/Central *tnenhepenheme*, roughly 'to repeatedly stop and stand while going along'. If this is so, Strehlow's analysis of this word suggests that he was unable to distinguish the /n/ and /nh/ sounds of Aranda.

The remainder of this section considers some of the issues of definition, and how Strehlow has handled them. Compare Strehlow's translation of *kekatalama* above with Breen's below which has a different definitional strategy: a statement of the underlying meaning plus example contexts where the word might apply.

13 There are two separate entries for this verb in Strehlow's dictionary with slightly different definitions.

kikertelheme, kiketelheme

not liking what someone does to you: *for example, talking about you or criticising you.* (Breen et al. 2000: 26)

Strehlow's definition would seem to involve expressing to someone that they have acted wrongly or badly, though perhaps not necessarily behaving badly to the person expressing that view. Breen's definition is focused on an individual's mental state. A corresponding expression to *kikertelheme* in Eastern/Central Arrernte is described as 'not wanting to talk to people or being unco-operative because you didn't get what you want; sulking, in a huff' (Henderson and Dobson 1994: 67). These three attempts at definitions clearly have something in common, and if there is in fact a single underlying meaning across these dialects and times, then it still remains to develop an accurate definition. A proper evaluation of Strehlow's definitions will only be possible when such fine-grained work is completed. The case of *kekatalama* also demonstrates a general point that part of the continuing value of Strehlow's definitions is that they challenge lexicographers of Aranda and Luritja to refine their understanding of the underlying meanings of an expression.

In relation to botanical and zoological terms, Strehlow sometimes provides scientific names as well as general or local common terms, and in some cases—particularly birds—fairly detailed descriptions, as in the following example. In such cases, and where cultural detail is provided, he is going beyond a narrow model of a dictionary in the direction of an encyclopedia.

nturuta {*nturrurta*/ / *nturrerte*}	Pigeon, brown with bonnet, rock pigeon, (*Lophophaps leucogaster*).—Red-brown wings with black stripes, black beak, grey-blue {…?}, red around the eyes, red-brown bonnet, white stripe from under the beak to under the eye, below this stripe a black ring which reaches up to the eye. White belly mixed with brown, growing darker towards the tail. Back brown with black bars. The long wing feathers brown with black tip, the internal wing feathers violet black.

As some of the examples above illustrate, Strehlow and other lexicographers face a range of issues because the range of meaning of a word in one language is not exactly the same as the range of meaning of the nearest word in another language. One way to appreciate the task is to examine categories of words which typically have relatively clear-cut systematic components of meaning. Such categories include pronouns and kin terms. The following is a relatively complex example drawn from the Aranda pronoun system. Strehlow glosses the Aranda second person pronoun *rankara* {*rraangkarra*//*rrangkerre*} and Luritja *nurungari* {*nyurrungarri*} as German *ihr*, but in fact *ihr* only overlaps to a limited degree with *rankara* and *nurungari*. Firstly, German *ihr* refers to two or more people whereas *rankara* and *nurungari* refer specifically to three or more people. Put differently, German *ihr* can refer to two people, roughly 'you two', but *rankara* and *nurungari* do not. Aranda and Luritja both have separate pronouns for 'you two', *mpaala*//*mpale* and *nyupali* respectively.

Secondly, German *ihr* has a number of different grammatical functions. *Ihr* does match *rankara* and *nurungari* in one particular function of that word: second person plural nominative—roughly parallel to English plural 'you' in subject contexts like 'you sat down'. However, *ihr* has other functions that do not match *rankara* or *nurungari* at all: third person singular feminine possessive (parallel to 'her (food)'), third person singular feminine dative (parallel to '(wave) to her'), third person plural possessive (parallel to 'their (food)'), and the formal second person possessive both singular and plural.

Thirdly, in general, Aranda has different forms of each non-singular pronoun according to the kin category of the people referred to. These distinctions in pronouns are falling out of use in much of the Arandic area. They are probably no longer used in Western Aranda but they were recorded from elderly Western Aranda speakers in the 1990s (Breen 1998). They were therefore presumably known in Strehlow's time, though only a few of these pronouns are in the dictionary. The first form, *rraakarriyanga*//*rrakerreyenge*, means 'you who are all in the same patrimoiety but in the opposite generation moiety'. This can refer, for example, to a father and his children but not to a mother and her children, or to a group of siblings. The second form, *rraantharriyanga*//*rrantherreyenge*, means 'you who are not all in the same patrimoiety'. This can refer, for example, to a mother and her children, but not to a father and his children, or to a group of siblings. The third form, *rraangkarra*//*rrangkerre*, is Strehlow's *rankara*. It means 'you who are in the same patrimoiety and the same generation moiety'. It can refer, for example, to a group of siblings, but not to a father and his children, or to a mother and her children. In some other dialects where these kin-based pronouns are still in use, the pronoun in this last category is also used when kin distinctions are not being made, and so can be considered generic in terms of kin. Assuming that Aranda *rankara* also had such a generic meaning in Strehlow's time, his gloss is not incorrect in relation to kin categories; it simply does not include the kin-based meaning that the pronoun also has.

Finally, in some dialects of Aranda the second person plural can also be used as a singular pronoun in an indirect way to address just one person if they are in a specific respected kin category (Wilkins 1989: 46). This also needs to be included in an account of the meaning of this pronoun.

Strehlow was clearly sensitive to the quite different system of kin terminology in Aranda, and able to investigate the meaning of each kin term to some depth. We see this in the following example, in his definition strategy of listing the (German) expressions for all the relationships that are subsumed under Western Aranda *tjia*.

itia (Southern dialect), *tjia* {*irteye* (S), *tjiya*//*tyeye*}	younger brother, younger sister, father's younger brother's son, mother's younger sister's son, woman's younger sister's husband, man's younger sister's husband, father's younger brother's daughter, mother's younger sister's daughter, woman's younger brother's wife, man's younger brother's wife.

The definition given for this word by Breen et al. (2000) is simply 'younger brother or sister'. At first sight, this seems very incomplete by comparison, but it may capture the fact that all the relationships listed by Strehlow actually involve only the Aranda concepts of BROTHER OR SISTER and, in the kin sense, YOUNGER. So while Strehlow's definition suits a technical description or a practical work for learners of Aranda, Breen's definition may better suit users who are familiar with the kin concepts of Aranda and perhaps other Aboriginal languages.

Meanings also reflect the introduced culture in a few cases. The missionary role of Strehlow and his colleagues in seeking terms to express Christian concepts and texts was a major project of translation (see Moore 2015). For example, a central concept in Aranda cosmology is *altjirra*//*altyerre*, a complex term that might be glossed as the creation and continuing underlying fabric of the world. It is sometimes translated as 'the Dreaming' in some contexts today but it has been the established translation of 'God' in Lutheran practice since Kempe. (See Green 2012 for a discussion of the meaning and translations of this term.) As an entry on its own, Strehlow gives only the Christian meaning for Altjira, but recognises its original meaning where it occurs within other expressions:[14]

Altjira {*Altjirra*//*Altyerre*}	Gott, der Unerschaffene	God, the Uncreated One
Altjirangamitjina {*Altjirrangamatjina*// *Altyerrengametyene* lit. '*from/in the altjirra*//*altyerre*'}	Totem-Götter (die ewigen Unerschaffenen)	Totem-Gods (the eternal Uncreated Ones) {dreaming beings}

There is of course a wealth of other information in the definitions in the dictionary which this discussion has only touched upon.

Conclusion

Strehlow's dictionary is a valuable historical resource that has made significant contributions to modern dictionaries of Arandic and Western Desert languages, and to other research. It was a remarkable personal achievement that came from Strehlow's intellect and training, and from the broader cultural description and translation work he also undertook. This chapter has examined Strehlow's dictionary from a linguistic perspective in order to understand his achievement, the nature and value of the work as it stands, and its potential contribution to future linguistic research and practical dictionaries. The details of his work will perhaps best be appreciated only when a historical dictionary of the Arandic languages is published. This will require careful interpretation of the entries, taking into account the nature of the dictionary as described in this chapter, and especially the detailed information which would need to be consistently made explicit in each entry. In the meantime, the presentation of the dictionary in this volume, and hopefully in a digital form, will be available for the study of Aranda language, culture and history.

14 Also note that he capitalises both Aranda words, apparently giving both concepts similar status. Most of the few other Aranda words capitalised in the dictionary are place names and interjections, and the remainder are a miscellaneous group.

6

The Mission Orthography in Carl Strehlow's dictionary

David Moore[1]

Introduction

This chapter provides an analysis of the orthography used for Aranda in the Carl Strehlow dictionary, and places this system in its historical context. Readers who are primarily interested in the immediate issues of pronouncing the Aranda words from their spelling in this dictionary should consult the separate Pronunciation Guides provided at the front of the dictionary in this book. Readers who wish to learn to use the current spelling of Aranda words should consult the modern dictionaries and other resources.

The first Arandic orthography for practical use emerged with the establishment of the Hermannsburg mission in central Australia in 1877 and the subsequent codification of the language in a range of written materials. The name of the language came to be written as 'Aranda' at that time, and this convention is followed throughout this chapter. The orthography, which I shall call the 'Mission Orthography', evolved over time and endured for around a century as a means of written communication for speakers of the Western Aranda language. The Mission Orthography was phonetic in character and was subject to the limitations

1 With contributions, and editing, by John Henderson.

of that type of orthography. It was finally replaced in the 1970s by basically phonemic orthographies, the type currently used for writing all the languages of central Australia. The two modern orthographies for the Western Aranda dialect are called here the Finke River Mission (FRM) orthography and the Institute for Aboriginal Development (IAD) orthography (which follows the Common Arandic approach).[2] The language name is written *Arrarnta* in the FRM orthography and *Arrernte* in the IAD orthography. This chapter does not seek to address all the issues involved in community, institutional and individual choices between these two modern Western Aranda orthographies. See Breen (2005) and Kenny (2017b) for discussion of some of the relevant issues. Kral (2000) discusses the use of literacy in the Western Aranda community.

The Mission Orthography was developed as a practical orthography for use in the Lutheran Western Aranda community, and was used in educational and religious works, a scholarly grammar and dictionary, and in personal correspondence. It was a regular orthography in that it attempted to consistently represent the sounds of Aranda, at least as they were perceived by the missionaries.

In contrast, some other early attempts to write Aranda words were basically ad hoc spellings of each word. In most cases, they were almost certainly intended to give only a rough indication of the pronunciation of just a few words rather than to establish a spelling system for extended writing for a range of purposes. Willshire (1891), and some others, made short wordlists with just a few items, without regular spelling across the words in the list. For example, Willshire gives 'Quasha Un-jew-ma' for what is written as *kwatja ntjuma* 'drink water' in the modern FRM orthography. This example illustrates some common properties of ad hoc spellings of the era. Firstly, these spellings were often based on hearing the words as sounds of English and applying the English orthography. Secondly, a given sound may be represented differently in different words: Willshire's <sh> in his 'Quasha' and his <j> in 'Un-jew-ma' actually represent the same sound (consistently represented by <tj> in the FRM orthography). Thirdly, ad hoc spellings sometimes relied on the spelling of specific English words, such as *Jew* here. Given that the English orthography is moderately irregular, with complex relationships between

2 Using the names of these institutions is just one way that the two orthographies are labelled. There is of course a more detailed history of the people, places and institutions involved. See below, and Breen (2001, 2005).

sounds and letters, the result is a highly irregular system of spelling Aranda words. Finally, hyphens are often used in an unsystematic way to try to compensate for the inconsistency of the relationships between letters and sounds.

The remainder of this chapter examines the details of the letter–sound correspondences for consonants and vowels in the Mission Orthography, and the subsequent development of the later phonemic orthographies. Some technical linguistic terms and symbols are necessary for the discussion but are introduced in a way that will hopefully be useful for a broader readership.

Orthography

Developing a practical orthography, or evaluating one, is a complex matter which involves taking into account the sounds and structure of the language in question, levels of bilingualism in the community, literacy skills in other languages, the functions of literacy in the language, community perceptions of existing or earlier orthographies of the language, social identity, power relations within a community, and other factors. Before considering the details of the Mission Orthography, it is useful to review some concepts which are important to understanding the sound systems of languages and the nature of writing systems. Readers who are familiar with these areas could skip to the next section.

A practical orthography is generally intended as a conventional writing system for everyday community use, that is, where people broadly agree to write the words of a language in the same way. It is a standard which allows individuals to communicate with each other in writing. In general, a practical orthography also aims to be regular or uniform, that is, to be consistent across a language by writing each word of the language according to general principles established for that language. As Gudschinsky (1973: 124) puts it, 'one cannot make an arbitrary decision [on spelling] for each word'.

For regular alphabetic orthographies, the general principles need to specify the relationships between individual sounds and letters. These are often summarised in a general pronunciation key of the kind found in bilingual dictionaries, grammars and language learning materials, as opposed to having to indicate the pronunciation of each word separately.

Some alphabetic orthographies are highly regular in that the relationships between sounds and symbols are essentially one-to-one, that is, each letter (or specific combination of letters) represents a single sound, and each sound is represented by a single letter (or specific combination of letters). The more regular an orthography is, the simpler its pronunciation key. If an alphabetic orthography is not very regular, it will not be straightforward to accurately pronounce a word from its spelling, or to accurately write the word from its pronunciation. Users of the orthography then just have to learn the idiosyncratic spelling of each word.

Establishing a regular alphabetic orthography requires identifying the sounds in all the known words of the language before any decisions can be made about how letters can be assigned to these sounds. In contrast, an ad hoc spelling of a word is typically produced without considering what sounds need to be represented in words overall, and without considering the overall regularity of the orthography. An ad hoc spelling may seem simplest for a limited purpose—just a few words, perhaps a name, or for a sign—but it does not take into account the broader issues in the learning and development of literacy in a community. Such inconsistent spellings may make it harder for people other than the writer—the community as a whole—to read the word in that specific use. They may also make it harder to learn to read and write in the language because they reduce the regularity of the orthography. Of course, a degree of irregularity is not a fatal weakness in an orthography, as the English orthography demonstrates, but it does affect the difficulty of learning to read and write in the language, especially for a minority language with limited resources.

Sounds and graphemes

The symbols of an orthography are graphemes, and in an alphabetic orthography, these are the letters or specific combinations of letters (and accent marks etc.) which represent the sounds of the language. A standard convention in discussing orthography is to use bracketing notation to distinguish different uses of symbols. Graphemes are represented in angle brackets, for example <sh> in the English orthography, in order to distinguish between the graphemes and the sounds they represent. This bracketing also distinguishes orthographic representation from the use of symbols for other purposes, such as phonetic transcription using the International Phonetic Alphabet (IPA) which is indicated by square brackets, and in which [sh] represents a sequence of two sounds.

At this stage, it is necessary to recognise that the term 'sound' in language actually covers two quite distinct concepts, phone and phoneme. Phonetics considers a sound for its objective physical properties, including how it is articulated by the organs of speech. The term 'phone' is used for a sound in this sense. The physical properties of an individual phone can be described, and can then be represented in transcription by the symbols of the IPA. In that function, the IPA symbols are therefore a kind of shorthand for a description of those particular physical properties. For example, [n] represents a phone that is voiced, a nasal, and produced with the tip of the tongue in contact above the upper teeth. The phone [n] occurs in English, Aranda and many other languages. Phonetic transcription represents the physical events of actual speech, but it can be broad(er) or narrow(er) depending on how precise or detailed the description is intended to be. A phonetic transcription may be narrow or precise enough to represent small differences in the way a single individual pronounces the same word on different occasions. A broad(er) transcription represents only larger phonetic differences.

Phonetic transcription identifies individual phones, but beyond this there is the question of how a language uses its phones to constitute its vocabulary. A central fact in this regard is the way that words of the vocabulary are differentiated by particular phonetic differences in a language. For example, in Aranda there are two phones, represented phonetically as [n] and [n̪] (a diacritic added below plain n). The phone [n] is as described above, while [n̪] is a different phone, a dental nasal, that is produced with the tongue against the back of the upper teeth. The difference between these two phones is used in Aranda to differentiate words of the vocabulary, for example [nəmə] 'sit, be' vs [n̪əmə] 'to rain, to wet (something)'. (These words are written in the FRM orthography as *nama* and *nhama*, respectively.) The difference between [n] and [n̪] is significant in Aranda because it can be the only difference in pronunciation between a pair of words, and is therefore crucial to correctly distinguishing words and their meanings in speech. The difference is said to be contrastive in Aranda.

The same two phones, [n] and dental [n̪], also occur in the pronunciation of English words. For example, 'ten' is typically pronounced [ten] whereas dental [n̪] occurs before the dental [θ] in a pronunciation of words like 'tenth', [ten̪θ] (Cox 2012: 137). Although these two phones occur in both English and Aranda, they are used very differently in English. Unlike Aranda, there are no English words that are differentiated just by this phonetic difference between [n] and [n̪]. This is never the only difference between words of English vocabulary. This means that in English the difference between [n] and [n̪] is not significant for speakers to differentiate distinct words. The difference is not contrastive in English.

This fact about English can be expressed by recognising [n] and [n̪] as minor variations of the same 'sound' in a special sense. This is expressed in technical terms by saying that [n] and [n̪] are allophones (or members) of the same phoneme in English. Bracketing notation uses slash brackets to indicate when an IPA symbol is being used to label a phoneme. Thus the English phoneme /n/ has the allophones [n] and [n̪] (and others). In Aranda, the fact that the difference between [n] and [n̪] differentiates words is expressed by recognising distinct phonemes, which can be labelled /n/ and /n̪/. In this way, the phoneme concept represents not just what phones occur in a language, but which differences between phones differentiate words of the vocabulary of the language. The way that speakers conceive of the sounds of their language tends to correspond to the phonemes that can be analysed from the phonetic facts of word pronunciation. For example, speakers of English are generally not aware that they are producing different phones [n] and [n̪] in words like 'ten' and 'tenth', and generally recognise these distinct phones as instances of the same sound in some sense. In contrast, speakers of Aranda are quite conscious of the sound difference between words like [nəmə] 'sit, be' vs [n̪əmə] 'rain, to wet (something)'. However, speakers' sense of the distinctness or sameness of sounds is not always exactly the same thing as determining what the phonemes of the language are, and needs to be considered separately in developing an orthography.

Analysis of the phonemes of a language allows the words of the vocabulary to be represented in terms of the phonemes in the word. For example, /ænθɹəpɔlədʒi/ is a phonemic representation of the word 'anthropology' in Australian English. Note that this includes the phoneme symbol /n/, by which there is no indication of the actual detail of pronunciation as dental [n̪] in this context. Speakers unconsciously know that the phoneme /n/ can be realised as the dental phone [n̪] in such words because of the following dental sound /θ/. Such phonetic differences which do not play a role in differentiating words in the language are effectively suppressed in a phonemic transcription. Of course, the concepts introduced in the discussion here are relevant to all the consonant and vowel phones of a language: we have only focused on [n] and [n̪] as an example.

In a phonemic orthography, the basic principle is that each grapheme represents a phoneme, which is sufficient information for speakers of a language to match spelling to pronunciation to identify a word. However, there are also additional factors that can play a role in designing a phonemic orthography, and as a result there is often not always a perfect correspondence between graphemes and phonemes.

These concepts can now be applied to consider the Mission Orthography and subsequent phonemic orthographies.

The Mission Orthography: Phonetic, uniform and continental

The Mission Orthography was developed by Hermannsburg missionaries so that they could translate the Bible and other materials into the local languages (Moore and Ríos Castaño 2018). It followed the 'continental' spelling system, according to Carl Strehlow (Kenny 2013: 98), and was an attempt at a uniform orthography. This was clearly a considered and systematic approach to developing a practical orthography for community use, in contrast to the ad hoc approach of authors such as Willshire, as discussed above. The 'continental' approach categorises the simple vowel phones with the letters <a>, <e>, <i>, <o> and <u>. In general terms, this simple approach offers at least the potential for greater consistency in spelling than trying to categorise the vowels of Aranda according to the many distinct vowel sounds distinguished in English orthography. The options for uniform orthographies available to linguistic and other fieldworkers in central Australia in the late 1800s and early 1900s are discussed in Moore (2013). Edward Stirling, for example, used the Royal Geographical System in the 1896 *Report on the work of the Horn Scientific Expedition to Central Australia* (Breen 2005: 94). The science of phonetics was developing at that time, and this was reflected in the evolving approaches to developing orthographies.

The Mission Orthography was founded in the system used by Pastor Hermann Kempe, and summarised in his phonetic key (1891a: 2). By the time Carl Strehlow was compiling the dictionary, the Mission Orthography was already used in teaching at the Hermannsburg school and in religious services. Primers, a worship book (Kempe 1891b), a grammar and vocabulary (Kempe 1891a) had already been published using it. Strehlow largely followed Kempe's approach, but made some modifications. Oberscheidt (1991: iii) considers that Strehlow 'continued to employ the basic form of the first orthography, creating a kind of orthographic continuity'. John Strehlow (2011: 739) adds, from a different point of view, that '[Carl Strehlow] did not attempt to modify the problematic spelling used by Kempe'. Strehlow (1908) clarified some points about the Mission Orthography, but did not produce any further explicit discussion of Aranda phonetics or orthography.

Some of the differences in Strehlow's spelling reflect his greater ability to discriminate between sounds than his predecessor's. Some other differences can be attributed to dialect variation, as Kempe and Strehlow consulted different speakers who appear to have pronounced some words differently. According to Kempe (1891a: 1–2):

> The vocabulary is that of the tribe inhabiting the River Finke, and is also, with only slight variations in the dialect, that of the tribes in the MacDonnell Ranges eastward to Alice Springs, but not far westward of the River Finke, and extending southward to the Peake.

Strehlow focused on what he saw as a different dialect, 'to use *Aranda aratja*[3] forms spoken by most of the people on the Station in place of the *Aranda ulbma* used by Kempe' (J. Strehlow 2011: 739). For some words, Strehlow specifies a specific dialect. In Kempe's list there are a number of words that appear to be from dialects away from the immediate Hermannsburg area, but are not annotated as such. In some cases, these differences between dialect forms involve an initial vowel. For example, Kempe gives *auma* 'hear', with an initial vowel, whereas Strehlow gives *wuma* without an initial vowel, and attributes *aūma* to a Northern dialect.

Analysis of the Mission Orthography

This section examines Kempe's orthography and its development in Strehlow's work. The Mission Orthography was a broad phonetic representation, rather than phonemic, in that it did not specifically attempt to represent only those phonetic differences which are significant in Aranda because they differentiate words. The Mission Orthography makes some sound distinctions which are not significant in Aranda, and

3 Carl Strehlow glosses *aratja* as 'straight, upright, just' and *ulbma* as 'tight, narrow'.

does not represent some distinctions which are significant. There are three factors to consider in this. Firstly, there is the question of which phonetic distinctions Kempe and Strehlow were able to discriminate, and whether they could discriminate them reliably in different words. To a large degree this can only be assessed against the fact that all the evidence indicates that the individual sounds of Aranda have not changed significantly since Kempe's time, though some individual words may have changed in their pronunciation over that time. There is evidence that the Hermannsburg missionaries modified the orthography as their ability to discriminate sounds improved. Secondly, there is the question as to whether there are phonetic distinctions which they were able to discriminate, but chose not to represent in the orthography in consideration of other factors. There is unfortunately relatively little recorded information on this point. However, there is some evidence that Kempe was in general conscious of the separate tasks in discriminating the sounds of the language and choosing letters to represent them: 'to make the number of written characters as few as possible, [a long vowel] is indicated by a small stroke over the letter, as [in] *lāda* ['point']' (1891a: 2). Thirdly, even where the orthography makes a distinction between sounds, there is the question of whether it is consistently applied in the spelling of individual words, both in Kempe's and Strehlow's dictionaries and in their other works. Kempe's representation of long vowels, discussed below, is such a case. In addition to these three factors, there is also the usual possibility of an accidental error in writing a word.

Kempe's phonetic key distinguishes 15 consonant graphemes, six simple vowel graphemes (and vowel length) and three diphthong graphemes. He characterises the sounds these represent by making comparisons to specific English spellings in example words, and therefore indirectly compares them to phonemes of English. This is of course appropriate for a grammar and vocabulary published in English. There is evidence of influence from both English and Kempe's and Strehlow's native German in the discrimination of individual phones, in the choice of letters to represent them, and in the choice of the comparison examples in English.

Consonants

The basic phonetic representation of consonant sounds in the Mission Orthography is shown in Table 1, with its correspondence to Aranda phonemes and the modern phonemic orthographies. The following sections provide more detailed discussion of other specific aspects of the representation, including consonant doubling. This table deals only with consonant phones as they occur singly in words: specific sequences of consonant phones in words are discussed later.

The first column in Table 1 gives a representation of the basic consonant phonemes using IPA symbols. This follows the phonemic analysis of consonants by Breen (2001) and Wilkins (1989). The table then indicates the representation of each phoneme in the FRM (Roennfeldt et al. 2006) and IAD (Breen et al. 2000) orthographies, which differ here in only a couple of respects. The orthographies in Kempe (1891a) and the Carl Strehlow dictionary are listed separately because there is a small number of differences between them. The way that the correspondences between the three orthographies are represented in Table 1 can be understood from the following example. The Mission Orthography (i) does not make the important distinction between the phonemes written as <t>, <th> and <rt> in the modern orthographies, and (ii) it does make a distinction between <t> and <d> which is not significant in Aranda because the difference between [t] and [d] does not differentiate words.

Table 1. Basic consonant phonemes and their orthographic representations.

Phonemes (IPA)	FRM & IAD	Mission Orthography	
		C Strehlow	Kempe
/p/	< p >	< p >, < b >	< p >, < b >
/k/	< k >	< k >, < g >	< k >, < g >
/t/	< t >	< t >, < d >	< t >, < d >
/t̪/	< th >		
/ʈ/	< rt >		
/c/	< tj >(FRM) < ty > (IAD)	< tj >	< tj >
/j/	< y >	< j >	< j >
		< i >	< i >
/l/	< l >	< l >	< l >
/l̪/	< lh >		
/ɭ/	< rl >		
/ʎ/	< ly >	< lj >	< lj >
/m/	< m >	< m >	< m >

<table>
<tr><th rowspan="2">Phonemes (IPA)</th><th rowspan="2">FRM & IAD</th><th colspan="2">Mission Orthography</th></tr>
<tr><th>C Strehlow</th><th>Kempe</th></tr>
<tr><td>/ ɲ /</td><td>< ny ></td><td>< nj ></td><td>< nj ></td></tr>
<tr><td>/ n /</td><td>< n ></td><td rowspan="3">< n ></td><td rowspan="3">< n ></td></tr>
<tr><td>/ n̪/</td><td>< nh ></td></tr>
<tr><td>/ ɳ /</td><td>< rn ></td></tr>
<tr><td>/ ŋ /</td><td>< ng ></td><td>< ng ></td><td>< ng ></td></tr>
<tr><td>/ ɹ /</td><td>< r ></td><td rowspan="2">< r ></td><td rowspan="3">< r ></td></tr>
<tr><td>/ ɾ /</td><td>< rr ></td></tr>
<tr><td>/ ɰ /</td><td>< h > (IAD)</td><td>< ŕ ></td></tr>
<tr><td>/ ᵖm /</td><td>< pm ></td><td>< tm ></td><td>< tm ></td></tr>
<tr><td>/ ᵗn /</td><td>< tn ></td><td rowspan="3">< tn >, < dn ></td><td rowspan="3">< tn >, < dn ></td></tr>
<tr><td>/ ᵗn̪/</td><td>< thn ></td></tr>
<tr><td>/ ᵗɳ /</td><td>< rtn ></td></tr>
<tr><td>/ ᶜɲ /</td><td>< tny ></td><td rowspan="2">< kn ></td><td>< kn ></td></tr>
<tr><td>/ ᵏŋ /</td><td>< kng ></td><td>< gn ></td></tr>
<tr><td>/ w /</td><td>< w ></td><td>< w >, < u >,
< o ></td><td>< w >, < u >,
< o ></td></tr>
</table>

In Kempe's phonetic key, he describes 15 consonant graphemes, shown in Table 2, as representing 'primitive' sounds of Aranda, that is, the original sounds of Aranda as opposed to the additional letters <f>, <s> and <z> used to represent sounds in biblical names.

Table 2. Consonant graphemes in Kempe (1891a).

'B b, like b in be'	'N n, like n in near'
'D d, like d in do'	'Ng ng, like ng in ring'
'G g, like g in go'	'P p, like p in pipe'
'H h, like h in here'	'R r, like r in roam'
'J j, like y in year'	'T t, like t in to'
'K k, like k in king'	'Tj tj, like g in gentle'
'L l, like l in long'	'W w, like w in wife'
'M m, like m in more'	

Most of the stop consonants are over-differentiated with respect to the phonetic property of voicing: <b> vs <p>, <d> vs <t>, and <g> vs <k>. In each of these pairs, the sounds are contrastive in German and English, that is they differentiate words, for example as demonstrated by *bush* vs *push*, *do* vs *to*, and *kill* vs *gill*. However, these pairs of phones are not contrastive in Aranda, in that there are no such pairs of words where the only difference in pronunciation is the difference between [b] vs [p] etc. It was therefore not necessary to distinguish them in the orthography. This type of over-differentiation is not necessarily a significant issue in an orthography provided that speakers of the language can consistently discriminate such non-contrastive sounds. However, this is often not the case, as noted above for [n] and [n̪] in English. Where two phones, such as [b] and [p], are frequently interchangeable within some words, this raises issues for a phonetic approach such as the Mission Orthography. It would result in multiple spellings of a single word according to the phonetic facts of each occasion of a speaker pronouncing that word. This occurs (perhaps accidentally) where Kempe has two distinct vocabulary entries for what appears to be the same word: *damba* 'loose, breakable' and *tamba* 'loose, shaking, perishable, fading'. The alternative is to make an arbitrary decision on which letter to use on a word-by-word basis, and to fix that as the idiosyncratic spelling of that word regardless of how it is actually pronounced on any given occasion. Kempe and Strehlow have in fact done this in many cases, for example with [b] and [p] in *banama* 'to build, to paint' vs *parama* 'to stop, to bar', where there is not a consistent difference in the first sound. The same applies in numerous words for [t] vs [d] and [k] vs [g]. The effect is that the spelling of individual words is more idiosyncratic, and the orthography overall is less regular.

The <h> in Kempe's phonetic key is unnecessary: it does not represent a contrastive sound in Aranda, and in fact does not appear in any of the words in his wordlist. Strehlow (1908: 698) states explicitly that he does not know the 'consonant h' in Aranda, meaning the initial sound in an English word like 'here'.

Kempe's key clearly recognises that the velar nasal [ŋ] occurs in Aranda and represents it as <ng>. However, this phoneme is represented quite variably in his writings, in part because the ability to discriminate a specific sound can depend on the position it occurs in within a word. In his grammar and vocabulary (1891a), Kempe consistently discriminates the velar nasal when it is the first sound in a word, for example in *ngapa* 'crow'. But his worship book (1891b) shows this phone being represented as <n> at the beginning of words. Compare:

> *Etna najila* 'they are hungry' (Kempe 1891b: 12)
> *Etna ngaiala*. [ditto] (Strehlow 1904: 14)

It would appear that Kempe's ability to discriminate the velar nasal in this position developed over time, but the initial variability on this point can be attributed to the influence of German and English. The velar nasal also occurs in both German and English, however, in these languages the velar nasal does not occur as the first sound in a word, and speakers of these languages tend initially to have difficulty in both recognising and pronouncing it in this position. The influence of German or English though is clearly not the same for everyone in this regard: the same issue with the velar nasal had earlier been encountered by the Dieri mission at Killalpannina but it was nonetheless written consistently by missionary Flierl.

Kempe and Strehlow also use <n> for a velar nasal in two other contexts where the key would mandate <ng>: before or after <k>. They use <kn> or <gn> for the sequence of these two consonant phones in for example *wolkna* 'grave', instead of <kng>, and they use <nk> where the key would have <ngk>, for example in *inka* 'foot'. It is not clear whether these reflect an inability to recognise the velar nasal in these contexts, or reflect influence from English or German spellings such as in *drink/trinken*, or reflect a considered spelling 'shortcut'. It could possibly be such a shortcut because Kempe seems to have been prepared to consider the number of letters required for a spelling, as suggested by his discussion of vowel length (1891a: 2), mentioned above. Further, Kempe's and Strehlow's use of <nk> for /ŋk/ in words like *inka* 'foot' does not distinguish /ŋk/ from the distinct sequence of alveolar nasal plus velar stop /nk/ in words like *imanka* 'long ago'.

Kempe's use of <r> is a complicated case. He uses it to represent three distinct phonemes of Aranda: the retroflex approximant /ɻ /, the alveolar tap/trill /ɾ/ and the back approximant /ɰ/ (discussed below). These phonemes are all represented in distinct ways in the modern orthographies, as Table 1 shows.

Double consonant letters

Both Kempe and Strehlow use double consonant letters in some words, but this does not appear to be consistent. In some cases, it appears to be an attempt to distinguish different phonetic properties, but it is not clear which phonetic properties. Aranda distinguishes dental, alveolar, post-alveolar (retroflex) and palatal places of articulation. Thus there are four lateral phonemes represented by <lh>, <l>, <rl> and <ly> respectively in the modern orthographies. There are four corresponding stops and four corresponding nasals at these places of articulation. Kempe's phonetic key significantly under-differentiates all these consonants in their place of articulation. Thus his <l> represents all of the four distinct phonemes represented in the modern orthographies as <lh>, <l>, <rl> and <ly> (which he also represents as <lj>). In English and German there is of course only one lateral phoneme, at the alveolar place of articulation, and it is common for speakers of these languages to have difficulty discriminating the other distinct lateral phonemes in Aranda: they tend to hear them all as alveolar /l/. Doubling of consonant letters in Kempe's and Strehlow's work seems to indicate a non-alveolar place of articulation without specifying which one, at least for the nasals. Kempe's vocabulary has an instance, *mballa* 'heat', where doubled <ll> represents a dental lateral (<lh> in the modern orthographies). In Strehlow's dictionary <ll> is not common but those that do occur are split relatively evenly between alveolar, retroflex and dental laterals. The tendency seems clearer with doubling of <n> in Strehlow's dictionary: the instances of <nn> there all seem to be retroflex or dental nasals, as opposed to alveolar and palatal.

The letter-doubling strategy also extends to some instances of <rr>. Kempe uses it in one case to distinguish two words, *garra* 'clay-ground' vs *gara* 'meat' where the former has the alveolar tap/trill /ɾ/ and the latter has the retroflex approximant /ɻ/. Strehlow's dictionary has many instances of <rr> vs <r> but there is no real consistency: both options represent the alveolar tap/trill /ɾ/ and the retroflex approximant /ɻ/ in different words. The modern orthographies both consistently represent the alveolar tap/trill as <rr> and the retroflex approximant as <r>.

Palatal sounds

The palatal[4] sounds are not consistently represented in the Mission Orthography. Kempe's phonetic key only has the palatal stop <tj>, and he thus appears to take the palatal nasal and lateral as a sequence of <n> or <l> respectively followed by <j>. This in itself presents no particular issue for the orthography.[5] More importantly, as noted in the previous section, both Kempe and Strehlow are inconsistent in distinguishing the palatal nasal and lateral from their alveolar counterparts, particularly at the beginning of words: they are written as <n> and <l> respectively in many

4 These are better characterised as alveopalatal but the more general term is sufficient here.

5 In fact T.G.H. Strehlow (1944: 14) later analysed all the palatals in this way as consonant clusters: 'j is very frequently met with as the final element of the consonant combinations lj, nj, tj, tnj, ntj'.

cases. For example, *ninta* 'one' (FRM *nyinta*). In the Luritja words in the dictionary Strehlow takes a different approach, drawing on the Spanish use of a tilde above <n>, for example *ngalatarbañi* 'hereinkommen, come into'. He presumably does not use the tilde in Aranda words because the spelling system for Aranda had already become established in use.

Kempe and Strehlow clearly use <nj> to represent two distinct things, (i) a single palatal nasal /ɲ/ and (ii) a sequence of a palatal nasal followed by a palatal stop /ɲc/, although they both also use <ntj> for the latter in other words. It is also possible that in some cases their <nj> represents a sequence of an alveolar nasal followed by a palatal stop /nc/, since this is known to occur in Arandic dialects. Thus it is not clear how to read <nj> in a given word. For example, Strehlow's <nj> in both *njuma* 'drink' (FRM *ntjuma*) and *itinja* 'near' vs *etintja* 'branch' (FRM *etinya* vs *etintja*).

The velar approximant

There is also variability in the representation of the voiced 'unrounded back approximant /ɰ/ articulated in the velar and uvular regions' (Henderson 2013: 20–21), a phoneme with approximant and weak fricative allophones. This is one of the phonemes that Kempe represented with <r>, for example *ara* 'wrath' (Kempe 1891a: 38). This Aranda phoneme is similar to /r/ phonemes in many modern varieties of French (Henderson and Dobson 1994: 22) and allophones of /r/ in German (Moulton 1962: 35) and it is therefore not at all surprising that German speakers represented this Aranda phoneme as <r>. Strehlow (1908: 699) describes its pronunciation and its representation in his work as follows:

> Den Konsonanten h kenne ich im Wonkaranda nicht, dagegen kommt ein gutturales r vor, das ich im Unterschied zum gewöhnlichen r mit einem Spiritus asper versehe (r̔). Es erfordert für den Weissen einige Übung, diesen Laut hervorzubringen; man versuche den Laut ch (wie in ach!) mit dem sanften, nicht rollenden r zu verbinden; z. B. rarka zu sprechen rcharka.

> [I do not know of the consonant h in Wonkaranda, however there is a guttural r, which in contrast to the usual r, I give with the Spiritus asper ʽ [i.e. r̔]. For a white person it takes practice to produce this sound. One attempts to make the ch sound (as in ach!) combined with a soft and non-rolled r, for example to pronounce rarka as rcharka.]

The *spiritus asper*, a Latin translation of 'rough breathing', is a symbol < ʻ > which appears in Greek linguistic tradition to indicate /h/, the glottal fricative. The Aranda velar approximant was later represented as <r̲> by T.G.H. Strehlow (1944). In the dictionary, Carl Strehlow also recognises the velar approximant as a distinctive sound in another way, by giving it a distinct place in the alphabetical order, placing the 44 entries after the entries starting with plain <r>. The velar approximant has been gradually lost from Western Aranda speech, and is not represented at all in the modern FRM orthography. Its loss in words has generally resulted in a long vowel sound, which Strehlow represented with a macron, as in *ā* 'anger'.

Simple vowels, diphthongs and semivowels

The representation of simple vowels, diphthongs and semivowels is one of the most obvious differences between the Mission Orthography and the modern phonemic orthographies, and indeed it is the major difference between the two modern orthographies. This section examines the representation of the simple vowels first in the Mission Orthography, and then the phonemic orthographies, before discussing the diphthongs.

The vowel letters in Kempe's (1891a: 2) phonetic key are used individually to represent simple vowel phones (and in some cases semivowels), and in combinations to represent diphthongs. They do not match closely to the phonetic distinctions that differentiate Aranda words, and thus cannot easily be correlated with a phonemic analysis of the vowels.

Simple vowels

Kempe's key to simple vowels is shown in Table 3. Because the phonetic representation in the Mission Orthography is broad, these vowel letters do not represent five specific vowel phones in Aranda. In fact, it is possible to discriminate a wide range of vowel phones in Aranda words. Rather, these five vowel letters represent a categorisation of that wide range of vowel phones into five broad phonetic categories. For a vowel phone in a given word to be represented in writing, the writer has to make a decision as to which phonetic category a particular vowel phone fits into.

Table 3. Simple vowels in Kempe (1891a).

'A a, like a in father, are'	'O o, like o in more'
'E e, like e in there, were'	'U u, like u in dull, or o in more'
'I i, like i in tin'	

The categorisation of vowel phones in this way explains certain types of inconsistency in the spelling of words in the Mission Orthography. Firstly, a vowel phone in a particular word can be borderline between two or more of the five categories, and since writers are basically forced to categorise it, they may categorise the same phone differently in writing the same word on different occasions. Secondly, in any language it is normal that there is a certain amount of variability in the pronunciation of a given word, even by the same speaker. So the same word may have slightly different vowel phones in it on different occasions. These points account for some cases in Strehlow's dictionary where there are two distinct entries for the same word, with a vowel phone represented differently, for example *ritjalama* and *ritjilama* 'see on the go'. In just a few cases, he gives two possibilities in the same entry, for example, *irkulambetninama* or *erkulambetninama* 'preserved'. Thirdly, there can be differences between individuals in how they categorise the same vowel phones, and therefore choose different letters to represent them. For example, Kempe's *ewoluma* 'to lean against' vs Strehlow's *iwulama* are very likely to represent basically the same pronunciation, even though three of the four vowel letters in the word are different in the two spellings. Strehlow and Kempe appear to have made different judgements of the best category for each of the vowel phones in the pronunciation of this word, even though both of them were using the set of letters in Table 3. In all of these examples, it is not that one of the spellings is necessarily an error; this variability in spelling is inherent in the way that the Mission Orthography works.

To turn now to the details of the vowels, Kempe's account of how these letters represent the vowel sounds is rather confused. With regard to the length of the vowel sounds, he describes the simple vowel phones as short; however, the majority of the English vowels that he gives as comparisons are in fact long, at least in modern Australian English: in 'father', 'are', 'were' and 'more'. This is complicated by his statement that the corresponding long vowel phones are represented by a macron diacritic over the relevant vowel letter. Kempe's key gives only one example: *lāda* 'point' where he says that <ā> represents the long vowel as in 'far'. This is then further complicated because, in his vocabulary, very few of the long vowel phones of Aranda are actually represented with the macron. Strehlow's dictionary makes greater use of the macron, with all five vowel letters <ā> <ē> <ī> <ō> <ū>, but it is used infrequently and is used to represent only a relatively small proportion of long vowel phones in words. He also occasionally uses a breve diacritic to indicate a short vowel, for example <ă>.

Kempe's <e> represents a broad phonetic category for which the two comparison vowels are as in *there* and *were*, /eː/ and /ɜː/ respectively in modern Australian English. Providing more than one comparison vowel is entirely consistent with the phonetic category approach since it serves to better indicate the phonetic range of the category. His treatment of <u> similarly has two comparison vowels. In fact, in his vocabulary Kempe also uses <u> to represent a vowel phone like the one in English *dull* in only a few words such as *kumerrama* 'to rise, get up', which Strehlow changed to *kamerama*. Given the spelling of words in Kempe's vocabulary, a better comparison in the phonetic key would have been the vowel in English *put* (and he could also have added 'like w in wife' for <u>). It is also problematic that he gives the comparison vowel in *more* for both <u> and <o>, since this means that the same vowel phone can be represented by either letter. This is presumably because the categorisation as <o> and <u> was not a good match to the actual vowel phones. T.G.H. Strehlow (1944: 8) similarly noted—albeit within his rather different vowel categorisation—that 'it becomes a matter of doubt whether to write u or o in a given instance'.

Simple vowels in the FRM and IAD orthographies

The correspondence between the Mission Orthography and the phonemic orthographies is complex with regard to vowels, and the details are more difficult to represent in a single table than for the consonants above. Table 4 shows the representation of simple vowels in the three orthographies. An obvious difference is that the Mission Orthography makes the most distinctions and the IAD orthography the least. This is a consequence of the phonetic basis of the former versus the phonemic basis of the latter. Another obvious difference is that the FRM and IAD orthographies do not use <o>. More important though than listing the vowel letters used in each orthography, is the fact that each orthography uses these letters in different ways, to represent different types of categorisation of the vowel phones that occur in the words of the language.

Table 4. Basic vowel distinctions in the orthographies.[6]

Mission orthography	< a > < e > < i > < o > < u > < ā > < ē > < ī > < ō > < ū >
FRM orthography	< a > < e > < i > < u > < aa>
IAD orthography	< a > < e > < i > < u >

Sources: Mission orthography: Kempe (1891a) and Strehlow (1910a); FRM orthography: Roennfeldt et al. (2006); IAD orthography: Breen et al. (2000).

The basic correspondence in vowels between the FRM and IAD orthographies is given in Table 5, leaving aside some details for the sake of an overview. The Aranda words in the table can be taken as examples of specific vowel phones and their representation, underlined for clarity. Table 5 shows how in some cases the same phone is categorised in different ways in the two orthographies. For example, the first vowel in the Aranda words for 'foot' and 'east' are categorised differently in the FRM orthography and represented as <i> and <e> respectively, whereas they are categorised the same and both represented as <i> in the IAD orthography. Note that due to the complexity of the correspondences in the table, the details of <e> in the IAD orthography have to be split into two separate parts in the table.

The IAD orthography is based on Breen's (2001) phonemic analysis of Aranda, and the aspect that most results in differences between the IAD and FRM orthographies is that in his phonemic analysis there is a phoneme /ə/ which has a wide range of allophones. This range occurs because /ə/ is much influenced by the articulation of its neighbouring phonemes in a given word. The context information in Table 5 gives the general flavour of how this operates, that is, how a given phoneme is realised as the specific phone in the example words. The main factors involved are the effects of (i) a neighbouring palatal consonant, or (ii) a neighbouring rounded consonant. In relation to the latter, Breen (2001) analyses not only the consonant phonemes listed in Table 1 above, but also a set of corresponding consonant phonemes which can be described as rounded or labialised, and represented in IPA as /t^{w}/ for example. This is pronounced

6 As noted above, Kempe (1891a) also occasionally uses a breve diacritic to indicate a short vowel, for example <ă>. Strehlow uses a circumflex diacritic in a few words, mostly <ê>. It is not clear what this is intended to indicate but he may have been experimenting with making a particular distinction that he decided not to proceed with.

with [w] if it is followed by certain vowels, including a word-final vowel. The IAD orthography represents these phonemes with the plain consonant representation plus <w>, for example <tw>.

Table 5. Vowel correspondences between the FRM and IAD orthographies.

FRM orthography		IAD orthography		Phoneme and context	
arrua 'rock wallaby'	< u >	(< w >)	arrwe	/C^w/	rounded consonant
ura 'fire' purta 'round'		< u >	ure purte	/u/	/u/ in all contexts. Alternative analysis: /ə/ before a rounded coronal consonant /C^w/[1]
ntjuma 'drink'		< e >	ntyweme	/ə/	after a rounded consonant /C^w/
wurra 'boy'			werre		after /w/
ntjwia 'corkwood'	< i >		ntyweye		after /C^w/ & before /j/
irrauwia 'weapons'			irraweye		after /w/ & before /j/
pitjima 'come'			petyeme		next to palatal consonant, except before / j /
mia 'mother'			meye		before / j /
ilkuma 'eat'		< i >	irlkweme	/i/	before a retroflex consonant
ingka 'foot'			ingke		
ekngarra 'east'	< e >		ikngerre		
erritja 'eagle'	< a >	< e >	irretye	[2]	vowel at end of word
katjia 'child'			ketyeye	/ə/	next to palatal consonant, except before /j/
kara 'meat'			kere		elsewhere
impatja 'track'		< a >	impatye	/a/	
kwaarra 'girl'	< aa >		kwarre		

[1] Breen (2001) offers these two analyses of the vowel in words such as these examples, depending on some specific details that are beyond the scope of this discussion.

[2] Wilkins (1989) analyses the word-final vowel [ə]~[ɐ] as the /ə/ phoneme. Breen's analysis of word-final vowels is more complex. When a word is at the end of a phonological phrase this non-contrastive and quite variable final vowel is analysed as a non-phonemic vowel associated with the phonological phrase, rather than the /ə/ phoneme.

Sources: FRM orthography: Roennfeldt et al. (2006); IAD orthography: Breen et al. (2000); Phoneme and context: Breen (2001).

Some of the categorisation of vowel phones in the early phonetic orthographies would appear to have been influenced by the native languages of their creators. One result is that the native German speakers Kempe and Strehlow write the language name as Aranda, while the native English speakers Spencer and Gillen write it Arunta. T.G.H. Strehlow (1944: 9) identified a back unrounded vowel [ɑ̩] which he identifies with the <u> in English *cut* and *butter*, and a German short sound, <a> as in *kann* and *Mann*. He notes that 'English research workers regularly identify [this Aranda vowel] with their [<u>] sound, whereas German writers regard it as the equivalent of their a sound'. In German orthography, <a> represents both /a/ and /ɑ̩/ (as in *Stadt*), a contrast which is not found in English (Moulton 1962: 99).

Diphthongs and semivowels

Kempe's representation of the semivowels /w/ and /j/ shows parallels to both English and German. His 'J j, like y in year' is clearly influenced by his native German, where the similar phoneme is written <j>, rather than the corresponding <y> in English. Strehlow (1908: 699) admits that his predecessors would have done better to use <y> instead of <j> but suggests that it was by then difficult to change since <j> was already in use in translations for the Aranda community. Conversely Kempe's and Strehlow's use of <w> in words like *iwuna* 'what?' shows no influence from German, where <w> represents the phoneme /v/.

Kempe recognises three diphthongs, as shown in Table 6. The letters that he chooses to represent these phones follow straightforwardly from the letters that he uses to represent the five simple vowel phones. The representation of the diphthongs happens to partially match German orthography and partially match English orthography. German has three diphthong phonemes: /aʊ/ written <au>, /ɔʏ/ written <eu> or <äu>, and /aɪ/ mostly written <ei> and <ai>. Both Kempe's <au> and <ai> match the German orthography, although <ai> is actually a less common spelling of the German diphthong phoneme /aɪ/. His choice of <oi> does not parallel German, but it does of course parallel the English representation of the diphthong in words like *coin*.

Table 6. Diphthongs in Kempe (1891a).

'Ai ai, like i in light'	'Oi oi, like oi in oil'
'Au au, like ow in now'	

Strehlow (1908: 698) takes the notion of diphthong slightly differently, adding <ui> and <ua>: 'In the Aranda language, only the following diphthongs are known to me: ai, au, oi, ui, ua. The vowels a and e, e and a, etc., may occur side by side, but are never pronounced as diphthongs'. Kempe (1891a: 2) and Strehlow both use, albeit rather inconsistently, a diaeresis diacritic < ¨ > over a vowel to mark it as distinct from the preceding vowel rather than a diphthong, for example Strehlow's *inkaïmbatja* 'footprint' which is a compound consisting of *inka* 'foot' and *imbatja* 'track'.

Most of the differences in this area within and between the Aranda orthographies depends on two related things, (i) whether a phone is taken to be a vowel or a semivowel (a vowel-like consonant), and (ii) how the syllables within a word are distinguished. By standard definition, a diphthong is a complex sound which can be analysed as a transition between two vowel phones within a single phonetic syllable.

In the Mission Orthography, <ai> and <au> are the only sequences of two vowel letters that represent true diphthongs, that is, occurring within a single syllable. Examples are given in Table 7 below. In words such as *jainama* 'send', the diphthong is followed by a retroflex consonant, and the pronunciation of <ai> actually varies between the diphthong indicated by Kempe and a long [a] vowel, at least in current Western Aranda speech. The modern orthographies treat this variation in different ways.

Table 7. Comparison of diphthongs in the Mission Orthography and modern orthographies.

	Strehlow Dictionary	FRM Orthography[1]	IAD Orthography
< ai >	jainama 'send' inkainama '(to) erect'	yairnama ingkairnama	yarneme ingkarneme
	Emphatic ending, e.g. lai! 'go!'	lhai!	lhaye!
< au >	Emphatic ending, e.g. lakitjau!		lheketyawe!

[1] The absence of FRM spellings of words in this table and the following ones is simply because these words do not appear in any available source that uses the FRM orthography.

In a much larger number of cases, illustrated in Table 8, a sequence of two vowel letters in the Mission Orthography represents a phonetic transition between the vowels of two syllables. For example, Strehlow's *jia* 'story' can be analysed as two syllables [ji:|a].

Table 8. Digraphs in the Mission Orthography and their representation in modern orthographies.

	Strehlow Dictionary	FRM Orthography	IAD Orthography
< ai >	(none)		
< au >	bāuma 'push' lauma 'hide'	pauwuma	paweme laweme
< ea >	erea, iria 'saltbush'		irreye
< ia >	jia 'story'	yia	yeye
< iu >	tākiuma 'spread out'	taakiwuma	takiweme
< oa >	itoa 'bush turkey' nóa 'spouse'	itua nua	irtewe newe
< oe >	ntoérama 'vomit'		ntewirreme
< oi >	boilama 'blow'		pewileme
< ou >	erouma 'shake'	rruwuma	rreweme
< ui >	ruilkara 'bird sp.'		rrewirlkere

In the type above, the IAD orthography, and to some extent the FRM orthography, show a different analysis of phonetic transition between the vowels of two syllables: a semivowel /w/ or /j/ is taken to occur between the two vowels. For example, where Strehlow has <au> in *bauma* 'push', the IAD orthography has <awe> in *paweme*. In this case, the FRM orthography combines both strategies, the sequence <au> plus the semivowel represented as <w>, *pauwuma*. An alternative strategy that is similar to this is also used in some words in the Mission Orthography: the transition between the vowels of two syllables is represented by three vowel letters, as illustrated in Table 9. German orthography also uses the same general strategy, for example in words like *feiern* /faiɐn/ 'celebrate' or *misstrauische* /mɪstrauɪʃ/ 'mistrustful'.[7]

Table 9. Trigraphs in the Mission Orthography and modern orthographies.

	Strehlow Dictionary	FRM Orthography	IAD Orthography
< aia >	taia 'moon'	taiya	taye
< aie >	irkaierama 'fade'		irrkayirreme
< aii >	irkaiïrkaia 'faint'		irrkayirrkaye
< aua >	taua 'bag' raualelama 'scatter'	thauwa	thawe rawelhileme

7 Much less commonly, German orthography also uses a semivowel symbol in representing such transitions, for example *Bayern* (Bavaria) /baiɐn/.

	Strehlow Dictionary	FRM Orthography	IAD Orthography
< aue >	rauerama 'disperse'		rawirreme
< aui >	rauilama 'scatter, sow'		rawileme
< eoa >	réoa, reowa 'entry'		rriwe, arriwe
< oiu >	ilboiuma 'deny'		ilpuyeweme

The strategy of a sequence of vowel letters is also applied to transitions between vowels over more than two syllables, for example the three syllables represented by <auia> in Strehlow's *errauia* 'weapons'. Compare IAD *irraweye.*

Note that Strehlow's alternative spelling *reowa* 'entry' in Table 9 exemplifies a combined strategy which parallels the FRM spelling of *pauwuma* with transitional <w>. This occurs in only a couple of other words in Strehlow's dictionary. Overall, these different strategies constitute a degree of inconsistency in the Mission Orthography.

As noted above, Strehlow (1908) also listed <ui> and <ua> as representing diphthongs. In fact his dictionary includes the range in Table 10 below. In terms of Breen's phonemic analysis of Aranda, these all involve the same phenomenon, a rounded consonant, written for example as /t^w/ using IPA, represented in the IAD orthography as <tw>. This is pronounced with [w] if it is followed by certain vowels, including a word-final vowel. The FRM orthography also represents this as a consonant plus <w> (except for some words where it has consonant plus <u>, as in *arrua* below). Strehlow is more inconsistent, representing this in different words as consonant plus <w> or <u> or <o>.

Table 10. Representation of rounded consonants in the Mission Orthography and modern orthographies.

	Strehlow Dictionary	FRM Orthography	IAD Orthography
< ua >	lankua 'bush banana'	langkwa	langkwe
< uia >	inguia 'old'	ingkwiya	ingkweye
< wa >	kwata 'egg'	kwaarta	kwarte
< we >	kwenja 'windbreak'	kwintja	kwintye
< oa >	aroa 'rock wallaby'	arrua	arrwe

Use of the Mission Orthography

The Mission Orthography can be examined as a system that developed over its time, and as the predecessor of the modern phonemic orthographies. Its origin and development can be understood in terms of the individuals who contributed to it, notably Kempe and Strehlow, but it must also be considered in terms of its intended users and their responses to it. As already noted, the Mission Orthography was used in educational and religious works, a scholarly grammar and dictionary, and in personal correspondence. It was used by Aranda people, though perhaps mostly within the school and church contexts.

The Mission Orthography was clearly intended to be a practical orthography, and its details were established by Kempe and Strehlow with practical considerations in mind. This is evidenced by Kempe's explicit attempt to keep the 'number of written characters as few as possible' (1891a: 2), and Strehlow's (1908) reluctance to make significant changes to the orthography once it had become established in the Hermannsburg community. There was also recognition of the importance of the broader context of English literacy in Australia in Strehlow's (1908) comment on the greater suitability of <y> over <j> in the Aranda orthography. T.G.H. Strehlow continued that sensitivity to context in justifying his later phonetic orthography (1971: l).

If the importance of making a distinction between a practical orthography for use in the language community and an orthography for scholarly or 'scientific' description of a language now seems obvious, it is because of more than 100 years of experience in the creation of new orthographies, a history in which Kempe and Strehlow played an early role. The tension between the development of a 'scientific' (phonetic) alphabet and a practical writing system can be seen with the adoption, and later abandonment, of the Lepsius Standard Alphabet (1863) for writing the Dieri language at the Bethesda mission, which was also founded by missionaries from Hermannsburg, Germany, in the late nineteenth century. The Standard Alphabet was specifically developed for use with hitherto unwritten languages, as opposed to situations where there was (as with Sanskrit) an existing orthographic tradition. One of the principles of the Standard Alphabet was that 'every sound must be defined physiologically before being given a place in the alphabet'. In the view of Kneebone (2005: 356), the main weaknesses of the Standard Alphabet were the tension between collectors of data and specialised scientific researchers, together with the complexity of the diacritic system, which gave rise to problems for the 'writer, reader and printer'. A similar story took place later in the Finke River mission's abandonment of T.G.H. Strehlow's phonetic orthography with its rich use of diacritics. Oberscheidt (1991) characterises that change as the rejection of a 'purely academic orthography', a criticism he directs not only to T.G.H. Strehlow's phonetic orthography but to the modern IAD orthography as well.

Scholarly interpretation

Missionaries trained in philology were the primary translators and collectors of linguistic data for scholarly analysis throughout the nineteenth century, but they also benefited from that analysis. Kempe (1891a) explicitly invited scholars to advise him on the analysis of Aranda, and Strehlow had a productive long-distance research relationship with the scholar von Leonhardi. Lepsius ([1863] 1981: 1) claimed that,

> An intimate relation exists between linguistic science and Missionary labours. The latter, especially in new and hitherto unwritten languages, supply the former—chiefly by means of translations. Vocabularies, Grammars and Specimens—with rich, and in some cases the only, materials for further investigation and comparison.

The Mission Orthography was under-differentiated in some aspects and over-differentiated in others. In this respect, it was like other orthographies of that time, for example Black's use of the International Phonetic Alphabet to record a Western Desert language (Black 1915). However, independently of the significance of this under- and over-differentiation for practical use in a language community, in some cases it resulted in misinterpretation of written materials by outsiders, including scholars.

Planert (1907: 552) lists 13 simple vowels, 18 complex vowels (diphthongs) and 3 triphthongs in Aranda—far more than his contemporaries had recorded. His overestimation of the diphthongs was caused by his lack of firsthand experience of the language and his reliance on documents written in the Mission Orthography. Planert also includes <ü> among his vowels, which Strehlow (1908) disputes, and claimed that 'triphthongs are not uncommon'. This may refer to the vowel letter sequences in the printed materials to which he had access and from his language informant, returned missionary Nicolai Wettengel. In response Carl Strehlow (1908: 698) stated:

> I am only familiar with the following diphthongs in the Aranda language: ai, au, oi, ui, ua. While the vowels a and e, e and a etc can certainly occur next to each other, they are never pronounced as diphthongs.

Planert claimed that he did not have access to Kempe's (1891a) grammar, however, J. Strehlow (2011: 962, 1018) believes that Planert relied upon the written language in Kempe's work to make his analysis.

Similar misinterpretation of the Mission Orthography has led in some cases to broader misunderstanding of the language. Alf Sommerfelt's (1938) analysis of Aranda is based upon the work of Kempe and Strehlow, as well as the work of Spencer and Gillen. In an attempt to show how Aranda was a primitive language Sommerfelt claimed that Aranda lacked categories found in Indo-European languages and supported his points with false etymologies (Wilkins 1989: 18; McGregor 2008: 6). One such etymology which involved *nama*, supposedly meaning both 'sit' and 'grass', was based upon an under-differentiation in the Mission Orthography. These are in fact two distinct words, with distinct pronunciations, represented as *neme* and *name* respectively in the IAD orthography.

Major developments in Aranda orthography

From Kempe's establishment of the Mission Orthography, its phonetic basis was seen as adequate for the purpose of practical communication between speakers of the language. They were able to recognise words even though not all the significant sounds of the language were distinguished in writing. Oberscheidt (1991: iv) notes that in reading, 'speakers of the language had continued to pronounce the dentals and retroflexes even when the missionaries failed to provide symbols for them'. This is to be expected for fluent readers because, once fluent, the processes of reading rely more on the recognition of whole words than on composing a word from its individual sounds.

During the period of phonetic orthographies, developments in phonetics and in orthography design increased the ability of researchers to discriminate and represent speech sounds. The Mission Orthography was one of a number of phonetic systems for Australian languages. These include Black (1915) and later, the Adelaide University Phonetic System (AUPS) in the 1930s (Monaghan 2008). T.G.H. Strehlow used a version of the AUPS orthography for his fieldnotes and scholarly works.

He produced an academic description of Aranda phonetics and grammar with a narrow phonetic transcription (1944) which, among other features, distinguished 23 vowel phones [iː ɪ ɩ y eː e ɛː a ɑː ɑ ɑ̣ ɔː ɔ oː uː ʊ ə ĭ ĕ ă ɑ̣̆ ŏ ŭ]. Following standard practices in phonetic transcription, many of these narrow phonetic distinctions were represented using diacritics. A simplified version of this scheme was then used in T.G.H. Strehlow's translation of the New Testament (1956) and in the Aranda Lutheran hymnal (1964). In comparison to the Mission Orthography, this system removed the major under-differentiation of place of articulation in consonants, and modified the categorisation of the vowels. A small sample from the hymnal gives the flavour of this orthography: 'Jíŋaṇa ŋū́ḷilāí, Iŋkā́ṭai, Ŋuā́ŋ' Uŋgwā́ŋaṇ̦ibḗra'. (IAD 'Yengenhe ngwerlilaye, Ingkartaye, Ngwange ngkwangenhiperre.')

As a practical orthography, however, T.G.H. Strehlow's orthography was disliked by the Hermannsburg mission staff who thought it made it difficult to write Aranda. The extensive use of the diacritics also presented technical issues for the printing technology of the day, and had also caused major delays in the printing of T.G.H. Strehlow's major works (Breen 2005: 94). A revised orthography was used in Albrecht's (1979) catechism, where diacritics played a more limited role, only distinguishing the place of articulation of some consonants, for example 'ṇ̦aṇ̦ibera aṭa ragaŋkarauṇa' (IAD 'nhanhiperre athe rrekangkerrewerne'). The fate of the diacritics was sealed by the advent of personal computers, as the early models did not readily handle all the diacritics used for Aranda (Oberscheidt 1991: iv).

The development of the theory of the phoneme extended understanding of the sound systems of languages by expressing which phonetic differences are used to differentiate words in a language. Sounds in a language that are contrastive in this way are expressed as the phonemes of the language. The phoneme concept was used in language description in American Structuralist linguistics, and many Australian linguists were first introduced to it by the first schools of the Summer Institute of Linguistics (SIL), held in Melbourne in the 1950s. SIL linguist Sarah Gudschinsky was instrumental in developing orthographies for languages as a way of encouraging literacy among speakers of those languages. These were based upon the identification of the distinctive phonemes of the language, considering the 'functional load' of each in relation to the whole language system (Gudschinsky 1973: 120). Pastor John Pfitzner, who was based at Hermannsburg mission from 1969 to 1984, attended a workshop run by

Gudschinsky in the summer of 1972–73. Pfitzner reanalysed the sounds of Aranda and created the modern FRM orthography, which then replaced both the Mission Orthography and the later phonetic orthographies. Pfitzner replaced the consonant diacritics with digraphs and reanalysed the vowels (Breen 2005: 95). As no words are differentiated by the voicing of stops, and speakers generally make no distinction between voiced and unvoiced stops, this distinction was no longer represented: the stops were represented as <p>, <t> and <k>, and <b>, <d> and <g> were dropped.

The development of the FRM orthography was paralleled by Breen's phonemic analysis of firstly Antekerrepenhe and then other Arandic languages, and the subsequent development of a phonemic orthography on this basis by the then School of Australian Linguistics (Breen 2005). Through the IAD, Breen and other researchers began to develop orthographies for Arandic languages including Western Arrernte, Eastern and Central Arrernte, Anmatyerr, Alyawarr and Kaytetye. The process involved meetings to consult with speakers of the languages over a number of years. These orthographies are distinct to each language, according to the differences between these languages and the preferences of their speakers, but they all follow similar principles, thus the Common Arandic approach. These orthographies have been used to produce dictionaries including the *Eastern and Central Arrernte to English Dictionary* (Henderson and Dobson 1994), the *Introductory Dictionary of Western Arrernte* (Breen et al. 2000), the *Central & Eastern Anmatyerr to English Dictionary* (Green 2010), the *Kaytetye to English Dictionary* (Turpin and Ross 2012) and the *Alyawarr to English Dictionary* (Green 1992; second edition by Blackman et al., forthcoming).

As summarised above, the most significant differences between the FRM and IAD orthographies of Western Aranda are the representations of vowels and diphthongs. The FRM orthography, and some orthographies in the Common Arandic approach, have undergone minor modifications since their inceptions but are now generally considered to be stable. A change made to the FRM orthography was to drop <o> from the orthography (Roennfeldt et al. 2006), recategorising these vowel phones with the other vowel phones represented by <u>. This brought it closer to the IAD orthography. In Wilkins's phonemic analysis of Mparntwe Arrernte (1989: 78) the phoneme /u/ has allophones [o] [ʊ] [ɔ] [ɔː] and [u] in different contexts. For a short period the school at Ltyentye Apurte

(Santa Teresa) introduced <o> into its orthography, but withdrew it so that there was a consistent orthography for Eastern/Central Arrernte in all the communities in which it is spoken.

Concluding remarks

The Mission Orthography was a uniform phonetically-based orthography of the late nineteenth century which was used for practical purposes by speakers of the Aranda language, both Aboriginal and non-Aboriginal. In the view of Gudschinsky (1973: 117), it is never possible to devise an orthography in a social vacuum, that is, apart from social pressures, for example dominant national languages such as English and their writing systems. This continues to be true for Western Aranda. Major languages impinge upon minor languages, and often force the orthography of the latter to compromise.

In the development of an orthography, the language of the creator is important. This means that we have had to consider German phonology and orthography in understanding how the Mission Orthography was devised by its German-speaking inventors.

The Mission Orthography was in use over a century from 1877 to the 1970s, during which it was a functional means of written communication for those who could understand Aranda, despite distinguishing only a minority of the phonemes of the language. A relatively large amount of material was written in the Mission Orthography, particularly religious materials that were used regularly by the entire mission community, and educational materials. A relatively high degree of consistency in the writing of the language is evident from missionary publications and letters. As a result, there was resistance to changing the orthography when T.G.H. Strehlow developed a phonetic orthography based on the IPA from the 1930s on, in order to publish works about Aranda language and culture. The Mission Orthography of Kempe and Carl Strehlow, and its descendant in T.G.H. Strehlow's phonetic orthography, coexisted into the 1970s when both were replaced by phonemic orthographies.

References

Adams, W.Y. 1998. *The Philosophical Roots of Anthropology*. Stanford: Centre for the Study of Language and Information Publications.

Albrecht, P.G.E. (ed.). 1979. *Araṇḍa–English Catechism: Luther's Small Catechism with Explanations*. Adelaide: Lutheran Publishing House.

Albrecht, P.G.E. 2002. *From Mission to Church, 1877–2002: Finke River Mission*. Adelaide: Finke River Mission.

Atlas of Living Australia. n.d. Access at: www.ala.org.au/faq/species-names/.

Austin, P. 2013. *A Dictionary of Diyari, South Australia*. London: SOAS, University of London. Access at: www.academia.edu/2491259/A_Dictionary_of_Diyari_South_Australia.

Austin-Broos, D. 2010. Translating Christianity. *The Australian Journal of Anthropology* 21(1): 14–32. doi.org/10.1111/j.1757-6547.2010.00065.x

Austin-Broos, D.J. 2009. *Arrernte Present Arrernte Past*. Chicago: Chicago University Press.

Berlin, I. 1976. *Vico and Herder*. London: Hogarth Press.

Black, J.M. 1915. Language of the Everard Range Tribe. In S.A. White (ed.), Scientific Notes on an Expedition into the North-western regions of South Australia. *Transactions of the Royal Society of South Australia* 39: 732–35.

Blackman, D., J. Green and D. Moore (forthcoming). *Alyawarr to English Dictionary*. 2nd edition. Alice Springs: IAD Press.

Breen, G. n.d. Arunta and Aranda and Arrernte: Why Do We Spell It Like That? Unpublished paper.

Breen, G. 1998. The Grammar of Kinship in Central Australia. Alice Springs. Manuscript.

Breen, G. 2001. The wonders of Arandic phonology. In J. Simpson, D. Nash, M. Laughren, P. Austin and B. Alpher (eds), *Forty Years On: Ken Hale and Australian Languages.* pp. 45-70. Canberra: Pacific Linguistics.

Breen, G. 2005. A short history of spelling systems in Arrernte. In A. Kenny and S. Mitchell (eds), Collaboration and Language, *Strehlow Research Centre Occasional Paper* 4: 93–102.

Breen, G. (compiler), with E. Rubuntja, G. Armstrong and J.C. Pfitzner. 2000. *Introductory Dictionary of Western Arrernte.* Alice Springs: IAD Press.

Bunzl, M. 1996. Franz Boas and the Humboldtian tradition: From *Volksgeist* and *Nationalcharakter* to an anthropological concept of culture. In G.W. Stocking (ed.), Volksgeist *as Method and Ethic: Essays on Boasian Ethnography and the German Anthropological Tradition.* History of Anthropology Vol. 8. pp. 17–78. Madison: The University of Wisconsin Press.

Cawthorn, M. and H. Malbunka. 2005. Hesekiel Malbunka. In A. Kenny and S. Mitchell (eds), Collaboration and Language, *Strehlow Research Centre Occasional Paper* 4: 71–75.

Cook, A.R. 1982. An Outline Grammar of Martutjarra Luritja. BA Honours dissertation, Monash University.

Cox, F. 2012. *Australian English Pronunciation and Transcription.* Cambridge: Cambridge University Press.

Eylmann, E. 1908. *Die Eingeborenen der Kolonie Südaustralien.* Berlin: Dietrich Reimer (Ernst Vohsen).

Foertsch, H. 2001. Missonarsmaterialien und die Entdeckung amerikanischer Sprachen in Europa: vom Sprachensammler Lorenzo Hervas y Panduro zum Linguisten Wilhelm von Humboldt. In R. Wendt (Hrsg.), *Sammeln, Vernetzen, Auswerten. Missionare und ihr Beitrag zum Wandel europäischer Weltsicht.* pp. 75–130. Tübingen: Gunter Narr Verlag.

Glass, A. and D. Hackett (compilers). 2003. *Ngaanyatjarra-Ngaatjatjarra to English Dictionary*. Alice Springs: IAD Press.

Goddard, C. (compiler). 1996. *Pitjantjatjara/Yankunytjatjara to English Dictionary.* Revised 2nd edition. Alice Springs: IAD Press.

Green, J. (compiler). 1992. *Alyawarr to English Dictionary*. Alice Springs: Institute for Aboriginal Development.

Green, J. (compiler). 2010. *Central & Eastern Anmatyerr to English Dictionary*. Alice Springs: IAD Press.

Green, J. 2012. The Altyerre story – 'suffering badly by translation'. *The Australian Journal of Anthropology* 23(2): 158–78. doi.org/10.1111/j.1757-6547.2012.00179.x

Gudschinsky, S.C. 1973. *A Manual of Literacy for Preliterate Peoples.* Ukarumpa, PNG: Summer Institute of Linguistics.

Hansen, K., with Luritja and Pintupi language speakers. 2011. *Luritja Picture Dictionary*. Alice Springs: IAD Press.

Hansen, K.C. 1984. Communicability of some Western Desert communilects. *Work Papers of the SIL-AAB* Series B, vol. 11: 1–112.

Hansen, K.C. and L.E. Hansen (compilers). 1992. *Pintupi/Luritja Dictionary.* 3rd edition. Alice Springs: Institute for Aboriginal Development.

Hawkins, J.A. 2003. German. In W. Bright (ed.), *International Encyclopedia of Linguistics*. pp. 61–69. New York: Oxford University Press.

Henderson, J. 2013. *Topics in Eastern and Central Arrernte Grammar.* München: Lincom.

Henderson, J. and V. Dobson (compilers). 1994. *Eastern and Central Arrernte to English Dictionary*. Alice Springs: IAD Press.

Humboldt, W.v. [1820] 1994. *Über die Sprache.* Tübingen und Basel: A. Francke Verlag.

Kempe, H. 1891a. A grammar and vocabulary of the language spoken by the Aborigines of the Macdonnell Ranges, South Australia. *Transactions of the Royal Society of South Australia* 14(1): 1–54.

Kempe, (F.A.) H. 1891b. *Galtjintana-Pepa: Kristianirberaka Mbontala*. Hannover: Hermannsburg Druck und Verlag der Missionshandlung.

Kenny, A. 2004a. Pmara Kutata – Pmerekwetethe. In M. Cawthorn (ed.), *Proceedings of the Strehlow Conference 2002*. pp. 20–25. Alice Springs: Northern Territory Government.

Kenny, A. 2004b. Western Arrernte pmere kwetethe spirits. *Oceania* 74(4): 276–89. doi.org/10.1002/j.1834-4461.2004.tb02855.x

Kenny, A. 2010. *Anthropology Report. Glen Helen Native Title Consent Determination, NT*. Alice Springs: Central Land Council.

Kenny, A. 2013. *The Aranda's Pepa. An Introduction to Carl Strehlow's Masterpiece* Die Aranda- und Loritja-Stämme in Zentral-Australien *(1907–1920)*. Canberra: ANU E Press.

Kenny, A. 2017a. Early ethnographic work at the Hermannsburg mission in central Australia, 1877–1910. In N. Peterson and A. Kenny (eds.), *German Ethnography in Australia*. pp. 169–93. Canberra: ANU Press. doi.org/10.22459/GEA.09.2017.07

Kenny, A. 2017b. Aranda, Arrernte or Arrarnta? The politics of orthography and identity on the Upper Finke River. *Oceania* 87(3): 261–81. doi.org/10.1002/ocea.5169

Kluckhohn, C. 1936. Some reflections on the method and theory of the Kulturkreislehre. *American Anthropologist* 38: 157–96. doi.org/10.1525/aa.1936.38.2.02a00010

Kneebone, H.M. 2005. The Language of the Chosen View: The First Phase of Graphization of Dieri by Hermannsburg Missionaries, Lake Killalpaninna, 1867–80. PhD thesis, School of Humanities, Adelaide University.

Kral, I. 2000. The Socio-historical Development of Literacy in Arrernte: A Case Study of the Introduction of Writing in an Aboriginal Language and the Implications for Current Vernacular Literacy Practices. MA dissertation, University of Melbourne.

Latz, P. 1996. *Bushfires and Bushtucker: Aboriginal Plant Use in Central Australia*. 1st edition reprint. Alice Springs: IAD Press.

Latz, P.K. 2014. *Blind Moses: Moses Tjalkabota Uraiakuraia, Aranda Man of High Degree and Christian Evangelist.* Alice Springs: P. Latz.

Lepsius, R. [1863] 1981. *Standard Alphabet for Reducing Unwritten Languages and Foreign Graphic Systems to a Uniform Orthography in European Letters.* 2nd, revised edition. Amsterdam Classics in Linguistics Vol. 5. Amsterdam: John Benjamins Publishing.

Liebermeister, B. 1998. Leben und Werk Carl Strehlows, des Erforschers der Aranda-und Loritja Stämme in Zentralaustralien. MA thesis, University of München.

Lohe, M. 1977. A mission is established at Hermannsburg. In E. Leske (ed.), *Hermannsburg: A Vision and a Mission.* pp. 6–41. Adelaide: Lutheran Publishing House.

Lucas, R. and D. Fergie. 2017. Pulcaracuranie: Losing and finding a cosmic centre with the help of J.G. Reuther and others. In N. Peterson and A. Kenny (eds.), *German Ethnography in Australia.* pp. 79–113. Canberra: ANU Press. doi.org/10.22459/GEA.09.2017.04

Marchand, J.W. 1982. Herder: Precursor of Humboldt, Whorf, and modern language philosophy. In W. Koepke (ed.) in cooperation with S.B. Knoll, *Johann Gottfried Herder, Innovator through the Ages.* pp. 20–34. Bonn: Bouvier Verlag Herbert Grundmann.

McGregor, W.B. 2008. *Encountering Aboriginal languages: Studies in the history of Australian linguistics.* Canberra: Pacific Linguistics, Research School of Pacific and Asian Studies, The Australian National University.

Monaghan, P. 2008. Norman B. Tindale and the Pitjantjatjara language. In W.B. McGregor (ed.), *Encountering Aboriginal languages: Studies in the History of Australian Linguistics.* Pacific Linguistics 591, pp. 251–72. Canberra: Pacific Linguistics.

Moore, D. 2013. A uniform orthography and early linguistic research in Australia. *History and Philosophy of the Language Sciences* Blog, 16 October, hiphilangsci.net/2013/10/16/a-uniform-orthography-and-early-linguistic-research-in-australia.

Moore, D. 2015. The Reformation, Lutheran tradition and missionary linguistics. *Lutheran Theological Journal* 49(1): 36–48.

Moore, D. and V. Ríos Castaño (2018). Translation in indigenous cultures. In S.-A. Harding and O. Carbonell Cortes (eds), *The Routledge Handbook of Translation and Culture*. pp. 241–52. London: Routledge.

Moore, D.C. 2003. TGH Strehlow and the Linguistic Landscape of Australia 1930–1960. Honours thesis, University of New England.

Morton, J. 1992. Country, people, art: The Western Aranda 1870–1990. In J. Hardy, J.V.S. Megaw and M.R. Megaw (eds), *The Heritage of Namatjira*. pp. 23–62. Melbourne: William Heinemann.

Moulton, W.G. 1962. *The Sounds of English and German: A Systematic Analysis of the Contrasts between the Sound Systems*. Chicago: University of Chicago Press.

Mühlmann, W.E. 1968. *Geschichte der Anthropologie*. Frankfurt am Main: Enke.

Oberscheidt, H.D. 1990. *Learning Arrarnta*. Hermannsburg: Finke River Mission. (Revision of *Learning Aranda* by J. Pfitzner and J. Schmaal 1975).

Oberscheidt, H.D. 1991. Western Arrarnta Analytical Dictionary. Unpublished Manuscript.

Penny, H.G. 2002. *Objects of Culture: Ethnology and Ethnographic Museums in Imperial Germany*. Chapel Hill and London: University of North Carolina Press.

Penny, H.G. and M. Bunzl. 2003. Introduction: Rethinking German anthropology, colonialism, and race. In H.G. Penny and M. Bunzl (eds), *Worldly Provincialism: German Anthropology in the Age of the Empire*. pp. 1–30. Ann Arbor: University of Michigan Press. doi.org/10.3998/mpub.17806

Pfitzner, J. and J. Schmaal. 1975. *Learning Aranda*. Hermannsburg: Finke River Mission. (Revised by H.D. Oberscheidt in 1985 and 1990 as *Learning Arrarnta*).

Pizzey, G. and F. Knight. 2007. *The Field Guide to the Birds of Australia*. 8th edition. Sydney: HarperCollins Publishers.

Planert, W. 1907. Aranda-Grammatik. *Zeitschrift für Ethnologie* 39(4/5): 551–66.

Reuther, J.G. 1899–1904. Diari Gramatik, Wörterverzeichnis, Taufordnung etc., Wankaguru-Sprache, Wörterverzeichnis Wonkanguru, luyani Nganmeni, Tirari, Wunkarabana-Jaurawurka-Jendruwonta-Wonkaranta, Jandruwonta Sprache, Volume 5. Manuscript. South Australian Museum, AA266/09/5.

Reuther, J.G. 1904–06. Wörterbuch. Volumes 1–4. Manuscript. South Australian Museum, AA266/09/1–4.

Roennfeldt, D. and members of the communities of Ntaria, Ipolera, Gilbert Springs, Kulpitarra, Undarana, Red Sans Hill, Old Station and other outstations (compilers). 2006. *Western Arrarnta Picture Dictionary*. Reprinted (with revisions). Alice Springs: IAD Press.

Sarg, F.C.A. 1911. *Die Australischen Bumerangs im Städtischen Völkermuseum*. Frankfurt am Main: Joseph Baer.

Schild, M. 2004. Heading for Hermannsburg: Notes on Carl Strehlow's early career path. In W. Veit (ed.), *Strehlow Research Centre Occasional Paper* 3: 51–58.

Schmidt, P.W. 1908. Die Stellung der Aranda unter den australischen Stämmen. *Zeitschrift für Ethnologie* 40(6): 866–901.

Schmidt, P.W. 1912–18. Die Gliederung der Australischen Sprachen und ihre Beziehungen zu der Gliederung des soziologschen Verhältnisse der australischen Stämme. *Anthropos* 7 (1912): 230–51, 463–97, 1014–48; 8 (1913): 526–54; 9 (1914): 980–1018; 12/13 (1917/1918): 437–93, 747–817.

Schulze, L. 1891. The Aborigines of the Upper and Middle Finke River: Their habits and customs. *Transactions and Proceedings of the Royal Society of South Australia* 14(2): 210–46.

Sommerfelt, A. 1938. *La Langue et la société, caractères sociaux d'une langue de type archaïque*. Oslo: H. Aschehoug & Co. (W. Nygaard).

Spencer, W. B. and F. J. Gillen. 1904. *The Northern Tribes of Central Australia*. London: Macmillan & Co.

Stockigt, C. 2015. Early descriptions of Pama-Nyungan ergativity. *Historiographia Linguistica* 42(2–3): 335–77.

Strehlow, C. 1904. *Galtjinjamea-Pepa Aranda-Wolambarinjaka*. Tanunda: Auricht.

Strehlow, C. 1907. *Die Aranda- und Loritja-Stämme in Zentral-Australien I. Mythen, Sagen und Märchen des Aranda-Stammes in Zentral-Australien*. Frankfurt am Main: Joseph Baer & Co.

Strehlow, C. 1907–20. *Die Aranda- und Loritja-Stämme in Zentral-Australien*. 7 Vols. Frankfurt am Main: Joseph Baer & Co.

Strehlow, C. 1908. *Die Aranda- und Loritja-Stämme in Zentral-Australien II. Mythen, Sagen und Märchen des Loritja-Stammes; die Totemistischen Vorstellungen und die Tjurunga der Aranda und Loritja*. Frankfurt am Main: Joseph Baer & Co.

Strehlow, C. 1910a. Comparative Grammar of Aranda and Loritja. Manuscript. Strehlow Research Centre, SP-46-47.

Strehlow, C. 1910b. *Die Aranda- und Loritja-Stämme in Zentral-Australien III (i). Mythen, Sagen und Märchen des Aranda-Stammes; die Totemistischen Kulte der Aranda-und Loritja- Stämme*. Frankfurt am Main: Joseph Baer & Co.

Strehlow, C. 1911. *Die Aranda- und Loritja-Stämme in Zentral-Australien III (ii). Mythen, Sagen und Märchen des Aranda-Stammes; die Totemistischen Kulte der Aranda-und Loritja- Stämme*. Frankfurt am Main: Joseph Baer & Co.

Strehlow, C. 1913. *Die Aranda- und Loritja-Stämme in Zentral-Australien IV (i). Das Soziale Leben der Aranda- und Loritja-Stämme*. Frankfurt am Main: Joseph Baer & Co.

Strehlow, C. 1915. *Die Aranda- und Loritja-Stämme in Zentral-Australien IV (ii). Das Soziale Leben der Aranda- und Loritja-Stämme*. Frankfurt am Main: Joseph Baer & Co.

Strehlow, C. 1920. *Die Aranda- und Loritja-Stämme in Zentral-Australien V. Die Materielle Kultur der Aranda- und Loritja*. Frankfurt am Main: Joseph Baer & Co.

Strehlow, J. 2004a. Shifting focus. In M. Cawthorn (ed.), *Proceedings of the Strehlow Conference 2002*. pp. 109–19. Alice Springs: Northern Territory Government.

Strehlow, J. 2004b. Reappraising Carl Strehlow: Through the Spencer–Strehlow debate. In W. Veit (ed.), *Strehlow Research Centre Occasional Paper* 3: 59–91.

Strehlow, J. 2011. *The Tale of Frieda Keysser. Volume I: 1875–1910.* London: Wildcat Press.

Strehlow, T.G.H. n.d. Unpublished Aranda to English Dictionary. Typescript held at the SRC.

Strehlow, T.G.H. 1932. Field Diary I. Strehlow Research Centre, Alice Springs.

Strehlow, T.G.H. 1944. *Aranda Phonetics and Grammar*. Oceania Monograph no. 7. Sydney: University of Sydney.

Strehlow, T.G.H. 1947. *Aranda Traditions*. Melbourne: Melbourne University Press.

Strehlow, T.G.H. 1956. *Testamenta Ljaṭinja, Aŋkatja Araṇḍauṇa Kŋatiwumala.* Adelaide: Council of the British and Foreign Bible Society in Australia.

Strehlow, T.G.H. 1965. Culture, social structure and environment in Aboriginal central Australia. In R.M. Berndt and C.H. Berndt (eds), *Aboriginal Man in Australia*. pp. 121–45. Sydney: Angus and Robertson.

Strehlow, T.G.H. [1967] 2005. Man and Language. Address to the Adelaide University Linguistic Society on 19 September 1967. In A. Kenny and S. Mitchell (eds), Collaboration and Language, *Strehlow Research Centre Occasional Paper* 4: 76–88.

Strehlow, T.G.H. 1969. *Journey to Horseshoe Bend.* Sydney: Angus and Robertson.

Strehlow, T.G.H. 1969–70. *Handbook of Central Australian Genealogies.* Adelaide: University of Adelaide. Typescript. Strehlow Research Centre, Alice Springs.

Strehlow, T.G.H. 1970. Geography and the totemic landscape in Central Australia: A functional study. In R.M. Berndt (ed.), *Australian Aboriginal Anthropology*. pp. 93–140. Perth: University of Western Australia Press.

Strehlow, T.G.H. 1971. *Songs of Central Australia*. Sydney: Angus and Robertson.

Strehlow, T.G.H. and P. Scherer (translators). 1964. *Ljelintjamea-Pepa Lutherarinja. Angkatja Arandauna Knatiwumala. [Aranda Lutheran Hymnal with Supplement of Occasional Prayers, Benedictions and Selected English Hymns]*. North Adelaide: Finke River Mission of the United Evangelical Lutheran Church in Australia.

Taplin, G. (ed.). 1879. *The Folklore, Manners, Customs and Languages of the South Australian Aborigines*. Adelaide: Government Printer.

Turpin, M. and A. Ross (compilers). 2012. *Kaytetye to English Dictionary*. Alice Springs: IAD Press.

Vatter, E. 1925. *Der australische Totemismus*. Hamburg: Museum für Völkerkunde.

Völker, H. 2001. Missionare als Ethnologen. Moritz Freiherr von Leonhardi, australische Mission und europäische Wissenschaft. In R. Wendt (Hrsg.), *Sammeln, Vernetzen, Auswerten. Missionare und ihr Beitrag zum Wandel europäischer Weltsicht*. pp. 173–218. Tübingen: Gunter Narr Verlag.

Wendt, R. 2001. Einleitung: Missionare als Reporter und Wissenschaftler in Übersee. In R. Wendt (Hrsg.), *Sammeln, Vernetzen, Auswerten. Missionare und ihr Beitrag zum Wandel europäischer Weltsicht*. pp. 7–22. Tübingen: Gunter Narr Verlag.

Wilkins, D.P. 1989. Mparntwe Arrernte (Aranda): Studies in the Structure and Semantics of Grammar. PhD thesis, The Australian National University.

Willshire, W.H. 1891. *The Aborigines of Central Australia: With Vocabularies of the Dialects Spoken by the Natives of Lake Amadeus and of the Western Territory of Central Australia*. Adelaide: Bristow, Government Printer.

Carl Strehlow's

1909 Comparative Heritage

DICTIONARY

How to use the dictionary

Carl Strehlow's spelling of: **Bold** = *Aranda* word; L = *Loritja*; D = *Dieri*
For the modern spellings of these words, see the dictionaries and sources in reference list.

Pronunciation guides and abbreviations used in the dictionary

These are only rough guides to pronouncing the Aranda and Loritja [Luritja] words in the dictionary on the basis of Carl Strehlow's spelling. Firstly, Strehlow did not distinguish all the sounds of these languages in his spelling. Secondly, he was not always consistent in writing an Aranda or Loritja sound the same way in all words. Thirdly, for simplicity's sake these guides do not deal with the details of all the various combinations of letters. Fourthly, the English comparison sounds given below are generally only similar to Aranda and Loritja sounds, not exactly the same.

If you are not a native speaker of Aranda or Luritja, these factors may lead you to pronounce some words wrongly if you rely only on these rough guides. You are advised to consult a speaker for the correct pronunciation of a word. For the modern spelling of Aranda and Loritja [Luritja] words, see the recent dictionaries and other materials.

Because this dictionary is an exact transcription of the original form of Carl Strehlow's handwritten manuscript, the accents and diacritics have been included. However, note that Strehlow uses them inconsistently in this dictionary (and sometimes does not use them at all in his other writing).

There are many issues in working out a spelling system for a language that has not been written before. Strehlow and other early missionaries used an approach that is now outdated. The modern writing systems for these languages take a different approach that respects the particular sounds found in these languages and how they differentiate words. For further discussion of the issues involved, and a comparison of the Arandic spelling systems, see Chapter 6.

Aranda rough pronunciation guide

Carl Strehlow	Similar sounds for English speakers
a	Represents a range of sounds: 1. The sound like the 'a' in English 'comma' or 'er' in 'father' 2. The sound like 'uh' in the English word 'but' 3. A sound like long 'ah' in 'fa̲ther' or 'can't'
ă	A breve on 'a' indicates a short sound. Like the sound 'uh' in the English word 'but' or 'a' in 'comma'
ā	Long 'ah' as in 'father'
b	Like 'p' or 'b'
d	Represents a number of sounds that are distinct in Aranda: 1. Like 't' or 'd' in English 'dot' 2. Like English 't' or 'd' but with the tongue tip curled higher in the mouth (something like the 'rt' or 'rd' in 'hurt' or 'herd' in many US dialects) 3. Like English 't' or 'd' but with the front of the tongue touching the back of the upper teeth
e	Like 'e' in 'every', 'there' or 'were'
ë	As for 'e' above, but the diaeresis indicates that the vowel is to be pronounced separately from an adjacent vowel in a word
g	Like 'k' or 'g'
i	Like 'i' in 'ink' or 'bit', like 'ee' in 'sheep' or like 'e' in 'every'
ī	Lengthened 'i' sound

ï	As for 'i' above, but diaeresis indicates that the vowel is to be pronounced separately from an adjacent vowel in a word
j	Like 'y' in 'you'
k	Like 'k' or 'g'
l	Represents a number of sounds that are distinct in Aranda: 1. Like 'l' in English 'like' 2. Like English 'l' but with the tongue tip curled higher in the mouth (something like the 'rl' in 'pearl' in many US dialects) 3. Like English 'l' but with the front of the tongue touching the back of the upper teeth. (A similar sound sometimes occurs in 'filth', 'wealth' etc.) 4. Like the 'lli' in English 'million'
m	'm'
n	Represents a number of sounds that are distinct in Aranda: 1. Like 'n' in English 'no' 2. Like English 'n' but with the tongue tip curled higher in the mouth (something like the 'rn' in 'burn' in many US dialects) 3. Like English 'n' but with the front of the tongue touching the back of the upper teeth. (A similar sound sometimes occurs in 'tenth', 'anthem' etc.) 4. Like the 'ny' in English 'canyon' 5. When followed by 'k', 'n' sometimes represents the 'ng' sound, like in English 'sinker'
n̄	Lengthened 'n' sound
ń	With the tilde on 'n'. Sounds like 'ny' in 'canyon'
ng	Like 'ng' in singer. (Not like 'ng' in 'finger')

o	Like 'o' in 'more'
ō	Lengthened 'o' sound
p	Like 'p' or 'b'
r, rr	Used interchangeably by Strehlow for two distinct Aranda sounds: 1. Normal Australian English 'r' as in 'rabbit' 2. Hard or rolled 'r'
r̔	'r' with spiritus asper. Sounds like a French soft 'r'
t	Represents a number of sounds that are distinct in Aranda: 1. Like 't' or 'd' in English 'dot' 2. Like English 't' or 'd' but with the tongue tip curled higher in the mouth (something like the 'rt' or 'rd' in 'hurt' or 'herd' in many US dialects) 3. Like English 't' or 'd' but with the front of the tongue touching the back of the upper teeth
tj	Like 'ch' in 'chin' or 'j' in 'jaw'
tm	Represents 'pm', like in 'topmost'
tt	Can represent English 't' or 'd' but with the tongue tip curled higher in the mouth
u	Like 'or' when stressed; like 'oo' in 'wood' when unstressed
ū	Lengthened 'u' sound
ŭ	With a breve on 'u', represents a range of sounds: 1. A short vowel sound like 'u' in 'put' 2. Like English 'w'
w	Like English 'w'

Loritja rough pronunciation guide

For Loritja, it is easier to relate Strehlow's spelling to the modern Luritja spelling system.

Carl Strehlow	Modern spelling	Similar sounds for English speakers
a	a	Like English 'a' in 'comma', 'uh' in 'but', or 'a' in 'father'
ā	aa	Long 'ah' like English 'a' in 'can't' or 'father'
b	p	Like English 'p' or 'b'
d	t	Like English 't' or 'd' in English 'dot'
	ṯ	Like English 't' or 'd' but with the tongue tip curled higher in the mouth (Something like the 'rt' or 'rd' in 'hurt' or 'herd' in many US dialects)
	tj	Like English 't' or 'd' but with the front of the tongue touching the back of the upper teeth. In many words, 'tj' is pronounced like 'ch' or 'j'
e	i	See 'i' below
g	k	Like English 'k' or 'g'
i	i	Like English 'i' in 'pink', like 'ee' in 'sheep', or like 'e' in 'end'
ī	ii	Lengthened 'i' sound
ï		As for 'i' above, but Strehlow's diaeresis indicates that the 'i' vowel is to be pronounced separately from an adjoining vowel in a word
j	y	Like English 'y' in 'yet'
k	k	Like English 'k' or 'g'

l	l	Like English 'l' as in 'let'
	l̲	Like English 'l' but with the tongue tip curled higher in the mouth. (Something like the 'rl' in 'pearl' in many US dialects)
	ly	Pronounced like 'lli' in English 'million'. In some words, 'ly' is pronounced with the front of the tongue touching the back of the upper teeth, like 'l' in English 'filth'
m	m	Like English 'm' like in 'mother'
n	n	Like English 'n' as in 'nothing'
	n̲	Like English 'n' but with the tongue tip curled higher in the mouth. (Something like the 'rn' in 'burn' in many US dialects)
	ny	Pronounced like 'ny' in English 'canyon'. In some words, 'ny' is pronounced with the front of the tongue touching the back of the upper teeth, like 'n' in English 'tenth'
n̄		Lengthened 'n' sound
ñ	ny	(with tilde on 'n') Pronounced like 'ny' in English 'canyon'
ng	ng	Like English 'ng' in singer
o	u (or uu)	Like English 'u' in 'put' or 'o' in 'more'
ō	uu	Lengthened 'u' sound. Can sound like the vowel sounds in English 'more' or 'caught'
p	p	Like 'p' or 'b'
r, rr	r	Australian English 'r' as in 'rabbit' or 'run'
	rr	Hard or rolled 'r'

t	t	Like English 't' or 'd' as in 'dot'
	ṯ	Like English 't' or 'd' but with the tongue tip curled higher in the mouth. (Something like the 'rt' or 'rd' in 'hurt' or 'herd' in many US dialects)
	tj	Like English 't' or 'd' but with the front of the tongue touching the back of the upper teeth. In many words, 'tj' is pronounced like 'ch' or 'j'
tj	tj	Like English 'ch' in 'chin' or 'j' in 'jaw'. In some words, 'tj' can be pronounced with the front of the tongue touching the back of the upper teeth
u	u	Like English 'u' in 'put'
ū	uu	Lengthened 'u' sound. Can sound like the vowel sounds in English 'or' or 'caught'
w	w	Like English 'w' in 'wait'

Abbreviations

The following list expands on abbreviations and additions found in the text of the dictionary.

c. alb.	with ablative (cum ablative)
c. genit.	with genitive (cum genitive)
cf./conf.	confer; compare, see
i.e.	that is (*id est*)
incl.	inclusive
intrs.	intransitive
lit.	literally
trs.	transitive
refl.	reflexive
postp.	postposition = after this and therefore owing to this
e.g.	for example (*exempli gratia*)

n./(n)	probably '*neu*', for example *Glocke* (n), *Tinte* (n)
s.	substantive (English)
b.	while (*beim*), for example *beim tragen* 'while carrying'
c./cr.	approximately, about (circa)
d.h.	that is (*das heißt*)
dupl.	duplication
fortw.	continually, continuously, constantly; means an action that keeps happening (*fortwährend*)
hl.	sacred (*heilig*)
od.	or (*oder*)
pl.	plural
spec.	species
u.	and (*und*)
z.B.	for example (*zum Beispiel*; English uses the Latin *exempli gratia*, e.g.)
?	question mark added by CS (Carl Strehlow)
[?]	question mark added by WA (Western Aranda people) and/or transcriber
[unclear]	comment on text added by transcriber
♀	symbol for female
♂	symbol for male

The following entries reproduce an exact transcription of the original orthographies and content of the entries in the handwritten manuscript, as is the wish of the Western Aranda people and to maintain its historical authenticity. Thus, to be true to the original some entries are out of order and one or the other entry is repeated in a slight variation.

A

ā; ā knara *Ärger, gewöhnlich mit knara (groß, sehr); z.B. sehr zornig.* ◇ irritation, anger; usually combined with knara (big, very), e.g. very angry. Ⓛ peka puntu, pata puntu

Aaí *keineswegs, sondern.* ◇ not at all, rather. Ⓛ aai! Ⓓ aaí

a͡i?; unta itja nukanga treritjika, aaí, unta nukanga kankitjika. *Interjektion der Verwunderung: wirklich?! Ists wahr?* ◇ interjection of astonishment: really?! True? Ⓛ omanti?; nuntu ngaiulunguru ngulurekuwia, aai, nuntu ngaiuku bukularekuntaku.

ambarknara *zornig.* ◇ angry.

ātaka *der Zorn.* ◇ anger.

āpa *außen, draußen, außerhalb (des Lagerplatzes).* ◇ outside (of camp). Ⓛ pila Ⓓ jelaua (?) ('?' added by CS)

āpala *außen, draußen, außerhalb (des Lagerplatzes).* ◇ outside (of camp). Ⓛ pilanka

adilka *weiß, noch nicht reife Körner (jelka).* ◇ white; unripe seeds (jelka: *Cyperus rotundus* now *Cyperus bulbosus*). Ⓛ talku

agia *ein Baum mit vielen kleinen eßbaren schwarzen Beeren (Canthium latifolium).* ◇ 1. bush currant tree with small edible black berries 2. bush currant, wild currant (*Canthium latifolium*). Ⓛ kauartji, aualuru

ailjerama *sich fortwährend besinnen (welchen Weg man gehn soll), unschlüssig sein.* ◇ assess constantly (which way to go), be undecided. Ⓛ unturingañi

ailpara *fortwährend.* ◇ constantly. Ⓛ ailpiri Ⓓ taijipaterina

ailpara ankama *fortwährend reden, schwätzen.* ◇ talk, chat constantly. Ⓛ ailpiri wonkañi

r̔akua; rākua *der weiche Saft; sehr weiche.* ◇ soft juice; the very soft. Ⓛ āuka

aráma [Northern dialect] *sehen.* ◇ to see. Ⓛ nangañi Ⓓ najina

arilalabuma *sich umsehen.* ◇ to look around. Ⓛ nakulaenni

ar̔ilatnama *spähend stehen.* ◇ to stand looking around. Ⓛ nakulakanjini

ar̔ilintatnama *erblicken.* ◇ to see. Ⓛ manakutalkañi, mananagañi

ajua *der alte Mann, der Alte, Vater.* ◇ old man, elder, father. Ⓛ tjilpi

āka *Bruder.* ◇ brother. Ⓛ kuta

aknua [Northern dialect] *cf.* **eknua** *vergeßlich.* ◇ forgetful. Ⓛ wătawăta

akua [Northern dialect] *[rechts] der rechte Arm.* ◇ [right] right arm. Ⓛ waku

akumbinjala *rechts.* ◇ right. Ⓛ wakūnka Ⓓ ngunari

akumbinja *das rechte (Gegensatz links).* ◇ right (opposed to left). Ⓛ wakupiti

ar̔inama [Northern dialect] *sehen.* ◇ to see. Ⓛ manangañi

akutnama *ausholen (zum Schlagen).* ◇ to raise (to hit). Ⓛ wakungarañi

  tnamagata *(mit dem Stock).* ◇ with the stick. Ⓛ wonnatara

akunintatnama *zerspalten (mit einem Schlag).* ◇ to split (with one blow). Ⓛ wakukitungarañi

āla *Erde, Land, Erdboden.* ◇ earth, soil, land, ground. Ⓛ manta, pana Ⓓ mita

  alankura *'Erdboden' oder fortwährend.* ◇ earth or continuously. Ⓛ manta nankuru

  alabotta *Erdkloß.* ◇ lump of earth. Ⓛ mantakaputu

  alarinja *Landbewohner (ala = Land, Erde; die Endung 'rinja' drückt aus: bewohnend, zu etwas gehörend).* ◇ land dwellers, people living on land, belonging to the land (ala = land, earth; rinja (suffix) = belonging to); one of the two patrimoieties (exogamous groups) of the Western Aranda. In Carl Strehlow's work the earth is described as an eternal presence in which at the beginning of time undeveloped humans were slumbering, they were already divided into moieties, called 'alarinja' and 'kwatjarinja' (of the earth and water respectively), and into a subsection system. According to Western Aranda mythology the moiety called 'alarinja' was divided into Purula, Kamara, Ngala and Mbitjana; and the other moiety 'kwatjarinja' into Pananka, Paltara, Knuraia and Bangata (Strehlow 1913). These anthropomorphic ancestor beings called 'altjirangamitjina' emerged from their underground dwellings (Strehlow 1907: 3) and wandered over the shapeless land, creating the landscape as it is still seen today, transforming themselves and establishing the world's structure and order. Ⓛ manta ngurara

alakarinja *erdig.* ◇ earthy. Ⓛ mantakarinja

alilirtja *Erdfurche.* ◇ earthen trench. Ⓛ manta ilirtji

alamanta *reine Erdboden.* ◇ pure or clean ground. Ⓛ mantakutu Ⓓ mita ngurru

ala ȓirka *weiche Erde, z.B. die Sandhügel.* ◇ soft soil, e.g. sandhills. Ⓛ manta tali Ⓓ dako

alalélama *mit Erde abreiben (tjatta).* ◇ rub off with soil (spear). Ⓛ mantankanani

alarkna *Lehm.* ◇ clay. Ⓛ manta artna Ⓓ puljuru? ('?' added by CS)

ala bulja *weiche Erde.* ◇ soft soil or earth. Ⓛ manta tula Ⓓ mita ngalara

alalibára *niedrig über dem Boden (fliegen).* ◇ low over the ground (fly). Ⓛ pantalpantalja

alaliwúnja *niedrig über dem Boden (fliegen?).* ◇ low over the ground (fly?). Ⓛ manta tununulala

alabatia *fruchtbar (Land), gute Zeiten [unclear].* ◇ fertile (land), good times. Ⓛ manta munupatu

alakaïwulama *Boden bedecken (Blüten).* ◇ cover ground (blossoms). Ⓛ mantaku matikatiñi

alarknakana *Töpfer (n).* ◇ potter (n).

alabanginja *Welt, die Erdbewohner.* ◇ world, people.

alatóppulba *Käfer (spec.), rot, mit Spitzen am Rücken.* ◇ red beetle with spines on back.

ăla *die Nase, der Schnabel (der obere Teil desselben).* ◇ nose, beak (upper part). Ⓛ mula Ⓓ mudla

alaltjura *das Nasenloch.* ◇ nostril. Ⓛ mula ala Ⓓ mudla wilpa

alalunjara *die Nasenscheidewand.* ◇ septum. Ⓛ mula lenjȇri

ala urba *das Nasenbein.* ◇ nosebridge. Ⓛ mula murbu Ⓓ mudla mokku

alaulta *verstopfte Nase.* ◇ blocked nose. Ⓛ mula ulta

alarentuerama *Nase (Gesicht) abwenden (schmollend).* ◇ nose (face) turn away (sulking). Ⓛ mula nelturingañi Ⓓ mudlapiti (*Nasenspitze*: tip of nose)

ălaăla *zornig, ärgerlich.* ◇ angry, annoyed. Ⓛ pekapeka

alerama *zornig werden.* ◇ get angry. Ⓛ pekaringañi

alalélama *mit Erde abreiben (tjatta).* ◇ rub with soil (spear). Ⓛ mantankanani

aláma [Northern dialect] *Leber.* ◇ liver. Ⓛ alu Ⓓ kalu

aláltankama *herausfließen (Saft oder Honig von den Blüten).* ◇ flow out (juice or honey from blossoms). Ⓛ mulbakañi

alateerama *mit Cermonie zum Abschluß bringen.* ◇ conclude with a ceremony. Ⓛ piribakani

alátilkama [Northern dialect] *Getöse, Musik machen.* ◇ make noise or music. Ⓛ tiltarani

alátitja [Northern dialect] *cf.* **latitja** *[lange Stecken], Balken.* ◇ (long stick), beam. Ⓛ alatatji

ala *sie beide.* ◇ those two. Ⓛ pula

alátara *sie beide.* ◇ both. Ⓛ pulakutara
alátunja *die beiden (Verstorbenen).* ◇ the two (deceased). Ⓛ pulapilku
albalta *sehr weiche Knie-Muskeln.* ◇ very soft knee muscles. Ⓛ palparkna
ilbilbariuma *(die Erde beim herausscharren) weithinstreuen.* ◇ scatter (dug out soil). Ⓛ wililpungañi
albaiara *bunte Raupe.* ◇ colourful caterpillar. Ⓛ anumara
albala *Schambedeckung.* ◇ pubic covering. Ⓛ matati Ⓓ nganpa, wirpa, ngampa? ('?' added by CS)
albulbinkama *herausscharren (Erde aus Loch).* ◇ dig out (earth out of hole). Ⓛ pulknarañi
ilbalelama *bedecken (die Sonne von der Wolke).* ◇ cover (sun by cloud). Ⓛ mamani Ⓓ parara
albalalbala *bärtig (Mund), mit Stacheln besetzt (nkualbila Fisch), faserig (Wurzeln).* ◇ bearded (mouth), covered with spikes (fish species), stringy (roots). Ⓛ albilalbili
albánalbaniláma *ausbreiten, weitererzählen.* ◇ spread, tell. Ⓛ bilabilarawonniñi
ilbañga *hoch (Bäume).* ◇ high, tall (tree). Ⓛ wara
albantiuma *ausstreuen, säen, auseinanderwehen.* ◇ scatter, sow, blow apart. Ⓛ tjintalwonniñi Ⓓ jaupana
albantinjiuma *abschlagen (die Schoten vom Baum).* ◇ knock off (pods from tree). Ⓛ wintalpungañi
albarankama *fortwährend ā ā ā sagen (Cultus).* ◇ say continually ā ā ā (ceremony). Ⓛ albiri wonkañi
albāra *jung, aufrechtstehend (Blätter).* ◇ young, upright (leaves). Ⓛ albara
albára *große Mulde, zum Sichten der jelka und zum Wasserholen gebraucht.* ◇ large bowl to winnow jelka and to carry water. Ⓛ kanilba
albartja *das lange, aufgelöste Haar.* ◇ long, open hair. Ⓛ aralta
albartjilama *kämmen (Haar), entwirren (Haar).* ◇ comb, detangle (hair). Ⓛ altakaltanani
albaua *unwohl, schwach (im Magen), schwächlich [unclear].* ◇ unwell, sick, weak (in stomach). Ⓛ alboa, nali
albauerama *unwohl werden, schwach werden.* ◇ become unwell, weak. Ⓛ naliringañi, alboaringañi
albatoppatuma *zerschmettern (die Halme).* ◇ to crush (grass blades). Ⓛ pulparātuni
albetjinba *der erstgeborene Sohn.* ◇ first born son.
albentintjiuma *weithin werfen, streuen (die Erde beim Scharren).* ◇ to throw, to scatter (soil when scratching or digging). Ⓛ wilipungañi
albentatnama *werfen, streuen.* ◇ to throw, to scatter. Ⓛ pulalknarañi
albelalbélelama *weiter sagen, ausbreiten.* ◇ to tell, to spread word. Ⓛ bilabilaringañi
albarinja *schön geschmückt (beim Cultus).* ◇ beautifully decorated (at ceremony). Ⓛ tjintjirinu
albérkuma *ausführen (den Willen eines Anderen).* ◇ execute (someone else's will). Ⓛ witikanjini
albérkulélama *fischen (mit Angel).* ◇ to fish (with a rod). Ⓛ ngalangamini
albéta [Southern dialect] *Schwanzende.* ◇ tip of tail. Ⓛ mani
albitja [Northern dialect], **inkaia albitja, irbanga albitja** *das Schwanzende; z.B. Bandicootschwänze oder Rattenschwänze (Schmuckgegenstand), Fischschwanz.* ◇ tip of tail; e.g. bilby or rat tails, tail of fish. Ⓛ mani, talku kuntu, talku mani
albitjalbélama *den Zauber entfernen oder herausziehen.* ◇ remove magic or pull it out. Ⓛ ngankarinani
albma *Kopfschmuck aus Kakadufedern.* ◇ headdress made of cockatoo feathers; branches at top of tree [?]. Ⓛ pokulu
albmelama *erzählen, sagen, antworten, nennen, melden.* ◇ to tell, say, answer, name, inform. Ⓛ wottani Ⓓ kalabana, dikana
albeltatuma *Auge stoßen (daß Wasser hervorkommt).* ◇ bump eye (causing it to water). Ⓛ wilpatakañi

albmelalama *refl. mit sich sprechen.* ◇ (reflexive) to speak with. Ⓛ wottaranani

albmelapalama *wieder erzählen.* ◇ to retell. Ⓛ wottawottani

albmelalawuma *nennen.* ◇ to name. Ⓛ wottaratalkañi

albmelitjalbuma *melden nach der Rückkehr.* ◇ to report after return. Ⓛ wottanikulbara

albma *ins Haar gesteckte Kakadufedern.* ◇ hair decorated with cockatoo feathers; hair bun [?]. Ⓛ pokulu

albōlba *Frühling (Monat vor der heißen Zeit, September).* ◇ spring (month before hot time, September). Ⓛ beukuara

albōlbaka *im Frühling.* ◇ in spring. Ⓛ beukuaraku

albōlja *enganeinanderliegende Zehen.* ◇ toes close to each other. Ⓛ lalpa

albōlja *sehr alt.* ◇ very old. Ⓛ nkebulba

alboritja *Bruder (mein).* ◇ brother (my). Ⓛ kalburuna

alboraworra *Schwarm, Haufe (Fliegen, Vögel, Tiere).* ◇ swarm, mob (flies, birds, animals). Ⓛ mingakurakura

alborananga *die beiden Brüder.* ◇ the two brothers. Ⓛ kalburura

albukanama *verschließen (eine Öffnung).* ◇ to close (an opening). Ⓛ bantani Ⓓ ngandrawalkaterina? ngenmana ('?' added by CS)

albōra *Bruder (auch von Tieren gebraucht).* ◇ brother (also used for animals). Ⓛ kulburu

alberuperuma *wieder heimkehren.* ◇ return home again. Ⓛ kulbanikulbañi

albula *(postp.) bis.* ◇(postposition) until. Ⓛ kutata

albulantanama *heimkehren in eine lange Linie, nur [unclear].* ◇ return home in a long line. Ⓛ kulbaratalkañi

albubalbuma *(duplick) heimkehren, umkehren.* ◇ (duplication) return home, return. Ⓛ kulbanañi

albuma *umkehren, zurückkehren.* ◇ to turn back, return. Ⓛ kulbañi Ⓓ tikana

albulantanama *zurückkehren.* ◇ to return. Ⓛ kulbaratalkañi

albutakalbuta *kleiner schwarzer Vogel.* ◇ small black bird. Ⓛ albutakalbuti

albuntara *Erdloch, in dem sich ein altjirangamitjina geschmückt hat.* ◇ hole (in which an ancestral dreaming being decorated itself). Ⓛ albantari

aldōla *Westen.* ◇ west. Ⓛ wilurara Ⓓ jentakara

aldolakua *nach Westen.* ◇ to the west. Ⓛ wilurarkarba

aldolataka *nach Westen.* ◇ to the west. Ⓛ wiluraralku

aldoparinja *in Westwinden einherfahrende böse Ratapa Kinder; das erstgeborene Kind von Zwillingen.* ◇ bad ratapa children who travel in west winds; first born twin. Carl Strehlow offers further meanings of this word, namely 'coming from the west' (Strehlow 1907: 14) and 'the evil [or bad] child coming from the west', i.e. aldola (the West) erintja (the bad or evil one) (Strehlow 1913: 1). Ⓛ wolbakujata, mamukututa

algábma (algōbma) *mager.* ◇ thin. Ⓛ wiltjiltji

alitja [Northern dialect] *langer Stecken, Balken.* ◇ long stick, beam. Ⓛ tabalpa

ālibuma *Haufen (Wall) machen, aufhäufen, sammeln.* ◇ make a heap, to pile up, to collect. Ⓛ utulutunañi

alinba tumanerama *am Erdboden kleben.* ◇ to stick to the ground. Ⓛ mantapuruna, ngalurapungañi

alínama [Northern dialect] *cf.* **linama** *zucken (beim Sterben).* ◇ to twitch (when dying). Ⓛ alurkuni

alkira toppa *jenseits der Wölbgung.* ◇ beyond the firmament. Ⓛ ilkari tana

alkira unkwana *Firmament.* ◇ firmament. Ⓛ ilkari tarka

alkira tjalka *Lufthimmel.* ◇ sky. Ⓛ ilkara iltana

alkira tnata *zwischen der Wölbung.* ◇ under the vault of the sky Ⓛ ilkari arila

alja, intuenta *kleines Steinmesser.* ◇ small stone knife. Ⓛ tilba, kanti

alítjilba *Bote.* ◇ messenger. Ⓛ puriñi

 For the modern spellings of these words, see the dictionaries and sources in reference list.

aljía [Northern dialect] *zugehörig (sex-totem).* ◇ belonging to. Ⓛ inánkutu (*Zwillings-pfl.*: twin plant)

alinga [Northern dialect] *cf.* **lenga** *Sonne.* ◇ sun. Ⓛ tjintu

alinja [Northern dialect] *cf.* **lenja** *Zunge.* ◇ tongue. Ⓛ talinji

alírra, alirra *Sohn, Tochter, Bruders Sohn, Bruders Tochter, Urgroßvater, Manns Schwesters Sohn, Manns Schwesters Tochter.* ◇ son, daughter, brother's son, brother's daughter, great-grandfather, husband's sister's son, husband's sister's daughter. Ⓛ katta untala, katta untalba Ⓓ ngatamura = offspring of opposite moiety, child of man (see Austin 2013: 23)

woialirra *Bruders Sohn, Mannes Schwesters Sohn.* ◇ brother's son, husband's sister's son. Ⓛ katta

kwaialirra *Bruders Tochter, Mannnes Schwesters Tochter.* ◇ brother's daughter, husband's sister's daughter. Ⓛ untala

alirratjurutja *Kinder (von Vater genannt).* ◇ children (term used by father). Ⓛ kattapiti

alirrukua *der alirra eines Anderen.* ◇ someone else's alirra. Ⓛ kattara

alirratja *mein Sohn (von Vater genannt).* ◇ my son (term used by father). Ⓛ kattana

alirratja *meine Tochter (von Vater genannt).* ◇ my daughter (term used by father). Ⓛ untalana

alinta [Northern dialect] *cf.* **linta** *Flamme.* ◇ flame. Ⓛ kala

alítjitja [Northern dialect] *cf.* litjitja. ◇ white ant larvae. Ⓛ alitjitji

alka *Körper, Block (Felsblock).* ◇ body, boulder. Ⓛ alala

álkabara *sehr alte, ausgelebte (Frau), vertrocknet (Frucht).* ◇ very old, worn out (woman), dried or shrivelled (fruit). Ⓛ warbalba, walkabara

alkábara *eßbare Knollen.* ◇ edible bulbs. Ⓛ alkabiri

alkāla *hell (neugeborene Kinder), bleich.* ◇ fair (newborn children), pale. Ⓛ alkali Ⓓ bulu

alkalkérama *mit dem Schwanz wedeln.* ◇ to wag tail. Ⓛ irkiñi

alkálalkála *dünn, wässerig (Speise).* ◇ thin, watery (food). Ⓛ kalturba Ⓓ danto

alkambalkangerama *nach jemanden aussehen [unclear].* ◇ look out for someone. Ⓛ kambalkambalariñi

alkama, auch relkama *cf.* **ŕelkama** *hell werden, Tag anbrechen.* ◇ dawn, daybreak. Ⓛ rakatiñi

alkanbubanbuma *hinüberspringen.* ◇ to jump over. Ⓛ tjilkalukatiñi Ⓓ tankarana (überschreiten)

alkanbuma *hinüberspringen.* ◇ to jump over. Ⓛ tjitakanbañi

akalbelama *reiben den Körper (von Zauberer).* ◇ rub body (by [?] magician). Ⓛ altakaltaniñi

alkanteriltjilama *sehr rein machen (tjilara).* ◇ clean thoroughly. Ⓛ pirapiraninañi

alkanta *kleine geschabte Holzblumen (der Bluträcher) [unclear].* ◇ small 'wood flowers' (of avengers). Ⓛ tarabanba

alkara *der Himmel, hell, hoch.* ◇ sky, bright, high. Ⓛ ilkari Ⓓ pariwilpa

alkarka [Southern dialect] *eine sehr kleine Ameisenart.* ◇ very small ant species. Ⓛ alkirki

alkaragata [Southern dialect] *hell.* ◇ bright, light. Ⓛ ilkariákata

alkaralkara [Southern dialect] *hell, klar, scheinend.* ◇ light, clear, shining. Ⓛ ilkarilkari Ⓓ kintjalkuru

alkarabinjánga [Southern dialect] *sehr hoch.* ◇ very high. Ⓛ ilkariwirili

alkaraka iwuma [Southern dialect] *in die Höhe werfen.* ◇ throw into the air. Ⓛ ilkariku wonniñi

alkaralkara (alkáralkára) *Blume mit blauen Blüten.* ◇ flower with blue blossoms. Ⓛ alkaralkari

alkāra *Fleisch zu beiden Seiten des Rückens.* ◇ flesh on both sides of backspine. Ⓛ wilara

alkaratjoratja *durchscheinend (von vielen Löchern), löchricht.* ◇ shine through (many holes), full of holes. Ⓛ alenkurukuru

alkaritjititjitiuma *alles durcheinander werfen.* ◇ throw everything into disorder. Ⓛ ilkari pinpintjiwonniñi Ⓓ terateribana

alkaruntuara *durchsichtig (Glas).* ◇ transparent (glass). Ⓛ mantawirili, ilkariwirili

alkiranjaranja *eine Hütte, bei der der Himmel hereinscheint; eine Hütte mit vielen Löchern.* ◇ hut into which the sky shines; hut with many holes. Ⓛ ilkariwirili

alkátua *glatter Stein, auf dem Sämereien gerieben.* ◇ smooth grinding stone. Ⓛ tjēwa

alkalteuma *ausspucken (Bissen Brot oder Fleisch).* ◇ spit out (morsel of bread or meat). Ⓛ (alkalteuma) burpungañi

alkauma *brechen, erbrechen.* ◇ to vomit. Ⓛ ulkabutunañi Ⓓ ngukoworrana

alkaulama *refl. sich erbrechen.* ◇ (reflexive) vomit. Ⓛ ulkabutunañi Ⓓ ngukoworrana

alkëuma [Northern dialect] *brechen, erbrechen.* ◇ to vomit. Ⓛ ulkabutunañi Ⓓ ngukoworrana

alkirambaranga *unbeständig in der Arbeit sein, vielgeschäftig.* ◇ inconsistent at work.

alkeerama (inka) *Füße ausstrecken.* ◇ stretch out feet. Ⓛ (tjinna) wararingañi Ⓓ ngurakatina

alkia *sehr groß (Menschen).* ◇ very big (humans). Ⓛ wara

alkielba *durchscheinend, löchricht, heilend (von Geschwüren).* ◇ shine through, holy, healing (ulcers). Ⓛ alkiilbi

alkérama *singen, schreien (Vögel).* ◇ to sing, to screech (birds). (Entry deleted by CS)

alkira [Northern dialect] *cf.* **alkara** *Himmel.* ◇ sky. Ⓛ ilkari, inimiri Ⓓ pariwilpa

alkirabinjánga [Northern dialect] *cf.* **alkarabinjanga** *sehr hoch.* ◇ very high.

alkirakeranama *zum Himmel auffliegen.* ◇ fly up into the sky. Ⓛ ilkarikura maparbakañi

alkirakerama *zum Himmel auffliegen, in die Höhe auffliegen.* ◇ fly into the sky, fly up high. Ⓛ ilkarikuparbakañi

alkirakerala nariraka, alkirakerala lariraka pl. *zum Himmel auffliegen, in die Höhe auffliegen.* ◇ plural fly into the sky, fly up high. Ⓛ ilkarikuparbakara wonningu

alkarurtjauia *das mit Fleisch umgebene, runde Rückgrat einer kleinen Schangenart.* ◇ backbone or spine of a small snake species that is surrounded by flesh. Ⓛ warurunkalba, nalburumbalburu

alkāra *das Fleisch zu beiden Seiten des Rückgrats (Raupe).* ◇ flesh on both sides of backspine (caterpillar). Ⓛ wilara

alknatnana *Wasserfläche, Wasserspiegel.* ◇ water surface. Ⓛ alknatnana

alkiranga mbalknininja *unter dem Himmel, wo die Vögel fliegen.* ◇ under the sky, where the birds fly. Ⓛ ilkarinku ngaiïkuru

alkenkarénama [Northern dialect] *beteuern (wahres und falsches).* ◇ reassure, affirm (wrong and false). Ⓛ turkulkata tunañi

alkútakálkuta *brechübel.* ◇ very sick. Ⓛ ulkabulkaba

alknala karama [Northern dialect] *einen beobachten, belauern.* ◇ observe, prey on someone.

alknakimanalinja *Triumphzug.* ◇ triumphal (display).

alknéljelja *Augapfel.* ◇ eyeball. Ⓛ kuru kalka

alkna *Auge.* ◇ eye. (May also mean 'seed' according to G. Róheim.) Ⓛ kŭru Ⓓ milki

alkna irkaia *kurzsichtig.* ◇ short sighted.

alkna ilbala *Augenwimpern (Augen-feder).* ◇ eyelashes (eye-feather). Ⓛ kuru nanbinba Ⓓ milki kutja

alkna jinba *(Augen-Haut), Augenlid.* ◇ (eye skin), eyelid. Ⓛ kuru panki

alkna junta *Augenhöhle.* ◇ eye socket. Ⓛ kuru ngadi Ⓓ milki wilpa

alkna kwata *(Augen-Ei), Augapfel.* ◇ (eye egg), eyeball. Ⓛ kuru kalka (kuru ngukuta deleted by CS) Ⓓ milki tandra

alknānda *Augenbrauenbogen, Stelle gerade über den Augenbrauen.* ◇ eyebrow (arch), line just above eyebrow. Ⓛ kuru ngarrkiri

alknandapunga *Augenbrauen.* ◇ eyebrows. Ⓛ kuru intu Ⓓ milkipilpa

alknatoppa *(Augenrücken), Augenlid.* ◇ eyelid. Ⓛ kuru tana

alkninkera *(Augen-wand), Stelle zwischen Augenlid und -brauen.* ◇ (eye wall), space between eyelid and brow. Ⓛ kuru ngankiri Ⓓ milki dirla (dirkala)

alknolja *Träne.* ◇ tear. Ⓛ tjirbmila Ⓓ milkigildi

alkna bojultja *das schwachsehende Auge.* ◇ eye with poor sight. Ⓛ kuru pujurpujura

alkna paraltja *das schwachsehende Auge.* ◇ poor sighted eye. Ⓛ kuru aparaltji

alkna iltélta *Weiße im Auge.* ◇ white of eye. Ⓛ kuru iltilti

alkna ilira *das gutsehende Auge.* ◇ eye with good sight. Ⓛ kuru palturuku

alkna terkaterka *(Schimpfwort) von Auge und grün = grünes Auge.* ◇ swear word meaning 'green eye' (see Strehlow 1913: 93). Ⓛ kuru ókiriókiri

alkna lurra *das entzündete Auge.* ◇ inflamed eye. Ⓛ kuru ngatinba

alkna bangalkureramala rama *zwinkern.* ◇ to wink. Ⓛ bambarekulanuganba nangañi

alkna irbalbirbuma *Augen abwenden, Anspielung auf alknarintji.* ◇ turn eyes away, avert eyes; reference to alknarintji (women who turn their eyes away (look away), who do not marry) (see Strehlow 1911: 46). Ⓛ kuru terbaterbañi

alknalanbánama *zornig dreinsehen.* ◇ look angry. Ⓛ kuru injini

alknalambatilama *alle nacheinander im Kreis ansehen.* ◇ everyone in a circle looks at each other.

alknalaraka inbuma *übersehen, nicht sehen.* ◇ overlook, not see. Ⓛ nakula kanjini Ⓓ wonpana

alknalaraka rama *übersehen, nicht sehen.* ◇ overlook, not see. Ⓛ ninkiltunkulá nangañi

alknalba, ntulba *Hüfte, Lende (= ntulba).* ◇ hip, loin. Ⓛ ankalba

alknala renama *belauern, mit dem Blick verfolgen, beobachten.* ◇ prey, observe, watch. Ⓛ meŕara irbini

alknalbatataka *Vogel (spec.)* ◇ bird species. Ⓛ mitiïti

alknalkama *intr. Augen öffnen, sich öffnen (Knospe).* ◇ (intransitive) open eyes, open (bud). Ⓛ pitaltjiriñi

alknalkinja *mit geöffneten Augen, wach.* ◇ with open eyes, awake. Ⓛ pitaltji

alknalkaralama *rollen mit den Augen (vor Zorn).* ◇ roll eyes (in anger). Ⓛ kurubakabakañi

alknaltara *rein, klar (Wasser), hell.* ◇ pure, clear (water), light. Ⓛ kaltaru Ⓓ milkitjari, woldankara, kulikiri

alknamburka *ausdrücklich.* ◇ explicitly, emphatically.

alknaltutja *Gras (mit eßbaren Samen).* ◇ grass (with edible seeds). Ⓛ alknultatji

alknankanjinkanja, alknankanjankanja *Auge schnell von einer zur anderen Seite wendend.* ◇ look quickly from side to side (see Strehlow 1913: 93). Ⓛ kuriñiltuniltu

alknalórriritjiláma *prüfend von allen Seiten ansehen.* ◇ examine from all sides. Ⓛ kuru unururingañi Ⓓ milkimilkiterkana

alknambalknamba *Pflanze mit rötlichen Stengel und fleischigen Blättern.* ◇ plant with red stem and fleshy leaves. Ⓛ alknambalknamba Ⓓ kanalkapana

alknambuma *intr. Augen aufmachen, blühen (andata).* ◇ (intransitive) open eyes, blossom. Ⓛ kururingañi Ⓓ milki tjenmana

alknambulelama *trs. Augen öffnen.* ◇ (transitive) open eyes. Ⓛ kuruni Ⓓ tiwitiwirina (*blühen*: bloom)

alknambatnitjinjima *Augen aufmachen und zum Himmel erheben (Frösche und Menschen).* ◇ open eyes and look up into the sky (frogs and humans). Ⓛ kururekula kalbañi

alknalambatilama *alle, die [unclear] dich ansehen.* ◇ all who look at you or each other [?]

alknantarba *einäugig.* ◇ one eyed.

alknalintarintara *das Schauspiel.* ◇ performance.

alkirapintjanga *Turmspitze (n).* ◇ spire.

alknalinama *vorhersehen (eine Tat).* ◇ foresee (a deed).

alknantáraltuma *Augenlicht vergehen, Dunkel vor den Augen werden.* ◇ fading eyesight, get dark before eyes. Ⓛ kuru mungaringañi

alknanta *Flamme, auch blutdürstig, grausam, mordgierig (Streithammel), feurig (im Kampfe).* ◇ flame, blood thirsty, cruel, murderous (thug), fiery (in battle). Ⓛ kala, teli (*Flamme*: flame); marari (*blutdürstig*: bloodthirsty)

alknantérama *Flamme emporschlagen.* ◇ rising flame. Ⓛ waru teliringañi

alknantélama *anzünden, anfachen (Feuer).* ◇ to light, to fan (fire). Ⓛ kalani telini

alknantérama *quälen (z.B. die Tiere), plagen.* ◇ to torture (e.g. animals), torment. Ⓛ marariríñi Ⓓ jupana

alknanterinja *die Plage.* ◇ torture, torment.

alknantalalangalanga *die vielen Feuer eines Lagerplatzes.* ◇ many camp fires. Ⓛ pintjiliri

alknantama *den Körper in zitternde Bewegung setzen.* ◇ set body into trembling motions. Ⓛ pinpitjingani

alknaralama *sich rot färben (vom Blut).* ◇ to colour or turn red (from blood). Ⓛ ngurkalngurkalaríñi

alknara *Abendrot, wenn nur noch das Abendrot im Westen leuchtet.* ◇ evening glow, when only the glow in the west is left; twilight; sunset. Ⓛ kalkara Ⓓ kalkaura

alknarakerama *Abend werden.* ◇ towards evening.

alknaraka *abends, zum Abend.* ◇ towards evening. Ⓛ kalkaraku

alknarambalknara *sich fortwährend umsehend.* ◇ look around continuously. Ⓛ nguntilnguntila

alknara, tataka *Abendrot.* ◇ evening red, dusk. Ⓛ kalkara ngurkalngurkal Ⓓ kalkamarana

alknaranturara *Abend werden.* ◇ become evening. Ⓛ kalkarapuru

alknarerama *Abend werden.* ◇ become evening. Ⓛ kalkararingañi

alknaralknarerama *Abend werden.* ◇ become evening. Ⓛ kalkara-kalkarariñi

alknaralama *sich umsehen, zurücksehen.* ◇ look around, look back. Ⓛ nguntilangarañi Ⓓ worrakalina

alknarbunarbunala rama *das eine Auge sieht durch [unclear], schielen.* ◇ be cross-eyed. Ⓛ talbankatalbanka nangañi

alknarintja (aragutja alknarintja) *mythische Weiber, die nicht heiraten dürfen.* ◇ mythical women who are not allowed to marry (see Strehlow 1907: 6, 97). Ⓛ alknarintji

alknarbana *Baum (spec.), aus dem Speere gemacht werden.* ◇ tree species from which spears are made. Ⓛ alknirbini

alknáta *ein Nadelbaum spec., Fichte, dufted wie eine Tanne (Callitris).* ◇ native pine tree, *Callitris glaucophylla.* Ⓛ wolknati

alknatnana *mitten auf dem See, Wasserspiegel.* ◇ in the middle of the lake, water surface; clear water. Ⓛ alknatnana

alknátera *öffentlich, augenscheinlich.* ◇ publicly, apparently; clear. Ⓛ kurunka Ⓓ dinkari

 For the modern spellings of these words, see the dictionaries and sources in reference list.

alkneljelja *Augapfel.* ◇ eyeball. Ⓛ kuru kalka

alknaterala rama *mit eigenen Augen sehen.* ◇ see with own eyes. Ⓛ kurunka nangañi

alknemeremerala rama *[unclear] mit dem Auge zwinkern.* ◇ to wink with eye. Ⓛ kuruterbaterbara nangañi

alknemanta *sehr lange Speer.* ◇ very long spear. Ⓛ kutukuna

alknatama *trs. verbrennen.* ◇ (transitive) burn. Ⓛ mululu kambañi

alknealknea *großer Strauch mit langen schmalen Blumen und schwarzen, nicht eßbaren Beeren.* ◇ large bush with long narrow leaves and black inedible berries. Ⓛ alknealkneï

alkneleruma (alkna jirama) *Gesicht vergehen vor Erschöpfung, verhungern.* ◇ face fades from exhaustion, starve. Ⓛ kuruwiaringañi

alknénera *Große rote Cikade spec. an Gummibäumen (Thopha colorata).* ◇ large red cicada (*Thopha colorata*) on gumtrees. Ⓛ alkneneri

alknemunta *lange Speer.* ◇ long spear. Ⓛ kutukuna

alknenta *seitwärts, nach einer Seite hin.* ◇ sideways, towards one side. Ⓛ talba Ⓓ worku

alknentala nama *an der Seite (jemandes) gehen.* ◇ walk beside (someone). Ⓛ talbanka ninañi

alknentala rama *zur Seite sehen.* ◇ look sideways. Ⓛ talbanka nangañi

alknentama *zur Seite sehen.* ◇ look to the side. Ⓛ talbani

alknenterama *seitwärts sehen.* ◇ look sideways. Ⓛ talbaringañi

alknerama *Augen aufschlagen (von neugeborenen Kindern).* ◇ open eyes (newborn children). Ⓛ kururingañi

alkniltala rama *schielen.* ◇ be cross-eyed. Ⓛ talbankatalbanka nangañi

alknipata *grüne Raupen, die sich an jipa-Ranken finden.* ◇ green caterpillars on jipa vine. Ⓛ kurungati

alknerkala *am Abhang (stehend).* ◇ on slope (standing). Ⓛ karbanka

alknerka *Abhang.* ◇ slope. Ⓛ karba

alkurbalkurberama (?) [Northern dialect] *aus: schäumen (Meer).* ◇ derived from the word 'to froth'. ('?' added by CS)

alkukalkurelama *schlagen, daß Striemen entstehen, zerschlagen.* ◇ to beat (causing laceration), to smash.

alknoljeruma *Schwarz vor den Augen werden, vor Erschöpfung.* ◇ faint from exhaustion. Ⓛ kuruwiaringañi

alknólja *Träne, Augenfett.* ◇ tear, eye fat. Ⓛ tjirbmilja, tjirbmila Ⓓ milkigildi

alknólknelama *trösten (einen Traurigen).* ◇ to comfort (a sad one, person in sorrow). Ⓛ utuututuni

alknólta [Northern dialect] *sterbend, Augen brechend (im Tode).* ◇ dying, eyes breaking (at death). Ⓛ atulta tutani

alknoljalawonturbma *viele Tränen [unclear].* ◇ many tears. Ⓛ urbmultala (ninañi)

alknôrtja *Embryo.* ◇ embryo. Ⓛ banganba

alknoljurbalknolja *große Tränen.* ◇ large tears. Ⓛ tjirmiltalatjirbmilta

alknotninja *eifersüchtig.* ◇ jealous. Ⓛ numbaiariñi Ⓓ mandrakarowali

alknunturuntu̓rula rama *großes rundes Auge.* ◇ large round eye. Ⓛ kuru teruterura nangañi

alknultinkama *intr. ertrinken.* ◇ (intransitive) drown. Ⓛ mulakuturingañi Ⓓ purujulkana

alknultinkalelama *trs. ertränken.* ◇ (transitive) drown. Ⓛ mulakutini Ⓓ purujulkana? ('?' added by CS)

alknuralknura *Strauch mit Schotenfrüchten.* ◇ shrub with pods. Ⓛ aljalji

alkōlja *die zerriebene Gummirinde.* ◇ ground gumtree bark. Ⓛ ulkulji

alknurbunana *Käfer, braun mit gelben Querstreifen.* ◇ brown beetle with yellow cross-stripes. Ⓛ kumburumburi

alkora *Strauch (spec.)* ◇ shrub species. Ⓛ alkuru

alkāra *frische (Eier), frischgelegte (Eier).* ◇ fresh (eggs), freshly laid (eggs). Ⓛ bakuburu

alkumala *Baum (spec.)* ◇ tree (species). Ⓛ wolkamala

alkulaia *Strauch mit ovalen Blättern.* ◇ bush with oval leaves. Ⓛ kubata

alkulbilama *durchgraben, durchbohren.* ◇ dig through, drill through. Ⓛ alkalkirini Ⓓ mirpana

alkulialkula lama *ziellos umherwandern.* ◇ wander around aimlessly. Ⓛ wapalpekura jennañi

alkuljalkulja *Nachahmung des Schreies des Adlers.* ◇ imitation of eagle's call. Ⓛ kuljakuljalba

alkuljalkulja *Wasservogel, der nach Fischen taucht.* ◇ waterbird who dives for fish. Ⓛ ulkuljulkulji

alkura *(postp.) mehr.* ◇ (postposition) more. Ⓛ nguanba

alkurumba *viele, überall umherliegend (Steine).* ◇ many (stones, boulders) scattered or lying around. Ⓛ alkurumbu

alkurilbanalanama *nach allen Richtungen auseinander laufen.* ◇ disperse in all directions. Ⓛ bakalarani

alkuta *Schild.* ◇ shield. Ⓛ kutitji Ⓓ piramara

alkutungalkuta *kleine Schilder mit denen die Kinder spielen.* ◇ small shields children play with. Ⓛ kutitjikutitji

alkuta unkwana *das Schulterblatt.* ◇ shoulder blade. Ⓛ kutitji tarka Ⓓ pilperipira, pilperi (*Schulter*: shoulder)

alkurulba *durchschichtig, fensterähnliche Öffnung, Fenster.* ◇ transparent, window. Ⓛ alawirili

alkurbanta *Blasen auf dem Wasser (untertauchen).* ◇ bubbles on water (submerge, dive). Ⓛ taljikutu

alkunarala *Larven (weiß) in alkunara-Wurzeln.* ◇ grubs (white) in alkunara roots. Ⓛ alkunari

alkunara *Baum spec.* ◇ tree species. Ⓛ alkunari

alta *Tag, Licht.* ◇ day, light. Ⓛ julta Ⓓ ditji

altamalta *täglich.* ◇ daily. Ⓛ jultamurkamurka

altérama *Tag werden, hell werden.* ◇ daybreak, dawn. Ⓛ jultaringañi

altabareratnama *Tag anfangen.* ◇ begin day. Ⓛ majultarekulatalkañi

altábatara *Zwielicht, Morgen- und Abenddämmerung, Zwielicht anbrechen.* ◇ twilight, sunrise and sunset. Ⓛ jultakutu Ⓓ parantjalku

alta [Northern dialect] *Haar der Menschen und des Wildes, Wolle (n).* ◇ hair of humans and game, wool. Ⓛ intu

altálama (altaluma?) *Haar ausfallen.* ◇ lose hair. Ⓓ kintjalkuru ('?' added by CS)

altakalta *auseinander, los, frei.* ◇ apart, loose, free. Ⓛ altakalta

altakaltérama *sich zerstreuen, los werden (von Krankheit), lösen (den Fötus bei Geburt).* ◇ scatter, get rid (of sickness), detach. Ⓛ altakaltariñji

altakaltilama *losmachen, befreien, lösen (den Fötus bei der Geburt).* ◇ separate, detach. Ⓛ altakaltanani Ⓓ kurakana

altakatjakatja *helle Mondschein (beim Vollmond).* ◇ bright moonlight (at full moon). Ⓛ irtnani

altarinja *erfunden, erdichtet.* ◇ invented, made up.

altarba [Northern dialect], **kwatja altárba** *clay-pan, clay-pan water.* ◇ claypan, claypan water. Ⓛ altarba

áltarama *durchspeeren (Bein), peitschen (sodaß die Haut zerschnitten wird).* ◇ pierced by a spear (e.g. leg), whip (to lacerate skin). Ⓛ wintarpungañi

altanatambuma *hin und her wehen mit (der Feder) spielen (Wind).* ◇ blow back and forth (wind) play with (a feather). Ⓛ pulknarañi

altalirgúraka *einig (Freunde).* ◇ in agreement (friends). Ⓛ ngalutu

altáltuka *Fremdling, in der Fremde sein.* ◇ stranger, to be abroad. Ⓛ barkara Ⓓ waiarka, marka

altanea *Larve (in Gummibaum Wurzeln).* ◇ grub (in gumtree roots). Ⓛ imbita

ultunta *eine Art Kalkstein.* ◇ kind of limestone. Ⓛ ultuntu

altankuma *gierig an sich raffen, reißen.* ◇ snatch up greedy, seize. Ⓛ tuljani, tulani Ⓓ pamapamana

áltara; manna itja, mantara itja *nichts habend, arm; ohne Eigentum.* ◇ have nothing, poor; without belongings. Ⓛ áltaru

altarka *der hervorsprossende Same.* ◇ sprouting seed. Ⓛ bulututu

altarama (altárama) *finden.* ◇ to find. Ⓛ tukarurunangañi Ⓓ mankamankana, dankana (*zufällig finden*: find by chance)

altaranama *laufen (Feuer), durchlaufen, durchschreiten.* ◇ run (fire), run or go through. Ⓛ arbani

alterama *conf.* **alta** *Tag werden.* ◇ daybreak. Ⓛ jultaringañi

alteuma *glatt, eben machen.* ◇ smooth, make even. Ⓛ tulkuwonniñi

altentuma *herabfließen (Blut sowie Saft von Baum).* ◇ flow down (blood, sap of trees). Ⓛ tutirapungañi

altentupentuma *Duplik.* ◇ Duplication of altentuma. Ⓛ tutirangariñi

altja, *z.B.* **noaltja** *zugehörig verbunden, z.B. die eigene Frau.* ◇ belong, e.g. own wife. Ⓛ wolta, e.g. kuriwolta, kurina Ⓓ milpara

altjiwata *wirklich zugehörig.* ◇ really belonging to. Ⓛ wollaltamantu

altjerama *zugehörig werden.* ◇ become part. Ⓛ woltaringañi

altáperinja *Böse, Teufel, der Arge.* ◇ bad spirit being, devil, evil one.

altinka *Name des Mondmannes.* ◇ name of moonman.

altjala *Mutters Vater (Großvater).* ◇ mother's father (grandfather). Ⓛ altjalina

altjalatja *mein Großvater (Mutters Vater), Enkel (Tochters Sohn), Enkelin, (Tochters Mann).* ◇ my grandfather (mother's father), grandchild (daughter's son), grandchild (daughter's daughter or son's daughter), (daughter's husband). Ⓛ altjilina wolalta

tjimia altjala *mein Großvater (Mutters Vater) oder Enkel, Enkelin.* ◇ my grandfather (mother's father) or grandchild. Ⓛ kunarbina

altjamaltjerama *eine andere Gestalt annehmen.* ◇ change shape (see Strehlow 1907: 5). Ⓛ maltjimaltjiringañi

altja *Tinte (n).* ◇ ink.

altjia *die Ranke der lankua, die eßbare Frucht.* ◇ lankua vine, edible fruit. Ⓛ altjiï

altjikaltjika *eingeschrumpft, gerunzelt.* ◇ shrunk, wrinkled. Ⓛ wiljiriwiljiri Ⓓ winjirinjiri

Altjira, altjira *Gott, der Unerschaffene.* ◇ God, the Uncreated One; dreaming being. The word 'Altjira' is used today to denote the Christian God, but in Carl Strehlow's time it was a polysemic key term. He wrote that the etymology of the word 'altjira' had not yet been found, but that Aranda people associated 'the word now with the concept of the non-created. Asked about the meaning of the word, they repeatedly assured me that Altjira refers to someone who has no beginning, who did not issue from another (erina itha arbmamakala = no one created him). Spencer and Gillen's claim (Northern Tribes of Central Australia p. 745) that 'the word alcheri means dream' is incorrect. Altjirerama means 'to dream', and it is derived from altjira (god) and rama (to see), in other words, 'to see god'. The same holds true for the Loritja language. Tukura nangani = 'to dream', from turkura (god) and nangani (to see). It will be demonstrated later that altjira and tukura in this context do not refer to the highest God in the sky but merely to a totem god which the native believes to have seen in a dream' (Strehlow 1907: 2). Carl Strehlow came to use the word in a number of different contexts. One attempt to solve the polysemy of 'altjira' was to use upper and lower cases, i.e. Altjira and altjira. Upper case 'Altjira' was used for a supreme being or high god; and in the Christian context of the mission, for

'God'. In lower case, 'altjira' was used in a vast array of contexts, assuming meanings in indigenous use and standing in stark contrast to the new meaning the missionaries had tried to impress on it. Today Western Aranda people use the word 'tnankara' to denote the Dreaming, dreaming ancestor, mythological past, birthmark, dreaming mark. Ⓛ Tukura (see Strehlow 1908: 1–2) Ⓓ Murra

Altjirangamitjina *Totem-Götter (die ewigen Unerschaffenen).* ◇ Totem-Gods (the eternal Uncreated Ones); dreaming beings. Ⓛ Tukutita; derived from 'tuku = tukura': 'the uncreated or unmade one' and 'tita': 'eternal' (Strehlow 1908: 2). Ⓓ Murra-murra

altjiroambala *unaufhörlich.* ◇ continuous. Ⓛ tukurita

altjirerama *(Gott sehen), träumen.* ◇ (to see God), to dream. Ⓛ tukura nangañi

altjirerinja *Traum.* ◇ dream. Ⓛ tukurbmanañi, tukurbmanami Ⓓ ngapitja

altjeta, patta altjeta *Stein mit denen Wurzeln abgeklopft werden.* ◇ stone used to clean roots.

altjimbaltjimba *undurchdringliches Dickicht.* ◇ impenetrable thicket. Ⓛ tatajerri

altjinka *zusammengereihte Blüten.* ◇ blossoms strung together. Ⓛ tatutu

altjinka *zusammengebunden, zusammen gereiht (Schwänze).* ◇ tied together, strung together (tails). Ⓛ tatutu

altjirkawuma *mit sich selbst sprechen.* ◇ speak with oneself. Ⓛ urukulini Ⓓ walkurali jatana

altjinka *Fadenspiel der Mädchen und Weiber.* ◇ thread game of girls and women. Ⓛ tatutu, kalbiri Ⓓ warawarapana

altjiuma *trs. überfließen machen (Wasser).* ◇ (transitive) make (water) flow over. Ⓛ totini, indeni

altjiulama *intr. überfließen (Wasser, Brotteig).* ◇ (intransitive) flow over (water, bread dough). Ⓛ indeni Ⓓ pinpiterina

altjota *Gras (spec.) (Panicum).* ◇ grass species (*Panicum*). Ⓛ iltjota

altjura *Loch (im Boden, im Holz, in Kleidern).* ◇ hole (in ground, in wood, in clothes); open. Ⓛ ăla Ⓓ wilpa, wilpawilpa (*zerrissen*: torn, *Kleid*: clothing, dress)

altjurerama *intr. öffnen.* ◇ (intransitive) open. Ⓛ alaringañi Ⓓ wilparina

altjurilama *ein Loch machen, öffnen (Tür).* ◇ make a hole, open (door). Ⓛ alani

altjuritjaltjurilama *durchlöchern.* ◇ perforate. Ⓛ alankurunkuruni Ⓓ titatita ngankana

altjuritjaltjura *löchricht, voller Löcher.* ◇ holy, full of holes. Ⓛ alankurunkuru

altjutnama *sich niederbücken (zum Fressen), sich niederlassen.* ◇ to bend down (to eat), settle down. Ⓛ bobañi

altjurankánama *wühlen (Maulwurf).* ◇ dig (mole). Ⓛ alawonkarabakañi

altjutnelélama *brüten (von Vögeln).* ◇ hatch eggs (birds). Ⓛ bobaljennañi Ⓓ purulkaterina

altjutnapitnama *sich ducken (Kamele, ilia), fortw. den Hals beugen (beim Gehen) Kamele.* ◇ to duck (camels, emu), constantly undulate (when walking) (camels). Ⓛ bobaranani

altólinama [Northern dialect] **(altalinama)** *ergreifen, erhaschen (Beute), umfassen (den Sterbenden).* ◇ grab (prey), embrace (the dying one). Ⓛ tulani

altolinanama [Northern dialect] *umfaßt halten.* ◇ hold tight. Ⓛ matulani

altólaltólinanama *dupl. erfassen, erhaschen.* ◇ (duplication) capture, grasp, hold. Ⓛ matulatularawonnañi

altuma *verstopfen, verschmieren, bedecken (Haut).* ◇ block, smear, cover (skin). Ⓛ pantani

altunta *weißer Stein.* ◇ white stone. Ⓛ ultunta

alturinja *Aufführungsplatz, der gereinigte.* ◇ ceremony ground, the cleaned or cleared one. Ⓛ urelba

ălua *Blut.* ◇ blood. Ⓛ ngurka, mitji Ⓓ kumara (*Blut*: blood, *Saft*: juice, *Flut ohne Fische*: flood without fish)

ālua *eßbare Wurzeln.* ◇ edible roots. Ⓛ ngalunba

alulúlama *bluten.* ◇ bleed. Ⓛ ngurka wararkatiñi Ⓓ kumarina

alua talalama *bluten.* ◇ bleed. Ⓛ ngurka totini Ⓓ kumara ngakana

alua ilkanama *Blut vergießen.* ◇ shed or lose blood. Ⓛ ngurka alani

alua ilkanalama *refl. sein Blut vergießen, sich verbluten.* ◇ (reflexive) to shed, lose or spill blood, bleed. Ⓛ ngurka palurunka alani

amala ankama *aufstoßen (Hickup).* ◇ burp (hiccup). Ⓛ ngetaninañi

tmarkinja *der gereinigte Platz (wo Zeremonien aufgeführt werden).* ◇ cleaned or cleared place (where ceremonies are performed); amboanta means 'cleared one'. Ⓛ amboanta

amāninta [Northern dialect] *Halbbruder, Halbschwester.* ◇ half-brother, half-sister. Ⓛ jakukutu

ámboa *alter Mann, lebensmüde, Neffe und Nichte von Seite des Vaters.* ◇ old man, weary of life, nephew and niece on father's side. Ⓛ burka

amba *Sohn oder Tochter von Seite der Mutter, cf. Verwandtschaftsbeziehungen.* ◇ child, son or daughter on mother's side (nephew or niece), see kinship terms (Strehlow 1913: 68). Ⓛ ukari (*Schwesters Sohn*), nankii Ⓓ ngatani (*Sohn oder Tochter v. Seite der Mutter*: son or daughter on mother's side)

ambekua *Neffe (eines Andern).* ◇ nephew (of someone else). Ⓛ ukarira nankiïra

ambua *Erdloch.* ◇ hole in ground. Ⓛ panaburka

āna *die Erde, der Erdboden.* ◇ the earth, the ground. Ⓛ pana

inánta *D. cf. nanta (überladen), [unclear]: erschöpft, ermüdet, überladen (Magen), fertig (Speisen), durchbacken, gar (Brot).* ◇ exhausted, done, finished. Ⓛ ananta

anbanaia *Larve der weißen Ameisen.* ◇ larvae of white ants. Ⓛ anbinii̇

ánbara (anbera) *weiter (räumlich), vorwärts.* ◇ further (space), forwards. Ⓛ wainta

anbarérama *vorbeilaufen, vorbeifließen (Saft), herabfließen (Süßigkeit).* ◇ run past, flow by (juice), flow down (something sweet). Ⓛ waïntariñi

anbara lama *weiter gehen.* ◇ to go on. Ⓛ waïnta jennañi

anbaela nama [Southern dialect] *weiter entfernt sein.* ◇ be further away. Ⓛ waintakata ninañi

anbarinjanbarerama *vorbeigehen (an etwas).* ◇ go past (something). Ⓛ waintawaintariñi

anbarindama *weiter geben.* ◇ pass on, give. Ⓛ waintanka jungañi

anbāra *weiße Stirn (Hunde, Pferde).* ◇ white forehead (dogs, horses). Ⓛ wiluna

anbarinjala *weiter (räumlich) hinfort.* ◇ further (space), onwards. Ⓛ waintanku

anbarinila *sofort (gehen).* ◇ (go) at once. Ⓛ waintakaru

anbarumaruma *viele weißgestirnt stehen (die ihre Stirn mit weiße Zeichen geschmückt haben).* ◇ many (persons) with foreheads painted white (decorated with white [de]signs) are standing. Ⓛ ululbi ngarañi

anbuma *befühlen, berühren, auflegen (Hand).* ◇ feel, touch, lay on (hand). Ⓛ pampuni Ⓓ karakarana

unbuma *weiter gehen.* ◇ walk on. Ⓛ jenbuni

unbubunbuma *dupl. weiter gehen.* ◇ duplication of 'walk on'. Ⓛ jenbujenbuni

anbalbánbalama *refl. sich selber überall befühlen.* ◇ (reflexive) feel, examine oneself everywhere. Ⓛ pampupampuni

anbalbanbarama *trs. überall befühlen, untersuchen (mit der Hand).* ◇ (transitive) feel, examine (with hand) everywhere. Ⓛ pampapampurapungañi

anbanalenjima *in einer Linie (nebeneinander anmarschiert kommen).* ◇ in one line (arrive side by side). Ⓛ ngalabilaringañi

anbentiuma *ausstreuen, aussäen (Samen).* ◇ scatter, sow (seeds). Ⓛ pinpaltjingañi

anbentintjiuma *zerbeißen und umherstreuen (der Kakadu die Sämerei und Rinde).* ◇ to bite to pieces and scatter (e.g. cockatoo seeds and bark). Ⓛ pinpaltjingarawonniñi

andara (andera) *fett, Fett, Mark, der Beine.* ◇ fat, fat or marrow of legs. Ⓛ niti Ⓓ mani, gildi

anangintja *kleine Raupe (spec. rötlich).* ◇ small caterpillar (reddish species). Ⓛ ngalankátuni

andaribana *('der mit Fett bestrichene'), der Junge (so genannt nachdem er bemalt ist).* ◇ boy (coated in fat) (see Strehlow 1913: 12). Ⓛ nitita

andata; (deba andata) *Blume, Blüte; (Daune, Vogeldaun).* ◇ flower, blossom; (down, bird down). Ⓛ tunku, wommulu; (*Vogeldaun*: wommulu, kudu) Ⓓ (tiwi) tui, tupu (*aufblühende Blume*: blossoming flower)

andata tata *Blumen.* ◇ flowers. Ⓛ untuntu

angna *Frucht, Same, Kern.* ◇ fruit, seed. Ⓛ kalka, alba Ⓓ tandra

ibatja angna *ibatja (Milch, Brust), angna (Frucht).* ◇ ibatja (milk, breast), angna (fruit); milky fruit, plant. Ⓛ ibi kalka

kwatja angna *weibliche Brust, Regentropfen.* ◇ woman's breast, raindrops. Ⓛ kapi kalka

angnélama *Samen reinigen.* ◇ clean seeds. Ⓛ kalkani

angna matataka *Früchte in Büscheln zusammen sitzend, sehr fruchtbar.* ◇ bunches of fruit, very fertile. Ⓛ kalka parapara

angnakaraba *unfruchtbar.* ◇ infertile.

angna intartnakintartna *Frucht dicht zusammen sitzend (Feigen).* ◇ dense fruit (e.g figs on tree), i.e. a lot of fruit on a plant. Ⓛ kalka tururu, kalkapalilkara

angna rurba *Obst (n).* ◇ fruit (generic); this appears to be a new term.

angnama *schlucken, verschlucken (einschlucken einen großen Bissen), in der Kehle stecken bleiben.* ◇ swallow, swallow the wrong way (stuck in throat). Ⓛ pulkurkmanañi (*einschlucken*: swallow), ngetaninañi

angnilitnama *(Herz)pochen (vor Zorn, Aufregung).* ◇ (heart) beat, throb or pound (from anger, excitement). Ⓛ ataiátuni

angna lalkinja *eine aufgehende Saat.* ◇ germinating crop.

ángnera *Gesicht.* ◇ face. Ⓛ junba Ⓓ mudla

angnera arentuerama *Gesicht abwenden.* ◇ turn face away. Ⓛ junba talbaringañi Ⓓ mudla walkina

angna tjintjirikana *unfruchtbar (Baum).* ◇ infertile (tree).

anjatima *frieren (refl.)* ◇ (reflexive) feel cold. Ⓛ perijerriñi Ⓓ katana (It is not clear in CS manuscript if this word belongs into this entry or the entry below.)

anja *Vater.* ◇ father. Ⓛ mama Ⓓ katana

ankallawotna; wotna *ein Mann, der begierig nach seiner ankalla ist; begierig.* ◇ man who is keen on his ankalla; keen, lusting. Ⓛ itirkila (*widerspenstig*: stubborn)

ankālla *rauhe Felsen.* ◇ rough or hard rocks. Ⓛ itirki

ankallankalla *kleine Eidechse.* ◇ small lizard. Ⓛ pintjalbatu

ankankilbara *halbroh, halbgar.* ◇ half-raw, half-cooked. Ⓛ wonkalwonkala

anka *unreif, grün, nicht gar.* ◇ not ripe, green, not done. Ⓛ wonka Ⓓ kati (*roh*: raw), puda (*unreif*: not ripe)

ánkala (ndolka) *Äste.* ◇ branches; lump on tree. Ⓛ antulka

ánkala *Stacheln (des Moloch horridess).* ◇ thorns (of thorny devil (reptile)). Ⓛ talta

ankāla *Regenwolke.* ◇ rain cloud. Ⓛ ngankali Ⓓ talara-palku

ankallankalla *hurerisch (blutschänderisch), fortwährend den Fußspuren der Weiber nachlaufen; Eidechse.* ◇ (incestuous) man who is always chasing women; lizard. Ⓛ winkiwinki

ankalla *Cousin.* ◇ cousin. Ⓛ wotjira
ankallukua *Cousin (eines Andern).* ◇ cousin (of someone else). Ⓛ wotjirara
ankallankalla (L), **uriakaljialjia** *Pflanze, auf Bergen wachsend, mit fasrigen rötlichen Blüten; Blume.* ◇ plant growing on mountain slopes with reddish fibrous blossoms; flower. Ⓛ ankallankalla
ankama *sagen, sprechen, reden, blöcken (Schaf), krähen (Vögel), rauschen (Bäume).* ◇ to say, speak, talk, bleat (sheep), crow (birds), rustle (trees). Ⓛ wonkañi Ⓓ jatana
bailba ankama *unverständig reden.* ◇ talk unintelligibly. Ⓛ wobalbi wonkañi
barbuta ankama *unverständig reden.* ◇ talk unintelligibly. Ⓛ kaualikura wonkañi
etatua ankama *sehr lange sprechen.* ◇ talk for a very long time. Ⓛ kutu wonkañi
erilkna ankama, entára ankama *laut sprechen.* ◇ speak loudly. Ⓛ kutururu wonkañi
ritjinja ankama *leise sprechen.* ◇ speak softly. Ⓛ talbiwonkañi, talwonkañi
ankanankana *Redner.* ◇ speaker. Ⓛ wonkami wonkami
ankalabuma *bitten, betteln, summen (Käfer).* ◇ ask for, beg, hum (beetle). Ⓛ wonkaraïni Ⓓ ngampararina
ankaúerama *sich beraten (Männer).* ◇ discuss (men). Ⓛ wonkawonniñi
ankalelama *trs. tönnen machen.* ◇ (transitive) make sound. Ⓛ wonkatjingani
ankaratnapallanama *im Chor sagen, im Chor zwitschern oder singen.* ◇ say in chorus, sing in chorus. Ⓛ wonkawonkarapungañi
inkana *(postp.) alle.* ◇ (postposition) all. Ⓛ tuta
ankankalintama *singend aufsteigen (Vogel).* ◇ ascend singing (bird). Ⓛ mawonkaraïni
inkanga *Achsel.* ◇ armpit. Ⓛ alipiri
ankāra *der Saft (der Raupen, von Beeren, Früchten).* ◇ juice (of caterpillars, berries, fruit), type of tree. Ⓛ ulkurknu
ankarutnarama; ankarutnarana *die Schelle schlagen (n); die Schelle (n).* ◇ strike the bell; the bell.
ankara *breit.* ◇ wide. Ⓛ bila
ankara *Baum (spec.)* ◇ tree species. Ⓛ ankara
ankarankara *Strauch (spec.), kleiner Baum.* ◇ bush species, small tree. Ⓛ ankarankari
ankaratja *herabrollendes Gestein.* ◇ rocks that are rolling down. Ⓛ tarara
ankata *Wolke.* ◇ cloud. Ⓛ matari
ankata *Eidechse (Egernja cohitu).* ◇ type of lizard, bearded dragon, cadney, jew lizard (*Egernja cohitu* now *Pogona vitticeps*). Ⓛ kanu
ankatanalakalama *intr. herabrollen (Stein).* ◇ (intransitive) roll down (stone). Ⓛ kutikutikatirokalïngañi
ankatala *durstig.* ◇ thirsty. Ⓛ marka Ⓓ tertieli
antatakua *sehr durstig.* ◇ very thirsty. Ⓛ markatara, manjiketára
ankatamea *Trank.* ◇ drink. Ⓛ nantupala
ankatanitjikalama *sich herabwälzen.* ◇ to roll down. Ⓛ tarara okalingañi Ⓓ kalikalibakana
ankatananama *sich rollen, sich fortwährend umrollen.* ◇ roll, continuously roll over. Ⓛ tarara jennañi Ⓓ walawalakana
ankatanala nama *trs. etwas fortwährend drehen (z.B. ein Rad).* ◇ (transitive) turning something continuously (e.g. a wheel). Ⓛ aririninañi
ankatitjanánama *sich umdrehend rollen (Scheibe).* ◇ to roll turning (disk). Ⓛ tararamajennañi
ankatäuma, ankatiuma *umdrehen, rollen, wälzen.* ◇ to turn around, to roll. Ⓛ tararawōniñi
ankatitjalama *refl. sich wälzen ?* ◇ (reflexive) to roll. ('?' added by CS) Ⓛ tarara jennañi

ankátnara *weiße Kakadu mit blauen Ring.* ◇ white cockatoo with blue ring. Ⓛ ankátnara Ⓓ naripinti

antineretnáma *schnell laufen, weiter schießen (Eidechsen).* ◇ to run quickly, to dart by (lizard). Ⓛ intingaráñi

ankatja; ankatja altarinja *Wort, Sprache; Märchen, Fabel, Mythe.* ◇ word, language; fairytale, fable, myth; 'ankatja' means today 'language, word'. Ⓛ wonka

ankeela, ankeëla *der Schuldner.* ◇ debtor; cousin.

ankeengera nama *schulden.* ◇ to owe.

ankatja kerintja *Geheimsprache.* ◇ restricted language. Ⓛ tamala anitji

ankatja kerintja *Geheimsprache.* ◇ secret language. Ⓛ tamala anitji

ankatja runka *Schimpfwort.* ◇ swear word.

ankéa *Gabe verlangend.* ◇ demand a gift, beg. Ⓛ ngatji

ankéankéa [Northern dialect] *cf.* **nkeankéa** *verlangend.* ◇ demanding. Ⓛ ngatjingatji

ankiebana [Northern dialect] *cf.* **nkéabana** *Gabe.* ◇ gift. Ⓛ ngatjita Ⓓ poto

ankéala nama [Northern dialect] *cf.* **nkeala nama** *nach der Gabe verlangen.* ◇ demand the gift. Ⓛ ngatjila ninañi

ankeengara-ilta *Wirtshaus, Herrberge.* ◇ pub, inn.

ankatjabaltura ankama *fortwährend reden (mit Worten zusetzen).* ◇ to talk continuously (urge with words). Ⓛ wonkatiwonkañi Ⓓ jatijatibana

ankielta *Gast, der eine Gabe verlangt.* ◇ visitor who demands a gift. Ⓛ ngatjintu

ankurutna *Larven (weiß) in lalba-Rinde.* ◇ grubs (white) in lalba-bark. Ⓛ ankurunu

ankua *schläfrig, schlafend, Schlaf.* ◇ sleepy, sleeping, sleep. Ⓛ anku Ⓓ mokka, mokkali

- **ankuérama** *schläfrig werden, einschlafen.* ◇ grow tired, go to sleep. Ⓛ ankuringañi
- **ankuíndama** *schlafen.* ◇ to sleep. Ⓛ anku ngariñi Ⓓ mokka turarana
- **ankuatnima** *in Schlaf fallen, einnicken.* ◇ fall asleep, doze off. Ⓛ kokururiñi

ankuankua *Widder (Kalb?).* ◇ ram (calf?) ('?' added by CS). Ⓛ mulkurumulkuru

unkuánkua *cf.* **nkuankua** *befriedigt, zufrieden.* ◇ satisfied, content. Ⓛ bokulba

ankurilama *befriedigt, einverstanden sein.* ◇ satisfied, to agree. Ⓛ unbaringañi

ankuerintja *Ostwind.* ◇ east wind. Ⓛ ankurintji

ankula *die Vertiefung im Boden, in der sie ihre Sämereien aufhäufen, Tenne.* ◇ depression in which to pile up seeds, threshing floor. Ⓛ wonkulu

anma *bald.* ◇ soon. Ⓛ wonnu Ⓓ wolja (kuperi)

ankuleetatétata *schwarz bemalt (wie Bluträcher).* ◇ painted black (like avengers). Ⓛ kituburutunu

anmangaletákata *lang lebend.* ◇ long living. Ⓛ wonnunkulenku

antanéranama *schnell gehen.* ◇ walk fast. Ⓛ wapakatiñi

antaka *weit, breit.* ◇ wide, broad. Ⓛ marari, bila, jakutamunu = ilbalaralerra Ⓓ marru, worita

- **antakerentjima** *sich ausbreitend niederlassen.* ◇ spread out and settle down. Ⓛ ngalabilaringañi
- **antakerama** *sich ausbreiten, sich zerstreuen.* ◇ spread, scatter. Ⓛ bilaringañi Ⓓ marrurina
- **lupara antakerama** *Beine auseinanderhalten.* ◇ keep legs apart. Ⓛ tunta bilaringañi
- **antakilama** *weit machen.* ◇ widen. Ⓛ bilani
- **antakakana** *die Breite.* ◇ width.
- **antakiuma** *trs. ausbreiten.* ◇ (transitive) spread. Ⓛ bilara wonniñi

antakauakaua *die weite Tür (Öffnung).* ◇ wide door (opening). Ⓛ bilalku

antāla *Zeit.* ◇ time. Ⓛ tunku

ántakara *Süden.* ◇ south. Ⓛ ulbarira Ⓓ kuankeri

 For the modern spellings of these words, see the dictionaries and sources in reference list.

antakarakula *im Süden (in trs. Sätzen).* ◇ in the south (in transitive sentences). Ⓛ ulbarir̃akarbanka

antakarakua *südlich, nach Süden.* ◇ to the south. Ⓛ ulbar̃iranku

antakarambinjala *südlich.* ◇ southerly. Ⓛ ulbar̃irakarba

antakaranitja *in südlicher Richtung.* ◇ in southerly direction. Ⓛ ulbar̃irapiti

antakarinja *der Südwind.* ◇ south wind. Ⓛ ulbar̃inelba

antálabuma [Northern dialect] *cf.* **ntalabúma** *beschleichen (Wild).* ◇ creep (up to game); pursue. Ⓛ urakatiraïni

antalélama [Northern dialect] *cf.* ntalelama. Ⓛ urakatini

antana [Northern dialect] *Opossum.* ◇ possum, *Trichosurus vulpecula.* Ⓛ wainta, witjulu

antalanama *lauernend weiterschleichen.* ◇ sneak preying. Ⓛ burtjikatiñi

antaläuma *lauern und horchen.* ◇ prey and listen. Ⓛ urakatiratalkañi

antanama *verfolgen.* ◇ pursue. Ⓛ māurakatiñi

antangalama *verfolgen (den rechten Weg).* ◇ follow (right path). Ⓛ munu jennañi

tátnama *sich nicht treffen, nicht begegnen, (belauern).* ◇ not meet, to miss each other, (prey on). Ⓛ urakatiñi

antátnama *belauern, lauern (aufs Wild).* ◇ prey (on game). Ⓛ urakatiñi

antanatopparba *kleiner gelbe Vogel.* ◇ small yellow bird. Ⓛ wolbatiti

ántara; antara tualtja; antara knara; antara larra; antarakua *Schwiegervater (Fraus Vater, Fraus Vaters Bruder) cf. Verwandtschaften; eigene Schwiegervater; Fraus Vaters ältere Bruder; Fraus Vaters jüng. Bruder; der antara eines Anderen.* ◇ father-in-law ◇ *cf.* kin relationships (see Strehlow 1913). Ⓛ wáputu; wapututaltji; waputu puntu; waputu wongu; waputura Ⓓ taru

antamantalama *sich ausbreitend weiter gehen.* ◇ to move on and spread out. Ⓛ bilalkujennañi

antamantarkama *sich ausbreitend weiter laufen (Raupen).* ◇ spreading as moving along (caterpillars). Ⓛ kunkujurini

antirtnankama *aufstoßen, den Schlucker haben.* ◇ belch, have hiccups. Ⓛ kaltara wonkañi

antáparperáma *sich winden, sich krümmen (Schlange).* ◇ twist (snake). Ⓛ munururiñi

antara *Strauch (spec.)* ◇ shrub species. Ⓛ tjuntala

antjalarama *(c. gen.) für etwas achten.* ◇ (c. gen.) pay attention to something.

antjibata *unfreiwillig.* ◇ involuntary.

anjibana *verlangend, liebend (Männer).* ◇ desiring, loving (men). Ⓛ úntuta

antjartjára *(Kehle weit) = heimweh haben.* ◇ (lit. wide throat), be homesick. Ⓛ untuwara

antja, aïntja *Kehle, Hals.* ◇ throat, neck. Ⓛ untu Ⓓ jerkala

antjabulja *(weiche Kehle), barmherzig, sanftmütig.* ◇ (lit. soft throat), merciful, gentle. Ⓛ untutula Ⓓ maramanju, manju

antja knara *(große Kehle) mutig, beherzt.* ◇ (large throat) courageous, brave. Ⓛ untupuntu

antjaltjura *(offene Kehle) nicht heiser, laut (warm).* ◇ (open throat) not hoarse, loud. Ⓛ untu ā̄la

antjarkaia (antja irkaia) *(geschlossene Kehle), heiser.* ◇ (closed throat), hoarse. Ⓛ untuarkaii Ⓓ ngarukura

antjulbma *(enge Kehle), heiser.* ◇ (narrow throat), hoarse. Ⓛ untutulu Ⓓ kurarina

antja-ntjirka *(trockene Kehle), durstig, blutdürstig.* ◇ (dry throat), thirsty, bloodthirsty. Ⓛ untubilti

antjalintia *hartherzig.* ◇ hard-hearted. Ⓛ untukubaibai

antja ekára *heiser.* ◇ hoarse, husky. Ⓛ untu opulu

antjatjita *sanftmütig.* ◇ gentle. Ⓛ untutula

antjantaka *volle Kehle (schreien).* ◇ full throat (scream). Ⓛ untubila

antjabma *Wille.* ◇ will. Ⓛ untukarikari

antjabatama *nicht wollen.* ◇ not wanting or willing. Ⓛ untu aruringañi

antja nama *wollen.* ◇ to want. Ⓛ untu ninañi Ⓓ jertapaterina

antjaantjerama *den Endschluß fassen.* ◇ to decide. Ⓛ untuunturingañi

antjerama *willend werden, willigen (in eine Sache).* ◇ become accepting, agree (in regard to a matter). Ⓛ unturingañi

antjalatnama *fort wollen.* ◇ wanting to leave. Ⓛ untunku mir̃ani

antja erkuma, antjerkuma *(Kehle umfassen), würgen, erwürgen.* ◇ (take by the throat), strangle, throttle. Ⓛ untu witini Ⓓ ngulina

antjatnama (antja utnama) *erwürgen, erdrosseln, (die Kehle beißen).* ◇ strangle, (bite throat). Ⓛ untu patani Ⓓ njulina

antjulbmerama *verdursten, ersticken.* ◇ die of thirst, suffocate. Ⓛ untutuluringañi

antjitatáka *gehörig, Geliebte die um einen sind und von demselben versorgt werden.* ◇ belonging, loved ones who surround someone and are looked after by same. Ⓛ ngalutu (ngalutumurka)

antja-irtjara *(weite Kehle), heimweh haben.* ◇ (wide throat), be homesick. Ⓛ untuwara

antjínama *kalt wehen (Wind), säuseln, kühl anwehen.* ◇ cold or cool blowing (wind). Ⓛ pipini

antjima [Northern dialect] *cf.* **ntjima** *(wärmen).* ◇ to warm. Ⓛ ngantjini

añtja *Nierenfett.* ◇ kidney fat. Ⓛ kabulita wolku

antjitatáka *Angehörigen.* ◇ kin. Ⓛ ngalutumurka

antjua *Nest, Wehr, Fischwehr.* ◇ nest, weir, fish weir. Ⓛ puni Ⓓ kunjila, wola? ('?' added by CS)

antjulbmérama *verdursten, ersticken.* ◇ die of thirst, suffocate. Ⓛ untutuluringañi

anuna [Northern dialect] *cf.* **nuna** *wir.* ◇ we. Ⓛ nganana

antjiïlbmara *lange Federn, lange Blätter.* ◇ long feathers, long leaves. Ⓛ okirilbatuni

antjilanána *Halsband.* ◇ neckband. Ⓛ untungana

antjantjara albuma *Heimweh habend, heimkehr.* ◇ be homesick, return home. Ⓛ jennalerikulbañi

apma *Schlange.* ◇ snake. Ⓛ wommi

apmátuna *getötete Schlange.* ◇ dead snake (a snake that was killed). Ⓛ wommi pungubaii

apú *Ausruf der Bestürzung.* ◇ exclamation of regret. Ⓛ jakka!

putiaputa *verschiedene Haufen, (von Männern oder Samen) Schichten.* ◇ different mobs, layers (of men or seeds). Ⓛ utulumurkamurka

apulla [Eastern dialect] *conf.* pulla. Ⓛ kaltuka

apúta [Northern dialect] *cf.* **pata, patta** *Stein.* ◇ stone, rock, hill, mountain. (No entry for 'pata', CS decided in the course of compiling his data to spell this word 'patta') Ⓛ puli

aralkalélama *aufhetzen, Aufruhr machen.* ◇ incite, stir up, cause a riot.

antjabialkara *cum. gen. wohlgefällig.* ◇ pleasing.

ăra *schnell.* ◇ fast. Ⓛ wolla

arábarkula [Northern dialect] *stumm.* ◇ mute. Ⓛ wonkakuraru

ărakunna *der schlecht laufen kann.* ◇ the one who cannot walk well. Ⓛ kujawolla

araungara *schnell (laufend).* ◇ (walking) fast.

arantemarantema *sehr schnell.* ◇ very fast. Ⓛ wollapattipatti, wollakawollaka

ăra (ā) *zornig.* ◇ angry. Ⓛ peka Ⓓ tiri

ar̃eratna nama *trs. ärgerlich machen, erzürnen.* ◇ (transitive) make angry. Ⓛ pekarekula talkañi

arankalélama *trs. zornig machen, erzürnen.* ◇ make angry, enrage. Ⓛ ulaljenañi Ⓓ tiririna

ar̃érama *zornig werden.* ◇ get angry. Ⓛ pekaringañi

 For the modern spellings of these words, see the dictionaries and sources in reference list.

arankarérama *knirschen mit den Zähnen.* ◇ grind with teeth. Ⓛ patakantiringañi

ar̔etiljawata *unversöhnlich.* ◇ irreconcilable. Ⓛ pekatimantu

ar̔ambirina *sehr zornig.* ◇ very angry. Ⓛ pekanbiriñi

āra *rote Känguruh (Macropus rufus).* ◇ red kangaroo (*Macropus rufus now Osphranter rufus*) (Atlas of Living Australia. n.d.) Ⓛ mallu Ⓓ tjukuru

ara-ara *Känguruh-Gras, mit büschelförmigen Halmen die sich rot färben. (Andropogon).* ◇ kangaroo-grass with tufted red blades (*Andropogon*). Ⓛ wirawiri

arabara *Grasart mit haferförmigen bläulichen Ähren.* ◇ grass species with oat-shaped bluish ears. Ⓛ arapara

aragata [Northern dialect] *Mund, Schnabel (Vogel).* ◇ mouth, beak (bird). Ⓛ ta, tamirka Ⓓ manna (*Mund*: mouth)

ara *(in Zusammensetzungen) der Mund, die Öffnung.* ◇ (in compounds) mouth, opening. Ⓛ ta

aragutja (arugutja) *Weib (mulier).* ◇ woman (wife). Ⓛ kunka Ⓓ widla, widlapirna (*alte Frau*: old woman), kaluka (*Frau in untergeordneter Stellung*: woman in subordinated position)

arailabuma *aussuchen, erwählen.* ◇ choose, select. Ⓛ ekuntarariñi

araknatataka *sich rötend (Früchte).* ◇ blush (fruit). Ⓛ kalakalangarañi

arákalaka; unta tmara rakalaka pitjalbai. jinga karalitjalbaimauna, botanta ilina inditjiaka. *vorher erwähnt, von früher bekannt; (der Platz) zu dem ein anderer bereits gegangen (ist), ausgesucht (Platz).* ◇ mentioned earlier, previously known; known (place) that someone has already gone to, chosen (place). Ⓛ banabakita

arakala; arakala ilkuma *ausgesucht; z.B. zuerst ein wenig essen, versuchen.* ◇ chosen; e.g. try a little bit of food. Ⓛ taku ngalkuñi

aralbmeltjalbmeltja *die mit weißen Haaren besetzten Ober-Lippen (Känguruh), weißer Schnurrbart (Känguruh).* ◇ upper-lip covered with white hair, white moustache (kangaroo). Ⓛ ta ilbmiltjilbmiltji

aralbuma [Northern dialect] *schmatzen, einziehen (Wasser).* ◇ smack, slurp (water). Ⓛ nuntalbmanañi

arelbuma [Northern dialect] *schmatzen.* ◇ smack, eat noisily. Ⓛ nuntalbmanañi

arálkama (aragata) *Mund aufsperren, gähnen.* ◇ open mouth wide, yawn. Ⓛ taluriñi, talangarañi Ⓓ manna terkana

arálkata *schwarze Beere (spec.)* ◇ black berry species. Ⓛ waiuka

aralbalalbala (ara-albalalbala) *der mit Stacheln besetzte Mund, der bärtige Mund.* ◇ mouth covered with stubble, bearded mouth. Ⓛ talbilalbili

aralinkinama *den Kopf (in den Schlamm) bohren (Fische).* ◇ to dig head into mud (fish). Ⓛ tukatunañi

araljilba *ungenießbar, verdorben, sauer.* ◇ inedible, rotten, sour. Ⓛ kaljilba, kidi

arálitja *Wüterich, der zum Messer greift.* ◇ choleric, brute who reaches for the knife. Ⓛ owilba

aralbarenkunama *sich fortwährend scheu umsehen.* ◇ constantly look around. Ⓛ ninaninarabakañi

araltama *verbieten, beschwichtigen.* ◇ forbid, appease. Ⓛ markuni Ⓓ daudauana, dauadauana

araltjiltja *Zahnlücke.* ◇ gap between teeth. Ⓛ patiri

araltutjaltutja [Northern dialect] *cf.* **raltutjaltutja** *sehr laut.* ◇ very loud. Ⓛ tēltara

aramanerîñja *festhalten in der Erde (Wurzel).* ◇ hold on to earth (roots). Ⓛ ngalulba

aramanga, aramána *stumm, fest.* ◇ silent, tight. Ⓛ tapatti

arámbalkama *den Mund (Schnabel) aufmachen, aufsperren.* ◇ open mouth (beak), open wide. Ⓛ talangarañi

arambilkuma *sehr viel fressen (Vögel).* ◇ to eat very much (birds). Ⓛ katurku ngalkuñi

aramatula *Schnabel (der Papageien).* ◇ beak (of parrots). Ⓛ tamatula

urámbia *überhitzt.* ◇ overheated. Ⓛ kambalkambal

urámbierama *sich erhitzen.* ◇ to heat (from anger). Ⓛ kambalkambalariñi

arámbouma *im Zorn (einen Schuldigen) schalten, lästern.* ◇ scold in anger (the guilty), to make nasty remarks. Ⓛ maiuni Ⓓ pankipankina, ngirkibana

ăránkara *sehr schnell.* ◇ very fast. Ⓛ ngaruta

arambara knara *sehr schnell, wütend.* ◇ very fast, furious. Ⓛ ngarupitjipitji Ⓓ kaldrintjariana? ('?' added by CS)

ăraărérenama *sehr schnell laufen.* ◇ run very fast. Ⓛ matalkaringañi

ăraăra *sehr schnell.* ◇ very fast. Ⓛ wollakawollaka

arakana *Laufbahn, Rennbahn.* ◇ racecourse. Ⓛ wollatura

arandilkanga *fest.* ◇ firm.

pepa arandilkanga; pepa *Pergament; Papier.* ◇ parchment; paper. 'pepa' is a new word deriving from the English word 'paper'. Carl Strehlow (1915: 70) recorded a handsign for pepa meaning 'book, letter'.

ararinja [Northern dialect] *richtige Geschwister (die alle denselben Vater und dieselbe Mutter haben).* ◇ siblings who all have the same father and mother. Ⓛ nakulapunguta

arángalkura *große Heuschrecken.* ◇ large grasshoppers. Ⓛ mallukuta

aranbilama *verteilen, austeilen.* ◇ distribute, deal out. Ⓛ bilani (verteilen)

Aranda *'scharf', ein Steinmesser spec, heftig, (schimpfen), zornig, wütend.* ◇ 'sharp', a type of stone knife, violently, (scold), angry; name of Arandic language. Ⓛ āranda (*Steinmesser*: stone knife, *schimpfen*: scold), áluna (*heftig*: violently), minga-mingantu

arángatja *mein Großvater (oder Enkel, Enkelin).* ◇ my grandfather (or grandson, granddaughter). Ⓛ tamuna

aránga, aranga; aranga knara; aranga larra; kwaia aranga; lorra aranga ♂; woia aranga; kwaia aranga *Großvater (Vaters Vater), Enkel, Enkelin; der ältere Bruder des Großvaters; der jüngere Bruder des Großvaters; die Schwester des Großvaters; Mutter des Schwiegervaters, Großneffe; Großnichte.* ◇ father's father (grandfather), grandson, granddaughter; older brother of father's father; younger brother of father's father; sister of father's father; mother of father-in-law; grandnephew; grandniece. One of the principal ways to acquire rights and responsibilities in relation to land is through one's aranga (father's father) in Western Aranda society. Other rights are obtained through one's tjimia (mother's father) as well as through one's palla (father's mother) and ebmanna (mother's mother), they are however not of the same order as those acquired through one's aranga. Ⓛ tamu; tamu punta; tamu wongu Ⓓ ngadada

arángukua *Großvater (eines Andern).* ◇ grandfather (of someone else). Ⓛ tamura

arangatappatuna *große rote Heuschrecken.* ◇ large red grasshoppers. Ⓛ toppulkira

aránga (erenga) *graues Kängaruh, Euro, Macropus robustus.* ◇ grey kangaroo, euro, *Macropus robustus* (Gould). Ⓛ kanala Ⓓ turu

aranjikama *zum Streit herausfordern.* ◇ challenge. Ⓛ arbmultakani Ⓓ pupana

aránkaia *Fächerpalme, Livistona Mariae.* ◇ palm tree (*Livistona mariae*). Ⓛ aranki

arankalitnima *prasselnd verbrennen (Sträucher).* ◇ burn cracking (scrub). Ⓛ ngarbmankulanañi

arankama *schreien, sehr laut rufen (vor Zorn und Wehmut).* ◇ cry, shout very loud (from anger and sadness). Ⓛ ngarbmanañi

arantjua *Wassersack (aus aroa-Fellen).* ◇ waterbag (made of wallaby skins). Ⓛ arantji

arantjuma (arantjurama?) *(Mund trinken), küssen.* ◇ kiss (lit. mouth drink). ('?' added by CS) Ⓛ nuntuni, ta nunjuni Ⓓ manna tapana, manna tapamalina (*einander küssen*: kiss each other)

arankara [Northern dialect] *cf.* **rankara** *ihr.* ◇ you (2nd person plural). Ⓛ nurangari

arankuia *wilde Kirschbaum.* ◇ wild cherry tree. Ⓛ kõpata Ⓓ manaura? ('?' added by CS)

arapóla *Haut des Mundes, inneren Lippen.* ◇ skin of mouth, inside lips. Ⓛ tapanki

arapmaramara [Northern dialect] *Gaumen.* ◇ palate. Ⓛ ngurk-ngurba

arapmarapma *Grasart.* ◇ grass species. Ⓛ arámarama

ararama *auslesen, wählen, abteilen.* ◇ pick out, choose, separate. Ⓛ ekuntani Ⓓ kalkalkana

arantiuma *sich ausbreiten (Bart um den Mund).* ◇ spread (beard around mouth). Ⓛ paraarintanañi

aranta *heiß (Platz).* ◇ hot (place). Ⓛ aranta

araratankama [Northern dialect] *cf.* **raratankama** *weiter sagen.* ◇ spread word. Ⓛ patjiri wonkañi

araratala tuma [Northern dialect] *cf.* raratala tuma. ◇ punish, avenge. Ⓛ patjirinku pungañi

araratilama [Northern dialect] *cf.* raratilama. ◇ appease. Ⓛ patjirenañi

ararkua [Eastern or Southern dialect] *cf.* **kuralja** *Siebengestirn.* ◇ Seven Sisters, Pleiades. Ⓛ okarála Ⓓ mankaraworra

arata *Strauch auf Bergen wachsend, spec. mit eßbaren Früchten.* ◇ bush with edible fruit that grows on mountains (*Eremophila freelingii*), native fuchsia. Ⓛ arata

aratalbalbiuma *verlieren.* ◇ to lose. Ⓛ batatjingani

arátama [Northern dialect] *cf.* **ratama** *herauskommen.* ◇ to come out. Ⓛ bakañi

arátalela nama [Northern dialect] *cf.* **ratalela nama** *herausführen.* ◇ to lead out. Ⓛ bakataljini

arátintjima [Northern dialect] *cf.* ratinjama. ◇ come out, open (sun). Ⓛ bakaratalkañi

aratinjtilama [Northern dialect] *cf.* ratinjalama. ◇ come out, step out, open up (star). Ⓛ ngalabakara talkañi

aratnatátama *reifen, rot werden (Früchte).* ◇ to ripen, to redden (fruit). Ⓛ turatjitjanañi, kalakalanganiña

aratjapura *senkrecht, gerade.* ◇ vertical, straight. Ⓛ tukaruru

aratja *gerade, aufrecht, gerecht.* ◇ straight, upright, just. Ⓛ tukáruru, turkula Ⓓ talku

aratjaratjilama; aratjaratjilalama; aratjaratjerama *trs. rechtfertigen (n); refl. sich rechtfertigen; pass. rechtfertigen.* ◇ (transitive) to justify; (reflexive) to defend; (passive) to justify, defend.

aratjimantataka *alles, was gerade oder gerecht ist.* ◇ all that is just. Ⓛ tukarurubábata

aratjaratjilȧnama *schnurstracks hinter einen herlaufen.* ◇ follow behind someone. Ⓛ turkulturkulbmanañi

aratjagata (aratjigata) *Zeichen-Stöcke, die in die Nähe des Lagerplatzes gesteckt werden; Richtscheit, Wegweiser, Zielscheibe.* ◇ signposts in vicinity of camps, sign, target. Ⓛ tukarurukata Ⓓ toa

aratjingala *Vorbild, Zeichen (Wunder).* ◇ symbol, sign (miracle). Ⓛ tukarurunka? ('?' added by CS)

áratnanka *sehr schnell (kommen), fleißig.* ◇ very quick (come), hard-working. Ⓛ wollatura

aratnolka *Strauch mit bläuliche weißen, glockenför. Blüten (auf den Bergen sich findend), (Aster Mitchelli).* ◇ shrub with bluish white bell-shaped blossoms (grows on mountains); mintbush, *Prostanthera striatiflora*. Ⓛ aranulku

aratnangiuma *(ins Wasser) werfen.* ◇ throw (into water). Ⓛ tululu wonniñi

aratnangiulaka *(in den Boden) hinein gehen.* ◇ to go into (the ground). Ⓛ lalkarukatiñi

arbantema *z.B.* **pitjarbantama** *oder* **pitjikarbantema** *postp. müssen, z.B. Du mußt kommen.* ◇ (postposition) must; e.g. you must come.

arelkutanama *treiben (etwas zu tun, hasten).* ◇ to drive (to do something; to hurry, to hasten).

arelkalelama *schimpfen, fortwährend zanken.* ◇ to scold, quarrel constantly.

arbábaka *vor langer Zeit, einst.* ◇ a long time ago, once upon a time. Ⓛ wombabaka

arbabakala *vor langer Zeit, einst.* ◇ a long time ago, once upon a time. Ⓛ wombamaninji

arbakura, arbekua *ein anderer.* ◇ someone else.

arbalama *nicht verstehen, nicht kennen.* ◇ not understand, not know. Ⓛ wombaputa Ⓓ worangana

arbaloárbala *unverständlich (ankama).* ◇ unintelligibly (talk). Ⓛ wobalbi Ⓓ ngarukura

arbauunja *glücklich?, zufrieden.* ◇ happy, satisfied. ('?' added by CS)

arbámaninja *einst (in der Zukunft), nach langer Zeit.* ◇ once (in the future), after a long time. Ⓛ ngulamaninja, wombamaninji

arpanalama *des Todes schuldig machen, sterben.* ◇ deserve death penalty, die. Ⓛ kurbani

arbauutérama *fehlen, nicht vorhanden sein, verschwinden.* ◇ to miss, not be present, to disappear. Ⓛ wombaringañi

arbauuta *verdeckt, unsichtbar (von der Sonne, die durch Wolken verdeckt ist), verschwunden, vor unbestimmter Zeit.* ◇ covered, invisible (sun covered by clouds), disappeared (a long time ago). Ⓛ womba, wombalta Ⓓ walu

arbérama *fehlen, abwesend sein, nicht da sein.* ◇ to miss, be absent, not be present. Ⓛ wombaringañi

arbmauanjima *ganz leer (Bauch) sein, sehr hungrig sein.* ◇ be completely empty (stomach), be very hungry. Ⓛ wilatularingañi

arbmánama *schaffen, hervorbringen (bei ihren religiösen Ceremonien).* ◇ to create, to produce (at ceremonies). Ⓛ baluni Ⓓ pantjimana

arbmanananana, arbmanarinja *Schöpfer.* ◇ creator. Ⓛ balunmibalunmi

arbmaninja *Schaffen.* ◇ create. Ⓛ balunta

arbmaninjamea *Geschaffene.* ◇ the created. Ⓛ baluntabala

arbmanka *schnell, gewaltsam entreißen, z.B. arbm. inama.* ◇ quickly snatch away with force. Ⓛ babaltubabaltu

arbuma *behauen, glatt schaben, z.B. tjatta, abschaben (mittels der mera).* ◇ trim, smooth, e.g. spear; scrape off or clean (with a spear thrower). Ⓛ tauani

areljeteljeta *die Nester der Honigameisen.* ◇ nests of honeyants. Ⓛ ariljitiljiti

arbuna *ein anderer.* ◇ another, other. Ⓛ kutuba, munu Ⓓ nguru

arbunakarbuna *verschieden machen.* ◇ make different.

arbunarba *jener da.* ◇ that one there. Ⓛ kutubarba

arbunarbuna *andere.* ◇ others. Ⓛ kutubakutuba

arbukarba *jene.* ◇ those. Ⓛ kutubakutubaku

arbukantarbukanta *jene anderen (nicht ich).* ◇ those others (not me). Ⓛ kálkikukálkikukutu

arbuntarba *die andern.* ◇ the others. Ⓛ kalki

arétjingatjinga *Felsbrocken.* ◇ rock, boulder. Ⓛ taltalba

arebalananama *intrs. auf dem Boden rollen (Wagen).* ◇ (intransitive) roll on surface (wagon).

arenba *scharf, spitz (Messer).* ◇ sharp, pointy (knife). Ⓛ iri

areba, arébba [Northern dialect] *cf.* **reba** *große Mulde.* ◇ large bowl. Ⓛ biti

 For the modern spellings of these words, see the dictionaries and sources in reference list.

arékua *Felsenufer (Gorge).* ◇ gorge. Ⓛ ju-tatulbi

arelkuma [Northern dialect] *fortschicken, drängen zum Weitergehen, zum Aufbruch.* ◇ to send away, urge to leave, urge to move on. Ⓛ tjingani Ⓓ walpamalina? ('?' added by CS)

arelkuta *Larven, weiß, in lupa-Wurzeln.* ◇ white grubs in lupa roots. Ⓛ arelkuta

arelpa *spitz, scharf.* ◇ pointy, sharp. Ⓛ talali Ⓓ tjerkara, tiri

arémakua *Lichtung (im Gehölz).* ◇ clearing (in the bush). Ⓛ ngurara

arenkuma *sich fortwährend umsehen, von einem zum andern.* ◇ constantly look around, from one to the other. Ⓛ talbatalbaringañi

aréoa *Tür, Eingang.* ◇ door, entrance. Ⓛ aréwa Ⓓ manna

aréola *vor der Tür, am Eingang.* ◇ in front of the door, at the entrance. Ⓛ aréwanka

aretnama *der spitzige Rückgrad (der spitzige oder der magere Rücken).* ◇ pointy backbone (pointy or lean back). Ⓛ talarara

aretna [Northern dialect] *Name.* ◇ name. Ⓛ ini

arentuerama [Northern dialect] *Gesicht abwenden.* ◇ turn face away. Ⓛ talbaringañi Ⓓ walkina

arémakula *tiefes Loch (Brunnen), Vertiefung.* ◇ deep hole (well), ditch. Ⓛ kubilji

arganakankua *Freudigkeit.* ◇ joy, joyfulness.

arganapanapa *willig, freudig.* ◇ willing, joyful.

argana *freudig, fröhlich.* ◇ joyful, cheerful, happy. Ⓛ iñka, piriña Ⓓ manju

arganabanánga *sehr fröhlich.* ◇ very cheerful. Ⓛ iñkapuntu (iñkakåratikårati)

arganabuljabulja *freundlich, gütig.* ◇ friendly, kind. Ⓛ iñka ibilja Ⓓ maramanju

arganérama *sich freuen, spielen.* ◇ be happy, to play, have fun. Ⓛ iñkañi, piriñi Ⓓ mankina, pirkina (*spielen*: to play)

arganalélama *trs. einen erfreuen.* ◇ (transitive) to please someone. Ⓛ iñkatjingañi

arganelenáma *trs. freudig machen, erfreuen.* ◇ (transitive) make happy, to please. Ⓛ maïnkatjingani

arganka *Baum, eine Art Eucalyptus (blood-wood).* ◇ type of eucalyptus tree, bloodwood, *Eucalyptus opaca.* Ⓛ arginki

argankunba *die mehr als faustgroßen Knollen der arganka Eucalyptus terminalis.* ◇ bulbs of arganka (*Eucalyptus terminalis* now *Eucalyptus opaca* (Latz 1996)) that are larger than a fist. Ⓛ arginki itirki

argeta *gelber Ocker.* ◇ yellow ochre. (Deleted here by CS and reinserted below with 'k' as 'arketa'). Ⓛ argita

arintapma *Busch mit langen Stracheln.* ◇ bush with long prickles. Ⓛ minjerka

argutilama *verhören.* ◇ to question, cross-examine. Ⓛ kulira wonnani

arilatambakana *Maus.* ◇ mouse. Ⓛ maluwonnalba

aríla [Northern dialect] *dort.* ◇ there. Ⓛ nara

arinkarinka (ara + inka) *Leiter.* ◇ leader.

ariltja *der Speichel, Blasen (auf dem Wasser).* ◇ spit, saliva, bubbles (on the water); froth, foam, dribble. Ⓛ talji, tjalji

ariltjantatnama *Blasen auf dem Wasser aufsteigen.* ◇ bubbles rising to water surface. Ⓛ taljikutungarañi

ar̉ilbaritjima [Northern dialect] *cf.* **rilbaritjima** *leise sprechen.* ◇ to speak softly. Ⓛ tāltalariñi

ariljatna [Northern dialect] *Lunge.* ◇ lung. Ⓛ ariljakiri Ⓓ buñga

ariljinga (aréljinga) *Kinnbacken.* ◇ jaw. Ⓛ arilingi Ⓓ mannakiri

arilkara *hell, weiß.* ◇ light, white. Ⓛ pirpirba

arilkama [Northern dialect] *cf.* **relkama** *Tag anbrechen.* ◇ daybreak, dawn. Ⓛ jultaringañi

ariltiltiltilta *das Gerätsch, das durch das Nagen (der Mäuse) hervorgeht, knabbern, knacken, zerknacken.* ◇ noise made by gnawing mice, to nibble, to crack, to crunch. Ⓛ ketunketun

ariltiltiltiltanáma *zerknacken.* ◇ to crack. Ⓛ ketunketunariñi

arina [Northern dialect] *cf.* **rena** *dort.* ◇ there. Ⓛ nara

ariltjialtjipa *frischen (Zeichen, die auf dem Körper gemalt sind).* ◇ fresh (designs painted on body). Ⓛ kuarita

arinama [Northern dialect] *cf.* **renama** *setzen.* ◇ to sit down. Ⓛ tunani

arinopinama [Southern dialect] *hinlegen, zusammenlegen, aufschütten, (Sämereien).* ◇ to lay down, to fold, to make a heap, (seeds). Ⓛ tunatunani

arinalama [Northern dialect] *cf.* **renalama** *sich setzen.* ◇ sit down. Ⓛ ninakatiñi

arinalalakalama [Northern dialect] *cf.* **renalalakalama** *sich niedersetzen.* ◇ sit down. Ⓛ ninakatira okalingañi

arinbinba [Northern dialect] *Oberlippe und Unterlippe.* ◇ upper lip and lower lip. Ⓛ tabinbinbi Ⓓ mannamimi (*Lippe*: lip)

arínjamboninja *märchenhafte Männer.* ◇ mythical men that feature in a narrative classified by Carl Strehlow as a 'fairytale' (Strehow 1907: 104). Ⓛ apuju

erinta [Northern dialect] *cf.* **ronta** *sehr kalt.* ◇ very cold. Ⓛ warri

arintja [Northern dialect] *das böse Wesen.* ◇ bad being, bad spirit (feared by people); derived from 'ara' meaning 'angry, bad, vicious, fierce' (Strehlow 1907: 11–13). In Western Aranda mythology, a place in the far west called Tatara was associated with these bad spirit beings. They appear in many different guises and have different names such as kokolura, who have the form of a dog but human hands and kangaroo legs (Strehlow 1907: 11). Today, they are also referred to as 'monsters' in English. Ⓛ mamu

aralelama (arilelama) *mit etwas davonlaufen.* ◇ run away with something. Ⓛ talkilijennañi

ar̔ira [Eastern dialect] *das rote Känguruh.* ◇ red kangaroo.

arirétnama *eilen, schnell laufen.* ◇ hurry, run fast. Ⓛ patantura jennañi

ariralurulánama *sehr schnell laufen.* ◇ run very fast. Ⓛ talkalukulakúlbañi

arirama *laufen, eilen, rennen.* ◇ run, hurry. Ⓛ talkalungañi Ⓓ mindrina

ariranama *laufen zu.* ◇ run to. Ⓛ matalkaringañi, mawollaringañi

arirentjima *herbeieilen, herzulaufen.* ◇ hurry to. Ⓛ ngalatalkalungañi, ngalatalkañi

áriralbuntama *entlaufen, wegeilen.* ◇ run away, hurry away. Ⓛ talkalukukatiñi Ⓓ kurkarina (*entlaufen*: run away, escape)

aritjalkanama [Northern dialect] *conf.* **ritjalanama** *aufbrechen (Schoten).* ◇ break open (pods). Ⓛ tambirpungañi

aritjima [Northern dialect] *cf.* **ritjima** *flüstern.* ◇ to whisper. Ⓛ tālarini

aritjintama [Southern dialect], **aritjintjima** *aufspringen.* ◇ jump up. Ⓛ nakula kalbiñi

arkama (?) *fortgehen.* ◇ go away. ('?' added by CS)

arkalalama *weiter wandern.* ◇ to wander on. Ⓛ majennañi

arkabarkama *mit fort wandern.* ◇ wander away with. Ⓛ matalkaniñi

arkalaworkala nama *schwindlig werden.* ◇ to get dizzy. Ⓛ kunku jurira ninañi

aritjalitjala *honey-eater (Acanthogenys rufigularis); hellbraunes Genick, weißgesprenkelte Brust und Bauch, graugefleckte Rücken mit weißen Schwanzspitzen (Vogel).* ◇ honeyeater (*Acanthagenys rufogularis*). Ⓛ aritjilitjili

arkanama *versuchen, schmecken, prüfen.* ◇ try, taste, test. Ⓛ atjini Ⓓ wontjana, namana

arkaninjebara, arkaninjikebara *Geschmack.* ◇ taste. Ⓛ atjilpuntu

arkalélama *erregen (Lust), bewegen (Herz).* ◇ excite, arouse (lust), move (heart).

 For the modern spellings of these words, see the dictionaries and sources in reference list.

arkapa *Unterbein nur der Vögel, vom Knie bis zum Fuß.* ◇ lower leg (only of birds), from knee to foot. Ⓛ arkapa

arkapa *Desert Oak.* ◇ desert oak (*Allocasuarina decaisneana*).

arknankama *groß wachsen, dick werden (Beine).* ◇ grow big, become fat (legs). Ⓛ unkañi

arkápala *voll (Mond).* ◇ full (moon). Ⓛ wilapuntu

arkatnaberuparama *(Duplik.) schnell heimkehren.* ◇ (duplication) to return home quickly. Ⓛ kutikulbanikutara

arkapitjala *Kniescheibe der Vögel (contra: arkapa-tjala).* ◇ kneecap of birds. Ⓛ mata

arkatnalbuma *schnell umkehren (an einen entfernten Ort).* ◇ turn back quickly (to a distant place). Ⓛ kutikulbañi

arkara *weiße Vogel spec.* ◇ white bird species Ⓛ wiratu, workerimba

arkára *Mann der verheirateten Schwester (♂).* ◇ husband of sister (♂). Ⓛ markaii

ankara *weit, ausgedehnt (Wasserfläche).* ◇ wide, expansive (water surface). Ⓛ bila

arkatnia *eifrig, schnell (lama).* ◇ eager, quick (walk). Ⓛ róutjibatjiba Ⓓ marapakapirna, worpanalu

arkēlba *Kopfschmuck von Eulenfedern.* ◇ headdress made of owl feathers. Ⓛ pokulu

arkéntera [Northern dialect] *conf.* **irkentera** *große Fledermaus.* ◇ large bat. Ⓛ arkentiri

arketa *gelbe Ocker.* ◇ yellow ochre. Ⓛ arketa

erutatja *australische Maikäfer.* ◇ Australian Maybeetle. Ⓛ arketunba

arkelkerala nama *sich sehnen (nach der Heimat).* ◇ long for (home country, *heimat*). Ⓛ atjikirikaniñi

arkelkerama *sich sehnen (nach Hause).* ◇ long for (home). Ⓛ atjikirikanini

arkna *Lehm.* ◇ clay. Ⓛ arkna Ⓓ puljuru

arkilbiluntuma *schnell weiter wandern.* ◇ walk on quickly. Ⓛ majanañi

arkerinjerama *weglaufen, fortlaufen (vom Mann).* ◇ run away (from husband). Ⓛ arkerinjeriñi

arknala; kata katjianga arknala tnama *(um es zu beschützen) vor einem stehend, schützend vor (einen stehen), (um es zu beschützen).* ◇ stand in front of somebody to protect. Ⓛ nguru (*vor uns*), ngananala; katu pipiringuru nguru ngarañi (*schützend vor einem stehen damit der Feind einen nicht schlagen kann*)

arkitjalbuma *von der Wanderung zurückkehren.* ◇ return from a walk. Ⓛ kulbanañi

arknamanangálama *schnell arbeiten, sich sputen.* ◇ work fast, hurry up. Ⓛ jurikatiñi

arknantaiuma *beschützen, abhalten (vom Schlagen).* ◇ protect, stop (from hitting). Ⓛ ngalkini

arknanterama *bewahren, beschützen, aufhalten.* ◇ protect, stop. Ⓛ ngalkilarini

arknáta *schützend, abhaltend (den Feind).* ◇ protect, keep away (enemy). Ⓛ anga

arkirintinama *einschlagen (Blitz).* ◇ strike (lightning). Ⓛ larapungañi

arknátarknáta *beschützend.* ◇ protecting. Ⓛ angaanga

arknaninja *hervorkommend (Regenbogen).* ◇ come out (rainbow). Ⓛ bakanta

arkuénama *Sitte sein.* ◇ customary.

arkueninja *die Sitte.* ◇ custom.

arknua urbula *Tinte (n).* ◇ ink.

arkerinja *unwissend.* ◇ ignorant.

arkerinja nama *unwissend sein.* ◇ be ignorant.

arknantiuma *beschützen, behüten.* ◇ protect. Ⓛ ngalkini Ⓓ ngamalkana

arknanuma *(aus dem Boden) hervorkommen (Regenbogen).* ◇ (rainbow) come (out of ground). Ⓛ bakani

arknanupanuma *(aus dem Boden) hervorkommen (Regenbogen).* ◇ (rainbow) come (out of ground). Ⓛ bakabakañi

arknōlta *dem Tode nahe.* ◇ close to death. Ⓛ atulta

arknarama *ansehen die Person.* ◇ look at a person.

arknata nama *bewahren, aufhalten.* ◇ protect, stop. Ⓛ anganinañi

arknaneuma *bleiben lassen, am Leben lassen.* ◇ to leave alone, to spare life.

arknatankama *beschwichtigen mit Worten (Streitende).* ◇ to calm with words (people who are quarreling or fighting). Ⓛ angawonkañi

arkunta *die Höhlung, die die Mäuse im Boden machen, Mauseloch.* ◇ mouse hole. Ⓛ urkuntu

arknataulama *fürsprechen.* ◇ intercede. Ⓛ arknatarini

arknenbanealama *Heimweh haben und gehen (nach Hause).* ◇ to be homesick and go (home). Ⓛ bakabakaltjingani

arknaterama *abhalten (von Tätlichkeiten), schlichten (Streit).* ◇ to restrain (from violence), settle (quarrel). Ⓛ angaringañi

arkularkua *eulenartiger Nachtvogel, der in der Nacht seinen Kuck Kuck artigen Ruf erschallen läßt, auch Mopoke genannt; Kuckucks-Eule.* ◇ owl-like nightbird with a cuckoo-like call; also called Mopoke (*Ninox novaeseelandiae*). Ⓛ kurr-kurr Ⓓ kapakaparunga

arkulta *Grasart (ähnlich altjōta).* ◇ grass species (similar to altjōta). Ⓛ mutimuta

ároa *Rock-Wallaby.* ◇ rock-wallaby. Ⓛ wāru Ⓓ kantu

arkāra *die frischen (Eier der Vögel).* ◇ fresh (bird eggs).

arolanbuma *streiten, disputieren.* ◇ quarrel, dispute. Ⓛ tularapungañi

aróralama *lang herunterwachsen (Bart).* ◇ long downwards growing (beard). Ⓛ wanpulakatiñi

arólta, arolta ankama *sehr leise (sprechen).* ◇ very quietly (speak), whisper. Ⓛ wimma, wimmaka wonkañi

arótna [Northern dialect] *das Kinn.* ◇ chin; jaw. Ⓛ ngotu

arótuma [Northern dialect] *cf.* **rotuma** *drücken.* ◇ press. Ⓛ puruni

arknarama *unterscheiden, Unterschied machen.* ◇ distinguish, make a difference.

arpa *(postp.) selbst.* ◇ (postposition) self. Ⓛ urpa Ⓓ munta

árpatnama *kratzen, scharren (Schlafplatz).* ◇ scratch, scrape (sleeping place). Ⓛ naiïrpungañi

arpánama *schuldig sein, Strafe verdient haben.* ◇ be guilty, deserve punishment. Ⓛ kurpani

arpánalama *sich schuldig machen (des Todes).* ◇ to deserve death. Ⓛ kurpani

artata *fest, hart (Lehm), stark, schwer.* ◇ firm, hard (clay), strong, heavy. Ⓛ artata Ⓓ kanpara (paratara)

artjábera *eine haferartige Grasart (Panicum).* ◇ an oat-like grass species (*Panicum*). Ⓛ irtjabiri

artja *auseinander, gespreizt (Beine).* ◇ apart, spread (legs). Ⓛ talka

artjȧnama *fortgehen, schnell fortlaufen.* ◇ go away, run quickly away. Ⓛ witjibakañi, talkaringañi, kartjilkañi Ⓓ puntina, palkana, danina (*sich verabschieden*: say goodbye)

artjalélama *verführen, mitgehen machen.* ◇ to seduce, to manipulate someone to do something. Ⓛ jertjatalinañi Ⓓ karkarkana

artjarankama, artjarilama *zureden, zu gehen; zureden zu gehen.* ◇ to encourage to go. Ⓛ wolkara wonkañi

artjarerama *sich entschließen zu gehen.* ◇ decide to go. Ⓛ wolkarariñi Ⓓ manungana? ('?' added by CS)

artjara lama *sehr weit wandern.* ◇ wander very far. Ⓛ worpara jennañi

ártjima *dringen in einen (um eine Erlaubnis), einen fortwährend bitten um etwas (z.B. die Erlaubnis um fortzugehen).* ◇ beg constantly someone for something (e.g. permission to leave). Ⓛ artani

artirtanténama *sich wälzen (vor Schmerzen).* ◇ roll (in pain).

arknatoppatoppa, arknatamuljamulja *Widerstand.* ◇ resistance.

arknatoppatopperama, arknatamuljamuljerama *Widerstand leisten.* ◇ resist.

artjaninjartjanama *sehr schnell laufen.* ◇ run very fast. Ⓛ mapantatunañi

 For the modern spellings of these words, see the dictionaries and sources in reference list.

artjalbáritja nama *ohne Aufenthalt weiter wandern.* ◇ continue walk without a stop. Ⓛ jertarabakani

artjelbmiuma *das Tagerslicht sich verbreiten (das Licht am Morgen).* ◇ dawn (light in the morning). Ⓛ turangarañi

artjalbáritjalélama *einen sogleich mit sich gehen heißen.* ◇ order someone to accompany at once. Ⓛ jertajertataljini

artjentuma *in Reihen auf und abgehen, dabei die Hände auf und niederbewegen.* ◇ walk up and down in line moving hands up and down. Ⓛ taiïrpungañi

artjara lama *mit fort gehen.* ◇ go away with. Ⓛ wopara jennañi

artjelbmiwia *die Zeit vor Tagesanbruch, Lichtstreifen breiter werden.* ◇ time before daybreak when it starts getting brighter, early in the morning (Strehlow 1915: 44). Ⓛ turangarañi

artjima *sich wärmen, sich sonnen.* ◇ to warm, to sun. Ⓛ ngantjini

artuartua [Northern dialect] *Nachthabicht.* ◇ night hawk. Ⓛ tūra

árua *Handgriff des Schildes.* ◇ handle of shield. Ⓛ ngaru

artjinama *scheinen (Sterne, Mond)?* ◇ shine (stars, moon). ('?' added by CS) Ⓛ irtnani

arugula *zuerst.* ◇ first (of all). Ⓛ kuranji, urunba, uruna Ⓓ ngopera

arugulerama *sich zuerst erheben.* ◇ rise first. Ⓛ urunbaringañi

arugulinja *der erste, das erstgeborene Kind.* ◇ the first, first-born child. Ⓛ kuranjikatara, urunkátarata

arugulabâkala *zuerst, einst.* ◇ first, once. Ⓛ urunkátara

arugulawotta, arugulapalkula *einstweilen, zunächst.* ◇ for the moment, in the meantime. Ⓛ urunbamantu, urunbamantu

arugutja *Weib, mulier.* ◇ woman. Ⓛ kunka

artnanta, urtnanta *abbröckelnde Erde.* ◇ crumbling soil. Ⓛ urtnaka

aruilkara [Northern dialect] *cf.* **ruilkara** *cookatoo-parrot (graue Papagei).* ◇ grey parrot. Ⓛ kurankurana

arumbala *Platz wo Ceremonien aufgeführt werden (ausgehöhlter Platz).* ◇ ceremony ground. Ⓛ unkara

arúkupakupa *Schnauzbart.* ◇ moustache. Ⓛ tabutu

arúmunta [Northern dialect] *kleine im Schlamm lebende Fische.* ◇ small fish who live in mud. Ⓛ urumuntu

arumba *die Schwester.* ◇ sister. Ⓛ narumba Ⓓ kaku, ? ('?' added by CS)

arumbananga *die beiden Geschwister (Bruder und Schwester).* ◇ the two siblings (brother and sister). Ⓛ narumbara

arumbukua *Schwester oder Bruder eines Andern.* ◇ sister or brother of someone else. Ⓛ narumbarara

arumbintjara *alle Geschwister.* ◇ all siblings. Ⓛ narumbarawaritji

arúnama [Northern dialect] *cf.* **runama** *(schlagen einen Unschuldigen).* ◇ hit an innocent. Ⓛ urtnuni

arungatja *mein zugehöriger.* ◇ my kin. Ⓛ woltara

arúnkulta *Gift, Zaubergift; (ara=böse, schnell, ulta=ultakama=brechen) = schnell zerbrechend.* ◇ poison, magic poison. Ⓛ irati

ata *oder* **ta** *ich (trs.)* ◇ I (transitive). Ⓛ ngaiulu Ⓓ ngato

arulurumba *der Monat, in dem es wieder heiß wird (October).* ◇ month in which it heats up (October). Ⓛ arulurumbu

atamba *niedrig, kurz.* ◇ low, short. (CS moved this word to 'r̔' entries) Ⓛ tar̔ta

atatamba *niedrig, demütig.* ◇ low, humble. (CS moved this word to 'r̔' entries) Ⓛ tar̔tapiti

atérama *sich erniedrigen.* ◇ to humiliate oneself. (CS moved this word to 'r̔' entries) Ⓛ tar̔taringanje

atatambílama *verkürzen.* ◇ shorten. Ⓛ tar̔tani

atalba *Baum (spec.)* ◇ tree (species). Ⓛ atalba

atánja *schon, bereits* ◇ already, e.g. unta tukala tanja, unta erina imbutjika. Ⓛ atanji, e.g. nuntu pungutu atanji, nuntu paluna wontintaku (On opposite page of manuscript CS noted 'punkuwialpi ninantaku'; it is not clear to which entry this relates.)

atja *Waffe zum Werfen.* ◇ throwing weapon. Ⓛ ātji

atjua *Regenstreifen, die herabfallenden Regentropfen.* ◇ rain, falling raindrops. Ⓛ worrala Ⓓ talarangura

atjara *aufgesprungene (Boden, Rinde am ntjuia Baum), unterirdische Gang (Maulwurf).* ◇ split (ground, bark of ntjuia tree), subterranean burrow (mole). Ⓛ atjiri

atna *Kot, Dung, Mastdarm, Vagina, Eingeweide.* ◇ excrement, dung, rectum, vagina, intestines. Ⓛ kunna Ⓓ kudna *oder* kunna

atnaltjura *Hintern.* ◇ bottom (behind). Ⓛ kunna ala Ⓓ kudnapiti (*Magen*?: stomach) ('?' added by CS)

atninturka *Magen.* ◇ stomach. Ⓛ kunna ituntu Ⓓ kudnawala, kudnapiti

atna tataka *(Schimpfwort) (vagina rubra).* ◇ swear word (red vagina). Ⓛ kunna itinitini

atna nilkna *(Schimpfwort) vaginae hur.* ◇ a swear word. Ⓛ kunna kankata Ⓓ kudnana

atnuluma *Exkremente lassen.* ◇ defecate. Ⓛ kunnarangáñi Ⓓ kudna tjurana (*Durchfall haben*: have diarrhoea)

atnunka [Northern dialect] *cf.* **tnunka** *Beutelratte.* ◇ rat kangaroo. Ⓛ malla

atna tnolka *die Exkremente der Wallabys.* ◇ wallaby dropping. Ⓛ kunna metu

atnéumala ilkuma *Haut fressen, häuten.* ◇ eat skin, to skin. Ⓛ kanbira ngalkuñi

atua; atua kutata *Mann.* ◇ man; in Western Aranda 'atua kutata' (composed of 'man, men' and 'always'). Strehlow (1907: 4) referred to spirit beings that are now called 'pmara (place, country, home) kutata (always)'. Ⓛ patu, watti Ⓓ materi

atua palkula *ich, ein Mann.* ◇ I, a man. Ⓛ wattimantu

aūma [Northern dialect] *cf.* **wuma** *hören.* ◇ to hear. Ⓛ kulini Ⓓ ngarana

aūla *Holzart aus der Speere gemacht werden.* ◇ type of wood from which spears are made. Ⓛ aūlu

aūmba *kleiner Busch (spec.)* ◇ small bush (species). Ⓛ aūmba, aiïmbi

atna tama *Flatus lassen.* ◇ pass wind. Ⓛ kunna tunmanañi, kunna punmanañi

atírka [Northern dialect] *grün.* ◇ green. Ⓛ okiri

B

ba *und.* ◇ and.

baka *postp. oder Fragepartikel, der nicht übersetzt wird.* ◇ postposition or question article that is not translated.

bábauma, bábeuma *anstecken (Krankheit).* ◇ infect (disease). Ⓛ bakajungañi

baiïmilama (n) *kaufen.* ◇ buy.

babuterama *sich verbreiten (Geschwür).* ◇ spread (abscess, ulcer). Ⓛ bilaringañi

baiakajaka ankama *sehr viele bau bau bau rufen.* ◇ call many bau bau bau calls. Ⓛ meratura

baialkintja *alle im Takt bau, bau, bau rufen.* ◇ together call in time bau bau bau. Ⓛ meratura

baiakalta *Eidechse.* ◇ lizard. Ⓛ katungantirpa

bailba (balba) *unverständlich z.B. ankama (reden), verkehrt (heiraten).* ◇ incomprehensible, e.g. talk, wrong marriage. Ⓛ wabalbi Ⓓ karpakarpa? ('?' added by CS)

bailbiuma *verstreuen, wegwerfen.* ◇ scatter, throw away. Ⓛ wabalbi wonniñi

bailberama, bailbilama *verlieren.* ◇ to lose. Ⓛ wabalbinañi Ⓓ tintana, tintaterina

balberama *sich irren.* ◇ to mistake; get lost. Ⓛ wabalbiringañi

bailka *(vom Engl. gebildet) Sack.* ◇ (derived from English) bag. Ⓛ bailki

bakaljerakaljera *getrost, zuversichtlich.* ◇ trustful, optimistic.

bailkiuma *abschälen (Rinde), abhäuten (das Wild).* ◇ peel off (bark), skin (game). Ⓛ pepungañi Ⓓ giltjana, kankana (*abschälen*: peel)

bakalama; bakama *einfallen (Haus); einreißen (Haus).* ◇ collapse (house); pull down (house).

baita *Schwanz (der Schlange).* ◇ tail (of snake). (Entry deleted by CS) Ⓛ wipu

bakkitara *sehr schlecht (Teufel).* ◇ very bad (devil). Ⓛ barkaltu

bakka; inguntabaka era litjina *(postp.) wohl, wahrscheinlich; z.B. vielleicht morgen wird er gehen.* ◇ (postposition) well, probably; e.g. he might go tomorrow. Ⓛ baka; mungatarabaka paluru jennana

era lakabaka *er ist vielleicht gegangen.* ◇ he might have gone. Ⓛ paluru jennabakka? ('?' added by CS)

bakaba *schwer (Zunge), unverständlich (reden).* ◇ heavy (tongue), unintelligible, incomprehensible (talk). Ⓛ tarbmala Ⓓ ngaru tadakani; ngantara? ('?' added by CS)

bakuta *gemischte Haufe (z.B. Mörtel), angehäufte Erde, Nest der Fasanen.* ◇ mixed heap (e.g. mortar), heaped up earth, nest of pheasant. Ⓛ bukuti

bakala *kleine Mulde zum Wasserschöpfen (aus ininta gefertigt).* ◇ small bowl (made of ininta wood) to scoop water. Ⓛ nangunba, nanguna

bala *Stein, mit dem die Sämereien gerieben; Reibstein.* ◇ grinding stone. Ⓛ tungari Ⓓ marda kaparu (*Klopfer*: pounding stone)

balla *unrecht, verkehrt.* ◇ wrong. Ⓛ munu, titu Ⓓ tjikatjika, tjautjau

  balla lama *in die Irre gehen.* ◇ go the wrong way. Ⓛ munu jennañi, titu jennañi

  ballilama *unrecht tun.* ◇ do wrong. Ⓛ mununi, tituni

-bala, nanabala *dieser, hier (postp.)* ◇ this one here (postposition), e.g. nana-bala. Ⓛ bala-nanga

balajurajura *sehr leicht (rukura indora), abgetragen (Kleider), sehr dünn (Kleider).* ◇ very light (rukura indora), worn out (clothes), very thin (clothes). Ⓛ rar̔irar̔i

balakȧlaka *sehr ungeschickt.* ◇ very clumsy. Ⓛ kauanku

bálataka *verkehrt machen.* ◇ wrongly made. Ⓛ kurakatilba

balbalauma *fehlen, nicht haben, ermangeln, versäumen.* ◇ lack, not have, wanting, miss.

balba *ohne Absicht, aus Versehen (etwas geben).* ◇ without intention, by mistake (give something). Ⓛ wabalbi

balbabartjima *plötzlich aufleuchten, umleuchten.* ◇ suddenly light up.

balkama *bleichen, verbleichen (Blumen).* ◇ fade (flowers). Ⓛ kerkambañi

balkala *vergeblich, unnützlich, unbemerkt, ohne Absicht.* ◇ in vain, useless, unnoticed, without intention. Ⓛ wabalku Ⓓ baku, bakueli

  balkitjalbalka *ganz absichtslos (z.B. arirama = rennen), einfältig, aufrichtig.* ◇ without purpose (e.g. run), simple, stupid, sincere. Ⓛ kaiiwara

balkara *bleich, rein, unbefleckt.* ◇ pale, pure, without blemish. Ⓛ titi

balla *Bauchfett.* ◇ belly fat. Ⓛ wila niti

balkinja *eitel, vergeblich.* ◇ in vain.

baltaruka *wolkenlos, klar (Himmel).* ◇ cloudless, clear (sky). Ⓛ kaltaru

baluka *Teig.* ◇ dough. Ⓛ miïbaluka

balupa toppingakula *Schulter nicht bewegen können.* ◇ cannot move shoulder. Ⓛ alibiri tanaparari

balupa *Schulter.* ◇ shoulder. Ⓛ alibiri

bana *postp. dieser, hier.* ◇ (postposition) this one here. Ⓛ tu, nkurangu

banama *trs. bemalen, einreiben, bauen (Haus).* ◇ (transitive) paint, rub in, build (house); decorate. Ⓛ jabani (n), unani (*einreiben*)

  banalama *refl. sich bemalen, sich einreiben.* ◇ (reflexive) paint, rub on. Ⓛ unani

atuabȧna *dieser Mann.* ◇ this man. Ⓛ wattitu, watti nkurangu

banalakama *widerraten (wohin zu gehen).* ◇ recommend not (to go somewhere).

banba *überall.* ◇ everywhere. Ⓛ tjowariwari Ⓓ paruparu

banbala *überall.* ◇ everywhere. Ⓛ tjowariwarinku Ⓓ paruparu

banbilama *treffen (beim Speer werfen).* ◇ hit (with spear). Ⓛ apunpungañi

banbinera *alle Dinge, alles Geschaffene.* ◇ all things, all creations. Ⓛ lewara Ⓓ [w]uduku [original damaged – word unclear] (*gesamt, alle*: all together, all)

banga *geschlossen (Auge), blind, alte Frau, Mutter.* ◇ closed (eye), blind, old woman, mother. Ⓛ bamba Ⓓ butju

alkna bangerama *Augen schließen (refl.)* ◇ (reflexive) close eyes. Ⓛ kuru bambaringañi Ⓓ milki parina

banga, luka *Steinmesser.* ◇ stone knife. Ⓛ abanga

bānga *cane-grass.* ◇ cane grass. Ⓛ abānga Ⓓ wilpera

bangata *eine Heiratsklasse.* ◇ marriage class, subsection, skin name. Ⓛ tabangati (♂), nabangati (♀)

baninjíbana *kleiner Wasservogel.* ◇ small waterbird. Ⓛ ibininjíbini

banjarérama *reifen (Früchte).* ◇ to ripen (fruit). Ⓛ unmeringañi

bankalanga *böses Wesen in Gestalt eines häßlich behaarten Mannes.* ◇ evil being in shape of an ugly hairy man; considered to be a dangerous hairy (male) spirit which may kill and devour humans. Sometimes this term is also used for an evil female spirit, called aragutja (woman) erintja (evil), i.e. 'bankalanga woman'. See Strehlow (1907: 42, 93, 103–4). Other ugly, hairy beings are called 'Leketaleka'. They are ugly people covered with hair and have a bird-like coccyx anus; they are named after the latter (Strehlow 1907: 31). Ⓛ bankalangu

bankuna *Stock zum Schlagen.* ◇ hitting stick. Ⓛ bankunu

banta *hölzerne Mulde, flach aus ininta verfertigt, zum Sichten des jelka, etc.* ◇ wooden flat bowl made of ininta wood used for winnowing jelka etc., coolamon. Ⓛ kanilba

bara *postp. jener (derselbe).* ◇ (postposition) that one (the same one). Ⓛ karu

katjiabara *jenes Kind da.* ◇ that child there. Ⓛ pipirikaru

barbuta *fremd (Sprache), unverständlich, unkundig (der Sprache).* ◇ foreign (language), incomprehensible, ignorant (of foreign language). Ⓛ wabalbi

barbutilama *unverständig reden.* ◇ talk unintelligibly. Ⓛ wabalbinañi

barbuterama *unverständig sein.* ◇ be unintelligible. Ⓛ wabalbiringañi

barguma *beschwichtigen (Streitende, indem man sie auf den Laib schlägt).* ◇ calm (quarrelling people by hitting their body). Ⓛ markuni

barinba *lang, weit (Wasserloch).* ◇ long, wide (waterhole). Ⓛ wipuwaralkara

barka *Kohle.* ◇ coal. Ⓛ jalta, alta [Western dialect]

barka tataka *glühende Kohle.* ◇ glowing coals. Ⓛ jalta intinítini Ⓓ turupila

barka ngula *ausgebrannte Kohle.* ◇ burnt coals. Ⓛ jalti warri Ⓓ nunko

barkintilja *der Kohlenplatz (wo ausgebrannte Kohlen liegen).* ◇ place of coal (where burned coals lie). Ⓛ altabatti

barkabarka *das innere Fleisch der Oberschenkel.* ◇ flesh on inside of upper thigh. Ⓛ marukuru wottánjeri

bartja *hell.* ◇ bright, light. Ⓛ tjitjaku

bartjima *scheinen, leuchten, blitzen.* ◇ shine, glow, flash, lightning. Ⓛ tjitjakambañi Ⓓ mintjina

kwatja bartjima *blitzen.* ◇ to flash, lightning. Ⓛ kapirtnáñi

bartjinja *Helle, Schein.* ◇ light, shine; glow. Ⓛ tjitjakuriñi

bartjinabartjina *Leuchten, Leuchtkörper (Sterne).* ◇ shine, luminous body (stars). Ⓛ tjitjakambami

bartja inenguka *Abglanz.* ◇ reflection.

băta (bŭta) *postp. begierig nach.* ◇ (postposition) desirous of. Ⓛ la

tnábata (atna+bata) *wollüßtig.* ◇ lustful. Ⓛ kunnala

batanga (butanga) *postp. voller-, bedeckt mit-.* ◇ (postposition) full of, covered with. Ⓛ banti

mendabatanga *voller Krankheit.* ◇ full of sickness. Ⓛ mekinbanti

batalelama *trs. einen umdrehen.* ◇ (transitive) turn someone around.

batakérama *sich drehen (Wind).* ◇ to turn (wind). Ⓛ kambapalaringañi

batakilama *einen anderen abbringen von seinem Beschluß.* ◇ dissuade someone from a decision. Ⓛ kambapalani

batakilalama *sich anders besinnen.* ◇ change mind. Ⓛ kambakutuparingañi

batakilentjima *einen anderen zurückbringen (von seinem Irrtum, Abwegen).* ◇ change someone's mind (about a mistake). Ⓛ ngalakambapalani

batama *nicht verstehend, nicht wollend, unvermögend sein.* ◇ not understanding, not wanting, unable to. Ⓛ untuwiaringañi

antjabatama *nicht wollen, keine Lust haben.* ◇ refuse, have no desire. Ⓛ untukuraringañi

litjika batama *nicht gehen wollen.* ◇ not wanting to go. Ⓛ jenkuntaku tomatiriñi

batéatapa *nicht vermögend, nicht wollend, unmöglich.* ◇ unable, not wanting, impossible. Ⓛ tarbitarbi

alabateatapa *nichts schlechtes vermögend, sehr gut.* ◇ unable to do bad, very good. Ⓛ manta indotatu

baterama *zurückgehen, sich abwenden.* ◇ go back, turn away. Ⓛ aruriñi

inka baterama *seine Füße zurückziehen (refl.)* ◇ pull back feet (reflexive). Ⓛ tjinna turburiñi

batubaterama *umkehren, zurückkehren.* ◇ turn around, turn back. Ⓛ aruáruriñi

batta *Beutel (der Känguruhs, etc.)* ◇ pouch (of kangaroos, etc.) Ⓛ buta

bauabauerama *sich stoßen (im Spiel), sich schubsen.* ◇ to bump (at play), shove, push. Ⓛ untuunturapungañi

bāuma [Southern dialect], **bēuma** [Northern dialect] *stoßen, fortstoßen, fortschieben.* ◇ push, push away, shove away. Ⓛ untuni

baua, bāula *ohnmächtig, bewußtlos.* ◇ unconscious. Ⓛ abaula

bāulerama *in Ohnmacht fallen, sich herunterfallen lassen (z.B. Raupen), sich herabstürzen (vom Felsen).* ◇ faint, fall down (e.g. caterpillars), throw oneself (from a cliff). Ⓛ abaularingañi

bealkarélama *ausführen (Befehl).* ◇ carry out (order).

bebatuma *zittern (sehr zittern).* ◇ tremble (tremble a lot). Ⓛ tjititipatapatañi

mburkimba bebatuma *am ganzen Leibe zittern.* ◇ tremble (whole body). Ⓛ anbaratawara tjititipatapatañi

belama *schenken.* ◇ to give.

belinja *das Geschenk.* ◇ present, gift.

belkua *aus Versehen, aus Verwechslung (etwas nehmen) ein anderer?* ◇ by accident take something. Ⓛ bilku ('?' added by CS)

beltama *lehren (die Tj. Gesänge den Novizen).* ◇ teach. Ⓛ punarpungañi

benta *salzig (Wasser), bitter (Wasser).* ◇ salty (water), bitter (water). Ⓛ apinta, muluru

bentja *Quelle.* ◇ spring. Ⓓ jukari

kwatja bentja; kwatja pintja [Northern dialect] *Quellwasser.* ◇ springwater. Ⓛ kapi nerru Ⓓ ngapajukari

birkna *schönes (Laub), schön grün.* ◇ beautiful (leaves), beautifully green. Ⓛ talta

boilama *blasen, anblasen (jem.)* ◇ blow, blow at (someone). Ⓛ puni Ⓓ pulkana

boïnkama *hauchen, ausatmen.* ◇ breathe, breathe out, exhale. Ⓛ ngalbmanañi

boïnka *Hauch.* ◇ small breath, whiff. Ⓛ ngālja Ⓓ jaola (*Hauch*)

bojultja (alkna) *schlecht sehend.* ◇ not able to see well, bad eyesight. Ⓛ péjurperjúrba (kuru)

bakkarabokkara *taumelnd (Betrunkener).* ◇ staggering (drunk). Ⓛ kurirkúriri Ⓓ paraparawarana

bakkarabokkarérama *taumeln.* ◇ stagger. Ⓛ kurirkuririríñi Ⓓ ditjiditjirina

bōkunja *Öffnung der vagina, (Scham).* ◇ female genitals. Ⓛ umbukulji

bokutakūta *rein (Kleid).* ◇ clean (dress).

bōla *Eidechse (spec.)* ◇ lizard species. Ⓛ bobula

bōlara *Junges, das noch im Beutel getragen wird.* ◇ young marsupial still carried in pouch. Ⓛ apulurungu

bōlatama *schüchtern, verlegen, Schande.* ◇ shy, embarrassed, shame. Ⓛ kundamatu

boldabolda *Blasen (in den Händen).* ◇ blisters (on hands). Ⓛ biltjinbiltjin

boldabolderama *Blasen bekommen.* ◇ get blisters. Ⓛ biltjinbiltjinariñi

boldankama *platzen.* ◇ burst. Ⓛ lapulapuriñi

bonta *stumpf.* ◇ blunt. Ⓛ patti

borrarenalama *verzagen, verzweifeln.* ◇ despair.

borra *verlegen, verschämt, zaghaft.* ◇ embarrassed, timid, shy, ashamed. Ⓛ kunda

borrerama *verlegen machen, sich nicht getrauen.* ◇ make embarrassed, not dare. Ⓛ kundaringañi

borrilentama *verlegen machen.* ◇ embarrass someone. Ⓛ kundawottani

borraperama *verlegen sein.* ◇ be embarrassed.

borkia, *z.B.* **jinga borkia** *sehr müde, z.B. ich bin sehr müde.* ◇ very tired, e.g. I am very tired. Ⓛ burkaia

borrentalama *ausschlagen (Pferd, wenn es angetrieben wird).* ◇ kick (horse when driven). Ⓛ manmarpungañi

borkerentjima *müde werden.* ◇ become tired. Ⓛ ngalaburkarekukatiñi

borkeranama *ermüden.* ◇ become tired. Ⓛ maburkarekukatañi, maburkaringañi

borka *müde, erschöpft, starr.* ◇ tired, exhausted, stiff. Ⓛ burka Ⓓ waltowarlto

borkerama *müde werden, erstarren.* ◇ become tired, stiffen, petrify. Ⓛ burkaringañi Ⓓ patana, patapatarana, walturina, mandaterina.

borkilama *müde machen, erstarren machen.* ◇ make tired, make stiff, petrify. Ⓛ burkani

botta *Klumpen, Kugel, Grasbüschel, dicke Masse vermischt mit Wasser* (Strehlow 1920: 4). ◇ lump, ball, tuft of grass, thick pulp mixed with water. Ⓛ kaputu Ⓓ tjaputjapura, dambura, dambudambura, taka (*Lehmkloß*: lump of clay)

inkabotta *Kurzfuß.* ◇ clumpfoot. Ⓛ tjinna kaputu

botterama *sich zusammenballen (Lehm), zumachen.* ◇ to clump, lump, press together (clay), to close. Ⓛ kaputuriñi

(iltja botterama) *sich sammeln, sich versammeln.* ◇ gather, assemble. Ⓛ mara kaputuriñi

bottilapílama *zusammenballen (der Zucker von den lalba Blättern).* ◇ form together (sugar of lalba leaves). Ⓛ kaputunkanáñi

bottilama *trs. zusammenballen.* ◇ (transitive) lump together. Ⓛ kaputunani

bottibottilama *zu Hauf bringen.* ◇ bring lots. Ⓛ kaputukaputuni, taputapuni

bottabotta *Versammlung, Haufe.* ◇ meeting, crowd. Ⓛ kaputukaputu

bottabotta nama *mitten im Haufen sein.* ◇ be in the middle of a crowd. Ⓛ kaputukaputu ninañi

bottatara *zusammen, miteinander (gehen, dual).* ◇ together, with each other (go dual). Ⓛ túngukutára

botjirama *sich versammeln (um Häuptling).* ◇ assemble (around chief). Ⓛ nujuringañi, tunguringañi

bottera *kurz.* ◇ short. Ⓛ murila

bŭla, (bala) *dagegen, hingegen, aber.* ◇ opposed, but. Ⓛ bula

bula *Speichel.* ◇ saliva. Ⓛ tjali, talji Ⓓ ngaltja

bulilélama *etwas bespucken.* ◇ spit at something. Ⓛ talji inkanani

buliuma *ausspeien, ausspucken.* ◇ spit out. Ⓛ talji wonniñi, tjaliwonniñi Ⓓ ngaltja worrana

bula ntjirkerama *Speichel vertrocknen, verschmachten, verdursten.* ◇ saliva dries out, be parched, die of thirst. Ⓛ talji parururiñi

 For the modern spellings of these words, see the dictionaries and sources in reference list.

bulalabulalerama (iltja) *sich in die Hände spucken.* ◇ spit in hands. Ⓛ talinkatalinkanañi

bulanta tnama *Blasen (über dem Wasser) aufsteigen, wo es hineingefallen ist.* ◇ bubbles rise up (from water) where it fell in. Ⓛ taljikutu ngarañi

bulja *weich (Erde, Fleisch), lose (Sand).* ◇ soft (earth, flesh), loose (sand). Ⓛ tōla Ⓓ ngalara, miltjamiltja

buljilama *biegen.* ◇ bend. Ⓛ tōlani

buljabuljilama *trs. erweichen durch fortwährendes Bitten, bitten.* ◇ (transitive) soften through constant begging, beg. Ⓛ tólatálani

buljinkara *Eidechse (spec.)* ◇ lizard (species). Ⓛ mutinka

bulkna *furchtlos, unbesorgt (gehen).* ◇ fearless, without a worry (walk). Ⓛ kauankauana

bulknala *furchtlos, unbesorgt.* ◇ fearless, carefree. Ⓛ kauankauanta

bunabuna *leer (z.B. Wasserloch), Gefäße?* ◇ empty (e.g. waterhole), vessels. Ⓛ bilti Ⓓ kala ('?' added by CS)

bunabunerama *austrocknen (Wasser).* ◇ dry out (water). Ⓛ biltiringañi

bunara *Bogen (Waffe).* ◇ bow (weapon).

bunalanála *allen insgesamt, ohne Ausnahme (geben).* ◇ (give) everything without exception. Ⓛ wapalkuninjánku

bunalanúla *Verschwendung.* ◇ waste. Ⓛ wapalkuninjanku jungañi

bunkata *Strauch (spec. ilbotilbota).* ◇ shrub (ilbotilbota species) Ⓛ bunkati

bunulanula irbuma *einbrechen.* ◇ break in.

bunulanulélama *verschwenden.* ◇ to waste.

buta *postp. begierig nach.* ◇ (postposition) desirous. Ⓛ la

tnabuta *wollüstig.* ◇ lustful. Ⓛ kunnala

butanga *postp. wollen -, bedeckt mit.* ◇ (postposition) want -, covered with. Ⓛ banti

ilkatabutanga *voller Schmerzen.* ◇ full of pain. Ⓛ mekinbanti

D

Danna *kalt.* ◇ cold. Ⓛ warri, peria Ⓓ kilpa, kilpali

dannatuma *frieren.* ◇ freeze, feel cold. Ⓛ warripini

dannunka *Kälte, kaltes Wetter.* ◇ cold, cold weather. Ⓛ warripilkara

dannankua *sehr kalt, Kälte.* ◇ very cold, coldness. Ⓛ warrimba

danna *Gefäß, Mulde.* ◇ container, bowl, carrying dish, coolamon. Ⓛ bunna, ankala

dalbadalba *Muscheln.* ◇ mussels.

dalbadalba lanjalanja *Perle (n).* ◇ pearl.

dantama *schließen (Tür), zumachen (Loch), verkleben, verstopfen.* ◇ shut (door), close (hole), paste, stick, block. Ⓛ pantani Ⓓ ngenmana (*zumachen*: close)

dantalinalina *Vorhang.* ◇ curtain. Ⓛ pantanmi

datintenama *hineinschlagen (Nagel), hindurchdrehen (Schraube).* ◇ hit in (nail), turn in (screw). Ⓛ balapungañi

deba rinbinba *Schnabel.* ◇ beak. Ⓛ tawaledi

deba *Vogel, alles was fliegen kann.* ◇ bird; everything that can fly. Ⓛ tjita Ⓓ paia

deba andata *(wörtlich: Vogel-Blumen), die Daunen der Vögel.* ◇ (literally: bird-flowers), bird down. Ⓛ tjita wommulu

debadeba *Geflügel (auch Käfer etc.)* ◇ fowl (also beetles etc.) Ⓛ tjitatjita

debama *untersinken, versinken, zu Grunde gehen.* ◇ submerge, sink, perish. Ⓛ tarbaraokalingañi Ⓓ kunakutina? ('?' added by CS)

detjantuka *Zahnschmerzen.* ◇ toothache. Ⓛ takutjilpa

detja, detta *Zahn.* ◇ tooth. Ⓛ kádidi Ⓓ mannatandra

detjalura *Zahnfleisch.* ◇ gums. Ⓛ kadidi wollura

detjiltárkama *Zähne klappern, Zähne knirschen (vor Kälte oder Zorn).* ◇ teeth chatter (from cold), grind teeth (with anger). Ⓛ kadidi tirkilbmanañi Ⓓ manna katakatangana

detja gaterama *die Zähne zeigen (von Hunden).* ◇ show teeth (dogs). Ⓛ kadidi ninjirangañi

detja relbmintalama *Zähne fletschen.* ◇ bare or fletch teeth. Ⓛ kadidi ninjirapungañi

detja rungulta *Giftzahn.* ◇ fang, poison tooth. Ⓛ kadidi piralji

talkua tnama *(nachmittags um 3 Uhr) abwärts stehend (Sonne).* ◇ (afternoon 3 o'clock), low standing (sun). Ⓛ katakutara

dōlta *müde.* ◇ tired. Ⓛ adulta

dolterama *müde werden.* ◇ become tired. Ⓛ adultaringañi

dorradorra [Southern dialect] *kurz, niedrig.* ◇ short, low. Ⓛ tarta, mutu Ⓓ wordu

dorradorralélama *kurz machen.* ◇ shorten. Ⓛ tartani

dorradorraléntjima *kurz machen.* ◇ shorten. Ⓛ ngalatartani

dorrinjilama *kürzen.* ◇ shorten. Ⓛ tartani, mutuni

dottadotta [Southern dialect] (= **tōtatōta**) *kurz.* ◇ short. Ⓛ kalkaturu

E

ebmangalimbuma *liegen lassen.* ◇ leave behind.

ebminjanana *unnütz (Knecht, der nichts taugt).* ◇ useless (servant, farmhand).

ebalérama *verlangen (einen zu sehen).* ◇ demand (to see someone).

eba *Widerhacken (am Speer und Speerwerfer).* ◇ barb (on spear and spear thrower). Ⓛ ngama, mokula Ⓓ ngami

ebmáta *Luftspiegelung.* ◇ mirage. Ⓛ ninga

ebalanga *Samen einer Grasart spec.* ◇ seeds of a grass species. Ⓛ ibilingi

ebmama (imbuma) *sein lassen.* ◇ let be. Ⓛ wontiñi

ebaltja *Freund.* ◇ friend. Ⓛ ngultu

ebaltjilarama *sich Freunde machen (durch Geben).* ◇ make friends (through gifts). Ⓛ ngulturapungañi Ⓓ tjampitjampibana

ebánama *Hund setzen auf imora (possum) mit Lauten: irr, irr, irr.* ◇ set dogs on possums with irr, irr, irr sounds. Ⓛ eritúnañi

ebmalkanga *undurchsichtig, gerüstet, fest, dicht, ohne Risse.* ◇ opaque, armed, solid, tight, without cracks. Ⓛ patti

ebmanna *Mutters Mutter, Mutters Mutters Bruder.* ◇ mother's mother, mother's mother's brother; people affiliated with a country through their mother's mother are called, in Western Aranda, kutungula. Their rights to country are usually not as strong as the rights that people gain through their father's father (aranga) and their mother's father (tjimia). However, there are exceptions. Ⓛ altali, inkilji

ebmanna *Mutters Mutter, Mutters Mutters Schwester, Mutters Mutters Bruder.* ◇ mother's mother; mother's mother's sister, mother's mother's brother. Ⓛ inkilji

ebmanna *Mutters Mutters Bruder, Mutters Tochters Sohn, Tochters Sohn, Tochters Tochter.* ◇ mother's mother's brother, mother's daughter's son; daughter's son (female perspective); daughter's daughter (female perspective). Ⓛ altali

lorra ebmannatja *Mutters Mutter.* ◇ mother's mother. Ⓛ kami inkiljini

lorra ebmanna *Mutters Mutters Schwester.* ◇ mother's mother's sister. Ⓛ kami inkiljini

kalja ebmanna, kiebanna *Mutters Mutters Bruder.* ◇ mother's mother's brother. Ⓛ altali, altjali

knaia ebmanna *Fraus Mutters Vater.* ◇ wife's mother's father. Ⓛ altali

kwaia ebmannatja *Tochters Tochter (♀).* ◇ daughter's daughter. Ⓛ inkilji

kwaia ebmanna *Schwesters Tochters Tochter.* ◇ sister's daughter's daughter. Ⓛ inkilji

woia ebmannatja *Tochters Sohn (♀).* ◇ daughter's son. Ⓛ altalina

woia ebmanna *Schwesters Tochters Sohn.* ◇ sister's daughter's son.

 For the modern spellings of these words, see the dictionaries and sources in reference list.

ebmannukua *conf.* **ebmanna** *der ebmanna (Mutters Mutter) eines Anderen.* ◇ someone else's mother's mother.

ebmálkua *Kammer, Furche, Aushöhlung (des Ufers), kleinere Abteilung einer Hütte.* ◇ small room, groove, hollow, eroded riverbank, small partition. Ⓛ mumutukutuku Ⓓ punga wapu

ebmaltja *kleiner roter Vogel.* ◇ small red bird. Ⓛ wonnapawonnapa

ebminjebminja *Auskehricht.* ◇ rubbish.

ebmintja *unbrauchbar, nutzlos, weggeworfene (Frau), entlassene (Frau), sein gelassen.* ◇ useless, disposed (wife), dismissed (wife); worn out, thrown away, discarded. Ⓛ emintji

ebmintjerama *unbrauchbar werden.* ◇ become useless. Ⓛ ebmintjiringañi

ebmíntjebmintja *ganz unbrauchbar.* ◇ completely useless. Ⓛ emíntjemíntji

ebmanebmana *Eidechse.* ◇ lizard. Ⓛ wiruwirurba

ebmannakerama *huren mit seiner ebmanna.* ◇ forbidden relationship with ebmanna. Ⓛ inkiljikirini

ebmannabuta *die sehr begierige ebmanna (die Frau).* ◇ the very eager ebmanna (woman). Ⓛ inkiljipanti

ēka *Grind, Schorf, Hülse, Kruste (von Schlamm).* ◇ scab, husk, crust (of mud). Ⓛ pita

ekérama *sich Schorf bilden.* ◇ form scabs. Ⓛ pitaringañi Ⓓ putarina? ('?' added by CS)

ekálla, ekalla *Teig, Brotteig.* ◇ dough, bread dough. Ⓛ numa Ⓓ bukatanka

ekallilama *Teig machen, kneten.* ◇ make dough, knead. Ⓛ numani

ekállaka *ganz, alle, überall.* ◇ whole, all, everywhere. Ⓛ lewara

ekaltalantema *wieder heftig.* ◇ again, violent. Ⓛ kantinkaka

ekalta *stark, mächtig, fest, zähe (Fleisch).* ◇ strong, powerful, firm, tough (meat). Ⓛ kanti, puti Ⓓ ngurru, ngurrungurru

ekaltatnúmuramura *sehr stark.* ◇ very strong. Ⓛ kantilenku Ⓓ ngurrungurru

ekaltilama *stärken, befestigen.* ◇ strengthen, fortify. Ⓛ kantini

ebmanga *gelassen.* ◇ calm.

ekara *leer, ausgetrocknet (Wasserlöcher).* ◇ empty, dried out (waterholes). Ⓛ ekeri

ekarérama *austrocknen (Wasser).* ◇ dry up (water). Ⓛ ekeririñi

ekarama *anziehen (Kleider), befestigen (z.B tjalanka an dem Speerwerfer).* ◇ put on (clothes), attach (e.g. tjalanka on spear thrower). Ⓛ partatunañi Ⓓ widmana

ekalba *vielmehr.* ◇ rather.

ekaralama *refl. sich ankleiden, sich etwas umwickeln.* ◇ (reflexive) dress, wrap. Ⓛ partatúnkanañi Ⓓ widmaterina

ekarkeuma *zusammenfügen, zusammenbauen.* ◇ join or build together.

ekarkarana nama *fortwährend bleiben.* ◇ stay constantly, remain. Ⓛ ngalutu ninañi Ⓓ ngamana

ekarkarananalanama *wohnen.* ◇ inhabit, live. Ⓛ ngalutureraninañi

ēkna *totkrank, tot; (jedenfalls Contraktion aus erilkna).* ◇ very ill, dead. Ⓛ ini

eknarbeknarba *verschiedene Weise.* ◇ in a different way.

eknamekna *verschieden.* ◇ different.

ĕkna *allein.* ◇ alone. Ⓛ kutulenku Ⓓ pilki

eknákekna *einzeln, zerstreut, beiseits.* ◇ single, scattered, apart. Ⓛ kututukututu Ⓓ pilkijapilki

eknákeknilama *trs. zerstreuen, auseinanderjagen (Schafe).* ◇ (transitive) scatter, chase apart (sheep). Ⓛ kututukututunañi

eknamalinja *besonders, z.B. einen besonders nehmen.* ◇ particular, e.g. take one in particular.

eknakalinja *verschieden.* ◇ different. Ⓛ munumariñi

eknarinja, *z.B.* **atua eknarinja pitjima.** *einzeln, allein; z.B. ein einzelner Mann kommt.* ◇ single, alone; e.g. a single man comes. Ⓛ kutuntariñi

eknóatjoatja *vereinzelt, zerstreut (Bäume) stehend.* ◇ isolated, scattered (trees). Ⓛ ngatakuru

eknajunta *Marktplatz (n).* ◇ marketplace.

eknara *Osten.* ◇ East. Ⓛ kakarara Ⓓ Tiriwa
eknarakua *östlich.* ◇ easterly. Ⓛ kakararalku
eknunitja *östlich (Geheimsprache).* ◇ easterly. Ⓛ kakarapiti
eknarbinala rama *nach der Seite sehen.* ◇ look to the side. Ⓛ kambakutanku nangañi
eknarbinarbinala rama *nach beiden Seiten sich umsehen.* ◇ look to both sides. Ⓛ kambakutakambakutanku nangañi
eknarbauma *trs. drehen, wenden, auf die andere Seite legen.* ◇ (transitive) turn, lay on the other side. Ⓛ kambakutubanañi Ⓓ karitjina
eknarbeknarba *von allen Seiten her, manigfaltige Weise.* ◇ from all directions. Ⓛ kambamurkamurka
eknarbunilama; *z.B.* **gara**
eknarbunilama *trs. umwenden.* ◇ (transitive) turn over; e.g. turn over meat. Ⓛ kambakutuwoniñi Ⓓ karitjimalkana
eknatiuma *trs. umkehren (einen Gegenstand).* ◇ (transitive) turn around (an object).
eknata *Raupe, behaarte.* ◇ hairy caterpillar. Ⓛ inarka, wonka Ⓓ panga, padi
ēknataratara *zweischneidig.* ◇ double edged. Ⓛ kambakutara
éknua *vergeßlich.* ◇ forgetful. Ⓛ pinnapatti
éknuma; noa-eknuma *zu sich nehmen; heiraten.* ◇ marry (noa-eknuma). Ⓛ jeltiñi
eknakilinja *Heiratsklasse.* ◇ marriage class. Ⓛ munu mariñi Ⓓ mardu, witta
eknulama *rufen, locken.* ◇ call, entice. Ⓛ amajeltiñi
eknunama *locken, rufen zu kommen.* ◇ entice, call to come. Ⓛ majeltiñi
eknulalbuma *zurückholen, zurückrufen (Menschen).* ◇ get or fetch back, call back (people). Ⓛ jeltirakulbañi
ekwalkulea *verschnitten (Eunuch).* ◇ castrated (eunuch).
ekuna *weiße Farbe (Trauer-und Rachezeichen).* ◇ white colour (sign of mourning and revenge). Ⓛ okunu
ekúngala *neben.* ◇ beside. Ⓛ aiïnka
ekunja [Southern dialect] *Asche.* ◇ ash. Ⓛ ulbulu, wauna Ⓓ puta
ekulitnima *neiden, beneiden.* ◇ to envy.
ekuratuja [Northern dialect] **(inkata)** *Häuptling.* ◇ chief. Ⓛ palunakutia
ekurangatjina [Northern dialect] *darauf.* ◇ thereupon, then. Ⓛ palulunguru
eler̔erama *fett werden (wenn man vorher mager war), größer werden.* ◇ become fat (when one was lean before), grow larger. Ⓛ aler̔eringañi
emintjira *Grasbüschel, die ins Wasser geworfen werden um Fische zu fangen.* ◇ grass thrown into water to catch fish. Ⓛ imintjiri
enta *(postp.) allein, nur.* ◇ (postposition) alone, only. Ⓛ –tu
atuénta *von atua-enta.* ◇ man-only. Ⓛ wattitu
entára *laut, deutlich (z.B. ankama), fest (z.B. irkuma).* ◇ loud, clear (e.g. to talk), firm (e.g. to hold). Ⓛ kutururu Ⓓ paraparali
erakimbara *er zuerst.* ◇ he first. Ⓛ paluruwaraka
erabȧna *jener.* ◇ that (one). Ⓛ paluruta
era *er, sie, es.* ◇ he, she, it. Ⓛ paluru Ⓓ nauja [nau] *er es*; nauia, nadruja? (*sic*) ('?' added by CS)
eramérama *die Gleichen, das Geschlecht.* ◇ same family, clan.
eratara *beide.* ◇ both. Ⓛ palurukutara
eratarabana *die beiden.* ◇ those two. Ⓛ pulatu
ekurangamarugula *vor ihm her, z.B. lama (gehen).* ◇ in front of him, e.g. walk in front of him. Ⓛ palumbakuranji
era ntema *er wieder.* ◇ he again. Ⓛ palurukaru
erabaleuma *umfallen, umstürzen (Mulde).* ◇ fall over (bowl). Ⓛ taru wonniñi
erabákama *herumgehen (um etwas), hervorkommen (hinter einem andern), sich hervorschleichen.* ◇ go around (something), come out from (behind someone), creep up. Ⓛ arewokkañi

erabakanama *im Kreis um etwas herumgehen.* ◇ go in a circle around something. Ⓛ marewokkañi

erabakalakalélama *um etwas herumgehen.* ◇ go around something. Ⓛ areráreritjíngañi, ajuntajuntitjingañi

erai! *sieh! seht!* ◇ see! Ⓛ nauai!

eráka *Tasche aus Fellen.* ◇ bag made of skins. Ⓛ éraka

erāka *ein sehr langer boomerang.* ◇ very long boomerang. Ⓛ panmara

erákama *im großen Bogen um die Frauen herumgehen, schamhaft gehen.* ◇ to walk around women to avoid them because of feeling shame. Ⓛ arewokkani

erákanama *sich heranschleichen im Bogen, z.B. an das Wild.* ◇ creep up circling (e.g. game). Ⓛ marurakatiñi

erákalaláma *jagen, sich heranschleichen.* ◇ hunt, creep up. Ⓛ marurakatiratalkañi

erakiljélama *intr. jucken (Geschwür).* ◇ (intransitive) itch (abscess). Ⓛ erëereñi

erákara *schamhaft.* ◇ modest. Ⓛ pekura Ⓓ ninta, nintali (nintapani, nintanguru *schamlos*: shameless)

erakarérama *sich schämen.* ◇ feel ashamed. Ⓛ pekuraringañi

erakarerelama *trs. beschämen.* ◇ (transitive) shame. Ⓛ pekurani

erakaralelama *trs. beschämen.* ◇ (transitive) shame. Ⓛ pekurani

erakarakajartuma *trs. beschämen.* ◇ (transitive) shame. Ⓛ pekurakutjitini Ⓓ ninta dangana

erakarilama *trs. einen beschämen.* ◇ (transitive) shame.

erakintja *schamhaftig, den Frauen aus dem Wege gehen.* ◇ (transitive) bashful, timidly, avoid women. Ⓛ pekurantu Ⓓ nintali

erakintjilama *trs. schamhaft machen (den zu Beschneidenden dem Einfluß seiner Mutter entnehmen).* ◇ (transitive) make timid, intimidate. Ⓛ arewakataljiñi

erakarerinja *die Schande.* ◇ disgrace.

erakulbuta *schamlos, der seine Schande frech leugnet; einer der sich schämt, seine Schande zu gestehen.* ◇ shameless, he who lies shamelessly about his disgrace; he who is ashamed to admit his disgrace. Ⓛ pekurala? Ⓓ nintapani, nintanguru? ('?' added by CS)

érama, érema; ta érama, era rella aratja namanga *glauben, dafür halten; ich halte dafür, dafür halten.* ◇ believe, reckon; in my view. Ⓛ ereñi; ngaiulu neriñi, paluru matu tukaruru ninantala.

erákutja *Strauch mit eßbaren Früchten.* ◇ bush with edible berries. Ⓛ erakutji

eralera *kleine, weiße Larven, unter der Erde der Gummibäume.* ◇ small white grubs under gumtrees. Ⓛ erali

erála *abgeworfene Haut (der apma, tjapa).* ◇ shed skin (of snakes and grubs). Ⓛ neri, liri

eramerama *langer boomerang zum Schlagen.* ◇ long hitting boomerang. Ⓛ erámeráma

erama *lange ulbar̄inja (Waffe zum Schlagen [boomerang]) von den südöstlichen Völkerschaften eingehandelt.* ◇ long ulbarinja (weapon to strike with) boomerang, traded from peoples in the south-east. Ⓛ erama Ⓓ kirra mara

eraleragunama *versiegen, einziehen (Flutwasser).* ◇ dry up (floodwater). Ⓛ lalarakani

eráma *mit Fett bestrichen.* ◇ coated in fat. Ⓛ nabañi

eramata *ein kleiner Strauch mit großen, hellgrünen Blättern, dessen Wurzeln geröstet gegessen.* ◇ small bush with large light-green leaves, its roots are roasted and eaten. Ⓛ eremati

erámatika *einer wie der andere aussehend (von gleicher Gestalt).* ◇ look alike (of same build). Ⓛ palurunguanba

eramitja *tiefe Grube.* ◇ deep ditch. Ⓛ ngadi Ⓓ dulkuru? kodu. ('?' added by CS)

eramatuna *kleine Vogel.* ◇ small bird. Ⓛ tjintiwili

erámeráma *gleichgestaltet, das Geschlecht.* ◇ same stock. Ⓛ palurunguánba

erambinja *Pflanze (spec.) ähnlich wie inmota.* ◇ plant similar to inmota (*Lepidium phlebopetalum*). Ⓛ erimbinji

eranbilama *austeilen (Brot, Geschenke).* ◇ distribute (bread, presents). Ⓛ munutumunutunañi

eránberama *verteilen (Wolken).* ◇ spread (clouds). Ⓛ munutumunuturiñi

erangera *Strauch mit eßbaren Früchten.* ◇ bush with edible fruit. Ⓛ erengeri

erangera *Larven in erángara Wurzeln.* ◇ grubs in erangera roots. Ⓛ erengeri

eranbatanama *verbreiten (Gerücht).* ◇ spread (rumour). Ⓛ mabilani

érapala *schräg abfallend, gewölbt, halbrund.* ◇ sloping, arching, semicircle. (CS added small drawing of two halfcircles above each other) Ⓛ erepali

erangakua *hinter (etwas versteckt, versteckt, verborgen hinter), z.B. eine Landschaft, die hinter einer Gebirgskette liegt.* ◇ behind (hidden), e.g. a landscape hidden behind a mountain range. Ⓛ parari

erāra *sehnsüchtig.* ◇ longing. Ⓛ wotjila, wotjilta Ⓓ wolkareli

erárerama *sich sehnen (nach seinem Heimatsort), sich entschließen (in die Heimat zurückzukehren) z.B. tmaraka.* ◇ longing for (home or heimat), decide (to return home) e.g. tmaraka. Ⓛ wotjilariñi Ⓓ wolkarina? ngaramarana ('?' added by CS)

erarerarélama *sich sehnen (nach Hause).* ◇ to long (for home). Ⓛ wotjilbwotjilbmanañi

erareranama *sich sehnen nach Hause.* ◇ longing for home. Ⓛ mawotjilariñi

eratunatuna *schädlich (Speisen), lebensgefährlich.* ◇ harmful (food), life threatening. Ⓛ punkurutunami

erarpa *er selbst.* ◇ himself. Ⓛ palurunata

erarpinja *von selbst (gewachsen).* ◇ by itself (grown).

eraritnima *laut tönen (intrs.)* ◇ sound loud (intransitive). Ⓛ kurangañi

eratara *sie beide.* ◇ those two. Ⓛ palurukutara Ⓓ pudla

erātja *lupa-Hülsen; den Kern umgeben.* ◇ lupa pods; surrounding the seed. Ⓛ eratji

eratja *leicht bewölkt, weiße Wolken.* ◇ slightly overcast, white clouds. Ⓛ merauru

erenkiwulama *mit dem Ellbogen hinwegstoßen, Ellbogen einhacken, sich sträuben loszukommen, mit dem Ellbogen stoßen.* ◇ push away with elbow, try to get away. Ⓛ marawiltalkañi

eraua *Lehmebene; das Nest von Ameisen auf Lehmebenen?; kurze harte Fläche, die weiße Ameisen hergestellt haben und ihre Neste darau bauen.* ◇ claypan, antnest on claypans?; surface prepared by white ants to built their nests on it. Ⓛ putu ('?' added by CS)

erauankunama *schnell die Flügel bewegen.* ◇ move wings quickly. Ⓛ apunpúngañi

erauia *Waffen.* ◇ weapons. Ⓛ urala

ererinjaknanama *herabströmen (Blut).* ◇ flow down (blood). Ⓛ ererikatiñi

erátnalama *abmagern.* ◇ lose weight. Ⓛ kebulariñi

erengna *bewußlos.* ◇ unconscious. Ⓛ tjilalka

erengnarama (?) *bewußlos werden.* ◇ faint. ('?' added by CS) Ⓛ tjilalkaringañi

erebilanga [Northern dialect] *großer weißer Vogel.* ◇ big white bird. Ⓛ erebilangu

erénga [Northern dialect] *conf.* **aranga** *graues Känguruh, Bergkänguruh.* ◇ grey kangaroo, mountain (hill) kangaroo. Ⓛ kanala

erauia *viele dicht zusammen stehende Stämme.* ◇ densely standing trunks. Ⓛ katatjilitjili

ereërentjerama *den Boden fegen (Zweige).* ◇ sweep floor (with branches). Ⓛ mantapitjiriwokkañi

erengenta *Nasenknochen (Schmuck).* ◇ nosebone (ornament). Ⓛ mulákiri

 For the modern spellings of these words, see the dictionaries and sources in reference list.

érereérelálbuma *nach kurzer Zeit umkehren.* ◇ turn around after a short time. Ⓛ wottilknurekulakulbañi

ererinka *öde Fläche.* ◇ desert. Ⓛ ererinki

erenka [Eastern dialect] *Hund.* ◇ dog.

erenka *schnell, flüchtig, furchtsam, ungestraft, entronnen.* ◇ fast, fleeting, anxious, unpunished. Ⓛ atjiki

erenkérama *sich scheu oder furchtsam umsehen.* ◇ look fearfully or anxiously around. Ⓛ atjikiriñi

eŕetarerama *verschütten, ausschütten (intrs.)* ◇ spill (intransitive). Ⓛ tarungariñi

ererakualama *zerstreut auf dem Boden liegen (abgefallene Blüten), den Boden bedecken.* ◇ scattered on the ground (fallen blossoms). Ⓛ utulungariñi

erera *für eine kurze Zeit.* ◇ for a short time. Ⓛ wotilknu Ⓓ woljaia

eréteratera *schnell bewegend (Körper).* ◇ moving fast (body). Ⓛ eretaritari

ererendama *leihen (jemandem).* ◇ to loan (someone something). Ⓛ wotilknujungañi Ⓓ woljaia jinkina

eriljilberelanama *mit gespreizten Fingern gestreckt daliegen.* ◇ lie stretched out with splayed fingers. Ⓛ eriljaliérekániñi

erilja *Larve (rötlich) in erilja Wurzeln.* ◇ (reddish) grub in erilja roots. Ⓛ antara

erilja *Strauch mit weidenähnlichen Blättern, gelben Blütenkätzchen und Schotenfrüchten.* ◇ bush with willow-like leaves, yellow flower catkins and pods. Ⓛ antara, tuntala

erilkna *tot.* ◇ dead. Ⓛ jupa Ⓓ nari

erilkna *laut, laut sprechen* ◇ loud, speak loud. Ⓛ kutururu

erilaualaua *(vom Wind) auseinandergeblasen (Federn).* ◇ blown away (feathers by wind). Ⓛ purulankani

erilkataka *das Sterben.* ◇ dying.

erilknatuma *töten, totschlagen.* ◇ to kill, to murder. Ⓛ jupapungañi Ⓓ narielu

erilknalama *blaß (der Tote).* ◇ pale (the deceased).

erenkiwulama *sich sträuben, loszukommen versuchen.* ◇ resist, try to get free. Ⓛ marawiltalkañi, rubiltalkañi

erilknabata *Vorfahren.* ◇ ancestors, the old people. Ⓛ jupantjiniri

eranka *grün (Gras).* ◇ green (grass). Ⓛ okiri

erinjakama *aufschlitzen (den Bauch).* ◇ slit open (stomach). Ⓛ wartnuni

erinjakalama *refl. sich den Bauch aufschlitzen.* ◇ (reflexive) slit open stomach. Ⓛ wartnuni

erinta [Southern & Eastern dialect] *cf.* **ponta** *sehr kalt.* ◇ very cold. Ⓛ warri

erintja *böse Wesen, Teufel.* ◇ bad or evil beings, devils, bad spirits, monsters. Ⓛ mamu Ⓓ kutji

erinjalba *(Cycas Palme) der dicke Stengel, am dem der Kolben sitzt.* ◇ (cycad) thick stem on which butt grows. Ⓛ para

eritja *Adler.* ◇ eagle. Ⓛ katuwara, wariti Ⓓ karawara

aritjilkanama *aufbrechen (z.B. Schoten).* ◇ open (e.g. pods). Ⓛ tapunpungañi Ⓓ pakina

eritjinka *(Adlerfuß), südliches Kreuz (Sternbild).* ◇ (eagle foot), Southern Cross (star constellation). Ⓛ Tjinnawariti Ⓓ paiatidna

eritjulba [Northern dialect] *roter Ocker.* ◇ red ochre. Ⓛ ulba katuwara

erkularulanama *ergreifen (jemanden) bei der Verfolgung.* ◇ capture (somebody). Ⓛ witiwitira wonnañi

erknērknerama *sich sehnen (nach Hause).* ◇ yearning (for home). Ⓛ wotjilariñi

etalénama *erschlagen (Feind).* ◇ kill (enemy). Ⓛ untutunañi

eroaljatuma *rächen.* ◇ avenge, revenge. Ⓛ jupapungañi

erkunama *erfassen, anpacken.* ◇ catch, seize, grasp hold, grab; hug. Ⓛ mawitini

erkuma *fassen, anfassen, umfassen, ergreifen, fangen, festhalten.* ◇ catch, seize, capture, hold tight. Ⓛ witini Ⓓ patana

erkuralelama *sich gegenseitig am kleinen Finger anfassen.* ◇ hold each other's small fingers. Ⓛ tintjirapungañi

erkurinja *gefaltet.* ◇ folded. Ⓛ tintjili

erkuruma *umarmen.* ◇ embrace. Ⓛ witirapungañi

erkuentjima *anfahren (auf einen), anpacken (von Hunden).* ◇ jump at, grab (by dogs). Ⓛ ngalawitini

erkulambetninama *erhalten bleiben.* ◇ preserved.

erkutjikérama *umfassen wollen; im Begriff stehen, ihn zu umfassen.* ◇ want to embrace, about to embrace him. Ⓛ witintakuriñi

eróa *rundes Loch oder Grube in dem Erdboden (in der viele Samen lagen)* (see Strehlow 1920: 18). ◇ round hole or ditch in ground (that had been filled with seeds). Ⓛ papipa

eroaljalkuma *die Erschlagenen verzehren.* ◇ eat the slain. Ⓛ jupangalkuñi

eroaljatuma *erschlagen (Feind).* ◇ killed (enemy). Ⓛ jupapungañi, meripungañi

eroámba *regenlose (Wolken) vorüberziehende.* ◇ rainless (clouds) passing by. Ⓛ kebularinta

eroámberama *verziehen (Wolken).* ◇ disperse (clouds). Ⓛ kebulariñi

eroánba *weiße Kranich.* ◇ white crane. Ⓛ eroanbi Ⓓ mulpa

erora *jung (Mann), dünn, frisch (Holz), geschmeidig, gelenkig, frisch (Fußspuren).* ◇ young (man), slender, fresh (wood), supple, flexible, fresh (footprints). Ⓛ erura

eroanbintarama *spielen, sich einander fangen, Fangspiel.* ◇ to play, to catch one another, a catchgame. Ⓛ wonkakunankunanariñi

erōra [Southern dialect] *cf.* **entára (ankama)** *laut.* ◇ loud (ankama: talk). Ⓛ erura (wonkañi)

eroatjeroatja *Grasart (haferähnlich).* ◇ grass species (oat-like). Ⓛ oratjorátji

erorunba *sehr schnell, flink.* ◇ very fast, agile. Ⓛ eruraka

erolitja *putaia Höhlen Eingang.* ◇ cave entrance (of a wallaby species). Ⓛ erulatji

erorula (erorula) *vor sehr langer Zeit; einst.* ◇ a very long time ago, once upon a time. Ⓛ erorita

erorútna *Muskeln schnell bewegend.* ◇ move muscles quickly. Ⓛ erorutni

eroutja *große Geschwulst (Aussatz).* ◇ large swelling. Ⓛ nunguru

erōtja *Absceß, Geschwür.* ◇ abscess.

eróara *frisch glänzend, fettig (Blüten).* ◇ fresh shining, greasy (blossoms). Ⓛ nitinkuru

erōta *Brustbein (der Vögel und Kamele).* ◇ chestbone (of birds and camels). Ⓛ metutu

erouma *zittern, beben (vor Furcht oder Kälte).* ◇ shake, shiver (from fright or cold). Ⓛ tjititingañi

ilútjikatjíla erouma *vor dem Tod zittern.* ◇ fear death. Ⓛ iluntakita tjitjitingañi

roubouma *(Dupl.) fortwährend zittern (z.B. Sehnsucht nach der Heimat).* ◇ (duplication) shake continuously (e.g. from longing for home, from being homesick). Ⓛ tjititikanañi

erŭátnama *schwarz sein.* ◇ be black. Ⓛ mungawonniñi

erakúnjerama *nicht wollen, Bitte abschlagen, keine Lust haben zum Geben.* ◇ refuse, deny request, have no desire to give. Ⓛ tomatiriñi

erulanga *Grevillea junctifolia.* ◇ *Grevillea juncifolia* (Latz 1996). Ⓛ ultukunba

erulanganana *eine sehr lange, gestreifte Schlange, sehr giftig.* ◇ a very long, striped and very poisonous snake. Ⓛ erúlanganínami

erulba *Strauch (spec.) mit hellen Blättern.* ◇ bush species with light-coloured leaves. Ⓛ arulba

erulja *ganz eingefallen (vor Alter oder Hunger), Gestalt zusammengeschrumpft (Haut).* ◇ emaciated (of age or hunger), shrivelled (skin). Ⓛ kebulba, kebula

erulinja *ein Mann, dem ein langer Bart wächst.* ◇ man who is growing a long beard. Ⓛ murbu

eruljarulja *abgemagert, eingetrocknet (Körper).* ◇ emaciated, dehydrated or shrivelled (body). Ⓛ bukirbukira, kebulkebulba

 For the modern spellings of these words, see the dictionaries and sources in reference list.

eruljeruljerama *verziehen (Gesicht, zum Weinen).* ◇ screw up (face to cry). Ⓛ wiljurwiljurariñi Ⓓ ngininginirina

erultja *reisig, trockene Büsche.* ◇ twigs, dry scrub. Ⓛ malara

erula *schwarze Schwanzspitze (der aroa).* ◇ black tail end (of wallaby). Ⓛ omulkni

eruma *schwarz sein, braun sein.* ◇ be black, be brown. Ⓛ maru

erūntja *freigebig.* ◇ generous. Ⓛ munta Ⓓ munta [?]

erúntja *dunkle Erdhöhle, Nische (des Grabes).* ◇ dark cave in ground, niche (in grave). Ⓛ nulu, narkulta

erúntjanga *dunkle Erdhöhle.* ◇ dark cave in earth. Ⓛ nulu

erúntjatna *dunkel (farbig).* ◇ dark (coloured). Ⓛ marukuru

erultja tanama *durchlöchern (Fleisch vom Speer), zerfleischen.* ◇ perforate (meat with spear), lacerate. Ⓛ bailkarpungañi

erunka *furchtlos.* ◇ fearless. Ⓛ nintingánara

erunkura *sehr schnell (im Laufen).* ◇ very fast (run). Ⓛ erunkuru

erunkurunkura *sehr schnell.* ◇ very fast. Ⓛ erunkurunkuru

erunkurunkuraerer etnalbuma *sehr schnell davonlaufen.* ◇ run away very fast. Ⓛ wolbankawobakatiñi

erúntara *ausweichend.* ◇ evasive. Ⓛ arintji

eruntarérama *ausweichen (der Gefahr), zur Seite springen (vor dem tjatta).* ◇ avoid (danger), jump to the side (to avoid spear). Ⓛ arintjiriñi Ⓓ warkurina

erutatja *australischer Maikäfer.* ◇ Australian Maybeetle. Ⓛ arketunba

erōtjabata *Vorfahren.* ◇ ancestors, the old people.

ēta, eta *conf.* **antja** *Schlund, Hals, Speiseröhre.* ◇ throat, neck, oesophagus. Ⓛ eta Ⓓ ngaiipiltji

etérama *wollen.* ◇ want. Ⓛ unturingani Ⓓ purkaljerina

eterinja *Wunsch, Wille.* ◇ wish, will. Ⓛ untuta

etakama *Gewissensbisse empfinden.* ◇ remorseful, feel remorse. Ⓛ kurbani Ⓓ purkaljerina

etakintja *Gewissensbiß.* ◇ gilt, remorse. Ⓛ kurbanta Ⓓ purka

etalerama *denken, meinen.* ◇ think, reckon, opine. Ⓛ urukuluni Ⓓ ngundrana

etaleṙelabuma *gedenken, erinnern.* ◇ think of, remember. Ⓛ urukúlerariñi

etatnama *erdrosseln, erwürgen.* ◇ strangle, throttle. Ⓛ untuwitini

etulbmerama *(Schlund eng werden) verdursten, ersticken.* ◇ die of thirst, suffocate (narrowing of throat). Ⓛ untutúluringañi

etátagáta *keine Lust haben, widerspenstig.* ◇ have no desire, refractory. Ⓛ untukainkaina

etirkuantirkuanta *eigensinnig, widerspenstig, apathisch.* ◇ obstinate, refractory, apathetic. Ⓛ untukánankánana

etakama *siehe oben eta.* ◇ See above: eta.

etalerama *denken, meinen, überlegen.* ◇ think, reckon. Ⓛ urukuluni Ⓓ ngundrana

etaleṙelábuma *cf.* eta.

eta tanama *Schlund ausstrecken (die Schlange beim Laufen).* ◇ stretch out neck (snake when moving). Ⓛ untu tunañi

etalingetala *Verstand.* ◇ mind, intelligence. Ⓛ kulilkulilba Ⓓ manu, tjuru

etalingetalalama *verstehen.* ◇ understand. Ⓛ kulilkulilbajennañi

etalingetala nama *verstehen.* ◇ understand. Ⓛ kulilkulilba ninañi

etulukaluka *vertieft (sein in eine Arbeit).* ◇ absorbed (in work). Ⓛ urukulilba

etalinja; *z.B.* **era etalinja nguanga nama**. *immerfort, fortwährend; er ist immer freundlich.* ◇ continually, constantly; he is always friendly. Ⓛ ṙata

etalukalukalélama *etwas erwägen, fortwährend an etwas denken.* ◇ consider something, continually think about something. Ⓛ urukulira wottañi

etama *bauen (Haus).* ◇ build (house). Ⓛ paltani

etama *anzünden, anfachen (Feuer).* ◇ light a fire, fan (fire). Ⓛ kutani Ⓓ japina, wagana

etalama *anfachen (großes Feuer machen).* ◇ fan (make big fire). Ⓛ kutarangarañi

etanétana *Heizer, der immer Feuer anzündet.* ◇ he who always lights fire. Ⓛ kutalpuntu

etamintja *eßbare Wurzeln (rübenähnlich) spec.* ◇ edible roots (carrot-like) species. Ⓛ etimintji

etapikana *unverbesserlich, sehr schlecht.* ◇ incorrigible, very bad. Ⓛ kujamatu

etantara *Pflanze mit rübenartigem Kraut und eßbaren Wurzeln.* ◇ plant with carrot-like tops and edible roots. Ⓛ etantiri

etata *lebendig.* ◇ lively, alive. Ⓛ wonka, kana Ⓓ tepi

etaterama *lebendig werden.* ◇ become alive. Ⓛ wonkaringanje, kanaringañi Ⓓ tepirina

etatilama *lebendig machen.* ◇ make alive, lively. Ⓛ wonkani, kanani Ⓓ tepi ngankana

étatakáta *gesund, kräftig.* ◇ healthy, strong. Ⓛ kanatara

etátakia *(von etata-kama = Leben abschneiden) giftig, nicht genießbar, gefährlich.* ◇ poisonous, not edible, dangerous (gun); derived from 'life' and 'cut off'. Ⓛ ilupaiï

etătja *faul, träge, sehr langsam (gehen).* ◇ lazy, indolent, sluggish, very slow (walk). Ⓛ tālu

etatjilama *trs. einen müde machen sodaß er langsam geht.* ◇ (transitive) tire out someone. Ⓛ kanenkujennañi Ⓓ ngurali

etatjetta *lebenslang, immer; (von etata+tjetta).* ◇ lifelong, always (derived from life + long, far away). Ⓛ kanaruntu

etatnama *siehe oben 'eta'.* ◇ see above 'eta'.

etátua *lange (zum reden, singen).* ◇ long (to speak, sing). Ⓛ wonkalara

eterama *wollen (siehe oben 'eta').* ◇ want (see above 'eta'). Ⓛ unturingañi

eterinja *Wille, Wunsch (siehe oben 'eta').* ◇ will, wish (see above 'eta'). Ⓛ untuta

etétarenama *eingeben (Worte).* ◇ suggest (words). Ⓛ tintinpungañi

etintja *Arm, Zweig (eines Baumes), Ärmel.* ◇ arm, branch (of tree), sleeve. Ⓛ jerri

etokuwiïlama *festsitzen (Speer in der Wunde).* ◇ stuck (spear in wound). Ⓛ tunkurpungañi

janna etokuwiïlama *nicht herausziehen können.* ◇ cannot pull out. Ⓛ butu tunkurpungañi

etnantambala *gleich viele.* ◇ equal amount.

ētna *dicht (Bäumen), Dickicht.* ◇ dense (trees), thicket. Ⓛ tāta

etnabana *diese.* ◇ these. Ⓛ tanatu, palurungari

ĕtna *sie (pl.)* ◇ they (plural). Ⓛ tana Ⓓ tana

etninkaraka *sie alle.* ◇ they all. Ⓛ tanápuara

etnakarajinga *Familie (die Familie von Anderen).* ◇ family (of others). Ⓛ tananakarpa

etnakaratitja *sie insgesamt, Häuptl.-Volk.* ◇ they all together (chief's people). Ⓛ tananukarpalta

etokerama *widerfahren (Leiden).* ◇ suffer (misfortune). Ⓛ ilaringañi

etnákarakia *jene Gruppe, die Abteilung der Gruppe, der ich nicht angehöre.* ◇ opposite moiety; those people or that kindred. See Strehlow (1913: 62, fn. 5) for an elaborate attempt on the possible etymology of this Aranda term. Ⓛ tananukarpitina

etóppa [Southern dialect] *Gürtel (= tjipa).* ◇ belt. Ⓛ nanpa

etoppalerkuma *trs. gürten.* ◇ (transitive) gird. Ⓛ nanpanku witini Ⓓ ngampibana

etoppalerkulama *refl. sich gürten.* ◇ (reflexive) gird. Ⓛ nanpanku karbini Ⓓ ngampina

etoppambenja *daneben, neben her.* ◇ beside, next to. Ⓛ pilawana

etoppa *Rand.* ◇ edge. Ⓛ iltji, pila

etóppala *abseits, daneben.* ◇ apart, beside. Ⓛ pilanka

 For the modern spellings of these words, see the dictionaries and sources in reference list.

etoppala lama *abseits von den andern gehen.* ◇ walk apart from the others. Ⓛ pilanka jennañi

etoppetoppa *in einer Reihe neben einander.* ◇ in a row beside each other. Ⓛ pilapila

etoppatíkana *weit entfernt (von einander).* ◇ distant (from each other). Ⓛ mantapalakutu

etoppaka *am Rande.* ◇ at the edge. Ⓛ iltjiku, pilaku

etua (= **itinja**) *nahe.* ◇ near, close. Ⓛ ila

etukuétua *sehr nahe.* ◇ very near. Ⓛ aiilkira

etua nama *zerstückt, in Stücke geschlagen (Fleisch).* ◇ cut up, cut into pieces (meat). Ⓛ itjili ninañi

etuélama *zerstückeln (Fleisch).* ◇ cut, carve into pieces (meat). Ⓛ itjilinañi

etuánama *eintreten für einen andern, den Tod für einen andern erleiden.* ◇ stand up for someone, endure death for someone else. Ⓛ tjitanguta, tjitangutatu

etuánga *geduldig, gelassen.* ◇ patient, composed. Ⓛ kaiuwara

etuáraetuára *faul, lässig.* ◇ lazy, slack. Ⓛ kanenkanenku

etuaraetuara ankama *mundfaul sein.* ◇ to speak unclearly, lazily. Ⓛ kanenkanenku wonkañi

etuia *Strauch mit eßbaren Früchten.* ◇ shrub with edible fruit. Ⓛ putuju

etuia *Larven (weiß) in etuia-Wurzeln.* ◇ grub (white) in etuia roots. Ⓛ putuju

etulbmerama *verdursten, ersticken (siehe oben eta).* ◇ die of thirst, suffocate (see above 'eta'). Ⓛ untutuluringañi

etúna *eine Art Kalk.* ◇ kind of limestone. Ⓛ lurru

étuna *sehr heiß.* ◇ very hot. Ⓛ lurru Ⓓ karareli, turuturu

etunaka *Sommer.* ◇ summer. Ⓛ lurrunka

étunétuna *große, rote Honig-Ameisen.* ◇ big red honeyants. Ⓛ etunétuna

etunintja *eßbare Frucht.* ◇ edible fruit.

etúta *Gras (art), Samen gegessen.* ◇ grass species with edible seeds. Ⓛ etuta

G

galtja *klug, wissend.* ◇ clever (intelligent), knowing, expert. Ⓛ ninti Ⓓ kiri

galtja nama *wissen.* ◇ to know. Ⓛ ninti ninañi

galtjéeama *klug werden, lernen, verstehen.* ◇ become clever, learn, understand. Ⓛ nintiringañi Ⓓ kiririna

galtjerinerina *der Lernende, Schüler.* ◇ pupil, student. Ⓛ nintiringamiringami

galtjindama *klug machen, unterrichten.* ◇ make clever, instruct in. Ⓛ nintini Ⓓ ngujangujara jinkina

galtjindanindana *Lehrer.* ◇ teacher. Ⓛ nintimanintinmi Ⓓ ngujangujara-jinkinietja

galtjindinjamea *Unterricht, Unterweisung.* ◇ lesson, instruction. Ⓛ nintilpuntu Ⓓ ngujangujara

galtjerana *der Schüler.* ◇ pupil.

kamba *süß (Speisen).* ◇ sweet (foods). Ⓛ ngumu

gar⊠ilkama *aufschreien, laut schreien.* ◇ cry out, scream. Ⓛ merawokkani

garra *Fleisch, Wild, Fleischspeisen.* ◇ meat, game. Ⓛ kuka Ⓓ nganti

garrataka *viel Fleisch, noch mehr Fleisch.* ◇ plenty of meat, some more meat. Ⓛ kukamari

gata *Ort, Stelle, Ende, - außen, sichtbar, flach, öffentlich.* ◇ place, spot, locality, position, end; outside, visible, flat, public; light; clear (speech, language). Ⓛ urelba, akata Ⓓ piri

gatala *draußen, sichtbar, offenbar.* ◇ outside, visible, obvious, in the open, evident; clear. Ⓛ urelta Ⓓ palarani

gaterama *offenbar werden.* ◇ become obvious. Ⓛ ureltaringañi Ⓓ pirirna

detja gaterama *Zähne zeigen (Hund, der beißen will).* ◇ show teeth (dog who wants to bite). Ⓛ kadidi ninjirangani

gatarenama *ein Ende machen, zerstören, einen umbringen.* ◇ put an end to, destroy, kill somebody.

gatilama *aufräumen, ausfegen (Haus), glatt-, eben machen, reinigen (Boden).* ◇ tidy up, sweep (house), smooth, make level, clean (ground), clear. Ⓛ ureni

gata arbanána *hin und wieder (an verschiedenen Plätzen).* ◇ now and again (at different places).

gatalelama *trs. aufdecken, bekennen (Unrecht).* ◇ (transitive) uncover, plead guilty. Ⓛ utitanani

gata mara *rein.* ◇ pure. Ⓛ urelpalla, akata palla

gatawollawolla *wütend auf dem Kampfplatz stehen, zum Kampf herausfordernd.* ◇ stand furious on battlefield, challenge to a fight. Ⓛ akatanguntunguntapungañi

gatalarumba *rein (Platz).* ◇ clean (place).

gatawotaúerama *verschwinden vom Erdboden, aussterben.* ◇ disappear from the face of the earth, die out. Ⓛ wialurrulurrungarañi, raungarañi

gitjala; irbangagitjala *postp. für, anstatt (c. gen.)* ◇ (postposition) for, instead of (c. gen.)

gōda [Southern dialect] *Ei.* ◇ egg. Ⓛ ngokuta Ⓓ kapi

godna *dumm, unwissend.* ◇ stupid, ignorant, unaware, not knowing. Ⓛ ngurba Ⓓ ko, manuko

gōla *langes Haupthaar.* ◇ long hair. Ⓛ manka Ⓓ para

gōla-tjima *Zopf.* ◇ plait. Ⓛ manka-wakitji

goltama *bedecken, zudecken, verhüllen.* ◇ cover, veil. Ⓛ waltuni Ⓓ walpana, walpadakana

goltalama *refl. sich zudecken.* ◇ (reflexive) cover. Ⓛ waltunañi

goltulta *kurze Schößlinge (neben dem Stamm).* ◇ short shoots (beside trunk). Ⓛ taltalta

gultjiletanga *mit verschränkten oder eingehackten Armen.* ◇ with crossed arms. Ⓛ wakunka-iti

gulatja *Halsband.* ◇ neckband. Ⓛ untungana Ⓓ jelkara

ultangátuta *der Kurze, Klein von Person.* ◇ short person, petite. Ⓛ gultumuta

gultja *Armschmuck, Armband.* ◇ armband. Ⓛ wakungana

gultjakuára *haarene Decke (mit der sich der Mond zudeckt).* ◇ blanket made of hair (the moon covers himself with it). Ⓛ merawara (?) ('?' added by CS)

gunama *hineinlegen, hineinstellen, hineinsetzen.* ◇ put into. Ⓛ irbini, tarbatunañi Ⓓ widmana, kibana? ('?' added by CS)

gui͡ [Southern dialect] *Ausdruck der Überraschung = ach.* ◇ expression of surprise = oh. Ⓛ pũta

gunakélama *behalten (im Gedächnis).* ◇ keep (in mind). Ⓛ urukulini

gunitjalbuma *hineinlegen (bei der Heimkehr).* ◇ lay into (on return home). Ⓛ irbini kulbara

gunalakalama *herunterlassen trs.* ◇ let down (transitive). Ⓛ irbirukwalingani

gunalalakalama *refl. herniederlassen.* ◇ (reflexive) let down. Ⓛ tarbatura okalingañi

goltinjamata *verdeckt.* ◇ covered.

gunja, gunja kwatja, litjina gunja *postp. verbunden mit Substantive und Verben: nicht mehr, kein, z.B. kein Wasser (mehr) da, nicht gehen werden.* ◇ (postposition with nouns and verbs) no more, none e.g. no more water (there), will not go. Ⓛ wiata, kapi wiata; jenkuntawia

gúnuta *kurz, nicht hoch (Sträucher).* ◇ short, not high (bushes). Ⓛ tarta

gúruna, guruna *Seele (im lebenden Menschen), Leben.* ◇ soul (in living human), life. The spirit or soul of a person is also called 'inka' in Western Aranda. No obvious distinction is made today between the words inka and guruna. While Western Aranda people use inka and guruna interchangeably today, the terms seem to have had a slightly different meaning in the past. Inka according to Carl Strehlow was used for the spirit of a living human being, who was in danger; and the word guruna was used for the soul of a living person (Strehlow 1907: 15). When a person dies,

 For the modern spellings of these words, see the dictionaries and sources in reference list.

the soul was called iltana, which means 'ghost' (Strehlow 1915: 23). Ⓛ gurunba Ⓓ mungara

gúrunga; gúrungatjína [Southern dialect] *danach, darauf.* ◇ after, following. Ⓛ palulanguru, kāna

gurúrkna *die aus den Haaren Verstorbener angefertigte Schnur (Gürtel oder Halsband).* ◇ string made of hair of deceased (belt or neckband). Ⓛ manjunuma Ⓓ ngaldra? ('?' added by CS)

I

ibara *der schwarz und weiß gestreifte Kranich.* ◇ black and white striped crane. Ⓛ ibari

ibalama *fasten.* ◇ to fast.

ibarkna *Netzfett, Netz.* ◇ fat. Ⓛ niti

ibalala *die Brust (im allgemeinen).* ◇ chest (in general). Ⓛ batta

ibatja *Milch, Brust.* ◇ milk, breast. Ⓛ ibi Ⓓ ngamatanka

ibatja-ndintja; ibatja-ndanandana *Säuger, Amme (eine Frau, die das Kind stillt); Säuger, Amme.* ◇ mammal, nurse (a woman who breast feeds); mammal, wet nurse. Ⓛ ibi Ⓓ ngamatanka

ibatjangna *(Milch-Frucht) weibliche Brüste.* ◇ (milk-fruit) female breasts. Ⓛ ibikalka Ⓓ ngama

ibarapa *kleine Eidechse.* ◇ small lizard. Ⓛ ibaripi

ibaraia *herabhängend (Brüste).* ◇ hanging down, sagging (breasts). Ⓛ ngarikatinta

ibebilama *fürbitten, fürsprechen.* ◇ plead for. Ⓛ alani Ⓓ jurajuralkana

ibalintja *nüchtern, nichts gegessen.* ◇ sober, not having eaten.

ibiljakua *wilde Ente.* ◇ wild duck. Ⓛ tjipijaku

ilalakalama *fortwährend reden.* ◇ talk continuously.

ibinja *fremd, der Fremde.* ◇ foreign, foreigner, stranger. Ⓛ urela

ilalapilala kalama *fortwährend reden.* ◇ talk continuously.

íbuma *ausdrücken (Därme).* ◇ empty (guts). Ⓛ nibini Ⓓ jikana

ilelengandama *trs. Rat geben, raten.* ◇ (transitive) to give advice, advise.

ila *der lange Leib (der Schlange).* ◇ long body (of snake).

ila, jerra-ila *Bau (der bull-dog ants).* ◇ bull ants' nest. Ⓛ piti, minga-piti

ilakuntja *Schutzzaun (aus Zweigen).* ◇ windbreak (made of branches). Ⓛ ju

ila relbma *glänzende Stamm.* ◇ shiny trunk. Ⓛ ngana, kaltaru

ila *Halm (Grashalm), Stamm (von Bäumen).* ◇ blade (grass blade), trunk (of trees). Ⓛ ngana

ililbirtja *helle Stamm (Tnima).* ◇ light coloured trunk (Tnima). Ⓛ ngana lililba

ilaka *wir beide; wenn der Vater von sich und seinem Sohn spricht (exclusiv).* ◇ we two; when father speaks of himself and his son (exclusively). Ⓛ ngalinba

ilama *sagen, erzählen.* ◇ say, tell. Ⓛ wottani Ⓓ kaukaubana

ilalama *einem ansagen, (bekennen?), Entschluss kundgeben.* ◇ announce (a decision). ('?' added by CS). Ⓛ palunku wottani

ilelarénama *erlauben (etwas zu tun).* ◇ allow (to do something). Ⓛ wottariani

ilelalbuma *sich verabschieden, (fortgehen, nachdem man gesprochen hat).* ◇ to farewell, (leave after speaking). Ⓛ wottarakulbañi

ilitjalbuma *wieder erzählen.* ◇ retell. Ⓛ wottara kulbañi

ilinílina *Redner.* ◇ speaker. Ⓛ wottalbaii Ⓓ jatanietja

ilanama *sehen auf einen, ansehen (z.B. als Schwiegervater).* ◇ regard (as father-in-law). Ⓛ nakánañi

ilapilama *wieder erzählen.* ◇ retell. Ⓛ wottaṙanáni, wottawottañi

ilanbilanga *fest, dicht, ohne Löcher, undurchsichtig.* ◇ solid, dense, without holes, not transparent. Ⓛ walupirpmari, walu lenku

ilalajinama *fortsenden mit den Worten.* ◇ send away with the words. Ⓛ wottaraijani

ilta ilanbilanga *Festung (n).* ◇ fortress.

ilangarakalkara *bis wann?* ◇ until when?

ilarinja *postp. nach.* ◇ (postposition) after.

ilarakúltakultérama *aufschwellen (der Leib von vielem Wasser trinken).* ◇ swell (from drinking a lot of water). Ⓛ unkarapatapatanariñi

ilangára? *wann?* ◇ when? Ⓛ jaltjiáranka?, jaltjinka? Ⓓ winta?, wintari?

ilantja *hohe Gras (art), Rohr-Gras (Phragmites communis).* ◇ tall grass (species), cane-grass. Ⓛ ilentji

ilantja *Eidechse (spec.), kleine Eidechse, häufig in Gärten.* ◇ lizard (species), small lizard, frequently in gardens. Ⓛ tuntalpini

ilanta *wir beide (Mann und Frau).* ◇ the two of us (man and woman); or we two (in opposite patrimoieties and one generation apart, as mother and child, uncle and nephew). Ⓛ ngali

ilanta [Northern dialect] *cf.* **lanta** *wir beide (Mann und Frau).* ◇ the two of us (man and woman/wife); or we two (in opposite patrimoieties and one generation apart, as mother and child, uncle and nephew). Ⓛ ngali

ílapa *Steinbeil.* ◇ stone axe. Ⓛ ilipi, wonnantu Ⓓ kalara

ilapa-ngantjingantjilama, ilapingantjingantjila *Steinbeil - Tragende = der Beil-Träger.* ◇ axe carrier (Strehlow 1910b: 91). Ⓛ ilipi ngalutangalutanku jennañi

ilaraperuma *sprechen einander.* ◇ talk to each other.

ilátuma *trs. niederwerfen, zu Boden werfen, seine Stirn an etwas schlagen, einen an den Füßen packen und mit dem Kopf an etwas schlagen.* ◇ (transitive) throw down, to the ground, hit forehead on something, grip someone by the feet and beat head against something. Ⓛ antawonnini, bailkupungañi

ilarrabilarra [Northern dialect] *Binsen.* ◇ rushes. Ⓛ ankarànkara

ilatoppatuma *trs. mit dem Kopf (an etwas) schlagen.* ◇ (transitive) hit with head (something). Ⓛ bailkupunkanañi

ilapanganjaganja *ein Insekt, das Honig trägt.* ◇ insect that carries honey. Ⓛ ilipinganjinganji

ilba *1. Ohr auch 2. Gebärmutter, Nachgeburt.* ◇ 1. ear 2. womb, afterbirth; uterus, placenta. Ⓛ 1. pinna, 2. ilpi Ⓓ talpa, kutjera (*Ohr*: ear)

ilbágata [Southern dialect] *Ohr.* ◇ ear. Ⓛ pinna

ilbatnata *vordere Seite des Ohres.* ◇ front side of ear. Ⓛ pinnawila

ilbatoppa *Ohr-rücken, hinter dem Ohr.* ◇ back of ear, behind ear. Ⓛ pinnatana

ilbakutáka *'ganz Ohr sein', willig hören.* ◇ listen willingly, intently. Ⓛ pinnali Ⓓ talpakaldruėli

ilbátilbata *willig, zuverläßig.* ◇ willing, reliable. Ⓛ pinnali

ilbaṙirbmankua *taub sein.* ◇ be deaf. Ⓛ pinnanji Ⓓ talpakuru

ilbatjaltjila *leicht lernend, verständig.* ◇ learn easily, quick to understand, intelligent. Ⓛ pinnawolla

ilbatjaltjilerama *leicht lernen, verständig werden.* ◇ learn easily, understand. Ⓛ pinnawollaringañi

ilbaleala *sicher (schlafen).* ◇ safe (sleep).

ilbamara (ilba + mara) *fruchtbare Frau.* ◇ fertile woman. Ⓛ ilbamari

ilbankama *sich besinnen, sich erinnern.* ◇ remember. Ⓛ nintibakani

ilbankalelama *trs. einen erinnern.* ◇ (transitive) remind someone. Ⓛ pinnankarani

ilba [Southern dialect] *Sandhügel.* ◇ sandhill. Ⓛ tali

ilbagatagata *boomerang mit Hacken (von Norden).* ◇ boomerang with hook (from the north). Ⓛ kiri, pinnantinanti Ⓓ ngamiringa (*boomerang mit Hacken*), kirra ngamiringa

ilbagata = mit (gata) dem Ohr (ilba) *ein boomerang mit Hacken.* ◇ boomerang with hook. Ⓛ kiri

ilbakutaka *willig hören.* ◇ listen willingly. Ⓛ pinnali

 For the modern spellings of these words, see the dictionaries and sources in reference list.

ilbala *Blatt, kleiner Zweig, Federn, Flügel, Flossen.* ◇ leaf, twig, feathers, wings, fins. Ⓛ kalbi Ⓓ talpa (*Blatt*: leaf), kutja (*Feder*: feather)

ilbala unkwalkna *Federseele.* ◇ feather soul (composed of *Feder*: feather and *Seele*: soul). Ⓛ urkalba Ⓓ kutja (*Federseele*: *Feder* = feather, *Seele* = soul)

ilbala ngala nama *fliegen.* ◇ fly. Ⓛ kalbajuritjingarabakani

ilbalankara *weites Blatt.* ◇ wide leaf. Ⓛ kalbilbila

ilbanabanama *laufen langsam (Emu).* ◇ run slowly (emu). Ⓛ kutijnennañi

ilbalauma *schnell fortgehen.* ◇ go away fast. Ⓛ jenkulatalkañi

ilbalama *abwehren (mit den Händen), sich ducken, ausweichen (der Gefahr), zur Seite springen, abhalten (den Speer mit dem Schilde).* ◇ ward off (with hands), duck, avoid (danger), jump out of the way, fend off (spear with shield). Ⓛ mamani

ilbakarenama *trs. einen beschwören, daß er etwas tun soll.* ◇ (transitive) implore/ beg somebody to do something.

ilbalandama *lehren, unterrichten.* ◇ teach, instruct. Ⓛ nintini

ilbálara *weit, (= antaka) weite Ebene.* ◇ wide, wide or vast plain. Ⓛ bila

ilbalelama *hindern (Land).* ◇ prevent (land).

ilbananánana *Verkläger.* ◇ accuser.

ilbalbarawuma *schlenkern (mit den Händen).* ◇ swing (hands). Ⓛ wililpungañi Ⓓ ngaringaribana? ('?' added by CS)

ilbalbariuma *etwas abschütteln (von sich), hin und her schütteln (der Hund seine Beute).* ◇ shake off something (from oneself), shake back and forth (dog its prey). Ⓛ wililpungañi

ilbalbarawulama, ilbalbariúlama *schütteln (Kopf), sich schütteln (wie ein Hund, der aus dem Wasser kommt).* ◇ shake (head), shake (like a dog who has come out of water). Ⓛ winanpungañi, pinpintipungañi

ilbaléala *cf.* **ilba** *sicher.* ◇ safe.

ilbálunga *große Höhle (Versammlungsort).* ◇ big cave (meeting place). Ⓛ kulbi

ilbalturaltura *Vogel (spec.) klein, schwarz und weiße Flügel, Kehle und Leib weiß, Rücken bläulich.* ◇ small bird (species), black and white wings, white throat and body, blueish back. Ⓛ ilbalturulturu

ilbaluntuma *fortlaufen, weglaufen.* ◇ run away. Ⓛ wollakajennañi

ilbámanna *Pfanze mit eßbaren Blättern.* ◇ plant with edible leaves. Ⓛ akulu, ilbamanni

ilba-manta *taub.* ◇ deaf. Ⓛ pinnapatti Ⓓ talpakuru, kutjeraburu

ilbamara *cf.* **ilba 2.** *die fruchtbare Frau.* ◇ fertile woman.

ilbalérama *vergessen (etwas mitzunehmen).* ◇ forget (to take something). Ⓛ watawatani

ilbamba *der entseelte Körper, aus dem ein böses Wesen die Seele herausgenommen hat.* ◇ soulless body from which an evil being stole the soul. The body can continue to live without the soul for several days (see Strehlow 1907: 14). The soul is called 'inka' or 'guruna' today. Ⓛ ultu Ⓓ pundupundu

ilbanala *laufend (langsam laufen).* ◇ walking (walk slowly). Ⓛ kutijennantu

ilbanabanama *umherlaufen, sehr schnell laufen (Emu).* ◇ run around, run very fast (emu). Ⓛ kutijennañi

ílbanama *verklagen, anschuldigen.* ◇ accuse. Ⓛ tukaruruni Ⓓ nguldru terkana

ilbangatertanga ankama *vergebens einem zureden.* ◇ beg/implore in vain. Ⓛ pinnankatananka wonkañi Ⓓ ngurrungurrubana

ilbangintála *störrig, widerspenstig, ungehorsam.* ◇ stubborn, obstinate, disobedient. Ⓛ kunjinji, pinna ŕama Ⓓ nginjaru? ('?' added by CS)

ilbambuma *sich röten (Rinde der Gummibäume), sich rot färben.* ◇ turn red (bark of gumtrees). Ⓛ taltirkambañi

ilbangurangura ankama *warnen (vor Gefahr).* ◇ warn (about danger). Ⓛ angaménmén wonkañi, urungurunga wonkañi

ilbangala *Eidechse.* ◇ lizard. Ⓛ kalamèra

ilbanka *Strauch mit langen, dicken Nadeln und sehr harten, mandelförmigen Früchten (needle-bush) Hakea Leucoptera.* ◇ bush with long, thick needles and very hard almond shaped fruit (needlebush), *Hakea leucoptera.* Ⓛ piripiri Ⓓ kulua

ilbankama *sich besinnen, sich erinnern.* ◇ consider, reflect, remember, recall. Ⓛ nintiwonkañi

ilbankalélama *trs. besinnen machen, erinnern (einen andern).* ◇ (transitive) make realise, remind (somebody). Ⓛ pinnankarani

ilbalkindama *schmeicheln.* ◇ to flatter.

ilbamankura *dickbäuchig.* ◇ fat bellied, potbellied, fat (abdominal). Ⓛ wila ngatinba

ilbanta *allgemeiner Regen.* ◇ general rain. Ⓛ ilbanta, irtjingi Ⓓ talara

ilantitnima *Regen fallen, regnen.* ◇ to rain. Ⓛ irtjingi patangarañi Ⓓ talara kodana

ilbaülkulelama, ilbaunkalelama *trs. erinnern.* ◇ (transitive) remember, recall.

ilbantatnima *regnen.* ◇ to rain.

ilbangaratuma *strafen (mit Worten).* ◇ punish (with words).

ilbeltatuma *züchtigen.* ◇ to discipline.

ilbara *Baum spec. mit langen schmalen Blättern.* ◇ tree species with long, narrow leaves. Ⓛ anuntu Ⓓ wirra? ('?' added by CS)

ilbara *Nasenbein, Känguruhknochen von den Weibern und Mädchen getragen.* ◇ nosebone, kangaroo bone worn by women and girls. Ⓛ ilberi

ilbarilbara *ebene (Fläche), glatte (Fläche).* ◇ level, smooth (surface). Ⓛ ilberilberi

ilbara ankama *glatt reden, verteidigen (mit Worten).* ◇ smooth talk, to defend (with words). Ⓛ batjiri wonkañi

ilbarabunja ankama *fürsprechen, verteidigen, in Schutz nehmen (gegen Verleumdung).* ◇ to advocate, to defend, to defend (from defamation). Ⓛ angawonkañi

ilbarka *ein flaches Schutzdach, ein glattes Dach.* ◇ flat protective roof, smooth roof.

ilbarindama *an etwas hängen.* ◇ to hang on something. Ⓛ waralknariñi

ilbaraléa *Schlange, giftig, spec circa 4 Fuß lang, Rücken grünlich gelb mit braunen Feldern, Bauch gelb.* ◇ poisonous snake species about 4 feet long that has a greenish-yellow back with brown spots and a yellow belly. Ⓛ pantirba

ilbaratja *Larven (weiß) in ilbara-Wurzeln.* ◇ grubs (white) in ilbara roots. Ⓛ wonnukutu

ilberarénanama *aufhängen (z.B. Wäsche).* ◇ hang up (e.g. washing). Ⓛ worraltunañi, worraltunkula katini (katibana) waruwarukana, (katibaterina) waruwarukijiribaterina

ilberarenalama *sich aufhängen.* ◇ (reflexive) to hang. Ⓛ palurunku worraltunañi

ilbarbaia *Habicht spec.* ◇ hawk species. Ⓛ talbuntji, talbutalbu

ilbaranama *sich anklammern (an etwas).* ◇ cling (to something). Ⓛ worralknarañi

ilbarinama; *z.B.* **kwatja ilbarinitjikai pitjai** *erzählen, lehren, unterrichten, zeigen; z.B. Zeig mir das Wasser.* ◇ tell, teach, instruct, show; show me the water! Ⓛ nintini (= pitjai); kapi nintintaku ngalajerrai!

ilbarilbanánama *herunterhängen.* ◇ to hang down. Ⓛ warawaralngariñi

ilbarilbaranama *sich fest an etwas klammern (Vögel an Ast); z.B. die Sonne kurz vor Untergang.* ◇ cling or hold tightly onto something (birds onto branches); sun just before setting. Ⓛ worra worralknarañi

ilbarilbara *ebene, flache Fläche.* ◇ level, flat surface. Ⓛ ilberilberi, waralwaral

ilbarilbara ngama *an der Kante (anfassend etwas) tragen, sodaß es herabhängt.* ◇ carry something by its edge, so it hangs down. Ⓛ waralwaral katiñi

ilbarinja *eine Larve, die sich an den tnurunga Büschen findet.* ◇ grub living on tnurunga bushes. Ⓛ ilbirinji

 For the modern spellings of these words, see the dictionaries and sources in reference list.

ilbar̃irbmankua *cf.* **ilba** *taub sein.* ◇ be deaf. Ⓛ pinnanji

ilbararénama *sich umwickeln (etwas Schnur).* ◇ to wrap around (some string). Ⓛ waraltunañi

ilbarka *klein, eingedrückt (Nase).* ◇ small, flat (nose). Ⓛ lalba

ilbarkerama *einfallen (Gestalt, Gesicht vor Alter).* ◇ to wither (body, face from age). Ⓛ beltaringañi, lalbaringañi

ilbérama *rötlich werden.* ◇ turn reddish. Ⓛ warknarañi

ilbartja (ilbirtja) *hell (Haar), weiß, grau, verwelkt.* ◇ fair (hair), white, grey, wilted. Ⓛ lililba

ilbata *Stoppeln, Baumstumpf.* ◇ stubbles, tree stump. Ⓛ tamala

ilbatilbata *cf.* **ilba** *willig, zuverlässig.* ◇ willing, reliable. Ⓛ pinnali

ilbatjaltjila *cf.* **ilba** *verständig.* ◇ intelligent, understanding. Ⓛ pinnawolla

ilbāta *Masern (überall am Körper verbreitet).* ◇ measles (all over body). Ⓛ mutu

ilbátuma *umstoßen (z.B. einen Tisch), umwerfen, zerstören (z.B. ein Haus).* ◇ knock over (e.g. table), overturn, destroy (e.g. house). Ⓛ patani Ⓓ kokoterkibana

ilbentjilama *herkommen (langsam).* ◇ approach (slowly). Ⓛ ngalakutijennañi

ilbatuna *Baumstumpf.* ◇ tree stump. Ⓛ tamala mutunta

ilbéuma *hinterlassen (des Verstorbenen, der sein Weib und Kinder zurückläßt).* ◇ leave behind (deceased man who leaves his wife and children behind). Ⓛ alapunkukatiñi Ⓓ delkina, gilbarina

ilbeulalama *verlassen (trotzig seine Eltern).* ◇ to leave (defiantly ones' parents). Ⓛ alapunkukatiñi, alawontikatiñi

ilberala *sehr schön (daliegen).* ◇ very beautiful (lie). Ⓛ taltirknarañi

ilberinja *sehr schön (aussehen, Farbe).* ◇ very beautiful (appearance, colour). Ⓛ taltirkumbani

ilbia *Strauch spec., nadelförmige Blätter und gelbe Blüten.* ◇ bush species with needle-like leaves and yellow blossoms. Ⓛ ilbii

ilbila *der an den Mulgazweigen befindlicher Honig.* ◇ honey on mulga branches. Ⓛ aultjiri

ilbirba *große Blätter (Gummiblätter), kleine Gummizweige.* ◇ big leaves (gum leaves), small gum twigs. Ⓛ balbira, taljira, taljirba

ilbirtja *rote Laus.* ◇ red lice. Ⓛ lililba

ilbitjalbélama *herausziehen (z.B. den Speer aus einer Wunde, oder das Zauberholz aus dem Kranken).* ◇ pull out (e.g. spear out of wound or magic-wood out of sick person). Ⓛ altakaltanani

ilbmára *Tau.* ◇ dew. Ⓛ intjilpi Ⓓ buru

ilbmara-ultunda *Tautropfen.* ◇ dewdrops. Ⓛ intjilpi ultundu

ilbmarka *unbeschnittener (Junge).* ◇ not initiated (boy). Ⓛ kurari

ilbmarauma *um Beistand bitten, bitten, flehen.* ◇ beg for assistance, beg, implore. Ⓛ wonkatiriñi Ⓓ juajuangana

ilbmaraulama *um Beistand bitten, bitten, flehen.* ◇ beg for assistance, beg, implore. Ⓛ wonkatiriraïni

ilbmilbmaka rama *mit den Augen drohen.* ◇ threaten with eyes. Ⓛ wombanji inkulanañi Ⓓ milki tekibana

ilbminja *Asche.* ◇ ash. Ⓛ tunba

ilbmana *schwarze Honig-ameise.* ◇ black honeyant. Ⓛ ilbmani

ilbminta [Southern dialect] *cf.* **ekalta** *mächtig.* ◇ powerful. Ⓛ kanti

ilbmānta *Honig-Tropfen (die Honig-Blüten, die auf den Boden fallen).* ◇ drops of honey (honey blossoms that fall to the ground). Ⓛ tjilpuntu

ilbilbaraiwulama *(Wasser) von sich abschütteln (Tiere).* ◇ shake (water) off (animals). Ⓛ pinpintapungañi

ilboiuma *leugnen, nicht glauben, zweifeln.* ◇ deny, not believe, doubt. Ⓛ woiawatani

ilbórata (auch ilbárata) *fleißig.* ◇ industrious. Ⓛ atamba Ⓓ jigleri (jiljeri)

ilbótilbota *Strauch spec. weiße, fliederähnliche Blüten und dunkelgrüne, nadelförmige Blätter.* ◇ shrub species with white, lilac blossoms and dark green needle-shaped leaves. Ⓛ mulili

ilbōtja [Southern dialect] *ringneck-parrot.* ◇ ringneck parrot.

ilbula *Strauch spec. feine nadelförmige Blätter (tea-tree, ti-tree, Melaleuca glomerata).* ◇ shrub species with fine needle shaped leaves (*Melaleuca glomerata*, tea tree, ti tree). Ⓛ ilbili

ilbulata *eine Mulgaart mit hellen Blättern.* ◇ mulga species with light coloured leaves. Ⓛ manjiri

ilbuma *auffangen (tjata oder jelka beim Reinigen).* ◇ catch (tjata or jelka when cleaning). Ⓛ mamani

ilbunkura *schmutzig, mit Asche besudelt, nicht gereinigt.* ◇ dirty, soiled with ash, not cleaned. Ⓛ titi

ilelinkinaí? [Eastern dialect] *und* [Northern dialect], **ilakinaí?** [Northern dialect] *Was? (iwunai?).* ◇ what? (iwunai?). Ⓛ nai?

ilenga [Northern dialect] *weit.* ◇ far. Ⓛ wonma

ilengakilenga *weit von einander entfernt.* ◇ far apart from each other. Ⓛ wonmakuwonma

ilirerama *wachsen machen, schwellen machen (Brüste).* ◇ make grow, make swell (breasts). Ⓛ unkañi

ilenkuma *hervorkriechen aus dem Boden, aufsteigen gen. Himmel (z.B. die Larven).* ◇ crawl out of the ground, ascend to the sky (e.g. grubs). Ⓛ piralankȧñi

ilenkupenkuma *dupl. hervorkommen, aufsteigen (wie oben).* ◇ (reduplication) come out, ascend. Ⓛ piralankanȧñi

ilentja *Kakadu.* ◇ cockatoo. Ⓛ ilentji

ilia *Emu.* ◇ emu, *Dromaius novaehollandiae.* Ⓛ kalaia Ⓓ warugatti

iliapa *Emu-Schwanzfedern, lange Emufedern.* ◇ emu-tailfeathers, long emu feathers. Ⓛ aturu

ilia punga *(Emu-Haare), die kurzen Federn des Emu.* ◇ (emu hair), short emu feathers. Ⓛ kalaia ngalbu

iliakwata *Emu-Ei.* ◇ emu egg. Ⓛ kalaia ngokuta

iléngа *Emu-(penis).* ◇ emu-(penis). Ⓛ kalu

ntjiïkaputa *kleines Emu.* ◇ small emu. Ⓛ akala, akalba Ⓓ ilbula

ilelta *der Bast.* ◇ fibre. Ⓛ ilelta Ⓓ ilbula

ilíara *junge Männer.* ◇ young adult men. Ⓛ maliara Ⓓ ilbula

iliárra *Verwandtschaft, Vaters Schwesters Tochters Mann und Mutters Bruders Tochters Mann.* ◇ kinship, father's sister's daughter's husband and mother's brother's daughter's husband. Ⓛ altali? ('?' added by CS) Ⓓ ilbula

ililbera [Northern dialect] *der graue Stamm (der ilbula) (ila-ilbera).* ◇ grey trunk (of ilbula) (ila-ilbera). Ⓛ ngana lililba

ililbmarilbmara *vielstandig (Strauch).* ◇ bulky (shrub). Ⓛ ngana intjilbatara

ilina *wir beide (ein Bruder zum andern Bruder).* ◇ we two (brother to a brother). Ⓛ ngali

ilinanta *wir beide (ein Mann zu. s. Frau).* ◇ we two (husband to his wife). Ⓛ ngalita

ilinbinja *Anführer der Bluträcher.* ◇ leader of revenge party. Ⓛ teïra, teïrba Ⓓ mudlakutja? ('?' added by CS)

ilinja *Bund, Bündel.* ◇ bunch, bundle. Ⓛ tetirba

ilinjiuma [Northern dialect] *einwickeln, umwickeln, zusammendrehen (Schnur).* ◇ wrap, wind around, roll together (string). Ⓛ tetirpungañi

ilinjatuma [Northern dialect] *binden, fesseln.* ◇ tie, shackle. Ⓛ karbini, tetirpungañi

ilintarinja (ila+intarinja) *dicht zusammen stehende Stämme.* ◇ trunks standing densely together. Ⓛ alukuru

ilintarintara (ila+intarintara) *vielstandig, vielstämmig.* ◇ dense (tree trunks, stems, bushes). Ⓛ tȧtapȧrapara

ilirra *hell (Auge), gutaussehend, schön (Gestalt) (?), klar (Wasser).* ('?' added by CS). ◇ bright (eye), good looking, beautiful, clear (water). Ⓛ kaltaru

 For the modern spellings of these words, see the dictionaries and sources in reference list.

ilirrerama *hell werden, sich sonnen.* ◇ become light, sunbathe. Ⓛ kaltaruriñi

ilirrilama *hell machen (Auge), sich den Schlaf aus den Augen reiben, sich sonnen.* ◇ make bright (eye), rub sleep out of eyes, sunbathe. Ⓛ pitaltjiriñi, kaltaruriñi

ilirka *zusammengetrocknetes Aas (von Tieren), trockener Kadaver.* ◇ shrivelled carrion (of animals), dry carcass. Ⓛ tikila

alkna ilírra *ein halb-blindes oder ausgelaufenes Auge?* ('?' added by CS). ◇ Possibly meaning 'half-blind or run out eye'.

ilirtja *Furche, Rinne, Graben, Schlucht.* ◇ furrow, channel, ditch, gorge. Ⓛ woltara, ilirtji

ilirtjilama *Furche machen, Rinne machen.* ◇ make a channel. Ⓛ woltaranañi, ilirtjini

ilirtjibama *den Grund graben.* ◇ dig in the ground.

ilita [Northern dialect] *testiculi.* ◇ testicle. Ⓛ tulkur

ilitakama [Northern dialect] *kastrieren.* ◇ castrate. Ⓛ tulkur kuntani

ilitja [Southern dialect] *grün (Früchte), unreif, ungar (Fleisch).* ◇ green (fruit), unripe, not yet cooked (meat). Ⓛ wonka

ilitjera [Southern dialect] *kräftig, gesund.* ◇ strong, healthy. Ⓛ linkira

jilitjiïla *Rauschen (der Flügel), Flattern, Knarren (der Räder).* ◇ flapping (of wings), flutter, creaking (of wheels). Ⓛ tirkilwarañi

ilka *ruhig, windstill, seßhaft (Mensch).* ◇ quiet, calm, settled (human). Ⓛ kilki

alka *Felsplatte, Felsblock?* ◇ rock plate. ('?' added by CS). Ⓛ palpa

ilkanga *Felsplatte (Palm Creek), Felsblock.* ◇ rock plate, boulder, name of Palm Creek. Ⓛ walu

ilkarinjatua *böse Wesen, die sich unter Felsplatten aufhalten.* ◇ evil beings or bad spirits who live under rock plates; i.e. 'the ones living under rock plates' (Strehlow 1907: 12). Ⓛ katu bankalangu

ilkaia *Backe, Wange.* ◇ cheek. Ⓛ kanta, kantja Ⓓ ngadla

ilkaialta *Backenbart.* ◇ side burns. Ⓛ kantaïntu

ilkainama *sichten (Sämmereien).* ◇ winnow (seeds, grain). Ⓛ anparangañi

ilkalurkna *Ader.* ◇ artery, vain. Ⓛ ilkalurknu

ilkala *Sodabusch.* ◇ saltbush. Ⓛ tjilkala Ⓓ malto

ilkalatja *rot und weiß gestreifte Larven in den ilkala-Büschen.* ◇ red and white striped grubs in ilkala bushes. Ⓛ tjilkala

ilkakutja *Sturm.* ◇ storm.

illkaltaltua *sehr leicht, nicht schwer.* ◇ very light, not heavy. Ⓛ pirambi

ilkalabareria *Rückkehr-Bumerang.* ◇ returning boomerang. Ⓛ kikirikunu

ilkaiïlkaierama *aufständig werden.* ◇ become rebellious.

ilkama *schreien, brüllen, krähen.* ◇ scream, roar, crow. Ⓛ merañi Ⓓ maritjina

ilkalbilkama *fortwährend schreien.* ◇ scream continuously. Ⓛ meramerañi

ilkákama *einem nachschreien.* ◇ shout after someone. Ⓛ tjitini

ilkalélama *schreien machen, brüllen machen.* ◇ make cry, make roar. Ⓛ merataljini

ilkatjintjima, ilkatnatjintjima *schreien (Vögel) (beim Aufstehen), krähen (Hahn).* ◇ squawk (birds when awaking); crow (rooster). Ⓛ merarakalbañi, meramerarakalbañi

ilkatnitjitnitjalbuma *fortwährend schreien z.B. nach Brot.* ◇ scream constantly, e.g. for bread. Ⓛ meramerañi kulbara

ilkinja *Geschrei.* ◇ racket. Ⓛ meranji Ⓓ miritja

ilkamilkama *arm.* ◇ poor. Ⓛ maŕalba

ilkánama *vergießen.* ◇ spill, shed. Ⓛ alani

alua ilkanama *Blut vergießen.* ◇ shed blood. Ⓛ ngurka alani

ilkanjindama *auf dem Ellbogen gestützt liegen, sich auf den Ellbogen stützen.* ◇ lie propped up on elbow; prop up on elbow. Ⓛ nukupiti ngariñi, ngunanpiti ngariñi Ⓓ tintiterkana, nankaterina

ilkánkula *sehr schnell (Sturmwind, Pferd).* ◇ very fast (storm wind, horse). Ⓛ wollatura

ilkántuántua [Southern dialect] (**ilkaltaltua**) *sehr leicht.* ◇ very light. Ⓛ pirambi

ilkarkama [Southern dialect] *erschrecken.* ◇ get a fright. Ⓛ kokurkanȧñi

ilkaralama *ausstrecken (Glieder, Hände oder Füße) refl.* ◇ (reflexive) stretch out (limbs, hands or feet). Ⓛ tjiraratunañi Ⓓ ngurakatina

ilkartja *schuldig.* ◇ guilty. Ⓛ tali, talji

ilkatnanama *einen langen Schrei ausstoßen.* ◇ utter a long cry. Ⓛ meraratalkañi

ilkatoa [Northern dialect] *Pflanze mit gurkenähnlichen Früchten.* ◇ plant with a cucumber-like fruit. Ⓛ ilkuta

ílkata; patta ílkata; inka ílkata *fig. Rücken z.B.* ◇ figurative 'back'. Ⓛ taltu

patta ílkata *Bergrücken.* ◇ mountain ridge. Ⓛ puli taltu

inka ílkata *Knöchel.* ◇ foot knuckle. Ⓛ tjinna taltu

ílkata *Mulde aus Gummiholz.* ◇ bowl made of gumtree wood. Ⓛ biti

ilkáta *schmerzend, Schmerz.* ◇ painful, pain. Ⓛ mekina, mekinba

ilkatérama *Schmerzen, wehe tun.* ◇ in pain, hurt. Ⓛ mekinariñi Ⓓ ketjaketjana, pandrarina

ilkatintjama *anfangen zu schmerzen.* ◇ starting to hurt. Ⓛ mekingarañi

ilkatilkatoa [Northern dialect] *Pflanze spec.* ◇ plant species. Ⓛ ilkutilkuta

ilkelkerindama *auf der Seite liegen.* ◇ lie on side. Ⓛ ngilingili ngariñi, kultupiti ngariñi

ilkilja *das, was man gegessen hat, das Gegessene; das Verdaute, der Mist.* ◇ food eaten; digested food, stool. Ⓛ ilkilji

ilkēnama *überragen, größer machen als ein anderer.* ◇ tower over, make taller. Ⓛ alaủrkuni

ilkinja *Zeichen (am Körpe angebracht).* ◇ designs. Ⓛ (wolkatunata), wolka

ilkínjana *eine aus Kalk und kemba Blüten hergestellte Masse.* ◇ mixture of limestone and kemba blossoms. Ⓛ taṙitaṙi, aretaṙitaṙi

ilkitjera *Strauch (dead finish) mit kurzen Stacheln und gelben Blüten.* ◇ shrub (dead finish) with short needles and yellow flowers. Ⓛ kurara Ⓓ pararaka

ilkna *naß, feucht, weiß (Zahn).* ◇ wet, damp, white (tooth). Ⓛ tōpi Ⓓ ngapali, ngapatjanka

ilknamboba *mitten auf dem Wasser.* ◇ in the middle of the water. Ⓛ ilknangururba Ⓓ kunakalu

ilknilknilara *herabfließende Saft.* ◇ juice flowing down. Ⓛ kurungátangȧta

ilknama *trs. waschen, reinigen (streicheln).* ◇ (transitive) wash, clean (stroke). Ⓛ urini, paltjiñi Ⓓ kulirkana

ilknalama *refl. sich waschen.* ◇ (reflexive) wash. Ⓛ uriranañi Ⓓ kulirkaterina

ilknákama *absondern, abteilen, auslesen, auswählen, abspenstig machen.* ◇ separate, partition, select, choose, remove. Ⓛ akatatauani Ⓓ mulkana, tjirimalkana

ilknakatnétnama *zusammenzählen, auslesen und zusammenzählen, rechnen.* ◇ add together, select and count together, calculate. Ⓛ intjiiṅtjiñi Ⓓ windamana

ilknálama *sich aufrichen (nach dem Schlaf), sich strecken, sich dehnen (nach dem Schlaf).* ◇ get up, stretch (after sleep). Ⓛ watuni Ⓓ warpina, ngutana

alkna ilknalama *sich den Schlaf aus den Augen reiben.* ◇ rub sleep out of eyes. Ⓛ paltjiñi

ilknárintja *ein Speer aus agia Wurzeln verfertigt.* ◇ spear made of agia roots. Ⓛ mulu

ilknara *nackt, bloß.* ◇ naked, bare. Ⓛ ilknari, utita (nackt) Ⓓ palu

iknarilama *trs. von den Hülsen entblößen (jelka-Körner).* ◇ (transitive) strip off husk (jelka-seeds). Ⓛ ilknarinani

 For the modern spellings of these words, see the dictionaries and sources in reference list.

ilknariuma *abhäuten (Tiere), abklopfen (die Rinde von den Bäumen).* ◇ skin (animals), knock off (bark from trees). Ⓛ ngiripungañi

ikneléruma [Southern dialect] (= **alkneleruma**) *Gesicht vergehen vor Erschöpfung, verhungern.* ◇ fade from exhaustion, starve. Ⓛ kuruwiaringañi Ⓓ wariwarina

ilknua *testiculi.* ◇ testicle. Ⓛ ngambu

ilknuiltuma *kastrieren.* ◇ castrate. Ⓛ ngambu kuntani

ilknuinama *kastrieren.* ◇ castrate. Ⓛ ngambu manjiñi

ilkobana *Amme, Ernährer.* ◇ wet nurse, provider.

ilkóta *kleine gurkenähnliche Frucht.* ◇ small gherkin-like fruit. Ⓛ ilkuta, unbati

ilkótilkóta *rankende Pflanze mit roten Beeren (nicht gegessen), Melothria maderaspatana.* ◇ vine with red berries (not edible), *Melothria maderaspatana* now *Mukia maderaspatana* (Latz 1996). Ⓛ ilkutilkuta

alkúlialkúla lama *kreuz und quer wandern.* ◇ walk aimlessly. Ⓛ wabalbiwabalbi jennañi

ilkuma *essen, fressen.* ◇ eat. Ⓛ ngalkuñi Ⓓ táïna (tajina)

ilkulilkulalama *eilig essen (vor dem Aufbruch).* ◇ eat in a hurry (before departure). Ⓛ ngalkungalkukatiñi

ilkubilkuma *fortwährend essen.* ◇ eat continuously. Ⓛ ngalkungalkuñi

kwakala ilkuma *fortwährend essen, viel essen.* ◇ eat continuously, eat a lot. Ⓛ kututu ngalkuñi

tnolbala ilkuma *unmäßig essen.* ◇ eat excessively. Ⓛ bulbanka ngalkuñi

ilkurkna *der dicke Saft (der Larven und Beeren).* ◇ thick juice (of grubs and berries). Ⓛ alkurknu

ilkwátera *zwei zusammen (sitzen), beide zusammen, ein Paar, Gesellschaft, Gemeinschaft.* ◇ two together (sit), both together, a couple, society, community. Ⓛ malpa, malparara Ⓓ milpara

ilkwaterilama *mit einem anderen gehen.* ◇ go with someone else. Ⓛ malpantanañi

iloa *viele, cr. 20.* ◇ many, circa 20. Ⓛ nguangua

iloamiloa *zu 20 u. 20.* ◇ 20 and 20. Ⓛ nguanguakanguangu

iloamulkurantema *sehr viele (wieder).* ◇ very many (again). Ⓛ nguanguatara

ilóara *Salz, Salzkruste, Salzsee; in Tjur. Gesängen: weißes (Stirnband).* ◇ salt, salt crust, salt lake; Lake Lewis. Ⓛ pando, muluuru

ilóatja *hilflos, sterbenskrank.* ◇ helpless, very sick. Ⓛ aratalenku

iltinjingambura *Zwietracht.* ◇ discord.

ilóra *Eidechse, sp. (mit großem Kopf).* ◇ lizard species (with big head). Ⓛ wollura

ilta ilanbilanga *Festung.* ◇ fortress.

ilta *Haus, Hütte.* ◇ house, hut, humpy. Ⓛ minta, kanku Ⓓ punga

ilta-toppa *Dach (flache Dach).* ◇ roof (flat roof). Ⓛ minta-tana Ⓓ punga ngalpa

ilta-kaputa *Dach.* ◇ roof. Ⓛ minta-katalara

iltaljiltalja *einsam (im Lagerplatz zurückbleiben).* ◇ lonely (stay back at camp). Ⓛ kutuntu

iltairama *klingen, tönen, lauten (intrs.), schnalzen (mit dem Munde).* ◇ sound, ring, toll (intransitive), smack with mouth. Ⓛ nguntalmanañi

iltairatuma *klagend zusammen schlagen.* ◇ hit together wailing. Ⓛ timbilbmanañi, timbilpungañi

iltinkiltinka *Glocke (n).* ◇ bell.

iltama *schalten, zanken.* ◇ scold, quarrel; growl, swear; burn (wood); bark (dog). Ⓛ warkiñi Ⓓ jatibana, jatijiribana

iltarama *sich streiten (mit Worten).* ◇ fight (with words). Ⓛ warkirapungañi Ⓓ jatamalina

iltalbatuma *klatschen (mit den Händen).* ◇ clap (with hands). Ⓛ pantulbmanañi

iltama *ausziehen (Federn), abstreifen (Tjur. Schmuck).* ◇ pluck (feathers), strip. Ⓛ puntani

iltariltara *das Klappern, Stampfen (der Hufe).* ◇ clatter, stomp (of hoofs).

iltára *klappern, dröhnen, lauten.* ◇ clatter, roar, sound; sound of feet when someone is coming. Ⓛ talala

iltarkama *klappern, knarren (Ästen), ächzen (Stämme im Winde).* ◇ rattle, creak (branches), groan (trunks in the wind). Ⓛ tirkilbmanañi, tirkiltukariñi

iltarbakaturuma *klappernd aneinaderschlagen (Speere, Früchte), ächzend sich reiben (Wurzeln).* ◇ clattering against each other (spears, fruit), rub groaning against each other (roots). Ⓛ tirkiltukatiñi

iltarkatnauma *klappern (der Speer auf der Felsplatte).* ◇ rattle (the spear on the rock plate). Ⓛ tirkilbmara okalingañi

iltariltarauma *erschallen lassen, läuten (trs.)* ◇ let ring, toll (transitive). Ⓛ takaltakaltjingañi Ⓓ katangiribana (*läuten*: to ring)? ('?' added by CS)

iltariltara *stampfen (der mit den Füßen beim gehen stampft).* ◇ stomp.

iltjakilama *ausrüsten (zur Reise).* ◇ prepare (for a journey); go on a long journey, going camping a long way away.

iltjantarba *einhändig.* ◇ one handed.

iltemba *eine kleine Mulde aus ininta angefertigt, mit welcher Teig in Asche geschoben wird.* ◇ small bowl made out of ininta wood, used to push dough into ashes. Ⓛ altimbi

iltjikélama *auf die Hand legen (Tjur. z.B.)* ◇ lay on hand. Ⓛ marankanañi

iltaratuma *klopfen (an der Tür), zerklopfen (Samen).* ◇ knock (on the door), grind (seeds). Ⓛ takaltjingañi Ⓓ nandranandrana, tatangiribana

iltjambiltjanga *Blasen (in der Hand).* ◇ blisters (on hand). Ⓛ biltjinbiltjin

iltankutja *friedlich, nicht zanksüchtig.* ◇ peaceful, not quarrelsome. Ⓛ ngalutu

iltankua *mit Wasser sich bespritzend, sich abkühlend.* ◇ to cool with splashes of water. Ⓛ altunka

iltariuma *kneifen, zwicken.* ◇ pinch, nip. Ⓛ mintini Ⓓ milkana

íltira *Steinmesser (spec.)* ◇ stone knife (species). Ⓛ kaltjiti

iltátuma *ausrotten, alle umbringen, erschlagen.* ◇ exterminate, kill everybody, slay. Ⓛ muriripungañi

iltira *hell, weiß, Hornhaut auf dem Auge.* ◇ white, cornea (on eye). Ⓛ kaltjiti, tinku

iltirerama *weiß werden, hell werden.* ◇ turn white, lighten. Ⓛ kaltjitiriñi

ilta [Northern dialect] **alta** *Tag.* ◇ day. Ⓛ julta

ílterama [Northern dialect] *conf.* **álterama** *Tag werden.* ◇ become day, daybreak. Ⓛ jultaringañi

iltjerkniltjerkna *rötlich sein (Känguruh Haare; Früchte z.B. Feigen).* ◇ be reddish (kangaroo hair; fruit e.g. bush figs). Ⓛ taltirtaltira

iltirbminjatuma *Takt schlagen.* ◇ beat time. Ⓛ tirkiltipungani, timbilbmanañi

iltiákama, iltíltakama *schnell töten, zaubern.* ◇ kill quickly, make magic. Ⓛ putulbmanañi, kutukanañi

iltjalura *Handballen.* ◇ hand ball. Ⓛ marawollura

iltja *Hand.* ◇ hand. Ⓛ măra

- **iltja ulbura** *die Finger (mit Ausnahme des Daumens).* ◇ fingers (except thumb). Ⓛ mara walpuru
- **iltjakantja** *Finger.* ◇ finger. Ⓛ maraakantji
- **iltjatjenja** *Mittelfinger.* ◇ middle finger. Ⓛ marawara
- **iltjatnata** *Handteller.* ◇ palm of hand. Ⓛ marawila
- **iltjakurkakurka** *der kleine Finger.* ◇ little finger. Ⓛ mara ngali
- **iltjatoppa** *Handrücken.* ◇ back of hand. Ⓛ maratana
- **iltjamákura, iltjanékua (iltjamēkua)** *Daumen.* ◇ thumb. Ⓛ maramámara, marapantji
- **iltjatuatja** *[Fingertal] Raum zwischen den Fingern.* ◇ [finger valley] space between fingers. Ⓛ maratinki

iltjingiltjala *auf [mit] den Händen z.B.* ◇ on (with) the hands. Ⓛ maranka

 For the modern spellings of these words, see the dictionaries and sources in reference list.

iltja tulama *Hände klatschen.* ◇ clap hands. Ⓛ mara pulpanjinañi

iltjingiltjala ngama *auf den Händen tragen.* ◇ carry in hands. Ⓛ maranka katiñi

iltja irkulumbatninama *zwei Personen halten ihre Hände zusammen.* ◇ two people holding their hands together. Ⓛ mara witira kanjini

iltja rakuinerama *Hände halten.* ◇ hold hands. Ⓛ mara tintjirapungañi

iltja irkuruma *Hände halten.* ◇ hold hands. Ⓛ mara witirapungañi

iltjangantaléa *freigebig, Spender, der wirklich austeilt, Wirt (n).* ◇ generous, true giver, host. Ⓛ maramunta

iltjamiltja *früh, beim Aufgang der Sonne (die Strahlen der aufgehenden Sonne).* ◇ early, at sunrise (rays of rising sun). Ⓛ karawollawolla, purupuru

iltjéltja *mantis, starkes Vorderbein, grüne Heuschrecken.* ◇ mantis, strong foreleg, green grasshoppers. Ⓛ wiltjiltji

iltjantja *Baum, spec. (beefwood), schmale, lederartige Blätter (cr 25 cm lang, ½ cm breit), Grevillea striata.* ◇ tree species (beefwood), narrow leather-like leaves (appr. 25 cm long, ½ cm wide), *Grevillea striata.* Ⓛ iltilba

iltutjarenalama *zerbrechen (intrs.), umbrechen (Baum), verfallen (Mauer).* ◇ break (intransitive), break (tree), collapse (wall). Ⓛ bultulukatiñi

iltjarkna *Darm, die dünnen Därme.* ◇ gut, thin guts. Ⓛ bilinji

iltuma *schneiden, zerschneiden (z.B. Fleisch).* ◇ cut, cut up (meat). Ⓛ kuntani

iltjatua [Northern dialect] *cf.* altjōta. ◇ grass species. Ⓛ iltjota

iltjeljera [Northern dialect] *Eidechse mit Schwanzstumpf.* ◇ lizard with knob tail. Ⓛ iltjiljari

iltjénma *Krebs.* ◇ yabby, crab, crayfish. Ⓛ iltjenmi Ⓓ kundidiri (kurundi?) ('?' added by CS)

iltjilitjaltjilérama *langsam heranschleichen (Katzen).* ◇ creep up slowly (cat). Ⓛ maratjila

iltjikiltjika, iltjinkiltjika *faltig, gerunzelt, häßlich, mager.* ◇ wrinkled, creased, ugly, scrawny. Ⓛ wiljiwiljirba Ⓓ winjiwinjiri

iltjerama *ausruhen, ruhen, sich erholen.* ◇ rest, recover. Ⓛ iltjaringañi Ⓓ pillari ngamana, ngara ngamana, datturu ngamana

íltura *[unclear].* Ⓛ ilturu

iltjulbura *10.* ◇ does not mean '10' today, but 'many hands'. Ⓛ marawalpuru

iltjulburaminkulbura *20.* ◇ 20. Ⓛ marawalpurubatjinna walpuru. (Today, the word 'pala' is used in Aranda and Loritja to indicate numbers, it follows an English number, e.g. 20 pala, 110 pala.)

iltminterama *sich steif fühlen.* ◇ feel stiff. Ⓛ tewilariñi

ilulama [Northern dialect] *herabsteigen.* ◇ descend. Ⓛ wararakatiñi

ilulintjilama [Northern dialect] *cf.* **lulintjilama**, *herunterkommen.* ◇ descend. Ⓛ ngalawararakatiñi

ilultara *Princess Alexandra parrakeet.* ◇ Princess Alexandra's Parrot (*Polytelis alexandrae*). Ⓛ ilulturu

ilúka *Fichte.* ◇ tree species. Ⓛ wolknati

iluma *sterben, auflösen, einziehen, austrocknen (Wasser), auslöschen (Licht).* ◇ die, disintegrate, dry out (water), extinguish, switch off (light), put out (a fire). Ⓛ iluñi Ⓓ palina

ilulinlama *tot am Boden liegen.* ◇ lie dead on the ground. Ⓛ ilura ngariñi

iltulbiuma *umbringen, trs. einem das Leben nehmen.* ◇ to kill, (transitive) to take someone's life.

ilunama *auslöschen (Feuer).* ◇ extinguish (fire). Ⓛ iluntanañi Ⓓ palimana

ilutjikilutjikérama *in den letzen Zügen liegen.* ◇ dying, passing away. Ⓛ iluntakiluntaku ngariñi

iloatja *hilflos, rettungslos.* ◇ helpless, doomed. Ⓛ aratalenku

ilulupuluma *langsam herabsteigen.* ◇ slowly descend. Ⓛ wararakatinánñi

iltulbailtuia *sehr kalt.* ◇ very cold. Ⓛ peria, kuntakuntara

ilumba *Baum spec. (lime-wood) weiße Rinde, Eucalyptus tesseralis.* ◇ tree with white bark (lime-wood), ghost gum, *Eucalyptus tessearis*? possibly *E. papuana* (Latz 1996). Ⓛ tōta úlupa

ilumbartja *Gummi des ilumba.* ◇ gum of ghost gumtree. Ⓛ úlumbartji

ilumbalitnana *giftige Schlange, cr. 3 Fuß lang. Rücken: grau-grünlich. Bauch: gelb.* ◇ poisonous snake, about 3 feet long. Back: grey-green. Belly: yellow. Ⓛ tota

ilunama *auslöschen (Feuer), verderben (trs.)* ◇ extinguish (fire), spoil (transitive). Ⓛ iluntanañi

ilulatanama *ersticken (vom Rauch oder wenn etwas [unclear]), verderben.* ◇ suffocate, spoil.

ilungángala inama *rauben.* ◇ steal. Ⓛ kunnabakaranka manjini

ilura *dick, stark (Mann), fett, fleischig, dicke Rinde (Baum).* ◇ thick, strong (man), fat, meaty, thick bark (tree). Ⓛ wolku

ilúrra *Vogel spec. (klein, weiß).* ◇ bird species (small, white). Ⓛ ilurru

ilura [Northern dialect]; **alkna ilura** *entzündet, geschwollen; entzündetes Auge.* ◇ inflamed, swollen; inflamed eye. Ⓛ iltilti, kuru iltilti

ilutjikilutjikerama *in den letzten Zügen liegen.* ◇ dying. Ⓛ iluntakiluntaku ngariñi

iltjabotta *Handballen, Faust, z.B. iltjabottala ilknima.* ◇ hand ball, fist.

ilunjunkuna *sterblich.* ◇ mortal.

ilunjalkua *sterblich.* ◇ mortal.

ima *zum Tod verurteilt, in Todesgefahr.* ◇ sentenced to death, in peril. Ⓛ meri

imilama *zum Tode helfen, verurteilen.* ◇ to sentence (to death). Ⓛ meeriwalkuni

imerinja *der Totschläger.* ◇ murderer. Ⓛ muranu

imalalkuja *in Todesgefahr, Trübsal.* ◇ in peril, sadness, sorrow. Ⓛ merimata

imalalkura *in Todesgefahr, Trübsal.* ◇ in peril, sadness, sorrow. Ⓛ meringuanba

imakimaka *Trübsal.* ◇ sadness, sorrow.

imambula *fast tot, dem Tode nahe.* ◇ nearly dead, close to death. Ⓛ jupataka

imakimakerama *sich verderben.* ◇ spoil (reflexive).

imanama *hinhalten (einen etwas zu geben).* ◇ offer. Ⓛ itoanáñi

imaninja *Preis, Kampfpreis.* ◇ price; olden times, long time ago, very old.

imanai *halt es ihm hin (um es ihm zu geben).* ◇ offer it to him. Ⓛ titalai! itōrai!

inkai! *halt deine Hand auf! (um zu nehmen)!* ◇ take it! Ⓛ inkai!

imankarbuna *vor cr. 5 Monaten.* ◇ circa five months ago; quite a while ago. Ⓛ raua kutuba

imankulkura *vor cr. 6 Monaten oder länger.* ◇ circa 6 months ago or more. Ⓛ raua nguanba

imanka knara *vor cr. 9 Monaten.* ◇ about nine months ago; long time ago. Ⓛ raua puntu

imanka indora *vor cr. 1 Jahr.* ◇ about one year ago. Ⓛ raua lenku

imankaparatoa *vor cr. 2 Jahren.* ◇ circa two years ago. Ⓛ rauakatoa

imankuntuara *vor cr. 4 Jahren.* ◇ circa four years ago. Ⓛ rauanka wirili

imanka *einst (vor mehreren Monaten, vor cr. 3–4 Monaten).* ◇ once (a few months ago, about 3–4 months ago); long ago; once upon a time, once; olden time. Ⓛ raua Ⓓ waru, warula

imankuntuarakala *vor cr. 10–16 Jahren.* ◇ about 10–16 years ago. Ⓛ rauanka wirilita

imankinja *einstig.* ◇ once, former. Ⓛ rauata Ⓓ warawaru

imankuramankura *weithin reichend (Äste).* ◇ far reaching (branches). Ⓛ tuntawoljiwolji

imankakata; imankulkura *vor sehr vielen Jahren; neulich, vor 6 Monaten.* ◇ many years ago. Ⓛ rauakata; raua nguanba

imara *Mistelzweig (Loranthus linophyllus).* ◇ mistletoe branch (*Loranthus linophyllus* now *Amyema* spp. or *Lysiana* spp. (Latz 1996)). Ⓛ nenkininba

 For the modern spellings of these words, see the dictionaries and sources in reference list.

imararinja *die in Mistelzweigen sich aufhalt. bösen Wesen.* ◇ wicked beings or bad spirits who dwell in mistletoe; 'mistletoe inhabitants' i.e. imara (mistletoe) -rinja (belonging to) (Strehlow 1907: 12). Ⓛ nenkingurara

imankangaaltjirangamballa *von Ewigkeit her.* ◇ an eternity ago, ages ago. Ⓛ rauantitalenku

imatiuma [Northern dialect] *cf.* matiuma. ◇ bind, wind around. Ⓛ juntunañi

imatubara *cf.* matubara. ◇ shackled. Ⓛ junba

imbalama *(einen) allein lassen, zurücklassen.* ◇ leave behind. Ⓛ wontira jennañi

imbakalama (imbama-kalama) *abfallen, sich ablösen.* ◇ fall off, detach. Ⓛ nalburtalkañi

imbalalama *zurücklassen, verlassen.* ◇ leave behind, abandon. Ⓛ wontikatiñi

imaturba [Northern dialect] *zusammen gewickelt, unentwickelt (Brüste).* ◇ not developed (breasts). Ⓛ mulbakanta

imbalalbuma *verlassen (Lagerplatz).* ◇ abandon (camp). Ⓛ wontirakulbañi

imanka-altjirangamuntuarakala *in grauer Vorzeit.* ◇ before time began. Ⓛ tukutita, wirilikata

imbalarénama *lassen (geschehen), erlauben.* ◇ let (happen), permit. Ⓛ wontirijenni

imba *Hülle, die die Larven zurück lassen.* ◇ cocoon left behind by larva. Ⓛ imbu

imbala(w)úma *gehen, scheiden (von Seite des Mannes), entlassen, erlassen.* ◇ go, depart, dismiss. Ⓛ wontiratalkañi Ⓓ worrani patana

imararutnitjalbuma *(viele Vögel) kreisen in der Luft.* ◇ (many birds) are circling in the sky. Ⓛ tariri ninañi kulbara

imararutnilitjilama *im Kreise herumfliegen (Vögel).* ◇ to circle (birds). Ⓛ tariripungañi-jenkula

imbalbimbuma *verlassen, im Stich lassen (die Angehörigen des Lagerplatzes).* ◇ abandon, forsake (kin of a camp). Ⓛ wontiwontiñi

imbákama *zurückhalten vom Gehen (durch Worte oder mit Gewalt).* ◇ hold back from leaving (with words or force). Ⓛ walitunañi

imbana *Eigentum, (das ein anderer zu lassen (imbuma) hat, nicht nehmen darf).* ◇ property that no other person may take; special, important. Ⓛ matubura

imankangala *je, jemals.* ◇ ever.

imbanakana *Almosen.* ◇ alm.

imbanama *vorbeigehen, vorübergehen.* ◇ pass by, go by. Ⓛ mawontiñi

imbánama *einen zurücklassen, ihm zuvorkommen.* ◇ leave someone behind, preempt. Ⓛ wontira bakañi

imbanimbana *gehörig, zu eigen sein.* ◇ belonging to. Ⓛ matuburamatubura

imbaljinama *trs. fortschicken.* ◇ (transitive) send away.

imbanintuma *verschonen, pflegen (einen Kranken).* ◇ spare, nurse (a sick person). Ⓛ purintunañi

imbara ngalakana *Vorbild.* ◇ (role) model.

imbara *Zeichen, Linie, Umriß, Abdruck (Fuß), Jahresringe.* ◇ sign, design, line, outline, imprint (foot), year rings. Ⓛ ninka Ⓓ malka

imbara knaragata *bunt, bemalt z.B. mantara.* ◇ colourful, painted, e.g. bag. Ⓛ ninka puntutara

imbarutnulama *Schmuck abstreifen.* ◇ remove decorations. Ⓛ puntani

imbarakama *stehen lassen, nicht umhauen (imperf. imbakaraka er lies stehen).* ◇ let stand, not cut down (imperf. he let stand).

imbariuma *die Zeichen eingravieren.* ◇ engrave designs. Ⓛ ninkawonniñi

initjinjima *wieder nehmen.* ◇ take again.

imbatja *Spur (Schlange), Fußabdruck, Eindruck.* ◇ track (snake), footprint, impression. Ⓛ ninka

inka imbatja *Fußabdruck.* ◇ footprint. Ⓛ tjinna ninka

imbatabiwuna *Spinne (kleinere Art).* ◇ smaller spider species. Ⓛ imbakunkun

inbatnalama *laufen lassen, fahren lassen (Kleid), nicht nachgehen.* ◇ let go, let slip (dress), not follow. Ⓛ wontirajennañi

imbátnama *einen laufen lassen, nicht nachlaufen.* ◇ let go, not go after. Ⓛ wontirabatani

imbembalbanáma *an einem vorbeigehen, ihn nicht mitnehmen.* ◇ go past somebody, not take him along. Ⓛ mawontiraïni

imboba *halbtot.* ◇ half dead.

imbouma *(reife Früchte) abschütteln.* ◇ shake off (ripe fruit). Ⓛ pinpintipungañi

imbuma *lassen, sein lassen, vorübergehen.* ◇ let, let be, pass by. Ⓛ wontiñi Ⓓ worrarana

imbalama *allein lassen.* ◇ leave alone. Ⓛ wontirajennañi

imbalalama *zurücklassen, liegen lassen (s. Eigentum).* ◇ leave behind (his property). Ⓛ wontikatini Ⓓ worrarijiribana

imbalalbuma *verlassen (den Lagerplatz) um Heim zukehren.* ◇ leave (camp) to return home. Ⓛ wontirakulbani

imbalarénama *erlauben.* ◇ allow, permit. Ⓛ wontirijenni Ⓓ manunikurana

imbalawuma *entlassen.* ◇ dismiss, discharge. Ⓛ wontiratalkañi

imbánama, imbaranama *einen zurücklassen, ihm zuvorkommen.* ◇ leave behind, beat him. Ⓛ wontira bakañi, wonkirapunkula bakañi

imbiltja [Northern dialect] *menschenleer (Platz).* ◇ deserted (place).

imbulkura *große graue Heuschrecke.* ◇ large grey grasshopper. Ⓛ ambulkuri

imbulkna *vernarbt, Narbe, Mal.* ◇ scared, scar, mark. Ⓛ mēlala Ⓓ tjinpiri

imbulknérama *vernarben, heilen.* ◇ scar over, heal (wound). Ⓛ melalariñi

imintjera [Northern dialect] *cf.* **mentera** *Fischwehr.* ◇ fish weir, fish trap. Ⓛ imintjiri

ímpopa *angespeert, zu Tode verwundet.* ◇ speared, mortally wounded. Ⓛ impepi

imitjima *vor langer langer Zeit.* ◇ a long, long time ago. Ⓛ iwaritamunu

imora, antana *Opossum.* ◇ possum, *Trichosurus vulpecula.* Ⓛ waiuta, nunta, witjulú, witjulu Ⓓ pildra

inakitja = lalitja *Beere spec., Carrissa Brownii.* ◇ conkerberry, *Carissa lanceolata* (Latz 1996). Ⓛ ngamunburu

imuntunguntungérama [Northern dialect] *sehr alt werden (Mensch, Baum), zerschlissen (Kleider).* ◇ grow very old (human beings, trees), torn (clothes). Ⓛ lakalakaringañi

inalama *reifen (Früchte).* ◇ ripen (fruit). Ⓛ panjaruriñi

inaltjarerama [Northern dialect] *einander wiedersehen.* ◇ see each other again.

inalanga, tjili [Southern dialect] *Igel, Ameisenigel.* ◇ echidna, *Tachyglossus aculeatus.* Ⓛ inalingi, tjilka

inalbuma *zurücknehmen.* ◇ to take back. Ⓛ manjirakulbañi

inama *nehmen, holen, abpflücken, fangen.* ◇ take, fetch, gather, catch. Ⓛ manjini Ⓓ manina

inalama *aufnehmen.* ◇ pick up. Ⓛ manjirangarañi

inalbuma *zurücknehmen.* ◇ take back. Ⓛ manjirakulbañi Ⓓ manina tikana

inanama *mitnehmen.* ◇ take along. Ⓛ mamánjini

inátnanama *schnell nehmen, an sich reißen.* ◇ take quickly, seize. Ⓛ manjiratalkañi

initjika lama, kwatja initjika lai! *holen, hol Wasser!* ◇ get, get water! Ⓛ manjintaku jennañi Ⓓ manijiribana

inalala nama *sich weithin zerstreuen, um Wild zu holen.* ◇ spread out to hunt game. Ⓛ manjiri-ngarañi

inbentiuma *abwerfen (ein Baum die Früchte).* ◇ throw off (tree its fruit).

inbánama *einen hinhalten, warten lassen.* ◇ hold up somebody, let wait.

inarkama *glänzen (Sterne).* ◇ shine (stars).

inbarauma *nötigen (zum Schwatzen).* ◇ force (to talk).

inapa *ein breiter über der Brust gemalte Streifen.* ◇ broad stripe painted over chest. Ⓛ ngarkabāla

inangantarba *einarmig.* ◇ one armed.

inbakitnanama *trs. einen überreden, überzeugen.* ◇ (transitive) persuade someone, convince.

inilalama *bekommen, mitnehmen.* ◇ receive, take along. Ⓛ manjilkatiñi

inilalbuma *nachdem man erhalten umkehren, mit nehmen.* ◇ return after receiving (obtaining), take along. Ⓛ manjirakulbañi

ininilalbuma *etwas genommen habend, umkehren.* ◇ having taken something, turn around or leave. Ⓛ manjimanjirakulbañi

inilopalama *einsammeln (Cikaden).* ◇ collect (cicadas). Ⓛ manjimanjirangarañi

inilabuma *ablesen (z.B. Raupen).* ◇ pick off (e.g. caterpillars). Ⓛ muntupunkulaïni, manjiraïni

inanama *mitnehmen.* ◇ take. Ⓛ mamanjini

inangiwunjiwunja *dünne Arme (haben).* ◇ thin arms (have). Ⓛ jerrikewinjiwinji

inangatjulbara *dicke Arme.* ◇ thick arms. Ⓛ jerri-lunku (*sehr groß*: very big)

inangara *sehr fest, sehr hart (Felsen), streng (Haar).* ◇ very solid, very hard (rock), tight (hair). Ⓛ manga

inanga *Arm, Vorderbein, Flügel, Ast.* ◇ arm, front leg, wing, branch. Ⓛ jerri Ⓓ nguna (*Oberarm*), ngunakutja (*Schwungfeder*)

inangerelalama *Kreise ziehen, schweben (Vögel in der Luft).* ◇ circle, hover (birds). Ⓛ ngungarirekula jennañi

inangerelanama *fortwährend hin und her bewegen (Körper).* ◇ move continuously back and forth (body). Ⓛ ngungari ninarananñi

inangara nama *bleiben, sich aufhalten.* ◇ stay, remain. Ⓛ ngungari ninañi

inankala *weise, gelehrt, bekannt.* ◇ wise, learned, known. Ⓛ atirbi, taka (*weise*) Ⓓ milkila

inapakaltjia *Eidechse (Amphibolurus pictus).* ◇ lizard (*Amphibolurus pictus* now *Ctenophorus pictus* (Atlas of Living Australia. n.d.)). Ⓛ inapakaltji

inara *furchtlos, geduldig (die Strafe auf sich nehmen).* ◇ fearless, patient (endure punishment). Ⓛ inturku

inangararenalama *Hände auf den Rücken legen.* ◇ put hands on back. Ⓛ tananguntjiri ninakatiñi

inatnanama *schnell nehmen, an sich reißen.* ◇ take quickly, grab. Ⓛ manjiratalkañi

inatnama *abtun, wegnehmen, berauben, davontun.* ◇ take away, steal. Ⓛ manjiratalkañi

inangajerama *Zweige fortwährend bewegen.* ◇ move branches continuously. Ⓛ ngungaraninañi

inatjai! *interj. nach Konja = Arme, Bedauernswerter.* ◇ interjection after 'Konja' meaning 'poor thing!' Ⓛ alturunkai!

imbalalama *nachdem man den Lagerplatz verlassen hat, weiter gehen.* ◇ after leaving the camp, move on. Ⓛ matalkaringañi

inbuma *treten (auf etwas).* ◇ tread (on something).

inba *übrig geblieben, allein gelassen (Kind).* ◇ left over, left alone (child). Ⓛ kulu, umbanki

inbakama *verbinden, einhacken (Finger in Finger eines andern).* ◇ hold (with finger someone else's finger). Ⓛ wollitunañi

inbakama *abwendig machen (z.B. noa).* ◇ entice away (e.g. husband, wife). Ⓛ wollitunañi Ⓓ katjirimana

inbaratnuma *auseinanderziehen (Haar zum Spinnen).* ◇ pull apart (hair for spinning). Ⓛ erewiltjini

inbantakama *aushacken, auspicken (z.B. Augen).* ◇ peck out (e.g. eyes). Ⓛ wintalpungañi

inbaraparama *auseinanderziehen (Haar zum Spinnen).* ◇ pull apart (hair for spinning). Ⓛ erewiltjiwiltjini

inbanama *überschreiten, überspringen (über Zaun).* ◇ cross, jump over (fence). Ⓛ matabulukatiñi Ⓓ tankarana

inbánana *feuchte Boden, feuchte Erde.* ◇ damp ground, damp soil. Ⓛ anbununu

inbarka *Tausendfüßler.* ◇ centipede; an evil spirit being in the form of a gigantic centipede that comes with the south wind or in a storm from the south (Strehlow 1907: 14). When an inbarka bites a person three times, it is believed that death is imminent, because this was not an ordinary centipede, but an evil being in the form of an inbarka (Strehlow 1907: 13). Ⓛ kanbarka Ⓓ tiltiri

inbenba *kleiner Vogel, gelber Kopf, Rückenfedern grau, gelblicher Schimmer, Flügel und Schwanzfedern grau mit gelben Außenrand, schwarzer Schnabel, schmales weißes Halsband. 1) bee-eater; 2) yellow throated miner (Myzantha flavigula).* ◇ small bird with yellow head, grey back-feathers, yellow gleam, grey wing- and tail-feathers with yellow edge, black beak, small white neckband. 1. Bee eater 2. Yellow throated miner (*Myzantha flavigula* now *Manorina flavigula* (Pizzey and Knight 2007)). Ⓛ bilbil

inbititjititja *voller Narben, narbig.* ◇ full of scars, scarred. Ⓛ irbinirbini, irtalirtali

inbalauka *sich widerrechlich aneignen, Dieb (z.B. ebmanna).* ◇ acquire unlawfully, thief. Ⓛ wararakatinguta

inbilanama *hineinkriechen (in hohlen Ast).* ◇ crawl (into hollow tree). Ⓛ wararakatiñi

inbitjera, (arkularkua) *Kuckuck-Eule.* ◇ cuckoo-owl. Ⓛ kurr-kurr

inbentitnama *abfressen (Raupen), kahlfressend stehen.* ◇ (caterpillars) eat, eat bare. Ⓛ karpungañi

inbia ndarama *Frauen austauschen.* ◇ exchange wives. Ⓛ kutilba jungañi

inbora *schwer (Last).* ◇ heavy (burden); heavy, hard, difficult (language). Ⓛ lauanba Ⓓ mati

inbilinditjalbuma *hineinkriechen und sich in der Hütte niederwerfen (nach der Heimkehr).* ◇ crawl into hut and throw oneself down (after returning home). Ⓛ wararakatiñi kulbara

inbótna *Hagel.* ◇ hail. Ⓛ mankuta, kunada [Southern dialect] Ⓓ marda buru

inbótna rurla *das Hagelkorn.* ◇ hailstone.

imbulkura *schwarz-graue Heuschrecken.* ◇ black-grey grasshoppers. Ⓛ ambulkuri

indalbaka renama *über die Schulter legen (z.B. das erlegte Wild).* ◇ lay over shoulder (e.g. killed game). Ⓛ alinba tunañi

indalba ngama *auf der Schulter tragen.* ◇ carry on shoulder or carry something over shoulders (e.g. kangaroo). Ⓛ alinba katiñi

inbintja *der sich widerrechlich aneignet, Dieb.* ◇ one who acquires something unlawfully, thief. Ⓛ kankala

indeltja (intéltja) *Heuschrecken.* ◇ grasshoppers. Ⓛ tjintilka Ⓓ pindri

inbantatnima *herabfallen vom Himmel, regnen.* ◇ fall down from sky (rain).

indāltja *auseinander stehende (Zehen des Emu).* ◇ spread (toes of emu). Ⓛ andulka

inbalauma *sich widerrechlich aneignen, stehlen (z.B. eine Frau).* ◇ acquire unlawfully, steal (e.g. a woman). Ⓛ wararakatiñi

indanapanama z.B. **tjaia nana Utnadataka indanapanama** *führen (Weg).* ◇ lead (way). Ⓛ ngarirabakañi

indara *Vulva.* ◇ vulva. Ⓛ tuka

indama; *z.B.* **nuka mantara knara indama** *liegen, gehören, haben c. gen.; ich habe viele Kleider (wörtlich: meine Kleider groß liegt).* ◇ lie, belong, have c. gen.; e.g. I have many dresses (literally: my dresses much lie). Ⓛ ngariñi Ⓓ parana

inditjalbuma *bei der Rückkehr liegen.* ◇ lie down on return. Ⓛ ngariñi kulbara

indapindama *fortwährend liegen, fortwährend liegen, sich (dort) befinden, seinen Lagerplatz dort haben.* ◇ lie, be continuously. Ⓛ ngariánañi

ulbarindama *auf dem Bauch liegen.* ◇ lie on the stomach. Ⓛ watungariñi

indaláranama *überall sich lagern.* ◇ camp everywhere. Ⓛ ngariratalkanañi

toppalela indama *auf dem Rücken liegen.* ◇ lie on the back. Ⓛ tanapiti ngariñi

ultalela indama *auf der Seite liegen.* ◇ lie on the side. Ⓛ kultupiti ngariñi

indanama *daliegen (Platz).* ◇ lie there (place). Ⓛ mangariñi

indatnapitnama *auf der Seite liegen (Ochsen), sitzen, hängen.* ◇ lie on side (cattle), sit, hang. Ⓛ ngariránañi

inditjalama *sich niederlassen.* ◇ settle down. Ⓛ jenkula ngariñi

indatjerama *Freunde werden.* ◇ become friends. Ⓛ ngaluturingañi

indarka *weiße Ameise, Termite.* ◇ white ants, termite. Ⓛ mutuínba

indarkaputa *zerfressenes Holz.* ◇ wood eaten away (by ants). Ⓛ mutuinbanti

indata [Northern dialect] *cf.* **ndata** *still.* ◇ quiet, silent; name of place on Western Aranda territory. Ⓛ ŕata

indatoa *schön; schöner Mann.* ◇ beautiful; beautiful man (Strehlow 1907: 102–3). Ⓛ indota, kuninjatu

inditja *gelähmt (nachdem man mit einem Messer geschnitten worden ist).* ◇ lame, paralysed (after one has been cut with a knife). Ⓛ tanti

indoala *arganka-Blüten.* ◇ arganka-blossoms. Ⓛ tutunbiri

indora *sehr.* ◇ very. Ⓛ lenku

indotindóta *halbkreisförmig gebogen.* ◇ bent. Ⓛ nunkinunki

indóta *halbkreisförmig gebogen, schön.* ◇ bent into a semicircle, beautiful. Ⓛ nunki

indótilama *biegen, schmücken.* ◇ to bend, to decorate. Ⓛ nunkini (*biegen*: to bend), indotaniñi (*schmücken*: to decorate) Ⓓ tjirkatjirkana, tjirkatjirkaterina

inalopalama *sammeln (Cikaden).* ◇ collect (cicadas). Ⓛ manjira ngaranáñi

ínerra [Northern dialect] *cf.* **nerra** *rockhole.* ◇ rockhole; place (tree, rock or waterhole) where a person's spirit might have come from. Ⓛ wakula

inealatnuruma [Northern dialect] *umarmen, an sich drücken (2 Freunde).* ◇ embrace, squeeze one another. Ⓛ ngamankarapungañi

ingalama *empfangen (von Seite der Frau).* ◇ receive (from wife's side). Ⓛ barkani

inénkakũa *sehr hungrig.* ◇ very hungry. Ⓛ aïnmatara

inginja *Bart, Ziegenbart.* ◇ beard, goat's beard. Ⓛ ngankura, ngankurba Ⓓ nganka

antanatópparba *Vogel.* ◇ bird. Ⓛ wolbatítitítu

inguaparapara *abends, wenn die Sonne untergegangen ist.* ◇ in the evening, when the sun has set. Ⓛ mungapadu, mungaparapara

ingua *Nacht, finster.* ◇ night, dark (Strehlow 1915: 45). Ⓛ munga Ⓓ tinka

ingula *in der Nacht.* ◇ in the night. Ⓛ munganka

inguarinja *Nachtwanderler.* ◇ sleepwalker. Ⓛ mungala

ingueranama *Nacht werden.* ◇ become night. Ⓛ mamungarekukatiñi

inguarakua *Nachtwandler.* ◇ sleepwalker. Ⓛ mungaru

ingumurunka *sehr finster, dunkel.* ◇ very dark. Ⓛ mungawonniñi

ingumunka *sehr finster.* ◇ very dark. Ⓛ mungawonniñi

ingupuntja, inguapuntja *die tiefe Nacht, die schwarze Nacht (Zeit um Mitternacht).* ◇ deep night, black night (time before midnight) (Strehlow 1915: 45). Ⓛ mungakututu

inguia *alt.* ◇ old. Ⓛ rauata Ⓓ womala

inguatoppatoppala *während der ganzen Nacht.* ◇ during the whole night. Ⓛ mungawaritiji

ingunanga *große, weiße Larven unter der Rinde der eßbaren Gummibäume spec.* ◇ large white grub under gumtree bark (edible species). Ⓛ analtala

inguatoppalta *die Zeit nach Mitternacht.* ◇ time after midnight (Strehlow 1915: 45). Ⓛ munga ngururkultu

injitta urarankarama *Flamme lodert empor.* ◇ flame flares up.

injipinjatjina *Strauchart.* ◇ shrub species. Ⓛ apintapinta

inguntingunta *früh (vor Sonnenaufgang).* ◇ early (before sunrise). Ⓛ mungawapu

inguntawara *nach einigen Tagen.* ◇ a few days later (Strehlow 1915: 46). Ⓛ mungatara wiakutu

ingunta *(zusammengesetzt von ingua (Nacht) + enta (nur eine) morgen (nach Sonnenaufgang), morgens.* ◇ tomorrow (Strehlow 1915: 46), morning (after sunrise); compound: ingua (night) + enta (only one): only after one night. Ⓛ mungatara, unguntara Ⓓ tankubana

inguntakuia *übermorgen.* ◇ the day after tomorrow (Strehlow 1915: 46). Ⓛ mungatara, kutubaka

inguntarbuna *übermorgen.* ◇ the day after tomorrow (Strehlow 1915: 46). Ⓛ mungatara kutuba, ungutarakutuba Ⓓ tankubana nguru

inguntingunta *früh (vor Sonnenaufgang, wenn die Vögel zu singen anfangen).* ◇ early (before sunrise, when the birds start to sing). Ⓛ mungawapu Ⓓ tankutankubana

ingutnala *morgens, unmittelbar vor Sonnenaufgang.* ◇ in the morning, just before sunrise (see Strehlow 1915: 44). Ⓛ mungapurunka, mungawinki Ⓓ tinkangulu

ingutna *früh vor Sonnenaufgang.* ◇ early before sunrise (Strehlow 1915: 44). Ⓛ mungapuru

inguntulkura *nach mehreren Tagen.* ◇ after several days (Strehlow 1915: 46). Ⓛ mungatarangana, mungatara nguanba

inguntakalaka *nach cr 1 Woche.* ◇ circa 1 week later (Strehlow 1915: 46). Ⓛ mungatarakita

ingunta arbabaka *nach langer unbestimmter Zeit.* ◇ after a long indefinite time (Strehlow 1915: 47). Ⓛ mungatarakaputa, mungataramaninji

ingunta arbamaninja *nach langer unbestimmter Zeit.* ◇ after a long indefinite time (Strehlow 1915: 47). Ⓛ mungatararauamaninji, mungatara ngulamaninji

inguaparapara *Anbruch der Nacht, abends (nachdem die Sonne untergegangen ist).* ◇ beginning of night, evening (when sun has set). Ⓛ mungaparapara

injalirbuma *hinaufreichen (Wirbelwind oder Ranke).* ◇ reach up (whirlwind or vine).

inilalama *mitnehmen (Sachen).* ◇ take along (things). Ⓛ manjilkatiñi

ingutjika [Northern dialect] *cf.* **ngutjika** *eine Pflanze mit kleinen fleischenen Blättern, auf Bergen wachsen (ljaua ähnlich).* ◇ plant with meaty leaves, grows on hills. Ⓛ epiépi ('?' added by CS)

injalirbalbinama *hinaufreichen (Wirbelwind).* ◇ to reach up (whirlwind).

inilama *holen.* ◇ to get or to take with you. Ⓛ manjirangarañi Ⓓ maningana, manijiribana (*holen einen andern*: fetch someone)

inilarilaralbuma *vor sich hertreiben (Wild).* ◇ chase (game). Ⓛ mingakurakura kulbañi

inilalbuma *mitnehmen (bei der Heimkehr).* ◇ take with you (when returning home). Ⓛ manjirakulbañi

ininba *Same (sperma).* ◇ sperm. Ⓛ ngutu

iningukua *der Totem-Vorfahr.* ◇ totem ancestor; spirit double. Carl Strehlow (1908: 53–56, 81) called this spirit 'zweites ich' ('the second me'). This word appears not to be in use currently, although this type of spirit is known and called pmarakutata [Carl Strehlow's spelling: 'tmarakutata'] by Western Aranda people. In a more general context 'iningukua' was an alternative term for 'altjirangamitjina' (Strehlow 1910b: 7), which means 'dreaming ancestor'. Strehlow wrote that the altjirangamitjina from whose metamorphosed body the ratapa [spirit child] emerged was the iningukua of a person (Strehlow 1908: 53). Western Aranda people consider these spirits generally as friendly, they are 'good spirits' that 'look like you or us', every person has one of them. Ⓛ woltara

ininjininja *kleiner Vogel.* ◇ small bird. Ⓛ wonnapawonnapa

ininja *Feind, ein Mann mit Federschuhen, der einen andern erschlagen will.* ◇ enemy, man with feather-shoes, who wants to kill someone. Ⓛ wonnapa

inintalatuna (ininta-ilatuma) *kleine Beutelratte (Phascologale Macdonnellensis).* ◇ small marsupial rat (*Pseudantechinus macdonnellensis*) (Atlas of Living Australia n.d.) Ⓛ inintingalulba

ininjalkna *feindlich.* ◇ hostile. Ⓛ wōnapakuru

injikaleuma *zurückstoßen.* ◇ push back. Ⓛ tambirtalkañi

ininja *Hüfte, Schlegel (des Wildes).* ◇ hip, drumstick (of game); meat from hips and sides of animal. Ⓛ kantumi

ininta *Bohnenbaum, ein Baum, der (rote und gelbe) bohnen-förmige Früchte trägt (Erythrina vespertilio).* ◇ bean tree with red and yellow beans (*Erythrina vespertilio*). Ⓛ ininti

injatjinja ilkuma *alles kahl fressen.* ◇ eat everything bare. Ⓛ punarku ngalkuñi

injítama *fressen, viel essen (z.B. Fleisch).* ◇ eat a lot, eat (e.g. meat). Ⓛ aubakañi

injatjinja *kahl gefressen.* ◇ eaten bare. Ⓛ punarku

injama, injíma *hinaufsteigen, aufsteigen, reiten.* ◇ climb, mount, ride. Ⓛ kalbani Ⓓ dukana

injinja *Greis, alter Mann.* ◇ old man. Ⓛ tjilpi

injakara *schwer (Last).* ◇ heavy (burden). Ⓛ talili

injitta *Flamme.* ◇ flame. Ⓛ tī

injakarilama *sich aufladen (Last).* ◇ load (burden). Ⓛ tali tunañi

injitalama *Flamme emporsteigen.* ◇ rising flame. Ⓛ ti jennañi

injakariuma Ⓛ tali talini

injilalama or injilawoma *hinaufklettern.* ◇ climb up. Ⓛ kalbaratalkañi

injilinjilaworama *dual.* ◇ dual of 'climb up'. Ⓛ kalbaratalkañi kutara

injiltjinjiltja *kleiner Krebs.* ◇ small crab. Ⓛ injiltjinjiltji

injulabaterama *Witwer (der die Frau verloren hat).* ◇ widower (the one who has lost his wife). Ⓛ walukutaringañi

injiranga *eine Baumart (Mulgaart).* ◇ mulga species. Ⓛ injirangi

injínama *aufsteigen (Rauch), hinaufsteigen (auf den Berg, Leiter).* ◇ ascend (smoke), climb up (mountain, ladder). Ⓛ makalbañi

injipala *(trotzig), Mann der mit Tochter hurt.* ◇ (defiant) man, who whores with his daughter. Ⓛ injipali

injitjinjima *aufsteigen, auffahren.* ◇ climb up, ascend. Ⓛ kalbarabakani, kalbakatiñi Ⓓ tarana

injilarenama *hinaufklettern.* ◇ climb up. Ⓛ makalbawonniñi

injentjima *hinaufsteigen.* ◇ climb up. Ⓛ ngalakalbañi

injetnima *hinaufsteigen.* ◇ climb up. Ⓛ makalbañi

injitjera *Frosch, kleiner, in den Creeks sich aufhaltend (Heloporus pictus).* ◇ small frog who lives in creeks. Ⓛ ngangi

injitjinjitja *kleiner Vogel, sehr schlank, hochgewachsen (den Männern gehörend).* ◇ small, very slim bird (associated with men). Ⓛ injitjinjitji

injíninjína *der Reiter (n).* ◇ rider.

inka latinja *frische Fußspuren.* ◇ fresh footprints. Ⓛ tjinna kuarita

inka ngurukinja *gestrige Fußspuren.* ◇ yesterday's tracks. Ⓛ tjinna mungatita

inkanabana *zuletzt.* ◇ finally, last. Ⓛ ngantitu

inka tnuara *Hacke.* ◇ heel. Ⓛ tjinna tari

inka *Fuß, Fußspuren, Fußabdrücke (im Sand).* ◇ foot, footprints (in sand). Ⓛ tjinna Ⓓ tidna

inkantarba *einfüßig, einbeinig.* ◇ one-footed, one-legged.

inkakantja *Zehe.* ◇ toe. Ⓛ tjinnawalpuru Ⓓ tidnawutju

inkanerama *dahinterbleiben.* ◇ remain behind.

inkamákura *große Zehe.* ◇ big toe. Ⓛ tjinnamamara Ⓓ tidnangandri

inkanekunekua *große Zehe.* ◇ big toe. Ⓛ tjinna mamatura

inkanekua *große Zehe.* ◇ big toe. Ⓛ tjinna mama

inka albara *die mittleren Zehen.* ◇ the middle toes. Ⓛ tjinna walpuru

inkatnata *Fußsohle.* ◇ sole (foot). Ⓛ tjinnawila Ⓓ tidnamandra

inka kurkakurda *die kleine Zehe.* ◇ small toe. Ⓛ tjinna ngalli

inkatopa *Fußrücken.* ◇ ridge of foot. Ⓛ tjinnatana

inkatuatja *(Fußtal), Raum zwischen den einzelnen Zehen.* ◇ (foot valley), space between toes. Ⓛ tjinnatinki

inka róttukatúra *kurze Zehen.* ◇ short toes. Ⓛ ngali turbu Ⓓ tidna ngalki (*kleiner Zehe*: small toe)

inkalura *Fleisch an der Hacke.* ◇ flesh on the heel, trotter. Ⓛ tjinnawollura

inkaïta *harte Sohle (der Eingeborenen), Huf, Klaue (die feste Haut derselben).* ◇ hard sole (of natives), hoof, claw (hard skin). Ⓛ tjinnabakka

inkaltála *Krallen (bei Vögeln, Hunden und Katzen).* ◇ claws (of birds, dogs and cats). Ⓛ tjinnapiri

inkaltala *südliches Kreuz.* ◇ Southern Cross. Ⓛ waritipiri

inkaïmbatja *Fußeindruck, Fußspur.* ◇ foot imprint, footprint, track. Ⓛ tjinnaninka

inkantama *den Fußspuren nachgehen.* ◇ follow tracks. Ⓛ tjinnawonnañi

inkakatakata *Fußgelenk.* ◇ ankle. Ⓛ tjinna tata Ⓓ tidnapalka (*Fußgelenk*: ankle), (tidnaaipiri: *Fußschemel*)

inka intarinja *Schwimmfuß.* ◇ webbed foot. Ⓛ tjinna lapala

inkartja *weitauseinanderstehende Zehen (Emu).* ◇ spread toes (of emu). Ⓛ tararba Ⓓ ngarana? ('?' added by CS)

inkanambenjaka renalama *sich unter. setzen.* ◇ sit down behind or at the bottom of something.

inkainama *aufrichten, aufstellen.* ◇ erect, straighten. Ⓛ ngaratunañi Ⓓ terkibana

inka-kunna *ungeheuer steil.* ◇ enormously steep. Ⓛ nganka kuja

inkaia *Bandikut (rabbit-bandicoot) von der Größe eines Kaninchens, dessen Schwänze (albitja) von den Frauen getragen werden.* ◇ bilby, *Macrotis lagotis*. Ⓛ talku Ⓓ kapĭta

inkaia albitja *Bandikut Schwänze.* ◇ bandicoot tails. Ⓛ talku kuntu, mani

inkamanama *oben (sitzen), oben an (sitzen).* ◇ top (sit), at the top (sit). Ⓛ ngatara ninañi

inkakinkara *schlank, dünn, schmächtig.* ◇ slim, thin, slender. Ⓛ wirunkurunku

iñka *Geist eines lebenden Menschen, der in Gefahr ist.* ◇ spirit of a living human being, who is in danger; soul, spirit of a human being; people say that one has to lie in a certain position at night, so the spirit or soul is safe. The spirit or soul of a person is also called 'guruna' in Western Aranda. No obvious distinction is made today between the words inka and guruna. Inka like altjira (meaning 'God') and other Aranda words have been used by the Lutheran Church in their bible translations and have Christian connotations. Inka combined with the word alkngaltara means Holy Spirit, for example. While Western Aranda people use inka and guruna interchangeably today, the terms seem to have had a slightly different meaning in the past. Inka according to Carl Strehlow was used for the spirit of a living human being, who was in danger; and the word guruna was used for the soul of a living person (Strehlow 1907: 15). When a person dies, the soul was called iltana, which means 'ghost', and it was imagined to be white (Strehlow 1915: 23). The word iltana for ghost can also mean skeleton today. Ⓛ ngoa

inkalalama *auffliegen (Vögel).* ◇ fly up (birds). Ⓛ parpakani

iñka jirama *die Seele vergeht.* ◇ soul passes away. Ⓛ ngoa wiaringañi

inkalelama *anbieten zum Vertausch.* ◇ offer for exchange. Ⓛ wonkaltaltunañi

inkai! *gieb her! lange her!* ◇ give it to me! Ⓛ inkai!

inkama *conf.* ankama. ◇ say, speak, talk.

inkanakerama *sich hinten aufstellen, hintendrein laufen.* ◇ stand at the back, follow behind. Ⓛ ngantikurekukatiñi, ngantikuriñi Ⓓ ngatjina

inkana *alle zusammen.* ◇ all together. Ⓛ lewara Ⓓ warupoto

inkanangeralakalama *zuletzt hineinsteigen (ins Wasser).* ◇ climb in last (into water). Ⓛ ngantiwana rekukatiñi

inkana *der letzte, zuletzt, hinten.* ◇ the last, at last, at the back, behind. Ⓛ nganti, mala Ⓓ ngadani

inkananga *zuletzt, hinten.* ◇ last, at the back. Ⓛ ngantiwonna, ngantiwana

inkaninkana *zuletzt, zu spät.* ◇ last, too late. Ⓛ wantiwanti, ngantinganti

inkana nanginkanérama *hinter her laufen (zuletzt liegen machen).* ◇ walk (run) behind. Ⓛ ngantikungantikuriñi

inkanintalelama *huren, nachdem der Ehemann oder die Ehefrau fortgegangen ist.* ◇ (lie at the end); adultery after husband or wife has gone away. Ⓛ ngantingariljennani

inkanapinkana, taia inkanapinkana *der letzte, im letzten Monat.* ◇ last, last month. Ⓛ wantiwanti, pira wantiwanti

inkalakalama, inkalangurbalama *fortwährend bitten.* ◇ continuously beg.

inkankaulama *betteln.* ◇ beg.

inkankaulanalana *Bettler.* ◇ beggar.

inkalbinkama *fortwährend bitten.* ◇ to ask or beg continuously.

inkanga *Schulter, Achsel.* ◇ shoulder, armpit. Ⓛ jambila

inkanja *Mittag.* ◇ midday. Ⓛ kalala parpa Ⓓ tōda, tōda nagmana (*Mittags ruhe halten*: have a midday break)

inkanjubana *unverheiratet, ledig.* ◇ not married, single.

inkantama *den Fußspuren folgen, verfolgen.* ◇ follow tracks. Ⓛ tjinnawonnañi Ⓓ karina (*nachfolgen*), tajipaterina? warapana ('?' added by CS)

ïnkangankama *großer grauer Habicht.* ◇ large grey hawk. Ⓛ ngankarangankara

inkaparérama *ausweichen, zur Seite springen.* ◇ avoid, jump to the side. Ⓛ arintjikatiñi

inkapa *Fußstapfen.* ◇ foot imprints.

inkaninja *das jüngste Kind.* ◇ youngest child. Ⓛ malata

inkára *Baum (spec.)* ◇ tree species. Ⓛ ankara

inkāra *unsterblichen, sicher, geborgen, auch die Totem-Götter.* ◇ immortal, safe, Totem-Gods. Ⓛ wonkaruntu, kanaruntu

inkanjinkanja *vormittags um 9 Uhr.* ◇ in the morning. Ⓛ parpaparpa

inkaraka *alle.* ◇ all. Ⓛ apuara, kútuara, umuna Ⓓ pratjana

inkanjatnaka *nachmittags cr. 3 Uhr.* ◇ in the afternoon about 3 o'clock. Ⓛ parpakultu

inkarinjaka *alle zusammen, alles.* ◇ all together, everything. Ⓛ kutuli, tjiwariwari Ⓓ pratjaterina

inkaraka indora *alle ohne Ausnahme.* ◇ all without exception. Ⓛ apuaralenku

inkárama *rascheln.* ◇ rustle. Ⓛ lekiñi Ⓓ pirungana

ínkamáraranta *in einer Reihe nebeneinander (fliegen oder sitzen Vögel).* ◇ beside each other (birds flying or sitting). Ⓛ tapiri

inkaralelama *Geräusch machen, rascheln machen (vom Wind).* ◇ make noise, rustle (wind). Ⓛ lekitjingani

inkerbintja *das Umbiegen der kleinen Zehe des ininja.* ◇ bending of a man's little toe (with feather shoes). Ⓛ tjinnakata

inkarérama *Hände austrecken (um Gaben zu empfangen).* ◇ stretch out hands (to receive gifts). Ⓛ inkarawonniñi

inkárknerama *eifrig, hastig, aufgeregt sein (impulsiv handeln).* ◇ be eager, hasty, excited (act impulsively). Ⓛ ngaruriñi

inkaritníma *alles auslaufen (Wasser).* ◇ drain away (water). Ⓛ apuarapatangariñi

inkaualama *bitten (um eine Gabe).* ◇ ask (for a gift).

inkatjinka *blaß, bleich (vor Furcht).* ◇ pale (from fear).

inkarkara *menschenleer, öde.* ◇ deserted. Ⓛ munguna

inkartja *Fußspur, ausgetretene Spur, Fußweg (track).* ◇ footprint, track. Ⓛ ankirtji, tarara, wonbawonba

inkata *Häuptling, Herr (allgemein Vater).* ◇ chief, ceremonial leader. According to Strehlow (1915: 1), the chief of a traditional country was called inkata or 'father of all', but on a general level he was only a 'primus inter pares', and his position was only hereditary, i.e. not necessarily achieved through knowledge or wisdom. Today the word inkata is used for Lutheran pastor. Ⓛ tina, atunari Ⓓ kapara

inkata knara *große Häuptling.* ◇ great leader. Ⓛ atanipuntu

inkatitja *König.* ◇ king.

inkatintja *Kaiser.* ◇ emperor.

inkantitja *Gefolge eines Häuptlings, der Jüngere.* ◇ entourage of a chief, the younger one.

inkilirtja *Furche zwischen Steingeröll.* ◇ channel between boulders. Ⓛ múrulmúrula

inkatérama *schreien, heftig weinen.* ◇ cry, weep violently. Ⓛ urkantjiriñi

iñkénkantáma *furchtsam machen, Furcht einflößen.* ◇ make fearful. Ⓛ ngoatjiriñi

inkenínkena *großer grauer Habicht, auf Berge sich aufhaltend.* ◇ large grey hawk living on mountains. Ⓛ ngankarangankara

inkerara *in der Mitte dünn, zu beiden Seiten dick (Stein).* ◇ thin in the middle, thick on both sides (stone). Ⓛ kabajultu

inkerárarára *sehr dünn (Stamm eines Strauches).* ◇ very thin. Ⓛ inkerárirári

inkilja *zornig, entstellt, böse, sehr ärgerlich.* ◇ angry, furious. Ⓛ kiltji, mirbana

inkiljérama *entstellt werden vor Zorn.* ◇ become distorted from anger. Ⓛ kiltjiringañi, mirbanariñi

inkineritjalbuma *nach der Ankunft alle auf einen Haufen stehen.* ◇ after arrival to stand together. Ⓛ ngarakatinikulbara

inkinjalkua inkama *unverschämt bitten, betteln.* ◇ beg, demand. Ⓛ ngatjintu inkañi

inkeralama *fortwährend stehen (nicht weiter gehen).* ◇ to stand continuously (not move on). Ⓛ walenku ngarañi

inkéuma *hinabstürzen (vom Berge).* ◇ fall (down from mountain).

alankura, wolkna inkura *ausgehöhlte Boden, Nische.* ◇ niche. Ⓛ narkulta

nkura *ununterbrochen, unaufhörlich.* ◇ continuously. Ⓛ ratatura

inkua, manna inkua *Schilf, dessen Wurzeln gegessen werden.* ◇ reed with edible roots. Ⓛ unka

iñkua *Zelle (der Nester von Honigameisen), dunkle Erdhöhle.* ◇ cell (in honeyant nests), dark cave. Ⓛ nurri

inkua *fast, beinahe.* ◇ almost, nearly. Ⓛ nguana

inkualaka; ta manna ndakala, inkuálaka unta lakitjau *'damit ja nicht'.* ◇ under no circumstances. Ⓛ nguanba-puta; ngaiulu mii nuntuna junguta, nguanba jenkutjipinka putau

inkua ndama *hinhalten, doch wieder wegziehen, bevor der andere ergreift.* ◇ hold out, pull away again, before being taken away again. Ⓛ nguana jungañi

inkulkna *der kite-hawk.* ◇ kite-hawk. Ⓛ baninka Ⓓ kukunka

inkunalérama *sich umwenden (zurücksehen).* ◇ turn (look back). Ⓛ nguntila ngarañi Ⓓ worrakalina

inkulba *einheimisches Tabak (Nicotiana).* ◇ highly valued native tobacco (*Nicotiana*). Ⓛ minkula

inkulbinkulba *Pflanze, wilder Tabak (Nicotiana suaveoleus).* ◇ plant, wild tobacco (*Nicotiana suaveolens* /*N. gossei*; may possibly be *N. velutina* and *N.* spp. (Latz 1996)). Ⓛ minkulminkula

ínkunalérelabúma *sich umsehen.* ◇ look around. Ⓛ nguntilanguntila rekulariñi

inkunjera *Larven an Gummibaumrinden.* ◇ grubs in gumtree bark. Ⓛ unkunjeri

inkuriwuma *herabstreichen, herabdrücken, massieren (den Körper).* ◇ rub down, press down, massage (body). Ⓛ wonturpungañi

inkurinkura *unweglich, voller Löcher (Weg).* ◇ rough, full of holes (track). Ⓛ talatitalati

inkura *geschlossener (ausgehöhlter) Raum.* ◇ enclosed space. Ⓛ tunu

nkura *unaufhörlich (singen).* ◇ (sing) continuously. Ⓛ ratatura

inkurúkajatuntja *jemanden erwarten.* ◇ expect someone. Ⓛ unbaringanje

inkurbma *Mistelzweigfrüchte, die sich an Tnima Sträuchern finden.* ◇ mistletoe fruit on tnima bushes. Ⓛ wolkamali

unkutatja *gelbe Larven in den Wurzeln der inkuta.* ◇ yellow grubs in roots of inkuta bush. Ⓛ puntiti

inkuta *kleiner Strauch mit nadelförmigen hellgrünen Blättern und gelben Blüten (Cassia).* ◇ small bush with needle-shaped light green leaves and yellow blossoms (*Cassia* now *Senna artemisiodes* (Latz 1996)). Ⓛ punti

inkutinkuta *krumm.* ◇ crooked. Ⓛ kalikali

inkuta *krumm.* ◇ crooked. Ⓛ kali

inkutinkuta *krumm, schief, verkrüppelt.* ◇ crooked, crippled. Ⓛ nunkinúnki, kalikali Ⓓ kundikundi, kutiri, kutikutiri, kudiri

inkurkna *zerrissener Boden (vom Regen).* ◇ riven ground (from rain). Ⓛ unkurknu

inkutilama *biegen, krumm machen.* ◇ to bend. Ⓛ nunkini

inka inkutinkuta *krumme Beine.* ◇ crooked legs. Ⓛ tjinna kúnkalikúnkali

inmalinja *Fremdling, in der Fremde sein.* ◇ stranger, foreign. Ⓛ barkanta, barkara Ⓓ waiarka, marka

inmanmaraúlama *schütteln (Kopf).* ◇ shake (head). Ⓛ pinpintipungañi Ⓓ wiltjana

inmanmaraíwuma *schütteln (Baum).* ◇ shake (tree). Ⓛ pinpintipungañi

inmara *Wellen.* ◇ waves. Ⓛ inmari Ⓓ mandikila

inmaralama *kleine Wellen schlagen.* ◇ make small waves. Ⓛ inmarijennañi

inmatéolama *große Wellen schlagen.* ◇ make big waves. Ⓛ papararíñi

inmarakaturuma *alle zusammen wickeln, sich herumwickeln.* ◇ to wind (together or around). Ⓛ kulakularapungañi

inmátoa [Northern dialect] *cf.* **inmota, inmōta** *eßbare Pflanze (Lepidium phlebopetalum) mit kleinen lanzenförmigen Blumen.* ◇ edible plant with small spear-shaped leaves. Ⓛ inmuta

inmenmánkama *alle zusammen schreien.* ◇ shout together. Ⓛ ngeljurkani

inmérama *sich vermehren.* ◇ to multiply. Ⓛ tutaringañi

inma *sehr viele.* ◇ very many. Ⓛ tuta

inmōta *eßbare Pflanze (Lepidium phlebopetalum) mit kleinen lanzenförmigen Blumen.* ◇ edible plant with small spear-shaped leaves (*Lepidium phlebopetalum*). Ⓛ inmúta

ínola *Spinne.* ◇ spider. Ⓛ ínula Ⓓ marankara

inna *Baum, Holz.* ◇ tree, wood. Ⓛ ngana, punu Ⓓ pita

innabotta *Knorren am Baum.* ◇ knots on a tree. Ⓛ talta

inōta *sehr viele, ein großer Haufe (Vögel).* ◇ very many, big flock (birds). Ⓛ leñku

ínnopúta *Glieder am Leibe anliegend oder angewachsen, zusammengewachsen.* ◇ limbs joined to body, grown together. Ⓛ turbu

inpanama *sieben, sichten.* ◇ sieve, sift. Ⓛ winpungañi

inna kwalinja, inna inkulia *Ebenholz (n).* ◇ ebony, black wood.

inna retjingana *Ruder (n).* ◇ oar.

inkuenkua *das Rohr (n) (zum Messen und Schlagen).* ◇ stick (for measuring or hitting).

intatjila *allenthalben, unter.* ◇ wherever, under. Ⓛ banbanka

alkira intatjila *unter dem Himmel.* ◇ under the sky. Ⓛ ilkari banbanka

intalauma *in liegender Stellung sein (Mond).* ◇ be in a lying position (moon). Ⓛ mangariñi

inta *Spindel, Fischspeer, Stecken.* ◇ spindle, fish spear, stick. Ⓛ wili Ⓓ jadi

inta *Felsen (häufig gebraucht in Zusammensetzungen).* ◇ rock, cliff (often used in compounds). Ⓛ katu

intákata *eine kleine Mulde aus Gummiholz.* ◇ small bowl made of gumtree wood. Ⓛ arri

intálbmerama *Krampf haben.* ◇ have a cramp. Ⓛ tjilunariñi Ⓓ matata

intalelama *bemalen (Körper), Zeichen machen, schreiben.* ◇ paint (body), make (de)signs, draw, write. Ⓛ wolkatunañi

intalerakara *ehrbar, geehrt.* ◇ respectable, honoured.

intalelanelana *der Schreiber.* ◇ writer.

intalinja *Zeichen, Schrift.* ◇ signs, script, writing. Ⓛ wolka, ninka

intalja *Haube (Kakadus).* ◇ crest (cockatoo); crested cockatoo. Ⓛ pankupanku

intalinja knaragata; mantara intalinja knaragata *mit großen Zeichen; ein Druckkleid mit großen Feldern.* ◇ with large (de)signs; a printed dress with large patterns. Ⓛ wolkapuntutara; mantara wolkapuntutara

intela *jelka Halm.* ◇ jelka blade. Ⓛ katititara

intalinja irkaiagata *mit kleinen Zeichen.* ◇ with small (de)signs. Ⓛ wolkairkaiitara

intalinja lanjatara (mantara) *gestreift.* ◇ striped (dress). Ⓛ wolkaminpurutara

intalintátnama *ganz niedrig über das Ziel hinweg fliegen, vorüber fliegen (Speer), nicht treffen.* ◇ fly very low over target, fly past (spear), miss. Ⓛ mamangariratalkañi

intalta *viele Schößlinge: Feigenbaumschößlinge.* ◇ many saplings. Ⓛ nañi

intalurka *Grasart (spec. curly-grass, Eleusine aegypticea?).* ◇ curly grass species. Ⓛ intilirki

intaminja *lange Fischspeer.* ◇ long fish spear. Ⓛ wiliwara

intánga, intanga, intangatja *Schwägerin (F: die Frau des Bruders und die Schwester des Mannes), Manns Schwester cf. Verwandtschaftsbezeichnungen.* ◇ sister-in-law (brother's wife and husband's sister); see kin terms in Strehlow (1913). Ⓛ toari, toarina Ⓓ kamari

intanga knara *die Frau des älteren Bruders.* ◇ wife of older brother. Ⓛ toari puntu

intanga larra *die Frau des jüngeren Bruders.* ◇ wife of younger brother. Ⓛ toari wongu

intangukua *Schwägerin eines Andern.* ◇ sister-in-law of someone else. Ⓛ toarira

intánalauma *totstechen, totspeeren.* ◇ stab or spear to death. Ⓛ wakaratalkañi

intangatja *eigene Schwägerin cf. Verwandtschaftsbezeichnungen.* ◇ own sister-in-law, *cf.* kin terms. Ⓛ toarina

íntingéra *beim Spiel sich anstoßen, einen Klaps geben, fechten, spielen.* ◇ knock against (at play), give a slap, fence, play. Ⓛ kintingeri

intángarára *große, grüne Frösche.* ◇ large green frogs. Ⓛ intingarari

intama *sehr müde.* ◇ very tired. Ⓛ kobañi

intantjima [Southern dialect] *cf.* intjentjima. ◇ come up. Ⓛ ngalakalbañi

intarama [Southern dialect] *cf.* **ntjarama** *schnarchen.* ◇ to snore. Ⓛ ngurbmanañi

intára *mehr, weiter (gehen, arbeiten).* ◇ more, further (go, work). Ⓛ kutururu

intarinja *alle auf einen Hauf, allgemein (Regen), dicht (Wände), zusammengewachsen, aneinandergewachsen.* ◇ all in a mob, general (rain), solid (wall), grown together. Ⓛ intirintji, lewara (*alle zusammen*: all together)

intarinjilama *vereinigen, versammeln.* ◇ unite, assemble. Ⓛ intirintjinani

intarintara *viele zusammenstehend (Stämme), zusammengewachsen, verbunden (dicht Schwimmhaut).* ◇ many standing together (trees), grown together, joined. Ⓛ mintirbmintira

intátjatuma *spalten (Strauch um Speere zu verfertigen).* ◇ split (bush to make spears from it). Ⓛ patalpungañi

intjiíntjiá *süße Masse, die die iwunjiwunji in die argankunba legen, aus welcher die Larven hervorgehen.* ◇ sweet substance, which the iwunjiwunji lay into the argankunba (bulb); from which grubs hatch.

interarpa *Wespen.* ◇ wasps. Ⓛ jelili

interarparapa *Wespen.* ◇ wasps. Ⓛ intirirpirirpi

intata wollama *nachfolgen (wenn recht viele einen nachfolgen).* ◇ follow (when quite a few are following). Ⓛ wollankarini

intareuma *hochheben.* ◇ to lift up. Ⓛ untuni

intatala lama *nachfolgen (einige).* ◇ follow (some). Ⓛ wollanka jennañi

intauintaua *lang, langschwänzig.* ◇ long, long-tailed. Ⓛ kakunkakun

intatakérama *nachgehen, nachfolgen.* ◇ follow, pursue. Ⓛ wollankariñi

intatjintama [Southern dialect] *hinaufsteigen, hinaufklettern.* ◇ climb up. Ⓛ kalbarabakañi

intētnanama *sich ausstrecken (zum Schlafen).* ◇ stretch out (to sleep). Ⓛ lurkungarañi

inteïtnama *reichen, langen (bis).* ◇ reach (to). Ⓛ mangariñi

intia *Steinhöhle.* ◇ stone cave. Ⓛ kulbi Ⓓ minka? ('?' added by CS)

inteltja, intaltja *Heuschrecken.* ◇ grasshoppers. Ⓛ tjintjilka

intenbara *Gras (spec. Panicum).* ◇ grass (*Panicum* species). Ⓛ intenbiri

intentituruma *Farbe reiben.* ◇ rub paint. Ⓛ ularpungañi

intiïntia [intjiintjia] *kleine rote Beere, die an einem Busch mit sehr kleinen dunkelgrünen Büscheln/Blättern wachsen (eßbar).* ◇ small red berry that grows on a bush with very small dark-green leaves (edible). Ⓛ witiwita

intinerama *durchstechen, durchbohren (Nasenwand).* ◇ pierce (septum). Ⓛ wakarapungañi

intingera *fechten, sich mit dem Speer stechen.* ◇ fence, stab with a spear. Ⓛ kintingeri

intita *stinkend.* ◇ stink. Ⓛ bokka, ona

intiterama *stinkend werden, sein.* ◇ starting to stink. Ⓛ bokkaringañi

antinerétnama *schnell laufen, weiter schießen (Eidechse).* ◇ run fast, dart away (lizard). Ⓛ intingarañi

intjitakilama *annehmen (als etwas).* ◇ accept (as something).

intirtna *eingetrocknet (Ei).* ◇ dried up (egg); stinking, rotten. Ⓛ tamala Ⓓ tabalju

intiítjintítja *hinkend, Bein nachziehend.* ◇ limping, drag leg. Ⓛ tuñga

intitja *steif, Bein nachziehend.* ◇ stiff, drag leg. Ⓛ tanti

intitja [Northern dialect] *junger Mann.* ◇ young man. Ⓛ wongu

intitjera [Southern dialect] *conf.* **injitjera** *Frosch.* ◇ frog. Ⓛ ngangi

intitjiuma *unterrichten, unterweisen, 'einweihen'.* ◇ instruct, teach, show how something is done. Ⓛ tintinpungañi

intitatja *sehr große Larven (spec.)* ◇ very large grubs (species). Ⓛ intitatji

intitjimelanka *sehr schön gefärbt.* ◇ very beautifully coloured. Ⓛ kuninjatu

intitjeritjera *sehr viele, circa 40 Personen oder Gegenstände.* ◇ very many, circa 40 people or objects. Ⓛ taua alkarinji

intjanga *Wasseransammlung, Wasserloch, Pfuhl.* ◇ pool of water, waterhole. Ⓛ muruntu (pando) nindri

intiljabilapa [Northern dialect] *Schmetterling.* ◇ butterfly. Ⓛ pintapinta

intiljabarkaborka *flügellahm.* ◇ cannot fly, broken wing. Ⓛ pantalpantala

intjentjima *heraufkommen.* ◇ come up, come back; return. Ⓛ ngalakalbañi

intjima *aufsteigen (von Vögeln).* ◇ soar (birds). Ⓛ kalbañi

intjilama *aufwachsen (Bäume).* ◇ grow (trees). Ⓛ jerralbakañi

intjalka [Northern dialect] *Raupenart.* ◇ caterpillar species. Ⓛ kantila

intjika [Southern dialect] *cf.* ntjaka. ◇ gone, away.

intintilalbuma *heraufsteigen (bei der Rückkehr).* ◇ climb up (on return). Ⓛ makalbarakulbañi

intjinama *hinaufklettern.* ◇ climb up. Ⓛ makalbañi

intjikalauma *aushöhlen, brechen (Steine).* ◇ to hollow, to break (stones). Ⓛ tatunpungañi

intjira *Eidechse (spec.) cr 2 Fuß lang, schwarz.* ◇ black lizard species circa 2 feet long. Ⓛ nintjiri

intōta *unbrauchbar, wertlos.* ◇ useless, worthless. Ⓛ apunta

indóala *gelbe, honighaltige blood-wood Blüten.* ◇ yellow bloodwood blossoms with honey. Ⓛ tutunberi

intoa *Fraus Vaters Schwester.* ◇ wife's father's sister. Ⓛ nankiï

intola *Habicht.* ◇ hawk. Ⓛ tiltila, mentola

intjirintjira *sehr kleiner Vogel, schwarzer Schnabel, schwarze Beine, grauer Kopf und Flügel, grau und weiß gestreifter Vorderkopf, weiße Brust, – so groß wie Zaunkönig.* ◇ very small bird with black beak, black legs, grey head and wings, grey and white striped forehead, white chest (size of wren); bird that makes a sound to announce that the native truffle is coming out of the ground. Ⓛ intjirintjiri

intōtintōta *unbrauchbar, wertlos.* ◇ useless, worthless. Ⓛ apúntapúnta

intunama *abhauen (Bäume), fallen, abschneiden, beschneiden.* ◇ chop (trees), fall, cut off. Ⓛ mutuni Ⓓ karuwalli ankana, tita ngankana? ('?' added by CS)

intolintola *mantis (die sich an Gräsern aufhält).* ◇ mantis (who lives in the grass). Ⓛ intolintola

intólintola *Grasart.* ◇ grass species; spinifex grass. Ⓛ intolintola

intuénta *Steinmesser, mit dem sich die jungen Leute die Brust ritzen, um die Narben hervorzubringen.* ◇ stone knife that young people use to scar their chests. Ⓛ tilba

intolowintolerama *von allen Richtungen zu schreien.* ◇ to shout from every direction. Ⓛ ngaringariratalkañi

inturapurapa *dunkle Höhle (dunkle Steinhöhle).* ◇ dark cave (dark stone cave). Ⓛ munganmunganba

intonuranura *unbeweglich (dasitzen) im Camp, sitzen nicht fortgehen.* ◇ (sit) motionless in the camp, stay, not go away. Ⓛ nguramati

inturka *furchtlos.* ◇ fearless. Ⓛ nguluwia Ⓓ manubaku

intúrka *Magen, (L[oritja]) cf.* knarinja, latnara. ◇ stomach. Ⓛ antarka Ⓓ kudnapiti

intúrkuna *Schlange, nicht giftig (spec.)* ◇ snake species, not poisonous; carpet snake. Ⓛ inturkunu

inturkura *Grasart.* ◇ grass species; prickly and sticky grass. Ⓛ karra

inturkurinturkura *kurze Grasart, mit stachlichen Weizenähren-ähnlichen Blüten.* ◇ short grass species with wheat-like blossoms. Ⓛ karrakarra

inura *lahm.* ◇ lame. Ⓛ numbu Ⓓ tjunduru

ípita *tief, tiefes Loch, Grab, Schlucht.* ◇ deep, deep hole, grave, gorge. Ⓛ ngadi, tuku Ⓓ mikari, wali, kudu, dulkeru

ipitalama *tief machen, Grab machen.* ◇ dig deep, make grave. Ⓛ ngadini

intúngulúngula *wenn im Osten alles licht ist.* ◇ when the sun has risen and there is light in the east. Ⓛ jultaparapara

ipitalukaluka *uneben, holperig (Weg).* ◇ uneven, bumpy (road). Ⓛ ngadinkurungadinkura Ⓓ diladila?, dulkerudulkeru ('?' added by CS)

iralunba *Eidechse (spec.)* ◇ lizard species. Ⓛ utanki

irandinda *Enten (art).* ◇ duck species. Ⓛ urandandi

iranda *schwarze Kakadu.* ◇ black cockatoo. Ⓛ irandi

irándakaljíraljíra *Pfanze mit flachen Blüten.* ◇ plant with flat blossoms. Ⓛ irandikiljiriljiri

irbalalama *hineingehen, untergehen (Sonne).* ◇ to go into, to go down, to set (sun). Ⓛ tarbaratalkini

irbalakalama *(in die Erde) eingehen, untergehen (Sonne).* ◇ to go into (the earth), to set (sun). Ⓛ tarbaraokalingañi

irbaltala *kräftig sein, vermögend sein.* ◇ be strong, be able, be capable. Ⓛ irbaltanka

irandana *der Stamm des agia-Baumes.* ◇ trunk of agia tree. Ⓛ irandiñi

irbalterama *übertreffen, mehr vermögen als ein anderer.* ◇ surpass, be better than another. Ⓛ irbaltaringañi

irbalauma *hineingehen, sich verstecken, sich verstecken im Gebüsch.* ◇ go into, hide, hide in the bushes. Ⓛ tarbaratalkañi

irbaltangirbálta *kühn, waghalsig, sehr kräftig.* ◇ daring, very strong. Ⓛ irbaltankairbaltanka

irbaltangirbálterama *sehr kräftig sein, etwas wagen, etwas vermögen.* ◇ to be very strong, to risk, to be able, to be capable. Ⓛ irbaltirbaltaringani

inua *dick (Brei), steif (Bein etc.)* ◇ thick (paste), stiff (leg, etc.) Ⓛ ananta

intokula *Rauchgefäß.* ◇ smoking container.

irbana *sehr alt (Frau), abgelebt (aragutja), in Samen gegangen (Früchte).* ◇ very old (woman), worn out (woman), gone to seed (fruit). Ⓛ irbini

irbalarpa iwulama *sich bald hinwerfen, bald dort hinwerfen.* ◇ soon throw oneself down. Ⓛ waiapungañi

irbanama *hineingehen.* ◇ go into. Ⓛ matarbani

irbanga *Fisch.* ◇ fish. Ⓛ irbingi Ⓓ paru? ('?' added by CS)

irbangakarinja *Fischer.* ◇ fisherman.

irbanginjirkna *Habicht (spec.)* ◇ hawk species. Ⓛ irbanginjirkni

irbanta *Eidechse (spec.), Varanus eremius.* ◇ lizard species, *Varanus eremius* (pygmy desert monitor) (Atlas of Living Australia n.d.) Ⓛ tjirbanti

inturapa *ein schwarzer boomerang.* ◇ black boomerang. Ⓛ marukurra

irbantara *Kniegelenke.* ◇ knee joints. Ⓛ irbantiri

irbiltiltiltilta *Knacken des Kniegelenks.* ◇ cracking of knee joints. Ⓛ palturpalturba

irbaralelama *zusammenhäufen, aufhäufen (im Vorratshaus).* ◇ to pile up. Ⓛ kutulenani

irbaratnauma *hineinströmen (viele Menschen).* ◇ stream into (many people). Ⓛ tarbarangariñi Ⓓ jurborina

irbatarbéulama *sich wälzen (vor Vergnügen).* ◇ roll around (in glee). Ⓛ kutikutikatini

irbatatuma *zusammenbinden (Stricke), anspannen (Pferde).* ◇ tie together (ropes), harness (horses). Ⓛ titirpungani

irbirberama *ehren (cum genit.)* ◇ to honour (*cum genit.*)

irétatja *Stock, Stab, Zepter (n).* ◇ pole, stick, sceptre.

irbentjima *hereinkommen.* ◇ come in. Ⓛ ngalatarbañi

irbintinerinja *verflochten sein, verwachsen (2 Gummibäume nebeneinander).* ◇ intertwined, grow together (two gumtrees). Ⓛ waturwatutu

irbónba, *z.B.* **tmara irbonba** *leer, verlassen, z.B. verlassener Lagerplatz; ungewiß, zweifelhaft, verwüstet.* ◇ empty, abandoned, e.g. abandoned camp; uncertain, doubtful, destroyed. Ⓛ rumu

irbónberama *leer, verlassen werden; wüste werden.* ◇ empty, to become abandoned, deserted. Ⓛ rumuringañi

irbonbilama *wüste machen.* ◇ make deserted.

irbóta *gut, friedlich, gesund.* ◇ good, peaceful, healthy. Ⓛ indota

irboterama *besser werden.* ◇ get better; clever. Ⓛ indotariñi

irbilkira *grau (Macrop. robust) Haare, das große Känguruh.* ◇ grey (*Macropus robusta*) hair, big kangaroo. Ⓛ lililba

ireta *taub, fast.* ◇ deaf, closed; mad. Ⓛ rama

iretara *stark, heftig (Wind).* ◇ strong, severe (wind). Ⓛ turkara

irbuma *hineingehen, einziehen (Wasser), untergehen (Sonne), untertauchen.* ◇ go into, soak in (water), set (sun), disappear. Ⓛ tarbañi Ⓓ wirina

iretaleluma *einem etwas entfallen, aus der Hand fallen, aus dem Mund fallen.* ◇ fall (out of hand or mouth). Ⓛ patawollawollañi

irbalakalama *untergehen (Sonne), in die Erde eingehen.* ◇ sink (sun), go into the earth. Ⓛ tarbaraokaliñi

irbulélama *hineinführen.* ◇ lead into; put something in. Ⓛ tarbatunañi, tarbatiljinañi Ⓓ wirilkana

irbanama *hineingehen.* ◇ go into. Ⓛ matarbani

irbulintatnama *hineingehen.* ◇ go into. Ⓛ matarbaratalkani

irbutjikalama *hineingehen (ins Wasser), untergehen (Sonne).* ◇ go into (the water), set (sun). Ⓛ tarbaraokalingañi

iretinerama [Northern dialect] *fest zusammen halten (Wurzeln).* ◇ hold together firmly (roots). Ⓛ ngamirapungañi

iretinerinja [Northern dialect] *fest zusammen haltend (Wurzeln).* ◇ hold together firmly (roots). Ⓛ ngamirapunguta

irenma *Cikade.* ◇ cicada. Ⓛ mirin mirinba

irénmarenma *kleinere Cikade, gebl. Körper.* ◇ smallish cicada, faded, bleached or yellowish body. Ⓛ tjiririnba

iretatuma *anstarren (jemanden), fest ansehen.* ◇ stare at (somebody). Ⓛ nakulakanjini Ⓓ najina parana

iréta [Northern dialect] *Stock, Stecken.* ◇ stick. Ⓛ arata

irétatja *große schwarze Cikade, Macrotristria Hillieri.* ◇ large black cicada, *Macrotristria Hillieri* now *Burbunga hillieri* (Atlas of Living Australia n.d.) Ⓛ tjeraiï

iria (irea) *Salzbusch.* ◇ saltbush. Ⓛ iriï Ⓓ palkalara

iriaria *Cottonbusch.* ◇ cottonbush. Ⓛ iriïri

iriakurra = **jelka** *zwiebelartige, erbsengroße Frucht (Hauptnahrungsmittel der Frauen), Cyperus rotundus.* ◇ onion-like, pea sized bulb (main food of women), *Cyperus rotundus* now *Cyperus bulbosus* (Latz 1996). Ⓛ tanmati

irkaia *geblendet, nicht sehen können.* ◇ blinded, cannot see. Ⓛ arkaii

irkaierama *geblendet werden.* ◇ be blinded. Ⓛ arkaiiringani

irkaiïlama *trs. blenden (Sonne).* ◇ (transitive) blind (sun). Ⓛ arkaiini

irkaiïrkaia *kaum sichtbar, kaum erkennbar, unbemerkt.* ◇ hardly visible, hardly recognisable, unnoticed. Ⓛ arkáiarkáiï

irkāla *Wüste, Einöde.* ◇ desert, wasteland. Ⓛ munguna

irkelaualaua *verödet, öde.* ◇ desolate, deserted. Ⓛ leli

irkálanga *Gerippe, Skelett, abgemagert.* ◇ skeleton, emaciated; thin (hair or foliage); light (weight). Ⓛ iliri

irkelaualauerama *veröden.* ◇ become desert. Ⓛ leliringañi

irkelaualaua *zu Wüste werden.* ◇ become desert. Ⓛ leli

irkalentja *brauner Habicht (Sp. G.)* ◇ brown hawk (according to Spencer and Gillen). Ⓛ kirkilati Ⓓ kirki? ('?' added by CS)

irkalla *Steinmesser; der an der mēra befestigte spitze Stein.* ◇ stone knife, pointed stone attached to spear thrower. Ⓛ tula Ⓓ kutawonda, kuduwanda, kutuwonta

irkama *jucken (intrs.), kratzen.* ◇ itch (intransitive), scratch. Ⓛ irkini

irkanama *trs. kratzen (Katzen).* ◇ (transitive) scratch (cats). Ⓛ wirknani

irkanalama *(refl.) sich kratzen.* ◇ (reflexive) scratch. Ⓛ wirknani Ⓓ pununu parana, muruwara, muruana

irkarinjagata *aufgedeckt.* ◇ uncovered.

irkapa *Baum (desert-oak), Casuarina Decaisneana.* ◇ desert oak, *Casuarina Decaisneana* now *Allocasuarina decaisneana* (see Latz 1996). Ⓛ kurkara

irkapantenta *Desert-oak Dickicht.* ◇ desert oak thicket. Ⓛ kurkarakurkara

irkápara *die nächsten Verwandten des Beschnittenen.* ◇ close relatives of a boy who has been through 'business' (initiation). Ⓛ irkapiri

irkarutnuruma *klappern (Speere).* ◇ rattle (spears). Ⓛ tirkiltukatini

irkarama *fühlen, tasten nach etwas, scharren, kratzen (Vögel), umwühlen.* ◇ feel around for something, scratch (birds), uproot. Ⓛ jatini

irkarama *aufdecken (Decke wegnehmen).* ◇ uncover (take blanket away).

irkililkilelama *jucken (Brüste), kratzen machen.* ◇ itch (breasts), make itchy. Ⓛ irkiïrkini

irkatakama *beißen (kwata).* ◇ bite, burn (smoke). Ⓛ beurtunani

irkentera *große, weiße Fledermaus.* ◇ large white bat. Ⓛ irkentiri

irkelka *unnahbar, ausweichend.* ◇ unapproachable, evasive. Ⓛ arintji

irkelkerama *unantastbar werden (ein starker Mann, dem sich keiner naht), ausweichen (der Gefahr).* ◇ become unassailable (a strong man), avoid danger. Ⓛ arintjiriñi

irkintja *Syphilis.* ◇ syphilis. Ⓛ kirkni Ⓓ kududu

irkinjirkinja *kleiner Busch (sp.)* ◇ small bush species. Ⓛ irkinjirkinji

irkitja *Garn, Faden.* ◇ yarn, thread. Ⓛ puturu

irkitja womma *spinnen.* ◇ spin. Ⓛ puturu runkani Ⓓ turpana

irkebara (*oder* **arkēbara**) *Gummi an ilumba-, arganka- und iltjantja Bäumen.* ◇ gum on ilumba, arganka and iltjantja trees. Ⓛ arkebiri

irkna [*auch* **irtna**] *Hülsen, Schalen (Früchten), Schuppen, Gräten (Fischen), zwiebelartige Frucht (jelka), – auch Schorf.* ◇ husks, pods, peel (fruit), scales, fishbones, onion-like fruit (jelka), – also scab. Ⓛ neri Ⓓ paperi (*Hülse*: pod, husk), baka (*Schuppen*: scales)

irknéulama [irtnéulama] *Schorf entstehen, wenn die Wunde heilt; Hülle von sich werfen; Decke von sich werfen.* ◇ form scab when wound heals; throw off cover(ing); throw off blanket. Ⓛ neri pungañi

irknala *Rinde (von Bäumen).* ◇ bark (of trees). Ⓛ lekara Ⓓ pitji (*Baumrinde*: bark), *Schuppen*: scales

irknalbirknalba *eingekapselte Früchte (Cycas-Palme).* ◇ encased seeds (lit. fruit) (cycad palm); *Macrozamia macdonnellii* (Latz 1996). Ⓛ neriwinki

irknalakultára *eßbare, lange, rote Larven, die sich unter der Rinde der Gummibäume aufhält.* ◇ edible long red grub that lives under bark of gumtrees. Ⓛ irkniljikultari

itelínjagunja *unbedeckt (Kopf).* ◇ uncovered (head).

irkua *Eiter.* ◇ pus. Ⓛ urka Ⓓ pua

irkua nerkuma *Eiter ausdrücken.* ◇ squeeze pus out. Ⓛ urka tulkuni Ⓓ pua jikana, puapuarina (*verfaulen*: to rot)

irkurinja *das Joch.* ◇ yoke.

irkuanta *hartherzig, unbarmherzig, fest, still, klaglos (leiden), apatisch.* ◇ hard-hearted, merciless, firm, silent, uncomplaining (suffer), apathetic. Ⓛ kainkain

irkulambetninama *oder* **erkulambetninama** *erhalten bleiben.* ◇ preserved.

irtna *die Schale (des Krebses), die Haut (der Schlange)?* ◇ shell (of crab), skin (of snake). ('?' added by CS)

irtneulama *sich häuten.* ◇ shed skin. Ⓛ neri pungañi

irkungala *neben, zur Seite (cum abl.)* ◇ beside (with ablative) Ⓛ aiinka

irkungarbaka *daneben.* ◇ next to, beside. Ⓛ aiïkutuba

irkungala lama *neben einander gehen.* ◇ go beside each other. Ⓛ aiinka jennani

eróalawolla *kreisförmiges Zeichen am Körper, rundes Wasserloch.* ◇ circle design on body, round waterhole. Ⓛ taburita

irtjartirtjata *Strauch mit eßbaren Früchten.* ◇ shrub with edible fruit. Ⓛ irtjartirtjáti

irula *Schwanzspitze (von Wallaby).* ◇ tail tip (of wallaby). Ⓛ jauali, mulkni

irūla *Schwan (der sich jedoch hier nicht aufhält).* ◇ swan (not native in central Australia), *Cygnus atratus*. Ⓓ kuti

irulunba *Eidechse (spec.)* ◇ lizard (species). Ⓛ utanki

irura *zornig (Moskito).* ◇ angry (mosquito). Ⓛ ngaru

artnarankama *zwitschern (im Haufen) (grass-parrakeet).* ◇ chirp (in a flock) (grass parakeets). Ⓛ banbaworrañi

ita [Southern dialect] *conf.* **itja** *Laus.* ◇ louse. Ⓛ kulu

itaia [Southern dialect] *cf.* **tjaia** *Weg.* ◇ path. Ⓛ iwara

ita *taub.* ◇ deaf. Ⓛ rama

itaïta *taub, taubstumm, dumm.* ◇ deaf, deaf and dumb, stupid. Ⓛ ramarama Ⓓ pattipatti (*dumm*: dumb, stupid)

iterama *taub werden (vom Geschrei).* ◇ become deaf (from noise). Ⓛ ramaringani

itilama *betäuben (durch Geschrei), den Vestand rauben.* ◇ deafen (with noise), rob mind. Ⓛ ramani

itaïtilama *betäuben.* ◇ deafen, stun. Ⓛ rare wonniñi

itáka [Southern dialect] *conf.* **tjaka** *lose.* ◇ loose. Ⓛ ataki

itála [Southern dialect] *conf.* **tjala** *Kniescheibe.* ◇ kneecap. Ⓛ irbi Ⓓ pantjamata

itanja [Southern dialect] *cf.* **tjenja** *lang.* ◇ long. Ⓛ wara

itántara *Darmfett.* ◇ fat of intestine. Ⓛ ngututari

itárangama [Southern dialect] *cf.* **tjarangama** *herantragen.* ◇ to bring. Ⓛ itarikatiñi

itarinama [Southern dialect] *cf.* **tjarinama** *heranziehen.* ◇ to pull. Ⓛ itariñi

ītata *Zeit.* ◇ time. Ⓛ ántalu

itanterelama *warten (Zeit lang).* ◇ to wait (a long time). Ⓛ talbaninañi

itnáritjinjíma *hinaufklettern.* ◇ to climb up. Ⓛ mararakalbañi

itintjiuma [Northern dialect] *begraben.* ◇ to bury. Ⓛ totuni

itipmara, itapnara [Southern dialect] *Finger und Zehennägel.* ◇ finger and toe nails. Ⓛ piri, miltji

itelama *bedecken (Haut oder Schuppen), aufsetzen (Hut), werfen auf den Kopf (Staub).* ◇ cover (skin and scales), put on (hat), throw on head (dust). Ⓛ wattuni

itjalama? *oder nicht.* ◇ or not?

ítera *Saum, Rand, Ufer, Grenze.* ◇ seam, edge, riverbank, border, boundary. Ⓛ iñinji, ngaii, mimi Ⓓ wondiri (*Grenze*: border, boundary)

iteranga *am Ufer.* ◇ at the riverbank. Ⓛ iñinjinguru

iteela *am Ufer, am Abhang.* ◇ at the riverbank, at the slope. Ⓛ ngaiinka Ⓓ kalikali

itenétena *Überfluß.* ◇ overflow.

iteramitera *am Ufer entlang.* ◇ along the riverbank. Ⓛ ngaiïwonnawonna

iterekérama *am Ufer (Fuß des Gebirges) entlang gehen.* ◇ walk along the riverbank (foot of range). Ⓛ miminkarini

itelalbunama *bedecken (mit der Haut).* ◇ to cover (with skin). Ⓛ walturapatañi

itélelanáma *verhüllen, bedecken, umhängen.* ◇ veil, cover, cloak. Ⓛ mularanañi

itia [Southern dialect], **tjia** *jüngerer Bruder, jüngere Schwester, Vaters jüng. Bruders Sohn, Mutters jüng. Schwesters Sohn, Fraus jüng. Schwesters Mann, Manns jüng. Schwesters Mann, Vaters jüng. Bruders Tochter, Mutters jüng. Schwesters Tochter, Fraus jüng. Bruders Frau, Manns jüng. Bruders Frau.* ◇ younger brother, younger sister, father's younger brother's son, mother's younger sister's son, wife's younger sister's husband, husband's younger sister's husband, father's younger brother's daughter, mother's younger sister's daughter, wife's younger brother's wife, husband's younger bother's wife. Ⓛ malantu, malangu Ⓓ ngatata

itiukua *der itia eines Andern.* ◇ someone else's itia.

itia altjala (iltjala) *Vaters jüngere Schwesters Tochter (♀), Mutters jüngerer Bruders Tochter (♀).* ◇ father's younger sister's daughter, mother's younger brother's daughter.

itiïlatja; itiatja *'mein' jüngerer Bruder; mein jüngerer Bruder.* ◇ 'my' younger brother; my younger brother. Ⓛ malangulu

itinja, itinjawara *nahe, ganz in der Nähe.* ◇ near, very near. Ⓛ ila, ilakarka Ⓓ karakara

itinjilama, ilani itinjerama *einholen, sich nähern.* ◇ to catch up; approach. Ⓛ ilaringañi Ⓓ karakararina (*nähern*: approach)

itinbara [Southern dialect] *cf.* **tjinbara** *sehr heiß.* ◇ very hot. Ⓛ itinbiri

itinjerenama *sich nähern.* ◇ approach. Ⓛ ilarekukatiñi

itirka [Southern dialect] *Geschwür im Fleisch.* ◇ abscess. Ⓛ itirki

ititja *Mulga Baum (Acacia neura).* ◇ Mulga tree, *Acacia aneura* (see Latz 1996). Ⓛ kurku

ititjerama *ititja werden.* ◇ to become mulga. Ⓛ kurkuringañi

ititjintja *Mulga-Speer.* ◇ mulga spear. Ⓛ intiwirki

iteelaworrama *nachfolgen [unclear].* ◇ follow. Ⓛ wollankawollankaringañi

itolélama *hin und her schwenken (Zweige) hüpfend.* ◇ (branches) swing from side to side bouncing. Ⓛ kauanjingañi

itia (auch itja) *Laus (schwarze).* ◇ lice (black). Ⓛ kulu Ⓓ kata

itjaworra *einmals.* ◇ once.

itja; atua itja *nein, nicht, kein; z.B. kein Mann.* ◇ no, not; e.g. no man. Ⓛ wia Ⓓ wata (*nicht*: not), pani (*kein*: not, *nein*: no)

itinjitinja *nahe.* ◇ near. Ⓛ ilakarkakarka

itjima *nichts.* ◇ nothing. Ⓛ wiamba

iténa *Pflanzenkost.* ◇ plant food. Ⓛ unita

itjititjita *Strauch mit glockenförmigen Blüten.* ◇ shrub with bell-shaped blossoms. Ⓛ kaiurukaiuru

itninjalarenama *beweinen, weinen über.* ◇ cry over.

etnantambala *gleich viele.* ◇ as many. Ⓛ tanakutulenku

itnarama [Northern dialect], **itnaranama, itnarakama** *rutschen auf den Knien, kriechen.* ◇ to slide on knees, crawl. Ⓛ marani, mamarañi, marajuriñi Ⓓ marakana

itnima; itnima (iknima) *weinen; fallen.* ◇ cry, weep; fall. Ⓛ ulani Ⓓ jindrana

itnima (iknima) *fallen.* ◇ to fall.

itnilelama *fällen, fallen machen.* ◇ to fell, to make fall.

itninama *fallen auf, sich werfen auf jemanden.* ◇ fall on, throw oneself on someone.

itnilélama *zum Weinen bringen (durch traurige Botschaft).* ◇ make someone cry (with a sad message). Ⓛ ulajennañi

itninjilérama *sehr viel weinen, trauern.* ◇ cry a lot, mourn. Ⓛ ulanjinkanta

itninjalarenama *sich dem Weinen überlassen, trauern über, weinen über.* ◇ mourn, cry about.

itnilarenama *sehr viel weinen, jammern.* ◇ cry a lot, lament. Ⓛ ularawonnañi

itnetneuma [Northern dialect] *cf.* **tnetneuma** *fluchen, verwünschen.* ◇ swear, curse. Ⓛ iniwonini

itnáruparuma [Northern dialect] *hin und her rutschen, kreisen (Vögel).* ◇ slide back and forth, circle (birds). Ⓛ ngarañikutara

iwatnama *herauswerfen.* ◇ throw out. Ⓛ wonnirijenni

itnóra; knulja itnóra *wild, Wild; dingo.* ◇ wild, game; dingo. Ⓛ itnúra; papa itnúra Ⓓ jampa

itúkula *schnell (laufen).* ◇ fast (run). Ⓛ kutururu

iwulalakalama *sich hinwerfen.* ◇ throw. Ⓛ ngárikatira okalingañi

itoa *wilde Puter.* ◇ bush turkey, Australian Bustard, Plains Turkey, *Ardeotis australis*. Ⓛ nganuti Ⓓ kaladura

itunta [Northern dialect] *Magen.* ◇ stomach. Ⓛ ituntu Ⓓ kudnapiti

iwarakananma *weglaufen (in ein Versteck), sich verstecken.* ◇ run away (to a hidding spot), hide. Ⓛ mangalbarabakañi

iwōpa *Spinngewebe.* ◇ spider web. Ⓛ woñka Ⓓ karalja

iwuma *werfen, wegwerfen.* ◇ throw, throw away. Ⓛ wonniñi Ⓓ worrana

iwulijinama *zu Boden werfen, hinauswerfen.* ◇ throw to the ground, throw out. Ⓛ wonnirijennañi Ⓓ narrana

iwulama *sich hinwerfen, sich zurücklehnen.* ◇ throw (reflexive), lean back. Ⓛ ngarikatiñi Ⓓ worraterina

iwulitjalbuma *sich (nach der Rückkehr) niederwerfen.* ◇ throw oneself down (on return) (reflexive). Ⓛ ngarikatinikulbara

iwutjangera ntjalbanama *mit einem Ruck aufstehen.* ◇ get up with a jerk. Ⓛ wianku bakalkatiñi

iwuliuma *wegwerfen, verwerfen.* ◇ throw away, dismiss. Ⓛ woniritalkañi Ⓓ worrarijiribana

iwulítnanama *sich hinwerfen (auf den Boden).* ◇ throw (on the ground). Ⓛ kulbara ngaikatiñi

iwonba *kleine Stäbe (Zahnausschlagen, zum Zusammenschlagen).* ◇ small sticks (to knock out tooth and clap together). Ⓛ tururu

iworka *Dickicht.* ◇ thicket. Ⓛ tata

iwuna? iwunamá? *was? Was ist los?* ◇ what? What is the matter? Ⓛ naii? nāmba? Ⓓ minna?

iwolkulama *im Kreis (um etwas) herumgehen.* ◇ walk in a circle (around something). Ⓛ parakulbañi

iwuka? *weshalb? warum?* ◇ why? Ⓛ nāku? Ⓓ minnandru? Warum?

iwetnanama *wegwerfen (Strauch), wegreißen (Schutzzaun).* ◇ throw away (shrub), tear down (windbreak). Ⓛ wonniwonnirangariñi

iwutjintjima *vor sich hinwerfen (Schlange – ihren Kopf).* ◇ throw in front (snake – its head). Ⓛ wonnirakalbañi

iwũnja *Moskito.* ◇ mosquito. Ⓛ kewinji Ⓓ kunti

iwunjinbakalama *hineinströmen (z.B. in ein Haus).* ◇ pour (into a house). Ⓛ kutuwarakatarbañi

iwunjiwunja *fliegende Ameisen, die aus argankat. Gummibäumen hervorkommen.* ◇ flying ants that come out of gumtrees. Ⓛ iwinjiwinji

iwuta *nail-tailed wallaby.* ◇ probably crescent nailtailed wallaby *(Onychogalea lunata)*. Ⓛ tauala

iwutiwuta *schmal (Stirn).* ◇ narrow (forehead). Ⓛ wotjinkuru

J

jabataratara *sehr fett.* ◇ very fat. Ⓛ ngatinpuntu

jau! *Ja und! (so ists).* ◇ So! (that's it!). Ⓛ watu!

jabajaba *unkundig sein, nichts gehört habend.* ◇ be ignorant, not heard anything. Ⓛ kauaru

jabalpa *fett, Schmerbauch.* ◇ fat, potbelly, Aranda name of Glen Helen Gorge. Ⓛ ngatina

jabajabérama *sich erkundigen (nach etwas), sich befragen.* ◇ inquire (after something). Ⓛ kauaruriñi Ⓓ jekijekibana (*heimlich*: secretly)

jabea (*z.B.* **mannaka jabea**) *arm, bedürftig.* ◇ poor, needy. Ⓛ maralba (*z.B.* miïku maralba)

jábmama *beobachten, betrachten.* ◇ watch, observe; stare, look hard. Ⓛ wombantjinañi

jai! *heda! Sieh da.* ◇ hey! Look here! Ⓛ jai! Ⓓ mai!

jaia *Wassermoos.* ◇ watermoss, slime in water. Ⓛ aijaii

jaijurumba *mit grünem Wassermoos bedeckt (Wasser).* ◇ (water) covered with green algae or slime. Ⓛ aijaiïkutu

jainama; ekuranga inkananga jainama *wegschicken, wegsenden; ihm nachschicken.* ◇ send away; send after him. Ⓛ íjani Ⓓ jinpana, tadana

jainaninana *Absender.* ◇ sender. Ⓛ ijanmijanmi

jainala jinama *zurücksenden.* ◇ send back. Ⓛ ijérijani

jainuajainerama *sich einander zusenden (Geschenke).* ◇ send to each other (gifts).

Ijaiïnja *fauchend, zischend (Schlange).* ◇ hissing (snake). Ⓛ tulutulu

jakkai! *Ausruf der Verwunderung, der Überraschung (z.B. bei einem Kampf) oh! Ach!* ◇ exclamation of astonishment or surprise (e.g. in a fight) oh! Ah!; oh!, hey!, wow!, gee! ouch! Ⓛ jakko! Ⓓ jakkaijai!

jakkabai! *Ausruf des Schmerzes (Oh weh!).* ◇ exclamation of pain: ouch! Ⓛ jakkur!

jainalarenama *melden, einem sagen lassen (durch einen Boten).* ◇ notify, inform (by messenger).
jakama, jakalelama *zureden, überreden zu bleiben.* ◇ persuade, talk into staying; stop someone going. Ⓛ atekurani
jabalka *(auf dem Boden) gebreitete Sträucher.* ◇ branches of bushes spread out (on ground). Ⓛ ilkiwonni
jákota *Sack aus Fellen, in dem manna (Brot) getragen wird, Schlauch.* ◇ skin bag to carry bread. Ⓛ kunnapatti Ⓓ junga
jakularama *erforschen.* ◇ explore.
jakularélama *nachfragen, sich erkundigen (nach einem verlorenen Gegenstand).* ◇ inquire, search (for a lost object). Ⓛ turkulturkulbmanañi Ⓓ jakalkingana
jauluralura *die Säge (n).* ◇ saw (n).
jauluralurala tama *zersägen.* ◇ to saw.
jalama, tungalama *vielleicht.* ◇ perhaps, maybe. Ⓛ waputa
jalbijalba *lang herabhängende (Zweige, Haare), mit herabhängenden Zweigen.* ◇ hanging down (branches, hair). Ⓛ jalbajalbi
jalknajalkna *sehr weit entfernt, kaum sichtbar.* ◇ very far away, hardly visible. Ⓛ arkaiarkaii
jatajatilama *Last auflegen.* ◇ to load. Ⓓ jama (*Fischnetz*: fish net)
janna *nicht vermögend sein, nicht könnend.* ◇ not able to; not capable of. Ⓛ butu Ⓓ bulu
jartuma *mit Fragen belästigen.* ◇ trouble with questions. Ⓛ butunba, butu
jatuntja! *Sage! Sag an!* ◇ speak, speak up! Ⓛ tamili?
jartaka, juka *vielleicht, ich weiß nicht.* ◇ maybe, I do not know. Ⓛ wombalta
jatjulkara, jatjikuia *kleine Beutelratte, kleine Rattenart.* ◇ small marsupial rat (species) Ⓛ jatjulkuri
jaralama *suchen nach etwas (was er verloren hat).* ◇ search for something (that has been lost). Ⓛ wiakuwiakunangañi
jarka *Asche.* ◇ ash. Ⓛ epa
jartja *glatt (Stamm), astlos, schlank.* ◇ smooth (trunk), branchless, slim. Ⓛ wirunkurunku
jarejara *aufgesprungen (Zehen), rauhe oder rohe (Zehen).* ◇ cracked (toes), rough. Ⓛ kirikiri
játjara *Besuch, Gesellschaft.* ◇ visit, company. Ⓛ maiatari Ⓓ milpara
jartijarta *ermattet, ermüdet.* ◇ exhausted, tired. Ⓛ walenku
jatjara lama *besuchen.* ◇ visit. Ⓛ maiatari jennañi
jartuma *zu singen und zu sagen, vorsingen, vor-sagen (introitus), vorsprechen, herausfordern, preisen (was der Andere tun wird), auf die Probe stellen.* ◇ prompt, recite, intonate, begin, praise, test. Ⓛ takani
jatjara nama (ekurauna) *besuchen.* ◇ to visit. Ⓛ maiatari ninañi
jatu? *Nicht wahr? Ist es nicht so? (Sag ist es nicht so?) Frageartikel.* ◇ Isn't it? Question particle. Ⓛ panatoa?
jatuma *schwer sein, drücken, zusetzen (mit Fragen).* ◇ press, bother with questions. Ⓛ palini
jatajata *klagend (unter der Last).* ◇ complaining (under a load). Ⓛ ngalkarangalkara
jatutjalama *intr. drücken.* ◇ (intransitive) press. Ⓛ palinijenkula
ja͡u! *Interjection der Zustimmung: So ists! Wirklich!* ◇ interjection of agreement: Alright! Ⓛ watu
jearíbara *Gabe, Geschenk.* ◇ gift, present. Ⓛ waiïrita
jelabankura *unverwandt, fortwährend.* ◇ continually. Ⓛ ratatura
jelabankurala rama *unverwandt ansehen.* ◇ continually look at. Ⓛ ratatura nangañi
jelka (irkna) *zwiebelartige, erbsengroße Frucht (Hauptnahrungsmittel der Frauen), Cyperus rotundus.* ◇ onion-like, pea sized bulb (main food of women), *Cyperus rotundus* now *Cyperus bulbosus* (Latz 1996). Ⓛ tanmati, neri Ⓓ jaua
jatajatilama *auflegen Last.* ◇ to load.

jérendama *vertauschen, verkaufen.* ◇ exchange, sell. Ⓛ waïirijungañi Ⓓ jinkinmalina

jenkua *sehr alt (Kleid), der sehr alte Mann, Greis.* ◇ very old (dress), very old man. Ⓛ multamulta Ⓓ womala

jienkua *sehr alt, Greis.* ◇ very old, old man. Ⓛ mokunba

jentarpa *Vogel (spec.)* ◇ bird species. Ⓛ talburatalburu

jerratja *kleine, schwarze, fliegende Ameise.* ◇ small, black flying ant. Ⓛ mingata

jerra *Ameise.* ◇ ant. Ⓛ minga Ⓓ mirka

jerrabottabotta *der Ameisen-Haufe; Gruppe von Ameisen.* ◇ anthill; group of ants. Ⓛ mingakaputukaputu

jerrajerriwuma *unaufhörlich schreien (junge Vögel).* ◇ cry continuously (young birds). Ⓛ ngeangearbmanañi

jerrámba, jerramba *Honigameise, die den Honig im Leibe trägt.* ◇ honeyant (carries honey in its body), *Camponotus inflatus*. Ⓛ winaturu, mitala, tala Ⓓ wikana

jerríuma *glattschaben, glätten (tjatta), abstreifen.* ◇ to smooth (spear), strip off. Ⓛ wiripungani

jetnólkuma *stöhnen, klagen.* ◇ groan, moan. Ⓛ butukuluni

jerrijerriulama *(dupl.) einschrumpfen.* ◇ (reduplication) shrink, shrivel. Ⓛ wiriwiripungañi

jerarelama *die Hand auf die schmerzende Stelle legen.* ◇ lay hand on painful spot.

jia *Nachricht, Botschaft.* ◇ message; story, news. Ⓛ tjiri Ⓓ ninti

jentua *Schlafplatz.* ◇ sleeping place. Ⓛ lau

jialbmélama *Botschaft bringen, verkünden, verraten.* ◇ bring a message, announce. Ⓛ tjiri wottani Ⓓ jaura tikalkana, wondawondana

jerruntuma *um etwas herumlaufen.* ◇ walk around something. Ⓛ taiïrpungañi

jiatnankama *vorherverkünden.* ◇ announce (in advance). Ⓛ tjiri wirkani

jérrama *einen nicht antreffen (den man sucht), nicht finden (Wild zum Jagen).* ◇ miss (someone whom one is looking for), unable to find (game during hunt). Ⓛ ngokani

jellara *Faß (n), Kiste (n), Tonne (n).* ◇ barrel, box, drum.

jelitjajela *das Rasseln (der Räder).* ◇ rattling (of wheels).

jerrarelinja *übel.* ◇ sick.

jerrarelama *sich übel befinden, unwohl sein.* ◇ feel sick, unwell.

jibarinama *verneinen, verleugnen, abschlagen (Bitte).* ◇ deny, refuse (request). Ⓛ wia wottani Ⓓ kutikutibana

jibarinalama *sich entschuldigen.* ◇ apologise. Ⓛ wia wonkani

jibélama *auf und nieder bewegen, hin und her bewegen (danna) sichten.* ◇ move up and down or back and forth (bowl), sift, shake. Ⓛ kanini

jibuma [Southern dialect] *cf.* **ortjérama** *lügen.* ◇ to lie. Ⓛ nguntjiwonkañi

jibalélama *betrügen.* ◇ deceive. Ⓛ nguntijennañi

jibunakana *Lügner.* ◇ liar. Ⓛ nguntjiwonkamatu

jibuntja *Lüge.* ◇ lie. Ⓛ nguntjintji

jikala *kleine Mulde.* ◇ small bowl. Ⓛ nangunba

jikalumbalumba *Blätterbüschel (an Zweigen).* ◇ bunches of leaves (on branches). Ⓛ panmawórranmi

jilajila [Northern dialect] *cf.* **julajula** *sehr viele.* ◇ very many. Ⓛ mingakurakura

jilbijinama; *z.B.* **apma jilbijinama inka** *umwickeln, sich um etwas wickeln.* ◇ wind, wrap around something; e.g. snake winds itself around a foot. Ⓛ titirpungañi, karbikarbini

jilkara *grau, weiß (Emu).* ◇ grey, white (emu). Ⓛ kipara, mintalbi

jimajirka (jimajurka) *leicht zerbrechlich, weich.* ◇ fragile, soft. Ⓛ mokunba

jilbajinama *ranken (um etwas), z.B. Schlingpflanze.* ◇ entwine, wrap around something (climb, grow around something), e.g. creeper (plant).

jimbaltjilerāma *etwas durchsuchen, über etwas nachdenken, grübeln.* ◇ think about something, ponder. Ⓛ paraninangañi Ⓓ kurakurana

jinama *trs. binden, zusammen binden, verbinden (Wunde), umwickeln.* ◇ (transitive) tie, tie together, bandage (wound), wind or wrap around. Ⓛ waturpungañi, karbiñi Ⓓ karana

jinalama *refl. sich etwas umbinden.* ◇ (reflexive) tie something around. Ⓛ karbiñi

jinba *Haut, Fell, Schale, Rinde.* ◇ skin, fur, peel, bark. Ⓛ panki Ⓓ dala (*Haut*: skin), pitji (*Rinde*: bark)

jinbara *Schlangenhaut.* ◇ snakeskin. Ⓛ winbiri

jinbara *Strauchart, aus der Speere verf. werden (Tecoma australis).* ◇ shrub species from which spears are made (*Tecoma australis* now *Pandorea pandorana*) (Latz 1996). Ⓛ winbiri

jinga *ich.* ◇ I. Ⓛ ngaiulu Ⓓ ngani

jinilama *verweigern, abschlagen (Bitte), abhalten (vom Streiten).* ◇ refuse, deny (request), prevent (quarrel). Ⓛ tjirkani

jinilalama *refl. sich verweigern, nicht zu Willen sein.* ◇ (reflexive) refuse, not be willing. Ⓛ tjirkaraninañi

jipa *rankende Pflanze mit hellgrünen Blättern, kleinen Blüten, deren rübenartige Wurzeln gegessen werden (Boerhavia diffusa).* ◇ climber with light green leaves, small blossoms and edible tuber roots; tar vine, (*Boerhavia*) (see Latz 1996). Ⓛ wajipi

jipatja *Raupen, die sich an der jipa-Ranken finden.* ◇ caterpillars who live on jipa vines. Ⓛ anumara

jirama *aufhören, verschwinden, zu Ende sein, vergehen.* ◇ cease, disappear, end, pass. Ⓛ wiaringañi Ⓓ mudana

jiranama *verschwinden, vergehen; z.B. Wunden, etc.* ◇ disappear; e.g. wounds that heal etc. Ⓛ mawiaringañi

jirarerama, jurarerama *ausbleiben, fortbleiben.* ◇ stay away. Ⓛ wiarekula wonniñi

jirangeranga *vergänglich.* ◇ fleeting, ephemeral.

jiritjikalutja *dem Ende nahe (Aufhören).* ◇ dying, close to the end or to death.

jiranjalkua *vergänglich.* ◇ ephemeral.

jírara *Norden.* ◇ north. Ⓛ alintjara (alintara) Ⓓ tidnankara

jirarakua *nach Norden.* ◇ to the north. Ⓛ alintjinalba, alintjaralku

jirarambinjala *nördlich.* ◇ north, northerly. Ⓛ alintjarakarbaku

jirula *im Norden.* ◇ in the north. Ⓛ alintjara

jirknininja *Nordwind.* ◇ north wind. Ⓛ alintakata (alintjakata)

jirkna *gehässig, neidisch.* ◇ spiteful, envious. Ⓛ keltji

jirknerama *hassen.* ◇ to hate. Ⓛ keltjirangañi Ⓓ kalakalarina

jita *der herabhängende fette Bauch.* ◇ hanging potbelly. Ⓛ ngatin

jitala tnara *sehr fett (z.B. Schweine).* ◇ very fat (e.g. pigs). Ⓛ ngatinpuntu

jitinama *ziehen.* ◇ pull. Ⓛ ngaluni

joa *Hüfte, Taille.* ◇ hip, waist. Ⓛ kappa Ⓓ kappa

jóaja *Frau, die geboren hat; Wöchnerin.* ◇ woman who has given birth. Ⓛ ajoaji

joará nama *die Spuren der umkehrenden Schlange.* ◇ tracks of a returning snake. Ⓛ matotatura kulbanguta

jotuia (jatuia) *schwer, drückend.* ◇ heavy, pressing. Ⓛ palin

jotuma (jatuma) *drücken (Last).* ◇ to weigh down (load). Ⓛ palini

jotuma *auflegen (eine Last).* ◇ to load.

jountjia *der lange Hals der Vögel (der Emu, itoa und Pelican).* ◇ long neck of bird (emu, bush turkey and pelican). Ⓛ kaua

juka *ich weiß nicht.* ◇ I do not know. Ⓛ womba Ⓓ anaka (nganako)

jukukerinama *verziehen (Wolken), weggehen (für immer).* ◇ clear away (clouds), go away (for ever). Ⓛ wombarekula bakañi

jukutjikulélama, jakutjikulélama *Barmherzigkeit üben, jammern (eines Andern), Mitleid haben.* ◇ show pity, lament, have empathy. Ⓛ umbuumbuni Ⓓ kalumiltjamiltjarina

julajula (jilajila) *sehr viele.* ◇ very many. Ⓛ mingakurakura

janturbmanáma *sehr weinen.* ◇ cry very much. Ⓛ urbmuntala ninañi

jukutakuta nama *in Sterben liegen.* ◇ dying.

julta *Sache, Ding (ein von der Loritja Sprache herübergenommenes Wort).* ◇ thing (Loritja loan word in Aranda). Ⓛ julta

junta *Höhlung, Vertiefung im Boden.* ◇ hollow, depression in ground. Ⓛ laū

alknajunta *Augenhöhle.* ◇ eye socket. Ⓛ kurulaū

tmarajunta *Vertiefung im Schlafplatz (in der sie schlafen).* ◇ depression in sleeping place (in which they sleep). Ⓛ nguralau

juntama *suchen.* ◇ search. Ⓛ nguriñi Ⓓ wontina, kulpina

juntalama *(sich suchen), sich besinnen, sich orientieren.* ◇ (introspective), consider, orientate. Ⓛ ngurirariñi

juramba *Zucker an den lalba-Strauch.* ◇ sugar on lalba bush. Ⓛ albitalji

jura *Baum spec.* ◇ tree species. Ⓛ ujúru

jurajura *sehr leicht (Kleider), sehr dünn (Kleider).* ◇ very light (clothes), very thin (clothes). Ⓛ rambirambi Ⓓ tjankatjanka

jurankama *sausen (Wind), heulen (Sturm).* ◇ whistle (wind), howl (storm). Ⓛ kurangañi (*Rausch, Wind*)

jurankama *rauschen (Meer).* ◇ roar or sough (sea). Ⓛ lulumanañi

jurankama *fauchen (Schlange).* ◇ hiss (snake). Ⓛ wilijiri wonkani

jurankinja *Rauschen, Brausen.* ◇ roar. Ⓛ bobuwaranini, karanganmi

jurka *leicht zerbrechlich, zart.* ◇ fragile, tender. Ⓛ mokuna

jurkerama *zerbrechlich werden.* ◇ become fragile. Ⓛ mokunaringañi

jurankala renama *zu Boden stürzen (vom Speer getroffen).* ◇ fall to the ground (hit by a spear). Ⓛ wālawonniñi

juta *porcupine-grass.* ◇ porcupine grass, spinifex. Ⓛ untia Ⓓ kuramala

jutalbma *Spitzen des porcupine-grass Halme.* ◇ tips of porcupine grass. Ⓛ untia ipiri

jutabintja *porcupine-grass Halme.* ◇ porcupine grass blades. Ⓛ untia tanbi

jutapatta *Schlafplatz der aranga (Euro).* ◇ sleeping place of euro.

jutarka *schwer (zu tun).* ◇ difficult (to do).

jutia *Last.* ◇ burden, load.

K

ka *(in Zusammensetzungen) = Kopf, Spitze.* ◇ (in compounds) head, point.

kā *Bruder.* ◇ brother. Ⓛ kuta

kabana *zur Vergeltung, wieder.* ◇ in retaliation, again; back, in turn, in return. Ⓛ wakubita Ⓓ kalala

kabanenta *ganz umsonst, gratis.* ◇ completely free, gratis. Ⓛ wakurakutu

kabananta ndama *umsonst geben, schenken.* ◇ give away, give. Ⓛ wakurakutu jungañi Ⓓ bakueli jinkina

kātja *mein älterer Bruder.* ◇ my older brother. Ⓛ kutana

kabantalabantala *undurchdringlich (Busch).* ◇ impenetrable (bush). Ⓛ múnutúrtutúrtu

kabanalkura *hinwieder, dagegen.* ◇ on the other hand. Ⓛ wakuranguanba

kabia *leise, langsam.* ◇ quiet, slow. Ⓛ purinji

kabia lama *leise gehen, schleichen (langsam).* ◇ go softly, sneak, creep (slowly). Ⓛ purinji jennañi

kábila *arandisiertes englisches Wort 'hobble' [Pferd? unclear].* ◇ hobble derived from the English word 'hobble'. Ⓛ kabili

kabilja *Eidechse (spec.)* ◇ lizard species. Ⓛ daputa

kabiljalkuna *Pelikan.* ◇ pelican. Ⓛ kabiljalku Ⓓ tampangara

kabilúnama *hin und her stoßen (vom Wind).* ◇ push back and forth (by the wind). Ⓛ tatunpungañi

kabitjirka *voll sein, bedeckt (mit Wunden).* ◇ be full of, be covered with (wounds).

kabuluma *öffnen (Mund), öffnen (Buch), auftun (Ohr), aufmachen (Hand), losbrechen (Steine), abstreifen (Zucker von den Bäumen), aufmachen (Buch).* ◇ open (mouth), open (book), open (ear); open (hand); break of (stones); strip (sugar from trees); open (a book). Ⓛ tankapungañi Ⓓ piltana

kabulunja *oder* **kabilunja** *offen, aufgeschlagen (Buch).* ◇ open (e.g. book).

kaburkulta *Schlange (spec.), geringelte Schlange, rot und schwarz geringelte Schlange.* ◇ snake (species), banded snake, red and black banded snake. Ⓛ kaburpi

kaditjina [?] *conf.* **tnaminjalkna** *Jakobsstab.* ◇ Orion? (a star constellation). Ⓛ kaditjina

kaëla ilkama *bau bau bau schreien (Geschrei der Bluträcher).* ◇ cry bau, bau, bau (cry of revenge party). Ⓛ meratura merañi

kaíima *anfangen zu schlagen.* ◇ start to hit. Ⓛ tjitini

kaia *einsam, allein.* ◇ lonely, alone. Ⓛ kutuntari

kaiala *einsam; die Einsame.* ◇ lonely; the lonely one (a mythical female being in Strehlow 1907: 30–31). Ⓛ kutuntarinku

kaiaka *zufrieden, glücklich, friedlich.* ◇ content, happy, peaceful. Ⓛ maka

kajurka *weiche Stelle auf dem Kopf.* ◇ soft spot on head. Ⓛ katamokuna

kakabanama *sich fortwährend erkundigen, sich erkundigen ob einer eine Botschaft oder Arbeit übernehmen will.* ◇ to constantly enquire, enquire whether somebody wants to take a message or a job. Ⓛ wonkawonniñi

kakalala (L) *cf.* **nkuna** *weißer Kakadu.* ◇ white cockatoo. Ⓛ kakalala

kakaraïnbuma; Kakaraïnbaka *nicht durchschauen können, sich nicht zurechtfinden können; 'sie können sich nicht zurechtfinden' (Platzname).* ◇ not able to see through; place name (Strehlow 1907: 78). Ⓛ bainkatini

kákatnámakátna *den Kopf fortwährend emporhebend (Raupe).* ◇ continuously lift head (caterpillar). Ⓛ katakattu

kakatuma *den Kopf auf und nieder bewegen (beim kriechen, z.B. Raupen).* ◇ move head up and down (when creeping, e.g. caterpillar). Ⓛ peulukatini

kakara iwuma *nach einer Seite hin werfen (nicht in die Höhe).* ◇ throw sideways (not upwards). Ⓛ kikiri wonniñi

kakarakana *Rückkehr boomerang.* ◇ return boomerang. Ⓛ kikiri, kikirikunu

kakuma (kōkuma) *beißen, aufbeißen, kauen, nagen.* ◇ bite, crack, chew, gnaw. Ⓛ patani Ⓓ matana

kákuakákua *nagend, zerbeißend.* ◇ gnawing, biting. Ⓛ ketunketunba

kakura *Haufe, Vorrat (z.B. der Ameisen).* ◇ heap, store (e.g. of ants). Ⓛ akakuru

kakuta *Hut (aus dem Engl.[unclear]).* ◇ hat. Ⓛ mokkati Ⓓ kakabilli

kakutjikama *ans Herz drücken (aus Liebe).* ◇ embrace (out of love).

kăla (auch kalla) *genug, fertig, schon.* ◇ enough, finished, already. Ⓛ bokkana Ⓓ matja

Kalla! *fertig! getan!* ◇ done! Ok!

era kalla pitjima *er kommt schon.* ◇ he is coming. Ⓛ paluru bokkana ngalajennañi

kallabara *schon.* ◇ already. Ⓛ bokkanaka

kalaka *wilde Pfirsiche.* ◇ wild peaches. Ⓛ totu

kalaka *postp. wider, gegen z.B. tjinnakalaka.* ◇ (postposition) against; e.g. against friends.

kálakakála *unsinnig, verwirrt.* ◇ absurd, confused. Ⓛ kauankauana Ⓓ parapara

kálakakálerama *verwirrt werden.* ◇ become confused. Ⓛ kauankauanariñi Ⓓ parapara warana

kalama *fließen (Wasser), gießen (Samen in eine Schüssel).* ◇ flow (water), pour (seeds into a bowl). Ⓛ okalingañi

kalambankama *sich ausstrecken (nach dem Schlaf), sich aufrichten (Känguruh).* ◇ stretch (after sleep), get up (kangaroo). Ⓛ tantarknarañi

kalantja *auseinandergehende Schenkel (Scheide?).* ◇ spread thighs (vagina?). ('?' added by CS) Ⓛ kankala

kalantjakalantja *ein wenig hinkend (gehen), [unclear].* ◇ walk with a small limp. Ⓛ katarurkátini

kalatja *mein älterer Bruder.* ◇ my older brother. Ⓛ kutalamanku

kalatoppa *Wand, Mauer.* ◇ wall. Ⓛ tatulpi Ⓓ wondiri

kalbakaia *sehr kalt (schneidende Kälte).* ◇ very cold (biting cold). Ⓛ kuntakuntanmi

kalbakama *schneidende Schmerzen (im Leibe).* ◇ cutting pain (in abdomen). Ⓛ kuntakuntañi

kalbalja *aufgelöstes Haar (der rukuta).* ◇ loose hair. Ⓛ kátara

kálbalba *die weißen Wolken, die den schwarzen Regenwolken voranziehen.* ◇ white clouds preceding black rain clouds. Ⓛ akálbalbi

kálbara *auf eine Schnur gereihte Schwänze, z.B. aroa-parra.* ◇ tails strung on string; e.g. rock wallaby tails. Ⓛ akaringi

kalbara *Gras (art).* ◇ grass (species). Ⓛ akalbari

kalbaralbara *aufrechtstehende Blätter an den Zweigspitzen.* ◇ leaves sticking up on branch tips. Ⓛ akalbari

kalberama *im Sterben liegen, Kopf sinken lassen.* ◇ dying. Ⓛ ngualankañi

kalbatunama *in die Knie sinken (vom Speer getroffen).* ◇ sink to the knees (hit by a spear). Ⓛ tulalarani

kálbita *große Wagen (Sternbild).* ◇ Big Dipper (star constellation). Ⓛ toralba

kalbatuluma *in die Knie sinken.* ◇ sink to the knees. Ⓛ tulalarani

kalbminjalbminja *mit Blüten bedeckt.* ◇ covered with blossoms. Ⓛ untuntuwarapungu

kalbakalama *hinken.* ◇ to limp. Ⓛ tantikatiñi, kataiakatianañi Ⓓ kunkana

kalijatuja *Schlossen, sehr großer Hagel.* ◇ hailstones, very large hailstones.

kalibera *Wasserbinsen (Scirpus Meyenii).* ◇ rushes Ⓛ ikilibiri

kalintinima *mit dem Kopf aufschlagen (auf den Boden, beim Hinunterfallen).* ◇ hit head (on ground by a fall). Ⓛ multurtjingani

kalintinilama *mit dem Kopf aufschlagen (beim Fallen).* ◇ hit head (by a fall). Ⓛ multurtjingaraniñi

kalja *der ältere Bruder, Manns ält. Schwest. Mann, Vat. ält. Br. Sohn, Mutt. ält. Schwest. Sohn, Fraus ält. Schwest. Mann.* ◇ older brother, man's older sister's husband; father's older brother's son; mother's older sister's son; wife's older sister's husband. Ⓛ kuta Ⓓ neji

kekua *der ältere Bruder (eines Andern).* ◇ older brother (of someone else). Ⓛ kutara

kaljamba (*conf.* **amba**) *der Schwiegervater (der ♀).* ◇ father-in-law (of ♀). Ⓛ katta

kaljaua [Southern dialect] *conf.* **kabilja** *Eidechse.* ◇ lizard. Ⓛ daputa

kaljitia [Northern dialect], **kaljatjia** *der jüngere Bruder.* ◇ younger brother. Ⓛ kuta-malangu

patta alka *Steinbrocken, losgelöste Stein.* ◇ piece of stone, loose stone. Ⓛ puli kalka

kalkaluntuma *voll sein (von Menschen).* ◇ full (of people). Ⓛ perulkañi

kalkama *winseln (Hund).* ◇ whimper, whine, cry (dog). Ⓛ kelbmanañi

kalkata *Knospe.* ◇ bud. Ⓛ muti Ⓓ pumpo

kalkna *1) Schädel, 2) Felsenspalt.* ◇ 1. skull; 2. rock-cleft. Ⓛ 1) katawirra 2) puli ngara Ⓓ talta

kalkuma [Eastern dialect] *beißen, aufbeißen.* ◇ bite, crack. Ⓛ patani

kalkuralkura *herabhängend (Zweige, Blätter).* ◇ hanging down (branch, leaves). Ⓛ ngutungutura

kaloïnbara *Welt (Inbegr. alles Geschaffene).* ◇ world (including all creations); everybody and everything.

kalta *dicht mit Nadeln besetzt (Zweigspitze).* ◇ densely covered with needles (tip of branch). Ⓛ pulkumba

kaltia *dicht behaart.* ◇ very hairy. Ⓛ pulkumba

kaltala *Kopfhaar.* ◇ head hair. Ⓛ kata manilba

kaltarba *kahle Stelle auf dem Kopf, Glatze.* ◇ bald patch on head, bald head. Ⓛ katabinā

kaltuntja *halbkreisförm. Umzäunung von Büschen, hinter der sich der Eingeborene versteckt, um Emus zu speeren.* ◇ hideout made of bushes from which emus are speared.

kaltjirbuma *tauchen (intrs.), untertauchen (im Wasser).* ◇ dive (intransitive), dive under (water). Ⓛ lebuntarbañi Ⓓ multibana? ('?' added by CS)

kaltjirbulelama *trs. untertauchen.* ◇ (transitive) dive. Ⓛ lebultiljini, lebuntarbatiljini

kaltjikaltjirbuma *sich verkriechen (unter Steinen).* ◇ hide (under stones). Ⓛ lebulalebulariñi

kaltjirbulakunama *hineinströmen (in ein Gebäude).* ◇ pour (into a building).

kaltjirbulakuninjaka ilta *Versammlungshaus.* ◇ meeting house, meeting place.

kaluka *Bock, Hengst.* ◇ buck, stallion. Ⓛ kaluka, kaluntji

kalula *Mark der Knochen.* ◇ bone marrow. Ⓛ kounba Ⓓ turintji

kaluta *Baum (spec.) mit dicken, herzförm. Blättern u. glockenför. Samenkapseln.* ◇ tree (species) with thick heart-shaped leaves and bell-shaped seed capsules. Ⓛ kaluti

kama *schneiden, abhauen.* ◇ cut, chop off. Ⓛ kuntani, antánani Ⓓ damona

kanakana *einer der fortwährend schneidet, der Schnitter.* ◇ one who constantly cuts, cutter. Ⓛ kuntanmi

kentjalbuma *nachdem man etwas abgeschitten hat, zurückkehren.* ◇ to return after cutting something off. Ⓛ ngalaantara kulbañi

kamara *eine Heiratsklasse.* ◇ marriage class, subsection, skin name. Ⓛ takamara ♂, nakamara ♀

kamba *Süßigkeit, Honig.* ◇ sweets, honey. Ⓛ ngumu

kamburka *die mit Süßigkeit angefüllten Leiber (der Honigameisen).* ◇ bodies of honeyants filled with sweet substance. Ⓛ kamburki? ('?' added by CS)

kabalbanama *senkrecht in den Boden stecken (z.B. die tnatantja).* ◇ erect vertical in ground (e.g. ceremonial poles). Ⓛ malantanani

kambanka *neben (cum abl.)* ◇ beside (with ablative). Ⓛ aiïnka

kamboba *Dach (einer Hütte), Gebirgsrücken, gewölbtes Dach, die Kuppel (n).* ◇ roof (of hut), mountain ridge, arched roof, dome. Ⓛ katalara

kamerama *aufstehen (v. Boden), aufgehen (Samen), wenn (von vielen Menschen) Staub aufsteigt.* ◇ stand up (from the ground), sprout (seeds), rising dust (many people). Ⓛ bakani, touninañi Ⓓ jiritjina

kamalelama *aufwecken, aufheben.* ◇ wake (somebody up), pick up. Ⓛ bakatiljini Ⓓ jiritjibana

kamalelanjalbuma *nachdem man einen aufgeweckt hat zurückkehren.* ◇ return after waking someone up. Ⓛ ngalabakatiljira kulbañi

kamakamerama *(duplic.) sich erheben, aufstehen.* ◇ (duplication) get up, stand up. Ⓛ bakabakani

kámalamalérama *aufstehen, um Sämereien zu rösten.* ◇ get up to roast seeds. Ⓛ bakarangarañi

kamakameralbuma *aufstehen u. heimkehren.* ◇ get up and return home. Ⓛ bakarabakara kulbañi

kamatjoretjorérama *alle sich erheben.* ◇ get up (everybody). Ⓛ bakalbakariñi, bakalworrañi

kameralalalama *sich erheben.* ◇ get up. Ⓛ mabakalkátiñi

kameralalama *aufstehen, sich erheben (vom Schlaf).* ◇ stand up, get up (after waking up). Ⓛ bakalkatiñi

kameranama *aufstehen machen, aufwecken.* ◇ rouse, wake (somebody up). Ⓛ mabakani

kameratnatjintama *sich erheben (vom Schlaf).* ◇ get up (after sleep). Ⓛ bakaratalkañi

kameralbanama *auf der Heimkehr sich erheben (vom Schlaf).* ◇ get up on return home (from sleeping). Ⓛ bakarabatani

kamerentjima *aufgehen (Sonne).* ◇ rise (sun). Ⓛ ngalabakani

kameritjikérama *anfangen aufzustehen.* ◇ start to get up. Ⓛ bakantakitaringani

kanaka *Bürgschaft, Stellvertretung.* ◇ guarantee, representation, delegation.

kánakakàna *Bürger, Stellvertreter.* ◇ guarantor, representative, deputy, proxy.

kamuna *Onkel (Mutters Bruder und Vaters Schwesters Mann), Schwiegersohn (♂), Bruders Tochters Mann.* ◇ uncle (mother's brother and father's sister's husband), son-in-law (♂), brother's daughter's husband. Ⓛ kamuru

tnēkua *kamuna eines Anderen.* ◇ someone else's uncle. Ⓛ kamuru

kananga *die beiden Brüder.* ◇ the two brothers. Ⓛ kutarara

kanangananga, kanangatua *alle Brüder.* ◇ all brothers. Ⓛ kutararawaritji Ⓓ nejimara? ('?' added by CS)

kinberinja, inka kinberinja *verlassend (den Boden).* ◇ abandon (ground). Ⓛ purupurunta, tjinna purupurunta

kánaka *zu Hilfe (pitjima).* ◇ (come) to the rescue. Ⓛ tjingulku

kandatandata *Blüten an den Zweigspitzen.* ◇ blossoms on tips of twigs. Ⓛ kata untuntutara

kanga [Eastern dialect] *schlecht.* ◇ bad. Ⓛ kuja

kangalangalerama *nach Luft schnappen (Fische und Ertrinkende).* ◇ gasp for air (fish and drowning people). Ⓛ akanjinkiririñi

kangaamboa (kanga + amboa) *(alte + Mann), ein alter schwacher Mann, Greis.* ◇ (old + man), old weak man. Ⓛ kujatinaburka

kanala *(postp.) an statt (eines andern).* ◇ (postposition) instead (of someone else).

kaninka *faul.* ◇ lazy. Ⓛ kanenku

kangitja *Eidechse, spec.* ◇ lizard species. Ⓛ wiruwirurba

kanjankarerama *Kopf aus d. Wasser strecken (Fische), nach Luft schnappen.* ◇ stick head out of water (fish), gasp for air. Ⓛ akanjinkiririñi

kangerkuma *aufbewahren (etw. für jeman.)* ◇ keep (something for somebody).

kānka [Southern dialect] *still, ruhig.* ◇ still, quiet. Ⓛ rata

kanakarta *halb, zur Hälfte.* ◇ half.

kankiuma *läutern (Gold), reinigen, sieben, sichten.* ◇ purify (gold), clean, sieve, sift, inspect.

kankiá *faul, mundfaul.* ◇ lazy. Ⓛ kanantu

kankarta *schwerhörig.* ◇ hard of hearing.

kanaka ankama, kanaka ilama *zurückfordern.* ◇ reclaim.

kankama *lieben.* ◇ love; be happy, smile. Ⓛ bokulariñi Ⓓ ngantjana

kankanankana *Liebende.* ◇ lovers. Ⓛ bókulbókularini

kankakala *geliebt.* ◇ loved. Ⓛ bokularinguta

kankinja *freundlich, liebend.* ◇ friendly, loving; happy. Ⓛ bokulta Ⓓ ngantjalu

kankinjaka *liebenswert.* ◇ lovable. Ⓛ bokulbáku

kankuakankerama *einander lieben.* ◇ love one another.

kankindama *unmittelbar bevorstehen (Ereignis).* ◇ pending (event).

kankuerama *lauschen, horchen, gehorchen, aufmerksam hören.* ◇ listen, obey, listen attentively. Ⓛ kuliñi Ⓓ pankina

kankuma *schöpfen (Wasser).* ◇ scoop, ladle (water); mop up water. Ⓛ taiïrákani, katini

kankurkna *Kopf voller Risse (od. voller Wunden).* ◇ head full of cracks (or wounds).

kanta, kantala *Frost, Reif, Eis.* ◇ frost, ice (see Strehlow 1907: 19–20); Kantala is a place on the Ellery Creek. Ⓛ wolka Ⓓ taleri

kantala tuma *frieren.* ◇ feel cold, freeze. Ⓛ wolkanka pungañi

kanta *zusammengerollt (Schlange), zusammen gedreht (Schnur), eine auf Kopf befestigte Schnur, – der aus Gras zusammengedrehte Ring, der auf den Kopf gelegt wird, wenn Dinge getragen werden, der große Kopf.* ◇ coiled up (snake), twisted (string), string fastened to head, ring made of grass that is placed on head to carry things, wreath; big head. Ⓛ akanta Ⓓ dambura

kantakanta *rund, Kranz.* ◇ round, wreath, ring or pad (made of hair) to carry things on head. Ⓛ akantakanta Ⓓ dambudambura

kantakanterama *sich zusammenrollen (Igel oder Schlange).* ◇ curl up (echidna or snake). Ⓛ akantakantariñi

kantanama *drehen (Schnur), zusammenrollen.* ◇ twist (string), roll together. Ⓛ akantanínañi

kantala ngama *auf dem Kopf tragen.* ◇ carry on head. Ⓛ akantanka katiñi

kantama *unverwandt stumm vor sich hinsehen.* ◇ stare silently in front of oneself. Ⓛ kurkanini

kantatuma *befestigen, festnageln.* ◇ fasten, fix to, nail on. Ⓛ palapungañi Ⓓ warukana

kantiantoppanama *unverwandt niedersehen (auf etwas).* ◇ stare down (at something). Ⓛ kataburknarañi

kantamilinja *n. Zahl.* ◇ number.

kantaralama *heruntersteigen (von etwas).* ◇ climb down (from something). Ⓛ tarungarañi

kantamilama, n. *zählen (n).* ◇ count.

kantaralitjikalama *sich niederlassen (Vögel).* ◇ settle down (birds). Ⓛ tarungarala okalingañi

kantiltja *Haube (von Vögeln).* ◇ hood, crest (of birds). Ⓛ pokulu

kantirkna (kanta-irkna) *Brüste (der Mädchen).* ◇ breasts (of girls). Ⓛ akantirkni

kantja *Spitze (von Zweigen, Bäumen, Schwanz).* ◇ tip (of twigs, branches, trees, tails). Ⓛ akantji

parra kantja *Schwanzspitze.* ◇ tip of tail. Ⓛ wipu akantji

kantjira *weiße Wolken; die weiße Wolke, die bei Gewitterschauern den schwarzen Wolken vorangeht.* ◇ white clouds; the white cloud that precedes black rain clouds (see Strehlow 1907: 25). Ⓛ akantjirkni

kantjinja *die jüngeren (Brüder, Söhne, Onkel, etc.), das zweitjüngste Kind.* ◇ younger (brothers, sons, uncles, etc.), second youngest child. Ⓛ akantji

kanturuba *Regenbogen.* ◇ rainbow. Ⓛ kanturangu

kapaltarinja *Schlange, giftig.* ◇ snake, poisonous. Ⓛ unjuratji, katamaru

kapmanta *(n) mit Eisenblech ged. Dach.* ◇ sheet iron roof.

kapmara *Hinterkopf.* ◇ back of head. Ⓛ katawira Ⓓ kukati

kapmara tanalama *(refl.) s. Haupt hinlegen (zum Schlaf).* ◇ (reflexive) lay head down to sleep. Ⓛ katawira ngarikatiñi Ⓓ kukati terkana

kapmara tanama *trs. Haupt hinlegen.* ◇ (transitive) lay head down. Ⓛ katawira ngaritunañi Ⓓ kukati terkibana

kaputanta kamerama *den Kopf erheben.* ◇ lift head. Ⓛ katakutu bakañi

kaputa *Kopf.* ◇ head. Ⓛ kata Ⓓ mangatandra

kaputa tjaia *Scheitel (gekämmt).* ◇ parted hair (combed). Ⓛ kata iwára

kaputa kantama *Kopf wehe tun.* ◇ head is hurting. Ⓛ kata kobañi

kaputata *lange weiße Raupe an den tnima-Sträuchern.* ◇ long white caterpillar on tnima-bushes. Ⓛ akapatati

kaputa intóuma *Kopfschmerz haben.* ◇ have a headache. Ⓛ kata rariwonniñi

kaputa unkwana *Schädel.* ◇ skull, cranium. Ⓛ kata tarka

kaputa kalkna *Schädel.* ◇ skull. Ⓛ kata meka

kăra *Ebene, Lehmebene.* ◇ plain, claypan. Ⓛ ákiri, pitjiri Ⓓ palara, paluru, palparu, waru

karantaka *weite Ebene.* ◇ wide plain. Ⓛ akiribila

karatja *Grube auf der Ebene.* ◇ ditch in plain. Ⓛ eraua

kararinka *weite Ebene.* ◇ wide plain. Ⓛ akiriuntubila

karinbanga *feste Ebene.* ◇ solid plain. Ⓛ akiríti

karinbanga indama *auf hartem Boden liegen.* ◇ lie on hard ground.
kāra *flüssige Mark, Honig, dicke Saft.* ◇ liquid marrow, honey, thick juice. Ⓛ alkurknu Ⓓ turintji
kārapaltunta *Saft-Tropfen (an Bäumen).* ◇ drop of juice (on trees), sap. Ⓛ tjilpititara
kāranenta *feste Mark (Knochen).* ◇ solid marrow (bone). Ⓛ tamala
karakara *eine Art Trompete.* ◇ type of trumpet. Ⓛ akirakiri Ⓓ wimmakoko
ulbura karakara *eine Art Trompete.* ◇ type of trumpet. Ⓛ ulburu akirakiri
karakarilama *fordern (Gabe).* ◇ demand (gift).
kararkararka *kahlköpfig.* ◇ bald. Ⓛ katatali
karatja *Haube (v. Vögeln).* ◇ crest, hood (of birds). Ⓛ watjinkuru
karritja *Bündnis, Freundschaftsbund.* ◇ alliance, friendship, bond.
karatjerama *Freunde werden.* ◇ become friends. Ⓛ ngulturingañi
karbatarbatélama *kauen (Speise).* ◇ chew (food). Ⓛ karpungañi
kareraua *geronnenes Blut.* ◇ congealed blood. Ⓛ puturingañi
karbalama *vernachlässigen.* ◇ neglect.
kariteuma *Haare zu Berge stehen (vor Furcht).* ◇ petrified. Ⓛ kamarabakañi
karinbanga (indama) *auf hartem Boden liegen.* ◇ lie on hard ground.
karilbmuntuma *voll sein (z.B. Haus voller Menschen), bedeck sein mit (Menschen oder Tieren).* ◇ be full (e.g. house full of people), covered with (humans or animals). Ⓛ ninara wonnañi
karitjingakaritja *Kindermesser (Rinde).* ◇ child's knife (bark).
kariljibatnuma *herunterströmen (Regen).* ◇ pour down (rain). Ⓛ wirurukatiñi
karitjakalama *herunterrutschen (z.B. pattanga).* ◇ slide down (e.g. from a rock). Ⓛ kattunguru wirulwarañi
karinba *Speer (vom Norden eingehandelt).* ◇ spear (traded from the north). Ⓛ karinba Ⓓ kalti ngaminto
karitja, ntjerkinta *langes Steinmesser.* ◇ long stone knife. Ⓛ kanti, tula Ⓓ kutuwonda
karitjilama *ausgleiten, fallen.* ◇ slip, fall. Ⓛ wiruntalkañi
karitjánkitjánka *aufrechtstehendes Haar.* ◇ hair standing up. Ⓛ kata tálarára
karka *Lauben-Vogel (bower-bird), derselbe baut sich eine Art Laubeingang, indem er mit bunten Steinen spielt; dunkelbraun mit gelben Flecken, auf dem Kopf einen großen rosa Flecken, (Chlamydodera guttata).* ◇ dark brown bowerbird with yellow spots and a large pink spot on its head; it builds a kind of arcade and decorates it with coloured stones (*Chlamydera guttata*). Ⓛ akarki
karkarénama *verschmieren, verkleben.* ◇ smear, stick. Ⓛ pantani
karknanteulama *refl. sich anhängen, hängen bleiben (z.B. Schmutz an Kleidern), sich anhängen (Hunde und Schlange, wenn sich festbeist).* ◇ (reflexive) attach, keep hanging on (e.g. dirt on clothes), attach (dogs and snakes when biting). Ⓛ waluringañi
karkuma *zittern, den Körper in zitternde Bewegungen setzen (beim Cultus), Schwanz hin u. her bewegen (Schlange und manche Vögel).* ◇ tremble, set body into trembling motions (at ceremonies), move tail from side to side (snake and some birds). Ⓛ pinpitjingañi
karpalama *bereuen (eine schlechte Tat), vernachlässigen.* ◇ regret (a bad deed), neglect. Ⓛ tomatiriñi Ⓓ burkaljerina
karperama *abschneiden, schneiden (Getreide).* ◇ cut off, cut (wheat, crop).
karralelama *beobachten (trs.)* ◇ (transitive) observe.
karra *wach.* ◇ awake. Ⓛ kana
karrerama *wach werden.* ◇ wake up. Ⓛ kanaringañi
karralama *wachen, warten (auf jemanden).* ◇ keep watch, wait (for somebody). Ⓛ patañi Ⓓ ngulukana
karta *Stoppel, die Stumpfen und Halme; Abgebießene.* ◇ stubble (crop), stumps and stalks. Ⓛ mutu

 For the modern spellings of these words, see the dictionaries and sources in reference list.

karterama *abbeißen, abscheiden (Haar), abhauen, schneiden (Getreide).* ◇ bite off, cut off (hair), chop, cut (wheat). Ⓛ kartjingañi, takerpungañi

kartakarterama *zerbeißen, zermalmen (z.B. Rinde).* ◇ bite to pieces, crush (e.g. bark). Ⓛ tákirtákirpúngañi

karratinja *die Schlaflosigkeit.* ◇ insomnia.

kartjita nama *angefüllt, voll sein (z.B. das Haus mit Menschen).* ◇ full, filled (e.g. house with people). Ⓛ utulánbara ninañi

kartnagunama *Kalk auf das Grab streuen, stillschweigen auferlegen (dem neuen Zauberdoktor).* ◇ sprinkle lime on grave, impose secrecy (on the new witch doctor). Ⓛ apurawonniñi

karuntuma *stampfen (den Boden, beim Tanz).* ◇ stamp, stomp (ground when dancing). Ⓛ kantuni

kata *Vater, Vaters Bruder (Onkel).* ◇ father, father's brother (uncle). Ⓛ katu, tjatji Ⓓ ngaperi

kata knara *Vaters älterer Bruder.* ◇ father's older brother. Ⓛ katu puntu

kata larra *Vaters jüngere Bruder.* ◇ father's younger brother. Ⓛ katu wongu

kata kantjinja *Vaters jüngere Bruder.* ◇ father's younger brother. Ⓛ katu akantji

katamata *väterlich.* ◇ fatherly. Ⓛ katuta

kataltja (katiltja) *der eigene Vater.* ◇ own father, my own father. Ⓛ katuwolta

katana; era pitjitjina katana *wahrscheinlich, (postp.)* ◇ (postposition) probably; e.g. he or she will probably come.

kăta *Spitze (von Blüten).* ◇ tip (of blossoms). Ⓛ akata

kătakăta *kleine Stab, Zauberstab.* ◇ small stick. Ⓛ katakata

katakata; intakatakata *(Enden [unclear]), Gelenk, Fußgelenk; Zauberholz (altes Wort).* ◇ joint, ankle; magic wood (old word) (Strehlow 1910b: 128). Ⓛ tata Ⓓ tidnapalka (*Fußgelenk*: ankle)

kātanga *klein (von Person), kurz.* ◇ small (person), short. Ⓛ murila

katangamakatanga *zuletzt (kommen).* ◇ last (to come, arrive). Ⓛ akatangamakatanguru

katapantapanta *Ende der Nacht, Morgengrauen, Zwielicht.* ◇ end of night, dawn, twilight. Ⓛ urelariñi

kātapala *klein (von Person), kurz.* ◇ small (of stature), short. Ⓛ akatapati

katapantapanterama *Zwielicht werden.* ◇ twilight. Ⓛ kitjalkuriñi

katana - katana *entweder – oder.* ◇ either – or. Ⓛ kutura – kutura Ⓓ kara – kara

kātara *windstill.* ◇ calm (no wind). Ⓛ rata Ⓓ dalpuru

katarama (katerama) *hinteruntersehen.* ◇ look down. Ⓛ walunangañi

kataratja *Reihe (hinter einander).* ◇ row (behind each other), in a row. Ⓛ warata (worrata)

kataratja lama *hintereinander gehen.* ◇ walk behind each other. Ⓛ warata jennañi

katamaranka renalama *die Hände hinter dem Hinterkopf falten.* ◇ fold hands behind head. Ⓛ nguntimar̃alu tunañi

katarénama *zum Abschluß bringen (Arbeit).* ◇ finish (work). Ⓛ akatatunañi

katatala rama *gehend betrachten [unclear].* ◇ look while walking. Ⓛ paranangañi Ⓓ naijinaijibana

kataratjeramala albuma *eins [unclear].* ◇ one after the other is looking as returning or on return [?] Ⓛ waratararekula kulbañi

katatárerama *sich spalten (Menschen), sich teilen (Wasser).* ◇ split (people), divide (water). Ⓛ akatakutarariñi

kataterilama *trs. abschneiden, teilen, abreißen, zerreißen.* ◇ (transitive) cut off, divide, tear off, tear. Ⓛ akatakutarani Ⓓ puntibana

katatarerinja *die Sekte (die sich abgesondert hat).* ◇ sect (that isolated itself).

katatnama *teilen, halbieren.* ◇ to divide, to halve. Ⓛ akatatauani

katawuntawunta *uneins, geteilter Meinung.* ◇ disagree, different opinion.

katēla nama (katailanama) *Augen niederschlagen.* ◇ lower eyes. Ⓛ wollunakánani

katerkaterka *die gekrümmten Spitzen (der Blätter oder Zweige).* ◇ bent tips (of leaves or branches). Ⓛ núturnúturba

katimala *Kissen, Kopfunterlage.* ◇ pillow. Ⓛ kátatabála

katira *weiß gestreift (Anspielung auf einen gestreiften Hund).* ◇ striped white. Ⓛ katiri (*schwarz und weiß gestreifter Hund*)

katitja lama *auf allen Vieren gehen, rollen (Wagen).* ◇ walk on all fours, roll (wagon). Ⓛ manmiri jennañi

katitjatitja *weiße Kopf.* ◇ white head. Ⓛ kátawómmulutára

katjulbmanga *zuversichtlich.* ◇ optimistic.

katjawara, tjilpa *wilde Katze, Beutelmarder.* ◇ native cat, Western Quoll. Ⓛ malalbara

katjuirbuma *versiegen, vertrocknen (Wasser).* ◇ dry up (water).

katjira, katjiba *Busch mit gelben Beeren, Solanum ellipticum.* ◇ bush with yellow berries, desert raisin, *Solanum centrale* (Latz 1996). Ⓛ praitji, akitjiri, kamburara

katjia *Kind.* ◇ child. Ⓛ pipiri Ⓓ kupa

katjiamalkura *kindlich.* ◇ child-like. Ⓛ pipiri nguanba

katakatilama, katjikatjilama *kitzeln.* ◇ tickle. Ⓛ kitjikitjini

katjilka *Schlange (giftig).* ◇ snake (poisonous). Ⓛ akiltjílki

katjanbata *die überall angeklebten Daunen (Cultus).* ◇ feather down. Ⓛ leoara

katnatnainama *sich mischen (in die Arbeit von andern).* ◇ interfere (in the work of others).

katna *oben, oberhalb.* ◇ up, above, over. Ⓛ kattu Ⓓ miri

katnatoppa *aufwärts, gegen (den Strom).* ◇ upwards, upstream or against (the current). Ⓛ kattukutu

katnataka *in die Höhe, höher.* ◇ upwards, into the sky, higher. Ⓛ kattukutu Ⓓ taranalu

katnerama *erheben, hochheben (Kopf, Hände).* ◇ lift, raise (head, hands). Ⓛ katturingañi

katnerentjima *früh, wenn die Sonnenscheibe sich über den Horizont erhebt.* ◇ early, when the sun rises over the horizon. Ⓛ katturikulakalbañi

katnatakakana *(n) die Höhe.* ◇ height.

katninga *oben.* ◇ above. Ⓛ kattu Ⓓ miri

katningala *oben.* ◇ up, at the top. Ⓛ kattuwonna

katningerama *c. abl. obliegen, übereinander.* ◇ subdue, overcome (c. abl.) Ⓛ kattungururingañi

katningakatningala *oben, auf.* ◇ up, on. Ⓛ kattutakattuta

katnakatnérama *immer höher fliegen.* ◇ fly higher and higher. Ⓛ kattukatturiñi

katnalelama *aufrichten, hochheben.* ◇ erect, lift. Ⓛ kattuni Ⓓ miri ngankana

katningambenja *oben (am Tisch, im Buch).* ◇ at the top (of the table, of the book).

katnanga *fort (gehen).* ◇ away (go). Ⓛ akaningi

katningambenjaka renalama *sich obenan setzen.* ◇ to sit at the top.

katningakana ekaralama *über (etwas) anziehen.* ◇ put over (something).

kātnama *gebeugt sitzen, trauern, reuen.* ◇ mourn, remorse. Ⓛ katawonkañi

kātnalánama *gebeugt, traurig dasitzen.* ◇ sit hunched, wretched. Ⓛ katawonkánini Ⓓ munkuru

katnatnainama *sich einmischen (in die Arbeit von andern).* ◇ interfere (in the work of others).

katóatóa *unschlüssig, sich besinnend.* ◇ undecided, considering. Ⓛ kauarakauara

katua *Puppe (Chrysalide).* ◇ pupa (chrysalis). Ⓛ akuta

kātnua *die verdickten Honigtropfen (z.B. am ntjuia-Baum), Klumpen.* ◇ thickened honey-drops (e.g. on the ntjuia-tree), lumps. Ⓛ ngumu

katuluma *auflösen (Band, Ehe), scheiden (Ehe).* ◇ dissolve (tie, marriage), divorce (marriage).

kauakaua *sehr lang.* ◇ very long. Ⓛ tauitaui

kauakaua *die sehr hohe Stange mit dem Federbusch.* ◇ very long pole with a feather tuft. Ⓛ tauitaui

kaualama *schwanken, schwingen, sich hin und her bewegen in Winde.* ◇ sway, swing, move back and forth in the wind. Ⓛ wollirikatiñi Ⓓ wijawijarina

kauuta *das aufgelöste Haar (eines Beschnittenen).* ◇ loose hair (of novice). Ⓛ katarára

kawortjawortja *mit weißen Blütenköpfen bedeckt (Zweige).* ◇ covered with white blossoms (branches). Ⓛ kawirtjiwirtji

kebenintja *Versammlung, Schule.* ◇ gathering, school.

kebenintjaka ilta *Schule.* ◇ school.

kebintjibintja *aufgelöstes, nach allen Seiten herabhängendes Haar.* ◇ loose hair hanging down on all sides. Ⓛ kátamíntamínta

kebakeba *Versammlung.* ◇ gathering, meeting.

keïntitjeritjera *sterblich, in Todesgefahr.* ◇ mortal, in mortal danger. Ⓛ jupajupa

kejalbijalba *nach allen Seiten herunterhängendes Haar.* ◇ hair hanging down on all sides. Ⓛ katamintaminta

kekatalama *tadeln, Vorwürfe machen.* ◇ reprove, reproach.

kekua *der ältere Bruder (eines Andern).* ◇ older brother (of someone else). Ⓛ kutara

kekurutja *die älteren Brüder (eines Andern).* ◇ older brothers (of someone else). Ⓛ kutanbara

kekatalinjagunja *untadelig.* ◇ impeccable.

kelbakérama *Person ansehen?* ◇ look at a person?

kelbara *kleine Eidechse (spec.)* ◇ small lizard (species). Ⓛ tantalkátu

keluma *ausreiben (Samen), von den Schalen befreien.* ◇ rub (seeds) to remove husks. Ⓛ notuni

kelkna [Northern dialect] *Felsenspalt.* ◇ cleft in cliff. Ⓛ ngarra

keltja *halb, Hälfte.* ◇ half. Ⓛ woltara Ⓓ jurra

keltjilama *teilen, halbieren.* ◇ divide, halve. Ⓛ woltarpungañi

kelukeluka *aufgelöstes Haar.* ◇ loose hair. Ⓛ katawólknatiwólknati

kelupa *lange, schwarze Schlange, giftig.* ◇ long black poisonous snake. Ⓛ mulburtji

kemba *Strohblume (Polycalymma stuartii).* ◇ strawflower (*Polycalymma stuartii*). Ⓛ akimba

kembakemba *kleine Strohblume (verschied. spec.)* ◇ small strawflower (many different species). Ⓛ akimbakimba

kementerama *versinken (im Schlamm).* ◇ sink (in mud). Ⓛ tarbani Ⓓ punpina

kemintjira *Spitze der Zweige.* ◇ tip of branches. Ⓛ imintjiri

kenkala *postp. ähnlich, gleich.* ◇ (postposition) similar, identical. Ⓛ aránka

kenkunalerama *den Kopf nach rückwärts wenden, sich umsehen.* ◇ turn head backwards, look around. Ⓛ katangantikuturingañi

kerama *'im Halbkreis um sich sehen', sich scheuen, sich genieren.* ◇ 'look around in a half circle', be timid.

kintja, kentja *lange Schwanz (Vögel), lange Schwanzfedern.* ◇ long tail (birds), long tailfeathers. Ⓛ akintji

képetépata, kepetepeta *Hinterkopf (Stelle [unclear]).* ◇ back of head (Strehlow 1910b: 131). Ⓛ kata ngatinkuru

kêrakêra *schwarz.* ◇ black. Ⓛ ulêrulêra

jera kêrakêra *schwarze Ameisen.* ◇ black ants. Ⓛ minga ulêrulêra

keruma (ka + eruma) *Kopf schwarz sein.* ◇ have a black head. Ⓛ kata mungawonniñi

keritjala *unbemerkt (kommen).* ◇ (come) unnoticed. Ⓛ arewakawuia

kerbakerba *dienstfertig.* ◇ eager in one's duty.

kētja *Leben (in Zusammensetzungen).* ◇ life (in word compounds).

ketjultakama *(Leben-abbrechen), erschlagen, erschießen.* ◇ (end life), slay, shoot. Ⓛ aluru kátantánani

kēuma *anfachen (Feuer).* ◇ fan (fire). Ⓛ kurkaltunañi

kimbara *postp. zuerst, vorn.* ◇ (postposition) first, in front. Ⓛ warika

arakimbara laka *das rote Känguruh liefe vorn an.* ◇ the red kangaroo leads [?]. Ⓛ malluwarika jennu

erá kimbala *er zuerst.* ◇ he first. Ⓛ paluru warika

kirbminjambaralama *alles Gebüsch niedertretend weiter laufen.* ◇ treading undergrowth down while pressing or running on. Ⓛ multurkumulturku jennañi

kintja (kĕntja) *Blütenspitzen, Blüten.* ◇ blossom tips, blossoms. Ⓛ akintji

kinjinta *in Zusammensetzungen: Haupt.* ◇ in word compounds: head.

kítjamberutjámbara *ein sehr großer Haufe (aufgeschüttenen Samen).* ◇ very big pile (of seeds). Ⓛ alujúrbaalujúrba

kitjala, irkunjakitjala *postp. vor (zeitlich), vor dem Essen.* ◇ (postposition) before (temporal), before eating.

knaia *Vater (gewöhnlich so genannt von den erwachsenen Töchtern).* ◇ father (term commonly used by adult daughters). Ⓛ katu, mama Ⓓ nagperi

knaia knara *ält. Bruder d. Vat.* ◇ older brother of father. Ⓛ katu puntu, mama puntu

knaia larra *jüngerer Bruder des Vaters.* ◇ younger brother of father. Ⓛ katu wongu, mama wongu

knaia kantjinja *jüng. Bruder d. Vat.* ◇ younger brother of father. Ⓛ katu akantji

knaia palla *Vaters Mutters Bruder, Fraus Vat. Vater.* ◇ father's mother's brother, wife's father's father. Ⓛ katu bakali

knaia ebmanna *Fraus Mutters Vater.* ◇ wife's mother's father. Ⓛ katu inkilji

knaiïninta *Halbgeschwister (Kinder von ein und demselben Vater).* ◇ half siblings (children from one father). Ⓛ mamatungu

knaninja *ewig, rein, heilig (z.B. Sonnenlicht).* ◇ everlasting, pure, sacred (e.g. sunlight). Ⓛ tukutita? ('?' added by CS)

knanakala *Totem-Platz.* ◇ totem place; dreaming, father's dreaming. Ⓛ arata

knaritjilama *zu viel tun.* ◇ do too much.

knarabana *groß dies.* ◇ big (this). Ⓛ puntutu

knăra; manna knara *groß (Gestalt), viel z.B. viel Brot.* ◇ big (posture), much (e.g. a lot of bread). Ⓛ puntu Ⓓ pirna

knarerama *groß werden.* ◇ to grow up. Ⓛ punturingañi

knarilama *[groß machen] viel sammeln.* ◇ collect/gather much [make big]. Ⓛ puntuni

knarindora *sehr groß, sehr viel.* ◇ very big, very much. Ⓛ puntulenku

knarintjara *sehr viele (z.B. Leute).* ◇ very many (e.g. people). Ⓛ puntu tjikara

knararbekua *das zweitälteste Kind.* ◇ second oldest child. Ⓛ puntungakálara

knaribata *(zusammengesetzt von knara=groß und ata=atua=Mann), (inkata) der große Mann, der ältere Mann in angesehener Stellung; der Älteste.* ◇ big man, elder, the older respected man; the oldest. Ⓛ puntulara, (tina) Ⓓ pinaru

knarakata *viel (Geld).* ◇ much (money).

knaribatananga Ⓛ puntularakutara

knaruntulama *nicht vermögen, nichts ausrichten.* ◇ not able to (do, achieve something).

knarinja *lange Schlange, nicht giftig (spec.)* ◇ long snake, not poisonous (species). Ⓛ inturkunu

knaramanta *teuer, viel kostend.* ◇ dear, expensive.

knaritja *Vater (auch Häuptling, Urenkel ♂).* ◇ father (also chief, great-grandson); leader, big. In Carl Strehlow's work 'knaritja' is used for father, chief, old man and totem ancestor. Ⓛ katu

 For the modern spellings of these words, see the dictionaries and sources in reference list.

knaritja knara *Onkel, der ältere Bruder des Vaters* ◇ uncle, father's older brother. The word 'knara' with kin terms indicates a more senior individual of the particular kin category, e.g. father's older brother rather than closer or biological father. Ⓛ katu puntu

knaritja larra *der jüngere Bruder des Vaters.* ◇ father's younger brother. Ⓛ katu wongu

knaritja kantjinja *der jüngere Bruder des Vaters.* ◇ father's younger brother. Ⓛ katu akantji

knartija palla *Vaters Mutters Bruder, Fraus Vaters Vater.* ◇ father's mother's brother, wife's father's father. Ⓛ katu bakali

knaritja ebmanna *Fraus Mutters Vater.* ◇ wife's mother's father. Ⓛ katu inkilji

knaritjaknaritja *kleines Steinmesser zum Bearbeiten von Holz, z.B. eines Speerwerfers mera.* ◇ stone knife. Ⓛ katungana

knópaknópa *der winterliche Wind, der kalte Wind.* ◇ cold wind. Ⓛ bobabobarawonnañi

knubaknutjina *Gespräch, Geplapper.* ◇ conversation, chat. Ⓛ wátaiíta

knujilelama *grün machen (Bäume durch Kultus – hat den Zweck, daß die Bäume schön grün werden), Krönen (n).* ◇ make green (trees through ceremony), to crown (see Strehlow 1910b: 224). Ⓛ nukamununi

knúerama *cf.* **eknua** *vergessen.* ◇ forget. Ⓛ watawatariñi Ⓓ kurutarana

knujabaknuja *vergeßlich, töricht.* ◇ forgetful, foolish. Ⓛ kauankauan

knulja *der Hund.* ◇ dog. Ⓛ papa Ⓓ kintala

knulja nekua *der Köter.* ◇ mongrel. Ⓛ mama

knulja itnora *der Dingo.* ◇ dingo. Ⓛ papa palku

knuljalknanbulelana *Pflanze.* ◇ plant; yellow daisy. Ⓛ papakurulba

knuljaknulja *kleine Insekt, ähnlich der Maulwurfgrille.* ◇ small insect that resembles the mole cricket. Ⓛ papapapa

knuljamanina *Pflanze.* ◇ plant. Ⓛ papangalulba

knuraia *eine Heiratsklasse.* ◇ marriage class, subsection, skin name. Ⓛ tungaraii, nungaraii

knurara *eßbare Wurzel spec.* ◇ edible root species. Ⓛ ungurari

kualbaia *beleidigt.* ◇ offended.

kualbaierama *beleidigt werden.* ◇ become offended.

kula *das Felsenwasserloch, der Krug (n).* ◇ rock waterhole, jug.

kotilja *Schüssel, tub (n).* ◇ bowl, tub.

kollerinjalkua *der Übertreter.* ◇ trespasser.

kokolura *böse Wesen in Hundegestalt.* ◇ evil beings or bad spirits in dog shape; they sometimes travel with the west wind (Strehow 1907: 11–12, 13). Ⓛ kokoluru

koa? *betrübt, traurig.* ◇ sad. ('?' added by CS)

koerama *leid sein, betrübt sein.* ◇ sorrowful.

kokutjikama [Southern dialect], **kwakitjikama** [Northern dialect] *umarmen.* ◇ embrace. Ⓛ ambuljennañi Ⓓ munkamalina, munamana

kotilja *ein Gefäß, ?* ◇ vessel. ('?' added by CS)

kólera [Southern dialect], **ankólera** [Northern dialect] *Fischfett.* ◇ fish fat, fish oil. Ⓛ ankóluru

kólerama *übertreten (Gebot), nicht beobachten.* ◇ infringe, not observe. Ⓛ aliñi Ⓓ tankarana

kolbmaraïlkalélama *durch 2 Feuer die Nähe eines kl. Lagerplatzes ankünden.* ◇ announce with two fires the proximity of a small camp. Ⓛ pujútujútutjingañi

kōlja *Pflanze mit blätterlosen Stengeln, gelb-weißen Blüten, rübenartige Wurzeln (spec.)* ◇ plant with leafless stems, yellow-white blossoms and carrot-like roots (species). Ⓛ akulja

koltjilétanga *Äste, die sich (einander) umarmen, umschlingende (Äste).* ◇ intertwined branches. Ⓛ karbirárbiri

kōnja *leid (sein), betrübt, traurig, Bedauernswerter!* ◇ be sad, sad, poor thing! Ⓛ matjutu, matu Ⓓ purka, purkali

kōnjerama *intrs. leid tun, bertrübt werden.* ◇ (intransitive) feel sorry or sorrow, become sad. Ⓛ matjuturingañi Ⓓ purkaljerina, purkapurkarina

kōnjilama *trs. betrüben.* ◇ (transitive) sadden. Ⓛ matjutuni

kubitja (ala) *verschwunden vom Erdboden.* ◇ disappeared from the face of the earth. Ⓛ kurbalta

kopakopa *Pilze mit schwarz farbigen Inhalt, mit den sich die Knaben im Spiel Bärte machen.* ◇ mushrooms with black coloured substance that boys play with and use to paint beards on their faces. Ⓛ kopukopu

kotnakotna *weiße Masse, weiße Zucker (in Bäumen).* ◇ white mass, white sugar (on trees). Ⓛ ngumungumu

kótupa *Hof, Umgebung des Hauses.* ◇ court (yard), surrounding of house. Ⓛ tatulbi

kotjubitjuma *schnell zusammen lesen, aufraffen.* ◇ to gather quickly. Ⓛ minjiminjini

kotjima *sammeln, einsammeln, häufen.* ◇ gather, collect, pile up. Ⓛ munguni Ⓓ mapana, kampana

kotjilauma *auflesen, aufsammeln.* ◇ pick up, gather. Ⓛ munguratalkañi

kriteka [Southern dialect] *cf.* **kara** *Ebene.* ◇ plain.

kubitja *Grube, in dem Wasser sich ansammelt.* ◇ ditch in which water collects. Ⓛ nerru

kuȋ! *Ausruf = ach! (Ausruf der Überraschung).* ◇ Ah! (exclamation of surprise). Ⓛ puta!

kwatja kubitja *das Wasser in der Grube.* ◇ water in a ditch. Ⓛ kapi nerru

kujúrbmajurbmélama *wiederkäuen.* ◇ ruminate. Ⓛ tauurtánañi

kubitjabitjilama *in Stücke zerschlagen.* ◇ smash to pieces. Ⓛ katalkatálbmanani

kujulba *viele Haufen (v. Schoten).* ◇ many heaps (of pods). Ⓛ alujúrbalujúrba

kŭla; nanakula? *(postp.) vielleicht, wahrscheinlich (bei Fragen); ist es dies?* ◇ (postposition) maybe, probably (in questions); is it this? Ⓛ bilku, nangatabilku

kulamakula *wahrscheinlich, jedenfalls.* ◇ probably, in any case. Ⓛ bilkultabilku

kujakuja *Mastdarm.* ◇ gut. Ⓛ kalupiti

kukara *(von Dieri: kukuru) Wurfkeule.* ◇ (from Dieri: kukuru) throwing club. Ⓛ ukukuru Ⓓ kukuru

kula *tiefe Loch.* ◇ deep hole. Ⓛ wakula Ⓓ kudu

kula nerra *tiefe Felsenwasserloch.* ◇ deep rock waterhole. Ⓛ wakula nerru

kula rata; Kularata *weite Loch.* ◇ wide hole; name of place. Ⓛ wakula bila

patta kula *tief ausgehöhlter Felsen.* ◇ deep washed out rockhole. Ⓛ puli wakula

kwatja kula *tiefe Wasserloch.* ◇ deep waterhole. Ⓛ kapi wakula, tukula

kúlakulelárama *sich umfassen (im Zorn) von Hunden, die sich beißen wollen, u. v. Menschen (die sich schneiden wollen).* ◇ to clasp each other (in anger); dogs who are going to bite each other and humans who want to stab each other. Ⓛ kulakularapungañi

kulbakakulberama *auf dem Bergrücken sich aufhalten.* ◇ to dwell or be on the mountain ridge. Ⓛ tantatantariñi

kulbakúlbilalàma *den Rücken biegen (beim Fressen).* ◇ to bend back (while eating or to eat [?]). Ⓛ nuntununturiñi

kulbakunama *schnell ausschreitend (beim Gehen).* ◇ walk quickly. Ⓛ irbirbini

kulaia *mythische Wasser-Schlange (spec.)* ◇ mythical watersnake species; rainbow serpent. Ⓛ wonnambi, muruntu Ⓓ kadimarkara

kulba *Spitze (Berges).* ◇ summit (of mountain). Ⓛ tānta

kulbira *großes im Süden sich aufh. Kängaruh.* ◇ large kangaroo living in the south. Ⓛ kulbiri

 For the modern spellings of these words, see the dictionaries and sources in reference list.

akúljinga *links.* ◇ left. Ⓛ tambu Ⓓ worrangantju

kulalba *blind.* ◇ blind. Ⓛ kulalbi Ⓓ butju

kunkuma *darbieten, hinhalten (Preis).* ◇ offer, hold out (reward).

kultuntatuma *weiße Blüten tragen (Strauch).* ◇ with white blossoms (bush). Ⓛ kátatawáratirangañi

akualélberama *rechte Arm steif werden.* ◇ right arm is getting stiff. Ⓛ wakualilbariñi

kultúntultúnta *mit weißen (Blüten) bedeckt.* ◇ covered with white (blossoms). Ⓛ katatiti

kumata, noa *Ehegemahl.* ◇ spouse. Ⓛ kuri

kumalinja *unwissend; einer, (von selbst/ von Natur gemachten) der von etwas nichts gehört hat.* ◇ ignorant; someone who is ignorant by nature. Ⓛ kulelkulu

kunjunba *der kl. Steinhügel (z.B. bei stock-yard).* ◇ small stone hill (e.g. at stockyard).

kumia *süß (Früchte), wohlschmeckend (Wasser).* ◇ sweet (fruit), nice tasting (water). Ⓛ ulára Ⓓ madu

kumia ntjainama *wohlrichend sein.* ◇ be fragrant. Ⓛ ulara pantiñi

kumbala *niederhängend (Zweige, Büsche).* ◇ hanging down (branches, bushes). Ⓛ tarukutu

kumbura *Felsen, Felsblock.* ◇ rock, boulder. Ⓛ pokuti Ⓓ marda tjupatjupara

kumunka *nicht bemerkt, nicht beobachtet, unbemerkt.* ◇ not noticed, not observed, unnoticed. Ⓛ ngatapatti

kumunka nama *heimlich sitzen.* ◇ sit secretly. Ⓛ ngatapatti ninañi Ⓓ kurirpi wapana

kumunka lama *hinschleichen.* ◇ creep up. Ⓛ ngatapatti jennañi Ⓓ kurirpi wapana

kunna *schlecht.* ◇ bad. Ⓛ kuja Ⓓ modlentji (madlentji)

kunnunba *schlecht riechend, sauer.* ◇ bad smelling, sour. Ⓛ majokuja

kunnerama *schlecht werden.* ◇ become bad. Ⓛ kujaringañi Ⓓ modlentji pantjina

kunnilama *schlechtes tun.* ◇ do bad. Ⓛ kujani Ⓓ modlentji ngankana

kulbakotjima *auflesen (v. Boden), aufsammeln.* ◇ pick up (from the ground), gather up. Ⓛ mungumunguni

kunnabintjalama *zufällig treffen, ohne Absicht töten.* ◇ to hit by accident, kill unintentionally. Ⓛ kurakatiñi

kuniamba *auf einem Haufen stehend (Schößling).* ◇ to stand bunched together (shoots). Ⓛ tapánmara

kunba *müßig, untätig, unschuldig, unachtsam.* ◇ idle, inactive, innocent, inattentive, careless. Ⓛ kunbu, jutu Ⓓ baku

kunbalúnbala, kubalubala *bell-bird (Oreoica cristata).* ◇ crested bellbird, *Oreoica cristata* now *Oreoica gutturalis* (Pizzey and Knight 2007). Ⓛ banbanbállala

kŭnja *klein, wenig (postp.)* ◇ small, little (postposition) Ⓛ tjiri Ⓓ ngalje (*wenig*: little, not much)

kunkurunkura nama *mit gebeugten Kopf dasitzen, unbeweglich vor sich hinsehen.* ◇ sit with head lowered, motionless. Ⓛ unkurunkuru ninañi Ⓓ kutukurana

kunkultjakunkultjala tuma *sehr schnell schlagen.* ◇ hit very fast. Ⓛ papaltupapaltu pungañi

kura *Mädchen.* ◇ girl. Ⓛ ókara

kurala, ekungala *postp. neben.* ◇ (postposition) beside. Ⓛ aiinka

kurbarenalama *sehr stark regnen, hinunterschütten.* ◇ rain very heavily, pour down. Ⓛ jelbikulu ninakatiñi

kuralja *Siebengestirn.* ◇ Pleiades (seven stars), Seven Sisters (see Strehlow 1907: 19–20). Ⓛ okaralji Ⓓ mankaraworra

kurbula; kaputa urbula *schwarze Kopf.* ◇ black head; name of a place in the West MacDonnell Ranges. Ⓛ kata maru

kuraiaraíalalankama *verleumden.* ◇ slander, defame. Ⓛ kambawonnawonna wonkañi

kununílama *(den Tod eines Andern) mitansehen, Zeuge sein (von seinem Tod).* ◇ witness the death of someone. Ⓛ kurakutuni

kunbinja *zufällig, ohngefähr.* ◇ by chance, approximately.

kurkeriltjilelama *trs. mehren.* ◇ (transitive) increase.

kutala *nahe bei, ganz in der Nähe.* ◇ close by, nearby, very close.

kurbiltja *Vogel spec. [unclear].* ◇ bird species

kutunta *Vorläufer.* ◇ forerunner.

kunkuma *hinhalten (um ihm zu geben).* ◇ hold out (to give to him).

kurka *klein, wenig.* ◇ small, little, (not much). Ⓛ wimma Ⓓ wakka

kurka *(die Jungen des Wildes).* ◇ young wild animals. Ⓛ tabuna Ⓓ muluru? ('?' added by CS)

kurkakatuia *Verlobter, Bräutigam.* ◇ fiancé, bridegroom. Ⓛ wimmatara

kurkameria, kurkamerila *winzig klein, kaum sichtbar (Adler in d. Höhe).* ◇ tiny, hardly visible (eagle in the sky). Ⓛ wimmarekula

kurkibana (= kurka-nuka) *Verlobte, Braut.* ◇ fiancée, bride. Ⓛ wimmata, tabunita

kurkna *ästig, dicht belaubt, mit dichten Nadeln besetzt.* ◇ branchy, densely foliaged, covered thickly with needles. Ⓛ bulkuna

kurknalélama *trs. warnen, zur Vorsicht ermahnen, Warnung zurufen.* ◇ (transitive) warn, caution, call out a warning. Ⓛ kurkurkutjingañi

kurknalelama *trs. einem zustimmen, beistimmen.* ◇ (transitive) agree with someone.

kurkunta *Knecht, Nachfolger, Untertan.* ◇ servant, follower, subject. Ⓛ tábunbiti

kurunta *Ratte (ohne Beutel).* ◇ rat (without pouch). Ⓛ akuruntu

kurra *Beuteldachs.* ◇ marsupial species. Ⓛ muta

kuruntuma *aufkochen (Wasser) intr., hervorquellen (Wasser), aufgehen (Gras), hervorgehen.* ◇ boil (water) (intransitive), gush out (water), sprout (grass), emerge. Ⓛ mulbakani

kurunga *die Blüten der Gummibäume.* ◇ blossoms of gumtrees. Ⓛ akurungu

kuta *immer.* ◇ always. Ⓛ kutu Ⓓ milingeru

kutata *fortwährend.* ◇ continually, always. Ⓛ kututu, kutulenku

kuterama *bleiben.* ◇ to stay. Ⓛ kuturingañi Ⓓ ngamantina? ('?' added by CS)

kutetalérama *im Gedächnis behalten.* ◇ keep in mind. Ⓛ kutuurukuliñi

kutata ngambakala *ewig.* ◇ forever, eternal. Ⓛ kututu aranka

kotjirka *sehr klein (Fleisch, Kind), winzig.* ◇ very small (meat, child), tiny. Ⓛ wimmalitji, kalkaturu

kutakwa *linkshändig.* ◇ left-handed. Ⓛ tambupiti

kutara *lange Blüten (der erulanga Büsche), die Kolben der Grasbäume, Tannenzapfen.* ◇ long blossoms (of the erulanga-bushes), the cobs of the grass trees, pine cones. Ⓛ kalinkalinba, kuntu (*Zapfen*) Ⓓ wuduwudu? ('?' added by CS)

kutura *lang (Stock).* ◇ long (stick). Ⓛ kuturu

kutinja *Herr oder Besitzer (eines Hundes).* ◇ master or owner (of a dog). Ⓛ ungara

kutakuta *Nachtvogel (mit lockender Stimme) so groß wie ruilkara, von roter Farbe, frißt Fliegen und Käfer (kutukutukutukutu).* ◇ nightbird, spotted nightjar (*Eurostopodus argus*). Ⓛ kunkutukuta

kutulba *kleine weiße (Wolken).* ◇ small white (clouds). Ⓛ kutanpi

kutungula *Untertan, Diener.* ◇ subject, servant; traditional owner through mother's father, mother's mother or father's mother; i.e. belonging to country other than through father's father. This appears to be a Warlpiri term written in the Warlpiri language: kurdungurlu (see Kenny 2013). Ⓛ pipawonnu Ⓓ mili

kutungula nama *dienen.* ◇ serve. Ⓛ pipawonnu ninañi Ⓓ milili ngamana

kuwíljawiljinkínama *schütteln (einen Baum).* ◇ shake (a tree). Ⓛ kuwiluwiluni

kwaia iltjala (altjala) *Cousine (Mutters Bruders Tochter oder Vaters Schwesters Tochter).* ◇ cousin (mother's brother's daughter or father's sister's daughter). Ⓛ kankuru wotjira

kwaia intanga *Schwägerin (Schwester des Mannes).* ◇ sister-in-law (husband's sister). Ⓛ toari

kwaia *ältere Schwester, Vaters ältere Bruders Tochter, Mutters ältere Schwester's Tochter, Fraus ält. Bruders Frau (♂), Manns ält. Bruders Frau (♀).* ◇ older sister, father's older brother's daughter, mother's older sister's daughter, wife's older brother's wife, husband's older brother's wife. Ⓛ kuju kankuru

kwaiankura *die ältere Schwester.* ◇ older sister. Ⓛ kankuruna

kwaiankuratja *meine ältere Schwester.* ◇ my older sister. Ⓛ kankuruna, totuna

kwaiitia [Southern dialect] *jüngere Schwester.* ◇ younger sister. Ⓛ kuju malangu

kwaiatjia [Northern dialect] *jüngere Schwester.* ◇ younger sister. Ⓛ kuju malangu

kwaiatjiatja *meine jüngere Schwester.* ◇ my younger sister. Ⓛ malanguna

kwaiatumba *Gras (art).* ◇ grass (species). Ⓛ urúta, kwaiatumba

kwaka *unmäßig, unaufhörlich, fortwährend.* ◇ excessive, continuously. Ⓛ bulba

kwakala ilkuma *fressen.* ◇ eat. Ⓛ bulbanku ngalkuñi

kwakala etaberama *sorgen.* ◇ to worry.

kwakaetalingetala nama *sorgen, fortwährend (an etwas denken, weinen).* ◇ worry, continuously (think about something, cry). Ⓛ bulbankukulilkulilba ninañi

kwaka [Eastern dialect] *conf.* **arkularkua** *Eule.* ◇ owl. Ⓛ kurrkurr

kwala, *cf.* **kula** *eine tiefe Grube.* ◇ deep ditch. Ⓛ ókala

kwalba *graue Wallaby zwisch. Porcupine Gras.* ◇ grey wallaby between porcupine grass. Ⓛ okalbi

kwalinja *schwarz (Holz).* ◇ black (wood). Ⓛ nukali

kwaljakwalja *Emu Federschmuck.* ◇ emu feather decoration. Ⓛ okaljukalji

kwalukwala *das Fleisch (an den Armen, die fleischigen Teile derselben, femora).* ◇ flesh (on arms). Ⓛ okálukáli

kwalintukwala *krächzendes Geschrei.* ◇ croaking noises. Ⓛ wonkakúnankúnanariñi

kwalintukwalerama *krähen (Hähne, Krähen).* ◇ to crow (roosters, crows). Ⓛ wonkakúnankúnan

kwamalaria *tiefe Grube oder Loch.* ◇ deep ditch or hole. Ⓛ wottantari

kwalanga *Päderastin (unbeschnitt. Junge).* ◇ novice. Ⓛ tuka

kwalangilama *Päderastin treiben.* ◇ practice pederasty. Ⓛ tukani

kwalangilana *Päderast.* ◇ pederast.

kwana *innen.* ◇ inside. Ⓛ ungu

kwanala *drinnen.* ◇ inside. Ⓛ ungunka Ⓓ mandrani

kwananlantema *drinnen.* ◇ inside. Ⓛ ungunkakamba

kwanaka *hinunter.* ◇ down. Ⓛ unguku

kwaniralakálama *untersinken (Sonne).* ◇ to set (sun). Ⓛ ungurekula okalingañi

kwanerama *hinunterbücken, sich ducken.* ◇ to bend, to duck. Ⓛ unguringañi

kwala *Gruben in denen ara und aranga gefangen werden.* ◇ ditches in which red kangaroos and euros are caught.

kwanama *verschlucken, verschlingen.* ◇ to swallow, devour. Ⓛ kultunañi Ⓓ julkana

kwanaminja *totkrank, dem Tode nahe.* ◇ dying, close to death. Ⓛ tunamulala

kwanginja *links.* ◇ left. Ⓛ tambu Ⓓ worrangantju

kwaninga *unten.* ◇ below. Ⓛ wăta, (watta), wata Ⓓ ngarinalu

kwananganganga *unter, z. B. unter die Flügel nehmen, zwischen durch.* ◇ under, e.g. take under the wings, between. Ⓛ wottawonna, unguwana

kwaningauna *nach unten, hinunter.* ◇ down. Ⓛ wóttatakura, watatakura

kwananganángala *unter (z.B. Sonne).* ◇ under (e.g. sun). Ⓛ ungurara

kwaniralakálama *untersinken (Sonne).* ◇ to sink, set (sun). Ⓛ ungurekula okalkingani

kwatiwuma *belohnen.* ◇ to reward.

kwatiwunja *Lohn.* ◇ reward, payment.

kwatjamata *wassersüchtig.* ◇ retaining water, oedematous.

kwatja wapa *das in der Ngalta-Wurzel und in lonkura Stamm befindende Wasser.* ◇ water in ngalta roots and in the lonkura-trunk. Ⓛ kapi ngántapiri

kwanjilinjala ekaralama *über (etwas) anziehen.* ◇ pull over (something).

kwanjalinjala *aufeinander (liegend).* ◇ (lie) on top of each other. Ⓛ palilkara, atulkira

kwanjitarerama *sich aufeinander legen.* ◇ to lie on top of each other. Ⓛ katulkiriringañi

kwanjatara *ineinander (steckend).* ◇ (insert) into each other. Ⓛ katulkira

kwanjirbera *mitten drin (stehend, v. Baum), zwischen (etwas stehend).* ◇ (stand) in the middle (of tree), stand between (something). Ⓛ katulkirawaritji

kwata worraworrilama *große Rauch aufsteigend.* ◇ big rising smoke. Ⓛ pújutujútu tjingañi

kwara *Mädchen, kleines Mädchen.* ◇ girl, little girl. Ⓛ kujuna, wanji, mēta Ⓓ mankara

kwárakaljialjia *(aljia=altja=die, mit ihr oder ihm verbunden) Pflanze mit milchigem Saft, Symbol der Mädchen.* ◇ plant with milky sap, symbol of girls (Strehlow 1913: 98). Ⓛ ōkaro

kwarukwara *Pflanze mit milchigem Saft.* ◇ plant with milky sap. Ⓛ okarókari

kwara *Eidechse spec. (Geheimsprache).* ◇ lizard species (alternative or restricted term). Ⓛ talera

kwata (urakwata) *Rauch.* ◇ smoke. Ⓛ puju Ⓓ jukati, turudupu

kwata (deba-kwata) *Ei, kleine lankua-Früchte.* ◇ egg, small lankua fruit. Ⓛ ngokuta, ngambu Ⓓ kapi

kwatja *Wasser, Regen.* ◇ water, rain. Ⓛ kapi (kape) Ⓓ ngapa, talara

atua kwatja ◇ rain men (see Strehlow 1907: 25–28).

kwatjarinja *Wasserbewohner.* ◇ waterdwellers; 'belonging to water' or 'coming from the water' (kwatja = water, rinja (suffix) = belonging to); one of the two patrimoieties (exogamous groups) of the Western Aranda. In Carl Strehlow's work the earth is described as an eternal presence in which at the beginning of time undeveloped humans were slumbering, they were already divided into the moieties 'alarinja' and 'kwatjarinja' and into a subsection system. According to Western Aranda mythology the moiety called 'alarinja' was divided into the Purula, Kamara, Ngala and Mbitjana subsections or 'skins'; and the other moiety 'kwatjarinja' into the Pananka, Paltara, Knuraia and Bangata subsections or 'skins' (Strehlow 1913). These anthropomorphic ancestor beings called 'altjirangamitjina' emerged from their underground dwellings (Strehlow 1907: 3) and wandered over the shapeless land, creating the landscape as it is still seen today, transforming themselves and establishing the world's structure and order. Ⓛ kapingurara

kwatjakwatja *wässerig, dünn.* ◇ watery, thin. Ⓛ kapikapi Ⓓ ngapali? ('?' added by CS)

kwatja atjua *Regen, herabfallende Regentropfen.* ◇ rain, falling raindrops. Ⓛ kapiwarala

kwatjapara *Blitz.* ◇ lightning. Ⓛ winba Ⓓ talarapraitji, pildripildri

kwatja bartjima *blitzen (während des Gewitters).* ◇ lightning (during a thunderstorm). Ⓛ winbákañi

kwatjankama *(Wasser sagt), donnern.* ◇ (lit. water says), to thunder. Ⓛ kapi wonkañi Ⓓ talarajindrana

kwatja-urkulta *hellleuchtender Blitz.* ◇ bright lightning.

 For the modern spellings of these words, see the dictionaries and sources in reference list.

kwatjinkatja *Donner.* ◇ thunder. Ⓛ kapiwonka Ⓓ talarajildri

kwatjabartjinja *Blitz.* ◇ lightning.

kwatja kula *tiefe Wasserloch.* ◇ deep waterhole. Ⓛ kapi tukula

kwatjalŭralŭra *Regenguß, schwere Regen.* ◇ downpour, heavy rain. Ⓛ kapilenku Ⓓ talara kuditji

kwatjambenka *Flut.* ◇ flood. Ⓛ kapibīla Ⓓ ngapamila?

kwatjatóatoa *leichte Regen.* ◇ light rain. Ⓛ kapi toatoïnba

kwatja ínera *Wasser (in ausgehöhlten Felsen).* ◇ water (in washed out rock). Ⓛ kapi wakula

kwatjintjanga *Wasseransammlung in der Creek.* ◇ banked up water in creek, waterhole. Ⓛ kapi muruntu

kwatja ankala *Regenwolke.* ◇ rain cloud. Ⓛ kapi ngankali

kwatjaïnbanginba *Pflanze, mit hellgrünen Blumen und Samenkapseln; wurde als Medizin gegen Kopfweh gebraucht.* ◇ plant with light green blossoms and seedpods; remedy for headache. Ⓛ kapiïnbinginbi

kwēba *Beutelratte von der Größe einer Katze.* ◇ marsupial rat about the size of a cat. Ⓛ kujuka

kwatjalibára *ganz niedrig über dem Wasser.* ◇ very low over the water. Ⓛ kapinkuparuparu

kwenja *Schutzzaun, Einfriedigung.* ◇ windbreak, enclosure. Ⓛ unta

kwatja-erulinja *ein Mann, dem ein langer Bart gewachsen ist, wenn der Bart beim Trinken ins Wasser (kwatja) reicht.* ◇ a man who has a long beard that touches the water when drinking. Ⓛ paluruwarata

kwérama *winken, Zeichen geben.* ◇ wave, beckon, make a sign. Ⓛ wakujuriñi

kwerinja *Zeichensprache.* ◇ sign language. Ⓛ wakujurinmi

kwatja ntuma *Wasser fallen, regnen.* ◇ water falls, raining. Ⓛ kapi patangarañi

kwatja tuljatulja *schmutziges, schlammiges Wasser.* ◇ dirty, muddy water. Ⓛ kapi-paki

kwatukwata *die Wurzeln oder Früchte des latjia, die fleischigen Oberschenkel des Emu, Leistengegend.* ◇ roots or fruits of latjia (edible root), meaty emu thighs, groin region. Ⓛ akutákuta

L

lăba *Feuerbrand, Fackel.* ◇ blazing fire, torch. Ⓛ danni

lāba *heruntergetretene Erde.* ◇ flattened soil. Ⓛ nuru

labalélama *überwachsen (Gras), bedecken (den Boden).* ◇ overgrown (by grass), cover (ground). Ⓛ nuruni

lábarinja *mythische Weiber, die niemals heiraten.* ◇ mythical women who never marry. Ⓛ ilibirinji

labara (ljabara) *kleine Stücke Rinde (zum Spielen).* ◇ small pieces of bark (for playing). Ⓛ ngantapi

lábilama *intrs. hineinrollen (Sand ins Wasser), trs. heruntertreten (das Ufer), in den Boden stampfen.* ◇ (intransitive) roll (sand into water), (transitive) tread down (river bank), stomp into the ground. Ⓛ totuni

labilkabilka *das herabfließende Blut.* ◇ pouring blood. Ⓛ ngurkakarikari

labinbenba *überhängende Fels, abfallende Fels.* ◇ overhanging cliff. Ⓛ tarutaru

labulburérama *sehr hungern, verhungern.* ◇ be very hungry, starve. Ⓛ aluulturiñi

lāda *Baumstamm.* ◇ tree trunk. Ⓛ wollati

ladakara *Fußbank.* ◇ footstool. Ⓛ wollatata

ládna *sehr viele.* ◇ very many. Ⓛ tuta

ladnerama *sich vermehren.* ◇ multiply. Ⓛ tutaringañi

ladnerátama *sich vermehren.* ◇ multiply. Ⓛ tutawirkanañi

ladnilama *trs. mehren.* ◇ (transitive) increase.

lāga *Dorn, Stachel, Stacheln (des Echidna).* ◇ thorn, prickle, quills (of echidna). Ⓛ tjilka Ⓓ dilka

laia jikarikara *weiche Rand des Sees.* ◇ soft edge of a lake. Ⓛ wollaijikirikiri

laia *das Meer.* ◇ sea. Ⓛ wollaiï

laiila *sehnsüchtig wartend auf einen, ungeduldig auf (wartend).* ◇ wait longingly for someone, impatient (waiting for). Ⓛ alaialaiï Ⓓ wolkareli

laiilaiérama *sehnsüchtig oder ungeduldig (auf jemanden warten).* ◇ longingly or impatiently waiting for someone. Ⓛ alaialaiiriñi Ⓓ wolkarina (*sehnsüchtig warten*: wait longingly)

laiakama *fragen.* ◇ ask. Ⓛ tabini Ⓓ jekibana

laiïnkama *auffliegen.* ◇ fly. Ⓛ purbakani

laínama *abschütteln, abstäuben, abklopfen (Schoten), ausdreschen.* ◇ shake off, dust off, pat (pods, husks), thrash. Ⓛ patatjingañi, patapungañi, jelkani Ⓓ kantikantina

lainopinama *abschüttelnd nehmen (Fische).* ◇ take or grab (fish) shaking it. Ⓛ patapunkanañi

lainalama *refl. sich (den Staub) abschütteln, abfallen (die reifen Früchte vom Baum).* ◇ (reflexive) shake off (dust), fall off (ripe fruit from tree). Ⓛ patapunkanañi

lainalábuma *schütteln (den Baum).* ◇ shake (tree). Ⓛ patatjingarariñi

lakatalakata *mäßig (im Essen).* ◇ moderate (eating).

lakinjatjatalkara *so lange.* ◇ so long.

lākama *jagen (Wild).* ◇ hunt (game). Ⓛ wonnañi

lákabara *schwarze Habicht.* ◇ black hawk. Ⓛ alakabara

lakalama *fortgehen, fortwährend gehen (auch um zu jagen).* ◇ go (away), go continuously (e.g. to hunt). Ⓛ jurikunkuninañi

lakakía *ein Angehöriger derselben Gruppe.* ◇ member of same moiety. Ⓛ ngananakurpiti

ljākaljāka *Strauch (spec.) mit langen Blättern und roten Beeren (nicht gegessen).* ◇ bush species with long leaves and red berries (not edible). Ⓛ tjilkartjilkara

lakalérama *ertrinken, ersticken (im Brei).* ◇ drown, choke (in swampy waterhole). Ⓛ mulakuturingañi

lákerama *herbeiströmen, hin und zurückschwimmen (Fische).* ◇ stream together, swim back and forth (fish). Ⓛ kunkujuriñi

lakarélama *nicht kennen, nicht erkennen.* ◇ not know, not recognise. Ⓛ butu ekuntani

lakarúntuma *zittern (vor Furcht).* ◇ to tremble, shake (from fear). Ⓛ tjilkabakani

lakara (luákara), ulakara? *Vorsprung (des Felsens).* ◇ cliff overhang. Ⓛ ulakirulakiri

lakina *so, so sehr.* ◇ thus, this much. Ⓛ alatji Ⓓ jeruja

lakinibera *so gerade so.* ◇ just like that. Ⓛ alatjitaka

lakantúrtukantúrta *sehr nahe zusammen stehende Stämme oder Stauden.* ◇ trunks or shrub standing very close together. Ⓛ tumbutumbu

lakinakatutja *so groß.* ◇ so big. Ⓛ alatjikutáta Ⓓ jerunia

lakinaka *geradeso, auf diese Weise.* ◇ just like that, in this way. Ⓛ alatjikula, alatjika

lakinja (lakinja) *so viele.* ◇ this many. Ⓛ alatjiru Ⓓ jeruntjaia

lakinakalakina *gerade so wie ein [unclear].* ◇ just like a [unclear]. Ⓛ alatjimurkalátjimurka maramara

lakinantema *in gleicher Weise.* ◇ in the same way. Ⓛ alkitjika

lakinjakakata *so viele.* ◇ this many. Ⓛ alatjirumurka

lakua *Strauch spec., stachlicher, mit kleinen Blättern, gelben Blüten und Schotenkapseln (Akacienart).* ◇ bush species, prickly, with small leaves, yellow blossoms and pods (*Acacia* species); mimosa bush, *Acacia farnesiana* (Latz 1996). Ⓛ aluku

lakula *sumpfig, morastig.* ◇ swampy, marshy. Ⓛ tunmirtara Ⓓ kinkalju

lalaia kata *vor einem her (gehen).* ◇ walk in front of someone. Ⓛ múlankakata

lalaka *lieb, wert.* ◇ dear, worthy. Ⓛ ngultu

lalakerama *freundlich bleiben.* ◇ remain friendly. Ⓛ ngulturingañi

lalaka irkuma *lieb halten.* ◇ hold dear. Ⓛ ngultu witini

lálakakalálaka irkuma *wert behalten.* ◇ keep worthy. Ⓛ ngultangultu witini

lalbaralalbara *Erz, ehern (gelb).* ◇ brass ore (yellow).

lalbara *gelb (Geschwür, Blüten).* ◇ yellow (abscess, blossoms). Ⓛ malalbara

lālama *vertreiben (Feinde), verscheuchen, wedeln (Fliegen).* ◇ drive away (enemies), scare away, shoo away (flies). Ⓛ baltunañi

lalarkama *zittern (vor Kälte).* ◇ shiver (from cold). Ⓛ ilbiljingañi

lalba *1. Strauch (spec.), hellgrüne, ovale um den Zweig sich schließende Blätter (auf Sandhügeln wachsend), Eucalyptus gamophylla. 2. Eine Art Wattle (auf Steinbergen wachsend).* ◇ 1. *Eucalyptus gamophylla* (grows on sandhills) 2. kind of wattle (grows on stony mountains). Ⓛ alalba, ilulbu

lalba *Steinmesser (spec.)* ◇ stone-knife (species) Ⓛ ulalbi

lalbalánana *Schlange (giftig) spec.* ◇ poisonous snake species. Ⓛ alalbankaninami

lalbilalbila *viele Halme, Haufen von Halmen.* ◇ many blades, pile of blades. Ⓛ albilálbili

lalbalenkuélama *freigebig sein, gern geben.* ◇ be generous, give willingly. Ⓛ indotindotani

lálalálarama *vor sich hin stoßen (mit etwas).* ◇ push (with something) forwards. Ⓛ ngu͡uungu͡utunañi

lalarama *nach vorn bewegen, nicken [unclear].* ◇ move forward, nod. Ⓛ ngu͡utunañi

lálerama *1. drohen, warnen. 2. zielen (nach jemanden).* ◇ 1. threaten, warn. 2. aim (at someone). Ⓛ ngútunani Ⓓ dikidikibana

lalejinama *fortschicken.* ◇ send away.

laleragunama *zertreten (Brot) mit Füßen treten, (in den Boden) stampfen.* ◇ squash/stamp (bread) with feet, trample (into the ground). Ⓛ turirbini

lalina *so.* ◇ so. Ⓛ pallata

lálilama *hervorbringen (Früchte), wachsen lassen.* ◇ yield (fruit), produce. Ⓛ bakatiljini

lalinakaguia *damit, sodaß.* ◇ so that, in order. Ⓛ pallakumaiu Ⓓ punkibana

lálitja *ein Strauch mit schwarzen Beeren, nicht übel schmeckend, in Gestalt einer kleinen Bohne (Carissa Brownii).* ◇ bush with black berries, (*Carissa lanceolata*) (Latz 1996). Ⓛ ngamunburu, manikitji Ⓓ jendralia

lalja *Akacien Mehl, Akacien Samen (lupa).* ◇ acacia flour, acacia seeds. Ⓛ alalji

laljiuma *Akacien Mehl machen, Samen zerklopfen.* ◇ make acacia flour, grind seeds. Ⓛ alaljiwonnini

lálkara *Gras (art).* ◇ grass species. Ⓛ okarita

lalinatara *so zwei, beieinander.* ◇ two together. Ⓛ lalatakutara

lálkara *der Knochen, Vogelknochen (von Adler, itoa oder Pelikan), der durch die Nasenwand gesteckt wird (Nasenschmuck von den Männern und Jungen getragen).* ◇ bone, bird-bone (of eagle, bush turkey or pelican) worn by men and boys in perforated nose septum. Ⓛ telunku, mulalkari, marapinti

lalkintinerama *Nasenwand durchbohren, durchstechen.* ◇ perforate, pierce septum of nose. Ⓛ mulalkiri kulturapungañi

lalkinja *Keim, die aufgehende Same, (Embryo).* ◇ germ, sprouting seed. Ⓛ alelkintji Ⓓ kuri, kuri punkana (*keimen*: germinate)

lalkna *in gutem Zustand, in Ordnung, geschickt bereitet.* ◇ in good condition, in order, skilfully prepared. Ⓛ nuka

lalknarerama *weiß werden (Halme).* ◇ turn white (blades). Ⓛ perulkáni

lalknilama *in Ordnung bringen, bereit machen.* ◇ prepare, make ready. Ⓛ nukani Ⓓ mapana kurana

lalkuma [Northern dialect] *cf.* lolkuma. ◇ refuse (request), deny. Ⓛ ngunjipungañi

lalknama *durchdringen (Schwert).* ◇ pierce (sword).

lalta (ljalta) *Holzende (in hohlen Bäumen), Späne.* ◇ wood chips (in tree hollows) or shavings; place to the west of Mt Sonder. Ⓛ ilenba

laltakalbala *Schlange, giftig (spec.)* ◇ snake, poisonous (species). Ⓛ ilaltakalbali

lalurútnama *mischen, vermengen (z.B. etwas mit Wasser).* ◇ mix, blend (e.g. something with water). Ⓛ turitarbatunañi

lalantánama *weit gehen, entlang gehen.* ◇ go far, go along. Ⓛ matalkanañi

lalantanerama *weit gehen, entlang gehen (dual).* ◇ go far, go along (dual).

laltauma *weit gehen, entlang gehen (plural).* ◇ go far, go along (plural).

lăma *gehen.* ◇ go, walk. Ⓛ jennañi, majennañi Ⓓ wapana

lāma *wegtreiben, verscheuchen.* ◇ drive away, scare away. Ⓛ tjingani, tjiriñi Ⓓ dangina

lālama *gehen machen (Feinde), von sich treiben.* ◇ drive away (enemies). Ⓛ tjingani

lapalama *weitergehen.* ◇ move on. Ⓛ jenkuntanka jennañi

lamarinka *unbekannt (Person), [unclear].* ◇ unknown (person). Ⓛ ngatatjinba

lamanitjikana *(keine Leber haben) = sehr hungrig sein.* ◇ (have no liver), be very hungry. Ⓛ alu wiata

lambalaia *Meer.* ◇ sea. Ⓛ wollaiï

lama *Leber.* ◇ liver. Ⓛ alu Ⓓ kalu

lamaknarilama *froh machen (durch ein in Aussicht gestelltes Geschenk), verheißen.* ◇ make happy, promise. Ⓛ alupuntuni

lamaknarilinja *Verheißung.* ◇ promise. Ⓛ alupuntunmi

lambilkala *große, graue Ente, grau und weiß gefleckte Brust und schwarze Schwanz.* ◇ large, grey duck, grey and white spotted chest and black tail. Ⓛ alambilkiri

lambulamba *Säbler, Schnabel mit aufwärts gekrümmter Spitze (Recuvirostra).* ◇ bird with beak bent upward (*Recurvirostra* now *Recurvirostra novaehollandiae*), red-necked avocet (Pizzey and Knight 2007). Ⓛ ulambulambi

lamankauurbmala ndama *mitleidig etwas geben.* ◇ give something out of pity. Ⓛ ngaruta bakara jungañi

lama altjurerama *sehr betrübt werden.* ◇ become very sad. Ⓛ alu julturingañi

lánama *wegtreiben (aus dem Weg), freimachen (den Weg), wegscheuchen, vertreiben (Vögel).* ◇ drive (off the path), clear (path), scare away (birds). Ⓛ matjingani tjirini Ⓓ dangina

lamatnama *sich erbarmen.* ◇ have pity.

lănba *Achselhöhle.* ◇ armpit. Ⓛ ngakula Ⓓ kapura

lānba *geschabte Holzblumen.* ◇ wood-flowers. Ⓛ ilanbi

lanbulélama *überfließen machen (Wasser).* ◇ (transitive) cause to overflow (water). Ⓛ wiltjingañi

lamatnama *(Leber weinen) sich erbarmen.* ◇ have pity. (lit. liver cry).

lanbuma *überfließen (Wasser).* ◇ overflow (water). Ⓛ wilknaráñi Ⓓ pinpitarana, kinkaljerina

lanbulélama *überfließen machen.* ◇ cause to overflow. Ⓛ tulburtjingañi, wiltjingañi

landatandata *die an den Stauden (Stamm = ila) befindlichen Blüten.* ◇ blossoms on stems (trunk) of a bush. Ⓛ ngana-untuntutara

langama *hinzufügen, hinzuschütten, zusammenbinden, zusammenschütten, vereingen, zusetzen, c. genit (ekura).* ◇ add, tie together, unit, *c. genit* (ekura). Ⓛ tunguni Ⓓ punmana (zusammen legen)

langerintja *das Zusammenschütten, Mischen.* ◇ mixture. Ⓛ tungulka

langankaia ankama *durch die Nase reden?* ◇ speak through nose. ('?' added by CS) Ⓛ mula-urba wonkañi

langamaĕla rama *mit der Hand die Augen beschatten, um besser zu sehen.* ◇ shade eyes with hand, to see better. Ⓛ karawolkani

langinbanilama *bedungen or bedingen [?]* ◇ to condition, cause.

langara *gerade, aufrecht.* ◇ straight, upright. Ⓛ jukaruru Ⓓ ngaranan

langerkuma *gerade halten (in der Hand).* ◇ hold straight (in hand). Ⓛ jukaruru witini

lanja *Steinbeil.* ◇ stone axe. Ⓛ wonnanta Ⓓ kalara

lanjalanja *wertvoll, kostbar, geschätzt (z.B. ihre Waffen).* ◇ valuable, precious, valued (e.g. weapons). Ⓛ ánini

lanjarantunana *Schlange, giftig.* ◇ poisonous snake. Ⓛ ilinjimutulba

lanjaltja *Nasenknorpel, Nasenmurkel [?]* ◇ nose cartilage; beard. Ⓛ ngurngurba

lanjima *hertreiben, herführen.* ◇ drive together, bring. Ⓛ ngalatjingani

lanjantariworrama *von allen Seiten heranstürmen (auf die Feinde).* ◇ rush together from all directions (Strehlow 1915: 13). Ⓛ pilpipungañi

lankaia *übel zugerichtet (durch Schlagen).* ◇ badly hurt (from a beating). Ⓛ makamunu

lanmankama *schlechtes reden (über jemanden), verleumden.* ◇ speak badly (about somebody), defame.

lankama *schmähen, schimpfen.* ◇ abuse, scold. Ⓛ niñipungañi Ⓓ kalana

lankerinjagata *bekannt.* ◇ known.

laritnama *hoch stehen.* ◇ stand high.

larana *die Welt (Inbegriff. alle Menschen).* ◇ the world (including all people).

laranapa *die Welt.* ◇ the world.

lankualankerama *sich einander erkennen.* ◇ recognise each another.

lankerama *erkennen.* ◇ recognise. Ⓛ ekuntani Ⓓ ngujamana

lankalaria *bekannt.* ◇ known. Ⓛ ekuntara Ⓓ ngujangujara

lankiwulama *sich verstecken, sich verstellen.* ◇ hide, pretend. Ⓛ jerkatarbañi

lankibuma *trs. Riß machen, einreißen (Kleid).* ◇ (transitive) tear (dress). Ⓛ lambini

lankinjamekana *vorzeitig, Urzeit.* ◇ primeval. Ⓛ iwaritamunu

lankua *Pflanze mit birnenförmigen Früchten, in denen eine eßbare Blume miteingeschlossen ist.* ◇ bush banana. Ⓛ unturknu

lānkua *ein Junges (Kängaruh oder inkaia).* ◇ young kangaroo or bilby. Ⓛ tjila

lanta *Flamme.* ◇ flame. Ⓛ kala

lănta *unfruchtbar.* ◇ infertile. Ⓛ barkakutu

lantama *herschicken, übergeben, überbringen.* ◇ send to, hand over, deliver. Ⓛ tantajungañi

lantera *Honig der Bienen.* ◇ honey of bees. Ⓛ alántiri

kēnkunna *eine Nase mit pimples (Mitesser).* ◇ pimples on nose (blackheads). Ⓛ lăntinja

lāntja *Aufseher.* ◇ overseer. Ⓛ atāntji, alintji

lanjararantunana *Schlange, giftige spec.* ◇ snake, poisonous species Ⓛ ilinjimutulba

lăra *Sehne an den Beinen, Muskel.* ◇ sinew of leg, muscle. Ⓛ paltara

lapalama *fortwährend gehen, weiter wandern.* ◇ walk constantly, walk on. Ⓛ jenkuntanka jennañi

lāpata *gut (Brot), sauber (Platz).* ◇ good (bread), clean (place). Ⓛ wotinba

laraka rama *mit den Augen drohen.* ◇ threaten with eyes. Ⓛ intani Ⓓ milki tekibana

larra *Creek, Fluß, Milchstraße.* ◇ creek, river, Milky Way. Ⓛ karu Ⓓ kaiari

larra *Milchstraße.* ◇ Milky Way. Ⓛ karu, meṙawari, tukalba

Larrabenta *Salzfluß (Finke).* ◇ Saltriver (name of Finke River). Ⓛ karu-apinti

Larrambonta [Southern dialect] *große Fluß (Finke).* ◇ big river (Finke). Ⓛ karu-apinti

larrabilarra *Binsen (Cyperus vaginatus).* ◇ rushes (*Cyperus vaginatus*). Ⓛ ankarankara Ⓓ kalku

lānta *eine kranzförmig gewundene laga-Ranke auf dem Kopf.* ◇ head wreath made of laga runners. Ⓛ akanta

larrajilkara *weiße Fluß (= große Fluß).* ◇ white river (great river). Ⓛ karu tjilpi

larakulara *cf.* ularakulara. ◇ against, (stand) opposite each other. Ⓛ ngapara ngarini

lárrintjinga *kleine Creek.* ◇ small creek. Ⓛ karu papipi

larralélama *wegspülen, wegwaschen (Flut).* ◇ erode, wash away (flood). Ⓛ untartjingani

laranga *hoch.* ◇ high.

larralama *schwimmen (Menschen).* ◇ swim (people). Ⓛ katurujennañi Ⓓ tarakana

larridama *cf.* **larrapallanama, pallanama** *schwimmen (Vögel).* ◇ swim (birds). Ⓛ katurauuringañi

láralabúma *Treibjagd veranstalten.* ◇ organise hunt. Ⓛ ulurupungañi

larangerama *intrs. sich erhöhen.* ◇ (intransitive) elevate oneself.

lataka *für jetzt, für einen Augenblick.* ◇ for now, for a moment. Ⓛ kuariku

latakama *für jetzt, für einen Augenblick.* ◇ for now, for a moment. Ⓛ kuarikumba

latawara *erst jetzt, erst heute.* ◇ only now, only today. Ⓛ kuari wiakutu

larumbarumba *schwellenden Brüste.* ◇ swelling breasts. Ⓛ rumburumbu

larumba *schwellend, geschwollen (Brust).* ◇ swelling, swollen. Ⓛ rumbu

larrapallanama *umherschwimmen (Fische, Vögel, Menschen).* ◇ swim around (fish, birds, people). Ⓛ ararijenkániñi

lárawulára *Rand (des Nestes).* ◇ edge (of nest). Ⓛ atambatamba

larba *bekümmert, traurig, betrübt.* ◇ worried, sad, sorrowful.

larberama *sich bekümmern, trauern, Leid tragen (um einen Toten).* ◇ grieve, mourn (someone's death). Ⓛ altururiñi

lárenátnama *einritzen, einschneiden (Loch in das [unclear] des Zauberdoktors).* ◇ incise, engrave. Ⓛ wartnuni

larbiuma *mahlen, zerreiben auf Steinen.* ◇ grind on stones. Ⓛ ularpungañi Ⓓ turara ngankana

larbiwutjintjima *schlängelnd den Kopf werfend (Schlange).* ◇ fling head to move forwards (snake). Ⓛ ularpunkula kalbañi

larrerama *schwimmen (Menschen).* ◇ swim (people). Ⓛ katuringañi

larumbarumba *schwellende (Brüste).* ◇ swelling (breasts). Ⓛ rumburumbu

lária *furchtlos, kühn.* ◇ fearless, daring. Ⓛ ónara

larinja *Mond.* ◇ moon. Ⓛ kinara

lárierama *genesen, stark, gesund werden.* ◇ recover, become healthy. Ⓛ lenkirariñi

lároalara *zum gehen bereit, zum Ausflug bereit.* ◇ ready to go. Ⓛ atámbatámba

lárkama *wetterleuchten.* ◇ sheet lightning. Ⓛ pinbani

larkinja *Wetterleuchten.* ◇ sheet lightning. Ⓛ pinbami

larurbarurberama *gähren, aufgehen (Brotteig).* ◇ ferment, rise (bread dough). Ⓛ rārariñi

larra *schlummernd.* ◇ slumber. Ⓛ ārari

larra nama *schlummern.* ◇ to slumber. Ⓛ arari ninañi

laruntuma *spielend im Kreis herumgehen.* ◇ go playfully around in a circle. Ⓛ taiirpungañi

lătalăta *die obere Seite des Schenkels.* ◇ upper part of thigh. Ⓛ munturu

lata *jetzt, heute.* ◇ now, today. Ⓛ kuari Ⓓ karari

lata ntama *jetzt wieder.* ◇ now again. Ⓛ kuarikutuka

lāta *Speer mit breiter Spitze.* ◇ spear with broad spearhead. Ⓛ wolla

latalata *Holzart, aus der Speere gemacht werden.* ◇ wood species used to make spears. Ⓛ ilitiliti

latakuia *gerade jetzt.* ◇ just now. Ⓛ kuarilenku

latarbatura (ila-tarba-tura kurz) *kahlen Baumstumpfen.* ◇ bald tree stump. Ⓛ warpili

latakara nama *oben sitzen (auf dem Baum).* ◇ sit at the top (of a tree). Ⓛ wollatata ninañi

ladakara *Fußbank.* ◇ footstool. Ⓛ wollatata

latenba *scrotum.* ◇ scrotum. Ⓛ walakulu

laterala lama *verlassen (einen Ort).* ◇ leave (a place). Ⓛ jengarikula jennañi

latilkama [Southern dialect] *Getönn machen, schnurren (Spindel).* ◇ make sound, hum, purr, whirr? (spindle). Ⓛ tēltara wonkañi

latinja *neu, jung.* ◇ new, young. Ⓛ kuarita Ⓓ marra

latinjerama *neu werden.* ◇ become new. Ⓛ kuaritaringañi Ⓓ marrarina

 For the modern spellings of these words, see the dictionaries and sources in reference list.

latinjilama *neu machen.* ◇ make new. Ⓛ kuaritani Ⓓ marraribana

latitja *Stab (zum Gehen), Stütze.* ◇ walking stick. Ⓛ tukara

latia *der Monat, wenn die Kälte abnimmt (August).* ◇ month when the cold subsides (August). Ⓛ kutuwara (August)

latirkuma *zusammen halten (Wurzeln).* ◇ hold together (roots). Ⓛ ngalunbinañi

látitjikaláma *kreuzweise übereinander legen (Hände).* ◇ lay crosswise over each other (hands). Ⓛ wollatataku tunani

latambala *gegenwärtig (Zeit).* ◇ present (time).

latjia *eßbare Wurzeln (spec.)* ◇ edible root, yam, *Vigna lanceolata*. Ⓛ wapiti, ngalatji

latjingatjora *Schlange (giftig).* ◇ snake (poisonous). Ⓛ mulatitu

latjingatjura *mit weißer Stirn (z.B. Hund).* ◇ with white forehead (e.g. dog). Ⓛ ngalawilunta

latoa *dieser, jener.* ◇ this one, that one. Ⓛ alangata

latjintara, itirkitirki *(widerspenstig) ein Mann, der mit seiner Klassenschwester Gemeinschaft hat.* ◇ stubborn man (who has a forbidden relationship with his classificatory sister) (Strehlow 1913: 103). Ⓛ alutirkitirki, putalputalja

latjapurpa *versammelt (stehen), Haufen (gehen).* ◇ assembled (stand). Ⓛ ngaralawonnañi

latjarinka *böse Wesen in Menschengestalt.* ◇ evil beings in human shape.

latukuna *dorthin.* ◇ over there. Ⓛ alabanatu

latiltja *feige.* ◇ cowardly.

latna *Stirn.* ◇ forehead. Ⓛ ngala Ⓓ milperi

latea *vollendet.* ◇ accomplished.

latnama *den eigenen Finger auf eine Stelle legen.* ◇ place finger on something.

latnara *Schlange, nicht giftige spec.* ◇ snake, not poisonous species. Ⓛ inturkunu

lataburinja *kürzlich, vor Kurzem.* ◇ lately, not long ago.

látupuláta *(dupplik.) tiefe Sand in der Creek, Creek-Sand.* ◇ (reduplication) deep sand in creek, creek sand. Ⓛ ulatupulati

lauarenama *einen besänftigen, versöhnen.* ◇ calm someone, reconcile.

lauarenalama *sich besänftigen, in 'Gleichgewicht' bringen.* ◇ calm down, to bring into 'balance'.

laua, lauala, (alóala) *ähnlich, gleich.* ◇ similar, same. Ⓛ ekuntara Ⓓ jenildramata

laualintjanga *2 gleiche Seen.* ◇ two identical lakes. Ⓛ pulamuruntu

laualintjara *gleichgesinnt, einmütig.* ◇ like minded, unanimous. Ⓛ tanatanamurka

lauilaua *schwarz (Erde, Vögel).* ◇ black (soil, birds). Ⓛ marurmarura

lauma, lēuma *verbergen, verstecken.* ◇ conceal, hide. Ⓛ jerkatunani Ⓓ kutibana

laulama *refl. sich verstecken.* ◇ (reflexive) hide. Ⓛ kumbini Ⓓ kutina

laulinja *versteckt, verborgen, heimlich.* ◇ hidden, concealed, secretly. Ⓛ jerkata

léaka *unfruchtbar (Weib).* ◇ infertile (woman). Ⓛ putapatti

léalea (ljéaljéa) *Abendstern (= Zwillinge).* ◇ evening star (twins). Ⓛ mulati

lébmarilama *(sich) entschuldigen (zu kommen).* ◇ apologise (to come). Ⓛ ngutapiriñi

lĕba; pennaleba *halb; halfpenny.* ◇ half; halfpenny.

lebmaȑila renama *zurückweisen (etwas).* ◇ decline, reject (something). Ⓛ ngunjipunkula jenni

lébarenama *dichtes Gebüsch, verhindern (die Aussicht, den Ausblick), großer Regen verhindert das Weitergehen.* ◇ thick bushes obstruct (view), heavy rain prevents from proceeding. Ⓛ patini

lebmérama *wehren (zu kommen), verhindern am kommen.* ◇ resist (to come), prevent (from coming). Ⓛ ngunjipungañi

lebmintjerama *hinterlassen (seine Güter), verlassen (seine Verwandten, z.B. der Verstorbene).* ◇ leave behind (possessions), leave (relatives, e.g. the deceased). Ⓛ emintjiriñi

lēkara *Hülsen, Borke.* ◇ pods, bark. Ⓛ rarininañi

lékara (likira) *rein, schön glänzend, gut, schön gebogen (Regenbogen).* ◇ pure, beautifully shining, good, beautifully bent (rainbow). Ⓛ warikiri

lekitjulbitalama *Unordnung machen.* ◇ make a mess.

lekarélama *gutes sagen, gutes wünschen.* ◇ wish well; today used in the Lutheran context for 'bless'. Ⓛ pinjipinjini

lekarambartja ankama *gutes anwünschen.* ◇ wish well. Ⓛ pinjipinjira wonkañi

lélama *versprechen.* ◇ promise. Ⓛ tankuni Ⓓ talpadakana; talpadakaterina (*sich verloben*: get engaged)

lelbeuma *unschädlich machen [unclear].* ◇ make harmless, difuse.

lelangalatnáma *fortwährend versprechen, vertrösten.* ◇ continuously promise, put off. Ⓛ tankuntatankuntaninañi

lélangantama *ermahnen, antreiben zur Arbeit, unterrichten.* ◇ remind, drive to work, instruct, teach. Ⓛ tintinpungañi

lélara *Steinmesser.* ◇ stone knife. Ⓛ alelari

lelba *starr, steif.* ◇ rigid, stiff. Ⓛ alilba

lelberama *steif werden.* ◇ become stiff. Ⓛ alilbaringañi

lelbilama *steif machen.* ◇ make stiff, stiffen. Ⓛ alilbani

lelbmara *Eidechse spec. [unclear].* ◇ lizard species. Ⓛ akilbara

lelbankama *sich heben von seiner Stätte (Berg).* ◇ rise from one's site (mountain).

lelera *Busch (Cassia Sturtii).* ◇ bush (*Cassia sturtii* now *Senna artemisioides* (Latz 1996)). Ⓛ alelari

lelirtja *Steingeröll, Kies.* ◇ boulders, gravel. Ⓛ malkarmalkara

lelka *eben, glatt, schlüpfrig.* ◇ even, smooth, slippery. Ⓛ wirula, wirulba

lelkerama *ausgleiten.* ◇ slip. Ⓛ wirularingañi

lelkeranama *herausgleiten, geboren werden (Kinder).* ◇ slide out, to be born (children). Ⓛ mawirularingañi, mawirultalkañi

lelkilama *glätten, ausgleiten machen, massieren, den Leib drücken.* ◇ smooth, make slip, massage, press body. Ⓛ wirulanani, wirultungani

lĕlkara [Southern dialect] **(ululkara)** *Stirnband (aranga Fell).* ◇ headband (euro fur). Ⓛ erowara

lelkirbota *schöngeglättet, schöngestaltet.* ◇ smoothed, well formed. Ⓛ wirulpalla

lelknaralknara *die frischen Schößlinge, die neben den alten Büschen hervorkommen.* ◇ young shoots that appear next to the old bushes. Ⓛ ? talta

lelinjala *in Kurzem [Kürze?], in Zukunft.* ◇ shortly, in the future.

lelinja *bald (nach mehreren Tagen).* ◇ soon (after a few days). Ⓛ ngulaku

ljelinja (lēlinja) *Regenbogen.* ◇ rainbow (This Aranda word was not known; today the word 'mbulara' is used for 'rainbow'.) Ⓛ kanturangu

lēlta [Southern dialect] **(= lēltja)** *abnehmende (Mond).* ◇ wane (moon). Ⓛ tankili

leltankama *hervorsprossen (Saat).* ◇ sprout (crop). Ⓛ bulbulbakani

lēltja *abnehmend.* ◇ wane, diminish. Ⓛ tankili

taia lēltja *Mondsichel.* ◇ sickle moon. Ⓛ pira tankili

lĕltja *Feind.* ◇ enemy. Ⓛ tjinarki, wonnapa

leltjakaleltja *feindlich.* ◇ hostile. Ⓛ wonnapakuwonnapa

lēna (lēnja) *jener, dort.* ◇ that one, there. Ⓛ pallata

lengankana *dort! da!* ◇ over there! there! Ⓛ pallakutu

lenkana? danna nuka lenkana? – lengankana! *wo? Wo ist meine Mulde? – dort!* ◇ where? where is my bowl? – there! Ⓛ pallawata? punna ngaiuku pallawata? – pallakutu!

lengankana! *dort!* ◊ there! Ⓛ pallakutu!
lenatoa *jener.* ◊ that one there. Ⓛ pallatatoa
leona *dort überall.* ◊ there everywhere. Ⓛ pallatu
lénama *abschütteln (Früchte vom Baum).* ◊ shake (fruit from a tree). Ⓛ patatjingañi
lenárenára *Turm.* ◊ tower.
lênga, lenga; alinga [Northern dialect]; **tarka, rarka** [Eastern dialect] *Sonne.* ◊ sun (Strehlow 1907: 16). Ⓛ tjintu, nilba [Southern dialect] Ⓓ ditji pirna
lênga ntalta *Sonnenstrahlen (Schamhaare der Sonne).* ◊ sunbeams (pubic hair of sun) (Strehlow 1907: 17). Ⓛ tjintu uru
lênga iltjamiltja *die langen Strahlen (Hände) der aufgehenden Sonne.* ◊ long sunbeams (hands) of the rising sun. Ⓛ tjintu karawolla
lêngarenarena *Uhr.* ◊ clock. Ⓛ nilbanangami
lênga tjulkuma *Tag anbrechen.* ◊ daybreak. Ⓛ perulkañi, jultaringañi
lênga irbulakalama *Sonne untergehen.* ◊ sunset. Ⓛ tjintu tarbara okalingañi
lênja *Zunge.* ◊ tongue. Ⓛ talinja Ⓓ tali
lênja kantja *Zungenspitze.* ◊ tip of tongue. Ⓛ talinja akantji
lênja tnata *Zungenbauch [?], auf der Zunge.* ◊ tongue belly [?], on the tongue. Ⓛ talinja wila
lênja toppa *Zungenrücken?; unter der Zunge.* ◊ under the tongue. ('?' added by CS) Ⓛ talinja tana
lênjirkna *das Loch in der Zunge (der Zauberer).* ◊ hole in tongue (Spencer and Gillen 1904: 524). Ⓛ talinja-ala
lenjiuma *Zunge ausstrecken.* ◊ poke tongue out. Ⓛ talinmanani
lenjanberérama (lenja=Zunge, anbererama=austrecken und wieder einziehen) *Zunge (Raben cult).* ◊ poke tongue in and out. Ⓛ talina waintárini
lênja bakaba nama *stottern.* ◊ stammer. Ⓛ talinja burka
lênga ragata *das Steigen des Tages (Sonne [unclear]).* ◊ daybreak, sunrise.
linjiriuma *herausziehen (z.B. den Fischspeer).* ◊ pull out (e.g. fishspear). Ⓛ koinpungani
lenjilkna *dicke, feste Eiter (Eiterpfropfen).* ◊ thick, solid pus (pus plug). Ⓛ alínjilkni
lenkunja *hübsch, schön.* ◊ pretty, beautiful. Ⓛ kunjinji
lenkunjilama *schmücken, sich schmücken.* ◊ to decorate. Ⓛ kunjinjatuni
lenkuilama *schmücken, sich schmücken.* ◊ decorate. Ⓛ kunjinjatuni
lenkuinkupa *sehr hübsch.* ◊ very pretty. Ⓛ kunjinji lenkutu
lentama *führen (den Weg).* ◊ lead (the way).
léntanàma [Southern dialect] *heranschleichend (mit gebeugter Stirn).* ◊ creep up (with lowered forehead). Ⓛ mauurakatiñi
lentitjalama *heranschleichend.* ◊ creeping up. Ⓛ ngalaúrakatiñi
lentara *früh vor Sonnenaufgang, Lichtstreifen im Osten sich zeigen (Hähne krähen), Morgengrauen.* ◊ early in the morning, early before sunrise, first light in the east (when roosters crow), at the crack of dawn, dawn (Strehlow 1915: 44). Ⓛ ulentiri
leoa *unterhalb, stromabwärts.* ◊ below, downstream. Ⓛ wăta
leongantabána *von unterwärts (kommen).* ◊ from below (come). Ⓛ watangurukutu
leontoppa *unterwärts, stromabwärts.* ◊ downstream. Ⓛ watankutu
leotaka *stromabwärts.* ◊ downstream. Ⓛ watakutu
leotakeritjikalerama *stromabwärts hinabgehen.* ◊ go downstream. Ⓛ watakuturekula okalingañi
lêralêra *von Loritja: ulêratêra.* Ⓛ ulêratêra
lêrama *begehren, verlangen.* ◊ desire, demand. Ⓛ ulkañi
lera *Vogel, Wasservogel (spec.)* ◊ bird, waterbird (species). Ⓛ aleri Ⓓ milkirina

lêrra; lerra [Southern dialect] *Sohn, Neffe; Sohn, Tochter (♂), Bruders Sohn, Bruders Tochter, Urgroßvater (♀).* ◇ son, nephew; son, daughter, brother's son, brother's daughter, great grandfather. Ⓛ kata

woialêrra *Bruders Sohn.* ◇ brother's son.

kwaialêrra *Bruders Tochter.* ◇ brother's daughter.

lêrratjurutja *alle Kinder (von Vater so genannt).* ◇ all children (term used by fathers).

lêrrukua *Sohn, Neffe (eines Anderen).* ◇ son, nephew (of someone else). Ⓛ katara Ⓓ ngatamura

lêrrakunjêrra *die Kinder (Nachkommen).* ◇ children (descendants). Ⓛ kataramurka

lerrakunja *Taube spec. (Sinnbild der Frauen).* ◇ small pigeon species (symbol of women). Ⓛ kokoku

lerralama [Southern dialect] *sich sonnen, (den Leib glänzen machen).* ◇ sunbathe, (make body shine). Ⓛ tjilpatjilpañi

letakama *auslesen.* ◇ select. Ⓛ akatatauani

latilkama (letilkama) *brummen (mythische Wesen).* ◇ hum (mythical beings). Ⓛ tiltaramérani

letirba *kleiner Vogel (spec.)* ◇ small bird (species) Ⓛ aletirba

lētja [Southern dialect] *lange Stecken, Balken, Bahre.* ◇ long stick, beam, rafter. Ⓛ tabalpa

letjaletja *kleine latjia Früchte.* ◇ small latjia fruit. Ⓛ ilitjilitji

letoppetoppa *in einer Reihe (liegen), reihenweise.* ◇ (lie) in one row, in rows. Ⓛ palilkara (ngariñi)

leuma *umreißen, umstürzen, umhauen, umsägen, fallen.* ◇ pull down, overturn, cut down, saw down, fell. Ⓛ katawonniñi

leurbaléa *große Haufe, Vorrat (v. Samen).* ◇ big pile, provision (of seeds). Ⓛ utulánbara

lewerama *ringen, streiten.* ◇ wrestle, fight. Ⓛ antawonnirapungañi

limintjala ankama *plappern.* ◇ chatter.

limintja? *fortwährend.* ◇ constantly.

likebala *getrost.* ◇ confident, reconciled.

lgurba *Schaum.* ◇ foam. (Aranda entry deleted by CS) Ⓛ talji

lgurbilama *schäumen.* ◇ to foam. (Aranda entry deleted by CS) Ⓛ taljini

likira [Northern dialect] *gewölbt, halbkreisförmig gebogen (Regenbogen).* ◇ arched, shaped in a semicircle (rainbow). Ⓛ warikiri

libárkalabárkala *Zickzack des Blitzes.* ◇ zigzag of lightning. Ⓛ pinpakulantakulanta

libarkalabarkala nama *blitzen.* ◇ lightning. Ⓛ pinpakulantakulantariñi

libiljenkama *sich entfalten (Wolken), aufbrechen (Knospe).* ◇ unfold (clouds), burst open (buds) or to bud. Ⓛ biljalankañi

lilika *bald (nach mehreren Tagen).* ◇ soon (after a few days). Ⓛ ngula

liljaua *Cormoranart.* ◇ cormorant species. Ⓛ tjilewi

liljirkaratnuruma *fortwährend (pfeifen), laut miteinander sprechen.* ◇ continuously (whistle), speak loud with each other. Ⓛ ngaljerbmanáñi

liljaka (liljerka) *eßbare Beeren von der Größe einer Stachelbeere mit widerlichem Geschmack.* ◇ edible berries (size of gooseberry). Ⓛ aliljaki

liljemba (ljelimba) *ein Stück Holz mit geschabten Blättern.* ◇ piece of wood with carved leaves [?]. Ⓛ melili (meljilji)

liljoa *nackten (kleine Vögel).* ◇ naked (little birds). Ⓛ ililjóa

limba *Pflanze mit fleischigen eßbaren Blättern (Parakilia) Claytonia (art).* ◇ plant with fleshy edible leaves (species); parakeelya, *Calandrinia balonensis* (Latz 1996). Ⓛ tungi Ⓓ parakilja

linbaralinbara *ein auf Säulen ruhendes Dach, Halle.* ◇ roof resting on pillars, hall.

lingintjia *Wasservogel.* ◇ waterbird. Ⓛ alingintjiï

linama *zucken (nach dem Sterben), das Fleisch nach dem Schlachten.* ◇ twitch (after death), flesh after slaughter. Ⓛ numbañi

 For the modern spellings of these words, see the dictionaries and sources in reference list.

ljinga [Southern dialect] *penis.* ◇ penis. Ⓛ kalu

lingatjakua *linkshändig.* ◇ left handed. Ⓛ tambupiti

linjalenga *graue Habicht.* ◇ grey hawk. Ⓛ ilinjilingi

linjatuma *binden, fesseln.* ◇ tie, shackle. Ⓛ juntúnañi

linbilanga [Southern dialect] *cf.* elanbilanga. Ⓛ toturtara

linjiuma [Southern dialect] *einwickeln.* ◇ wrap. Ⓛ junmanáñi

linjirbma *Zweigunterlage, dichte Zweige (Adlersnest).* ◇ pad of twigs, dense twigs (eagle's nest). Ⓛ ilinjirbmi

linjiulama *sich einwickeln (refl.)* ◇ wrap (reflexive). Ⓛ paluru junmanáñi

lingintjira *dicht zusammen stehende Zweige, dichtbelaubt (Mistelzweige).* ◇ dense foliage (mistletoe branches). Ⓛ warbili

línjíriùma *ausringen (Kleider).* ◇ wring (cloths). Ⓛ kowinpungañi

ljurkna, (liorkna) *Reis, Schössling.* ◇ sprig, shoot. Ⓛ tabanba

lipa *Schnur, mittels deren die Mulden getragen werden, Hymen, z.B. lipa-kama.* ◇ string to carry bowls, hymen. Ⓛ ngarkinti

linjilinja *Ausschlag.* ◇ rash. Ⓛ puretu

linjírkuia *die Muskeln (am ganzen Körper), die das Fleisch zusammen halten.* ◇ body muscles that hold the flesh together. Ⓛ taratăra

ljola *bitter (Worte).* ◇ bitter (words).

ljaiinja *Flügelschlag.* ◇ beat of wing.

ljía [Southern dialect] *zugehörig (sex totem).* ◇ belonging to. Ⓛ inánkutu

lirtjina *kleiner grüner Papagai (spec.); (shell-parrot); Bauch und Rücken hellgrün, Kopf und Flügel gelb und grau gestreift, blaue Flecken an beiden Wangen, Schwanzfedern gelb und grau (Melopsittacus undulates).* ◇ budgerigar (shell parrot), *Melopsittacus undulatus* (Pizzey and Knight 2007). Ⓛ kuljirtji, ngatitjiri Ⓓ katátara

ljerra *Klopfstein.* ◇ grinding stone. Ⓛ ápata

litja *Speerwunde, Wunde (durch Stich oder Schlag hervorgebracht).* ◇ spear wound, wound (caused by a stab or blow). Ⓛ itila, itilba

litjitja *weiße Ameisen larven (spec.)* ◇ species of white ant larva. Ⓛ alitjitji

litjilba *Bote.* ◇ messenger. Ⓛ alurkuni

ljartjimbuma *vertrocknen, verdorren.* ◇ dry out, wither, shrivel. Ⓛ kērkambañi

ljartjinja *verdorrt.* ◇ withered. Ⓛ kērba

ljaba *die Löcher der Honigameisen.* ◇ nest of honeyants. Ⓛ piti

ljakaljaka *behaart.* ◇ hairy. Ⓛ meninjimeninji, tjilkatjilka

ljaiinja *das Rauschen, Rasseln (der Flügel), flattern (Federn).* ◇ rustle (of wings), flutter (feathers).

ljaiama *fauchen (Schlangen), flattern (die Federn im Winde).* ◇ hiss (snakes), flutter (feathers in wind). Ⓛ tuluni, karalbmanañi

ljalangareréa *Schlange (giftig).* ◇ snake (poisonous). Ⓛ warurunkalba

ljala; pata ljala *Steingeröll, lose Felsen; Kies.* ◇ boulders, loose rocks; gravel, pebbles. Ⓛ ilili, malka Ⓓ paltiri (steiniges Land)

ljala alkurúmba *umherliegende Felsblöcke.* ◇ rock boulders lying around. Ⓛ ilili alkurumba

ljartjilélama *verdorren (Äste), verwelken (Blätter) (von der Sonne).* ◇ dry out (branches), wither (leaves) from sun. Ⓛ kērkambatiljini

ljaua *Pflanze mit fleischigen, eßbaren Blättern (Claysonia Balonnensis nach Stirling).* ◇ plant with fleshy, edible leaves (*Claysonia Balonnensis* according to Stirling). Ⓛ wakati Ⓓ manjura (*auf clay-pans*: on claypans), winkara (*auf Sandhügeln*: on sandhills)

ljaualjaua *kleine schwarze Käfer mit erhobenen Rückenplatte (coakraches).* ◇ small black beetle with elevated backshield (cockroach). Ⓛ wakatiwakati

nēka *eßbare Frucht.* ◇ edible fruit. Ⓛ ljella

ljélama *singen.* ◇ sing. Ⓛ warañi Ⓓ wonkana

ljelinja *Gesang.* ◇ singing. Ⓛ waranka Ⓓ wimma

ljelinjamea *Lied.* ◇ song. Ⓛ waranta palla
ljelknánkama *krächzen, krähen.* ◇ croak, crow. Ⓛ ngelbmanañi
ljerka tnatanbuma *Gummizweige umherstreuen.* ◇ scatter gumtree branches. Ⓛ tjaljirba pulknaráñi
ljelta *Bast.* ◇ fibre. Ⓛ ilenbi Ⓓ jinkapitji
ljerka *Gummibaumlaub (trockenes und grünes).* ◇ gumtree leaves (dry and green). Ⓛ tjaljiri, tjaljirba
ljerba *ältere Bruder.* ◇ older brother. Ⓛ kuta
ljerra *Stein mit dem die Steinmesser abgespalten werden.* ◇ stone to work stone knives. Ⓛ apata
ljiljangerama *zischen (Wasser), anfangen zu kochen.* ◇ hiss (water), start to boil. Ⓛ tjiljiliïriñi Ⓓ tilitilingana
ljerkuerama *zusammen pfeifen (Vögel), schwätzen, viele Worte machen.* ◇ whistle in concert (birds), chatter, talkative. Ⓛ ngeljerbmanañi
ljerkueranerana *der Schwätzer.* ◇ gossiper.
ljerkuljerkuerama *pfeifen (viele).* ◇ whistle (many). Ⓛ ngeljerngeljerbmanañi
ljima *(Zauberworte) murmeln.* ◇ mumble (magic words, spells). Ⓛ initunañi
ljirra *gut, (besonders von Verstorbenen).* ◇ good (especially coming from the deceased). Ⓛ patupala
ljerruntuma *(um die Lagerbewohner) herumgehen.* ◇ walk around (people in a camp). Ⓛ areoakani
ljirraljirra *sehr kleiner Vogel, dunkelblau mit schwarz und weißen Rücken, Kopf und Brust dunkelblau oder lilablaue Brust, Schwanz lang blau, Flügel grau und weiß, mit schwarzen Streifen [unclear]; Malurus Melanopten? oder Malurus Leuconotu?* ('?' added by CS) ◇ very small bird, dark blue with black and white stripes, head and chest dark blue or lilac blue, tail long blue, wings grey and white, with black stripes (now *Malurus (Musciparus) leucopterus* (Atlas of Living Australia n.d.)). Ⓛ iljirriljirri
ljirramea *sehr gut (Fleisch, Freunde).* ◇ very good (meat, friends). Ⓛ palamba
ljōla (lōla) *anus, Boden.* ◇ anus, ground. Ⓛ manna Ⓓ piti
ljirraljirra *sehr schön, sehr gut.* ◇ very beautiful, very good. Ⓛ palapala
ljōta (lōta) *zum Schein.* ◇ pretend.
ljota ndama *zum Schein geben, necken.* ◇ pretend, tease. Ⓛ iljota jungañi
lkurbilama *schäumen (aus dem Mund).* ◇ froth (from mouth).
lkurba *der Schaum.* ◇ froth.
lulba *Zucker auf den Lalba-Blättern.* ◇ sugar on lalba leaves. Ⓛ iljulbu
ljunga *agia-Beere.* ◇ agia berry. Ⓛ iljungu
ljurkna *Reis, Schößling.* ◇ sprig, shoot. Ⓛ tutula, tabanba
ljuntintja *viele (nebeneinander stehende) Schößlinge.* ◇ many shoots (beside each other). Ⓛ talta
ljéljentánama *grimmen im Bauch.* ◇ pain (in stomach).
(a)lkenkarenama [Southern dialect] *bezeugen, beteuern, fortwährend falsches bezeugen.* ◇ testify, affirm, constantly assert untruths. Ⓛ turkulkata tunañi
(a)lkútakalkúta *brechübel.* ◇ very sick. Ⓛ ulkabulkaba
(a)lkutakalkúterama *sich brechen.* ◇ vomit. Ⓛ ulkabulkabariñi
lkurbalkurberama *ausschäumen (Meer).* ◇ foam (sea).
loapatilama *gewinnen.* ◇ win.
ljoaljoa *schlecht schmeckend.* ◇ taste bad. Ⓛ kaljilkaljilba
loapata *Gewinn, Nutzen.* ◇ win, use.
loanilama *umrühren.* ◇ stir. Ⓛ wui͡tikini
loantawonta *aufgeschichtet (Felsen).* ◇ piled up (rocks). Ⓛ tálatitálati Ⓓ duldruwana
loatjira = ramaia *Eidechse, gelb mit schwarzen Streifen (varanus gouldii).* ◇ *Varanus gouldii* (yellow lizard with black stripes). Ⓛ kurkati, larkiti, panka
lola *conf.* **ljōla**. ◇ anus.
lōlandama *unterweisen, unterrichten.* ◇ instruct. Ⓛ tintinpungañi
lolja *Maus, in Felsspalten sich aufhaltend.* ◇ mouse that lives in rock cracks. Ⓛ ulila

lolkuma *abschlagen (Bitte), verweigern.* ◇ refuse (request), deny. Ⓛ ngunjipungañi

lóalóalelama (tmatala) *heimtückisch handeln.* ◇ act treacherously.

lolouma *auswählen, verschmähen (das nicht Gewünschte).* ◇ choose, scorn (the undesired). Ⓛ ekuntani

loaloala *Mühe.* ◇ trouble.

loltalaúma *mit Ausnahme, ausgenommen.* ◇ except. Ⓛ markuratalkañi Ⓓ kalitakali?

loltama *fest drücken, auf etwas, niederdrücken.* ◇ press (hard) down on something. Ⓛ paliñi

loltalelama *eindrücken.* ◇ press in. Ⓛ paliranáñi

loai! *(Ausruf) o!* ◇ o! (exclamation).

lumba *Waise.* ◇ orphan. Ⓛ tjitula Ⓓ ngamuru, matjumatju

lōna *dick, breit.* ◇ thick, broad. Ⓛ lauanba Ⓓ wondre

lōnga *der mit Honig angefüllte Leib der jerramba.* ◇ honey-filled body of honeyant. Ⓛ piti

longa (ilenga) *weit entfernt.* ◇ far away, distant. Ⓛ wonma Ⓓ worita

longakalonga, ilengakilenga *weit von einander entfernt.* ◇ far from each other. Ⓛ wonmakuwonma

longalinja *sehr weit, tagesweite, (cr. 15 engl. Meilen).* ◇ very far, day trip away (appr. 15 miles). Ⓛ wonmakatu

loñga *Höhle (eines inkaia oder Kaninchen).* ◇ burrow (of a bilby or rabbit). Ⓛ piti

longilama *sich versöhnen.* ◇ reconcile. Ⓛ neuñi

longulambaia *halbreif, halbgrün.* ◇ half ripe, half green. Ⓛ katalarakambanta

longulpura *forellenähnliche Fische.* ◇ trout-like fish; Spangled grunter (*Leiopotherapon unicolor*). Ⓛ ilongulpuru

lonkunka *Nasenbein.* ◇ nosebone. Ⓛ murburiri

lonkura *Grasbaum (Hanthorrhoea).* ◇ grass tree (*Xanthorrhoea*). Ⓛ ulunkuru

longateta *weiße Streifen quer über der Nase.* ◇ white stripes across nose. Ⓛ mulatitu

ilúra (lorra); alkna ilura *entzündet; entzündetes Auge.* ◇ inflamed, inflamed eye. Ⓛ iltilti, kuru iltilti

lôra *kleine Eidechse, spec.* ◇ small lizard species. Ⓛ waluru

lŭrralŭrra *Larve spec.* ◇ grub species. Ⓛ uluruluru

ilarakúltakúltérama *anschwellen [von [unclear]).* ◇ swell. Ⓛ unkarapata patanáriñi

lorinja *fremd (Sprache), Fremder.* ◇ foreign (language), stranger. Ⓛ urila (*fremde Sprache*), ngatari (*fremde Mann*) Ⓓ tula

lurka *trübe Himmel, leicht bewölkt, trübe (Wasser), unrein.* ◇ dull (sky), cloudy, muddy (water), unclean. Ⓛ ulbata Ⓓ murka

lurkiulama *sich reinigen, entleeren (Samen).* ◇ to clean, empty (seeds). Ⓛ kaltarurini

lorra *voll, satt (vom Trinken).* ◇ full (from drinking). Ⓛ tjiuri Ⓓ kaljura

lorrerama *voll.* ◇ full. Ⓛ tjiuriringañi Ⓓ turibaterina

lorrilama *tränken, bewässern.* ◇ to water. Ⓛ tjiurinani Ⓓ turina, turibana

lorrambartjalama *reichlich überlaufen, überschwemmen (Land).* ◇ flooded, inundated (land). Ⓛ alurumburtjijennañi Ⓓ tundribana

lorra *Großmutter.* ◇ grandmother. Ⓛ kami Ⓓ kami

lorra aranga *Fraus Vaters Mutter.* ◇ wife's father's mother. Ⓛ tamu

lorrakana *Tränke (n).* ◇ watering place.

lorra ebmanna *Mutters Mutter, Mutters Mutters Schwester.* ◇ mother's mother, mother mother's sister. Ⓛ kami inkilji Ⓓ kanini

lorra ebmanatja *Mutters Mutter.* ◇ mother's mother. Ⓛ kami inkiljina

lorra palla *(Großmutter) Vaters Mutter.* ◇ father's mother. Ⓛ kami bakali

lorra pallatja *meines Vaters Mutter.* ◇ belonging to my father's mother. Ⓛ kami bakalina

lurrulelanama *kräftig umfassen (trs.)* ◇ clasp firmly (transitive). Ⓛ kapulkumawitiñi

lūrailknálama (lorraīlknalama) *sich reinigen; sich den Schlaf aus den Augen reiben.* ◇ clean, rub sleep out of eyes. Ⓛ paltjini; kuru úrini Ⓓ turibaterina

louma *baden, waschen, auslöschen (Geschriebenes).* ◇ bath, wash, erase (writing). Ⓛ urini Ⓓ ngapangana, kulirkana

loulama *sich baden.* ◇ to bath (reflexive). Ⓛ urinánani

lotjungutjura [Southern dialect], **latjingatjura** [Northern dialect] *weiß bemalte Nasenrücken, mit weißer Stirn (ula).* ◇ nose bridge painted white, with white forehead (ula). Ⓛ ngalawilunba, ngalawilunta

ltaberama *einladen, den Gast auffordern, sich zu setzen.* ◇ invite, ask guest to sit down. Ⓛ pailbmanañi

ltaba *Fußaufschlag (des aroa), auf den Boden.* ◇ foot thump (of rock wallaby) on ground. Ⓛ pantulba

ltairama [Southern dialect] *in die Hände klatschen, läuten.* ◇ clap hands. Ⓛ takalbmanañi Ⓓ totungana, deltjingana

ltairama *knistern (die Finger).* ◇ crackle, crack (fingers). Ⓛ pultapungañi

ltala *kleine Wolke.* ◇ small cloud. Ⓛ iltali

iltalbatuma *klatschen (mit den Händen).* ◇ clap (hands). Ⓛ pantulbmanañi

ltala *Haare (des Wildes).* ◇ hair (of animals). Ⓛ iltali

ltalaltala *behaart, rauh.* ◇ hairy, rough. Ⓛ iltaliltali

ltaltuka nama *sich zu einem halten, bei ihm bleiben.* ◇ stay close to somebody, stick to him.

iltáljiltalja *einsam, allein?* ◇ lonely. Ⓛ kutuntu

tulunkalunka *voller Geschwüre.* ◇ covered in ulcers. Ⓛ altartji, nunguru

ltaltua [Northern dialect] *cf.* **ltolta** *verfault.* ◇ rotten. Ⓛ ultultu

ltalterama [Northern dialect] *cf.* **ltolterama**. ◇ to rot. Ⓛ ultulturingañi

ltana, iltana *Geist (losgelöst vom Körper).* ◇ spirit or soul (detached from body), ghost; when a person died, the soul was called iltana and it was imagined to be white (Strehlow 1915: 23). The word iltana for ghost can also mean skeleton today. Ⓛ ngōa Ⓓ jaóla

ltanaka tmara *Geisterland, Toteninsel.* ◇ land of the spirits, island of the dead. (tmara kutata) Ⓛ ngoaluruku-ngura

ltambiwomma [Southern dialect], **ultambiuma** [Northern dialect] *viele Brote machen.* ◇ make many breads. Ⓛ nummawonnini

ltarama *knistern (Feuer).* ◇ crackle (fire). Ⓛ arbañi

ltarbamenta *sehr traurig.* ◇ very sad.

iltarba *betrübt, traurig.* ◇ sad. Ⓛ alturu Ⓓ purka

ltarberama *betrübt werden.* ◇ become sad. Ⓛ altururiñi

(a)ltarba [Southern dialect], **kwatja altarba** *clay-pan.* ◇ claypan. Ⓛ altarba, kapi altarba

(a)ltarba [Southern dialect] *kahl, haarlos, kahle Fläche, kahle Boden.* ◇ bald, hairless, bare landscape, barren ground. Ⓛ altarba

ltarbakaturuma *aneinanderstoßen, Geräusch machen.* ◇ knock together, make noise. Ⓛ tarkulti pungañi

ltarkama *klappern (Speere), tönen.* ◇ clatter (spears), sound. Ⓛ tirkilbmanañi Ⓓ darringana?

ltarkalelama *Geräusch machen.* ◇ make noise. Ⓛ tirkiltjingañi

ltatjiltatja *einsam.* ◇ lonely.

ltarkna *gesund, kräftig, laut.* ◇ healthy, strong, loud. Ⓛ lénkira Ⓓ katukatu, jiltara, katitepi

ltarknerama *gesund, stark werden.* ◇ healthy, become stong. Ⓛ lénkirariñi, lénkiraringañi Ⓓ katukaturina

ltarknilama *gesund machen.* ◇ make healthy. Ⓛ lénkirbmanani Ⓓ katukatu ngankana

ltāta *Tanz, kurz vor der Einweihungsfeiern aufgeführt.* ◇ public dance performed not long before initiation ceremony; public ceremony (also called 'ndapa' meaning women's dance that is part of the initiation ceremonies). Ⓛ pulapa

ltátama *plätschern (Regen).* ◇ patter (rain). Ⓛ palkurbmanani

ltemba, ltembaltemba *Fisch spec.* ◇ fish species. Ⓛ altimba, altimbaltimba

ltauirbala *geschnürt, mit Schnüren geschmückt.* ◇ laced, decorated with strings. Ⓛ warbilinji

áltarama *Speerwunde beibringen, blutig schlagen, Schlag (so das die Haut durchschnitten wird).* ◇ wound with spear, beat bloody, blow (that cuts skin). Ⓛ witarpungañi

altárama *finden.* ◇ to find.

ltjarkula *eine kleine weiße Larve in lupa-Wurzeln.* ◇ small white grub in lupa roots. Ⓛ katati

iltjambiltjanga *Blasen (in der Hand).* ◇ blisters (on hand). Ⓛ biltjinbiltjin

ltjárama, ltjérama *zerteilen, durchschneiden z.B. den Ochsen halbieren, zertrennen, abtrennen, aufschneiden (der Länge nach).* ◇ divide, cut e.g. cut ox in halve. Ⓛ woltarpungañi

ltjarilkna ala *Toteninsel.* ◇ island of the dead. Ⓛ tupaku-ngura

ltjikiltjika *häßlich, mager.* ◇ ugly, thin, scrawny. Ⓛ wiljiruwiljiru

ltjeljera *Eidechse mit Schwanzstumpf.* ◇ lizard with a knob tail. Ⓛ iltjiljeri

iltjamiltja *die aufgehende Sonne.* ◇ rising sun. Ⓛ karawollawolla

(i)ltjerknambuma *rot, rötlich, rufus sein (das Känguruh).* ◇ red, reddish. Ⓛ taltirkambañi

ltjerkniltjerknambuma Ⓛ taltirtaltirkambañi

altjiroambala *unaufhörlich.* ◇ incessantly, never ending. Ⓛ tukutita, tukurita

iltjerkniltjerkna *von rot, rötlich sein (Känguruh), die Früchte rot sein.* ◇ be red, reddish (kangaroo). Ⓛ taltirtaltira

ltjumburkerama *aufhören zu wachsen.* ◇ to stop growing. Ⓛ nitiraringañi

ltjumbarka *verdorrt (Hand).* ◇ withered (hand).

ltulba *Knöchel, Enkel, Geschwulst.* ◇ knuckle, tumour, growth. Ⓛ taltu Ⓓ kima

ltulberama *aufschwellen, zunehmen (Mond).* ◇ swell, wax (moon). Ⓛ talturingañi Ⓓ kimarina

ltólbambarinja *unversöhnlich.* ◇ irreconcilable. Ⓛ ataltukulu

ltolta *faul (Holz).* ◇ rotten (wood). Ⓛ ultultu

ltolta *verfault, verrottet.* ◇ rotten, decayed. Ⓛ ultultu

ltolterama *verfaulen.* ◇ to rot. Ⓛ ultulturingañi Ⓓ puapuarina

ltólinama *umfassen (den Sterbenden), der Hund das Wild anpacken.* ◇ embrace (dying person), catch (dog the game). Ⓛ matulani

ltolinanáma *erhaschen (der Hund das Wild).* ◇ catch (dog the game). Ⓛ matularabakañi

ltulama *verbergen, trs oder intrs?* ◇ hide (transitive or intransitive?). ('?' added by CS)

iltúma *schneiden, abschneiden, zerstücken.* ◇ cut (off or into pieces). Ⓛ kuntañi

iltúlama *sich ritzen, sich schneiden (refl.)* ◇ scratch, cut (reflexive). Ⓛ palurunku kuntañi

iltulbatuja *sehr frieren.* ◇ feel very cold. Ⓛ kuntakantaranganañi

ltumba *rauflustig, geschickt im Werfen.* ◇ rowdy, skilled throwing. Ⓛ ultumbu

lturbarenama *durchschneiden, durchdringen, tödlich treffen (tjatalela).* ◇ cut, penetrate, hit mortally. Ⓛ bulturpungañi

lturkarawúma *warnen (mit Worten), Du wirst bald sterben; den Tod androhen.* ◇ warn (with words) 'you will die soon'; threaten with death. Ⓛ jupairbini

ltulberitjintjima *aufgehen (Brotteig).* ◇ rise (bread dough). Ⓛ talturekulakalbañi

lturkitjara *dem Tod nahe sein, in Todesgefahr sein.* ◇ be close to death, be in mortal danger. Ⓛ jupakuru

lturkna *löchrich (Schilde, Mulden), rissig (Kleider).* ◇ full of holes (shields, bowls), torn (clothes). Ⓛ lāra ulturknu

lturtnarenalama *sich etwas zerbrechen (z.B. Bein beim Fallen).* ◇ break something (e.g. leg from a fall). Ⓛ nalburtalkañi

lturuma *reinigen (mit den Händen).* ◇ clean (with hands). Ⓛ lauani

luákara, lākara (pata) *Felsen.* ◇ cliff. Ⓛ alala

luálba, lālba *Fremder, Feind.* ◇ stranger, enemy. Ⓛ tanba

luánja *dem Tode nahe, totkrank.* ◇ close to death, dying. Ⓛ tjilunba

luára *Bräutigam, der Verlobte.* ◇ bridegroom, fiancé. Ⓛ ngaru

luátninja *sehr gut (Gott, Mensch).* ◇ very good (God, human). Ⓛ kunjinji (kunjinjatu)

luatninjilama *gut machen.* ◇ make good. Ⓛ kunjinjinani

lubaluba, lībalība *ganz erschöpft sein, am Verschmachten.* ◇ completely exhausted, parched. Ⓛ wolbawolba Ⓓ warriwarrina

lubulubalerama *aus dem Versteck den verfolg. Feind beobachten.* ◇ from hiding watch enemy. Ⓛ kumbila ninañi

lubunbara *sehr viele, sehr viel.* ◇ very many, very much. Ⓛ pankiṙiri

luétnakaluétna *verschiedenartig, die Partei verschiedene (Arten), allerlei (Krankheiten).* ◇ diverse.

ulenta nama *nachschleichen, schleichend verfolgen (Katze den Vogel).* ◇ sneak, creep up, prowl, hunt (cat the bird). Ⓛ maúrakatini

luétna *Gegner, Gegenpartei.* ◇ opponent, opposing party. Ⓛ akatakutara Ⓓ kana jutjunto

lujalupa *mehr als …, sehr viele.* ◇ more than, very many. Ⓛ tjikaralenku

luka *Steinmesser sp.; Australische Fichte.* ◇ type of stone knife; Australian pine. Ⓛ iljuku

lukadúradura *Wasserhuhn.* ◇ waterfowl. Ⓛ pititálili

lukulbura kwananganganga *zwischen die Beine hindurch.* ◇ between the legs. Ⓛ alaṙara watawana, wottawona

lulelama *herunternehmen.* ◇ take down.

lukara *kleine Maus mit schwarz und grauen Punkten (ohne Beutel).* ◇ little black and white speckled mouse without pouch. Ⓛ iljukuru

lukata *eine Scheibe aus Gummiholzrinde rollen lassen.* ◇ to roll a gumtree bark disk. Ⓛ tukatta

lukatnérama *schnarchen.* ◇ snore. Ⓛ ngurpiltipiltiñi

lúkultmunta *der heranziehende Regen, der alles weiß einhüllt.* ◇ approaching rain that envelopes everything in white. Ⓛ bujulutu

lukulumbalumba *Blätter-Büschel (tea tree).* ◇ bunches of leaves (tea tree). Ⓛ ljikilimbilimbi

lukumúkuma *Dunst, dunstig (Hohenrauch?).* ◇ haze, hazy. Ⓛ anutumuru

lukalukanjima *brünstig sein, Verlangen nach vielen Männern haben.* ◇ in heat, have desire for many men. Ⓛ ngalakukalbani

lukuna *dort, anderswo.* ◇ there, elsewhere. Ⓛ panata, narata

lukura *Witwen oder unverheiratete Mädchen.* ◇ widows or unmarried girls. Ⓛ alukuru

tmara lukara *Witwen-Lagerplatz, Platz der unverheirateten Frauen.* ◇ widows' camp, camp of unmarried women; women's camp. Ⓛ ngura alukuru

lukurarinja *Witwen (Bewohner der tmara lukura).* ◇ occupants of women's camp. Ⓛ alukurita Ⓓ mangawaru

lukúrkuna *Waise (vaterlose Halbwaise).* ◇ orphan (fatherless half orphan). Ⓛ tjitulu Ⓓ matjumatju

lukuta *eine Pflanze mit fleischigen Blättern.* ◇ plant with fleshy leaves. Ⓛ atauilba

lulama *heruntersteigen.* ◇ climb down. Ⓛ wararakatiñi Ⓓ ngarina

lulalakalama *hinuntersteigen.* ◇ climb down. Ⓛ wararakatira okalingañi

lulelalakalama *hinterunterlassen.* ◇ let down. Ⓛ wararataljiru okalingañi Ⓓ ngarilkana

lulintjilama *herunterkommen.* ◇ descend, come down. Ⓛ ngalawararakatiñi

lulitnénama *heruntersteigen.* ◇ climb down. Ⓛ wararakatira talkañi

lulitjatnakalama *herunterklettern (vom Baum).* ◇ climb down (from a tree). Ⓛ okulikula talkañi

lulknumbaralama *sehr schnell davonlaufen.* ◇ run away very fast, hurry away. Ⓛ totijennañi

lulura *stark, mächtig (Mann, Anführer).* ◇ strong, mighty (man, leader). Ⓛ aluluru

lulurabaterama *mächtig werden.* ◇ become mighty. Ⓛ alulururiñi

lularenama *Streifen von der Schulter zum Gürtel malen, herabmalen.* ◇ paint stripes from shoulder to belt. Ⓛ ngaratunañi

lulbalulba *voll.* ◇ full. Ⓛ katawiliwili Ⓓ mannamiri

lulbara *Baum (spec.)* ◇ tree (species). Ⓛ ilulburu

lúljeribama *Grund legen, in eine Furche einen Stein stellen.* ◇ lay foundation, put a stone in a groove. Ⓛ alukuluriñi

(lu)lkurtjúlkura *salzigen Schleim auf dem Wasser.* ◇ salty slime on water. Ⓛ taljitalji

lulkara [Southern dialect] *Stirnband.* ◇ headband. Ⓛ roara

lultja *Eis, Reif.* ◇ ice, frost. Ⓛ walka, ngiñga

lulentjilama *herunterkommen.* ◇ come down. Ⓛ ngaláwararakatiñi

lulitjikalama *heruntersteigen.* ◇ descend. Ⓛ ngalawararakatina okalingañi

lultara *conf.* **ilutara** *Papagei.* ◇ parrot. Ⓛ ilulturu

(i)lulama *sich herniederlassen.* ◇ descend (reflexive). Ⓛ wararkatini

lultultaturuma *hineindrücken.* ◇ press in (Strehlow 1910b: 137). Ⓛ tartarani

luluruka *mit Blut überströmt.* ◇ covered in blood. Ⓛ ngurkaburu

luma *lösen, erlösen, auflösen, ausziehen (trs.) Kleider, öffnen (Buch), aufmachen, aufrollen, abbrechen (Haus).* ◇ loosen, release, undo, take off (transitive) clothes, open (book), open, unroll, break off, pull down (house). Ⓛ arañi Ⓓ dukarana? pirakana.

lulama *sich ausziehen (refl.), abnehmen (Hut).* ◇ undress (reflexive), take off (hat). Ⓛ palurunku arañi

luma *postp. vielleicht.* ◇ (postposition) perhaps, maybe. Ⓛ puta Ⓓ kara?

lumaka *graublau (Känguruh).* ◇ grey blue (kangaroo). Ⓛ tarutu

lumanama *Knospe hervorbrechen.* ◇ to bud. Ⓛ buturtninañi

lumanama *beobachten, ausgucken, einen aus einem Versteck ausspähen, hervorsehen.* ◇ observe, look out, spy on (from hiding), peer out. Ⓛ milini

lumba (lômba) *mutterlose Halbwaise.* ◇ motherless half-orphan. Ⓛ apunta

lumaninjila rama *beobachten (die Stirn vorstreckend).* ◇ to observe, to watch. Ⓛ ngalamilini

luminka *unbekannt (niemals zuvorgesehen).* ◇ unknown (never seen before). Ⓛ nulurba

lumintiltjarénama *auf der Lauer liegen, aus dem Loch hervorlugen (Maus).* ◇ ambush, peep out from a hole (mouse). Ⓛ kuruwokkíñi

lumunjamunja *voll sein (von Leuten).* ◇ crowded (with people). Ⓛ ngeljingeljini

lunakalantalunama *fortwährend verfolgen.* ◇ pursue continuously. Ⓛ wonnantanka wonnañi

ulúna *Brot, Pflanzenkost, Mahlzeit.* ◇ bread, plant food, meal. Ⓛ mirka

lunama *verfolgen, jagen, nachspüren (inka).* ◇ pursue, hunt, track (inka). Ⓛ wonnañi Ⓓ tajipaterina, tirikaripaterina

lunintjilama *verfolgen, hintreiben.* ◇ pursue, drive. Ⓛ ngalawonnañi

lunbatunbata *mürrisch, unzufrieden.* ◇ surly, discontented. Ⓛ mularamúlara

luninjilama *entgegen fliegen (Vögel).* ◇ fly towards (birds). Ⓛ ngalawonnañi

lunerama *fangen, erhaschen.* ◇ catch, capture. Ⓛ wonarapungañi

lungulalungulelama *sich erbarmen.* ◇ take pity. Ⓛ nujunujuni

lunja *Schatten (von Bäumen, Laubhütte).* ◇ shadow; shade. Ⓛ puri, watuti Ⓓ pungala, pungalkuru

lungerama *zusammenkommen.* ◇ gather. Ⓛ tunguringañi Ⓓ dankamalina (*zusammen kommen*: gather, *sich begegnen*: meet), manduina.

lunka *Haken, Widerhaken (am Speer), Anker.* ◇ hook, barb (on a spear), anchor. Ⓛ nangu Ⓓ ngami

lunkagata *postp. = gata = mit (cum), Speer mit Widerhaken.* ◇ spear with barb. Ⓛ nangutara (*mit dem Widerhaken*)

lunka [Southern dialect], **mannalunka** *mit [unclear].* Ⓛ mitara

lunkata *große Mulde, in der z.B. kleine Kinder getragen werden aus ininta Holz.* ◇ large bowl made of bean tree wood; small children are carried in them. Ⓛ ulunkati

lunkultja *Gewürm, Insekten und Schlangen, Tiere.* ◇ worms, insects and snakes, animals. Ⓛ wimmalara Ⓓ tjutju

lunkerama *hervorkommen, zum Vorschein kommen.* ◇ to come out, to appear. Ⓛ wiiwïirkani

lungura *gemischt, gemischte Gesellschaft.* ◇ mixed, mixed company. Ⓛ tungunmannu

lungurilama *mischen, vermengen.* ◇ to mix, blend. Ⓛ tunguni Ⓓ duldruwana, duldrungana, ngokibana.

lungurútnama *vermengen.* ◇ to mix. Ⓛ turitarbatunañi

lunkulbélama *zerstören.* ◇ to destroy.

luntalélama *aufbieten (zum Kampf).* ◇ to summon (to fight). Ⓛ tjipatjipani

lupa *Strauch mit hellgelben Blüten und Schotenfrüchten, wilde Akacia, von den Eingeborenen gesammelt, geröstet und gegessen.* ◇ shrub with light yellow blossoms and fruit-pods, wild acacia; roasted and eaten. Ⓛ úlupu Ⓓ kalju

lupalupa *Akacien-Strauch (klein).* ◇ acacia (small). Ⓛ ulupulupu

lupalupa *Larven in den lupalupa Wurzeln.* ◇ grubs in lupalupa roots. Ⓛ ulupulupu

lupatja *weiße Larven in Akacien-Wurzeln.* ◇ white grubs in acacia roots. Ⓛ ulupiti

libaliba (lubaluba) *sehr müde.* ◇ very tired. Ⓛ wolbawolba

lupaia *Ratte (ohne Beutel), Hapalotis Mitchilli.* ◇ rat (without pouch), hopping mouse, *Notomys mitchellii* (Atlas of Living Australia n.d.) Ⓛ ulkunba

lupara *Oberschenkel, Ober-Beine, Rebe, Ranke.* ◇ thighs, upper legs, vine. Ⓛ tunta Ⓓ tara

lupata *bleibend, beharrlich.* ◇ lasting, persistent. Ⓛ ngatala

lupaterama *bleiben, verharren.* ◇ stay. Ⓛ ngatalariñi

lupatilama *behalten.* ◇ keep. Ⓛ ngatalanani, ngatalmanañi

lurilknalama *sich waschen, sich reinigen, sich den Schlaf aus den Augen reiben.* ◇ wash, cleanse, rub sleep out of eyes. Ⓛ kuru urini, paltjini (*sich waschen*)

luraïlknama *reinigen, waschen (trs.)* ◇ clean, wash (transitive). Ⓛ paltjini

luralura *geschwollen, wülstig.* ◇ swollen, thick. Ⓛ uluruluru

lurba *kalte Wind, kalte Zeit (Winter).* ◇ cold wind, cold time (winter). Ⓛ wonta Ⓓ kilpa

lurbaka *im Winter (Mai-August).* ◇ in winter (May–August). Ⓛ wontaku Ⓓ kilpali

lurbakata *der Monat, in dem es wieder kälter wird (Herbst, April und Mai).* ◇ month, in which it gets cold again (autumn, April and May). Ⓛ wontakata

lurbitja *Sehne, Muskel.* ◇ sinew, tendon, muscle. Ⓛ bilku Ⓓ tiltja

(lurbutja) *Sehne.* ◇ sinew, tendon.

lurbmeritjilama *nicht weiter gehen.* ◇ go no further. Ⓛ ngutapiriñi

lurka *hell, bleich, scheinend (Sonne umkehren [auf oder untergehen?]).* ◇ light, pale, shine. Ⓛ alurka, púnura

lurkereulama *sehr hell scheinen (Mondschein = der Mond reinigt sich), sich mit roter Farbe bemalen.* ◇ shine very bright (moonshine = moon cleans himself), paint oneself with red colour. Ⓛ topirpungañi

lurkna *Ader, Sehne.* ◇ vein, artery, sinew. Ⓛ bilku Ⓓ tilja (*Sehne*)

lurknalurkna *sehnig.* ◇ sinewy, stringy. Ⓛ bilkubilku Ⓓ tiltjatiltja

lurknibata *Kniekehle.* ◇ hollow of knee. Ⓛ bilku ngati Ⓓ tiltjagandri

lurkiuma *reinigen, Schmuck entfernen, entleeren (Samen?).* ('?' added by CS) ◇ cleanse, remove dirt, empty (seeds). Ⓛ pitaltjinani

lurkninama *zaubern, Zauber (Sehne) entfernen; z.B. ein Gespeerte.* ◇ make magic, remove magic (sinew); e.g. [from] someone who has been speared. Ⓛ bilku manjini

lurka *helle, bleich (Hoingameisen).* ◇ light, pale (honeyants). Ⓛ alurku

lurka *Flecken (an der Kleidung).* ◇ spots (on clothing).

lurkumba *Zucker (auf den Gummiblättern).* ◇ sugar (on gum leaves). Ⓛ albitalji

lurkagunja *unbefleckt.* ◇ spotless, untainted.

lurkuta *undeutlich, unverständlich (Sprache), fremd.* ◇ unclear, incomprehensible (language), foreign. Ⓛ wabalbi

lurkutilama *alle durcheinander sprechen.* ◇ all talk at once. Ⓛ kaualkaualbmanañi

lurpma *Frosch (auf clay-pans).* ◇ frog (on claypans). Ⓛ ulurpmu

lurkutankama *verleumden, schlechtes berichten von Abwesenden.* ◇ defame, slander (in the absence of others). Ⓛ kaualikurawonkañi Ⓓ warawarapana, ngultuterkana

lurumbalknilama *sich waschen, sich baden.* ◇ (reflexive) wash, bath. Ⓛ paltjini

lururkna *sumpfig, morastig, (ala).* ◇ swampy, marshy (soil, ground). Ⓛ ngalngalba

lurralurra *ein Busch.* ◇ bush, shrub.

lurralura, lurralurra *eine weiße Larve.* ◇ white grub. Ⓛ ulurrulurru

lūta *kleines Wallaby (spec.)* ◇ small wallaby (species). Ⓛ meteki

lutitjala nama *die Beine übereinanderschlagen.* ◇ cross legs. Ⓛ alatatji ninañi

lutankama *stampfen, klopfen mit d. Füßen, sich erheben.* ◇ stamp, beat with feet, stand up. Ⓛ totuni

lutjala *hinten, zuletzt (kommen).* ◇ behind, the last (to arrive). Ⓛ nganti

lutnarinka *Stirn der Berge, Gebirgskamm.* ◇ mountain face, mountain ridge. Ⓛ pulingali

lutula *kurz, niedrig.* ◇ short, low. Ⓛ murilji, tarta

luta *immer, ewig.* ◇ always, everlasting. Ⓛ kutu

lutantjia *Honig der Honigameisen.* ◇ honey of honeyants. Ⓛ alutantjiï

lurrulelama *fest umfassen.* ◇ hold tightly. Ⓛ ngamini

lutunta *ohne, nicht mitgerechnet.* ◇ without, not included.

M

ma! *Nimm hin! Da!* ◇ take this! there!

maia *Mutter, Tanta (Schwester der Mutter).* ◇ mother, aunt (mother's sister). Ⓛ jaku

maia knara *ältere Schwester der Mutter.* ◇ mother's older sister. Ⓛ jaku puntu

maia pmalatja *die ältere Schwester der Mutter.* ◇ mother's older sister. Ⓛ jakuna puntu

maia larra *jüngere Schwester der Mutter.* ◇ mother's younger sister. Ⓛ jaku wongu

makura [Southern dialect] *die Mutter eines Andern.* ◇ mother of somebody else (of a male person). Ⓛ jakura

matjinga *meine Mutter.* ◇ my mother. Ⓛ jakuna

mēkua [Northern dialect] *Mutter einer Andern.* ◇ the mother of somebody else (a female person). Ⓛ jakura

maiamaia *große weiße Raupe, die sich an den tnurunga Sträuchen aufhält.* ◇ large white caterpillar that lives on tnurunga bushes. Ⓛ kowiawia

maiïnga [Southern dialect] *cf.* **mara** *gut.* ◇ good. Ⓛ pala

māninta *Halbgeschwister (dieselbe Mutter).* ◇ half-sibling (same mother). Ⓛ jakutungu

mainama *festhalten.* ◇ hold tight. Ⓛ ngaluni

mainalama *sich in etwas verwickeln, hängen bleiben.* ◇ get tangled up in something, get caught up. Ⓛ ngaluni

māka *Ellenbogen.* ◇ elbow. Ⓛ neku

makamaka *Greuel, Abscheu, Grauen.* ◇ horror, fear, dread; dangerous, dangerous place, sacred site.

makalaría *gefährlich, ungenießbar, unnahbar (den Feinden).* ◇ dangerous, inedible, unapproachable (the enemy), blameless, feared (by the enemy). Ⓛ amákalari

makamakerama *sich grauen.* ◇ to dread.

makerama *verschonen, unterlassen, nicht ausrichten.* ◇ spare, fail (to do), not accomplish. Ⓛ akangarañi

makerelalbuma *unverrichteter Sache.* ◇ without having achieved anything. Ⓛ amekenakula kulbañi

mákeřelaùma *zurückkehren, schmollen, launig sein, eigensinnig sein.* ◇ return, sulk, be moody, be obstinate. Ⓛ akapatiratalkañi

makulba *Stock zum Schlagen.* ◇ hitting stick. Ⓛ kuturu

makura [Southern dialect] *cf.* mekua. ◇ mother of somebody else. Ⓛ jakuru

makuta *der hohle Ast, das Loch im Stamm des Baumes.* ◇ hollow branch, hole in a tree trunk. Ⓛ amakuta

mala *schon, postp. einst, einmal.* ◇ already, (postposition) once, once upon a time.

măla *weiblich.* ◇ female. Ⓛ jaku

kutungula mala *Dienerin.* ◇ female servant. Ⓛ jaku pipawonnu

knulja mala *Hündin.* ◇ bitch (female dog). Ⓛ papa jaku

malalitjina *rankende Pflanze mit milchigem Saft.* ◇ plant with milky sap. Ⓛ malalitji, ibiïbi

malamalauma *sich stoßen in Gedränge.* ◇ bump into each other in a crowd. Ⓛ tumutumuni

mélanka *sehr gut (Menschen, Häuptling).* ◇ very good (humans, chief). Ⓛ pala

malankaia *sehr erhitzt, erschöpft.* ◇ very hot, flushed, exhausted. Ⓛ rukurkatji

malla (inka) *sehr kurz und breit (Füße).* ◇ very short and broad (feet). Ⓛ (tjinna)-tata

málakaljialjía *Pflanze mit milchigem Saft, Symbol der Weiber und Mädchen (aljia=altja=zugehörig).* ◇ plant with milky sap, symbol of women and girls (belong to). Ⓛ ngutanguta, okara

malla *Löcher, Gruben der wilden Hunde.* ◇ holes, pits of wild dog.

malbamala *heiser.* ◇ hoarse, husky. Ⓛ amalbamili

maljanuka *die Angehörigen der anderen Heiratsgruppe = meine Freunde.* ◇ the ones belonging to the other marriage-group, my friends; 'them', meaning the people in the opposite patrimoiety. One of the basic divisions of Aranda society organises all people into two groups, i.e. exogamous moieties. These patrimoieties were called 'Nákarakia' (our kindred or people) and 'Etnákarakia' (those people or that kindred) or 'Maljanuka' (my friends) by the Aranda. These terms were not names for one or the other moiety but were reciprocally used by both groups (Strehlow 1913: 62). Today Arandic people still refer – from an egocentric point of view – to such groupings that are maljanuka and nákarakia. Maljanuka means 'them' or 'our in-laws' while nákarakia means 'us'. In one's own patrimoiety, that is 'us', are one's actual and classificatory fathers and their siblings, father's fathers and son's children, and also one's mother's mother's patriline which is part of nákarakia [or ilakakia], i.e. 'us'. In the opposite moiety, maljanuka, in addition to one's spouse and brothers-in-law there are one's actual and classificatory mothers, mother's brothers and mother's fathers and also one's father's mother. Like the Aranda, the Loritja used particular terms for the members of these groups reciprocally. All relatives of an ego's group (own patrimoiety) were called

'Ngananukarpitina' meaning 'all of us'; and all relatives of the opposite moiety were called 'Tananukarpitina' meaning 'all of them' (Strehlow 1913: 79). In societies organised in this way one should always marry someone from the opposite moiety. Ⓛ tananukarpitina

maljurkurra *Beutelratte.* ◇ marsupial rat, rat with pouch. Ⓛ muta

maljurutnama *peitschen oder treiben (Sturm, die Wasserwellen).* ◇ whip or drive (storm, waves).

malkura *postp. wie, ähnlich.* ◇ (postposition) like, similar. Ⓛ nguanba

nunamalkura *wie wir.* ◇ like us. Ⓛ ngananangunaba

katjiamalkura *wie ein Kind, kindlich.* ◇ like a child, child-like. Ⓛ pipiri nguanba

malkura *flügge, ausgewachsen (nur Vögel).* ◇ fledged, fully grown (birds only). Ⓛ maraka

malla *Höhle (eines wilden Hundes oder Känguruhs).* ◇ cave (of a wild dog or kangaroo). Ⓛ turalba, narkulta

malta *Arm.* ◇ arm. Ⓛ ngakulta

maltala ngama *auf der Hüfte tragen, auf dem Arm tragen, unter dem Arm tragen.* ◇ carry on hip or arm, carry under the arm. Ⓛ ngakulta katiñi

maltala inama *unter dem Arm nehmen.* ◇ take under the arm. Ⓛ ngakulta manjini

maltala *unterm Arm.* ◇ under the arm. Ⓛ totunka

mamantara *zerschlagen, verwundet durch Schlagen.* ◇ break or smash to pieces, wounded from a beating.

malturamba *Gummi (auf den Lalba Sträuchen).* ◇ gum (on lalba-bushes). Ⓛ ilulbu

mamuntulama *formen, gestalten.* ◇ form, shape.

mámiluma *Schrof von der Wunde lösen.* ◇ remove scab from wound. Ⓛ peka arañi

măma *Wunde (Name).* ◇ wound, (Name of a person) (Strehlow 1920: 28). Ⓛ peka Ⓓ dapa

mamilama *verwunden.* ◇ to wound. Ⓛ pekani

manaltja *Schwanzfett (des Känguruhs).* ◇ tail fat (of kangaroo). Ⓛ nilji

mananga (*conf.* **maia**) *Mutter und Kind.* ◇ mother and child. Ⓛ jakurara

manánganánga *Mutter und 2 Kinder.* ◇ mother and two children, place name. Ⓛ jakurarawaritji

manangatua *Mutter mit 3 Kindern (seien es Söhne oder Töchter).* ◇ mother with three children (irrespective of gender). Ⓛ jakutíturára

manantja *Schaum, Gischt.* ◇ foam, spray. Ⓛ amanantji, talji Ⓓ ngulongaltja

manerinja *zusammengewachsen, dicht neben einanderstehend (Bäume), in einander verschlungen (die Wurzeln zwischen Bäumen).* ◇ grown together, standing close to each other (dense stand of trees), intertwined (tree roots). Ⓛ ngalurupunguta

rella manerinja *zusammengewachsene Menschen.* ◇ undeveloped human beings (at the beginning of time the bodies of the rella manerinja were grown together). Ⓛ matu ngalulba

manga *Fliege.* ◇ fly. Ⓛ amangi, punpun Ⓓ muntju

mangilama *Fliegen wedeln.* ◇ wave flies away. Ⓛ amangi bailtunani

mannaka pallerinja *Teuerung (von Brot).* ◇ price increase (of bread).

mangaparra *böse Wesen in Gestalt von großen, schwarzen Vögeln, die in der Nacht besonders den kleinen Kindern nachstellen.* ◇ evil beings or bad spirits in the shape of large black birds who mainly stalk small children in the guise of night; they travel in hot winds from the west and may cause death because they take peoples' souls away among other things (Strehlow 1907: 12, 13–14). Ⓛ marali

mangalkna *eben angesetzten (kleine) Früchte.* ◇ budding (small) fruit. Ⓛ amangikuru

mangala *unter, im Schatten.* ◇ under, in the shade. Ⓛ wollanka, luntawolla

para mangala *unter einem Gummibaum.* ◇ under a gumtree. Ⓛ itara wollanka

mangarabuntja *Fliege.* ◇ fly. Ⓛ amangarabuntji

mangarkunjarkunja *eine kleine Eidechse (spec.); mythisch: der Former der Menschen.* ◇ a small lizard species; in mythology: the maker of humans. Ⓛ namunaurkúnjurkunju (*Schöpfer der Menschen*: creator of humans), amungurkunjurkunju (*kleine Eidechse*: small lizard)

manjirama *sich verstellen.* ◇ disguise.

mannatulkatulka *Drüse, Geschwulst?, Schwären?* ◇ gland, tumour, growth. ('?' added by CS)

manginta *Eule, große Eule (spec.)* ◇ owl, large owl (species). Ⓛ wiratu

manjerkuma *vorbeiwerfen, verfehlen.* ◇ throw past, miss. Ⓛ wakupinpani

manjerkulawuma *vorbeiwerfen.* ◇ throw past. Ⓛ mawakupinpani

manjima *eßbare Beere von der Größe einer Stachelbeere, gelb mit widerlichem Geschmack.* ◇ yellow edible berry. Ⓛ kanba

manjura *conf.* **ilbalata**. ◇ type of tree. Ⓛ minjura

manka *beendet, fertig (gebaut).* ◇ finished, ready (built). Ⓛ bokkanita

manjarpa *Schlangengestalt, Schlange (genus).* ◇ shape of a snake, snake (genus). Ⓛ wonjirpi

mankalankala *erwachsen, flügge (Vogel).* ◇ grown up, fully fledged (birds). Ⓛ parpakajennañi

mankama *wachsen.* ◇ grow. Ⓛ unkani Ⓓ punkana

mankalelarama *groß wachsen machen.* ◇ to make grow large. Ⓛ unkaljirapungañi

mankalelama *aufziehen (Kinder).* ◇ raise (children). Ⓛ unkaljennani

mankitjintjama *aufwachsen.* ◇ grow up. Ⓛ unkarakalbañi

mankarankarerama *anwachsen (Wolke).* ◇ increase, grow (clouds). Ⓛ tambarknarañi

mankerama *aufwachsen, nachwachsen (Nachwuchs).* ◇ grow up (offspring). Ⓛ unkarawoniñi

mankinja *ausgewachsen (Bäume), erwachsen (Menschen).* ◇ fully grown (trees), grown up (humans). Ⓛ unkanta

mankilama *beendigen, vollenden.* ◇ bring to an end, finish, complete. Ⓛ patini

mankurara *Gewühl, Gewimmel, Durcheinanderlaufen, Durcheinanderlaufen (beim Spiel).* ◇ bustle, throng, milling crowd, confusion (at play). Ⓛ aririninañi

mankarama *hindern am Weitergehen (Gebüsch).* ◇ prevent from moving on (bushes). Ⓛ amikinangañi

manna *Pflanzenkost, Sämerei, Früchte, Brot.* ◇ plant food, seeds, fruit, bread. Ⓛ miï, mai Ⓓ buka

mannetanetana *Säamann.* ◇ sower. Ⓛ miïkutanmi

manna unkwaltja *Brocken.* ◇ piece, lump (bread, food). Ⓛ miï pitjili Ⓓ buka worduwordu

manna ulba *Mehl.* ◇ flour. Ⓛ mii pulba Ⓓ buka turara (*Mehl*: flour)

manpa *die ersten Funken, die beim Reiben des Feuers in das trockene Gras fallen.* ◇ first sparks that fall into the dry grass when rubbing fire. Ⓛ ngutulba

manna urkna *Brotteig, dicke Brei.* ◇ bread dough, thick paste. Ⓛ miï altji

manna ilbala *das Gemüse, Kohl (n).* ◇ vegetables, cabbage.

manta *dicht, geschlossen (Tür), stumpf (Messer), taub (Ohr), stumm (Mund).* ◇ tight, closed (door), blunt (knife), deaf (ear), mute (mouth). Ⓛ patti Ⓓ njeni (*Stumpf*), patu (*Stumpf*)

mantumanta *eingeschlossenes (Wasserloch), Damm.* ◇ enclosed (waterhole), dam. Ⓛ manguri

mantamanta *geschlossener Raum.* ◇ closed room. Ⓛ pattipatti

mantilama *schließen (Tür), verschließen, zumachen, zuhalten (Ohr).* ◇ shut (door), lock, close, cover (ear). Ⓛ pattini

mantamaleuma *trs. drängen (im Gewühl).* ◇ (transitive) pushing (in crowd).

mantara *Tasche in Kleidung, inkulba, Kleid.* ◇ pocket (in garment). Ⓛ mantari Ⓓ kati

mantaragata *bekleidet.* ◇ dressed. Ⓛ mantaratara

mantaramantara *den Boden bedeckend (Blüten)?* ◇ cover ground (blossoms). ('?' added by CS)

matakai [Southern dialect], **makuia** [Northern dialect] *nimm dies! (das ich Dir hinhalte).* ◇ take this! (that I hold out to you). Ⓛ imamaju

marajerama *sich zerstreuen, um Fleisch zu erjagen.* ◇ spread out to hunt for meat. Ⓛ parajuriñi

măra *gut.* ◇ good. Ⓛ păla Ⓓ ngumu

marerama *gut werden.* ◇ become good. Ⓛ palaringañi Ⓓ ngumu pantjina

marilama *gutes tun.* ◇ do good. Ⓛ palani Ⓓ ngumu ngankana

maralkura *besser.* ◇ better. Ⓛ palanguanba Ⓓ morla nguma

marulkura *in guter Ordnung niederlassen.* ◇ settled down into good order. Ⓛ palanguanba

mārala, marala *böses Wesen in Gestalt eines großen Schwarzen Vogels, der in Heißwinden daherfährt.* ◇ evil being or bad spirit in the shape of a large black bird, who travels in hot winds; 'marala' appears to have been used interchangeably with mangaparra (Strehlow 1907: 13). Ⓛ marali

marpara *Frucht des Gummibaumes.* ◇ fruit of gumtree. Ⓛ amirpiri Ⓓ paua

marra *Schulterknochen.* ◇ shoulder bone. Ⓛ alipiri

marrukabuta *die wohllüstige Schwiegermutter, begierig nach dem Schwiegersohn [unclear].* ◇ lusting mother-in-law, desirous of son-in-law. Ⓛ omarripanti

marra *Schwiegermutter (M), Schwiegersohn (F), Schwesters Tochters Mann (♂).* ◇ mother-in-law (m), son-in-law (f). Ⓛ omarri Ⓓ paiara (*Schwiegermutter* (M): mother-in-law, *Schwiegersohn* (F): son-in-law)

marra *Fraus Mutter, ♂.* ◇ wife's mother. Ⓛ mokuli, ngomaiï

marra tualtja *eigene Schwiegermutter, ♂.* ◇ own mother-in-law. Ⓛ tutaltji

marra knara *Fraus Mutters ältere Schwester.* ◇ wife's mother's older sister. Ⓛ mokuli p.

marra larra *Fraus Mutters jüngere Schwester.* ◇ wife's mother's younger sister. Ⓛ mokuli w.

marra *Tochters Mann, ♀.* ◇ daughter's husband. Ⓛ tutaltji

marra *Schwesters Sohns Frau, ♂.* ◇ sister's son's wife. Ⓛ ngomaiï

marra *Fraus Bruders Sohns Frau, Fraus Bruders Tochters Mann.* ◇ wife's brother's son's wife, wife's brother's daughter's husband.

marrukua *Schwiegermutter, -sohn (eines Andern).* ◇ mother-in-law, son-in-law (of someone else). Ⓛ omarrira

matalkulama *(zusammenkommen von verschiedenen Richtungen), sich vereinigen.* ◇ come together (from all directions), unite, assemble (Strehlow 1907: 69). Ⓛ tintjirapungañi

matara *Halsschmuck.* ◇ neck ornament. Ⓛ amatara Ⓓ jelkara (*Faden*: thread), kaldrati (*Halsschmuck*: neck ornament)

mataramatara *kleine auf Bergen wachsende Pflanze mit ovalen kleinen sich gegenüberstehenden Blättern.* ◇ small plant with little oval leaves that sit opposite of each other, grows on hills. Ⓛ amataramátara

matera *leichte, weiße Wolken.* ◇ fluffy white clouds. Ⓛ matari

mata, raninjamata *(posp.) mit; mit Gerät oder Sachen.* ◇ (postposition) with; with utensils, things. Ⓛ tara, jultatara

matakatáka *eine Kreuzweise über der Brust gebundene Schnur.* ◇ string tied crosswise over chest (used by women). Ⓛ amitikitiki

matiuma, matitjiuma *binden, umwickeln, umbinden, fesseln, zusammenwickeln, zumachen (Buch), kräuseln.* ◇ to tie, bind, wind, tie around, wrap together, close (book), curl. Ⓛ juntunañi, tetirpungañi Ⓓ dupudupu ngankana, workumandrana

matubara *gefesselt.* ◇ tied up, shackled. Ⓛ tetirba

maturba *zusammen gewickelt, unentwickelt (Brüste).* ◇ wrapped up, not developed (breasts). Ⓛ umuturba

matjintara *sehr trotzig, widerspenstig.* ◇ very obstinate, refractory. Ⓛ alutirkitirki, putalputalja

matunja-konja *betrübt, traurig oder Bedauerswert! (der Arme).* ◇ sad or poor thing! Ⓛ matutu

matjaunga *ausgestorben (Leute).* ◇ extinct, died out (people). Ⓛ merimatu

matja *Feuer, Brennholz.* ◇ fire, firewood. Ⓛ waru Ⓓ turu

matjakauma, matjakëuma *Feuer anfachen.* ◇ fan fire. Ⓛ waru kurkaltunañi

matjakapa *Feuerbrand, Fakel.* ◇ blazing fire, torch. Ⓛ warutani

matjangera *feurig.* ◇ fiery. Ⓛ warunguanba

matjatāra *großes, auflodherndes Feuer.* ◇ big, flaring fire. Ⓛ kurkala, waru kurkalta, waru kurkalba

matja-ilirtja *Grube, in der Feuer angezündet wird.* ◇ fire pit. Ⓛ waru ilirtji

matja-taba, matja tuāba *heiße Asche.* ◇ hot ash. Ⓛ waru epa

matja-kwata *Rauch.* ◇ smoke. Ⓛ waru puju Ⓓ turudupu (*Rauch*: smoke), turukunna *Rauchwolke* (fern)

matja-alknanta *Feuer Flamme.* ◇ lit. fire flame. Ⓛ waru kala, waru teli

mbabuta *eine trockne Stelle (wenn sich das Wasser verläuft).* ◇ dry spot (when water has subsided). Ⓛ mbababi

maůia *Gift (das Männer und Frauen mit sich tragen) vom Norden (von Tennants Creek kommen).* ◇ poison (carried by men and women from the north, from Tennant Creek). Ⓛ mauiï

mbabutérama *verlaufen (Wasser), trocken werden Erde.* ◇ subside (water), dry out (ground). Ⓛ mbabibiriñi

maramoka, maramokala tuma *Faust zum [Schlagen].* ◇ fist (to hit).

marurkábuma *sich freuen (über die Arbeit und Vorsicht eines Anderen).* ◇ be pleased (about someone's work and diligence). Ⓛ palalkunku palani

mbáljilkaljílka *sehr glatt (Stein), eben (Boden).* ◇ very smooth (stone), even (ground). Ⓛ wiŕul, wiŕulba Ⓓ pankara

mbaiamba *sehr eben, sehr gut (Weg).* ◇ very even, very good (path). Ⓛ bauali

mbaia *heiß, warm.* ◇ hot, warm. Ⓛ aranta

mbaieléela *sehr heiß.* ◇ very hot. Ⓛ arántaránta Ⓓ karareli

mbaia artjima *sich wärmen, sich sonnen.* ◇ to warm, to sun (reflexive). Ⓛ arantakambañi

mbanambana *Kochgefäß (n), Topf (n).* ◇ cooking pot, pot.

mbaka *anlehnend (an etwas).* ◇ lean (against something). Ⓛ ngambal

mbaka indama *(sitzend) sich anlehnen.* ◇ lean against something (sitting). Ⓛ ngambalngariñi

mbaka tnama *(stehend) sich anlehnen.* ◇ lean on (standing). Ⓛ ngambaltnarañi

mbakanama *sich anlehnen.* ◇ lean against or on. Ⓛ ngambalninañi Ⓓ jenina

mbakerenama *zusammenfügen, -halten, -drücken, vereinigen, übers Kreuz halten (Hände), fest an etwas drücken, aufmalen (Schmuck).* ◇ join, hold together, press together, unite, cross (hands), press hard on something, paint (decoration). Ⓛ ngambaltunañi Ⓓ jelaribana, manduibana

mbakiwunja renama *zusammenfügen, zusammendrücken, fest vereinigen, verbinden.* ◇ join, press together, unite, connect. Ⓛ ngimbingimbi = ninakatiñi

mbakama *trs. ausreißen, abbrechen (Früchte), abbeißen, abpflücken, abtrennen (Beine).* ◇ (transitive) pull or tear out, break off (fruit), sever (limbs). Ⓛ warpuni Ⓓ tampurinbana? ('?' added by CS), murtjana (*abfressen*)

 For the modern spellings of these words, see the dictionaries and sources in reference list.

mbakalama *intr. zerreißen (Kleid), einstürzen (Haus), abfallen (Frucht).* ◇ (intransitive) tear (dress), collapse (house), fall off (fruit). Ⓛ nalburtalkañi Ⓓ tampurina

mbakata [Southern dialect] *offen (Land), holzarm, kahl.* ◇ open (land), treeless, bare. Ⓛ urela, urelba

mbákatàla *außen, auf dem offenen Land.* ◇ outside, on open land. Ⓛ ureltanka Ⓓ palarani

mbakatnénama *schnappen (nach etwas), z.B. Hund nach Fleisch.* ◇ snap (at something), e.g. dog snaps at meat. Ⓛ warpuratalkañi

mbalanama *sich teilhaftig machen [unclear].* ◇ [unclear]

mbāla *ihr beide.* ◇ you two. Ⓛ numbali, nubali Ⓓ judla

mbalbaka rama *den ganzen Körper und Person selbst sehen.* ◇ to see the whole body as well as the person. Ⓛ ratatura nangañi

mbălla *schlecht, sehr schlecht.* ◇ bad, very bad. Ⓛ kulantu

mballataka *sehr schlecht (Mann), Hurer der seine maia begehrt, heiratet oder mit ihr verkehrt.* ◇ very bad man who has intercourse with his maia (Strehlow 1913: 93). Ⓛ kulantu

mbalilama *unrecht tun.* ◇ do wrong. Ⓛ kulantunani

mballumballa *die Hure, die ihren Sohn begehrt oder mit ihm verkehrt.* ◇ whore who has intercourse with her son (Strehlow 1913: 93). Ⓛ kulantukulantu

mbaleȓalera *weite Creek.* ◇ wide creek. Ⓛ untupila

mbalka; *z.B.* **pata mbalka** *Stein zum zerklopfen von Sämereien, Klopstein.* ◇ grinding stone. Ⓛ umbalki

mbalkaralkara *rein, glänzend.* ◇ clean, pure, bright. Ⓛ ilkarilkari Ⓓ woldankara

mbalknaninja *hoch, himmelhoch.* ◇ high, sky high. Ⓛ ngaiuwila

mbalkninama *brechen, lösen, hauen (Steine).* ◇ break, loosen, hew (stone). Ⓛ tambirpungañi

imbiltja, mbaltja *menschenleer.* ◇ deserted. Ⓛ ambiltji

mbiltjilkélama *zustopfen (Loch).* ◇ fill, plug (hole). Ⓛ ambiltjini

mballatama *Onarie treiben.* ◇ masturbate.

mballa *heiß, die heiße Zeit (Oct-Febr.)* ◇ hot, hot time period (October to February). Ⓛ lurru Ⓓ woldra

mballaka *im Sommer.* ◇ in summer, in the hot time (Strehlow 1915: 47). Ⓛ lurruku Ⓓ woldrakanja

mballilama *wärmen (Sonne).* ◇ to warm, heat (sun). Ⓛ lurruni

mbalambala *Hitzeausschlag.* ◇ heat rash; duplication of heat. Ⓛ etunítuni

mbalangambálilama *sich mit Farbe schmücken, sich bereiten.* ◇ adorn with paint, prepare. Ⓛ irbotirbotanañi

mbalangambala *bereitet, geschmückt.* ◇ ready, decorated.

mballatana *Onarist.* ◇ masturbator.

mbámara *gute Ruf, Name.* ◇ good reputation, name. Ⓛ măka

mbana knara *Mann der älteren Schwester (♂).* ◇ husband of older sister. Ⓛ marutu puntu

mbana larra *Mann der jüngeren Schwester (♂).* ◇ husband of younger sister. Ⓛ marutu wongu

mbana *Schwager (Fraus Bruder ♂).* ◇ brother-in-law. Ⓛ marutu Ⓓ kadi

mbanukua *Schwager (eines Andern).* ◇ brother-in-law (of somebody else). Ⓛ marutura

mbánama *schnell weiter brennen (Feuer).* ◇ continue to burn fast (fire). Ⓛ kambarabakañi

mbānama *gebären, legen (Eier).* ◇ give birth, lay (eggs). Ⓛ wolkani Ⓓ dankana, kantji patana

mbangara *Busch mit roten tomatenähnlichen Früchten.* ◇ bush with red tomato-like berries, name of outstation in West MacDonnell Ranges. Ⓛ itunbu

mbanga *reif (Früchte).* ◇ ripe (fruit). Ⓛ unmi

mbangara *neben einem andern, zur Seite.* ◇ next to someone. Ⓛ ambangara

mbangarilama *neben einen stellen oder legen.* ◇ stand or lay next to someone. Ⓛ ambangaranañi

mbangaratarilama *nebeneinanderstellen (2 Personen).* ◇ stand beside each other (two persons); get married. Ⓛ ambangarakutaranan

mbangarirbera *zusammen sein (viele).* ◇ together (many); together after marriage. Ⓛ ambangarara waritji

mbanja katuluma *ehebrechen.* ◇ adulterous.

mbanja *Ehe.* ◇ marriage. Ⓛ wongi Ⓓ pinta

mbanjagata *ehelich, verheiratet.* ◇ married. Ⓛ wongita

mbanja eknuma *heiraten.* ◇ marry. Ⓛ wongini

mbanja katululinja *Ehebrecher.* ◇ adulterer.

mbanjambanja *Porcupine-Maus.* ◇ porcupine-mouse. Ⓛ umbanjumbanji

mbanja katulunja *der Ehebruch.* ◇ adultery.

mbanka *übrig, übriggelassen (z.B. Brot).* ◇ left, left over (e.g. bread). Ⓛ winki, kulu umbanki

mbankinja *der übrige Raum.* ◇ remaining space, empty camp or place. Ⓛ kulupukuru

mbankangaruka *das Übrige.* ◇ rest, left over.

mbankama *klagen, seufzen, stöhnen.* ◇ lament, sigh, groan, moan. Ⓛ nariñi, ngarbmanañi Ⓓ kidakidana

mbantaka *eben, Ebene, große.* ◇ even, plain, big. Ⓛ umbantiki

mbantua *die Creek.* ◇ creek; Arandic name of Alice Springs today (see ulbaia (creek; fine sand)).

mbara *Maden, (Wurm).* ◇ maggots, (worms). Ⓛ katilka Ⓓ miriwiri

mbarangaranga *Ordnung (keine Unordnung).* ◇ order, tidiness (not a mess); process, protocol.

mbarama *fühlen, befühlen, machen, tun.* ◇ feel, touch, make, do. Ⓛ pampuni Ⓓ karakararina, warpibana

mbatta *kleine Beutelratte (Phasologale cristicauda).* ◇ small marsupial rat (*Phascologale cristicauda* now *Dasycercus cristicauda* or *D. blythi* (Atlas of Living Australia nd.)). Ⓛ murta

mbarkama *scheinen, glänzen.* ◇ shine, glitter. Ⓛ tjoalkambañi Ⓓ tjintina

mbatjalkatiuma *hervorbringen, fruchtbar machen, in einen besseren Zustand versetzen.* ◇ bring about, produce; to bing about, make fertile, improve conditions of. Ⓛ kutintjingañi

mbata *Stengel, Stoppel, Strunk.* ◇ stalk, stubble, stem, stump. Ⓛ mutu Ⓓ mokku

mbátara *Bauchfett.* ◇ belly fat. Ⓛ umbatjiri

mbatjamba *Bauchfett.* ◇ belly fat. Ⓛ umbatjimbi

mbekéuma *aufhäufen, auf einen Haufen werfen.* ◇ heap up, throw on a heap. Ⓛ ngambawonniñi

mbélkalama *sich freuen, in froher Erwartung.* ◇ to look forward to. Ⓛ inkapalaringañi

mbelkalélama *trs. erfreuen (durch ein Geschenk).* ◇ (transitive) to please (with a present). Ⓛ inkapalarini

mbewarenama *verbinden (miteinander), in Verbindung bringen.* ◇ join (together), bring together, connect. Ⓛ ngambawonniñi

mbenbalalbuma *überschreiten (Gebirge), auf der anderen Seite des Gebirges heruntersteigen.* ◇ cross (mountain), descend on the other side of mountain range. Ⓛ mawararakatirakulbañi

mbenja *postp. vor (örtlich).* ◇ (postposition) in front (locational).

mbenka *sehr groß, sehr viel.* ◇ very big, very much. Ⓛ tjoariwari

roambenka *eine große Flut.* ◇ big flood. Ⓛ juru tjoariwari

kwatjambenka *ein großes Wasser (See).* ◇ big water (lake). Ⓛ kapitjoariwari

matjambenka *ein großes Feuer, Feuersbrunst.* ◇ big fire, conflagration. Ⓛ warutjoariwari

mbéruma *sterben.* ◇ to die. Ⓛ iluñi

mberakeraka *hochmütig, hoffärtig.* ◇ arrogant, haughtly. Ⓛ mberakeraka [?]

mbinja (mbunja) *Rück-(Weg); den Weg, den einer gekommen ist; der zurückgelegte Weg.* ◇ (way) back, path someone has covered; distance covered. Ⓛ tou

mbinjala (mbunjala) *zurück, heim, z.B. zurückkehren auf dem Wege, den man gekommen ist.* ◇ go back, go home; e.g. return on path that one has come on. Ⓛ tounka, ngaparba

mbinjala lama *herumkehren.* ◇ turn around. Ⓛ tounka jennañi

mbitja *leer, verlassen (Platz).* ◇ empty, deserted (place). Ⓛ tou

mbitjana *eine Heiratsklasse.* ◇ marriage class, subsection, skin name. Ⓛ tambitjinba (♂), nambitjinba (♀)

mbóanta [Southern dialect], **ambóanta** *Versammlungsplatz der Frauen (wo Frauentanz).* ◇ women's meeting place (where they perform dances); amboanta means 'cleared one'. Ⓛ amboanta

mbōba *Mitte.* ◇ middle. Ⓛ ngururu Ⓓ terti

mbobala *in der Mitte, zwischen.* ◇ in the middle, between. Ⓛ ngururanka Ⓓ tertieli

mbobantema *mitten durch.* ◇ through the middle. Ⓛ ngururbaka

mbobulkura *mitten hinein.* ◇ straight into the middle. Ⓛ ngururungana

mboba indora *ganz in der Mitte.* ◇ right in the middle. Ⓛ ngururkultu

mbobanga ndama *weiter geben, vermitteln (das Geschenk).* ◇ pass on, give (gift). Ⓛ ngururungurujungañi

mbobalta *Stamm, Baumstamm (mittlern Teil des Baumes).* ◇ trunk, tree trunk (middle part of tree). Ⓛ ngururkultu

mbóbipatípata *eine große Menge, mitten in einer großen Menge.* ◇ large amount or crowd, in the middle of a large crowd. Ⓛ ngururupatupatu

mbobakilama *umschließen, einschließen.* ◇ surround. Ⓛ ngururkutúnani

mbobalta *Stamm (mittlern Teil des Baumes).* ◇ trunk (middle part of tree). Ⓛ ngururkultu

mbutatjinama *biegen (halbkreisförmig).* ◇ bend (semicircle). Ⓛ niliwitini

mbobipatipata *eine große Menge.* ◇ a large amount, mob or crowd. Ⓛ ngururupatupatu

mbobara *kl. Beutelratte.* ◇ small marsupial rat. Ⓛ ambabara

mbobitjilóla *in der Mitte (des Lagerplatzes).* ◇ in the middle (of the camp). Ⓛ ngururpati

mbobudora *Insel.* ◇ island. Ⓛ tuntōru Ⓓ watiwati

mbobulja *Kaulquappe.* ◇ tadpole. Ⓛ tjupulupulu Ⓓ Jundajunda

mbokulba *kurz, niedrig.* ◇ short, low. Ⓛ murila, murilba

mbokulberama *sich erniedrigen.* ◇ humiliate (reflexive), degrade (reflexive). Ⓛ muriljariñi

mbobunginja *das 3. älteste Kind.* ◇ third oldest child. Ⓛ ngurumatata

mbobutinja *das 4. älteste Kind.* ◇ fourth oldest child. Ⓛ ngururita

mbobuntunga *(= der mittelste), der kälteste Monat (Juli).* ◇ (middle), the coldest month (July). Ⓛ ngururkultu

mbomberama *behutsam sein (mit einem Kranken), warten, pflegen.* ◇ gentle (with a sick person), attend (to), nurse. Ⓛ umbuúmbuni Ⓓ dentjudentjumana

mbomberélabuma *auf der Hut sein (vor dem Feinde).* ◇ be weary (of the enemy). Ⓛ umbuumburiñi

mbonta; larrambonta *breit, groß; Finkefluß (der große Fluß).* ◇ wide (broad), big; Finke River (the big or wide river). Ⓛ kultu

mbontja *satt.* ◇ full. Ⓛ aubákanta Ⓓ jerto

mburpa *beweglich, lose, gewandt, ausweichend (dem Hindernis), ausgleitend, dahingleitend, eilig.* ◇ flexible, loose, agile, avoid (obstacle), slippery, glide along, speedy (Strehlow 1920: 26). Ⓛ titjuru Ⓓ kekilju

mburperama *ausgleiten, lose werden, hinfallen.* ◇ slip, come loose, fall (down). Ⓛ titurtiturjenañi Ⓓ kekiljerina

mburpamburpa *schnell dahin schreitend, sehr beweglich.* ◇ stride fast, very agile. Ⓛ titjurutitjuru

mbulara *Regenbogen.* ◇ rainbow. Ⓛ kanturangu Ⓓ kurikira

mbulbambakama *trs. hin und her zerren, an sich reißen, zerren.* ◇ (transitive) pull back and forth, seize, tear. Ⓛ warpuwarpuni Ⓓ diadialkana

mbulbuma *pfeifen (wie Mäuse).* ◇ whistle (like mice). Ⓛ mumbulbmanañi

mbulbuta renama *falsches beteuern, leugnen, bestreiten.* ◇ perjure, deny, dispute. Ⓛ palitunañi

mbulkna *Narben.* ◇ scars. Ⓛ melala

mbulknerama *vernarben.* ◇ heal. Ⓛ melaláringañi

mbulja *unschuldig.* ◇ innocent. Ⓛ ambiltji

mbultarenama *durchschneiden, durchhauen, durchsägen.* ◇ cut through, hew through, saw through. Ⓛ katurpungañi

mbultjérama *heilen (Wunde).* ◇ heal (wound). Ⓛ ambiltjiringañi Ⓓ putarina

mbultjinja *Diarrhöe.* ◇ diarrhoea. Ⓛ tjilpinmi Ⓓ kapaljerina

mbultjima *Durchfall haben, Diarrhoe.* ◇ have diarrhoea. Ⓛ tjilpini Ⓓ kudna tjurana

mbultjita *wilde Orangenbaum, (capparis), (Capparis Mitchelli).* ◇ bush orange, *Capparis mitchellii.* Ⓛ mbultjati

mbultuma *beißen (Rauch – die Augen).* ◇ sting (smoke in the eyes). Ⓛ kaltjini

mbuma (wumbuma), mbalanama *brennen.* ◇ to burn. Ⓛ kambañi

urambuma *das Feuer brennt.* ◇ the fire is burning. Ⓛ waru kambañi

tnatambuma *entbrannt sein (vor Ärger).* ◇ very angry. Ⓛ wila kambañi

mbunjala *cf.* **mbinjala** *zurück, heim, z.B. zurückkehren auf dem Wege, den man gekommen ist.* ◇ return, (go back), home; e.g. return the way one has come on. Ⓛ tounka, ngaparba

mbumindama *einem obliegen (etwas zu wählen), liegen vor einem zur Auswahl.* ◇ obliged (to choose something), have a choice.

mburberama (mpurperama?) *ausgleiten, hinfallen.* ◇ slip, fall. ('?' added by CS)

mburka *Leib, Körper.* ◇ body. Ⓛ anbara, anangu Ⓓ palku, palkumarra (*fettleibig*: fat)

mburtamburta *Körper hin und her bewegend.* ◇ move body back and forth. Ⓛ ngamburngámburu

mburkagatala *offenbar, ersichtlich.* ◇ obvious, evident. Ⓛ anbarautita

mburkagatalélama *offenbar machen.* ◇ make obvious. Ⓛ anbara utitanani Ⓓ kutiri ngankana

mbutitjilama *biegen (z.B. Stock).* ◇ bend (e.g. a stick). Ⓛ nutinutini

mekua *weiblicher Vogel (spec.), weibliche Larven.* ◇ female bird, female grubs. Ⓛ jakura

mekua *Mutter (eines Andern).* ◇ mother (of somebody else). Ⓛ jakura

melanka; andata melanka *sehr schön, sehr gut; die schöne Blume.* ◇ very beautiful, very good; the beautiful flower. Ⓛ watinba, untuntu watinba Ⓓ tintipidi

melba *Unterarm, Unterarmknochen.* ◇ forearm, forearm bone. Ⓛ amelbi

mburperama *verfehlen (das Ziel).* ◇ miss (target).

meltjenterkunja *gefaltet (Hände).* ◇ folded (hands). Ⓛ marawiti

mimbara *Zeichen (auf dem Körper gemalt).* ◇ designs (painted on body). Ⓛ mimburu

mimbara knaragata *bemalt.* ◇ painted. Ⓛ mimburu puntutara

meminérama *blitzen.* ◇ lightning. Ⓛ ngaralinbiñi

menda *krank.* ◇ sick. Ⓛ urini Ⓓ muntja, muntjala

menderama *krank werden.* ◇ fall sick. Ⓛ uriniriñi

mentera [Southern dialect] *Fischwehr.* ◇ fish weir. Ⓛ amintiri

mēra *Speerwerfer.* ◇ spear thrower. Ⓛ meru Ⓓ mankurara

merakalakala *Speerwerfer zum Spielen.* ◇ toy spear thrower. Ⓛ kalamerumeru

mewara *Mitternacht.* ◇ midnight. Ⓛ tukalba

merankanka *ein böses Wesen in Hundegestalt.* ◇ bad spirit or evil being in the shape of a dog. Ⓛ merankanka

notuta *tiefe Mulde.* ◇ deep bowl. Ⓛ metuta

miniera *mythische Weiber der Vorzeit.* ◇ mythical women of the Dreaming. Ⓛ minieri

miamia *vorsichtig z.B. lama.* ◇ cautious, e.g. go, walk. Ⓛ tákantákan jennañi

minkaltarana *Schlange, giftig.* ◇ snake, poisonous. Ⓛ mantaúntupúlpu, minkiringurara

malbamanalama *intr. sich hindurchzwängen, z.B. durch ein Loch.* ◇ (intransitive) force through, e.g. through a hole. Ⓛ ngalungaluni

minka *Syphilis.* ◇ syphilis. Ⓛ minki, kirkni

malbamanalélama *trs. hindurchdrücken, -schieben.* ◇ (transitive) press through, push through. Ⓛ ngalungaluni

monanga *Giftstrauch (Duboisia Hopwoodii).* ◇ poisonous bush (*Duboisia hopwoodii*). Ⓛ tulungu

monja *langsam, geduldig.* ◇ slow, patient; careful. Ⓛ purinba, purinja Ⓓ mankali

monjamonja *langsam, vorsichtig, geduldig, langmütig.* ◇ slow, careful, patient, forbearing. Ⓛ purinpurinba

monjamonjilama *Geduld haben, warten (Kinder).* ◇ be patient, wait (children). Ⓛ purinpurinmanañi

monjikana *mildtätig.* ◇ charitable.

monjikínila ndama *milde Gaben geben.* ◇ give alms. Ⓛ purinmatunka jungañi

monjamokilama, monjamokilai! *behalten, nicht herausgeben, zurückbehalten (den Lohn); behalte es!* ◇ retain, keep, refuse to give; keep it! Ⓛ ngatalbmanañi

monjarelama *sich in Acht nehmen.* ◇ be watchful, be on guard. Ⓛ purinjarekula nangañi

motjamotjilama *alles zermalmen (z.B. die Larven, die die Wurzeln zernagen).* ◇ gnaw everything (e.g. grubs gnawing roots). Ⓛ kerumútumútuni

mpurakata *die Kniescheibe.* ◇ kneecap. Ⓛ mutiwotta

mpara (mpura) *Knie, untere Ende des Schenkelknochens.* ◇ knee, lower part of thigh bone. Ⓛ muti urkuralji Ⓓ panja

mpura katnilama *Knie hochheben.* ◇ lift knee. Ⓛ muti kattuni

mpaṙela ntjitara nama *knieen.* ◇ kneel. Ⓛ mutinkatúra ninañi Ⓓ panju terkana

mpaṙela tunkara nama *nieder knieen.* ◇ kneel down. Ⓛ mutituru ninañi Ⓓ panju terkana ngarina

mpaṙela ntjitara tnama *auf den Knieen stehen (Emu).* ◇ stand on knees (emu). Ⓛ tantarangarañi, mutitunkula ngarañi

mparampara *gewunden, gebogen, krumm (der Lauf des Creek).* ◇ winding, curved, bent (course of creek). Ⓛ nunkinunki

mpurperama *ausgleiten, hinfallen.* ◇ slip, fall.

mulknara *Garn (aus Haaren gesponnen).* ◇ thread (spun of hair). Ⓛ amulknuru

mulata, tjatta mulata *Holzart, Speere.* ◇ kind of wood, spears. Ⓛ mulati, katji mulati

mulkumara *Schmeißfliege.* ◇ blowfly. Ⓛ murumulku, pubuléri Ⓓ muntjurunga

mungilama *trs. dämpfen (Feuer).* ◇ (transitive) damp (fire).

mungerama *dämpfen.* ◇ dampen.

multjamalawuruma *sich drängen.* ◇ push, crowd, thrust. Ⓛ untuúnturupungañi

mulunga *boomerang von südöstlicher Völkerschaft eingehandelt (ein Queensland Wort = Leben abschneidend).* ◇ boomerang (Queensland word meaning 'cut life off') traded from south-eastern tribes; killer-boomerang. Ⓛ amulúngu

mulurkulurka *rauh, uneben (Feile, Erdboden).* ◇ rough, uneven (file, ground). Ⓛ umulúrkulúrku

multjeratnalama *stoßen hin und her (die Wellen ein Schiff).* ◇ move back and forth (waves a ship).

munta; rula munta *dicht; Dickicht.* ◇ thick, dense; thicket. Ⓛ tata, punu tata

muntunguntungerama *eintrocknen (Wasser in der Creek), vertrocknen, eingehen (Bäume), altersschwach werden.* ◇ dry up (water in creek), dry out, die (trees), decrepit. Ⓛ lakalakaringañi

mururuta *cr. Zehn (Personen und Gegenstände).* ◇ circa 10 (persons and objects). Ⓛ kutuluru

murilja *Vogel (spec.)* ◇ bird (species) Ⓛ murila

murulunga *Gift, [unclear].* ◇ poison. Ⓛ irati

murukarinja *Vogel (spec.); scharren wie die Hühner nach Sämereien.* ◇ bird (species) that scratches like a chicken for seeds. Ⓛ marapurunba

muruanga *große braune Entenart.* ◇ large brown duck species. Ⓛ marawungi

conf. **arkulta** *Gras (Art), Samen.* ◇ Grass (species), seeds. Ⓛ mutimuta

mutja *Stumpf.* ◇ stump. Ⓛ patti

muturba *eine kleine angesetzte lankua.* ◇ small lankua fruit; name of an ancestor. Ⓛ amulungu

N

Nábinbàra *ödes, ausgebranntes Land.* ◇ desolate, burnt out land. Ⓛ urela

nakabakala *Mangel (an Gütern), unverständig, ohne Verstand.* ◇ lack (of goods), ignorant, without reason or sense, senseless.

nabantúruma *brummen, summen (Insekten, Fliegen).* ◇ to buzz, hum (insects, flies). Ⓛ betubetuni

nairama *kūku-ku schreien, gurren (Taube).* ◇ call kuku-ku, coo (pigeon). Ⓛ ngunarariñi

narilanama *Augen aufheben (zum Himmel).* ◇ look up (to the sky). Ⓛ eranakanáñi Ⓓ naiïna tarana

nakabánantáma *hier an diesem Platz.* ◇ here at this place. Ⓛ nangatakalbi

nakaguia *deswegen.* ◇ for this reason. Ⓛ nangakatulbi Ⓓ jendrangundria

nakantema *hier wieder.* ◇ here again. Ⓛ nangakuka

nāka *hierher, hier.* ◇ here. Ⓛ nangaku

nakanara pitjima *entgegen kommen, hierher kommen.* ◇ come to meet, come here. Ⓛ álaúla ngalajénnani, alaala ngalajenañi

nakerama *begegnen [zu einem kommen].* ◇ meet. Ⓛ patupatuni Ⓓ manduina

nakakata *so groß.* ◇ so big. Ⓛ nangakutáta

nakara, nuákara *Sippschaft, Camp-Genossenschaft.* ◇ clan, camp, residential group. Ⓛ ngananakuarpa

nakaratitja *wir alle zusammen, wir insgesammt.* ◇ we all together, all of us. Ⓛ ngananakuárpalta

nākua *gesättigt, satt.* ◇ satisfied, satiated, full. Ⓛ aubakana

nakarakia, nákarakia *unsere 'Sippschaft', unsere 'Gruppe'.* ◇ our clan, our group, our kindred or people; 'us', meaning the people belonging to one's own patrimoiety. One of the basic divisions of Aranda society organises all people into two groups, i.e. exogamous moieties. These patrimoieties were called 'Nákarakia' (our kindred or people) and 'Etnákarakia' (those people or that kindred) or 'Maljanuka' (my friends) by the Aranda. These terms were not names for one or the other moiety but were reciprocally used by both groups (Strehlow 1913: 62). Today Arandic people still refer – from an egocentric point of view – to such groupings that are maljanuka and nákarakia [or ilakakia]. Maljanuka means 'them' or 'our in-laws' while nákarakia [or ilakakia] means 'us'. In one's own patrimoiety, that is 'us', are one's actual and classificatory fathers and their siblings, father's fathers and son's children, and also one's mother's mother's patriline which is part of nákarakia [or ilakakia], i.e 'us'. In the opposite moiety, maljanuka, in addition to one's spouse and brothers-in-law there are one's actual and classificatory mothers, mother's brothers and mother's fathers and also one's father's mother.

Like the Aranda, the Loritja used particular terms for the members of these groups reciprocally. All relatives of an ego's group (own patrimoiety) were called 'Ngananukarpitina' meaning 'all of us'; and all relatives of the opposite moiety were called 'Tananukarpitina' meaning 'all of them' (Strehlow 1913: 79). In societies organised in this way one should always marry someone from the opposite moiety. See Strehlow (1913: 62, fn. 5) for an elaborate attempt on the possible etymology of this reciprocal term. Ⓛ ngananukarpitina

nakuna [Southern dialect] *jener, dort.* ◇ that one, there. Ⓛ naratanu

nā *Vater (in Zusammensetzung).* ◇ father (in compounds). (See also ninanga below)

nākura [Southern dialect] *Vater (eines andern).* ◇ father (of somebody else). Ⓛ mamara

nātja *mein Vater.* ◇ my father. Ⓛ mamana

nekua *Vater (eines Andern).* ◇ father (of somebody else). Ⓛ mamara

nala *hier.* ◇ here. Ⓛ nanganka Ⓓ ninkia, ninkida

nakua *dorthin.* ◇ there, over there. Ⓛ naraku

nakua inkana *jener, der zuletzt kommt.* ◇ the one, who comes last. Ⓛ narata nganti

nalabuma *schwimmen (Vögel).* ◇ swim (birds). Ⓛ ninarariñi

nalakélama *umarmen.* ◇ embrace. Ⓛ ambuni Ⓓ munkamalina

nalalama *fahren, reiten, währen, dauern (Leben).* ◇ drive, ride, last, continue (life). Ⓛ manjináñi, ninaratalkañi

nálangalalama *fortwährend sein.* ◇ be continuously.

nalaüma *ein wenig bleiben, (um dann weiter zu gehen).* ◇ stay a while (to then travel on). Ⓛ ninaratalkañi ?

nalitja *Unterlage (von Stecken und Zweigen – Adlersnest).* ◇ base, pad, underlay (of sticks and twigs – eagle's nest). Ⓛ nalitji

nalbanama *Blutschande treiben (Bruder und Schwester).* ◇ commit incest (brother and sister). Ⓛ murarapatañi

nalka *satt, Bauch gefüllt.* ◇ full stomach. Ⓛ palta Ⓓ jerto

nalkerama *satt werden.* ◇ become full. Ⓛ paltaringañi

naltarérama *zusammentreffen (von 2 feindlichen Parteien).* ◇ meet, encounter (two hostile parties), clash.

naltjarérama, naltarérama [Southern dialect] *cf.* **inaltjarérama** [Northern dialect] *wiedersehen (von Freunden).* ◇ see again (friends). Ⓛ ngaparku nangañi, nakula pungañi Ⓓ naiïmalina

naltanalterama *röcheln (Sterbenden).* ◇ groan (at death). Ⓛ unúltunúlturiñi

inaltjinaltja-érama *(viele) einander sehen, wieder sehn.* ◇ see again. Ⓛ nakunakulapungañi

namalelama *verdolmetschen, übersetzen.* ◇ translate.

naltauma *beisammen sein, versammelt.* ◇ be together, assembled. Ⓛ ninara woniñi

naltjambaranánama *hinaufklettern (auf Baum).* ◇ climb up (tree). Ⓛ kulbarawonniñi

nanama *dahinfahren.* ◇ travel (along).

nalanama *sitzen bleiben.* ◇ remain seated. Ⓛ ninaniñi

nama *sein, sitzen.* ◇ to be, to sit. Ⓛ ninañi Ⓓ nganana, ngamana

natnanama *sitzen bleiben, zurückbleiben (während die andern fortgehen).* ◇ remain seated, stay behind (whilst the others go away). Ⓛ ninaninañi

natnapatnama *dransitzen (Brust).* ◇ sit at. Ⓛ ninaranañi wongu

natnitjinjima *hervorkommen (Brustknospen/warzen?).* ◇ emerge (nipples). ('?' added by CS) Ⓛ ninara kalbañi

ñama *Gras.* ◇ grass. Ⓛ buta Ⓓ kanta

ñama terka *das grüne Gras.* ◇ green grass. Ⓛ buta okiri

ñama ntjirka *Spreu, Stroh.* ◇ hay, straw. Ⓛ buta bilti

nama ntjama *die Grasunterlage, die auf dem Kopf gelegt wird, um etwas zu tragen.* ◇ head pad of grass to carry something, wreath. Ⓛ buta banta, buta tăta

nametna *dicht stehendes Gras, Weide.* ◇ dense grass, pasture.

nalangalalama *sich aufhalten (längere Zeit).* ◇ stay, dwell (for a longer time period).

namaltulbatia *abends wenn es dunkel ist, wenn die Nacht das Gras (nama) bedeckt.* ◇ in the evening when it is dark, when the night envelops the grass. Ⓛ butata waltuwaltulba

nama bottera *Stoppeln (n).* ◇ stubbles.

namalélama *verlegen (Hütte, Wohnort).* ◇ shift (hut, camp). Ⓛ ararakatiñi

namintjera *geflügelte Ameisen (tonanga).* ◇ flying ants. Ⓛ watunuma

namanáma *unstät, bald hier, bald dort.* ◇ unsteady, fickel. Ⓛ atambatamba

namantia *kleine rote fliegende Ameisen.* ◇ small red flying ants. Ⓛ namantiï

namaneúlama *sich wälzen.* ◇ roll, wallow. Ⓛ kutikutikatiñi

namapálanga *die mit Gras bestandene Ebene.* ◇ grass covered plain. Ⓛ akátabílanka

namara *Schwiegervater, Vater des Ehemannes, Manns Vater (♀), Sohns Frau (♂), Bruders Sohns Frau.* ◇ father-in-law, father of husband, son's wife, brother's son's wife. Ⓛ katana

namaratja *eigene Schwiegervater (♀).* ◇ own father-in-law.

namarukua *Schwiegervater eines Andern.* ◇ someone else's father-in-law.

namarkulta *dick, korpulent, schwerfällig.* ◇ fat, corpulent, slow, sluggish, clumsy. Ⓛ ninakutakuta

namerama *Platz wechseln, verändern.* ◇ change place, alter, vary. Ⓛ mabakani Ⓓ warkurina

namilama *Platz machen (einem Andern).* ◇ make room (for somebody). Ⓛ mauntuni Ⓓ piri pinina, warku ngankana

naminama, namakantja *auf dem grünen Gras liegen, 'der auf dem Gras liegende'.* ◇ to lie on green grass, 'the one lying on grass' (Strehlow 1913: 92). Ⓛ putapanti, wongupanti

namintitintita *Maus (Porcupine [unclear]).* ◇ mouse species. Ⓛ untiapurilba

nanatitja *diese.* ◇ this one (female). Ⓛ nangataIta

nanabara *dieser.* ◇ this, this one (male). Ⓛ nangataka

nana *dies, dieses-hier.* ◇ this, this one here. Ⓛ nangata, ngāta

nanakantéma *hier.* ◇ here. Ⓛ nangankaka Ⓓ ninkida (*hier*: here)

nanatara *dual, diese beiden.* ◇ dual, these two. Ⓛ nangatakutara

nanakabara *dort.* ◇ there. Ⓛ nangakuka

nanankana, nanirbera *plural diese.* ◇ plural those. Ⓛ nangatatuta, nangatamurka

nanatóa *dieser.* ◇ this one. Ⓛ nangatakamba Ⓓ naupini

nanilka *zunächst, vorläufig.* ◇ first, at this stage. Ⓛ nangatatauára

nangantema *darauf (zeitlich).* ◇ thereon (temporal). Ⓛ ngānguruka

nanga *damals als, – damals.* ◇ at that time, then. Ⓛ pána Ⓓ jendranguta (*damals*: then)

nangara *jene (bekannten?).* ◇ those (known?). ('?' added by CS) Ⓛ panapaluru

nanka *Brust.* ◇ chest. Ⓛ ngarka Ⓓ munampiri, munakadra (*Brustkasten*: chest)

nánama *rutschen (auf dem Hintern), sich auf das Hinterteil stellen, sich erheben (Schlange).* ◇ slide (on behind), sit on backside, raise (snake). Ⓛ ninarabakañi

nanatnalbuma *rutschend heimkehren.* ◇ return home sliding. Ⓛ ninaninarabakañi

nankala [Southern dialect] *hungrig.* ◇ hungry. Ⓛ ainma

nanalintjima *emporlodern (Feuer), auffahren (Äste, Feuer).* ◇ flare up (fire), bounce up (branches). Ⓛ ninarakalbañi

nanankama *stampfen (den Boden).* ◇ stamp, pound (ground). Ⓛ popuwarañi

nankama *klopfen, Aufschlagen mit den Füßen (wenn die Känguruh laufen), stampfen.* ◇ beat, pound with feet (when kangaroos hop). Ⓛ popuwonkañi

nankapankama *fortwährend stampfen.* ◇ stamp continuously. Ⓛ totutotuni

nankalélama *klopfen (an die Tür), stampfen (mit den Füßen).* ◇ knock (at the door), stamp (with feet). Ⓛ talaltjingañi ([unclear]), mamaltjingañi (*mit Füßen*)

nankilindama *im Liegen stampfen (mit d. Füßen).* ◇ stamp when lying (with the feet). Ⓛ mamaltjingara ngariñi

nankinja; nankinjalbuma *Schall (Stampfen); Stampfen kommt her.* ◇ sound, thump; a thumping is nearing (Strehlow 1907: 35). Ⓛ totu

nankana *hier.* ◇ here. Ⓛ nangakutu

nankara *postp. cum. abl. diesseits.* ◇ (postposition, with ablative) this side. Ⓛ tangati

nankaranitja *diesseits.* ◇ this side. Ⓛ tangatipiti

nankurbala *(die geschwollene Brust).* ◇ swollen chest. Ⓛ ngarkabala

nankarákara *Brustschmerzen.* ◇ chest pains. Ⓛ ngarkar̈akar̈aka

inankuma *auffliegen, hochfliegen (von flüggen Vögeln).* ◇ fly up. Ⓛ parpakañi

nanjankama *klatschend an den Leib schlagen (Speer).* ◇ clap on body (spear). Ⓛ mutultjingañi

nanta *erschöpft, ermüdet, überladen (Magen), fertig (Speisen), durchbacken, gar (Brot).* ◇ exhausted, tired, overloaded (stomach), ready (dish), backed (bread). Ⓛ ananta

nanterama *fertig werden, erschöpft sein.* ◇ finished, exhausted. Ⓛ anantariñi, tamalariñi

nantalerama *nichts mehr essen können (weil voll; z.B. zu essen zu geben).* ◇ cannot eat any more (full). Ⓛ tomatiriñi

nantatnama *aufstoßen (nach dem Essen).* ◇ burp, belch (after eating). Ⓛ ngetaninañi

nantawuma *trs. drücken, drängen, schieben (einen andern).* ◇ (transitive) press, push, shove (somebody). Ⓛ tanakunañi

napalariwontjima *wellenförmig fliegen.* ◇ to fly in wave formation. Ⓛ ngalakaturikukatiñi

nantinanta *sehr hoch (Bäume).* ◇ very high (tree). Ⓛ wirunkurunku

nanto *Pferd.* ◇ horse.

nateatapa *ratlos.* ◇ puzzled, at loss.

natinja *Rat, Beschluß (den man selber fasst).* ◇ advice, (own independent) decision.

natalka *vorn, im Vordergrund.* ◇ at the front, in the foreground.

nárama *nach oben sehen, aufblicken.* ◇ look up. Ⓛ eranangañi Ⓓ najina tarana

naritjara *trappeln, stampfen.* ◇ trample, stomp. Ⓛ kunawonkañi

naranarérama *Rad schlagen Truthahn.* ◇ open its tail (turkey). Ⓛ ngúnaringúnarariñi

narangawonna *Pardalotus striatus: schwarze Streifen von dem Schnabel über den Kopf, gelbe Streifen über jedem Auge, fast weiße Brust, schwarz und braune gesprengelte Flügel mit Reihen von roten Punkten. Der Rest ist meistens grau oder hellbraun.* ◇ *Pardalotus striatus*: black stripes from the beak over the head, yellow stripes over each eye, breast is almost white, black and brown speckled wings with rows of red dots. The rest is usually gray or light brown. Ⓛ inaringiunja

naritjula *sehr hoch, steil (Felsen, Berg).* ◇ very high, steep (cliffs, mountain). Ⓛ wararabulka

arumbananga *Geschwisterpaar.* ◇ sibling pair. Ⓛ narumbara

narknulérama *gar braten, weich braten (intrs. das Fleisch).* ◇ roast until done, roast tender (intransitive, the meat). Ⓛ nanarúriñi

nátama *unentschlossen sein, sich überlegen, mit sich selber zu Rat gehen, mit sich selber sprechen.* ◇ undecided, think about, talk to oneself. Ⓛ untukururiñi

natanatawórrama *disputieren, sich besprechen.* ◇ debate, confer. Ⓛ untukururiñi

natalélama *trs. einem abraten, ihn unschlüssig machen.* ◇ (transitive) advise against, make irresolute. Ⓛ untukurarapungañi

natjerama *Leid tragen.* ◇ suffer.

nátalatálelérama *trs. fortwährend abraten, Wunsch abschlagen.* ◇ (transitive) constantly advise against, refuse request. Ⓛ untukurakurarapungañi

natiuma *sich nicht erweichen lassen (durch Flehen), einen nicht zu Willen sein, fortwährend die Bitten abschlagen.* ◇ not give in (to pleads), refuse request. Ⓛ tanakunañi

natiá *verstockt, ungehorsam, eigensinnig, nicht zu Willen.* ◇ stubborn, disobedient. Ⓛ tomatitara

natnitjinjima *herauskommen, hervorkommen (Samen).* ◇ come out, sprout (seeds). Ⓛ ninarakalbani

natalauma *drängen, bestürmen (mit Bitten), sich nicht abweisen lassen, immer wieder bitten oder betteln.* ◇ urge, plead. Ⓛ tomatinañi

nātja *jämmerlich, bedauernswert, Leid.* ◇ miserable, pitiable, sorrow. Ⓛ matutu

natnapatnama *oben an sitzen, über etwas sitzen, dransitzen (Brüste), an der Spitze sitzen.* ◇ sit at or over something, sit at the front. Ⓛ ninarakatiñi

natnanama *bleiben, zurückbleiben (im Lagerplatz).* ◇ remain, stay back (in camp). Ⓛ ninaninañi Ⓓ ngamantina

natnawuma *von einem Platz zum andern hopsen (das Känguruh beim Fressen).* ◇ jump from one place to the other (kangaroos when grazing). Ⓛ ninaninarakulbanañi

nāurba *Streifen (auf dem Rücken, Eidechse).* ◇ stripes (on the back of a lizard). Ⓛ kuntera

natoa *ohne Mangel, zufrieden, satt.* ◇ without want, satisfied, full. Ⓛ ambaru

nauaia *weiße Punkte von Kalk (Männer und Frauen).* ◇ white lime spots (men and women decorate themselves with these spots). Ⓛ anauai

nbunba *Feuerplatz; die Stelle, wo Sämereien geröstet werden; der Platz, wo die Speere geglätted werden, Fabrik (n).* ◇ fireplace; place where seeds are roasted or spears smoothed; factory; (working place). Ⓛ unbunbu

ndalama *[sich geben], stillen, Brust geben.* ◇ (lit. give self) breast feed, nurse (baby). Ⓛ etetunañi

ndalama *übergeben, einweihen.* ◇ hand over, initiate.

ndalkarinja *Eidechse, kleine ilantja spec.* ◇ small lizard species. Ⓛ tuntalpini

ndalbarkanama *sich hinsetzen mit untergeschlagenen Beinen.* ◇ sit with folded legs. Ⓛ ngatarbaninañi

ndalbarkanitjalama *sich niedersetzen.* ◇ sit down. Ⓛ ngatarba ninañi talkala

ndama *geben.* ◇ give. Ⓛ jungani Ⓓ jinkina

- **ndalama** *[sich geben], stillen, Brust geben.* ◇ (lit. give self) breast feed, nurse (baby). Ⓛ etetunañi, etejungañi
- **nditjalbuma** *zurückgeben.* ◇ give back. Ⓛ kulbarajungañi
- **ndentjima** *hergeben.* ◇ give up, part with. Ⓛ ngalajungañi

ndalangurbalama *pflegen zu geben.* ◇ in the habit to give.

ndalkeërama *fortwandern, verlassen (eine Gegend für immer).* ◇ wander away, leave (an area for good). Ⓛ wolkarariñi

ntuárakalérama (untuára=Jungfrau=virgin) *nach mehr verlangen.* ◇ ask for more. Ⓛ wirilikataringañi

indáta, ndata *schweigsam, betrübt, ruhig.* ◇ silent, dejected, quiet. Ⓛ rata Ⓓ kurukutukutu

- **indaterama** *ruhig werden (Meer) oder aufgeregt (Mensch).* ◇ calm down (ocean), or become excited (human). Ⓛ rataringañi Ⓓ dalpuru

ndartjima *(die Sonne) scheinen.* ◇ (sun) shine. Ⓛ turangarañi

indapindapakarama *schweben (Vögel).* ◇ hover (birds). Ⓛ mararukatañi

nditjalbuma *zurückgeben.* ◇ return, give back. Ⓛ kulbarajungañi

ntoltatuma *zerbrechen (die Schenkel).* ◇ break (thighs).

ndolja *Bild, Schatten (von Menschen).* ◇ image, shadow (of humans), film, photograph. Ⓛ undulu

ndoljambala *Schatten (Laubdach).* ◇ shade (canopy).

ndolka *Ast, quer.* ◇ branch. Ⓛ antulka Ⓓ kunarku

ndolkakilama *kreuzigen.* ◇ crucify. Ⓛ antulkakunañi

ndolkarenama *übers Kreuz legen.* ◇ lay crosswise. Ⓛ antulkatunañi

ltōtama *der Länge nach aufspalten (Baum).* ◇ split lengthwise (tree). Ⓛ katapungañi

ndolkartjawuja *ästig, verzweigt, in viele Arme zerteilt (Creek).* ◇ branched, divided, (e.g. a creek with many tributaries). Ⓛ antulka, murkamurka

ltōtalama *intrs. der Länge nach sich spalten (Bäume).* ◇ (intransitive) split lengthwise (tree). Ⓛ laratalkañi

ndulbmara *Rauch, Weihrauch (n).* ◇ smoke, incense. Ⓛ tōtō

ndulbmara renama *Rauch machen, räuchern.* ◇ make smoke, smoke. Ⓛ toto tjingañi, pujurtunañi

ndōra *zusammen getrocknete Früchte (Samen).* ◇ dry, shrivelled fruit (seeds). Ⓛ warurba

ndórerama *zusammen trocknen (von Hitze).* ◇ dry out (from heat), shrivel. Ⓛ warurbaringañi

neka *große Erdfrüchte.* ◇ large tuber. Ⓛ jella

néana *beieinander (Eheleute, 2 Freunde).* ◇ together (married couple, two friends). Ⓛ alangata

neanabara *beieinander (leben, von Eheleute gebraucht), beieinander wohnen (eheliche Umarmung).* ◇ with one another (live, used by married couples), live together (conjugal embrace). Ⓛ alangatakaru

neanatararpa ntema *beieinander, zusammen Leben (Eheleute).* ◇ together, live together (married couple). Ⓛ alangatakutaraka

nealatnáma *begrüßen (den Freund), an sich drücken.* ◇ greet (friend), embrace. Ⓛ ngamiñi

nēka *Schlangenart.* ◇ snake species. Ⓛ ániki

nealatnarama [Southern dialect] *dual, sich gegenseitig begrüßen (sich mit verschränkten Armen den Oberkörper hin u. her bewegend, gegenüberstehen als Freunde), an sich drücken.* ◇ dual, greet each other, welcome (friends standing opposite of each other with crossed arms and moving upper body back and forth), embrace. Ⓛ ngamirapungañi, ngamankarapungañi

nēka *eßbare Frucht (spec.)* ◇ edible fruit (species). Ⓛ ljella

nekua *conf.* **kata** *Vater (eines Andern).* ◇ father (of someone else). Ⓛ mama (der Köter), mamara

iltjanekua *Daumen.* ◇ thumb. Ⓛ maramamara

garra nekua = deba nekua *männliche Tier oder Vogel.* ◇ male animal or bird. Ⓛ kuka mamara

nénkakua *sehr hungrig.* ◇ very hungry. Ⓛ ainmatara

nelkunelkuna *gehorsam.* ◇ obedient.

nenkama *verachten (Menschen).* ◇ despise, hold in contempt (humans).

nēla *Entzündung (der Augen).* ◇ inflammation (of eyes). Ⓛ nēla

nelarénama *unten an sitzen.* ◇ sit at the bottom.

nelbanelba *ungehorsam.* ◇ disobedient. Ⓛ tanakutanaku Ⓓ delkijila

nelbéuma *verachten (Rat eines Andern, einen Befehl), nicht gehorsam.* ◇ defy (advice, order), disobedient. Ⓛ tanapungañi Ⓓ delkina

nelkuma *gehorsam, ausführen (den Befehl).* ◇ obey, execute (order). Ⓛ ngalangalariñi

nenka *Diamant Sperling.* ◇ diamond finch. Ⓛ nimanka, tjika Ⓓ tiwilitji, tuwilitja

nenkanenka *eine Grasart mit sehr feinen Halmen und Blüten (Ziergras).* ◇ grass species with very fine blades and blossoms. Ⓛ nenkanenka

nenta *verständlich, offenbar, sichtbar.* ◇ understandable, obvious, visible. Ⓛ nenti Ⓓ miltiri

nentarama *verstehen.* ◇ understand. Ⓛ nentiringañi

nentilama *erklären.* ◇ explain. Ⓛ nentini Ⓓ miltiri ngankana

nentilélama *verständig machen.* ◇ make clear, explain. Ⓛ utitanañi

nentila *großer Frosch (spec.), clay pan-frog (Chiroleptes platycephalus?).* ◇ large frog (species), claypan frog (*Chiroleptes platycephalus*?). Ⓛ anintili

nentala *unwillig, keine Lust haben.* ◇ unwilling, have no desire. Ⓛ tomati

nentalerama *unwillig werden.* ◇ grow reluctant.

nēra *Fieber.* ◇ fever.

nērka *das Junge (von Tieren).* ◇ young animal. Ⓛ wimma Ⓓ kuparu

nērkama *a) sich freuen (über ein Geschenk, über die Ankunft eines Freundes; b) wedeln mit dem Schwanz (Hund).* ◇ a) be pleased (about a present or the arrival of a friend); b) wag tail (dog). Ⓛ unbaringañi, wollarariñi Ⓓ mankina, wondiwondina

nėrama *huren (Vater mit seiner Tochter).* ◇ incest (father with his daughter). Ⓛ murañi

nēria *Mann (dessen Körper sich auf der Brust mit langem Haar bedeckt).* ◇ man (whose chest is becoming hairy). Ⓛ murpu

nérarara *Vogel (spec.)* ◇ bird (species). Ⓛ nerarari

nerkunjakana *Kälter (n).* ◇ [meaning not clear].

nerkuma *ausdrücken, auspressen (Saft).* ◇ squeeze out (juice). Ⓛ tulkuni, tuniñi Ⓓ jikana

neragata *offenbar, ersichtlich, erkennend.* ◇ clearly. Ⓛ ekuntari

nerra *angesammeltes Wasser im Felsen.* ◇ water collected in rockhole. Ⓛ wakula

nerra *Schwiegertochter (F), Schwiegermutter, Mutter des Mannes.* ◇ daughter-in-law (W), mother-in-law, mother of husband. Ⓛ nganari

nerra *Mannes Mutter ♀, Sohns Frau ♀, Schwesters Sohns Frau ♀, Mannes Bruders Sohns Frau.* ◇ husband's mother, son's wife, sister's son's wife, husband's brother's son's wife. Ⓛ ngunari

nerratja *eigene Schwiegermutter ♀, eigene Schwiegertochter.* ◇ own mother-in-law, own daughter-in-law. Ⓛ ngunarina

nerrukua *Schwiegermutter (= Tochter), eines Anderen.* ◇ mother-in-law (= daughter) of someone else. Ⓛ ngunarina

nerroa *Vogel spec.* ◇ bird species. Ⓛ nēro

nētanéta *reich, Überfluß haben.* ◇ rich, have an abundance. Ⓛ unetuneta

neulurra *blutige Maul (des Hundes).* ◇ bloody muzzle (of a dog). Ⓛ úrkilkúrkilka

neulbuta *sehr schlecht, sehr böse, sehr krank.* ◇ very bad, very wicked, very sick. Ⓛ urubúta

nga *du.* ◇ you. Ⓛ nuntu

nĕrara *Samenstrang (Funiculus spermat.)* ◇ funiculus spermatozoon. Ⓛ injíriri

ngabitjauma *umwenden (z.B. Fleisch).* ◇ turn over (e.g. meat). Ⓛ kambakutiwoniñi

ngaiïntalama *entrinnen.* ◇ escape.

ngaiamia *sehr hungrig.* ◇ very hungry. Ⓛ ainmapála

ngaiala *hungrig.* ◇ hungry. Ⓛ ainma Ⓓ mauali

ngaiïka-búta *sehr hungrig.* ◇ very hungry. Ⓛ ainmatara (*Geheimsprache*)

ngalkinja *das Los.* ◇ lot, fate.

ngalkitjala wuma *losen, das Los werfen.* ◇ draw.

ngaljakatara *sehr kleiner Same.* ◇ very small seed.

ngalakana *Beispiel, Gleichnis, Exempel, Vorbild.* ◇ example, parable.

ngákilkiùma *widersprechen.* ◇ contradict. Ⓛ tanapungañi Ⓓ tjakakana

ngakurakitjala (von ngama) *nach circa 5 Tagen.* ◇ after about 5 days. Ⓛ angapalumbakita

ngakuralaka (von ngama) *nach circa 6 Tagen.* ◇ after about 6 days. Ⓛ angapalumbakita

 For the modern spellings of these words, see the dictionaries and sources in reference list.

ngalangala *Rachen.* ◇ throat. Ⓛ ngotulngotula

ngalangalatnalbuma *hin und her bewegen (Schwanz), wedeln.* ◇ move from side to side (tail), wag. Ⓛ pirtjipirtjirariñi

ngala *Heiratsklasse.* ◇ marriage class, subsection, skin name. Ⓛ Nangala ♀, Tangala ♂

ngalabuma *mit sich nehmen/tragen (Waffen etc.)* ◇ take (weapons etc.) Ⓛ katiánañi

ngalalbuma *umhertragen, mitnehmen (bei der Rückkehr).* ◇ carry around, take along (on return). Ⓛ kulbajennañi

ngálalama *etwas (im Maul tragen) gehen (Hund); z.B. ein Stück Fleisch im Maul haben.* ◇ walk and carry something (dog walking and carrying something in mouth); e.g. have a piece of meat in mouth. Ⓛ katiratalkañi Ⓓ wijiwijibaterina

ngalama *zwinkern (mit den Augen), bewegen (Zweige im Winde).* ◇ wink (with eyes), move (branches in wind). Ⓛ juriñi Ⓓ wijiwijirina, (milki terkibana)

ngalalarulanama *hin und her bewegen.* ◇ move back and forth. Ⓛ pirtjirawonnañi

ngalanbuntuma *aufstehen (um weiter zu gehen).* ◇ get up (to move on), set out. Ⓛ jurikatiñi

ngalinka *eßbare Beeren.* ◇ edible berries. Ⓛ angilinki

ngálbangalaláma *dupl. aufstehen (um weiter zu gehen).* ◇ (reduplication) get up (to move on). Ⓛ jurijuririjennañi Ⓓ wijawijabaterina

ngalilbilba *Moskito (spec.)* ◇ mosquito (species). Ⓛ ngaliïlbilbi

ngáljawaljaúa *(weiche Sand) in der Creek.* ◇ (soft sand) in creek. Ⓛ karu tula

ngaljera *Gras (spec.) mit rötlichem Samen und einseitigen, weizenartigen Halmen.* ◇ grass (species) with reddish seeds and one-sided wheat-like blades. Ⓛ angiljiri

ngalelama *abschütteln (Früchte vom Baum).* ◇ shake off (fruit from a tree). Ⓛ pinpintipungañi

ntēmba *Baum, aus dessen weichen Holz Schilde gemacht werden.* ◇ tree (shields are made from its soft wood). Ⓛ angalta Ⓓ mulja

ngaltangalta *Blume mit gelben, löwenzahn artigen Blüten.* ◇ flower with yellow dandelion-like blossoms. Ⓓ punku

ngalta *ein Busch (Wasser in Wurzeln).* ◇ bush (stores water in its roots). Ⓛ angiltji

ngama *tragen.* ◇ carry; take. Ⓛ katiñi Ⓓ mandrana

ngalalbuma *mitnehmen (bei der Rückkehr).* ◇ carry, take along (on return). Ⓛ kulbajennañi

ilbarilbara ngama *am Rande (fassend) tragen.* ◇ carry at edges. Ⓛ waralwaralkatiñi Ⓓ tikalkana?

ngalabuma *mit sich nehmen (Waffen etc.)* ◇ take with, along (weapons etc.) Ⓛ katiánañi

iltjingiltjala ngama *mit (auf) den Händen tragen.* ◇ carry with (on) hands. Ⓛ marangurkunka katiñi Ⓓ munamana?

ngalangalélama *fortwährend bewegen (trs.)* ◇ move constantly (transitive).

indalba ngama *über der Schulter hängend [etwas] tragen.* ◇ carry something over shoulder. Ⓛ alinji katiñi Ⓓ wilimana

ngamanga *geduldig, gelassen (im Leiden), langmutig.* ◇ patient, composed (in suffering), silent, forbearing (in sorrow).

ngaléangála *Körner, Weizen (n).* ◇ grain, wheat.

kantala ngama *auf dem Kopf tragen.* ◇ carry on head. Ⓛ akantanka katiñi Ⓓ waltana

maltala ngama *unter dem Arm tragen, auf der Hüfte tragen (kleine Kinder).* ◇ carry under arm, carry on hip (small child). Ⓛ totunka katiñi Ⓓ mandrana

tangantangantala ngama *über einen Stecken etwas tragen (2 Männer).* ◇ carry something over a stick (two men). Ⓛ katatjititjitinka katiñi Ⓓ mandrana

tjibala ngama *auf der Hüfte tragen.* ◇ carry on hip. Ⓛ nanpanka katiñi Ⓓ munkana

ulkwalala (ulkálala) ngama *auf der Schulter tragen.* ◇ carry on shoulder. Ⓛ ulkalinka katiñi Ⓓ mandrana

unjila ngama *auf dem Hals reiten lassen (Kinder), auf dem Nacken tragen.* ◇ carry on neck. Ⓛ pininka katiñi Ⓓ mandrana

ngama *(in Zusammensetzungen) weiter entfernt.* ◇ (in compounds) further away. Ⓛ ngama

ngama nguruka *vor circa 3 Tagen.* ◇ about 3 days ago. Ⓛ ngama mungatu

ngama untuara *vor circa 4 Tagen.* ◇ about 4 days ago. Ⓛ ngama wirili

ngama untuarakala *vor circa 5 Tagen.* ◇ about 5 days ago. Ⓛ ngama wirilikata

ngama untuarulkura *vor circa 6 Tagen.* ◇ about 6 days ago. Ⓛ ngama wirilita

ngama ingunta *nach circa 3 Tagen.* ◇ about 3 days ago. Ⓛ ngama mungatara

ngamara *Fasan.* ◇ pheasant. Ⓛ wontu

ngamboba *5 Kind einer Familie von 8 Kindern.* ◇ fifth child in a family of eight children. Ⓛ ngurutita

ngambobibera *6 Kind einer Familie von 8 Kindern.* ◇ sixth child in family of eight children. Ⓛ mangururita

ngambakala *ewig.* ◇ eternal, everlasting. Carl Strehlow writes that 'The Aranda language has four words to describe eternal = ngambakala, ngambintja, ngamitjina, and ngarra' (Strehlow 1907: 1). Ⓛ tukurita Ⓓ ngurali

ngapuntara *weiter, noch mehr (sprechen).* ◇ further, even more (speak).

ngambintja, ngambitja *ewig.* ◇ eternal, for ever. Ⓛ tukurita Ⓓ ngurali

ngamitjina *ewig.* ◇ eternal. Ⓛ tukurita Ⓓ ngurangura

ngama *Du selbst.* ◇ yourself. Ⓛ nuntu

ngamilai *Du selbst sagen.* ◇ say it yourself. Ⓛ nuntuku wottalai!

ngamurkabai *tu es selber.* ◇ do it yourself. Ⓛ nuntuku manapirtji

nguamanna, ngamina *große jelka-Knollen.* ◇ large jelka bulbs, place in Palm Valley (Strehlow 1907: 87). Ⓛ ungamini

ngamiuma *hinbreiten (z.B. ein Kleid).* ◇ spread out (e.g. dress).

nganalélama *hin und her bewegen, schütteln.* ◇ move back and forth, shake. Ⓛ juritjingani Ⓓ wijawijabana

ngánama *ausgraben (Steine).* ◇ dig out (stones). Ⓛ ngatini

ngañka *Krähe, Rabe.* ◇ crow, raven. Ⓛ kanka Ⓓ kaualka

ngapuntara *noch mehr (sagen).* ◇ (say) more.

ngankara *Zauberdoctor, Zaubersteine.* ◇ medicine man, magic stones; healer, witch doctor. Ⓛ ngankari Ⓓ kunki

ngankariwuma *den Zauber entfernen vom Kranken.* ◇ remove magic, spell (from a sick person). Ⓛ ngankariwonniñi

ngarangara *Narr, Tor.* ◇ fool.

ngankariwuma *zaubern.* ◇ make magic. Ⓛ ngankariwoniñi, ngankarinañi

nantala tjunama *Luftspiegelung.* ◇ mirage.

nganta *Luftspiegelung, Fata Morgana.* ◇ mirage, fata morgana. Ⓛ anganta, niñga Ⓓ nili

nganta *Raupe, die Zucker auf die Blätter legt.* ◇ caterpillar that deposits sugar on leaves. Ⓛ anganta

ngantinganta *lange Beine (Vögel).* ◇ long legs (birds). Ⓛ wirunkurunku

nganta *eine Gras-Unterlage auf dem Kopf.* ◇ grass pad for head. Ⓛ akantakanta

ngantja *in der Erde verborgen, unterirdisch.* ◇ hidden in the ground, subterranean, underground. Ⓛ angintji

kwatja ngantja *das in der Erde verborgene Wasser, Quellwasser, soakage.* ◇ hidden underground water, spring water, soakage; rockhole. Ⓛ kapi angintji Ⓓ ngapa dirtji

rella ngantja *die in der Erde lebenden Menschen.* ◇ people living underground (see Strehlow 1907: 31–32). Ⓛ matu nguana

nganuna *wir (incl.)* ◇ we (inclusive). Ⓛ nuntugánana, nurangánana

ngapa *schwarze Krähe, Rabe.* ◇ black crow, raven. Ⓛ tankilka, kanka Ⓓ kaualka

takula *dunkle Muschel.* ◇ dark mussel. Ⓛ ngapulupula Ⓓ kuri

ngara *mal.* ◇ once, for example. Ⓛ kata
nintangara *einmal.* ◇ once. Ⓛ kutukata
ngarbeuma *trs. verändern, anders machen.* ◇ (transitive) change, alter.
ngaraka *Ranke mit bohnenartigen Schoten, die innen eine Blume enthalten (eßbar).* ◇ vine with bean-like pods containing blossoms (edible). Ⓛ mangaraka
ngarbeulama *sich verändern, anders werden, sich verstellen (Gesicht, Gestalt).* ◇ change (reflexive), become different, disguise (face, shape).
ngároa *tiefes Wasserloch, Brunnen.* ◇ deep waterhole, well. Ⓛ angaròu Ⓓ ngapapitjeri, ngapatjilli
ngarambinja *billig (nicht viel kostend).* ◇ cheap (not expensive).
ngatota *Panzer des Kriegers.* ◇ armour of warrior.
ngerarelama *sich spiegeln.* ◇ reflect.
ngerarélana *der Spiegel.* ◇ mirror.
nuna ngerarelanala tjorerelama *wir besehen uns im Spiegel.* ◇ we look at ourselves in the mirror.
ngēna *sehr still (leiden), lautlos (leiden), stoisch.* ◇ very quiet (suffer), silent (suffer), stoic. Ⓛ kaiuwara
ngarra *Bäume, Felsen, Wasserlöcher etc., wo sich die ratapa aufhalten, = ewigen (kutata tnaka).* ◇ trees, rocks, waterholes etc., where ratapa dwell = eternal ones (kutata tnaka). Ⓛ angarra
ngeljikara; *z.B.* aldolataka ngeljikara antakarulkura *zwischen (zwei Richtungen); nach Südwesten.* ◇ between (two directions), e.g. in between the west and the south, i.e. south-west. Ⓛ karbakarba; wilura-ralku karbakarba ulbaiïra nguanba
ngāta; unta ngatambenja pitjai *diesseits; du etwas weiter hierher kommen, diesseits.* ◇ this side. Ⓛ kalkuni
ngatambenja *andere Seite.* ◇ other side. Ⓛ kalkuniwana
ngeljekatara *Fruchtansatz (Fruchtansätze der Feigen) [unclear].* ◇ fruit buds; name of a Loritja ancestor (Strehlow 1920: 24). Ⓛ kauatjipa
ngebeuma *aussuchen, austeilen, sortieren.* ◇ select, distribute, sort. Ⓛ paranangañi
ngēna *starr (sich nicht rühren).* ◇ rigid, stiff (not moving). Ⓛ kaiuwara
ngalawutjawutjerama *herbeilaufen, schnell herankommen.* ◇ come fast. Ⓛ juriwontawóntani
ngĕra *postp. ähnlich, gleich, wie, in Gestalt.* ◇ (postposition) similar, like (in form). Ⓛ nguanba Ⓓ jeribaka
katjia ngĕra *wie ein Kind.* ◇ like a child. Ⓛ pipiri nguanba
ngarangara, ngerrangerra *unsinnig, verrückt.* ◇ absurd, crazy. Ⓛ wapawapa
tjina; nananga tjina; worra nana knarailkura *oder* **knara nananga tjina** *comp. als.* ◇ as. Ⓛ nguru; nangata nguru
ngetjilbara *Eidechse (spec.)* ◇ lizard (species). Ⓛ kinkilbari
ngetjima *bringen.* ◇ bring. Ⓛ ngalakatiñi Ⓓ padakana
ngetjalbuma *zurückbringen.* ◇ bring back. Ⓛ ngalakulbaïnañi Ⓓ padakana tikana
relara ngetjima *herbeiführen.* ◇ lead to, bring. Ⓛ atakatini
ngelkniuma *rechnen als etwas; c. genit.* ◇ count as something; *c. genit.*
ngetnima, ngetnama *in den Lagerplatz tragen.* ◇ carry into camp. Ⓛ kulbaianañi
ngilaka *(Vater und Sohn incl.), Mann und Frau (incl.)* ◇ (father and son incl.), husband and wife (incl.) Ⓛ nuntungalinba
ngilanta *wir beide (d.h. du und ich).* ◇ the two of us (i.e. you and I). Ⓛ nuntungalintu
ngilina *2 Brüder (inclus.)* ◇ two brothers (inclusive). Ⓛ nuntungali Ⓓ ngaldra
ngōta *spärlich.* ◇ sparse.
ñima *beschlafen (geschlechtlich).* ◇ intercourse. Ⓛ murañi
ñirima *dual. treten (Vögel), begatten.* ◇ mate. Ⓛ murarapungañi
ngualka [Southern dialect] *cf.* **kurkna** *ästig, dicht belaubt.* ◇ densely covered with leaves. Ⓛ bulkuna

ngotjangotja *Pflanzenkost.* ◇ plant food. Ⓛ mutimuta

nguanga *freundlich, ruhig, zahm.* ◇ friendly, calm, tame. Ⓛ āla Ⓓ murlali, manju

nguakara *Eidechse (spec.)* ◇ lizard (species). Ⓛ ungakari

nguanta *vermögend, fähig.* ◇ capable. Ⓛ unba

ngōta *mehrere (6–9).* ◇ several. Ⓛ ánguta

nguénba [Southern dialect] *morgen.* ◇ tomorrow. Ⓛ mungatara

nguenbárbuna [Southern dialect] *übermorgen.* ◇ the day after tomorrow. Ⓛ mungatarakutaba

ngulangula *lau.* ◇ mild.

ngula *kühl, angenehm, heil.* ◇ cool, pleasant. Ⓛ warri Ⓓ malti

ngulerama *kühl werden.* ◇ cool down. Ⓛ warriringañi Ⓓ maltirina

ngulilama *kühl machen (Fleisch).* ◇ make cool (meat). Ⓛ warrini

ngulbatuma *vor dem Loch liegen (Schlange) um sich zu sonnen.* ◇ to lie in front of a burrow (snake) to warm up. Ⓛ tjilbatjilbani

ngūmba *Hügel.* ◇ hill. Ⓛ tulalu

ngulunba *das schöne Geschlecht (Mädchen und Frauen).* ◇ the fair sex (girls and women). Ⓛ ngulunba

nguna? *wer?* ◇ who? Ⓛ nganana? Ⓓ worra, worrana

ngula *wer (in trans. Sätzen).* ◇ who (in transitive sentences). Ⓛ nganalu? Ⓓ warle

ngunatara? *welche beiden? dual.* ◇ which two? Ⓛ ngananakutara

ngunankana? *wer, welche (pl.)* ◇ who, which ones (plural) Ⓛ ngananatuta

ngunirbera? *wer, welche (pl.)* ◇ who, which ones (plural) Ⓛ ngananamurka

nguntarakitjala (von ingunta) *nach circa 4 Tagen.* ◇ after about 4 days. Ⓛ unguntarakita

ngúrangura; (aus ingua + aragula) *gegen Abend, wenn die Sonne untergeht; (vor der Nacht).* ◇ towards evening, when the sun goes down; (before nightfall). Ⓛ mungartji

nguranguerelakalerama *gegen Abend, untergehen.* ◇ towards evening, at sunset, sink, go under. Ⓛ mungartjimungartji = rekula okalingañi

ngurbmalélama *überlegen, erwägen.* ◇ think about, consider. Ⓛ munturmunturmanañi

nguruka (von ingua+ruka=ruga=vorher) *gestern.* ◇ yesterday, before. Ⓛ mungatu Ⓓ woldrawirdi

ngurukarbuna *vorgestern.* ◇ the day before yesterday. Ⓛ mungatu kutuba Ⓓ woldrawirdi nguru

ngurukakuia *vorgestern.* ◇ the day before yesterday. Ⓛ mungatu kutubaka Ⓓ woldrawirdi nguru

ngurukulkura *vor mehreren Tagen.* ◇ several days ago. Ⓛ mungatu nguanba

ngurukawara *vor einigen Tagen.* ◇ some days ago. Ⓛ mungatu wiakutu

ngutjika *eine Pflanze mit kleinen fleischenen Blättern, auf Bergen wachsen (Ijaua ähnlich).* ◇ plant with small fleshy leaves that grows on mountains (similar to Ijaua). Ⓛ ungutjiki

nuturatura *sehr niedrig (Strauch z.B.)* ◇ very low (e.g. bush). Ⓛ kalkaturu

nia *Schweiß.* ◇ sweat. Ⓛ akuri Ⓓ kangu

nilanilauna *Hurer, Ehebrecher.* ◇ whorer, adulterer. Ⓓ nilanila (*Luftspiegelung*)

nilauma *huren, verbotenen Umgang mit einem Weibe aus der richtigen Klasse haben.* ◇ have forbidden intercourse with a woman of the right marriage class. Ⓛ murara talkani

nilalbuma *wiederholten, verbotenen Umgang mit einem Weibe aus der richtigen Klasse haben.* ◇ repeated forbidden intercourse with a woman from the correct marriage class or subsection. Ⓛ murara kulbañi

nilinilauma *wiederholt mit ein und demselben Weibe Umgang haben.* ◇ repeatedly have intercourse with the same woman. Ⓛ muramarani

nilkna *heimlich.* ◇ secretly. Ⓛ ngurtu, kanka, mulata Ⓓ kurukuru

nilknala inama *heimlich nehmen, stehlen.* ◇ take secretly, steal. Ⓛ mulatanka manjini Ⓓ kurieli manina

nilknamba *Dieb.* ◇ thief. Ⓛ kankala Ⓓ kurikantji

nilknérama *verheimlichen, heimlich halten, verschwiegen.* ◇ conceal, keep secret, hide. Ⓛ ngurturingañi

nilknalintalélama *[heimlich niederlegen, machen] huren.* ◇ (secretly lie down) to have intercourse with someone you are not married to. Ⓛ kankanku ngariljennañi Ⓓ kurirpi ngamana (heimlich sitzen)

niltja = **iningukua** *der Schutzgeist.* ◇ spirit that looks after his or her human, spirit double; today these spirits are called pmarakutata (pmara meaning 'place, country, home', kutata meaning 'always'), spelled in Carl Strehlow's spelling 'tmara kutata'. Ⓛ kutubara

ñima *(beschlafen).* ◇ have intercourse. Ⓛ (tuka) murañi

ñirima *sich paaren (Vögel).* ◇ mate (birds). Ⓛ murarapungañi

nimba *Bild, Bildsäule, Gestalt.* ◇ picture, bust, gestalt, shape or form. Ⓛ nguana

relaka nimba *Stein, der die Gestalt eines Menschen hat.* ◇ stone or boulder that has the shape of a human. Ⓛ matunguana

iliaka nimba *Emu-Gestalt.* ◇ emu shape. Ⓛ kalaia nguana

nimbutnuma *arbeiten, bauen, herstellen, loosen.* ◇ work, build, make. Ⓛ aljikirináñi

nimurkurka *feuchte Erde (in Mäuselöchern).* ◇ damp soil (in mouse holes). Ⓛ muntuna

ninanga *Vater und sein Kind.* ◇ father and his child; father(s) and child(ren); a group of two or more people, one of whom is father to the other(s); father(s) and their child(ren) (of a particular subsection pair); a group of people in a ninanga relationship who are traditional owners of a country or estate (a traditional local group country); patricouple. Ⓛ mamarara

ninangananga *Vater und seine 2 Kinder.* ◇ father and his two children. Ⓛ mamararawaritji

ninangatua *Vater und seine 3 Kinder.* ◇ father and his three children. Ⓛ mamararamurka

ningalarama *dulden (ein Leiden).* ◇ endure, suffer (pain).

ningalarenama *aushalten (ein Leiden).* ◇ stand, bear (pain).

ningalauma *willig hinnehmen, erleiden, ertragen (Schmerzen etc.)* ◇ willing to suffer, endure (pain etc.) Ⓛ urukuliñi Ⓓ ketjaketjana

ninbinjerkama *ehren, hochhalten.* ◇ honour.

ningalarelbarenama *zurücklassen, nicht mitnehmen (z.B. ein Kind, das gern mitgehen möchte).* ◇ leave behind, not take along (e.g. a child, who would have liked to join). Ⓛ tulbatunañi

ninganinga *heimtükisch, heimlich [Anspielung auf Ningara? unclear].* ◇ treacherous, secret. Ⓛ kajuwara Ⓓ ngaruni

ninjalkna *seßhaft, nicht umherstreunend.* ◇ settled, not roaming around. Ⓛ wanabakuru

ninjira *Anführer der Bienen ('Königin' der Bienen).* ◇ queen bee; native bee. Ⓛ anjínjiri

ninjerbminjera *Brustbein.* ◇ sternum. Ⓛ mitjermitjera

ninjalapalapalla *Vogel, rote Brust, rötliche Federn.* ◇ bird, red chest, reddish feathers. Ⓛ miteïtú

aninjirkni *Schwalbenähnlicher Vogel.* ◇ swallow-like bird. Ⓛ ninjirkna

ninkabuta *mit weißer Farbe beschmiert zum Zeichen der Trauer (Frauen).* ◇ smeared with white paint (sign of mourning). Ⓛ mar̂alaringu

ninkara *leer (von Häusern), leer (d.h. ohne Früchte).* ◇ empty (houses), empty (i.e. without fruit).

ninkarauma *geheim halten (z.B. heilige Lieder).* ◇ keep secret. Ⓛ kutitunañi Ⓓ kurukurumalkana

ninkararinja *geheim gehalten, Geheimis.* ◇ kept secret, secret. Ⓛ jerkata

nintakaninta *einer nach dem andern.* ◇ one after the other.

njambala rename; njambala reninja *Versammlung abhalten; Ratsversammlung.* ◇ hold a meeting; counsel.

nitjigunja *abwesend.* ◇ absent.

ninkia *eigensinnig, widerspenstig, verschlossen, lieblos.* ◇ wilful, obstinate, reserved, unkind. Ⓛ tomati

ninkarerama *eigensinnig sein, nicht Folge leisten (den Befehlen oder Wünschen).* ◇ obstinent, not obey. Ⓛ jerkajerkaringani

nirka = **nērka** *ein Kleines, Junges (von Tieren).* ◇ young animal. Ⓛ wimma

nirilauma *Frau eines andern Mannes.* ◇ with wife of another man. Ⓛ muraratalkañi

ninta *eins, einer.* ◇ one. Ⓛ kutu Ⓓ kulno

nintamaninta *einzeln, einer um dem andern.* ◇ single, one after the other. Ⓛ kututukututu

nintarinjagata *mit nur einem Begleiter.* ◇ with only one companion. Ⓛ kútuntáritara

nintaranga, nintangara *einmal.* ◇ once. Ⓛ kutukata, kutukata

nintenta *allein.* ◇ alone. Ⓛ kututa Ⓓ kulnolu

nintarinji *allein, einsam.* ◇ alone, lonely. Ⓛ kutunta

nintakanintélama *zerstreuen, auseinandersprengen.* ◇ scatter, disperse. Ⓛ kututukututanañi

nintarabanantema *inner Eine.* ◇ inner one. Ⓛ kutubanabaka

nintérama *eins werden, zusammentreffen.* ◇ unite, join. Ⓛ kuturingañi

ninta arbuna *eine andere.* ◇ another one (female). Ⓛ kutukutuba

ninteritjitnénama *einholen (beim Laufen).* ◇ catch up (when running). Ⓛ kutuluriñitalkala

nintakaia *einziggeborener.* ◇ only born. Ⓛ kutukuru Ⓓ kunakulno

nintja *Akacienschoten.* ◇ acacia pods. Ⓛ worbma, apúlu

nitakatáka *Schlüsselbein.* ◇ collarbone. Ⓛ ngantili

njantinjanta *hoch, schlank.* ◇ tall, slim. Ⓛ wirínkuru

nitia *junger, unverheirateter Mann, nach Inkura-Aufführung.* ◇ young, unmarried man after ceremony. Ⓛ nitaiï

nitiera *sehr viele.* ◇ very many. Ⓛ nitaiïra

nitjinjima *hinaufklettern (auf einen Baum).* ◇ climb up (on a tree). Ⓛ ninarakalbañi Ⓓ katina

njaia *abgefallene (Früchte).* ◇ fallen (fruit). Ⓛ intaiï

njaialutnuma *schnauben (Pferde).* ◇ snort (horse). Ⓛ noaltawarkiñi

njaiïtnima *abfallen (Früchte v. Baum).* ◇ fall off (fruit from tree). Ⓛ intaiïpatangarañi

njatnaúma *sich niederlassen (zum huren).* ◇ settle down (to have intercourse with forbidden person). Ⓛ muntupungañi

njakeérama *beweinen, beklagen.* ◇ weep or cry over, lament. Ⓛ urkantjiriñi

njatjaurkérama *hervortreten (Augen vor Zorn oder vor Begierde nach Fleisch).* ◇ bulge (eyes when angry or from desire for meat). Ⓛ kuruturintalkañi

njakeérala nama *beklagen.* ◇ lament. Ⓛ urkantjurikaniñi

ñamakurka *der saftige, fettige Platz.* ◇ lush, rich spot. Ⓛ muntuna

namatuáta *feuchte Erde.* ◇ damp soil. Ⓛ tjipiïntiñi

njarama *cf.* **ntjarama** *schnarchen.* ◇ to snore. Ⓛ ngurbmanani

njārtna (inārtna) *Schwalbe, Flügel schwarz, Bauch weiß.* ◇ swallow, wings black, belly white. Ⓛ ininjirkni, inartiri

njarkuma *verbieten.* ◇ prohibit. Ⓛ markuñi

njoa *die Seite (des Flusses).* ◇ side (of river).

njoatara *auf beiden Seiten (des Flusses).* ◇ on both sides (of the river).

náltjamànna *rote (Früchte).* ◇ red (fruit). Ⓛ ngurkalngurkala

 For the modern spellings of these words, see the dictionaries and sources in reference list.

ntjaua *Krume (Brot), Klumpen (Blut).* ◇ crumb (bread), clot (blood). Ⓛ lungu Ⓓ pandra (*gestandene Blut*)

ntjaua *die rot angestrichene (Kemba) Blüte mit denen die Karakara geschmückt wird.* ◇ red blossom to decorate a karakara-trumpet. Ⓛ injaua

njerama, ntjerama *den Boden fegen (Zweig).* ◇ sweep floor (with branches). Ⓛ untuni

njiljarka *Kneuel, um das das eigene Haar gewunden wird.* ◇ ball used to tie one's hair around. Ⓛ intjiljirki

njirranga *Vogel, klein, schwarz, rote Brust.* ◇ bird, small, black, red chest. Ⓛ intjiringi

njilkilkila *zischend (von jungen Vögeln).* ◇ hiss (young birds). Ⓛ ngenmanañi

ntjilkiïlkibaánkama *zischen (wie ganz kleine Vögel).* ◇ hiss (like very young birds). Ⓛ ngēnngēnmanañi

njitta [Southern dialect] *cf.* **injita** *Flamme.* ◇ flame. Ⓛ ti

njóanjoa *böse Geister.* ◇ bad spirits. Ⓛ njoïnjoï

njiltja *der Stamm der agia-Bäume.* ◇ trunk of agia tree. Ⓛ kauartji

njōka *selbstsüchtig.* ◇ selfish, egotistic. Ⓛ mañga

njokala ilkuma *alles allein verzehren.* ◇ consume everything alone. Ⓛ manganka ngalkuñi

ñórerama *bewundern (einen Bau, eine Person), sich wundern, sich verwundern.* ◇ admire (a construction, a person), be astonished. Ⓛ nerariñi

njilkama *zischen (wie ein Bandikut = tnunka).* ◇ hiss (like a bandicoot). Ⓛ tenmanañi

ntjualelama? (ntjuma = ?), njualinjuala *über, übertreffend.* ◇ above, surpassing. ('?' added by CS)

njualélama *verfehlen (Ziel), nicht treffen, ungerecht beschuldigen, einen überholen (beim Laufen).* ◇ miss (target), accuse wrongly, overtake someone (running). Ⓛ malamalani

njualelalama *die Schuld von sich wälzen.* ◇ shift blame. Ⓛ palurunku malamalani

njumataka *das hintere (Zimmer), Hinterteil (von Raum), das Innere (Zimmer).* ◇ back (room), back part (of a space).

njualelanáma *vorbeilaufen (einem andern) vor demselben das Ziel erreichen, übertreffen, ungerecht beschuldigt.* ◇ overtake and reach the finish first, surpass, unjustly accused. Ⓛ mamalamalani

njuminjuma *einer hinter – andern (gehend).* ◇ one behind the other (walk). Ⓛ tangatanga

njuma *trinken, rauchen (Pfeife).* ◇ drink, smoke (pipe). Ⓛ tjikiñi, matjikiñi Ⓓ tapana

njunjingambura *Säufer.* ◇ drunk. Ⓛ tjikinmatuta

njurula *durstig.* ◇ thirsty. Ⓛ nantunka

njuruméa *Trank.* ◇ drink. Ⓛ nantupala

njumerererama *empfangen (geschlechtlich).* ◇ conceive (sexually). Ⓛ tangarekurbariñi

njurala nama *sehr durstig sein (auf der Reise).* ◇ very thirsty (on journey). Ⓛ nantunka ninañi Ⓓ manjarina

nkalbankétnama *wiederholt sagen, lesen.* ◇ say repeatedly, read. Ⓛ mauankara kulbánañi

njutupa *Opossum Magen.* ◇ possum stomach. Ⓛ waiutu ituntu

kanjántua *Mittags-Regen (Gewitter Regen).* ◇ midday rain (storm rain). Ⓛ parpawaritji, parpakaiakaiïta

njukelinja *der ältere Bruder, die ältere Schwester.* ◇ older brother, older sister. Ⓛ pinita

njukelerinja *die älteren Geschwister.* ◇ older siblings. Ⓛ pinirapúnkulapúngata

njuleninja *der jüngerer Bruder, die jüngere Schwester.* ◇ younger brother, younger sister. Ⓛ pininta

njulenerinja *die jüngeren Geschwister.* ◇ younger siblings. Ⓛ punirapunguta

njukelarinja *das höchste Stockwerk (n).* ◇ highest level.

(a)nkánkalálbuma *nachsprechen, nachsagen.* ◇ repeat (something someone has said). Ⓛ wottawottarakulbánañi

(a)nkánkawórrama *beratschlagen (die Versammlung).* ◇ discuss (the assembly). Ⓛ pinjipinjirapungañi Ⓓ warawarapana? manumanungana?

(a)nḱankaúlama *bitten, betteln.* ◇ ask, beg. Ⓛ wonkawonkiñi Ⓓ kaukau wapana

nkarba *ein anderer.* ◇ another one. Ⓛ kalki Ⓓ worku? pilki?

nkarindana *Wasservogel (spec.)* ◇ waterbird (species). Ⓛ unkarindini

(a)nkarankara [Southern dialect] *Strauch (spec.)* ◇ shrub (species). Ⓛ ankarankari

nkátintjara *schrecklich.* ◇ terrible.

nkarkna *eifrig, schnell, aufgeregt.* ◇ eager, quick, excited. Ⓛ ngaru

nkarknérama *aufgeregt werden.* ◇ get excited. Ⓛ ngaruringañi Ⓓ patijiritjina

nkarknilama *(trs.) aufregen.* ◇ (transitive) excite, stir up. Ⓛ ngaruni Ⓓ patijiritjibana

(a)nkáuerama *beraten, besprechen.* ◇ advise, discuss. Ⓛ aiṙatapirapungañi

(a)nkáuma *sich erkundigen (ob eine mit gehen will).* ◇ inquire (if someone wants to go along). Ⓛ aiṙatapini

(a)nkauulama *einem ankündigen, daß man zu ihm kommen will, seinen Besuch in Aussicht stellen.* ◇ announce to someone, that one would like to come, announce a possible visit. Ⓛ wonkarakulbañi Ⓓ tjampatjampana

nkauurbma *sehr schnell (kommen zum Unterricht).* ◇ very quick (come to instruction). Ⓛ ngaruta

ankéankéa *verlangend (nach Speise), bittend (um Brot).* ◇ demanding (food), asking (for bread). Ⓛ ngatjingatji

(a)nkéabana *Gabe.* ◇ gift. Ⓛ ngatjita

nkēbara *Cormoran (Graculus Carbo).* ◇ cormorant (*Phalacrocorax carbo*) (Pizzey and Knight 2007). Ⓛ ankibara Ⓓ malura

(a)nkélalanama *wartend (auf die Gabe) dastehen.* ◇ stand waiting (for a gift). Ⓛ etinka

nkenkala *ähnlich.* ◇ similar. Ⓛ aranka

nkēra *Ufer, Rand.* ◇ shore, bank, edge. Ⓛ ngankeri Ⓓ dirkala

nkēla, nkēlala *am Ufer, neben, daneben.* ◇ at the river bank, beside it. Ⓛ ngaiï, ngaiïnka

nkeramantataka *sich lang hinziehen Ufer.* ◇ a long stretching river bank. Ⓛ ngankeriparapara

nkerarélama *unterwaschen (Ufer).* ◇ washed out, eroded (river or creek bank). Ⓛ narkani

nkintja *Männer (in Zusammensetzungen).* ◇ men (in compounds). Ⓛ ankintji

nkintjibana *unverheiratet, Witwer.* ◇ not married, widower. Ⓛ ankintjita

tmarankintja *Männer-Lagerplatz.* ◇ men's camp. Ⓛ ngurankintji

nkintjirinja *ein Bewohner des tmarankintja.* ◇ resident of men's camp; single man. Ⓛ ankintjingurara

nkintjalerama *Witwer.* ◇ widower. Ⓛ ankintjinkariñi

nkólinama *viel geben, reichlich geben.* ◇ give plenty, give ample. Ⓛ junkulu patañi

(a)nkólera *Fischfett.* ◇ fish fat. Ⓛ unkolari

nkōpia *Termitenhaufen.* ◇ termite mound. Ⓛ akururu

nkuálbila *Fisch mit spitzigen Stacheln (bony-bream).* ◇ fish with spines (bony bream). Ⓛ unkalbili

(u)nkuánkua *freundlich, liebevoll.* ◇ friendly, loving. Ⓛ bokulba

(u)nkuánkua *Midder.* Ⓛ mulkurmulkura

nkura *immerfort (z.B. singen).* ◇ continually (e.g. sing). Ⓛ ratatura

nkurunkura [Southern dialect] *fortwährend, wiederholt (singen).* ◇ continuous, repeatedly (sing). Ⓛ rataturaratatura

nkulba *Tabak (einheimisch).* ◇ tobacco (native). Ⓛ minkula

nkulbinkulba [Southern dialect] *Blume, dessen Blätter dem einheimischen Tabak ähnlich sind.* ◇ flower whose leaves resemble the leaves of native tobacco. Ⓛ kumalta

inkulbinkurilama *sehr erfreut sein (über die Ankunft eines Freundes etc.)* ◇ to be very pleased (about the arrival of a friend etc.) Ⓛ unbaunbaringañi

nkura *die ältere Schwester.* ◇ older sister. Ⓛ kankaru

inkuléa *sehr dunkel, schwarz.* ◇ very dark, black. Ⓛ marukura, jaltapiri

ankúnjera *Holzwurm spec.* ◇ woodworm species. Ⓛ ankunjeri

nkuna *weißer Kakadu mit roter Brust.* ◇ white cockatoo with red chest. Ⓛ kakalala

nkuratja *meine ältere Schwester.* ◇ my older sister.

nkura *die ältere Schwester.* ◇ older sister. Ⓛ kankuruna

nkarbmana *Baum (spec.)* ◇ tree species. Ⓛ ankarbmana

kurbiltja *elsterähnlicher Vogel (spec.)* ◇ bird species. Ⓛ kurbiltji

nkurkuturkuta *alle zusammen.* ◇ all together. Ⓛ apuara

nkúrkna *zerrissen (Boden), voller Risse (Kopf).* ◇ cracked (ground), covered with scratches (head). Ⓛ inkurknu

nkurbmúrbma *vertrocknet, dürr (Sträucher).* ◇ dry (bushes). Ⓛ kirbmurbmu

nkuabara [Southern dialect] *Tanz (vor Einweihungsfeiern aufgeführt).* ◇ dance (performed before initiation ceremonies). Ⓛ inma

nkunaburka *die ganz kleinen (noch weißen) Cikaden.* ◇ very small (still white) cicadas. Ⓛ maliera

nkurananga *die zwei Schwestern (ältere und jüngere).* ◇ two sisters (older and younger). Ⓛ kankurura

nkurintjara *alle (meine) Schwestern.* ◇ all (my) sisters. Ⓛ kankururawaritji

nkunulbunulba rename *aufschlitzen (den Bauch).* ◇ slit open (belly). Ⓛ wartnuni

nkúlknunkuàra iluma *husten.* ◇ cough. Ⓛ kuntalbmanañi

nkurbmunkuara iluma *sich räuspern.* ◇ clear throat. Ⓛ kuntulpungañi, urkalba iluni

nkurbmunkuarérama *sich räuspern.* ◇ clear throat. Ⓛ urkalariñi

noakatuia *Bräutigam.* ◇ bridegroom. Ⓛ kurikatuia

noakama *heiraten.* ◇ marry. Ⓛ kuriwalkuni

noa knara *Fraus ältere Schwester, Manns älterer Bruder.* ◇ wife's older sister, husband's older brother. Ⓛ kuri puntu

nóa *Gemahl, Gatte, Frau, Schwager (Schwesters Mann), Schwägerin (Bruders Frau).* ◇ husband, spouse, wife, brother-in-law (sister's husband), sister-in-law (brother's wife). Ⓛ kuri, minma [Western dialect] Ⓓ noa

- **noa lárra** *Schwägerin, Schwager, (Fraus jüngere Schwester, Manns jüngerer Bruder).* ◇ sister-in-law, brother-in-law. Ⓛ kuri wongu
- **noagata** *ehelich.* ◇ conjugal. Ⓛ kuritara
- **noukua** *Frau (eines Andern).* ◇ wife (of somebody else). Ⓛ kurira
- **noatja** *eigene Frau, eingener Mann.* ◇ own wife, own husband. Ⓛ kurina
- **noataltja** *die rechtmäßige Frau.* ◇ rightful wife. Ⓛ kuriwóltaràra
- **noa eknuma** *heiraten.* ◇ marry. Ⓛ kuri manjini

noankuwonka *Schein, Sonnenschein, Feuerschein.* ◇ shine, sunshine, shine of fire. Ⓛ irtnani

noankuwonkilama *beleuchten (Feuer), bescheinen (Sonne).* ◇ light up (fire), shine on (sun). Ⓛ irtnairtnañi

noarkama *blinken, glühen (Eisen), funkeln (Sterne).* ◇ twinkle, glow (iron), glitter (star). Ⓛ turakambañi Ⓓ makapari (Abendrot), nguramarana (Morgenröte)

nōbma *Pech, das Siegel (n).* ◇ pitch, seal. Ⓛ kiti Ⓓ kandri

- **nobmalélama** *verpichen.* ◇ pitch over. Ⓛ kitinkánañi, kitini

nopana *'der immer bleibt' Sklave.* ◇ 'one who always remains' a slave.

nombía *widerspenstig, ungehorsam.* ◇ rebellious, disobedient. Ⓛ tomati

- **nómberama** *nicht kommen, zögern.* ◇ not come, hesitate. Ⓛ rauaringañi

nómbuma *widerspenstig sein, nicht gehorchen.* ◇ be rebellious, not obey. Ⓛ tomatinañi

nombeulkura *widerwillig, ganz langsam (kommen).* ◇ reluctant, come very slowly. Ⓛ tomatitara

nopanama *(duppl. von nama) immer sein, haben, gehören, sich aufhalten, sitzen bleiben.* ◇ (duplication of nama) always be, have, belong, dwell, remain, stay. Ⓛ ninaninañi

nota [Southern dialect] *Schoß.* ◇ lap. Ⓛ ambu Ⓓ ngalpa

ntailpara, ntailpura *Stern.* ◇ star. Ⓛ pintiri

ntailpura ingutnakana *Morgenstern.* ◇ morning star. Ⓛ tjiltjana Ⓓ ditji wakka

notuta *eine kleinere Mulde aus Gummiholz.* ◇ small bowl made of gumtree wood. Ⓛ metuta

ntainama *speeren.* ◇ to spear. Ⓛ wokkañi

nturbilama *den Speer gerade werfen (um zu töten).* ◇ throw spear straight (to kill). Ⓛ munturbmanañi

ntaiuma *huren, ehebrechen (mit verschiedenen Frauen oder Mädchen).* ◇ commit adultery (with a number of different women or girls). Ⓛ nenkilanani

ntakalama *Haar ausfallen.* ◇ lose hair.

ntakakata *wie groß?* ◇ how big? Ⓛ jaltjikutáta

ntakata *kleine Mulde.* ◇ small bowl. Ⓛ wilkiri

ntakatna (*inta: Hals, Genick katna: oben, aufgerichtet, erhoben) weißer Stein, erhobener Hals.* ◇ white stone, raised neck, place name (Strehlow 1907: 26). Ⓛ intakatni

ntákana [Southern dialect] *wie?* ◇ how? Ⓛ jaltji

ntakina *wie?* ◇ how? Ⓛ jaltji Ⓓ wordaru

ntakinakatutja *wie groß.* ◇ how big? Ⓛ jaltjikutáta Ⓓ wordajendrania

ntakinangakáta *wie viel (Geld, Mehl).* ◇ how much (money, flour). Ⓛ jaltjingurutáta Ⓓ worderuntja

ntakinja *wie viele?* ◇ how many? Ⓛ jaltjiru, jaltjiri Ⓓ worderuntja

ntakinja ranga *wieviel mal? wie oft.* ◇ how many times? how often? Ⓛ jaltjirara? Ⓓ worderuntja

ntakina namai? *wie ist es?* ◇ how is it? Ⓛ jaltji ninañai?

ntakinjatjatalkura *wie lange.* ◇ how long?

ntala? *wo?* ◇ where? Ⓛ jalla, jalkutu Ⓓ woderi

ntálama? *wo ist er (es)?* ◇ where is he (it)? Ⓛ jaltanka, jallanka

(a)ntalabuma *beschleichen (Wild).* ◇ creep up on (game). Ⓛ urakaterariñi

ntálanama *mitgehen, begleiten.* ◇ go with, accompany. Ⓛ wollankariñi

ntalama *mitgehen, begleiten.* ◇ go with, accompany. Ⓛ wollakuriñi

ntalarenama *lassen, an sich geschehen lassen, sich unterziehen.* ◇ allow, let it happen (to oneself), undergo. Ⓛ junkuliañi

ntalanama *belauern (Katze), lauern.* ◇ lie in wait (cat), lurk.

ntalbantánkama *nötigen zu kommen.* ◇ force to come. Ⓛ antaántawónkañi

ntalbmintalbma *ästig, mit vielen Ästen.* ◇ branchy, with many branches. Ⓛ taratutatuta

ntálelama *jagen (wenn der Wind weht).* ◇ hunt (when wind blows). Ⓛ antalunañi

ntálerama *wachsen, größer werden (Bäume).* ◇ grow, become bigger (trees). Ⓛ antaluriñi

ntalja *ins Haar gesteckte Vogelfedern.* ◇ bird feathers or bundle of tall feathers in hair. Ⓛ pokulu

ntalja *die Ähre.* ◇ ear (wheat). Ⓛ (pokulu?)

ndolkatara *Kreuzförmig (Ast).* ◇ cross shaped (branch). Ⓛ antulkatara

ntalka *Spreu, Zwiesel, Ast, Zweig.* ◇ chaff, branch, twig. Ⓛ antalka

ntalkaliwunja *der mit Spreu vermischte Samenhaufe (die am Boden liegenden Zweige).* ◇ pile of seeds mixed with chaff (i.e. small twigs lying around on the ground). Ⓛ antalkamulala

ntalkalawunama *huren (eine Ehefrau hat mit einem andern Gemeinschaft, mit ihrem Cousin Gemeinschaft).* ◇ wife having intercourse with her cousin. Ⓛ maantalkankarunkañi

 For the modern spellings of these words, see the dictionaries and sources in reference list.

ntalkawotna *(nalka = Spreu; wotna = sehr begierig) eine Frau, die mit ihrem Cousin; 'begierig auf Spreu zu liegen'.* ◇ woman who is eager to have intercourse with her cousin; 'desiring to lie on chaff'. Ⓛ antalkapanti

ntalkilama *eine Frau mit einem Mann Gemeinschaft haben.* ◇ a woman having intercourse with a man. Ⓛ antalkani

ntalkalawuma *huren, ein Mann mit seiner Tochter, wonna oder tjirkawotna.* ◇ to have intercourse with a wrong (classificatory) kin (e.g. a man with his daughter or father's sister). See Strehlow (1913: 93). Ⓛ antalkankarunkañi

ntalkinjala tuma *(in Zusammensetzungen mit pronom verbunden) schlagen (Feinde), besiegen.* ◇ (in compounds with pronouns) hit (enemies), defeat. Ⓛ katungururiñi Ⓓ kalalu ngankana

rantalkinjala tuma *er besiegt.* ◇ he defeats. Ⓛ palurukatungururiñi

tantalkinjala tuma *ich besiege.* ◇ I defeat. Ⓛ ngaiulu katungururiñi

ntalkur̔ulba *durchsichtig (Felsenöffnung), klar (Wasserspiegel).* ◇ clear (gap in cliff face), transparent (water surface). Ⓛ alawirili

ntalta *mannbar.* ◇ marriageable. Ⓛ uru

lenja ntalta *Sonnenstrahlen.* ◇ sunbeams. Ⓛ tjintu karawollawolla Ⓓ ditjimaramara

punga ntalta *Schamhaar.* ◇ pubic hair. Ⓛ tnañi

ntalpa *nach auswärts setzend (Zehen, z.B. Emu).* ◇ place outwards (toes, e.g. emu). Ⓛ ngata

ntāma *verfolgen, belauern, nachstellen.* ◇ pursue, prowl, hunt, track. Ⓛ wonnañi Ⓓ tirikaripaterina

inkantama *der Spur folgen.* ◇ follow the track, track. Ⓛ tjinna wonnañi

ntānama *heranschleichen.* ◇ creep up. Ⓛ mawonnañi

ntambuma *sich rötlich färben (Blätter, Rinde).* ◇ turn reddish (leaves, bark). Ⓛ warngarañi

ntambubambuma *sich färben, sich rötlich färben (fliegende Ameisen).* ◇ to colour, turn red (flying ants). Ⓛ warwarngarañi

ntamintana *Fisch mit silbergrauen Schuppen und schwarzen Querstreifen.* ◇ fish with silver-grey scales and black cross-stripes. Ⓛ intamintini

ntambalanama *gerötet sein [unclear].* ◇ reddish. Ⓛ warngaraniñi

ntana? *wo?* ◇ where? Ⓛ jalla Ⓓ wodéri?

ntananga? *woher?* ◇ where from? Ⓛ jalkutunguru Ⓓ wodérindru?

ntanauna? ntauna? *wohin?* ◇ where to? Ⓛ jalkutukutu Ⓓ wodajeri?

ntanaka? *wohin?* ◇ where to? Ⓛ jalkutuku? Ⓓ wodaninki?

ntanibera *woher.* ◇ where from. Ⓛ jallata

ntauna nga lamai? *wo gehst du hin?* ◇ where are you going to?

ntānama *heranschleichen.* ◇ sneak up. Ⓛ mawonnañi

ntama *(postpost) auch, gleichfalls.* ◇ (postposition) also, likewise. Ⓛ -lbi

ntanga *Sämerei, Gras-Samen.* ◇ seeds, grass seeds. Ⓛ intoku

ntángaltárangáltara *sehr weiche Früchte, aus denen Saft herausfließt.* ◇ very soft fruit from which juice drips out. Ⓛ tjilpitítara

ntanganparana *große Frosch.* ◇ large frog. Ⓛ intangarari

ntangerama *intrs. untertauchen.* ◇ (intransitive) dive, submerge. Ⓛ túlaringañi

ntangilama *trs. untertauchen.* ◇ (transitive) dive under, submerge. Ⓛ tulani

ntintjalérama *vor seinem Ende alle seine Sachen verschenken.* ◇ before death give away all possessions. Ⓛ junkukatiñi

ntánkama *rufen.* ◇ call. Ⓛ antawonkañi Ⓓ karkana

ntankalama *zu sich rufen, locken.* ◇ summon, entice. Ⓛ antawonkanáñi

tankalélama *einem zurufen, der in Gefahr ist; warnen.* ◇ warn. Ⓛ tankawokkáñi

ntankatnauma *nötigen zu kommen.* ◇ urge to come. Ⓛ jeltijeltini

ntanta *leer, z.B. Mulde.* ◇ empty, e.g. bowl. Ⓛ antanti

ntantiuma *nachlegen (beim Feuer).* ◇ stoke (fire). Ⓛ ultuúltuni Ⓓ darana, wangana

ntanteranama *aufpassen, bewachen.* ◇ watch out, be on the watch, guard. Ⓛ maántaántani Ⓓ tarkalkana (*wachen in der Nacht*: guard during the night)

ntanterama *bewachen, bewahren, aufpassen.* ◇ guard, take care, watch. Ⓛ antaántani

(u)ntántua *leicht (nicht schwer).* ◇ light (not heavy). Ⓛ rambi

ntapa; ntaperama *Taube (spec.)* ◇ pigeon (species), important women's dance; perform the ntapa dance. Ⓛ manpi

ntápara *Schwiegersohn (F).* ◇ son-in-law (W). Ⓛ urati

untába [Northern dialect] *Gummirinde.* ◇ gumtree bark. Ⓛ wontapi

ntáperama *tanzen (Frauen), Frauentanz.* ◇ perform the ntapa, dance (women). Ⓛ untiñi, wipiariñi, nanpini Ⓓ wimakilina (?)

ntapalaunama *fortwährend auf- und abtanzen (Frauen).* ◇ continuously dance back and forth (women). Ⓛ untira ïnkatjïngañi

ntapikna *11 Zoll lang, 4 Zoll breit. Karpfenähnl. Fischart.* ◇ carp-like fish, 11 inches long, 4 inches wide. Ⓛ antipini

ntápintápa karama *schaarenweise herumfliegen.* ◇ fly around in flocks. Ⓛ waangariñi, joangariñi

ntaputatalelena *stachliche Eidechse mit Schwanzstumpf.* ◇ prickly lizard with knob tail. Ⓛ papangarpa

ntaramantarauma *adv. von allen Seiten.* ◇ adverb, from all sides. Ⓛ wirilakatawirilakata

ntaramantaraumala ankama *von allen Seiten eine Sache besprechen, beraten.* ◇ discuss thoroughly. Ⓛ wirilakatawirilakatarekula wonkañi

ntaparperama *fallen, ausgleiten?* ◇ fall, slip? ('?' added by CS)

ntarata *Eidechse (spec.) grünl. braun, cr 1 Fuß lang, schwarze Streifen über den Augen u. breite bläulich-schwarze gespaltene Zunge.* ◇ blue tongue lizard, *Tiliqua*. Ⓛ lunkata, mita Ⓓ jidna

ntarbatareērala lama *auseinander gehen, sich trennen (von vielen).* ◇ separate (from crowd). Ⓛ tarabantara jennañi

ntarba *einäugig, taub (auf einem Ohr), lahm auf einem Fuß.* ◇ one-eyed, deaf (on one ear), lame on one foot. Ⓛ antarbi Ⓓ kutikuteri

ntarbatarirama *sich trennen, scheiden.* ◇ to part, to separate. Ⓛ tarakutarariñi

ntarbukama *trs. zerreißen, zertrennen.* ◇ (transitive) tear, separate. Ⓛ tarantanañi Ⓓ purana

ntarbukalama *intrs. zerreißen (Kleid).* ◇ (intransitive) tear (dress). Ⓛ tarantakatiñi Ⓓ puraterina

ntarbukantarba *zertrennt, zerstreut.* ◇ torn, scattered. Ⓛ antarbikantarbi Ⓓ piltjaru

ntélanélana *der Schwefel (n).* ◇ sulphur.

ntárinama *anzünden, z.B. ein Feuer, eine Hütte.* ◇ to light, e.g. a fire, a hut. Ⓛ kalañi

ntariltuma *beschatten (von den Wolken).* ◇ shaded (by clouds).

ntaringama *folgen, verfolgen, nachfolgen.* ◇ follow, pursue. Ⓛ wonnañi Ⓓ karina, karipaterina

ntareuma *wegtreiben (der Wind die Wolken).* ◇ drive away (wind the clouds).

ndartjima *Sonne scheinen.* ◇ to shine (sun). Ⓛ turongarañi

ntartilama *schmerzen, Schmerzen haben.* ◇ to hurt (intransitive), to suffer, have pain. Ⓛ antartanáñi

ntartjibartjuma *sich wärmen (am Feuer), sich sonnen, sich bescheinen lassen.* ◇ warm oneself (by the fire), to sunbathe, bask in the sun. Ⓛ irtnaranáñi

ntaritja *Bergzüge, Gebirgskette, steil, senkrecht.* ◇ mountain ranges, steep, perpendicular. Ⓛ antirtji

ntaritjinbara *viele spitzige Bergzüge.* ◇ many sharp mountain ranges. Ⓛ táltál

(i)ntartnérama *zuheilen, verheilen.* ◇ heal. Ⓛ pulpuráriñi Ⓓ parara

 For the modern spellings of these words, see the dictionaries and sources in reference list.

ntatarka *Schlange, nicht giftig spec.* ◇ non-poisonous snake species. Ⓛ inturkunu

ntatjatuma *spalten (der Länge nach).* ◇ split (lengthwise). Ⓛ patalpungañi

ntátna *steif, unbiegsam, hoch.* ◇ stiff, rigid, tall. Ⓛ arata

ntatnerama *steif werden (vom langen Sitzen).* ◇ get stiff (from sitting too long). Ⓛ arataringañi

ntatatnama *Schlucker haben, knurren (Magen).* ◇ have hiccups, rumble (in stomach). Ⓛ ngetaninañi Ⓓ ngankinkuna terdana

ntata *drückenden Schmerz empfinden (im Innern).* ◇ have pressing pains (inside). Ⓛ walenku

ntátupuntáta *tief eingesunkene Füße.* ◇ deep sunk-in feet. Ⓛ tunirtunirba

ntauērama *weinen, klagen.* ◇ cry, lament. Ⓛ urkantjiriñi Ⓓ ngirikidana, juajuangana

ntaueritnenkama *flöten (Emus).* ◇ warble, whistle (emu). Ⓛ bulupungañi

ntēlpara *das eine Knie erhoben (das andere Knie am Boden).* ◇ kneel on one knee. Ⓛ talkawaral

ntelpara irkuma *mit einem erhoben Bein stehen (Vögel).* ◇ stand on one leg (birds). Ⓛ talkawarilknaráñi

ndebuma *auslesen (Beeren).* ◇ pick out (berries). Ⓛ alaurkuni

andéëlerama *sich bestreichen (mit Fett).* ◇ rub (with fat), (reflexive). Ⓛ nitinkariñi Ⓓ jurborina

ntemba *Baum (spec.)* ◇ tree (species). Ⓛ antimbi

ntélama *anzünden (Feuer), anfachen (Feuer).* ◇ light (fire), fan (fire). Ⓛ kutañi

ntema; era pitjima ntema *wieder (postp.), zum zweiten und dritten Mal; er kommt wieder.* ◇ again (postposition), for the second and third time; he comes again. Ⓛ karu, ka; palaru ngalajennani karu

ntelauma *wetterleuchten.* ◇ sheet lightning. Ⓛ pinpani Ⓓ tjintina

ntentilalbuma [Southern dialect] *behutsam, schleichend umkehren.* ◇ cautious, turn back creeping. Ⓛ úraúrakátirakulbañi

ntenta *dicht (von Bäumen) zusammen stehend.* ◇ standing densely together (trees). Ⓛ tatajerri

interirperírpa *rote Libelle.* ◇ red dragonfly. Ⓛ interériréri

intérkuma *zusammenbinden, anspannen (Pferde).* ◇ tie together, hitch (horse). Ⓛ tintjini

ntēna *graue Maus (ohne Beutel).* ◇ grey mouse (without pouch). Ⓛ iljukuru

ntatna *hoher Baum (gen).* ◇ tall tree (gen). Ⓛ téwila

ntilja *großer pig-toed Bandikut.* ◇ large pig-toed bandicoot. Ⓛ walina

ntiljabilapa [Southern dialect] *Schmetterling.* ◇ butterfly. Ⓛ pintapinta Ⓓ kalibilibili

ntitja [Southern dialect] *junger Mann.* ◇ young man. Ⓛ wongu

ntitjimelanka *schön gefärbter Mann.* ◇ nicely coloured man. Ⓛ wongu-watinba

ntitja, tutja *ein Sternenpaar (2 junge Männer die einst auf Erden Kanguruhs jagten).* ◇ pair of stars (representing two young men, who once hunted kangaroos on earth). Ⓛ induta, indutakutara

titja *was bedeutet? Was ist?* ◇ what does it mean? What is? Ⓛ pitinja

ntitjétérintjéra *kleiner Vogel (spec.), Flügel schwarz, Brust weiß, Schwanz fortwährend hin und her bewegend.* ◇ willie wagtail: small bird species, black wings, white chest, moves tail constantly from side to side. Ⓛ tjintiratjintira

ntitjetjérina *Schlange, giftig (spec.)* ◇ poisonous snake species.

(a)ntjá *Gift, Schlangengift.* ◇ poison, snake poison. Ⓛ antjikantji

ntjikantja *Giftdrüse der Schlange.* ◇ venom gland of snake (see Strehlow 1907: 20–24). Ⓛ antjikantji

ntjabera *ganz.* ◇ all, entire, whole, complete. Ⓛ antapiri Ⓓ purru

ntjainama *riechen.* ◇ smell. Ⓛ pantiñi Ⓓ panina, panimana, pantamana

ntjainanama *riechen (fortwährend).* ◇ smell (constantly). Ⓛ mapantiñi

kumia ntjainama *gut riechen.* ◇ smell good. Ⓛ ulara pantiñi

unba ntjainama *schlecht riechen.* ◇ smell bad. Ⓛ unbu pantiñi

ntjaininja *Geruch.* ◇ smell, odour, scent. Ⓛ pantinma Ⓓ kuli

ntjilbintjainama *schnüffeln (von Hunden).* ◇ sniff (dogs). Ⓛ pantipantiñi

ntjaka *fort, weg.* ◇ gone, away. Ⓛ antjaki

ntjákama *nicht mehr antreffen (Gesuchte), verfallen, nicht mehr zu sehen bekommen, weggegangen, gestorben, nicht mehr am Leben finden.* ◇ not encounter, find or meet no more; deceased; separate. Ⓛ malantánañi

ntjakalama *fortgehen.* ◇ go away, leave. Ⓛ antjaki jenañi

ntjakilarbérama *lange ausbleiben, lange abwesend sein.* ◇ stay away for a long time, be absent for a long time. Ⓛ antjakiriñi

ntjakubma *Moloch horridus (Mountain Devil).* ◇ Thorny Devil, *Moloch horridus*. Ⓛ miniri

ntjala *Zauberknochen, Wadenbein.* ◇ magic bones, calf bone (fibula). Ⓛ kuru Ⓓ panji

ntjala *Wadenbein.* ◇ calf bone (fibula). Ⓛ kuru

ntjalintjala *Wadenbein.* ◇ calf bone (fibula). Ⓛ kurukuru

ntjalinama *Zauber entfernen.* ◇ remove magic. Ⓛ kuru manjini

ntjalbiuma *stoßen (sich an etwas), stolpern.* ◇ knock (against something), stumble, trip. Ⓛ tarbipungani

ntjalbiwótnama *staucheln, stolpern machen, fast zu Fall bringen.* ◇ stumble, cause to stumble, nearly trip (someone). Ⓛ parirtalkañi

ntjalka *Raupe, die sich von den tnelja-Ranken nährt.* ◇ caterpillar that feeds on tnelja-vines. Ⓛ kantila, intjalki, nimiri

ntjama *ausgebreitet (Zweige oder Decken), Bett.* ◇ spread out (branches or blankets), bed. Ⓛ panta

ntjamiuma *ausbreiten (z.B. die Decken, um darauf zu schlafen).* ◇ spread out (e.g. blankets to sleep on). Ⓛ pantatunañi Ⓓ jauibana, pirakana?

tjétjima *einsammeln (den Zucker an Blättern).* ◇ collect/gather (sugar from trees). Ⓛ intjini

ntjaramarbekua *viele andern.* ◇ many others.

ntjara *viele.* ◇ many. Ⓛ tjikara, tuta Ⓓ marapu

ntjaraknara *sehr viele.* ◇ very many. Ⓛ tutalenku, tjikaralenku

ntjaelatnama *schnauben (Pferde).* ◇ snort (horses).

ntjāra *Tal (zwischen Sandhügeln).* ◇ valley (between sandhills). Ⓛ luntu

ntjarama *schnarchen.* ◇ snore. Ⓛ ngurbmanañi Ⓓ kandrungana

ntjarerkuma *festbinden, zusammenbinden, zus. fassen, anspannen.* ◇ fasten, tie together, gather together, harness (horses). Ⓛ tintjini Ⓓ tjilpi ngankana, worku mandrana

ntjarra *der Schlafplatz der ara (Känguruh).* ◇ sleeping place of kangaroos.

ntjarra *eine weite Fläche (zwischen 2 Gebirgszügen).* ◇ wide plain (between two mountain ranges). Ⓛ unatjíri

ntjartnatnima *niesen.* ◇ sneeze. Ⓛ nurtjiñi Ⓓ duntjirina

ntjaua *Blutklumpen, mit Blut gefärbt, Krumme (Brot).* ◇ blood clot, coloured with blood, crumb (bread).

ntjauintjaua *blutrot, Purpur (n), rosenfarben.* ◇ blood red, purple.

ntjelba, (ntjilba) *taub (Frucht), leer (von Samen), schlaff, nicht saftig (Gras).* ◇ empty (fruit), empty (e.g. no seeds), limp, not lush (grass). Ⓛ bilta, kebula

ntjelberama *zusammentrocknen, einfallen.* ◇ shrivel up, cave in. Ⓛ biltaringañi

ntjiballa *zuchtlos.* ◇ immoral.

ntjérama *fischen (mittelst Graswehr).* ◇ fish (using a grass weir). Ⓛ untuni

ntjibarkabara *die Hure.* ◇ whore.

ntjeranama *ziehen (Wolken), abziehen (Fische).* ◇ move (clouds), move on (fish). Ⓛ unturabakani

ntjibantja *Bett.* ◇ bed.
ntjerka *kleine Beutelratte.* ◇ small marsupial rat. Ⓛ tujalbi
ntjerkinta *Steinmesser (sp.)* ◇ stone knife (species). Ⓛ intjerkinti
ntjia *Schweiß.* ◇ sweat, perspiration. Ⓛ akuri, kulkari Ⓓ kanga
ntjiilbuma *schwitzen.* ◇ to sweat, perspire. Ⓛ akuribakañi, akuripunturingañi Ⓓ kanga ngakana
ntjíkaleùma *stolpern.* ◇ stumble. Ⓛ tanapungañi, tjuanpungañi Ⓓ deringana, taringana
ntjiila ilbanama *weiter traben (Pferde, Hunde).* ◇ trot along (horses, dogs). Ⓛ mamiri kutujennañi
ntjikantja *Giftdrüsen der Schlange.* ◇ venom glands of snakes. Ⓛ antjikantji
ntjila [Northern dialect] *Wadenbein.* ◇ calf bone (fibula). Ⓛ kūru
ntjilama *sich wärmen.* ◇ warm oneself. Ⓛ ngantjiranañi
ntjilbintjainama *schnüffeln (Hunde).* ◇ sniff (dogs). Ⓛ pantipantiñi
ntjilbinja *kleine Sumpfvogel (spec.)* ◇ small swamp bird (species) Ⓛ injilbini
ntjilbuta *aus Versehen, unabsichtlich.* ◇ by accident, unintentional. Ⓛ wotiba
  ntjilbutilama *aus Versehen treffen.* ◇ hit by accident. Ⓛ wotibarunkani
ntjilkama *zischen (kleine Vögel).* ◇ hiss (small birds). Ⓛ ngenmanañi
ntjilkinja *stachlicher Strauch (spec.), etwa 4 Fuß hoch, mit gelben Blüten und hellgrünen, ovalen Blättern, die in Stracheln auslaufen.* ◇ prickly bush species about 4 feet tall, with yellow blossoms and light green oval leaves with prickles at its tips. Ⓛ intjilkanji
ntjilkinja *Larve in ntjilkinja-Wurzeln.* ◇ grub in ntjilkinja roots. Ⓛ intjilkanji
ntjilpa *das auf Lehmebenen angesammelte Regenwasser.* ◇ rainwater collected in claypans. Ⓛ wonta, tjitjikaka
ntjima *trs. wärmen (Feuer).* ◇ (transitive) to warm (fire). Ⓛ ngantjini
  ntjilama *refl. sich wärmen.* ◇ (reflexive) to warm. Ⓛ ngantjirarañi Ⓓ talpina, ngarakalina, ngurkumaterina
ntjipera *kleine Fledermaus.* ◇ small bat. Ⓛ antjipiri, pintangari
ntjiltja *der Pfahl.* ◇ pole.
ntjinbinba *Nest der Emus.* ◇ emu's nest. Ⓛ intjinbinbi
ntjintjiriuma *steigen (Flutwasser).* ◇ rise (floodwater). Ⓛ kurutuntutuntuni
intjipintjátjina *Pflanze mit blauen Blüten (in der Nähe von Wasserlöchern wachsend).* ◇ plant with blue blossoms (grows in the vicinity of waterholes). Ⓛ apintapinta
ntjipintia *1. Stockwerk (n).* ◇ first level.
ntjira *lange Grasart (ähnlich dem Zittergras).* ◇ long grass species. Ⓛ antjiri
ntjiranga [Southern dialect] *Mulga (spec.)* ◇ mulga species. Ⓛ injirangi
(i)ntjirbma *Stiel einer ilapa (Steinbeil).* ◇ handle of a stone axe. Ⓛ intjirbmi
ntjirbmarenama *mit Steinen bedecken.* ◇ cover with stones. Ⓛ turultunañi
ntjirka *trocken (z.B. Gras).* ◇ dry (e.g. grass). Ⓛ pilti Ⓓ muja
  ntjirkerama *vertrocknen.* ◇ dry up. Ⓛ piltiringañi Ⓓ mujarina
ntjōka *habsüchtig.* ◇ greedy.
ntjorra *Buschfeuer ([unclear]).* ◇ bushfire. Ⓛ inana
ntjuára *der blaue Kranich.* ◇ blue crane. Ⓛ untjari Ⓓ wirru
ntjuia *Baum mit langen Nadeln, (Honeysuckle).* ◇ tree with long needles (honeysuckle). Ⓛ witjinti, pirūu
ntjuiamba *Blüte des Honeysuckle (Hakea flower).* ◇ blossoms of honeysuckle (*Hakea* flower). Ⓛ piru͡u Ⓓ pitjambu (honeycomb)
ntjulkuta *Vogel (spec.) rötliche Federn, den erhobenen Schwanz fortwährend hin und her bewegen, zwischen Porcupine sich aufhaltend.* ◇ bird species with reddish feathers that moves its raised tail continuously from side to side and lives in porcupine grass. Ⓛ tjintjiwili
ntjuma *vorbei, weg.* ◇ past, gone. Ⓛ tañga, titu Ⓓ wonta

ntjuma lama *vorbeigehen.* ◇ to go by, to pass. Ⓛ tañga jennañi, titu jennañi Ⓓ wonta wapana

ntjumala ndama *verschenken, weggeben.* ◇ give away. Ⓛ tañganku jungañi

ntjumalakintjumala lama *nach verschiedenen Richtungen auseinandergehen.* ◇ disperse into different directions. Ⓛ tangakutanga jennañi

ntjilkuma; lênga tjulkuma *bleichen (Gras); Sonne bleich (= weißlich) hervorkommen.* ◇ bleach (grass); a pale (whitish) sun emerges. Ⓛ perulkañi; tjintu terangañi

njúratja *lange Schlange mit schwarzem Kopf, sehr giftig.* ◇ long snake with black head, very poisonous. Ⓛ unjuratji

ntjurbmanama *berghohe Wellen, bewegt.* ◇ very high waves, swell. Ⓛ páparuṙiñi

ntjarkula (ntjurkula) *Käfer (schwarz) mit langen Fühlhörnern.* ◇ beetle (black) with long sensor horns. Ⓛ katati

ntjúta, ntjita [Southern dialect] *Kreuzbein.* ◇ sacrum. Ⓛ titi, mutu, tangántanga Ⓓ kuldru

ntoérama *sich erbrechen.* ◇ vomit. Ⓛ ulkabutúnañi

ntómintoma *Fliege (spec.)* ◇ fly species. Ⓛ intumintumu

ntótnama *überladen (Magen), überfressen.* ◇ overeat. Ⓛ ngetanínañi, ngétininanáñi

ntotnérama *voll werden (v. Fressen).* ◇ become full (with food). Ⓛ ngetaringañi

ntotnia *übervoll, überladen.* ◇ overfull. Ⓛ mulkiri

ntōtnera *die Stirn des lakabara (Habichts).* ◇ forehead of lakabara hawk. Ⓛ tabiti

ntuāba [Southern dialect] *Rinde des Gummibaumes.* ◇ bark of gumtree. Ⓛ wontapi

ntukantuka *zerstoßen.* ◇ pound.

ntuána [Southern dialect], **untána** [Northern dialect] *gelb.* ◇ yellow. Ⓛ kantawara, wonkawonka Ⓓ parru?

ntukantukilama *zerstechen.* ◇ stab.

ntuara [Southern dialect] *jenseits.* ◇ beyond. Ⓛ wirili

ntujantuja ankama *sehr freundlich reden.* ◇ to speak in a very friendly manner. Ⓛ inkapala wonkani

ntumuramurerama *sich rüsten (sich bereiten).* ◇ arm, prepare.

ntulba *Becken, Hüfte.* ◇ pelvis, hip. Ⓛ ankalla

ntulba ilkata *Hüftknochen.* ◇ hip joint, hip bone. Ⓛ ankalla taltu

ntulula *Beckenöffnung (nach unten).* ◇ pelvis opening (downwards). Ⓛ antululu

ntulbala *neben, zur Seite.* ◇ beside, to the side. Ⓛ ankalta

ntulbankama *den Boden durchbrechen (Samen).* ◇ break through surface (seed). Ⓛ pulututubakañi

ntúlbankama *klopfen (das Geräusch des Klopfens).* ◇ to knock. Ⓛ tutuni

ntuma *tanzen, stampfen (bei der Aufführung der Ceremonien).* ◇ to dance, stamp, stomp (at ceremonies). Ⓛ kantuni

(a)ltúlba *geschwollen.* ◇ swollen. Ⓛ taltu

ltulberama *schwellen.* ◇ to swell. Ⓛ talturingañi

ntōra *das erwachsene männliche Opossum.* ◇ mature male possum. Ⓛ ánturu

ntura *Felsenhöhle (in die sich die Wallaby verziehen).* ◇ stone cave (of wallaby). Ⓛ unturu Ⓓ talta

ntumanama *verachten (Befehl).* ◇ ignore (order).

nturantura *faltig, rissig, runzlig (Gesicht).* ◇ wrinkled (face). Ⓛ wiljiriwiljiri Ⓓ winjirinjeri

nturanturerama *entstellt werden, zornig aussehen, faltig werden.* ◇ become distorted, look angry, become wrinkly. Ⓛ wiljiriwiljiriringañi

nturba *wahr, gewiß.* ◇ true, certain. Ⓛ munturu Ⓓ morlalu

nturbankama *wahr reden.* ◇ speak truthfully. Ⓛ munturu wonkañi Ⓓ morlalu jatana

 For the modern spellings of these words, see the dictionaries and sources in reference list.

nturbilama *Wahrheit reden.* ◇ speak the truth. Ⓛ munturanáñi

nturbaka *ins Sichere, ins Centrum (treffen).* ◇ (hit) the mark. Ⓛ munturaku

nturkna *Gehirn.* ◇ brain. Ⓛ unturu Ⓓ pua

nturkna *traurig, betrübt.* ◇ sad. Ⓛ alturu Ⓓ ngaurongauro

nturknerama *trauern, Totenklage halten, beweinen.* ◇ mourn, cry. Ⓛ altururingañi Ⓓ milamilarina, kalu pakina

nturkneranama *trauern, klagen (Heimweh).* ◇ mourn, feel sorry, lament (homesick). Ⓛ maálturuñi

nturknanturkna [ankama] *niedergeschlagen, sehr betrübt [sprechen].* ◇ dejected, (speak) very sadly. Ⓛ alturualturu wonkañi

tutibuma *dröhnen (hohlen Gummibaum schlagend).* ◇ resound, boom (beating hollow gumtree). Ⓛ bulupungañi

nturuma *knurren (Hund), grunzen (Schwein, Emu).* ◇ growl (dog), grunt (pig, emu). Ⓛ ngunturbmanáni (emu), nganjiririñi (*Hund*: dog), bulupungañi (emu)

nturuta *Taube, braun mit Haube, rock-pigeon, (Lophophaps leucogaster). Rotbraune Flügel mit schwarzen Streifen, schwarzer Schnabel, graublauer Vorderkopf, rote Stelle um die Augen, rotbraune Haube, weißer Streifen von unter dem Schnabel bis unter das Auge, unterhalb dieses Streifens ein schwarzer Ring, der bis an das Auge reicht. Weißer Bauch vermischt mit braun, zum Schwanz hin dunkler werdend. Rücken braun mit schwarzen Querstreifen die langen Flügelfedern braun mit schwarzer Spitze, die inneren Flügelfedern violet schwarz.* ◇ spinifex pigeon (*Geophaps plumifera*) (see Pizzey and Knight 2007). Ⓛ eburu

ntutaméa *Nahrung.* ◇ food. Ⓛ paltapala

ntutilama *speisen, füttern.* ◇ eat, feed. Ⓛ paltani

ntutakana *Futterplatz (n), Krippe (n).* ◇ feeding place, crib.

ntutjaraúma, ntutjiriúma *eine freudige Botschaft bringen (z.B. große Flut kommt).* ◇ bring good news (e.g. a big flood is coming). Ⓛ merawonniñi

nuántja *Geklapper, Getöne.* ◇ rattle, clatter, sound. Ⓛ tōla

unāra *stinkend.* ◇ stink. Ⓛ unna Ⓓ dunka, pundo pundo (*Gestank*: stink, reek)

unarintjima *stinken.* ◇ to smell bad, to stink. Ⓛ unnapantiñi Ⓓ dunkarina

nújuna *gebeugt, gebückt.* ◇ bent, stooped. Ⓛ nuntununtu

nuátnima *zögern, langsam kommen.* ◇ hesitate, come slowly. Ⓛ rauaringañi

nuka *mein.* ◇ my. Ⓛ ngaiuku Ⓓ ngujawakana

nukanalai *du bist mein Freund (Wohltäter).* ◇ you are my friend (benefactor). Ⓛ ngaiukunitalu Ⓓ ngakani

nulanulilama *zerhauen (in viele Stücke), zerstücken (Fleisch), in Stücke zerschlagen.* ◇ smash (into many pieces), cut into pieces (meat), break or smash to pieces. Ⓛ putaputani

nultanulta *voll (von Menschen).* ◇ full (of people).

nultanulterama *voll werden (v. Menschen).* ◇ fill up (with people).

numba *Lahme.* ◇ lame. Ⓛ numbu Ⓓ kutikuteri

numatata *die weiche, feuchte Erde.* ◇ soft, moist earth. Ⓛ topilkna

nuna *wir.* ◇ we. Ⓛ nganana Ⓓ ngaiani

nunata *wir (incl.), wir alle.* ◇ we (inclusive), all of us, we all. Ⓛ ngananalta

ñúngañúngerama *bereiten, mahlen (Grassämereien).* ◇ prepare, grind (grass seeds). Ⓛ ngunjingunjiringañi

nunjununja *gierig, hastig (essen, fressen), beim Gehen essen.* ◇ greedy, hasty (eat), eat on the move. Ⓛ tatjilitatjili (kaiuala)

nunkara *diesseits.* ◇ this side. Ⓛ tangati

nunkarakua *diesseits.* ◇ on this side. Ⓛ tangatinguanba

ñunta *Felspitze.* ◇ top of rock. Ⓛ kutinba

nuntiuma *stützen, unterstützen (die Hände eines Andern), anstoßen (Schiff am Lande).* ◇ support, prop up (hands of somebody), push (beached boat). Ⓛ toppaltunañi Ⓓ jenina

nunkarapuntuara *diesseits und jenseits, sehr vereinzelt.* ◇ this side and that side, very occasionally. Ⓛ ngatakurapawirili

nuntjima *richen, duften (Blumen intrs.), Brot.* ◇ smell, have a scent (flowers) (intransitive), bread. Ⓛ pantirpantirngarañi

nungurérama *sich (beim Sitzen) nach einer andern Seite umdrehen.* ◇ (when sitting) turn to a different direction. Ⓛ anungururiñi

inúra *lahm.* ◇ lame. Ⓛ inúru

nuranura *lahm, gelähmt.* ◇ lame, paralysed. Ⓛ inúrinúru

nuranurerama *lahm werden.* ◇ become lame. Ⓛ inúrinurufiñi

nurknunúrerama, nurknunárlrama *stinkend werden, verderben.* ◇ become smelly, go off. Ⓛ arknultatalkañi

nurra *unbeweglich, still (Menschen), still (Wasser).* ◇ motionless, still (human beings, water). Ⓛ unuru Ⓓ panpana, dapina, dapidapina, datturu

nurralélama *aufhalten, stehen machen.* ◇ stop, to bring to a halt. Ⓛ unurunáni

nuruma *ausreiben (Samen) mit den Händen.* ◇ rub (seeds) with hands. Ⓛ ularpungani

nururka *Ferse.* ◇ heel. Ⓛ mōku, (muku) Ⓓ tidnawarda

nūtara *lahm, an der Ferse gelähmt.* ◇ lame, paralysed heel. Ⓛ turbu

O

irkua *Leichensaft.* Ⓛ ōka, tulburu

okua [Southern dialect] *rechts, rechtshändig.* ◇ right, right-handed. Ⓛ waku Ⓓ ngunari

ortalinja *Schlangenfett.* ◇ snake fat. Ⓛ lurknupa

ortja *falsch, nicht wahr.* ◇ wrong, not true. Ⓛ ngunji Ⓓ jedi

ortjalta *Lüge, Lügner.* ◇ lie, liar. Ⓛ ngunjinju Ⓓ jedi[-jaura]

ortjataka *(ortja: falsch, talka: groß) Lügner.* ◇ liar. Ⓛ ngunjiwóttalba Ⓓ jedikantji

ortjérama *lügen.* ◇ to lie. Ⓛ ngunjinjiriñi

ortjerinérina *Lügner.* ◇ liar. Ⓛ ngunjiwottanmi

ortjaiabiéba *treulos, bundbrüchig.* ◇ disloyal. Ⓛ ngunjimatula

ortjabebilama, ortjajibalelama *betrügen (durch falsche Berichte).* ◇ deceive (with false reports). Ⓛ ngunjilinañi, ngunji ibilbmanañi Ⓓ jedibana

ortjerelélama *betrügen (durch falsche Berichte), falsches berichten.* ◇ deceive, report falsely. Ⓛ ngunji jennañi

ortjaijibijiba *betrügerisch, Betrug.* ◇ deceitful, fraudulent, fraud. Ⓛ ngunjiwonka

ortjunbuma *verleugnen.* ◇ deny. Ⓛ ngunjimaturingani

ortjaninganinga *heimtückisch, List.* ◇ malicious, treacherous, cunning. Ⓛ ebilngúntilku Ⓓ ngaruni

ortjerilba tnelanama *falsch zeugen, falsches Zeugnis reden (v. Andern).* ◇ perjure, tell lies about others. Ⓛ ngunjiwottara talkánañi

ortjána, tjatta ortjana *Sträucher, Holzart, Speere aus ortjana Holz.* ◇ shrubs, wood species; spears made of ortjana wood. Ⓛ ortanu, katji ortanu

ortjikaléuma *sich verstellen, heucheln.* ◇ disguise, fake, feign, be a hypocrite. Ⓛ ngunji jennañi

ortjajibalélama *betrügen.* ◇ cheat, deceive. Ⓛ ngunjilinañi

ortjitinjerama *hinterlistig sich einem nähern.* ◇ approach with treacherous intentions, pretend. Ⓛ ngunji ilaringañi

ortjitinjilama *trs. hinterlistig jemanden heranlocken.* ◇ (transitive) lure someone. Ⓛ ngunji ilañi

ortjitinjilélama *sich täuschen (in Betreffs eines andern).* ◇ be mistaken (about somebody). Ⓛ ngunji ilawetini

ortjungna *lang anhaltender Regen.* ◇ long-lasting rain. Ⓛ ortungu

otóppeotóppa *Weg längs des Gebirgszuges, am Rand des Gebirges.* ◇ path along a mountain range. Ⓛ luntjukutaraluntju

P

paita *Schwanz der Schlange.* ◇ snake tail. Ⓛ apaiiti

palai! *geh aus dem Weg, sieh dich vor (vor einem Feinde).* ◇ get out of the way, be wary (of an enemy); watch out! Ⓛ palai!

bálaruka *blind, blind geboren.* ◇ blind, born blind. Ⓛ wapalku

palaia *sehr weit entfernt.* ◇ very far away. Ⓛ tutan

palkanga *Vogel schwarzbauner Kopf, dunkelgüne Flügel, rötlich braune Brust, rotbraune Rückenfedern (King-fisher), legt seine Eier im Erdboden, besonders an Creek-Ufern.* ◇ kingfisher; bird with a black-brown head, dark green wings, a reddish-brown chest and red-brown back feathers; it lays eggs in the ground, in particular in creek banks. Ⓛ lōna, lōnba

palkara *Taube (bläulich, auf Bäumen sich aufhaltend).* ◇ bluish pigeon (dwells in trees). Ⓛ apilkiri, arélakarinba Ⓓ mudlabara

palba *drei.* ◇ three. Ⓛ mankuru

balkalaka *verblendet, leiblich und geistig blind, unsinnig, verrückt.* ◇ physically and mentally blind, crazy. Ⓛ kauankauan

pallanapallanama *fortwährend herumlaufen.* ◇ continuously walk around. Ⓛ jenkanara jenkánañi

pallanama *cf.* **larrapallanama** *umherstreunen, umhergehen, umherkriechen, umherschwimmen (Enten).* ◇ roam, stray, crawl, swim around (ducks). Ⓛ jenkanañi, lerikatiñi Ⓓ wirarina

pallalama *umherstreunen.* ◇ to stray. Ⓛ monojenañi

palla *Nierenfett.* ◇ kidney fat. Ⓛ kabulita

Palla *'Gemahl' in der auf und absteigenden Linie; Großmutter (Vaters Mutter), Enkel (♀), Enkelin (♀).* ◇ father's mother; 'Husband' in 'ascending and descending' line (father's mother), grandson, granddaughter; people affiliated with a country through their father's mother are called, in Western Aranda, kutungula. Their rights to country are usually not as strong as the rights that people gain through their father's father (aranga) and their mother's father (tjimia). Ⓛ bakali

lorra palla *Großmutter, Großtante.* ◇ grandmother, grand-aunt. Ⓛ kami bakali

knaia palla *Großonkel (Vaters Mutters Bruder).* ◇ grand-uncle (father's mother's brother). Ⓛ bakali

woia palla *Enkel (♀), Großmutter (♀).* ◇ grandson, grandmother. Ⓛ bakali

kwaia palla *Enkelin (Sohns Tochter) (♀), Großnichte (♀).* ◇ granddaughter (son's daughter), grandniece. Ⓛ bakali

lorra pallatja *meine Großmutter.* ◇ my grandmother. Ⓛ kami bakalina

woia pallatja *mein Enkel.* ◇ my grandson. Ⓛ bakalina

kwaia pallatja *meine Enkelin.* ◇ my granddaughter. Ⓛ bakalina

pallaparitja *der Platz des Palla.* ◇ place of father's mother. Ⓛ bakaliparitja

pallukua *Personen, die einander heiraten drürfen (der Klasse nach, palla nach).* ◇ people who are allowed to marry each other. Ⓛ bakalira

pallaïtaïta *Vogel, rot, fortwährend schreit.* ◇ red bird that constantly cries/screams. Ⓛ miteïti

pallatama *auffliegen (Schaar Vögel), schaarenweise, voll sein (von Rauch).* ◇ fly up (flock of birds), in flocks; be full (of smoke). Ⓛ ngalamúlani

palleranama *abirren (vom rechten Weg).* ◇ stray off (the right path). Ⓛ mamonoringañi

pallakia *breit, groß (Füße der Vögel).* ◇ broad, large (feet of birds). Ⓛ tjoalpurungu

palpaparama *mit Gewalt wegnehmen, erobern.* ◇ take with force, conquer. Ⓛ angangaringañi

pallapalla *sumpfig (Boden).* ◇ swampy (ground). Ⓛ kurakura

pallitjula etalerama *irren (errare).* ◇ err, to be mistaken, be wrong.

pāltara *Federschuh (emu) und Schuh des Opossum.* ◇ feather shoe made of emu feathers or possum skin. Ⓛ tjinnakata Ⓓ wakambara

paltjima *aufmachen, zerreißen, zerbrechen (Eier, tjappa, [unclear]).* ◇ open, tear, rip, break (eggs, grubs). Ⓛ talantanáñi

păltara *Heiratsklasse.* ◇ marriage class, subsection, skin name. Ⓛ tapaltara (♂), napaltara (♀)

palupala *Busch mit blauen Blüten und gelben Beeren (nicht gegessen).* ◇ bush with blue blossoms and yellow berries (not edible). Ⓛ okalupalu

pankarapankarérama *taumeln.* ◇ reel, stagger. Ⓛ kujurkujurkatiñi

pananganangérama *schweben (Vögel in der Luft, Kreise ziehen).* ◇ hover, circle (birds). Ⓛ wolbangururingañi

pankamiltja (miltja) *gebogene Zweig [der Bluträcher?], (das ins Haar gesteckt wird).* ◇ small bent twig (stuck into hair). Ⓛ pankamiltja

pananka *Heiratsklasse.* ◇ marriage class, subsection, skin name. Ⓛ tapananka (♂), napananka (♀)

panja *Pocken.* ◇ pox. Ⓛ wapata Ⓓ witja

pantja *Vogelfedern, Gefieder, (Federbusch, Schmuck).* ◇ bird feathers, plumage, (featherplume, decoration). Ⓛ pokulu opantji

pantjinga *völlig befriedigt, friedfertig, vollkommen.* ◇ completely satisfied. Ⓛ māka

pantjuma *willig, aufpecken (Samen).* ◇ willingly, peck (seeds). Ⓛ munguni

pantjupantjuma *fortwährend aufpicken.* ◇ continuously peck, pick up. Ⓛ mungumunguni

pápapapa *kleine Fischart.* ◇ small fish species. Ⓛ papapapa

para *Gummibaum (Eucalyptus rostrata).* ◇ gumtree (*Eucalyptus camaldulensis* (Latz 1996)). Ⓛ itára, ngápiri Ⓓ patara

para ulkumba *die weich geriebene Rinde des Gummibaumes.* ◇ soft ground gumtree bark. Ⓛ itara mina, ulkulji

marpara *Früchte der Gummibäume.* ◇ fruit of gumtrees. Ⓛ imirpiri Ⓓ paua

paraltja *Zucker auf den Blättern des Gummibaumes (der von Pflanzenläusen dort niedergelegt wird).* ◇ sugar on gumtree leaves (deposited by plant lice). Ⓛ apiraltji

para irkilja *graue Heuschrecken an Gummibäumen.* ◇ grey grasshoppers on gumtrees. Ⓛ itara irkilji

paraljuka *kleeartiges Kraut.* ◇ clover-like herb. Ⓓ ngadu

parama *aufhalten, hemmen, hindern, im Wege stehen.* ◇ stop, stand in the way, hinder. Ⓛ angaringañi Ⓓ ngandrawalkana

parametarka *Käfer.* ◇ beetle. Ⓛ itirki Ⓓ piriwakana

parapara *Strauch (mit eßbaren Früchten).* ◇ bush (with edible fruit). Ⓛ apirapiri

papangulura *ein hundartiges Tier, Bär.* ◇ dog-like animal, bear.

pattalankualankua *steinicht.* ◇ stony.

paritjulka *Pilze.* ◇ mushrooms. Ⓛ mantangaljiri

patta latitja *Pfeiler, Säule (n).* ◇ pillar, column.

paranama *aufhalten, hemmen.* ◇ stop, inhibit. Ⓛ maángaringañi Ⓓ ngandrawalkaterina

patta mbaljilkaljilka *glatter Stein, Marmor (n).* ◇ smooth stone, marble.

patta toppangabunga *Mauer (n).* ◇ wall, (make a wall).

parpantema *schnell wieder.* ◇ repeat quickly. Ⓛ papaltuka

parpa *schnell.* ◇ fast. Ⓛ papaltu Ⓓ nurrujĕli

parraloatjira *Schlange (giftig).* ◇ snake (poisonous). Ⓛ wiputinitini

parra *das dünne Ende des Speerschaftes.* ◇ thin end of spear shaft. Ⓛ tapara

parra *Schwanz, Stiel (des Fruchtkolbens).* ◇ tail, stalk (of a cob). Ⓛ wipu Ⓓ nura

paëla tuma *mit dem Schwanz schlagen.* ◇ beat with the tail. Ⓛ wipunkupungañi

parraluka *Schwanzspitze des Känguruhs.* ◇ tail tip of kangaroo. Ⓛ wipuakantji

parritjirbirba *Schwanzeindrücke (des Känguruhs).* ◇ tail impressions (of kangaroo) in soft ground or sand. Ⓛ wipu-ninka

parra *männliches Glied, (penis).* ◇ penis, tail. Ⓛ kalu Ⓓ kidni

parralbeta, parralbitja *Schwanzspitze.* ◇ tail tip. Ⓛ wipu-mani

parritja *Schwanz (der Schlange).* ◇ tail (of snake). Ⓛ oparátji

parritja karkuma *Schwanz fortwährend hin und her bewegen (Schlange).* ◇ constantly move tail from side to side (snake). Ⓛ wipipirirakulbañi

patta *Stein, Felsen, Berg.* ◇ stone, mountain, rock. Ⓛ puli, apu Ⓓ marda

patta naritjula *hohe Berg.* ◇ high mountain.

patta knara *Berg, Gebirge.* ◇ mountain, range. Ⓛ puli puntu, apu pulka

patta intartja *Gebirgszug (Range).* ◇ mountain range.

patta urta *Hügel.* ◇ hill. Ⓛ puli urta Ⓓ mardawonpa

patta urba *Gebirgsrücken.* ◇ mountain ridge. Ⓛ puli murbu

patta kulba *Bergspitze, Felsrücken.* ◇ summit, mountain ridge, top of mountain. Ⓛ puli tanta Ⓓ mardatuluru (*Gebirgsrücken*: mountain ridge)

patta itera *Bergabhang.* ◇ mountain slope. Ⓛ puli ngaiï Ⓓ marda kalikali

pattintaia, patta intaia *Gebirgstor, Gorge.* ◇ gorge. Ⓛ puli intaiï

patta alua *Felsblock.* ◇ rock boulder. Ⓛ puli alala, gatu pulka

patta iltara *weiße Felsen.* ◇ white cliffs. Ⓛ puli lilili, puli kaltjiti

patta ïmbatja *Felsenmalerei.* ◇ rock paintings. Ⓛ puli ninka

pattarinja *Bergbewohner, z.B. das graue Känguruh.* ◇ mountain dweller, e.g. grey kangaroo. Ⓛ pulingurara

pattalakala *Felsvorsprung.* ◇ rocky outcrop. Ⓛ pulimula, mulamula

patta tenta *die Steinplatte.* ◇ stone plate. Ⓛ puli walu Ⓓ mardapaltiri

patta lakara (luakara) *Felsvorsprung.* ◇ rocky outcrop. Ⓛ puli ulákiri

patta artjunba *mit Steinen übersät (Charl. W.)* ◇ covered with stones (Charlotte Waters). Ⓛ puli múrulmurula

pattamanina *Schlange, nicht giftig (spec.)* ◇ non-poisonous snake (species). Ⓛ pulingalulba, tatalpa

pattantjentja *ein kleiner, elsternartiger schwarz und weiß gefiederter Vogel der sein Nest aus Lehm an die Baumzweige klebt (mud-mag-pie, Gallina picata).* ◇ mud magpie (see Strehlow 1907: 28–29); *Gallina cyanoleuca* (Latz 1996). Ⓛ aputantjentji

patamapatilama *anhäufen (Schätze), vollfüllen (mit Getreide, etc.)* ◇ accumulate (treasures), fill (with wheat, etc.) Ⓛ patirangarañi

patta alkarimbala *Edelstein.* ◇ gem.

pattintola = pattintjentja *mud magpie, Gallina picata.* ◇ mud magpie; *Gallina cyanoleuca* (Latz 1996). Ⓛ aputantjentji

patanba *Wade.* ◇ calf. Ⓛ aputala Ⓓ kulapalku

páterama *zusammensickern (Wasser in Brunnen).* ◇ seep together (water in well). Ⓛ mámbaluriñi

patatoka *unfruchtbar, kinderlos.* ◇ infertile, childless. Ⓛ putapatti

aralkulama *sich zusammenziehen (Muskeln), steif werden.* ◇ contract (muscles), become stiff. Ⓛ pateratera

patinja toperama *Knie beugen, niederknien.* ◇ bend knees, kneel down. Ⓛ turburingañi

patinja itinjilama *die Beine an den Leib ziehen, zurückbiegen (Toten).* ◇ pull legs against body, bend backwards (the deceased). Ⓛ turbuturbuni

pinta [Northern dialect], **larrapinta** *salzig; Salzfluß.* ◇ salty; salt river, Finke River. Ⓓ kaldri?, ngarana

patua *Schößling, Reis.* ◇ shoot, sprig. Ⓛ aputa Ⓓ kurri

báulama *fortfliegen (Vögel), fortgehen (Menschen).* ◇ fly away (birds), go away (people). Ⓛ pajennañi

periljíkaljika *eine junge Schlange.* ◇ young snake. Ⓛ wimmalara

tjingangarálbai *geht fort von mir!* ◇ go away (from me)! Ⓛ ngaililunguru nerknenini

piltjililtjilelama *aus dem Ei schlüpfen.* ◇ hatch (out of an egg). Ⓛ tēpungañi

pinpirapinpira *der miner-Vogel (Myzantha flavigula), pin-pin-pin.* ◇ miner bird (*Myzantha flavigula* now *Manorina flavigula*) (Pizzey and Knight 2007). Ⓛ pinpiripinpiri

pitjima *kommen.* ◇ to come. Ⓛ ngalajennañi Ⓓ wokarana, kaparau: *komm*, kaparanau/kaparalau: *kommt.*

pitjalbuma *zurückkommen.* ◇ to return, to come back. Ⓛ ngalakulbañi

pitjilama *kamen (dorthin).* ◇ came (to that place). Ⓛ ngalajennañi

pitjintjima *ankommen, herkommen.* ◇ arrive, come or get here. Ⓛ ngalakalbakatiñi

pitjikalama *herniederkommen, heruntersteigen.* ◇ to descend, come down, climb down. Ⓛ okalekukatiñi

pitjalbutjikalama *wieder herabkommen.* ◇ to come down again. Ⓛ kulbakatira okalingañi

pitjipitjima *herkommen (duplik).* ◇ to come. Ⓛ ngalajenkanáñi

ponta *sehr kalt.* ◇ very cold. Ⓛ warri

pmopuntja, pmapuntja *Tiefe (Wasser?).* ◇ depth (of water?). Ⓛ muruntu

pulla *der Platz, wo Beschneidung stattfindet.* ◇ ceremony ground. Ⓛ kaltuka

pulurunga *das Junge (von Tieren).* ◇ offspring (of animals). Ⓛ apulurungu Ⓓ kaparu (*Junge Wild* [?])

punga *Haar (kurze), Wolle.* ◇ hair (short), wool. Ⓛ ïntu Ⓓ para, njurdu (*Tieren* = animals), wulpuru: *ungepflegtes Haar* = unkept hair.

pungapunga (*z.B.* **ala**) *behaarte (z.B. Nase), von Haaren gemacht.* ◇ hairy (e.g. nose), made of hair. Ⓛ intuïntu

punga ntalta *Schamhaare.* ◇ pubic hair. Ⓛ intu tnañi

pulalta nama *hineingelegt (z.B. ein Stück Holz in den Sägebock), hineingesteckt (Sprossen der Leiter), zusammengefügt (die rails in Yard).* ◇ insert (into each other), join together (e.g. rails of stockyard). Ⓛ niljiputurtninañi

purpa *viele (Büsche), zusammenstehend (Büsche).* ◇ many (bushes), stand of bushes. Ⓛ wonkuru

purpitatanga *viele dicht zusammen stehende Bäumchen.* ◇ big stand of small trees. Ⓛ wonkurabaúrala

purpma *Strauch, spec.* ◇ bush species. Ⓛ purpmu

purula *Heirantsklasse.* ◇ marriage class, subsection, skin name. Ⓛ Tapurula (♂), napurula (♀)

pokula *Federbusch (Hauptschmuck).* ◇ feather plume (headdress). Ⓛ pokulu

pokuta *Haarzopf, Gebirgsrücken.* ◇ hair plait, mountain ridge. Ⓛ pokuti

pútaba *unvorbereitet, unreinlich.* ◇ unprepared, unclean. Ⓛ uruputu

putabala lama *unvorbereitet darauf gehen.* ◇ set off unprepared. Ⓛ uruputunka jennañi

pula *die weiße Laus.* ◇ white louse. Ⓛ pulli

popankátnuma *den Boden stechen [unclear].* ◇ stab ground. Ⓛ popuarañi

puntutitja *Mann mit Federschuhen.* ◇ man with feather shoes. Ⓛ puntutitji

putaia [*oder* **luta**] *kleines graues Wallaby, so groß wie ein Kaninchen.* ◇ small grey wallaby, as big as a rabbit. Ⓛ tunku, meteki

puelama [Southern dialect] *blasen [unclear].* ◇ blow. Ⓛ puni

putalunga *Herz.* ◇ heart. Ⓛ kutuduru

putanba [Northern dialect] *Wade.* ◇ calf (fibula). Ⓛ aputala

pmala *Heiratsklasse.* ◇ marriage class, subsection, skin name. Ⓛ okari
pmalintjara *Heiratsklassen.* ◇ marriage classes, subsections, skin names. Ⓛ okarirawaritji
pintja [Northern dialect] *Quelle.* ◇ spring. Ⓛ apinti

R

rabatanama *(v. ura + tanama); versengen.* ◇ (from ura + tanama); singe, scorch.
raba, *z.B.* **mannaraba** *postp. ohne, ohne Brot.* ◇ (postposition) without, e.g. without bread. Ⓛ maṙala, miïmarala
rabiuma *(etwas) ausspeien, schieß. (aus d. Munde).* ◇ spit out (something), eject (out of mouth).
rabalanga [Northern dialect], **(rebilanga)** *weiße Vögel spec.* ◇ white bird species. Ⓛ erebilangi
rāga [Southern dialect] *Hand.* ◇ hand. Ⓛ măra
rabalelama *warnen, Stille gebieten.* ◇ warn, order silence. Ⓛ markuni
rabartjima; *z.B.* **lengala rabartjima** *brennen, z.B. die Sonne brennt.* ◇ to burn, e.g. the sun burns. Ⓛ ngarakambañi, tjintunku ngarakambañi Ⓓ ngurkumana; ditjieli ngurkumana
rubarka *geröstete ititja Same.* ◇ roasted (mulga) seed (Strehlow 1920: 25).
rabarknúrkna *glühende Kohlen.* ◇ glowing coals. Ⓛ waru turkuru
rabinja *eßbarer Same (spec.)* ◇ edible seed species. Ⓛ tnukura
rabiulama *hineingehen, sich verkriechen.* ◇ go into, hide. Ⓛ apurukatiñi
ragata [Southern dialect] *Mund.* ◇ mouth. Ⓛ ta, tamirka Ⓓ manna
raiakutakutérama *schnell atmen, röcheln.* ◇ to breath fast, to gasp (for air). Ⓛ ngálkutungálkuturingañi Ⓓ pudlapudlangana
raiankinja intita *stinkende Atem.* ◇ stinking breath. Ⓛ ngalaūna
raiankama *hauchen.* ◇ to breathe. Ⓛ ngalbmanañi Ⓓ ngararankama (*atmen* = breath), ngara ngankana
raiankinja *Hauch.* ◇ breath, whiff, waft. Ⓛ ngāla Ⓓ jaola
raiankinja *Hauch.* ◇ breath. Ⓛ tamura
raiarerama *sich schlagen, sich prügeln.* ◇ (have a) fight, beat (up). Ⓛ mararariñi
raiawungawunga *großer Häuptling, reichlich (geben).* ◇ great chief, ample (give). Ⓛ atanari Ⓓ muntapirna
raiawungawungala *reichlich (z.B. geben).* ◇ ample, generous, plenty (e.g. give). Ⓛ atanarinku Ⓓ muntapirna
(u)raiilakuraiïla *ungleich (z.B. austeilen).* ◇ unequal(ly) (e.g. distribute). Ⓛ ekuntarakekuntara
(u)raiïlakuraiïla ndama *ungleich austeilen (für den Einen ein großes Stück aussuchen, für den andern ein kleines Stück).* ◇ distribute unequally (e.g. a large piece for one and for the other a small piece). Ⓛ ekuntarakekuntara jungañi
raiura *Regel (monatlich).* ◇ period (monthly), menstruation. Ⓛ uraiuri
rakálakàla *darbend.* ◇ suffering, starving; stranded.
(a)rakala *begierig (nach etwas).* ◇ greedy (for something). Ⓛ taku
rakilama *begehren.* ◇ desire. Ⓛ takuriñi
rakalakalerama *darben.* ◇ suffer, starve; stranded.
rakama *an sich reißen, entreißen, rauben.* ◇ seize, snatch away, take by force, steal. Ⓛ waiañi, tulani
rákalaláma *mit Gewalt an sich reißen.* ◇ seize with force. Ⓛ tulalkatiñi
ralinama *Preis anbieten? Ziel vorstecken?* ◇ offer a prize?, set a goal?
ralininja *Preis, der vorgesteckt ist, das Ziel.* ◇ price, goal, finish.
rākitja *Ausgang; das Loch, aus dem die Eidechse aus ihrem Versteck hervorgeht.* ◇ exit; exit hole of lizard burrow. Ⓛ katati
rakantakanta *Strauch, dessen Früchte giftig sind.* ◇ shrub with poisonous fruit. Ⓛ irikantikanti
rakanmanmérama *spielen, sich tummeln (Vögel).* ◇ play (birds). Ⓛ ínkankárariñi

rakara *eine Art Taube, Rücken und Gesicht: rotbraun, Brust und Bauch: bläulich, Kehle und Hinterkopf: schwarz, weißen Vorderkopf und weiße Flecken an der Kehle. Etwas größer als Tauben, die sich gewöhnlich in porcupine grass aufhalten.* ◇ pigeon species, red-brown face and back, bluish belly, bigger than pigeon that usually lives in porcupine grass. Ⓛ marukuru

rakaranánama *rollen, dahinrollen (Radscheibe), im Weiterrollen versieg.* ◇ to roll, roll along (wheel, disk), run dry. Ⓛ lanmalanmaninañi

rakilama *nach Fleisch verlangen.* ◇ demand meat. Ⓛ takuriñi

rakaránama; rakaranánama *Kreise auf dem Wasser bilden; im Weiterrollen versiegen.* ◇ form circles on water surface; seep in, run (eventually) dry (Strehlow 1910b: 133). Ⓛ rarininañi

rakaratnatjinjima *Wellenkreis bildend aufsteigen.* ◇ emerge forming a circle of waves. Ⓛ rarininarakalbañi

kimbara *zuerst, z.B. er hat mich 'zuerst' geschlagen.* ◇ first, e.g. he hit me 'first'. Ⓛ warika

rákuanerínja *die boomerangs mit ovalen Linien.* ◇ boomerang with oval lines. Ⓛ palilkara

rákuanérama, rakuanerama *übereinanderschlagen (Füße), falten (Hände), zusammenwachsen, über etwas (hinweg) wachsen.* ◇ cross (feet), fold (hands), grow together, overgrow (something). Ⓛ terbirapungañi Ⓓ workamandraterina

rákuarákuanérama *ineinanderwachsen (Wurzeln), sich miteinanderverflechten.* ◇ grow into each other (roots), interlace. Ⓛ terbiraterbirapungañi

rákuanerinja *übereinanderhinwegwachsend (Wurzeln).* ◇ grow over each other (roots). Ⓛ palilkara

(u)rálama [Southern dialect] *einsinken (im Wasser, im Schlamm).* ◇ to sink in (water or mud). Ⓛ turitarbiñi Ⓓ punbina, kunakutina, kunakudina

(u)ralitjikalama *untersinken.* ◇ to sink. Ⓛ terbaraokalingañi

(u)rálilelama *versenken.* ◇ to sink (something). Ⓛ turirbini Ⓓ kunakudibana

(u)raljaperuma *untertauchen (im Wasser Vögel/Enten).* ◇ to dive (birds, ducks in water). Ⓛ karakukatiñi

ralbarankama *weinen, schreien (kleine Kinder).* ◇ to weep, to cry (small children). Ⓛ ngarbmanañi

ralbaruntjuma *fortwährend küssen.* ◇ to kiss continuously. Ⓛ nuntununtuni

(u)ralbuma *sich teilen (Wasser), vertrocknen, einziehen (Wasser), versiegen (Wasser).* ◇ to part (water), to dry up, to soak in (water), run dry. Ⓛ nērtnínañi

ralekerinja *Schlangenlinie.* ◇ snake line. Ⓛ nunkinunki

raljelba *bitter (Wort, Wasser).* ◇ bitter (words, water).

raljuka *Baum spec.* ◇ tree species. Ⓛ iljirauü

ralkama [Southern dialect] *gähnen, aufsperren (Mund).* ◇ yawn, open wide (mouth). Ⓛ talangarañi Ⓓ manna terkana

rálerarálera *gerade (Rücken) (ein Mann, Pferd).* ◇ straight (back of a man or a horse). Ⓛ aráleraráleri

ralkulama *zurückziehen (Füße), einziehen (Hände).* ◇ pull, draw back (feet or hands). Ⓛ kaputuriñi

raljaralja *sehr heiß, glühend heiß (Wasser, Stein, Mensch).* ◇ very hot, burning hot (water, stone, human). Ⓛ malkárkura

raljelberinja *Verbitterung.* ◇ bitterness.

raltaralta *kleine Fischart.* ◇ small fish species. Ⓛ araltaralta

raltaralta *Marienkäfer.* ◇ ladybird. Ⓛ araltaralta

raltutja *laut (Stimme), klar.* ◇ loud (voice), clear. Ⓛ pei̇altara, teïltara

raltutjaltutja *sehr laut.* ◇ very loud. Ⓛ pei̇altarapei̇altara, teïltarateiltara

réruarérama *sich einander sehen.* ◇ see one another.

rentjima *(herankommen) sehen.* ◇ see (approaching). Ⓛ ngalanangañi

răma *sehen.* ◇ see. Ⓛ nangañi Ⓓ najina (naiïna)

alknátera rama *mit eigenen Augen sehen.* ◇ see with one's own eyes. Ⓛ kurultu nangañi

alknéntala rama *zur Seite sehen.* ◇ look to the side. Ⓛ talbanku nangañi

alkniltala rama *schielen.* ◇ be cross-eyed. Ⓛ kuru niltunku nangañi

alknalaraka rama *übersehen.* ◇ overlook. Ⓛ ninkiltunkula nangañi

rentjalbuma *bei der Rückkehr sehen.* ◇ see on return. Ⓛ ngalanakulakulbañi

rinama, arinama [Northern dialect] *(liegen) sehen.* ◇ to see. Ⓛ manangañi

rélintátnama *vor sich liegen sehen.* ◇ to see it in front of oneself. Ⓛ manakukatiñi

ramaia *circa 2 Fuß lange, gelbe schwarzgemusterte Eidechse.* ◇ yellow and black patterned lizard (about 2 feet long); *Varanus gouldii.* Ⓛ panka, larkiti

ritjalama *[unclear].* ◇ see 'ritjilama' below. Ⓛ nangañi-jenkula

ramara *Eidechse (im Norden sich aufhaltend).* ◇ lizard (lives in the north). Ⓛ ramiri

(erá)malkura *gleich, gleich groß.* ◇ equal, same, the same size. Ⓛ (paluru)perina

ramalkurantemilama *(aus ramalkura-ntema (wieder) – ilama (machen)) eins so groß wie das andere machen.* ◇ make one as big as the other. Ⓛ paluruperinmanani

ramanerinja (era-manerinja) *festhaltend im Boden (Wurzeln).* ◇ hold tight to the ground (roots). Ⓛ ngalulba

ramaramintama *mit den Flügeln schlagen (Vögel).* ◇ beat wings (birds). Ⓛ kalbi pilarikula

rámaráma *(von era-ma-era-ma) gleichen, Nachkommen, Geschlecht.* ◇ alike, descendants, descent group; family. Ⓛ palurunganpalurungan, palurunganbapalurunganba

ramaramilama *gleich machen, ebenso machen.* ◇ make equal, make likewise. Ⓛ palurukapaluru wottañi

ramantitja *alle nacheinander.* ◇ all one after the other.

rambaltaia *zornig (sprechen).* ◇ angry (speak). Ⓛ wonkati

rambarknara *wütend, tobend.* ◇ furious, raging. Ⓛ ngaropitjipitji

(u)rámbarkama *(Feuer) scheinen [unclear].* ◇ (fire) shine. Ⓛ turakambañi

rambarambatnánama *wegreißen, wegschwemmen (reißende Flut das Ufer).* ◇ tear away, wash away (raging flood the banks). Ⓛ nerkanerkara bakani

rambalkama *erweitern.* ◇ enlarge, widen.

rámintja *Lagerplatz der unverheirateten Männer.* ◇ camp of single men. Ⓛ ambiri

rambeuma *verhöhnen, verspotten.* ◇ deride, mock. Ⓛ ninjipungañi

rámurilja [Eastern dialect] *Witwenschmuck.* ◇ widow's decoration.

rambintárama *schreien (im Kampf), Kampfgeschrei machen.* ◇ shout (in battle), yell battle cries. Ⓛ ngiljirā́tuni

randa, iranda [Northern dialect] *Busch mit breiten Blättern und stachlichten Stengeln, dessen kirschengroße, grüne Früchte (bitter) gegessen werden (Solanum ellipticum).* ◇ bush with broad leaves, prickly stems and cherry-sized green fruit (bitter) that are eaten (*Solanum ellipticum*). Ⓛ warandi, wanki

ranga *mal, dort.* ◇ once, there. Ⓛ kata Ⓓ pota

ninta ranga *ein mal.* ◇ one time. Ⓛ kutukata

ranguntérama *Hände aufhalten (um Gaben zu empfangen).* ◇ hold hands open (to receive gifts). Ⓛ marangurkuringañi

rangantanguma *treiben (der Wind das Schiff).* ◇ drive (wind the ship).

rangarangauma *nicht schlichten können (den Streit zwischen Kämpfenden), ohnmächtig zusehen.* ◇ not able to settle (a quarrel or a fight), look on powerless. Ⓛ ngambangambaninañi

rangataputa *Moskito (spec.)* ◇ mosquito species. Ⓛ kanalapatalba

rangiuma *fallen lassen (vor Müdigkeit), aus den Händen fallen.* ◇ drop (due to tiredness), fall out of hands. Ⓛ (mara) wirintalkañi

rangininja *Ziel, Preis, Ende.* ◇ goal, price, finish.
rangiltja; *z.B.* **tjata rangiltja itnima** *unvermögend, nicht halten könnend; z.B. der Speer entfällt ihm.* ◇ unable, cannot hold, e.g. drops spear. Ⓛ wirintalka; kata wirintalkañi
ranganama ◇ this time.
rangintarangala (ngama) *alle in Reihen (hintereinander) stehend (tragen).* ◇ standing in a row (behind each other) (carry). Ⓛ márangúrkungúrkunka (katini)
rangutnantama *vollbringen (Arbeit).* ◇ accomplish, finish (work).
raninja *Gerät, Sachen.* ◇ utensil, equipment, gear, things. Ⓛ julta Ⓓ poto
ránjunganjúnga [Southern dialect] *Wasser, das sich auf den Ebenen angesammelt hat, das die Känguruh trinken.* ◇ water that collects on the plains and is drunk by kangaroos. Ⓛ aranjúnganjúngu
eránka [Northern dialect] *Hund.* ◇ dog. Ⓛ papa
rankaia *conf.* **arankaia** *Fächerpalme.* ◇ fan palm. Ⓛ aranki
rankara *ihr.* ◇ you (2nd pl. nom.) Ⓛ nurangari Ⓓ jura
rankaratitja *ihr alle, ihr insgesammt.* ◇ you all, you all together. Ⓛ nurangárilta
rankuia *conf.* **arankuia** *schwarze, eßbare Früchte (wilde Kirschen).* ◇ black, edible fruit (wild cherries). Ⓛ kopata
rankurankua *verrückt, taub (nicht hören können), unsinnig.* ◇ crazy, deaf (cannot hear), senseless. Ⓛ ramarama, walwal Ⓓ jirijiri
rankurankuabaruburkula *taubstumm.* ◇ deaf and dumb.
rantalkinja nama (era-ntalkinja) *überlegen sein, besiegen.* ◇ be superior, defeat. Ⓛ palurukutu ninañi Ⓓ kalalu ngankana
nunantalkinja nama *wir besiegen.* ◇ we defeat. Ⓛ ngananakutulenku ninañi
erántatara [erantatara] *beide, gleich groß.* ◇ both, same size or hight. Ⓛ pulakutara
rantjarantja *hitzig (vor Zorn), wild aufgebracht (reden).* ◇ hot tempered (anger), enraged (speak). Ⓛ múlakuiamúlakuia
rantjikama *zum Streit herausfordern.* ◇ challenge to a fight. Ⓛ jerrpungañi
rantjikanakana *der Herausfordernde.* ◇ the challenger. Ⓛ jerrpunganmi
rantambala nama *übereinstimmen.* ◇ agree.
rantambala (era-ntambala) *übereinstimmend.* ◇ in agreement.
erápara *schräg (wie ein Dach), abschüssig (Ufer).* ◇ slanting (like a roof), steep (riverbank). Ⓛ tarutaru
(u)rápmara (ura-pmara) *abgebrannte Land.* ◇ burnt out land. Ⓛ nunma, naru
urápurápa *vom Feuer geschwärzt.* ◇ blackened by fire. Ⓛ wárutumúnmún
(u)ráparénama *(urapa-Ofen, rename-legen) in den Ofen werfen, einheizen.* ◇ put in the oven, heat. Ⓛ peurtunañi
rápanáma *einem den Weg verstellen.* ◇ hinder someone from proceeding. Ⓛ angángárañi
rapmarapma *Busch (spec.)* ◇ bush species. Ⓛ arumaruma
rapmárapmára *Gaumen.* ◇ palate. Ⓛ támatùla
rārinja *richtige Geschwister [unclear].* ◇ proper siblings. Ⓛ nakulapunguta
raragunama *alles hineinstecken, vergraben, eingraben.* ◇ put all of it in, bury. Ⓛ apuarairbini
rāra *sehr leicht.* ◇ very light. Ⓛ rambi
rarata *Vergeltung.* ◇ retaliation, retribution. Ⓛ batjirinka Ⓓ kalala
raratala tuma *strafen, rächen.* ◇ punish, avenge, revenge. Ⓛ batjirinka pungañi
raratankama *beschwichtigen, zum Frieden reden.* ◇ pacify, appease. Ⓛ batjiri wonkañi
rarambuma *sich röten (sich abschälen Rinde [unclear]).* ◇ redden (when bark peels off a gumtree). Ⓛ rarakambañi
raratilama *beschwichtigen.* ◇ appease, soothe. Ⓛ batjirénani
rarauarára (era-rauara) *Altersgenossen.* ◇ peers. Ⓛ tunguta Ⓓ kalumara

 For the modern spellings of these words, see the dictionaries and sources in reference list.

raroaïnalama *Getümmel machen.* ◇ cause turmoil or a commotion.
rarkua *Siebengestirn.* ◇ Pleiades. Ⓛ okuralji
rarkubarkuma *klappern (Speere), knirschen (Sägen).* ◇ to rattle (spears), to grind (saw). Ⓛ rurbmankanañi
rarkuma *klappern, dröhnen, knirschen.* ◇ to rattle, to roar, to crunch, to grind. Ⓛ roropungañi
rarpa, *z.B.* **erarpa** *postp. selbst; z.B. er selbst.* ◇ (postposition) self; e.g. he himself. Ⓛ rurpa, palururpa
ratinama *heruntersehen (auf ein Wild) um dasselbe zu speeren, aufs Korn nehmen.* ◇ to look down on (game) to spear it, take aim. Ⓛ walingañi
rāta [Northern dialect] *conf.* **ŕāta** *Schlange spec.* ◇ snake species. Ⓛ mantaramantara
rantanala indatnama *heraussteigen.* ◇ climb out. Ⓛ matulbakañi
ratitjinjima *heraufsteigen [unclear].* ◇ climb up. Ⓛ wirkarakalbañi
ratama *herausgehen, aufgehen, entspringen, auskriechen.* ◇ to go out, rise, emerge, crawl out; come out. Ⓛ bakañi Ⓓ dunkana
ratalela nama *herausführen.* ◇ to lead out. Ⓛ mawirkatiljini Ⓓ dunkalkana
ratintjima *herauskommen, aufgehen (Sonne).* ◇ to come out, rise (sun). Ⓛ wirkanañi Ⓓ dunkana tarana
ratintjilama *herauskommen, heraustreten, aufgehen (Stern).* ◇ to come out, to step out, to rise (star). Ⓛ ngalabakañi, ngalawirkanañi Ⓓ dunkana tarana
ratanama *hervorkommen.* ◇ to come out. Ⓛ mawirkani
ratankama *erheben (Wind).* ◇ to pick up (wind). Ⓛ múnmulukátini Ⓓ wilparina
ratapa *Ursprung der Menschen, Totem.* ◇ origin of humans, totem, dreaming being, mythical twins. In Carl Strehlow's work ratapa means child spirit, offspring, baby, child, conception dreaming, 'totem'. In T.G.H. Strehlow's work it means mythical children or Twins of Ntaria (Strehlow 1947: 118; 1971). Spencer and Gillen (1927: 623) use the word ratapa for a child to which a kuruna has given rise in the mother and for a baby immediately after birth. According to Carl Strehlow the word ratapa derives from the verb ratana meaning 'coming from, originating'. The ratapa, which he also calls 'Kinderkeime (child-seed)' (Strehlow 1908: 52) and 'Ursprung der Menschen (origin of human beings)' (Carl Strehlow's unpublished dictionary), were said to be invisible but fully developed children with reddish skin colour (Strehlow 1908: 52). The human soul begins its existence when a spirit child enters a pregnant woman giving the embryo a soul (Carl Strehlow 1908: 53–56; T.G.H. Strehlow 1971, 1978). Ⓛ aratapi
ratnilenja *Auszehrung, Schwindsucht.* ◇ consumption. Ⓛ kebulariñi
ratnangiwuma *hinunterfallen, hinunterstürzen, hineinpacken (den Toten in ein Loch), hineinstoßen, versinken (im Meer), hineinstoßen einen Stock in ein Loch.* ◇ fall down, put or pack (deceased into a grave), push in, sink (in the sea), push a stick into a hole. Ⓛ karalawonniñi Ⓓ kibana
ratnitjilama *hindurchgehen, sich hindurchzwängen.* ◇ go through, force or push through. Ⓛ tarungariñi talkala
rátoppa *Brust vor stehen, sehr gerade stehen.* ◇ stand very straight. Ⓛ nanártnanára
ratulélama *streifen (beim Werfen) [unclear].* ◇ to brush, to graze (with something, e.g. spear). Ⓛ pulmanañi
rátuntja *abgeschlagen, abgespalten (Steinmesser).* ◇ to knock off, to split off (stone knife). Ⓛ telpa
raua *frei, los, abgewickelt.* ◇ free, loose, unwound. Ⓛ altakalta
rauerama *los werden, sich abwickeln, sich zerstreuen, auffliegen, aufbrechen (Knospen), sich entrollen.* ◇ to get rid of, to unwind (reflexive), to disperse (reflexive), to fly up, to open (buds), to unroll (reflexive). Ⓛ altakaltariñi

rauilama *trs. hinstreuen, säen.* ◇ (transitive) scatter, sow. Ⓛ altakaltanañi Ⓓ teribana

raualelama *trs. hinstreuen, hinwerfen, auspacken (Sachen), säen.* ◇ (transitive) scatter, throw down, unpack (things), sow. Ⓛ altakaltanañi Ⓓ teriteribana

raueritnenkama *sehr laut sprechen (Mensch), sehr laut singen (Vögel).* ◇ speak very loud (people), sing very loud (birds). Ⓛ kultuúngutu wonkañi

raúerèlaláma *sich zerstreuen (Menschen).* ◇ disperse, scatter (people). Ⓛ altakaltarira jennañi

rauwiawia *große Häuptling.* ◇ big chief. Ⓛ inanari

rauntérama *pfeifen.* ◇ whistle. Ⓛ winpurangañi Ⓓ wilpina

raualélama *auswickeln (Federn).* ◇ unwrap (feathers). Ⓛ altakaltanañi

rebatarerama *einmal auf eine Seite, dann auf die andere Seite etwas herunterschießen (Habichte und Adler).* ◇ drop down alternating from one side to the other (hawks and eagles). Ⓛ tarutaruríngañi

rebba *große Mulde (von Gummiholz).* ◇ large bowl (made of gumtree wood). Ⓛ wirra Ⓓ ngampura pirna

rebilanga *großer, weißer Vogel.* ◇ large white bird. Ⓛ erebilangi

raunteranérana *der Pfeifer.* ◇ whistler.

arílla *dort.* ◇ there. Ⓛ nara

relabuma *umhersehen, nachsehen (einem).* ◇ look around, look after (someone). Ⓛ nakulajenkanañi

relakarelánkama *(fortwährend ansehend sprechen) lesen.* ◇ (constantly look at something while speaking) read. Ⓛ nákulakánakula wonkañi

relalabuma *sich besehen, beschauen.* ◇ look, examine (reflexive). Ⓛ nakulariñi

relareknuma *sich berufen (auf jemanden).* ◇ refer to (someone).

relinama *reichen (bis zu etwas).* ◇ to reach (to something).

rĕlama; rĕlai! *sich vorsehen, vor sich hingehend sehen, vorsichtig sein; sieh dich vor!* ◇ be careful, cautious; look out! Ⓛ palurunka nangañi; nauai! nangami

relbukinja *der Raub (den man dem Feinde abnimmt), die Beute.* ◇ loot (taken from enemies).

relara ngetjima *herbeiführen (vom Wind).* ◇ to bring (wind). Ⓛ wollakatini

ar̉ilaùma *zielen (nach einem Ziel).* ◇ to aim (at something). Ⓛ nakulatalkañi

releuma *ansehen (als etwas).* ◇ to regard, to consider (as something).

ar̉ilintáranàma *erblicken [unclear].* ◇ to see. Ⓛ makurbaraïnini

relbaritjima *leise sprechen.* ◇ to speak softly. Ⓛ talbatalbiriñi

relbma *glänzend (Stamm der ilbula), scheinend.* ◇ shiny (trunk of ilbula). Ⓛ tjilba

relbmarelbma *sehr glatt, glänzend.* ◇ very smooth, shiny. Ⓛ tjilbatjilba

relbmintalama *zeigen (Zähne), fletschen [unclear].* ◇ to show (teeth), bare teeth. Ⓛ ninjirani

relbakama *entreißen, mit Gewalt nehmen.* ◇ to snatch away, take with force. Ⓛ waiañi Ⓓ mamana

relbarelbakama *sich reißen um etwas, ringen miteinander (um etwas).* ◇ to scramble for something, to wrestle (something from someone). Ⓛ waíawaíani

relkatantuma *Leibschmerz haben.* ◇ to have stomach pain. Ⓛ nganurknarañi

relbuma [Southern dialect] *schmatzen.* ◇ to smack (lips), eat noisily. Ⓛ nuntalbmanañi

relbubélbuma [Southern dialect] *fortwährend schmatzen.* ◇ continuously smack. Ⓛ nuntalbmankániñi

rĕlea *dort.* ◇ there. Ⓛ naranka

reljinga [Southern dialect] *Kinnbacken.* ◇ jaw bone. Ⓛ arilingi, kadidi Ⓓ mannakira (*Kinnlade*)

reljatna *Lunge.* ◇ lung. Ⓛ tariljakiri Ⓓ buñga

relkuma *wegschicken, drängen (daß jemand gehen soll).* ◇ to send away, to urge (someone to go). Ⓛ uluni Ⓓ walpamalina (*einander drängen* = urge each other)

rella *Mensch.* ◇ human, person. Ⓛ matu Ⓓ kana
rella ngantja *die unterirdischen Menschen.* ◇ subterranean humans or people, i.e. people living inside the earth, rella (meaning 'person') ngantja (meaning 'the one hidden in the earth' or 'subterranean' (Strehlow 1907: 5). These hidden people are called today pmarakutata spirits. According to a creation narrative, a long time ago the people living inside the earth, the rella ngantja, did not know anything about fire, but one day a man from another place came who showed them how to make fire (Strehlow 1907: 31–32). Ⓛ matu nguanba
rella manerinja *die zusammen gewachsenen Menschen.* ◇ undeveloped people or beings, i.e. rella (people) manerinja (grown together); at the beginning of time the limbs of the rella manerinja were grown together (see Strehlow 1907: 2–3). Ⓛ matu ngalulba
rellaka nimba, rella intarinja *die aneinandergewachsenen Menschen.* ◇ grown together people (see Strehlow 1907: 3). Ⓛ matu mintirbmintira
reltaléa *Ente (art).* ◇ duck species. Ⓛ arelteleï
rellinja *böse Wesen in Gestalt von inkaia (Bandikut).* ◇ evil beings or bad spirits in bilby shape (Strehlow 1907: 12). Ⓛ tounita
relpa [Southern dialect] *scharf, spitz.* ◇ sharp, pointed. Ⓛ iri Ⓓ tjerkara, tiri
relpilama *schärfen.* ◇ sharpen. Ⓛ irini Ⓓ tjerkara ngankana, tiri wikana, dingana
relparenama (inka) *schnell gehen.* ◇ to walk fast. Ⓛ (tjinna) tunatunañi
remankura *breit (Stirn).* ◇ broad (forehead). Ⓛ ngala bilalku
rĕna *da, dort.* ◇ there. Ⓛ nara Ⓓ jerra
renama *trs. legen, hinlegen, bellen (Hunde).* ◇ (transitive) put, lay, lay down, bark (dogs). Ⓛ tunañi Ⓓ kurana
renalanama *sich setzen.* ◇ sit down. Ⓛ maninakatiñi
renalama *refl. sich setzen.* ◇ (reflexive) sit down. Ⓛ ninakatiñi Ⓓ ngamana ngarina
renalelama *trs. auffordern, sich zu setzen, begrüßen (den Ankömmling).* ◇ (transitive) invite, to sit down, welcome (someone who has just arrived). Ⓛ ninatunañi
renalalakalama *sich niederlegen.* ◇ lie down. Ⓛ ninakatira okulingañi
renalitjikalama *sich niedersetzen.* ◇ sit down. Ⓛ ninakatira okalingañi Ⓓ ngamana ngarina
renitjalbuma *niederlegen (bei seiner Rückkehr).* ◇ lie down (on his return). Ⓛ tunañikulbara
renalitjilama *sich niederlassen.* ◇ settle down, sit down. Ⓛ ninakatira talkañi
renalitjalbuma *sich niedersetzen.* ◇ sit down. Ⓛ ninakatirikulbañi
renitjálbanama *niedersetzen (nach der Rückkehr).* ◇ sit down (after return). Ⓛ tunañi jenkula
renamalkurantemilama [rena-malkura-ntama-ilama] *genau so setzen oder lernen, wie es gesetzt ist.* ◇ to learn exactly how it is (and was) laid down and transmitted. Ⓛ palununguanba kanani
reñkulindama *nach allen Seiten ausschauen.* ◇ look in all directions. Ⓛ minkiltunkula ngariñi
renarenalbuma *umstellen (Wild).* ◇ surround (game). Ⓛ tunkutunkula kulbañi
renopinama *hinlegen.* ◇ lay down, put down. Ⓛ tunkanañi
renapatupatalama *alle sich am Boden hinsetzen.* ◇ everybody sits down. Ⓛ ninaninakatiñi
renapalla *wenige.* ◇ few. Ⓛ narapili
renkinja nama *nötig sein.* ◇ be necessary.
renga *Podargus.* ◇ *Podargus strigoides*; tawny frogmouth. Ⓛ ngungi, nguri
renginja *Fisch (spec.)* ◇ fish species. Ⓛ erengini
rengaralama *den verkehrten Weg gehen (den rechten Weg verfehlen).* ◇ take the wrong path (miss the right one). Ⓛ kambanka jennañi

renkama *(c. gen.) bedürfen (etwas), willig sein?* ◇ (*c. gen.*) need or want (something).

renjamarenja ankama *(genau ansehend sprechen) lesen.* ◇ (speak looking closely, exactly, precisely) to read. Ⓛ nakulakanakula wonkañi

rentérama *schimpfen.* ◇ scold. Ⓛ tareriñi

rentekula *der ring-neck-parrot.* ◇ ringneck parrot. Ⓛ támatùla

rentua [Southern dialect] *vorbei, seitwärts.* ◇ past, aside, sideways. Ⓛ talba

rentuerama [Southern dialect] *vorbei sehen, seitwärts sehen.* ◇ look past, look to the side. Ⓛ talbaringañi Ⓓ mudla walkina

rentitjerama *heilen (Wunde), heil werden.* ◇ heal (wound).

renkuma *richten (sein Angesicht richten auf etwas, hinwenden sein Gesicht).* ◇ turn (face towards something).

réoa, reowa *Tür, Eingang.* ◇ door, entrance. Ⓛ árewa Ⓓ manna

rentunama *abschneiden.* ◇ to cut off.

rentúnana *Sichel (n).* ◇ sickle (n).

retjinama *zähmen, im Zaun halten.* ◇ tame, keep in check.

retjingana *Zaum (des Pferdes).* ◇ bridle (of horse).

rererérа *herabfließend (Saft).* ◇ flow down (juice, sap). Ⓛ iriríri *oder* iriri?

rēra *Wurzel.* ◇ root. Ⓛ ngaturu Ⓓ kapara

rérinjiwulàma *untertauchen, tauchen (Vögel).* ◇ dive (birds). Ⓛ iriritumbingarañi

(a)r̔erama [Southern dialect] *neidig sein, neiden.* ◇ be envious, envy. Ⓛ pekaringañi Ⓓ nguntjina

rĕrka *kahl, haarlos.* ◇ bald, hairless. Ⓛ talli

reruperuma *eingehen und wieder ausgehen, aus u. eingehen, hin und zurück schwimmen, hin und her wandern.* ◇ go in and out, swim back and forth, wander around. Ⓛ totulbakanáñi

reta [Southern dialect] *stecken, steif, fest.* ◇ stuck, stiff, solid. Ⓛ arata

ureta *graublau, blau.* ◇ greyish blue, blue. Ⓛ urutu

retjinga *Kamm (bei Vögeln, Gebirgen).* ◇ crest (of birds, mountains). Ⓛ aretjingi

retinga *in einer Linie stehend.* ◇ stand in one line. Ⓛ tabiri

retinja *hervortreten (Rückgrat).* ◇ protrude (backbone, spine). Ⓛ aretinji

retjingama *führen, leiten.* ◇ guide, lead. Ⓛ atakatiñi Ⓓ wapalkana

retinerinja [Southern dialect] *fest zusammenfaltend.* ◇ fold tightly together. Ⓛ ngamirapunguta

retna *Namen, Tj: Gesang.* ◇ name. Ⓛ ini Ⓓ tala, pinti

areknuma *beim Namen (z.B. rufen).* ◇ by name (e.g. call). Ⓛ amaialtiñi

retna laulinja *Geheim-Name.* ◇ secret name. Ⓛ ini jerkata

retjabaretja *Anführer.* ◇ leader.

rilera *friedlich, versöhnt, freundlich, zahm.* ◇ peaceful, reconciled, friendly, tame. Ⓛ ngultu Ⓓ murlali

retnangiuma *auswerfen (Anker).* ◇ to throw out (e.g. anchor).

rilararilara *sehr friedlich, sehr ruhig.* ◇ very friendly, very quiet. Ⓛ ngultungultu

rilarérama *sich versöhnen.* ◇ reconcile. Ⓛ ngulturingañi

rilarilama *versöhnen.* ◇ reconcile. Ⓛ ngultuni Ⓓ murlali ngankana

rinba *vor langer Zeit.* ◇ a long time ago. Ⓛ rauanta

rinbinba *Oberlippe, gerade Schnabel.* ◇ upper lip, straight beak. Ⓛ tabinbinba Ⓓ mannamimi

rinjiltjilinama *mit dem Schnabel erfassen (die Vögel die Fische), mit dem Speer speeren (die Fische).* ◇ grab with beak (birds, fish), to spear with a spear (fish). Ⓛ ariltjiltjinka manjiñi

rintjingankama *murmeln.* ◇ murmur.

rintjarela *Augenschein (nach d. A. richten).* ◇ appearance.

rinkarinka *Leiter, die Einschnitte im Baum, an denen man hinaufklettert (langer Stamm mit Ästen, [unclear]).* ◇ ladder, tree notches for climbing it, (long trunk with branches). Ⓛ bintalba

rentuarentua *abgewandt (Gesicht).* ◇ averted (face). Ⓛ talbatalba

rirtja *trocken (Erde).* ◇ dry (earth). Ⓛ paruru

rirtjerama *trocknen, trocken werden.* ◇ to dry, become dry. Ⓛ parururingañi

rirtjilama *trs. abtrocknen.* ◇ (transitive) dry, wipe (dry). Ⓛ parurunani

rinjiltja *Stoßzähne, Hauer, Schnabel.* ◇ tusks, beak.

aritjilkanama *trs. aufbrechen (Früchte), aufmachen (das Maul).* ◇ (transitive) break open (fruit), open (mouth). Ⓛ ninjirpungañi Ⓓ pakina

(a)ritjánkitjánka *aufrechtstehend.* ◇ stand straight. Ⓛ eriljánkiljánki

karitjankitjanka *aufrechstehendes Haar der Menschen und der Kakadu.* ◇ upright standing hair of humans and cockatoos. Ⓛ kata eriljankiljanka

(a)ritjima *flüstern.* ◇ to whisper. Ⓛ tailberiñi

ritjilama *auf der Wanderung erblicken.* ◇ to see on the go or move. Ⓛ nangañi jenkula

ritjinjankama *flüsternd reden.* ◇ talk in whispers. Ⓛ tailbiwonkañi

rōa *fließendes Wasser, Flut.* ◇ flowing water, flood. Ⓛ juru

roambenka *große Flut.* ◇ big flood. Ⓛ jurutjoariwari Ⓓ ngarimata, ngapa-kumari (*ohne Fische* = without fish)

roalama *fließen (Wasser).* ◇ flow (water). Ⓛ jurujenañi Ⓓ ngakana

roamba *wenig (essen), mäßig (im Essen).* ◇ (eat) little, moderate (eating). Ⓛ kuljangalka Ⓓ kalungeru

roambérama *wenig essen.* ◇ eat little. Ⓛ kujangariñi

roarka [Northern dialect] *abschüssig, senkrecht.* ◇ steep, vertical. Ⓛ kaljilkaljil

roarkitjunama *senkrecht abfallen (Felswand).* ◇ vertically fall away, sheer (rock wall). Ⓛ kaljilkaljil ngarañi

roarkna *schnell (gehen, kommen).* ◇ quick, fast (go, come). Ⓛ roatjibatjiba

roinja *Schlange (giftig).* ◇ snake (poisonous). Ⓛ arantji

rŏka *ruhig, schweigsam, still.* ◇ quiet, silent. Ⓛ rata Ⓓ dauru

rŏkerama *ruhig werden.* ◇ to become calm. Ⓛ rataringañi

rokilama *beruhigen.* ◇ to calm down. Ⓛ ratani

(a)rolta *sehr müde, steif (Glied), stumpf (Messer).* ◇ very tired, stiff (limb), blunt (knife). Ⓛ punuru

ronnaronnilama *umschließen, umzingeln.* ◇ to surround, encircle. Ⓛ tulutuluni

ronta *satt, gesättigt, anderen sein Essen überlassen, nähren.* ◇ full, leave food to others, feed, nourish. Ⓛ uranba

rontaronta *sehr satt.* ◇ very full. Ⓛ úranúranba

roralelama *ausschütten, verschütten, schütteln (Baum).* ◇ pour out, spill, shake (tree). Ⓛ pinpintitjingañi

ororínjaróralama *fortwährend auf und abgehen, fortwährend hin und zurück gehen.* ◇ continuously walk up and down. Ⓛ parajenkaniñi, ngurilingurilijenkaniñi

rowatowata *Mitleid.* ◇ empathy, pity.

rorkintjilama, rurkintjilama *geräuschvoll kommen.* ◇ come noisy. Ⓛ ngalararbmanañi

rowatowaterama *c. gen. mitleidig sein.* ◇ have pity.

rurkuma *Geräusch machen (beim Gehen), klappern, kratzen.* ◇ make sound (when walking), clatter, scratch. Ⓛ rarbmanañi

rorouma *langsam dahinschleichen (vor Schmerzen).* ◇ creep along slowly (due to pain). Ⓛ tarikatijennañi

roroulja *Horn, Hörner.* ◇ horn, horns. Ⓛ roroulji Ⓓ jurietja

rotnulama *reißende Schmerzen haben (als wenn alles entzwei ist).* ◇ have great pains (as if torn into pieces). Ⓛ bakurtjingañi

rotna *Kinn.* ◇ chin. Ⓛ nguttu Ⓓ ngankatjendra (Kinn), mannakira (Kinnlade)

rotnerama *drückende Schmerz empfinden.* ◇ feel pressing pain. Ⓛ murtalkañi

rottuma; *z.B.* **inka rottuma** *drücken, erdrücken, quetschen, treten; z.B. auf den Fuß treten.* ◇ press, crush, squeeze, tread; e.g. tread on foot. Ⓛ kantuñi puruñi; *z.B.* tjinna puruni

rŏtupa *gemalte Streifen um den Leib (Streifen).* ◇ stripes painted around body (stripes). Ⓛ taiïtopi

erŏtupma *Landzunge, Streifen Landes zu beiden Seiten vom Wasser umgeben.* ◇ spit of land. Ⓛ tunturu

roulta *lange Hals, lange Genick (der Vögel) auch Emu und Kamele.* ◇ long neck or nape (of birds as well as of emus and camels). Ⓛ kaua

roubouma *fortwährend zittern.* ◇ shake continuously. Ⓛ tjitítikanañi

ruálba [Southern dialect], **uralba** [Northern dialect] *Ranke mit eßbaren Früchten.* ◇ vine with edible fruit. Ⓛ uralbi

ruatnanga [Southern dialect], **uratnanga** [Northern dialect] *dorniger Bush mit großen rosenartigen weissen Blüten, Capparis nummularia.* ◇ thorny bush with large rose-like white blossoms (*Capparis nummularia*); wild passionfruit. Ⓛ uratningi

rubulubula *ohmächtig, betäubt (durch Stoß, Hagel), schwindlig, verwirrt.* ◇ unconscious, dizzy, confused, stunned (from a blow or hail). Ⓛ punkurupunkuru, kurerekurere

rubulubulerama *schwindlig werden, ohnmächtig werden, verrückt werden.* ◇ get dizzy, faint, go crazy. Ⓛ kurerekurereriñi

ruanbierama *sich ängstigen.* ◇ be afraid, be anxious, worry.

rubottabotterama *alle schnell zusammenlaufen, sich zusammenrotten.* ◇ run or band together quickly. Ⓛ kaputakaputariñi

ruburkula [Southern dialect] *stumm.* ◇ mute. Ⓛ wonkakuraru, tapatti

rubarabarerama *aufschwellen (Wunde, Teig aufgehen).* ◇ swell (wound), rise (dough). Ⓛ raráringañi Ⓓ nilji terkana

rubaruba *Wirbelwind.* ◇ whirlwind. Ⓛ unbalara Ⓓ watara wondru

rourkna *nachgiebig, sich sagen lassen.* ◇ compliant.

ruilkara *grauer Papagai mit gelblich-rötlichen Federn am Kopf und einzelnen weißen anderen an den Flügeln (cockatoo-parrot).* ◇ grey parrot with yellowish-reddish head feathers and single white wing feathers; cockatoo-parrot or cockatiel, *Nymphicus hollandicus* (Pizzey and Knight 2007). Ⓛ kurankuranba Ⓓ kurinjawiliwili

rakantakanta *der runde Erdwall, den die knuljaknulja an ihren Löchern machen.* ◇ earth mounds that insects make around their burrows. Ⓛ arakántakánta

rukatilama *versprechen (etwas zu geben).* ◇ promise (to give something). Ⓛ ngulakutankuni

ruka *zuerst.* ◇ first, to begin with. Ⓛ wara, wari

rúkulurúkulaláma *eine weite Strecke (gehen).* ◇ (walk) a long distance. Ⓛ rauankarauajennañi

rukantema *zuerst.* ◇ first (of all). Ⓛ warika

rukuntukunta *Aufenthaltsort der Teufel erintja, Ort der Qual, Hölle, wo es sehr heiß ist.* ◇ place of evil erintja beings, place of torment, hell, where it is very hot. Ⓛ pekalatjingani, paltipalti

rukuntukuntilama *quälen, fortwährend schlagen, foltern.* ◇ torment, constantly hit, torture. Ⓛ pekalatjingani

rukulba (ura & ulba) *die fleischige Brunst.* ◇ lust.

rukutaliuma *durch 4 angezündete Feuer die Nähe eines größern Lagerplatzes ankündigen.* ◇ indicate with four fires the position of a larger camp. Ⓛ warupunturingañi

rukunjerama *ehren.* ◇ to honour.

rukura *leicht.* ◇ light (opposite of 'heavy'). Ⓛ rambi, ranku Ⓓ ngaua

rukuntukuntilama *verderben.* ◇ to spoil, rot.

rukurkuatja *Ort der Qual, Aufenthaltort der Teufel, wo es sehr heiß ist.* ◇ place of torment, very hot place of devils. Ⓛ pekalatjingani

rukurkuátja *Fieber.* ◇ fever. Ⓛ nanarangañi

rukuta *('der Versteckte') beschnittener junger Mann, der sich verstecken muß (= laualinja); Männer so genannt.* ◇ ('the hidden one') young man, who must hide himself (laulinja = hidden); men who are hidden are called laulinja (Strehlow 1907: 41). Ⓛ tátata

rukútukúta *sehr große innere Hitze (im Leibe), Pein, Qual.* ◇ very big internal heat (in body), agony, torment. Ⓛ waralurkambañi

rukutukuta *Lohe (von Feuer), großer aufsteigender Rauch.* ◇ blaze (of fire), big rising smoke. Ⓛ pulkátakáta

rukutukutilama *quälen, peinigen.* ◇ torture, torment. Ⓛ kambalbmanañi

rukuntukunta *sehr zornig sein.* ◇ be very angry. Ⓛ wilawarutarani

rukuntukuntilama *sehr zornig machen, zum Zorn reizen.* ◇ make very angry, provoke.

rulaperinja *dichtes Gehölz.* ◇ dense wood, forest, thicket. Ⓛ nganapuru

rula *Holz.* ◇ wood, tree. Ⓛ ngana Ⓓ pita

rula munta *Dickicht.* ◇ thicket. Ⓛ ngana tata

rulbmerama *sich schließen (Wunde), verheilen (eine Wunde).* ◇ heal (wound). Ⓛ bottirbottirariñi Ⓓ parara

rulkalitnuma *rauschend hinunterfließen (Wasser), (über Felsplatten, in die Tanks).* ◇ flow down rushing (water), (over rock plates, into tanks). Ⓛ karalbmanañi

ruljarulja *Papagei spec. Kopf, Brust und Rücken grün, Flügel = grün, blau und schwarze Spitze, rotgelb am Vorderkopf und am Flügelgelenk, unten am Schwanz gelb, Schwanzfedern grün mit blauen Spitzen (Psephotus multicolour).* ◇ parrot species: green head, chest and back, green wings with blue and black tips, yellow-red forehead and wing joints, underside of tail yellow, green tail feathers with blue tips; mulga parrot (*Psephotus varius*). Ⓛ tjuriltjurilja

rulkumbara *sehr schnell (gehen).* ◇ (walk) very fast. Ⓛ manmiri

rultuma *sammeln, einsammeln.* ◇ collect, gather. Ⓛ pankiririñi Ⓓ kampana

rultanultana *Sammler.* ◇ gatherer. Ⓛ pankiririnma Ⓓ kampanietja.

rultulalbuma *wieder mitnehmen.* ◇ take away again. Ⓛ pánkirírirakúlbañi

ruljaperanama *fallen (unter die Mörder).* ◇ fall (amongst the murderers).

rulukurula *Nebel.* ◇ fog. Ⓛ urulukurulu Ⓓ tataru, kunmi

rumbara *Speer zum Töten von Menschen gebraucht.* ◇ spear used to kill people. Ⓛ intiwirki

rumerama *erscheinen, sich zeigen, zum Vorschein kommen.* ◇ appear, show oneself, turn up. Ⓛ wirkanañi Ⓓ wondraterina (*sich zeigen*: appear)

rumeritjalbuma *wiedererscheinen, wieder zum Vorschein kommen.* ◇ reappear, turn up again. Ⓛ kulbarawirkanañi

rumunta *kleiner (cr. 10 cm lang) schwarzer Fisch spec. im Schlamm sich aufhaltend.* ◇ small black fish species (circa 10 cm long) that lives in the mud. Ⓛ urumuntu

rumbinama *sich schließen (Wunde).* ◇ to close (wound). Ⓛ opuni

rumbinelanapanama *trs. schließen machen (durch Medizin).* ◇ (transitive) make close (heal with medicine). Ⓛ opuranani

runama *den Tod eines anderen verursachen (wenn sich z.B. der Mörder versteckt und der Bluträcher den Vater des Mörders dafür umbringt). Schuld sein (am Tode eines Andren).* ◇ cause someone else's death (e.g. when murderer hides and avenger kills father of murderer instead), be responsible for someone's death. Ⓛ urtnuni

rumarumerama *ein Geheimnis verraten (ein Geheimnis).* ◇ give away a secret. Ⓛ kurukururiñi

runbarunga *eine schlangenähnliche Eidechse (mit 2 Füßen).* ◇ snake-like lizard (with two feet); legless lizard; burrowing skink (*Lerista* species). Ⓛ urunburungu

runga *zugehörig.* ◇ belong. Ⓛ wolta

rungatja *mein, mir zugehörig.* ◇ my/mine, belonging to me. Ⓛ woltara

rungalura *mehrere.* ◇ several.
Ⓛ angutalitji

rúmbinama *tief atmen.* ◇ breath deeply.
Ⓛ goltunañi

rungara *auch.* ◇ also. Ⓛ puruna
Ⓓ bakana

rungarankama *zu Boden fließen (Saft).*
◇ flow to the ground (juice, sap).
Ⓛ tulbintiñi

rungarunga ankama *verbieten (etwas zu tun), ermahnen.* ◇ forbid (to do something), admonish. Ⓛ angamēnmēn wonkañi

rungultilama *Zauberei treiben, Giftmischerei treiben.* ◇ engage in witchcraft.

rungulta [runkulta] [Southern dialect] *Gift, Zaubergift* ◇ poison, magic-poison.
Ⓛ irati

rungúltjangùla *kühler Wind, Säuseln.*
◇ cool wind, rustle. Ⓛ warrinkuru
Ⓓ katakatana

runguntala ngama *mit beiden Händen umfaßt tragen (z.B. Beere und Früchte und die tnatantja).* ◇ carry with both hands clasped around (e.g. berries, fruit, ceremonial pole). Ⓛ marangurkunka katini

rungurkungurka *vorschichtig (mit beiden Händen etwas tragen).* ◇ carefully (carry something in both hands). Ⓛ katatjititjiti
Ⓓ dentjudentjumana

rungurkungurkala ngama
Ⓛ katatjititjitinku katini

rungúrpa *die Putenhenne.* ◇ turkey hen.
Ⓛ nganuti jakukata

runka *geübt, geschickt, gewohnt.*
◇ practised, skilful, used to. Ⓛ ninti
Ⓓ milkila

runkandama, runkundama?
unterrichten, üben (trs.) ◇ to instruct, to practise (transitive). Ⓛ nintini

runkerama *erlernen, sich üben, verbrauchen.* ◇ to learn, to practise, to use up. Ⓛ nintiringañi

runkapata *die Gewohnheit.* ◇ habit.

runtunerela *sich schlängelnd.* ◇ wriggle.
Ⓛ karbikarbira

rungultilinja *Zauberei, Giftmischerei.*
◇ magic, witchcraft. Ⓛ jerati

rontia *Feuershitze (rontia).* ◇ heat of fire.
Ⓛ ngarakambanmi

runtalkniwuma *abladen (Güter), verschenken, austeilen (Gaben).* ◇ unload (goods), give away, distribute (gifts).
Ⓛ utulutúnañi, utuluwónniñi

runuraïrbuma *durchdringen (Sauerteig).*
◇ penetrate (sourdough). Ⓛ kŭru wókkariïni Ⓓ pulkurutjerina

runtjama *küssen.* ◇ to kiss. Ⓛ nunjuni, nuntuni Ⓓ tapamalina

runtunerama *schlängelnd weiter wachsen (Wurzeln), nach verschiedenen Seiten laufend (Wurzeln).* ◇ keep growing winding (roots), grow in different directions (roots). Ⓛ karbikarbini, karbirarbiriñi

rupia *abgebrannt, mit abgesengtem Haar.*
◇ burnt down, with singed hair (Strehlow 1920: 33). Ⓛ naru

rupiïlama *Haar absengen.* ◇ singe hair off. Ⓛ nunmani, naruni

rurba, *z.B.* **jelka rurba** *großes (Korn), z.B. große jelka-Zwiebel, dick (Leib), große Tropfen, große Tränen.* ◇ big, fat, e.g. big jelka-bulb, fat body, big drop, large tear.
Ⓛ palpa

rurbmarura *faul, verdorben (Frucht).*
◇ rotten (fruit).

rurbmunka *ganz taub, verwirrt.*
◇ completely numb, confused. Ⓛ wala
Ⓓ talpakuru

rurkuma *Geräusch machen (beim Gehen), klappern, kratzen, Geräusch machen mit den Füßen.* ◇ make noise (walking), clatter, scratch, rattle, rustle.
Ⓛ tarulbmanañi, rarbmanañi

rurkuburkuma *Dupplikation d.v. poltern (plätschern).* ◇ duplication: clatter, lapping. Ⓛ rarbmankánani

rurkintjilama *geräuschvoll kommen.*
◇ come noisily. Ⓛ ngalararbmanañi

rurra *Raum, Abteilung, Löcher der ramaia Eidechse.* ◇ space, division, ramaia lizard holes, shelf-like spaces in ground where honeyants are lodged. Ⓛ ururru

Rutapuruta *sagenhafte Weiber.* ◇ mythical women, wives of arinjambóninja men. According to a narrative, classified as a fairytale by Strehlow (1907: 104), many arinjambóninja men and their rutapuruta wives lived in the north-east of Western Aranda territory. Ⓛ urutupurutu

rutja *große Mulde.* ◇ large bowl, dish. Ⓛ tartu, tātu

rurbmanknilama *rauschen (im Winde).* ◇ rustle (in the wind). Ⓛ rirbmipungañi

rutjarutja *sehr große Mulde, Kasten.* ◇ very large bowl, box. Ⓛ tartutartu, tatutatu

ruputupunga *sehr heiß (vom Feuer) z.B. Fleisch.* ◇ very hot from fire, e.g. meat. Ⓛ waru-lunkulunku

rutjibma *Berg Sonder, so genannt, weil auf diesem Berge vor Zeiten große Mulden (rutja) gestanden sind, die der kulaia Altjira gemacht hat (cr. 4496 Füße).* ◇ Mount Sonder named after rutja (meaning bowls) that were made by kulaia altjira (the rainbow serpent dreaming being) and stood on top of the mountain a long time ago. Ⓛ urutjíbmina

rurkuma *klappern, poltern, knarren, plätschern (Regen), das mit den Füßen hervorgebrachte Geräusch, knirschen, klappernd herabfallen (Stein).* ◇ clatter, splash, noise made by feet. Ⓛ rurbmanañi, rarbmanañi

runkunja *das Klappern der Mühle (n).* ◇ noise made by a mill.

ŕākua *sehr weich (die Larven vor der Verwandlung).* ◇ very soft (grubs before transformation). Ⓛ auka

ŕada *bald.* ◇ soon. Ⓛ ngulaku

ŕadalama *aufbewahren, aufheben (um es später zu verteilen).* ◇ keep, store (to distribute later). Ⓛ ngulaku ngariñi

ŕaiankinjaŕaiakinja *keuchend.* ◇ panting. Ⓛ ngālkulangālkula

ŕakua *roter Ocker.* ◇ red ochre. Ⓛ mokuna, mokurkuru

ŕālpara *unterirdische Höhle.* ◇ subterranean cave. Ⓛ ŕalpiri

ŕarka [Eastern dialect] *Sonne.* ◇ sun (Strehlow 1907: 16). Ⓛ tjintu Ⓓ jiraua

ŕăta *Platz zum Reinigen des jelka, Tenne.* ◇ place to clean the jelka, threshing floor. Ⓛ āta

ŕatamba *niedrig, kurz.* ◇ low, short. Ⓛ tatapiti

ŕatatamba *demütig.* ◇ humble. Ⓛ tatapiti

ŕatarata *kleiner Busch auf Bergen wachsend.* ◇ small bush that grows on mountains. Ⓛ talkutalku Ⓓ mulpa

ŕataŕata, ratarata *Strauch mit kleinen silbergrünen Blättern, sowie weisse Raupe auf ratarata Strauch.* ◇ bush with little silver-grey leaves; this term is also used for the white caterpillars that live on this bush. Ⓛ talkutalku

ŕātarāta *Vogel (spoonbill).* ◇ bird (spoonbill). Ⓛ talkutalku (spoon-bill)

ŕāta; tjaia ŕata *kurz (sprechen); cr ½ englische Meile.* ◇ short (talk); circa ½ an English mile. Ⓛ kutuwara

ŕaterama *kurz werden, einziehen [unclear].* ◇ become short, draw in. Ⓛ tatariñi

ŕāta *Schlange spec. cr. 3 Fuß lang, rötlich braun mit gelben Ringen, giftig.* ◇ snake species circa 3 feet long, reddish brown with yellow circles, poisonous. Ⓛ mantaramantara

ŕāta *conf.* **inkaia** *rabbit-bandicoot.* ◇ rabbit bandicoot, bilby. Ⓛ talku

ŕātajibalélana = inkaia jibalelama *d.h. die Bandikuts verkriechen sich in ihre Löcher, die Zeit vor Tagesanbruch, cr. 3 Uhr nachts.* ◇ when bandicoots crawl into their holes before daybreak at about 3am. Ⓛ talku nguntiljinami

ŕatambilama *verkürzen.* ◇ shorten. Ⓛ tatani

ŕātara, rátara *Westwind.* ◇ west wind. Ⓛ turkara

ŕatjileuma *sich rüsten (um die Feinde zu schlagen).* ◇ prepare, arm oneself (to defeat the enemy). Ⓛ untunkátuni

ŕātjara *der gerade Weg.* ◇ straight path. Ⓛ ŕātjiri

ŕātjinaŕátjinalama *den anus schnell von einer Seite zur andern bewegt gehen.* ◇ walk moving bottom quickly from one side to the other. Ⓛ nununtunununtu jennani Ⓓ tiltjangura

ŕatjua *Kniekehle.* ◇ back of knee. Ⓛ bilkungadi

ṙatérama *sich einziehen, sich kurz machen, sich zusammen ziehen.* ◇ shorten, contract (reflexive). Ⓛ tatariñi, tataringañi

ṙatīlama *übrig bleiben.* ◇ left over. Ⓓ kinkalju, mita jeljujelju

ṙeaṙea *weich, Fontanellen, Schläfe, sumpfig.* ◇ soft, fontanelle, temple, swampy. Ⓛ ngālngāl Ⓓ pilpa, ngalki (*Schläfe*: temple)

ṙatarka *schlangenartiger Wurm.* ◇ snake-like worm. Ⓛ wonnatjirki

ṙāltja *Zauberdoktor.* ◇ witch doctor. Ⓛ ngankari

ṙeberama *zusammenfließen, zusammenziehen (Wolken).* ◇ flow together, draw or come together (clouds). Ⓛ kutuluriñi

ṙedilja *wütend.* ◇ furious. Ⓛ pekati, pekala

ṙelinjataranama *(abgeleitet von rama) erblicken (einen Ankommenden).* ◇ to see (someone arriving).

ṙelkama [Northern dialect] *Tag werden, Morgen grauen.* ◇ dawn. Ⓛ rakatiñi

  ṙelkinja [Northern dialect] *Tagesanbruch.* ◇ daybreak. Ⓛ jultaringañi

ṙēlara *Horizont (vor sich erblicken).* ◇ (see) horizon (Strehlow 1910b: 39). Ⓛ ujuru

ṙembantama *fortwährend schlechtes tun, schlechte Arbeit leisten.* ◇ continuously do bad, perform bad work. Ⓛ katurtúnañi

ṙena *Eidechse (Varanus gilleni).* ◇ lizard (*Varanus gilleni*). Ⓛ inari

ṙenba [Southern dialect] *vor langer Zeit.* ◇ a long time ago. Ⓛ raua

ṙēna *störrisch, widerspenstig, gefühllos.* ◇ stubborn, obstinate, without feelings. Ⓛ ilbintji

ṙenina *Schlange cr. 4 Fuß lang, nicht giftig.* ◇ snake circa 4 feet long, not poisonous; woma, sandhill carpet snake. Ⓛ kunnea

ṙérama [Southern dialect] *(von aṙérama) neiden.* ◇ to envy. Ⓛ pekaringañi

ṙéunja *Luft, Windzug.* ◇ draft (wind). Ⓛ nguru Ⓓ ngarana

ṙeuntama *sich üben.* ◇ to practice.

ṙirka *Sandhügel.* ◇ sandhill. Ⓛ tali Ⓓ dako

  ṙirkamulka *Spitze des Sandhügels.* ◇ top of sandhill. Ⓛ talimanta

  ṙirkalurka *die roten Sandhügel.* ◇ red sandhills. Ⓛ taliïtina

ṙirtankama *laut den Boden stampfen mit seinen Füßen.* ◇ stamp ground loudly with feet. Ⓛ karalárañi

relara ngetjima Ⓛ atakatini

T

Ta [ăta] *ich, verbunden mit verb transitiem.* ◇ I, connected with transitive verb. Ⓛ ngaiulu Ⓓ ngato

tā *Frageartikel: 'was soll ich'?* ◇ question particle: 'what shall I (do)?'. Ⓛ atū?

tabala *ich (verstärkt).* ◇ I (emphasised). Ⓛ ngaiuluka

tabana *ich (verstärkt).* ◇ I (emphasised). Ⓛ ngaiulutu

tāba; matja taba *verloschen; z.B. verloschene Feuer, heiße Asche.* ◇ spent, e.g. spent fire, hot ash. Ⓛ ēba, waru-eba

tabataba *finster.* ◇ dark. Ⓛ mungaparapara

tabilja *Mahlstein.* ◇ grinding stone. Ⓛ tjiwa (Mahlstein)

tabitja *das eine Bein flach über das andere Bein legend.* ◇ put one leg flat on top of the other. Ⓛ turbu

tabitja [Eastern dialect] *pig-toed Bandikut.* ◇ pig-toed bandicoot. Ⓛ takana

taia *Mond.* ◇ moon (Strehlow 1907: 17–18). Ⓛ pira, kinara (W) Ⓓ pira, kota

  taia borkerama *der Mond nimmt ab.* ◇ the moon is waning. Ⓛ pira patanariñi, pira burkaringañi

  taia knarerama *der Mond nimmt zu.* ◇ the moon is waxing. Ⓛ pira punturingañi Ⓓ pira parina, pira kodana (*zunehmen*)

  taia lorka *abnehmender Mond, Mondsichel.* ◇ waning moon, sickle moon. Ⓛ pira alurka

 For the modern spellings of these words, see the dictionaries and sources in reference list.

taia lelta *oder* **leba** *zunehmender Mond.* ◇ waxing moon. Ⓛ pira tankili Ⓓ pira worra

taia arkapala, taia tnata knara *Vollmond.* ◇ full moon. Ⓛ pira arkápala, pira wilapuntu Ⓓ pira parina

taia borka *müde Mond.* ◇ tired moon. Ⓛ pira patanba

taiandama *leihen.* ◇ lend.

taiataia *runde Schneckenhaus.* ◇ round snail shell; moon grub. Ⓛ pirapira

tada, jinga tāda *postp. sogleich, folgend.* ◇ (postposition) following. Ⓛ karu, ngaiulu jennano karu

taiapitaia ilkama *bau, bau, bau rufen (um böse Einflüsse fernzuhalten).* ◇ call out 'bau, bau, bau' (to keep away evil influences). Ⓛ meratura merañi Ⓓ bau, bau, bau

taiaúma *leihen.* ◇ lend.

tailbilèlama *stoßen (Fuß an etwas), stolpern.* ◇ knock (foot against something), stumble. Ⓛ tarbikurañi Ⓓ dankaterina, dakaterina.

taia ilata *Neumond.* ◇ new moon.

taia ngumunta *Neumond.* ◇ new moon.

tāka *sehr groß (Holzblock, Baumstamm).* ◇ very big (block of wood, tree trunk). Ⓛ limalima, lunku

takaba *für kurze Zeit.* ◇ for a short time.

tăka; ekurataka; nunataka? *postp. verbunden mit Gen.: nötig sein; z.B. er hat etwas nötig; verbunden mit Nom: sollen, auch, mit: Was sollen wir tun?* ◇ (postposition) associated with genitive case: it is necessary, be in need of, e.g. he is in need (of something); associated with nominative case: shall, also, with: what shall we do? Ⓛ marri; palumbamarri; ngananamarri?

tjatatăka *mit einem Speer.* ◇ with a spear. Ⓛ katjimarri

tākama *ein Loch in einen hohlen Baum hauen (mit dem Beil).* ◇ chop a hole in a hollow tree (with an axe), smash, break. Ⓛ alani

tākalama *(refl.) zerbrechen, in Stücke zerbrechen (wenn ein Baum umfällt und zersplittert).* ◇ (reflexive) break, break into pieces (when a tree falls over and breaks into pieces). Ⓛ kirbmuntukatiñi

tăkabuma *zurückziehen (z.B. den Fuß).* ◇ pull back (e.g. foot). Ⓛ antangarani

takalama *zerfallen (Haus), einfallen (z.B. Haus) und Dach in Stücke.* ◇ fall apart (building), collapse (e.g. house and roof). Ⓛ kirbmuntukatiñi Ⓓ tampurina

tākalama *sich schnell bücken, sich ducken.* ◇ duck quickly. Ⓛ aparukatini, pelukatiñi Ⓓ puruna

tākilélama *umwerfen, einreißen (z.B. Wind).* ◇ push over, overturn, tear down (e.g. wind). Ⓛ peluntanáñi Ⓓ tampuribana

tăkalélama *antreiben (z. Arbeiten).* ◇ drive (to work). Ⓛ ngalanggalani

tākinjilama *umwerfen (z.B. der Wind).* ◇ push over (e.g. wind). Ⓛ ngalapeluntanáni Ⓓ tampuribana

tākalalakalama *sich ducken.* ◇ to duck (reflexive). Ⓛ lebulukatiñi

tākara *Wurzel.* ◇ root. Ⓛ ngaturu Ⓓ kapara

tákarantùnga *sehr groß, ungeheuer, riesig.* ◇ very big, huge, gigantic. Ⓛ pintalba

tăkerama *schnell sein (im Kommen), eifrig sein (bei der Arbeit), unablässig (schlagen).* ◇ quick (to come), be eager (at work), unremitting (beat). Ⓛ ngalangalariñi

tākiuma *ausbreiten (Wäsche zum Trocknen), breiten (Fleisch über Feuer).* ◇ spread out (to dry washing), spread (meat over fire). Ⓛ tjitjaku tunañi

takiwúnama *aufhängen (Wäsche zum Trocknen).* ◇ hang up (washing to dry). Ⓛ tjitjaku tunkula bakani Ⓓ witjibana, katibana

takinbuma *erben.* ◇ inherit. Ⓛ marakunani Ⓓ maratunka ngamalkana

takinbuninbúna *Erbe.* ◇ heir. Ⓛ marakunanmi

takintjara *Eidechse (spec.)* ◇ lizard species. Ⓛ bilanba

takitja *auf etwas gebreitete Stecken, Stuhl, Tisch.* ◇ spread over something (stick, chair, table), lay down. Ⓛ atakitji

takitjinbanba *große rote Ameise (bull-dog–ant).* ◇ large red ant (bull ant). Ⓛ kaltuka

tākua *die aus Laub hergestellte Umzäunung, Laubhütte.* ◇ enclosure or hut made of branches. Ⓛ unta

takula *weiße Muscheln, die von Norden eingehandelt.* ◇ white shells traded from the north. Ⓛ takulu Ⓓ kuri

takurindama *sich auf etwas stützen, auf etwas lehnen.* ◇ lean on something. Ⓛ njukupiti ngariñi

takutja *mein Onkel (Mutter's Bruder).* ◇ my uncle (mother's brother). Ⓛ kamuru

tálabànga *die Augen fest geschlossen (im Schlaf).* ◇ eyes closed tightly (while sleeping). Ⓛ kuru ngalulba

tālaka *lang.* ◇ long. Ⓛ raua

etata talaka *langes Leben.* ◇ long life. Ⓛ kana raua

talakaúma *lange zuhören.* ◇ listen for a long time. Ⓛ rauakuliñi

talakirkuma *lange festhalten, umfassen, umspannen.* ◇ hold tight, embrace, grasp for a long time. Ⓛ rauanku witiñi

talambata *sehr lange, fortwährend.* ◇ very long, constantly. Ⓛ rauakaiïkaiï

talambata ankama *fortwährend sprechen.* ◇ talk continuously. Ⓛ rauakaiïkaiï wonkañi

(i)talalanama *etwas bedecken, über etwas breiten.* ◇ cover something, spread over something. Ⓛ walturanañi

talama *ausgießen, ausschütten.* ◇ pour out, spill. Ⓛ tutiñi Ⓓ nangana

talalama *herabfließen (Wasser, Blut).* ◇ flow down (water, blood). Ⓛ tutiránañi Ⓓ nangaterina

talbatákalinja *der zerbröckelte (Felsen).* ◇ crumbled (rock). Ⓛ pilupilukatinta

talbatébama *hineinstecken (in den Boden oder ins Wasser).* ◇ stick (in the ground or into the water). Ⓛ rurarurarigañi

talba *fortwährend, wiederholt.* ◇ continuously, repeatedly.

(i)talbatama *ausbreiten, niederlegen, der Länge nach auf etwas legen (trs.)* ◇ spread out, lay down, lay lengthwise on something (transitive). Ⓛ mámamámani

talbatánama *strecken, gerade biegen (Speer).* ◇ to stretch, to straighten (spear). Ⓛ ngaritunañi

talbatakálama *einsinken (in tiefen Sand).* ◇ to sink (e.g. in deep sand). Ⓛ pilupilukatini

talbiulama *vor Zorn den Staub in die Luft werfen.* ◇ in anger throw dust into the air. Ⓛ tunumúlalariñi

talja *ruhig, besänftigt, leise (singen).* ◇ calmingly, soothingly, softly (sing). Ⓛ talu

taljerama *ruhig werden, sich legen (Zorn).* ◇ to become calm, to calm down, subside (anger). Ⓛ taluringañi

taljilama *beschwichtigen, besänftigen.* ◇ appease, calm. Ⓛ taluni Ⓓ wadlimana

taljilinilina *Friedensstifter.* ◇ peacemaker. Ⓛ talunmi Ⓓ wadlietja

talbatankama *schnell auffliegen (ein Vogel).* ◇ fly up quickly (a bird). Ⓛ titjurtitjura ninara jennani

talkua *Strich, Linie (über den Augen gemalt).* ◇ line (painted above eyes). Ⓛ kattakutara

tulkartja *roter Vogel, Art Wachtel [?].* ◇ red bird species. Ⓛ murukarinji

talpatalpa *kleine Muscheln, längliches Schneckenhaus.* ◇ small shells, longish snail shells. Ⓛ pirapira

talkutanama *den Speer auf das Genick (der in einer Reihe steht) legen.* ◇ lay spear on the back of neck (on the one who is standing in the row). Ⓛ katakutara tunañi

talbatantama *picken nach jemanden (Vögel nach Schlangen).* ◇ peck someone (birds snakes). Ⓛ wokkawokkañi

talpa [Southern dialect] *Mond.* ◇ moon. Ⓛ pira

taltja *unreif, grün, weich, frisch.* ◇ unripe, green, soft, fresh. Ⓛ tula Ⓓ waltowalto, tjanka

taltjilama *biegen.* ◇ bend. Ⓛ tulani
alkna tiltjatiltja *große (Augen) = (Eule).* ◇ big eye (= owl). Ⓛ kuru pintiri
taltjagula *Mulgaäpfel.* ◇ mulga apples. Ⓛ takatura, tarulki
taljiuma *(ins Wasser) springen.* ◇ jump (into water). Ⓛ tapulukatiñi, tulukatiñi
taljiunama *ins Wasser springen.* ◇ jump into the water. Ⓛ matululukatiñi
talua *Ende (z.B. der Arbeit, des Lebens).* ◇ end (e.g. of work, of life). Ⓛ talumba Ⓓ dia
tālerama *intrs. aufhören, fertig werden, ein Ende nehmen.* ◇ (intransitive) cease, end. Ⓛ taluriñi Ⓓ mudana
taluilama *trs. beendigen.* ◇ (transitive) (bring to an end) finish. Ⓛ taluni
talutaliïbuma *schruppen (den Boden), scharren [?].* ◇ scrub (floor), scrape. Ⓛ turbi, turbipungañi
tăma *abfließen.* ◇ drain, flow off. Ⓛ tāni, ngurka tāni
tămma *knallen (Peitsche).* ◇ crack (whip). Ⓛ tāni
tăma *reiben (auf Steinen), zerreiben, mahlen.* ◇ grind, rub (on stones). Ⓛ runkani
tánkalánkala lama *auffliegen (viele Vögel 2?).* ◇ fly up (many birds). Ⓛ pārbakarajennañi
tāmana *eßbare Pflanze spec.* ◇ edible plant species. Ⓛ utamini
taluwia *endlos, eine sehr lange Zeit.* ◇ endless, a very long time.
tamalka *die leeren eriltja Hülsen.* ◇ empty eriltja pods. Ⓛ atamalka
tamba *lose, beweglich, watschlig (Enten), schnell, fleißig.* ◇ loose, flexible, waddle (ducks), quick, industrious. Ⓛ ataki atamba (?)
tamberama *anbieten (zum Verkauf), los werden, feilbieten (Sache).* ◇ offer (for sale), get rid of. Ⓛ atambariñi
tanalama *sich aufrichten (aus liegender Stellung).* ◇ stand up (from a lying position).
tanalbanama *sich ausstrecken (Regenbogen).* ◇ stretch (rainbow). Ⓛ ngaritúnkula patani
tăna *dort, da, jener.* ◇ there, that one. Ⓛ nara Ⓓ naka, jera
tanauna *dorthin.* ◇ there, to that place. Ⓛ narakutu Ⓓ jerana
tananga *von dort.* ◇ from there. Ⓛ naranguru Ⓓ nakandru, jerandru
tanama *gerade biegen (Speer), glätten (Speer), niederdrücken (Kopf in die verschränkten Arme), durch die Nase stecken (den Nasenknochen).* ◇ to straighten (spear), to smooth (spear), to press (head in folded arms), to insert (nose-bone). Ⓛ ngaritunañi Ⓓ ngutana?
tanalama, tanalanama *sich strecken, sich dehnen (nach dem Schlaf), der Länge nach hinlegen, sich ausbreiten [unclear].* ◇ to stretch (after sleep), to spread. Ⓛ watuni, mawaturabakañi Ⓓ ngurakatina
tanalarulanama *sich ausbreitend vorgehen [unclear], in einer geschlossenen Linie vorgehen.* ◇ advance spreading out, advance in a closed line. Ⓛ ngaritunkula wonnañi
tánalanáma *sich umbinden (tjilara).* ◇ to tie (e.g. headband around head). Ⓛ ngaritunkanáñi
tananama *sich ausbreiten (Wolken), überziehen (der Himmel), sich ausbreiten (Fische) nach verschieden Richtungen.* ◇ to spread (clouds), become overcast (sky), scatter in different directions (fish). Ⓛ ngaritunkula bakañi
tanitjalama *sich ausbreiten (Fische).* ◇ to spread (e.g. fish). Ⓛ ngaritunani jenkula
tanbananbanga *Vogel (spec.), schwalbenartig.* ◇ swallow-like bird species. Ⓛ inertni
tanbatanga *undurchsichtig, dicht, taub, stumm, blind geboren.* ◇ opaque, dense, deaf, mute, born blind. Ⓛ patti, pinnawala, kurupatti, tapatti
tanga *conf.* **tjuanba** *ein Baum, iron-wood.* ◇ ironwood tree. Ⓛ untari
tangatja *gelbe Larve, die sich an den Wurzeln des tanga aufh.* ◇ yellow grub in the roots of ironwood. Ⓛ untari

tangaltja *Steingeröll, mit Steinen bedeckt.* ◇ boulders, covered with stones or boulders. Ⓛ atangaltji

tangamalauma *umfassen (jemanden), umarmen, zusammenfassen (etwas).* ◇ to clasp or hold (someone), to embrace, to hold or gather (something). Ⓛ ambutuljiñi

tanbatanga *stocktaub, garnichts hören können.* ◇ completely deaf, cannot hear at all. Ⓛ wāla, pinnawāla

tanganka *nunlich, vor kurzem, vor einer halben Stunde.* ◇ recently, a short time ago, half an hour ago. Ⓛ atanganki

tangantánama *umschließen, umzingeln, umstellen.* ◇ surround, enclose, encircle. Ⓛ tatulbinañi

tangantja *zu hilfe (pitjima).* ◇ come to help, come to the rescue. Ⓛ tatu (ngalajennañi)

tangántangantala ngama *mit beiden Händen vor sich tragend (z.B. lange Stecken).* ◇ carry with both hands in front of oneself (e.g. long stick). Ⓛ kattatjititjiti katiñi, kataparpanku katiñi

tanba *ein kleiner Flußlauf mit hartem Untergrund (nicht Sand).* ◇ hard bed of a small stream (not sandy). Ⓛ tartarba

tangaparama *im Kreise umstellen, umzingeln, aufhalten, nicht entweichen lassen.* ◇ to surround, to trap. Ⓛ arknatariñi

tangamatanga *Abteilung, Ordnung, (Luc. 1), (Nacheinander des Dienstes).* ◇ section, order.

tangatanga *Kreuz (Kreuzbein).* ◇ sacrum. Ⓛ akurúrbmurúrbmu

tanganbanganba bartjima *umleuchten.* ◇ shine.

tanganbanganba *um-herum, im Kreise herum.* ◇ around, around in a circle.

tangerama *herumlaufen (um etwas).* ◇ walk around (something). Ⓛ kaltupungañi

tangilama *Platz machen, einem zuvorkommen (z.B. der Erstgeborene von Zwillingen), umwechseln (Plätze).* ◇ make space, precede somebody (e.g. the first born of twins), change (places). Ⓛ alini

tangitja *im Kreis.* ◇ in a circle; gang up. Ⓛ tatu Ⓓ ngokana, ngokibana, kapikapi belagern

tangitjalama, tangitja pitjima *einschließen, im Kreis umstehen.* ◇ enclose, surround; gang up. Ⓛ tatujenañi, tatungalajennañi Ⓓ kapikapina

tangitjala pitjima *zu Hilfe kommen.* ◇ come to the rescue. Ⓛ tatungalajennañi Ⓓ marangokana

tangitjerama *umstehen etwas.* ◇ surround something. Ⓛ taturingañi

tangitjala ntankalama *zu Hilfe rufen.* ◇ to call for help. Ⓛ tatunku antawonkañi

tangitjama *umstellt, umzingelt.* ◇ surrounded. Ⓛ tatumba

tangutangilama *abwechseln, abwechselnd etwas tun.* ◇ take turns, alternate. Ⓛ alilkara alilkarariñi

tanka *große ramaia – Eidechse.* ◇ big ramaia lizard. Ⓛ larpati

tankanama *– Hinterteil, – Boden wühlen (Frösche).* ◇ backside, dig in the ground (frogs). Ⓛ tjilinjinañi

tanka *schnell, hurtig.* ◇ quick, swift. Ⓛ atamba

tankerama *schnell sich erholen.* ◇ recover quickly. Ⓛ atambaringañi

tankalélama *schnell zu Hilfe kommen, erretten (aus der Gefahr).* ◇ come quickly to the rescue, rescue (from danger). Ⓛ atambanañi Ⓓ kulkana

tankama *entwischen, entschlüpfen.* ◇ slip away, escape. Ⓛ titurtninañi

tankalélanilana *Retter.* ◇ saviour. Ⓛ atambanmi Ⓓ kulkanipirna

tantanantana *Stachel (des Skorpion).* ◇ sting (of scorpion).

tankuma *schöpfen (Wasser).* ◇ scoop, draw (water). Ⓛ katiñi Ⓓ kaluana, kaluwana

tantama *stechen, hineinstoßen (in das Brot).* ◇ stab, push (into bread). Ⓛ kultuni Ⓓ dakana (*stechen*: stab), karpana (*nähen*: sow)

tantana *schwarzer Reiher.* ◇ black heron. Ⓛ átantànba

tāntja; era nukalela tantja nama *bei ihm seiend, Gesellschaft leistend.* ◇ be with him, keep company. e.g. he or she is accompanying me. Ⓛ alintji

tarakalaka *nach circa 2 Wochen.* ◇ after about 2 weeks. Ⓛ kutarakita

tāra *abgestumpft, steif, gefühllos, gichtbrüchig oder der große Junge.* ◇ stiff, unfeeling, decrepit or the big boy (Strehlow 1907: 87). Ⓛ lanmalanma

tāratāra *taubstumm.* ◇ deaf and dumb.

tapatapa *finster.* ◇ very dark. Ⓛ mungulmungul

tĕratĕra *Netz, Netzfett.* ◇ tissue fat. Ⓛ atiïnti

tăra *zwei.* ◇ two. Ⓛ kutara Ⓓ mandru, mandruluko (*zu zweien* = in twos).

taramininta *drei.* ◇ three. Ⓛ kutarabakutu Ⓓ parkulu, parkuluko (*zu dreien* = in threes), parkuluntja (*nur drei* = only three).

taramatara *vier.* ◇ four. Ⓛ kutarabakutara Ⓓ mandrujamandru

taramapulba *fünf.* ◇ five. Ⓛ mankurkata, mankurabakutara

tarataraka *zum 2. Mal (z.B. geben).* ◇ for the second time (e.g. give). Ⓛ kútarakútaraku

tara-ma-tara *zu zweien.* ◇ in twos. Ⓛ kutarabakútara

tāra *lang, hoch.* ◇ long, high.

tara kurkindora *das sehr kleine Kind.* ◇ very small child. Ⓛ tjitji tokutoku

worra tara *der große Junge.* ◇ big boy. Ⓛ tjitji

tara knara *das große Kind.* ◇ big child. Ⓛ tjitji katu

matja tāra *ein hochaufflackerndes Feuer.* ◇ big flickering fire. Ⓛ waru kurkala/kurkalba/kurkalta

tarabanba *große geschabte Holzblumen (Schmuck der Bluträcher).* ◇ large wood flowers (decoration of avengers). Ⓛ ilanbi

tāraeróra *der junge Mann.* ◇ young man. Ⓛ wonguerora

tara, tāra *die langen (Emu)federn, Federbausch (Kopfschmuck), die langen Haare/die langen Federn (der Emus oder Adler), die langen Haare (von Hunden), zottig, Federbusch (Kopfschmuck bei den Ceremonien).* ◇ long (emu or eagle) feathers, plumage (headdress), long hair (of dogs). Ⓛ aturu Ⓓ watawata

tara *Adlerfedern, lange Federn, zottig, lange Adlerfedern.* ◇ eagle feathers, long feathers, shaggy, long eagle feathers. Ⓛ aturaturu

tărama *lachen, wiehern (Pferde).* ◇ laugh, neigh (horses). Ⓛ inkañi Ⓓ kinkana

tarinjaranga *fröhlich, ausgelassen.* ◇ merry, frolicsome. Ⓛ inkabi

tarilbatarilba ankama *Gelächter ausstoßen, lachend erzählen.* ◇ laugh, tell laughingly. Ⓛ inkapuntuinkapuntu wonkañi

tarakélukélua *lange Federn ins Haar gesteckt.* ◇ long feathers in hair. Ⓛ aturu taltaku

tăratăra *taub.* ◇ deaf; closed. Ⓛ patti

tarinjima *hinaufklettern.* ◇ climb up. Ⓛ kalbarawonnañi

taréuma *heruntersteigen, sich herniederlassen.* ◇ climb down, descend. Ⓛ taruwonniñi

taraunama *hinabsteigen.* ◇ climb down. Ⓛ mataruwonniñi

tarangaltja [Southern dialect?]. *Schambedeckung.* ◇ pubic covering. Ⓛ tarangaltji

tareranama *herabsteigen.* ◇ climb down. Ⓛ matarungarañi, matarurekukatiñi

tareratnama *heruntersteigen (vom Berg), herabkriechen, herabrutschen.* ◇ to descend, to climb down, to crawl down, to slide down. Ⓛ tarungarala okalingañi

tarauma *auf und nieder bewegen (Wasser).* ◇ move up and down (water). Ⓛ taretunañi

tarinjinama *hinaufsteigen.* ◇ climb up. Ⓛ makalbarawonnañi

taraunjinama *Feuer anmachen, aufflackern, anfachen.* ◇ fan fire on, light fire. Ⓛ pintjijungañi

tāratāra *abschüssig, herunterhängen.* ◇ steep, hang down. Ⓛ tarukutu

tarerama *herauskommen, heruntergleiten, geboren (Kind).* ◇ come out, slide down, born (child). Ⓛ tarungarañi

tareritjikalama *hinabsteigen.* ◇ to descend, to climb down. Ⓛ tarungarala okalingañi

taretnama *herunterhängen, sinken lassen (Hände).* ◇ to hang down, to sink (e.g. hands). Ⓛ tarungarañi

tarerama *herabschießen (Habicht), hinunterschießen (Fische), sich stürzen ins (Wasser), herunterhängen, abfallen (Ufer), herabfallen.* ◇ to shoot or drop down (e.g. hawk), dart down (e.g. fish), plunge into (the water), hang down, fall away (bank), fall down. Ⓛ tarungarañi

tarerinja *herniederhängend (z.B. Ast).* ◇ hanging down (e.g. branch). Ⓛ tarungaranmi

taruwara *nach unten gebogen (z.B. Ast).* ◇ bent down (e.g. branch). Ⓛ tarukutu

taritja *windstill.* ◇ calm (no wind). Ⓛ rata

taritjerama *Wind sich legen.* ◇ to abate (wind). Ⓛ rataringañi

taretambuma *rot werden, sich röten.* ◇ turn red, redden. Ⓛ tariltingañi

tarta *flach (Wasser).* ◇ flat (water). Ⓛ atárta Ⓓ buta (flach)

tarta *Blume, Blüte.* ◇ flower, blossom. Ⓛ muntu

tartatarta *(duplikat) Blumen.* ◇ (duplication) flowers. Ⓛ untuntu

tarinama; *z.B.* moggetalela tarinama *schießen.* ◇ shoot, e.g. shoot with a gun. Ⓛ wilitunañi

tāta *naß, feucht.* ◇ wet, damp. Ⓛ topi

tatagunama *ins Wasser werfen.* ◇ throw into water. Ⓛ turirbiñi

tatilama *naß machen.* ◇ make wet. Ⓛ topini

tatala lama Ⓛ topilkatiñi

tăta *Funke.* ◇ spark. Ⓛ ti Ⓓ turotiwilka

tarabara *schwarze Flecken auf der Stirn (Schmuck) (der Zauberer).* ◇ black spots on forehead (decoration of witch doctor). Ⓛ tatabara

tarumbara *schräges Dach.* ◇ slanting roof.

tataka *rot, scharlachrot.* ◇ red, scarlet. Ⓛ taltiritaltiri, itinitini Ⓓ maralje

alknara tataka *Abendrot.* ◇ evening red, sunset. Ⓛ kalkara ininitini

tatakama *schalten, Vorwürfe machen, bedrohen.* ◇ scold, reproach, threaten. Ⓛ arawolkuñi

tātala *sehr schnell (schlagen).* ◇ very fast (hit). Ⓛ wollarini

tatama *glühen.* ◇ glow. Ⓛ ininmanañi Ⓓ waluwalungana

tatara *Hölle, Wohnung der bösen Wesen.* ◇ hell, home of evil beings. Ⓛ wottatari

tataramba *Zucker auf den lalba-Sträuchern.* ◇ sugar on lalba-bushes. Ⓛ albitalji

tātata *unmündig.* ◇ underage. Ⓛ átatáta

tateúlama *den Kampf für einen andern bestehen.* ◇ fight for someone else, stand in. Ⓛ parpatariñi

tātja *Bandicoot (pig-toed) mit rotem Fell, zwei langen Zehen an jedem Fuß und langen Ohren (choeropus castanotis).* ◇ pig-toed bandicoot with red fur, two long toes on each foot and long ears (*Chaeropus castanotis* now *Chaeropus ecaudatus*) (Atlas of Living Australia n.d.) Ⓛ takana

tatnara *lau.* ◇ lukewarm, mild.

tatóa [ta-toa] *ich selbst.* ◇ I myself. Ⓛ ngaiulurpa

tatura *Vogel (spec.), der immer Emueier frist.* ◇ bird (species) that always eats emu eggs. Ⓛ etátura

taua *Tasche.* ◇ bag. Ⓛ ataua Ⓓ billi

taualama *sich aufblähen (Frösche).* ◇ inflate (frogs).

taúatàra *ich selbst (verstärkt).* ◇ I myself (emphasised). Ⓛ ngaiulukaúala

taualawollintama *sehr schnell laufen.* ◇ run very fast. Ⓛ taualknaríñi

tauatjipa *schwarzer Kopf, rote Kehle, weiße Brust, so groß wie eine Schwalbe.* ◇ bird with black head, red throat, white chest, size of a swallow.

teelabia nama *sich scheuen, sich fürchten.* ◇ dread, fear (reflexive). Ⓛ ngulukurkuriñi

teelabulabulélama *furchtsam machen, warnen.* ◇ to make anxious, to warn. Ⓛ ngulungulutjingañi

teelabultjabula *voll Furcht.* ◇ full of fear, fearsome, anxious. Ⓛ ngúlugúlutu
teelabultjabula nama *sich fürchten (vor der Strafe).* ◇ be afraid (of punishment). Ⓛ ngúlutungúluturiñi
teelantama, teelintama *Furcht einflößen, bange machen.* ◇ to scare, to make anxious. Ⓛ ngulutjingarapungañi, ngulujingañi
tekua *Ratte (ohne Beutel).* ◇ rat (without pouch); mouse. Ⓛ pátiki
telaëlaláma *fliehen, entlaufen.* ◇ flee, run away. Ⓛ ngulunakukatiñi
telama *zeigen.* ◇ show; teach. Ⓛ nintini Ⓓ wondrana
telaláma *sich zeigen.* ◇ show oneself (reflexive). Ⓛ itoniñi Ⓓ wondraterina.
telekélaka *Schlüsselbein.* ◇ collarbone. Ⓛ ngantuluru
tēlja *die hintere Hälfte (des erlegen Wildes), das Hinterteil, anus (ohne den Schwanz).* ◇ hind quarter (of game), back part (without tail). Ⓛ kar̃ila
telkiuma *sich stützen (auf den Ellbogen).* ◇ lean on (elbow). Ⓛ ngunanpiti ngariñi
tembanama *aufheben (Gebot), abschaffen.* ◇ abolish (order).
ténama [Southern dialect] *zeugen, hervorbringen, aufgehen (Saat), heraufbringen (der Sturm die Wolken).* ◇ produce, bring out, germinate, sprout (crop, seed), bring about (the storm the clouds). Ⓛ paluni
tentapentama *sich ausbreiten (Botschaft).* ◇ to spread (a message). Ⓛ wonka-taualknariñi
tenjima [Northern dialect] *cf.* **tenama**. ◇ produce, bring out, sprout (seed), bring about.
tentalelama *schräg vor sich haltend (beim Tragen).* ◇ carry something at an angle (in front of oneself). Ⓛ taualtunañi
tenkuérama [Northern dialect] *cf.* tangérama. ◇ go around (something).
tenkuilama [Northern dialect] *cf.* tangilama. ◇ make room, come first.
tenteratnama *abfließen.* ◇ drain, flow off. Ⓛ palungarañi
tenteranama *zusammenfließen, säuseln (Wasser), Laufe bilden, abfließen, herabfließen.* ◇ flow together, off or down. Ⓛ mapaluringañi
tēnta *glatt (Stein) Felsplatte.* ◇ smooth (stone or rock plate). Ⓛ wallu (wollu) Ⓓ pankara ('?' added by CS)
pata tenta *Felsplatte.* ◇ rock plate. Ⓛ puli wallu Ⓓ marda paltiri
tēntilama *glätten.* ◇ to smooth. Ⓛ walluni
tentatnama *fortwährend herabfließen.* ◇ flow down continuously, cascade. Ⓛ tutirapungañi
(tentama) *herabfallen (z.B. Baum).* ◇ fall down (e.g. tree). Ⓛ tultungarañi
tentia *seitwärts stehend (Ast), halbkreisförmig gebogen.* ◇ bent to the side (branch), bent in a semicircle. Ⓛ tarukutu
tentuma *gerade abfließen.* ◇ flow off evenly. Ⓛ tutirapungañi
tĕratĕra *Vogel spec. (schwalbenähnlich).* ◇ bird species (swallow-like). Ⓛ teruteru
(tăratăra) *gefühllos, abgestumpft, abgemattet.* ◇ numb, exhausted, flat. Ⓛ lanmalanma
(tarérama) *matt werden.* ◇ become exhausted. Ⓛ lanmalanmaringañi
taratarerama *abgestumpft werden, dickfellig werden, matt werden.* ◇ become indifferent, exhausted. Ⓛ lanmalanmaringañi
terēltjilama *sich fürchten, fliehen vor.* ◇ be afraid of, flee from. Ⓛ ngulukurkuringañi
tĕra, tēela *furchtsam.* ◇ fearful, anxious. Ⓛ ngulu, ngulunku
tĕralama *furchtsam gehen, fliehen.* ◇ to move or be fearful or anxious, to flee. Ⓛ ngulujennañi Ⓓ japamindrina
teralta, terélta *furchtsam, feige.* ◇ fearful, anxious, cowardly. Ⓛ nguluntu
terabuljabuljilama *trs. Furcht einflößen.* ◇ (transitive) scare. Ⓛ ngulungulutjingañi
terabanawata *sehr furchtsam.* ◇ very fearful, anxious. Ⓛ ngulutumantu
teratjankama *im Chor sagen (summen).* ◇ say in chorus (hum). Ⓛ terewonkañi

tērba *geschickt, erzogen.* ◇ agile, educated. Ⓛ takka

terbanama *erziehen, geschickt machen.* ◇ educate, make skilful.

teretankama *trrr schreien (quacken) (Cikaden) auch bei Kultus.* ◇ cry, croak, call trrr (cicadas). Ⓛ terewonkañi

terbinama *unterrichten, einpauken, fest eindrücken.* ◇ to teach, to instruct, to impress. Ⓛ tintinpungañi, takkapungañi

terelka *furchtsam.* ◇ anxious. Ⓛ nguluntu Ⓓ japali

terenta *größerer Frosch in Lehmebenen sich aufhaltend.* ◇ larger frog that lives in claypans. Ⓛ aterintji

terilkalama *(quaken) schreien (Frösche).* ◇ croak, cry (frogs). Ⓛ terbmanañi

terka *Strauch, an den Ufern der Wasserläufe wachsend, mit langen, schmalen, lederartigen Blättern. Wenn ein Insekt seine Eier in die Stengel niederlegt, nehmen die an demselben befindlichen Blätter eine längliche ovale Gestalt an. (Acacia saticina).* ◇ shrub with long, narrow, leather-like leaves that grows on the banks of watercourses. When an insect deposits its eggs in its stalks, its leaves take on a longish oval shape. The Loritja term 'Watarka' is the name of Kings Canyon. Its current scientific name is *Acacia ligulata* (Latz 1996). Ⓛ wottarka (watarka)

terbanánanana *Erzieher.* ◇ educator.

terkambilara *Grasdickicht, grüne Grasfläche.* ◇ grass thicket, green meadow. Ⓛ ókirípárapára

terka *grün, gelb.* ◇ green, yellow. Ⓛ okiri

terkaterka *grün, gelb.* ◇ green, yellow. Ⓛ ókirókiri Ⓓ kulja kulja.

alkna terkaterka *[grünes Auge], Schimpfwort, wenn der andere Teil Ehebruch [im Grünen d.h. draußen] getrieben hat.* ◇ (green eye) insult used for a marriage partner who has committed adultery (in the green, meaning outside). Ⓛ kuru ókirókiri

terkerama *grün werden.* ◇ to turn green. Ⓛ okiringañi Ⓓ kulja pandrina.

terkaluma *grün färben (Regenbogen).* ◇ to turn or colour green (rainbow). Ⓛ okiriltini

terkalama *grün und gelb werden (vor Zorn).* ◇ to turn green and yellow (from anger). Ⓛ okiriltini

tetnama *sich auf dem Boden setzen mit vor sich übers Kreuz geschlagenen Beinen.* ◇ sit down on the ground with crossed legs. Ⓛ tjilinínañi

terkateratera *ein kleiner grauer Taucher mit gespaltenen Schwimmfüßen.* ◇ small grey diver (bird) with split webbed-feet. Ⓛ itirkiteriteri

terkintaterkinta *gelb gestreift, gelb gezeichnet.* ◇ striped, marked yellow. Ⓛ okirilbátuni

téuma *abkratzen, abreiben, abschaben.* ◇ scrape off, rub off, scratch off. Ⓛ putipungañi

tingirkuma *umfassen (von hinten).* ◇ clasp, hold (from behind). Ⓛ niniwitini

teunama *ausfegen, reinfegen.* ◇ sweep out, sweep clean. Ⓛ maputipungañi Ⓓ darpana (*fegen*: sweep)

tingara *lange Stange, bei religiösen Ceremonien.* ◇ ceremonial pole. Ⓛ tingari

tia *böses Wesen, Teufel in Gestalt eines schwarzen Vogels.* ◇ evil being or bad spirit in the shape of a black bird; when this spirit being stands in front of the sun it causes an eclipse (Strehlow 1907: 17). Ⓛ mamakuia

tintjera *dicht (Gras, Sträucher).* ◇ dense (grass, bushes). Ⓛ tatulba

tilirkilirka *alle zusammen (kommen), alles (z.B. leugnen).* ◇ all (come) together, everything (e.g. deny). Ⓛ ápuàra

tĭnapalka *Schuhe.* ◇ shoes. Ⓛ tjinnapalka Ⓓ tidnapota

titjitjerina *Schlange (spec.) giftig.* ◇ poisonous snake species. Ⓛ kaiarakuntilba

tintjiuma *begraben.* ◇ bury. Ⓛ tunutunañi Ⓓ totina, nampana

titja *bedeutet.* ◇ signifies. Ⓛ pitiña

titjera [Eastern dialect] *conf.* **lirtjina** *grüne Papagei.* ◇ green parrot. Ⓛ kuljirtji

títjeritjera, titjeritjera *kleine Vogel (Art wag-tail) oben schwarz, Bauch weiß, Sauloprocta motacilloides.* ◇ small bird (willie wagtail species) with a black top and a white belly (Strehlow 1907: 100), *Rhipidura leucophrys* (Pizzey and Knight 2007). Ⓛ tjinteritjinteri Ⓓ tindritindri

tjaia *Weg.* ◇ path. Ⓛ iwara Ⓓ palto

tjaia mbinja *zurückgelegte Weg.* ◇ distance covered. Ⓛ iwara wonnu

tjaiïlama *Weg machen, Bahn machen, Scheitel kämmen.* ◇ make a path, cut a trail, part hair. Ⓛ iwarani

tjaia tjarilbinja *gerade Weg.* ◇ straight path. Ⓛ iwara warilkara

tjaíarama *aussehen (nach jemanden).* ◇ look out (for someone). Ⓛ iwara nangañi

tjaiarélama *warten (auf jemanden).* ◇ wait (for someone). Ⓛ iwara patañi

tilbaranama *hüpfen, hopsen (Känguruh, Kind beim Spielen).* ◇ skip, jump (kangaroos, children at play). Ⓛ maralkatini

tjaka *lose, beweglich.* ◇ loose, moveable. Ⓛ ataki

tjakilama *lose machen, hin und her bewegen, bewegen (durch anhaltender Bitten).* ◇ loosen, move back and forth; stir (through constant begging). Ⓛ atakanani

tjakalama *losgehen, davon fliegen (Vogel).* ◇ go or fly away (e.g. birds). Ⓛ ataki jennañi

titjagunja *silberhelle Wolke, Seide, seiden (n).* ◇ silvery cloud, silk, silken.

tjakama *töten (mit einem Schlag), nieder schlagen, nieder schießen, erschießen (Ochsen).* ◇ to kill (with one blow), to knock down, to shoot (down), shoot dead (e.g. bullock). Ⓛ butulbmanañi

tjakilinja *Zoll, Abgabe.* ◇ tax, duty, share.

tjakilinalina *Zöllner n.* ◇ tax collector.

tjala, itala [Southern dialect] *Kniescheibe.* ◇ kneecap. Ⓛ irbi Ⓓ pantjamata

patta tjăla *harter (Felsen).* ◇ hard (rock). Ⓛ manpamanpa

tjalanka *Pech (hergestellt aus Porcupine-grass).* ◇ resin, pitch (made from spinifex, i.e. porcupine grass). Ⓛ kiti Ⓓ kandri

tjalbalelama *sich anstoßen, Anstoß nehmen.* ◇ to knock (oneself), to take offence.

tjalapálapa *Nabel.* ◇ navel. Ⓛ puli Ⓓ bida

tjalbulelama *trs. stechen.* ◇ (transitive) stab. Ⓛ wiltjingani

tjalawunja *eßbare Wurzeln.* ◇ edible roots. Ⓛ itjaliwinji

tjálbmaraláma *die Rinde verlieren (dürre Äste).* ◇ shed bark (dry branches). Ⓛ lakalakaringañi

tjalbma (tjĕlbma) *Splitter.* ◇ splinter. Ⓛ lambi, pitjili, talbira Ⓓ pita tiwitiwi

tjalinja *das porcupine grass, von dem tjalanka Pech hergestellt wird.* ◇ porcupine grass used to make tjalanka resin or pitch. Ⓛ itjálinji

tjalka *Fleisch.* ◇ meat. Ⓛ iltana

tjalbakama *sich anstoßen.* ◇ knock (reflexive).

tjalknarérama *verwittern, weiß werden (Knochen).* ◇ weather, bleach (bones). Ⓛ pelumpurpuriñi

tjalbalakama *einen zu Fall bringen.* ◇ bring someone to fall.

tjalkuarénama *herabströmen [unclear].* ◇ flow down. Ⓛ éreringáriñi

tjamalarelka *ehrlich, ehrenhaft.* ◇ honest, honourable. Ⓛ wirulpala

tjamurilja *Witwenschmuck [unclear].* ◇ widow's decoration (Strehlow 1915: 23 (Fig. 3)).

tjambarambareleláma *sich schmücken, sich bemalen.* ◇ to decorate, paint (reflexive). Ⓛ irbotirbotartingañi

tjánatjánalánama *rücklings gehen.* ◇ walk backwards. Ⓛ murumurukatiñi

tjana *postp. durch, hindurch.* ◇ (postposition) through, cross. Ⓛ tatini

tjanama *überschreiten (Creek).* ◇ cross (creek). Ⓛ tatinínañi

tjananama *hindurchgehen (z.B. durch Wasser).* ◇ go through (e.g. through water). Ⓛ matatinínañi Ⓓ pararana

tjanalélama *hindurchführen, übersetzen.* ◇ lead through, transfer. Ⓛ tatiwonniñi

tjaninjalbuma *bei der Rückkehr hindurchgehen.* ◇ go through on return. Ⓛ tatinginara kulbañi, ngalatatinginarakulbañi

tjania *jenseits, am anderen Ufer.* ◇ beyond, on the other side of a river. Ⓛ wirilipiti

tjanalelalalbuma *herbeiholen.* ◇ to fetch, to bring. Ⓛ tatiwonnirakulbañi Ⓓ ?anina tikana pararana

tjanalelamala ngama *hindurchtragen.* ◇ carry something through.

tjandura *stark, hoch (Baum), steif (von Toten).* ◇ strong, high (tree), stiff (the deceased). Ⓛ tekila

tjanga *das Geliehene, Zins n.* ◇ loan, interest. Ⓛ alinji

tjania *jenseits, am andern Ufer.* ◇ beyond, on the other side of the river. Ⓛ wirilipiti

tjanka *Flechte, Haarflechte.* ◇ braid, hair plait. Ⓛ wakitji

tjánka *Kopfschmuck, Bohnen mit Pech befestigt.* ◇ headdress, beans attached with tar. Ⓛ wakitji

tjankutnuma *flechten (Haare).* ◇ to plait (hair). Ⓛ wakitjinañi

tjañka *bull-dog-ant.* ◇ bull ant. Ⓛ kaltuka

tjankala *zuletzt, Ende.* ◇ last, at the end, end. Ⓛ kutuwara

tjankalerama *fertig werden (Arbeit).* ◇ finish (work). Ⓛ kutukataringañi

tjanka *Ende, Spitze (Zweigen), die erulanga-Blüten.* ◇ end, tip (branches), *Grevillea juncifolia* blossoms. Ⓛ wakitji

tjankana *die Mistelzweige auf den tnima-Sträuchern und Mulga-Bäumen.* ◇ mistletoe on tnima bushes and mulga trees. Ⓛ itjankini

tjantinama *fortwährend (den Boden schlagen mit den Füßen).* ◇ constantly (hit the ground with feet). Ⓛ kantuni

tjantjurantjura *überströmt (mit Saft, mit Blut).* ◇ covered (with juice or blood). Ⓛ lurknulurknu

tjappa *Larve.* ◇ larva; witchetty grub, edible grub (generic). Ⓛ maku, ngalurba

tjapatía *der große Anführer (der Bluträcher), Hauptmann.* ◇ great leader (of revenge party). Ⓛ tëïra

tjaralbinja lama *schnurstracks weiter gehen.* ◇ walk straight ahead without stopping. Ⓛ waralkara jennañi

tjarandama *nachspüren, nachsehen.* ◇ to track, trace. Ⓛ nakulariñi

tjapinba *Schwäre, Geschwür.* ◇ abscess, ulcer. Ⓛ matinkíri

tjarangama *herantragen.* ◇ to bring. Ⓛ itarikatiñi

tjárinama *der Länge nach spalten (ein Strück Holz).* ◇ split lengthwise (a piece of wood). Ⓛ larapungañi

tjarinama *ziehen, heranziehen.* ◇ pull, draw close. Ⓛ itarinañi, itariñi Ⓓ parumana

tjaritíbuma *eine Furche im Sand ziehen.* ◇ make a line in the sand. Ⓛ totutunañi

tjarita *tiefer Einschnitt, Furche (Zeichen, Nachricht).* ◇ deep incision, groove (sign, message). Ⓛ itjariti, ninka

tjātjagata (tjartjagata) *Zeichen, Zeugnis, Wunder.* ◇ sign, testimony, miracle. Ⓛ turkalkata

tjātjagatilama *wahre Auskunft geben, bekräftigen, bezeugen.* ◇ give accurate information, confirm, testify. Ⓛ turkulkátanáñi

tjartja *(der Leib), Körner, Sämereien, (der Leib der Sämereien!).* ◇ (body), seeds, (the body of the seeds); person. Ⓛ anangu

tjātjatuma (tjartjatuma) *eingestehen (sein Unrecht) bekennen.* ◇ confess (admit to be wrong). Ⓛ turkulbmanañi

tjartjiuma *durch Rauch seine bevorstehende Ankunft anzeigen, Feuersignal geben.* ◇ to notify arrival with smoke, give smoke signal.

tjātjerama, tjōtjerama *sich dehnen (nach dem Schlaf), sich erheben, sich strecken.* ◇ rise, stretch (after sleep). Ⓛ watuni

tjatjeruma (tjātjerama) *sich erheben, aufstehen.* ◇ to get up, stand up. Ⓛ watuni

tjatjeruperuma *dupl. sich erheben.* ◇ reduplication of 'to rise'. Ⓛ waturánañi Ⓓ duntjirina

tjartjuatjartjatuma *einander ermahnen.* ◇ remind each other. Ⓓ tjātjerama

tjarantalama *nacheinander alles erzählen.* ◇ narrate everything in chronological order. Ⓓ tjātjerama

tjatjikata *cf.* tjartjagata. ◇ sign, evidence, miracle.

tjatna *conf.* iltjantja. ◇ tree species. Ⓛ iltilba

tjatta *Speer.* ◇ spear. Ⓛ katji Ⓓ kalti

tjauara *verschieden, Arten.* ◇ different, different species. Ⓛ alatjimurkamurka Ⓓ nguja, paka, talka

tjauerilja *Abgabe (an die knaribata oder an die Zauberdoktoren).* ◇ payment (to senior men or medicine men), share. Ⓛ itauerilji

tjēba *Stück, Glied, Teil, gespalten.* ◇ piece, limb, part, split. Ⓛ tăra Ⓓ burru, tjalatjala

tjebakintja *ein einzelnes Stück.* ◇ single piece. Ⓛ tarantanuta

tjebakama *in Stücke zerschneiden oder zerbrechen, spalten.* ◇ cut or break into pieces, split. Ⓛ tarantanañi Ⓓ tjelapalkana

tjebiatjeba *Glied (einer Kette).* ◇ part or segment (of a chain).

tjebakalama *intr. in Stücke zerbrechen.* ◇ (intransitive) break into pieces. Ⓛ tarantakatiñi Ⓓ tjalatjala ngankana

tjebarkatilama *zerscheitern, in 2 Stücke zerspalten.* ◇ split, split into two pieces. Ⓛ tarakútaranáñi

tjeberama *intr. zerbrechen, zerspringen.* ◇ (intransitive) break, crack. Ⓛ tarantariñi

tjebatarerama *in zwei Stücke zerbrechen oder zerspringen.* ◇ break or crack into two pieces. Ⓛ kutararíñi

tjebakata *zum Teil.* ◇ partly, in part.

tjebma *Rippe.* ◇ rib. Ⓛ nimiri Ⓓ bankitiri

tjebma ula *falsche Rippe.* ◇ false rib. Ⓛ nimiri akata

tjekua *der Großvater (tjimia) eines andern.* ◇ grandfather (tjimia) of someone else. Ⓛ tamura

tjelkunelkuna *gehorsam.* ◇ obedient.

tjekula *die Cycas-Palme.* ◇ Cycad. Ⓛ utukákili

tjelkuma *gehorsam.* ◇ obedient.

tjelja *kleine Mulde, mit der Wasser, Asche oder jelka geschöpft wird.* ◇ small bowl to scoop water, ash or jelka. Ⓛ kuntilba

tjengakata *Öffnung im Hause, Fenster.* ◇ opening in house, window. Ⓛ katati

tjenja indora (tingara) *sehr lang.* ◇ very long. Ⓛ warambatjipamunu

tjenja *hoch, lang.* ◇ high, long, tall. Ⓛ wottawara, watawara Ⓓ paieri, wirdi, wutju

tjenja indora *sehr lang.* ◇ very long. Ⓛ waralitji, wara

tjenkama *fortwandern (die Seele des Verstorbenen).* ◇ wander away (soul of deceased). Ⓛ piraljanbákañi

tjintja *die Spitzen der Zweige.* ◇ tips of branches. Ⓛ walpuru

tjentjima *aus einer Versammlung einen oder mehrere Personen besonders zu sich rufen (Geschichte [unclear]).* ◇ to call one or more persons specifically up at a meeting or gathering. Ⓛ alurkuni

tjerilkna *blaß (der Tote), fahl (Pferd).* ◇ pale (the deceased), pallid (horse).

tjeririnja *kleine Cikade.* ◇ small cicada. Ⓛ tjeririnba

tjeria *kleinere Cikade (an porcupine gras) (Burbunga venosa?).* ◇ smaller cicada (on porcupine grass). Ⓛ tjeraiï

tjerama *braten, backen [kochen].* ◇ roast, bake (cook); shoot. Ⓛ kuntini, bauañi Ⓓ ngurkumana, wajina [waiïna]

tjéritjéra *Stock zum Laufen, Stützen.* ◇ walking stick. Ⓛ tjukara

tjetta *weit entfernt.* ◇ far away. Ⓛ wonma

tjettakitjetta *weit von einander entfernt.* ◇ far away from each other. Ⓛ wonmakuwonma

tjerbatuma *zerteilen, Bahn brechen [unclear].* ◇ divide, make a passage. Ⓛ lalalpungañi

tjiala(lama) *auf allen vieren gehen.* ◇ walk on all fours. Ⓛ mamnirajennani

tjia [Northern dialect] *conf.* **itia** *jüngere Bruder (oder Schwester).* ◇ younger brother or sister. Ⓛ malangu

tjinkua *der itia eines Andern.* ◇ younger brother or sister of someone else. Ⓛ malangura

tjiankama *zischen.* ◇ hiss. Ⓛ tjoïnmanañi, winmanañi

tjiberawuma, tjiparawuma *nachspüren, untersuchen, richten.* ◇ track, investigate, judge. Ⓛ kutupinjinjiwonniñi

tjiberawunawuna, tjiparawunawuna *Richter.* ◇ judge. Ⓛ kutapinjinjiwonnimi

tjikara *rißig, gesprungen, aufgesprungen.* ◇ full of cracks, cracked, cracked open. Ⓛ ngara Ⓓ wirka

tjikatjira *Medizin, Heilpflanze.* ◇ medicine, plant remedy, bush medicine. Ⓛ tikitiki

tjila; era litjika tjila *postp. bald, z.B. er soll bald gehen.* ◇ (postposition) soon; e.g. he shall go soon. Ⓛ kita, palaru kenkuntakita

tjilala lunama *erjagen [unclear].* ◇ hunt. Ⓛ wotjilenku wonnañi

tjilara *Stirnband.* ◇ headband. Ⓛ wollaru, ngalilkiri Ⓓ tjarapu

tjilarala lorultaiwulama (lorulta-iwulama) *sich das Stirnband umbinden.* ◇ to tie on a headband. Ⓛ wollaru pilkungariñi

tjilararama *beobachten, nach allen Seiten Umschau halten, von allen Seiten betrachten.* ◇ observe, to keep watch in all directions, to look at from all sides. Ⓛ wollaranangañi

tjileuma *hineinpfropfen (Zweig), zusetzen (seine Länge etwas).* ◇ to graft into (branch), add (to length).

tjilarelalama *beobachten [unclear].* ◇ to observe, watch. Ⓛ ngirkikatiñi

tjilaritjalama *hervorlugen, aus einem Versteck hervorsehen.* ◇ to peer out from a hiding place. Ⓛ ngirkinijenkula

tjilarama *hinuntersehen (vom Berge), hineinsehen (in eine Höhle).* ◇ look down (from a mountain), look inside (a cave). Ⓛ ngirkiñi

tjilaralama *den Kopf von einer Seite zur andern bewegen.* ◇ move head from one side to the other. Ⓛ ngirkiranáñi

tjilba *grau (Haar).* ◇ grey (hair). Ⓛ tjilba

tjilpitjeria *(bratende Heißwind) der Monat, in dem es heiß wird, October und November.* ◇ (scorching wind) the month when it gets hot, e.g. October and November. Ⓛ kuntikuntira ngariñi

tjileulama *fortwährend verfolgen (z.B. Wild).* ◇ continuously pursue (e.g. game). Ⓛ watjilinañi

tjilpa *wilde Katze, Beutelmarder (Dasyurus) von brauner Farbe mit weißen Flecken.* ◇ native cat, western quoll, brown with white spots, *Dasyurus geoffroii*. Ⓛ malalbara, kuninka Ⓓ jikaura

tjilparatjilpara *kleiner Vogel, anthus Australis.* ◇ small bird, *anthus Australis* now *Anthus novaeseelandiae* (Australasian pipit) (see Pizzey and Knight 2007). Ⓛ tjalpuritjalpuri

tjilpita *Blume spec.* ◇ flower species. Ⓛ tjilpiti

tjima *Flechte, Haarflechte.* ◇ braid, hair plait. Ⓛ wakitji

tjimatnama [Southern dialect], **tjimutnuma** [Northern dialect] *flechten, zusammendrehen.* ◇ to plait (hair), wind together. Ⓛ wakitjipalañi Ⓓ wonjunkana

tjimara *Reihe, Linie (nebeneinander).* ◇ row, line (beside each other). Ⓛ tapiri

tjimaralama *nebeneinander gehen, in einer Linie gehen.* ◇ go side by side, go in one line. Ⓛ tapiri jennañi

tjimarandama *Rechenschaft geben, Rechnung tun.* ◇ be accountable, to give account.

tjimarantáma *eingestehen (Schuld).* ◇ confess (guilt). Ⓛ turkulbmanañi

tjimbarkna *böse Wesen in Weibergestalt.* ◇ bad spirits or beings in the shape of women (see Strehlow 1907: 12); today these female evil beings are usually called 'aragutja erintja' or in English 'wild women'. Such female spirit beings want a man and a baby, they are known to steal children and take men. To avoid an assault, a man having spotted such a spirit must not turn his back towards her. He has to move out of her way walking backwards. Ⓛ tjimbirkni

 For the modern spellings of these words, see the dictionaries and sources in reference list.

tjimbala *Zauberstäbe des Ulbaritja Stammes.* ◇ magic sticks of Ulbaritja tribe. Ⓛ tjimbili

tjimbili *Speer mit vielen Widerhaken (vom Norden und Westen).* ◇ spear with many barbs (from the north and west) or magic sticks carried about by the aranga. Ⓛ tjimbili

tjimia *Großvater (der Vater der Mutter), Großonkel, Enkel, (Tochters Sohn), Enkelin (Tochters Tochter), Großneffe, Großnichte.* ◇ mother's father (grandfather), grandchild, grandson (daughter's son), granddaughter (daughter's daughter), grand-nephew, grand-niece; people affiliated with a country through their mother's father are called, in Western Aranda, kutungula. They have right to country that are complementary to the rights that people gain through their father's father (aranga). Ⓛ kunarbi Ⓓ kalti windunto

tjimia altjala *mein Großvater (Mutters Vater).* ◇ my grandfather (mother's father). Ⓛ kunarbina

tjimia knara *Großvaters älterer Bruder.* ◇ mother's father's older brother. Ⓛ kunarbi puntu

tjimia larra *Großvaters jüngerer Bruder.* ◇ mother's father's younger brother. Ⓛ kunarbi wongu

kwaia tjimia *Großvaters Schwester.* ◇ mother's father's sister. Ⓛ puliri

kwaia tjimia *Bruders Tochters Tochter.* ◇ brother's daughter's daughter. Ⓛ puliri

woia tjimia *Bruders Tochters Sohn (m&w).* ◇ brother's daughter's son. Ⓛ kunarbi

lorra tjimia *die Mutter der Schwiegermutter.* ◇ mother of mother-in-law. Ⓛ puliri

tjimiatja *der eigene Großvater (resp. Großonkel, Enkel, Großneffe).* ◇ one's own grandfather (grand uncle, grandson, grandnephew). Ⓛ kunarbina

tjinama *hineinsehen (in eine Hütte).* ◇ to look into (a hut). Ⓛ njirkiñi

tjinanama *hineinsehen.* ◇ to look inside or into. Ⓛ manjirkiñi

tjinintjima *hereinsehen.* ◇ to look in. Ⓛ ngalanjirkiñi

tjinintjilama *hereinsehen.* ◇ to look inside. Ⓛ ngalanjirkikatiñi

tjinankerama *bald sterben.* ◇ to die soon. Ⓛ eralknaríña

tjinánkilàma *aufbewahren, aufheben (für einen andern).* ◇ keep, preserve (for somebody else). Ⓛ amalanáñi

tjipi *Schaf (n).* ◇ sheep.

tjipi-punga *Wolle.* ◇ wool.

tjinba *langsam, geduldig.* ◇ slow, patient. Ⓛ purina

tjinbalama *warten (auf jemanden).* ◇ wait (for somebody). Ⓛ patani Ⓓ kalkana

tjinbalélama *zutraulich machen (Kinder).* ◇ make trustful (children). Ⓛ purinmanañi

tjinnapalka *Schuhe, n.* ◇ shoes, n.

tjinbara *sehr heiß.* ◇ very hot. Ⓛ talkámbañi

tjipurkula *kostbar, Kleinod.* ◇ valuable, precious.

tjinganalai *'du bist sehr freigebig'.* ◇ 'you are very generous'. Ⓛ ngaiukúnitàlu

tjinnantuma *Ehre erweisen (den Alten).* ◇ honour (elders).

tjitja *Fleisch (von den kleinen Kindern so genannt).* ◇ meat (word used by children). Ⓛ tíita

tjintjurkna *Toten-Vogel.* ◇ the death bird (or the bird of the dead) is a small bird that calls at night tjitjurk, tjitjurk (Strehlow 1915: 6); people try to move such a bird on by calling out to it and throwing a stone at it. Ⓛ witjutjurkna

tjininja *Sachen, Eigentum.* ◇ things, property. Ⓛ pauali

tjininjinangala rama *von der Seite beobachten, Kopf auf die Seite legen und beobachten.* ◇ look at it sideways, tilt head sideways and observe. Ⓛ wàringirkira nangañi

tjinna *Freund, Wohltäter, Spender.* ◇ friend, benefactor, donor. Ⓛ wolta ngultu Ⓓ kamaneli

tjinnamanturka *Wohltäter, reiche Spender.* ◇ sponsor. Ⓛ woltantamantu

tjinnakatjinna *freigebig, wohltätig, freundlich mit einander.* ◇ generous, charitable, friendly with each other. Ⓛ woltakawolta

tjinkara *Pflanzenkost [?], Mahl [?].* ◇ plant food. Ⓛ itjinkiri

tjipantapantiuma *sich ausbreitend, lang machen (Bart).* ◇ spread, grow long (beard). Ⓛ wonpularañi

tjintalbintanintja *voller Flecken, gefleckt.* ◇ full of spots, spotted. Ⓛ níntaníntana

tjintatjinta *Blume mit kleinen weißen Blüten (Senfgeschmack).* ◇ flower with small white blossoms (mustard taste). Ⓛ tjintitjinta

tjintatnuma *zerfetzen, in kleine Stücke zerreißen.* ◇ tear into small pieces. Ⓛ pitjilenañi

tjintjiriuma *herausfließen (Blut bei der Regel), herabfließen.* ◇ flow out, flow down. Ⓛ topaltjingañi

tjiparipara *schnell laufend.* ◇ run fast. Ⓛ tjipiripiri

tjipa *Gürtel.* ◇ belt; piece, part. Ⓛ nanpà Ⓓ mandamanda

tjipala ngama *im Gürtel tragen.* ◇ carry on belt. Ⓛ nanpanka katiñi Ⓓ munkana?

tjipitja *Ein Stück Holz, zum Spuren und Figuren im Sand zu zeichnen. Ein Spiel.* ◇ a piece of wood, to draw tracks and shapes in sand; a game. Ⓛ ninka

tjipara *Eigentum, etwas, das mir gehört, das ich nicht weggeben will.* ◇ property, something that belongs to me and I do not want to give away. Ⓛ matupura Ⓓ judujudu

tjirpatjirpa *die mit der mera auf dem Fischspeer (inta) eingeritzten Ringe.* ◇ circles engraved with the 'mera' on fish spear called 'inta'.

tjipatjipa *fleißig.* ◇ hard working, industrious; energetic, lively, healthy. Ⓛ rotjípatjípa Ⓓ marapakapirna, maranurru

tjiratjirerama *den Todeskampf kämpfen [unclear].* ◇ agony, death throes. Ⓛ tjiritjiriringañi

tjiratjira *(Erde) stechend (mit einem Stock) beim Spazierengehen.* ◇ stab ground (with a stick) on a walk. Ⓛ túkaratúkara

tjiratjira *sterbend, dem Tode nahe, im Todeskampf.* ◇ dying, close to death, in death throes. Ⓛ tjiritjiri

tjirkererama *weiß reiben oder färben (Stirnband an der weißen Rinde des Gummibaumes).* ◇ to colour white (headband with the white bark of a gumtree) (Strehlow 1910b: 95). Ⓛ pirapirariñi

tjirka *kleine Geschwür im Fleisch.* ◇ small abscess in flesh. Ⓛ itirkĭ

tjirkoa *Entenart.* ◇ duck species. Ⓛ itjirkoa

tjita *weich, biegsam, klein, schwach.* ◇ soft, supple, small, weak. Ⓛ tola

tjitatjita *ziemlich klein.* ◇ quite small. Ⓛ tólatóla

tjitilama *biegen.* ◇ bend. Ⓛ tolani Ⓓ kutiri ngankana

tjirkawotna *(sehr widerspenstig) in Frau, die mit ihrem Vater hurt.* ◇ (very rebellious) a woman, who has intercourse with her (classificatory) father; (Strehlow 1913: 93). Ⓛ puta

tjitaminjaminja *Blume (der Kornblume ähnlich).* ◇ flower (resembling cornflower). Ⓛ tjitiminjaminja

tjirkawara *äußerst widerspenstig im Mann, der seine Schwester hurt.* ◇ (extremely rebellious) a man who has intercourse with his sister. Ⓛ itjirkitirki

tjitara *Schlange spec. nicht giftig.* ◇ non-poisonous snake species; bad spirit being in the shape of a large green snake that comes from the south. It may enter a person and devour his or her internal organs causing death. This evil being's name tjitara means 'the one with a small head' (Strehlow 1907: 13). Ⓛ nantala, tjitari

tjítalapárinja *Lerche (trillerend auf).* ◇ lark (rise warbling). Ⓛ tjituluperinji

tjiteraterélama *erziehen, wachsen machen.* ◇ to educate, to make grow, to grow up. Ⓛ unkaljenañi
tjitjina *die Schleuder.* ◇ sling.
tjitatja *kleiner Speer (womit Kinder spielen).* ◇ small spear (children's toy). Ⓛ tatjitatji
tjitjitánama *vorhersagen, weissagen.* ◇ predict, foretell. Ⓛ wottalbmanáñi
tjitjata nama *herrschen (Häuptling).* ◇ rule (chief). Ⓛ atani ninañi
tjiteratjitera *kleine gelbe Vögel.* ◇ small yellow birds. Ⓛ tjituratjitura
tjitjibura *lange, schmale (Stirn), lange schmale (Früchte z.B. ngaraka).* ◇ long narrow (forehead), long narrow (e.g. bean-like pod of a vine species). Ⓛ watjinkuru Ⓓ wirdi
tjitjatérama *herrschen, befehlen.* ◇ rule, command; rules. Ⓛ átanariñi
tjiuka *der jüngere Bruder (eines Andern).* ◇ younger brother (of someone else). Ⓛ malangura
tjitjirkuma *zusammen halten (Wurzeln).* ◇ hold together (roots). Ⓛ ngalunbinañi
tjitjinelama *etwas (z.B. ein Stock) gerade in der Hand halten, zielen (mit dem Gewehr).* ◇ hold something (e.g. stick) straight in the hand, aim (with rifle). Ⓛ tjerinpungañi
tjorrarenarena *Wage.* ◇ scale.
tjorrerama *sich ansehen, messen.* ◇ look at each other, size up.
tjorrerinja *das Maß.* ◇ the measure.
tjorrerinjaka inkuenkua *das Maßrohr (n).* ◇ measuring rod.
tjorrelelama *zwingen.* ◇ to force.
tjorrelarenama *zwingen.* ◇ to force.
tjoa *mager.* ◇ thin. Ⓛ nurka Ⓓ jeranja, jeltja, marki
  tjoatjoa *duplik. mager.* ◇ very thin. Ⓛ nurkanurka
  tjoerama *abmagern.* ◇ lose weight. Ⓛ nurkariñi
tjorrelarenama *zwingen.* ◇ to force.
tjoa *Zwillingsbruder.* ◇ twin brother; mate, friend; person born on the same day; two men who have been through 'business' together. Ⓛ ina
tjoarka *honighaltige Blüten des ntjiuia.* ◇ honey containing blossoms of honeysuckle. Ⓛ tjoarki
tjoankua *der Zwillingsbruder eines Andern.* ◇ twin brother of someone else. Ⓛ inanku
tjoananga *Zwillinge.* ◇ twins. Ⓛ inarara, mulati
tjointjara *Altersgenossen.* ◇ peers. Ⓛ inarara, mulati
tjontama *anfangen (zu arbeiten).* ◇ begin, start (to work). Ⓛ ngarutaríñi Ⓓ wonnina
  tjontinja *Anfang.* ◇ the beginning. Ⓛ ngarutarinmi
tjoarbánama *ranken (um einen Baum).* ◇ entwine, wind (around a tree). Ⓛ titirpungañi
tjôra *Schlange, giftig.* ◇ poisonous snake. Ⓛ mutuka
tjorra *Bein, Schienbein, Pfeiler (oder kleine rote Ameise).* ◇ leg, shin, pillar (or small red ant). Ⓛ eka; tjirara Ⓓ nguramokku
tjôra *kleine rote Ameisen.* ◇ small red ants. Ⓛ mutuka
tjŏra; era ilutjika tjora *postp. bald (Absicht, daß etwas geschehen soll); er soll gleich sterben.* ◇ (postposition) soon (intention that something shall/will happen); he shall die soon. Ⓛ ngula, paluru iluntakita ngula
tjorawunga *der Schlafplatz der aroa.* ◇ wallaby sleeping place.
tjŏrabitjŏra *Sonnenschein.* ◇ sunshine, warmth. Ⓛ linkirabura
tjorrerama *etwas besehen, gesehen, messen, [unclear] (Creek).* ◇ to look at something, to examine, to measure. Ⓛ ekuntani, intañi
tjorerama *sich sonnen, (Sonne).* ◇ to sun, (sun); sunbath. Ⓛ titakambañi Ⓓ nitaterina (*sich sonnen*).
Tjoritja, Tjorritja? *McDonnell Ranges.* ◇ West MacDonnell Ranges. Ⓛ eritni
tjotjikalama *um Hilfe bitten, flehen (um), um Hilfe rufen.* ◇ beg for help, implore, call for help.

tjortjikama, tjôtjikama *um Hilfe bitten, flehen (um), um Hilfe rufen.* ◇ ask or beg for help. Ⓛ arawolkuni Ⓓ winpana

tjôtjerama *sich strecken (nach dem Schlaf).* ◇ stretch (after sleep). Ⓛ watuni

tjotjerama *ausstrecken (Hand).* ◇ stretch out (hand).

tjuanba *Baum mit kleinen, in Büscheln herabhängenden Blättern, iron wood, (Acacia estrophiolata).* ◇ ironwood; *Acacia estrophiolata* (Latz 1996). Ⓛ untari, utanti, tanbana?

tjorulbma *der Stich eines Insekts (die Wirkung desselben).* ◇ insect sting (and its effect).

tjukara *Stock (auf dem man sich beim Gehen stützt).* ◇ stick; walking stick (Strehlow 1910b: 99). Ⓛ tukara

tjuára *Strauch mit glänzend grünen, linienförmigen Blättern und hopfenblütenähnlichen Blüten (Dodonaea viscosa).* ◇ bush with bright green, narrow leaves and blossoms like hop flowers; *Dodonaea viscosa* (Latz 1996). Ⓛ wottara, menjinka

tjueta *Schlange (spec.)* ◇ snake species. Ⓛ wommi-ngana

tjubmara *Fingernägel, Zehennägel, Krallen.* ◇ fingernails, toenails, claws. Ⓛ piri, miltji Ⓓ piri

iltja-tjubmara *Fingernägel.* ◇ fingernails. Ⓛ mara piri Ⓓ mara piri

inka-tjubmara *Zehennägel.* ◇ toenails. Ⓛ tjinna piri Ⓓ tidna piri

tjukugula *die Fruchkolben der Cycas-Palmen.* ◇ seeds of cycad. Ⓛ utukákili

tjukapulapula *dicht zusammen stehende Bäume.* ◇ dense stand of trees. Ⓛ tjúkupúlupúlu

tjukunja *ruhig, schweigsam, still.* ◇ quiet, silent, still. Ⓛ rata or rāta Ⓓ ngapu.

tjukunjerama *schweigen, ruhig werden.* ◇ be silent, say nothing, become calm. Ⓛ rateringañi Ⓓ ngapurina

tjukunjilama *trs. beruhigen.* ◇ (transitive) calm. Ⓛ rātani Ⓓ ngapu paribana?

tjukaralama *an Krücken gehen.* ◇ go on crutches. Ⓛ tukarajennañi

tjularka *mit weißer Stirn.* ◇ with white forehead. Ⓛ tularka

tjulbakama *beißen (Rauch – die Augen oder die Kehle).* ◇ bite (smoke in eyes or throat). Ⓛ nelkuni

tjulberama *ausstrecken (Füße).* ◇ stretch out (feet). Ⓛ watuni

tjulka *Kalk.* ◇ lime, limestone. Ⓛ kaltji Ⓓ tudna

tjulkulintama *bescheinen (Sonne), im Sonneschein liegen.* ◇ shine on (sun), lie in sun. Ⓛ bilbirangañi

tjulkura *weiß.* ◇ white. Ⓛ titi Ⓓ warru

ilknua? *testiculi.* ◇ testicles. Ⓛ tulkurba

tjunama *heben, aufheben, hochheben.* ◇ lift, lift up, raise. Ⓛ talini Ⓓ makumanina

tjunalama *sich selbst (Sachen) auf den Kopf legen.* ◇ put (things) on head. Ⓛ talilkatiñi

tjulitja *Pflanze mit großen gelben Blüten.* ◇ plant with large yellow blossoms. Ⓛ úntunúntana

tjunba *Große Eidechse, bis 6 Fuß lang, Haut teppichartig (Varanus giganteus).* ◇ large lizard, can grow up to 6 feet in length, carpet-like skin (*Varanus giganteus*, Perentie) (Atlas of Living Australia n.d.) Ⓛ pulalba, wongapa Ⓓ pirinti

tjunta *Magen.* ◇ stomach. Ⓛ ituntu

tjunkuna *Stock zum Schlagen.* ◇ hitting stick. Ⓛ tjunkunu

tjununkara *Totenopfer, bestehend aus Knochen, die auf das Grab der Verstorbenen niedergelegt werden.* ◇ offering for the dead, consisting of bones that are put on the grave of the deceased. Ⓛ itjárilkni

tjununkara ndama *Totenopfer geben.* ◇ give offering to the deceased. Ⓛ jungañi, itjarilkni

tjupularra *guter Weg, gerader Weg.* ◇ good path, straight path. Ⓛ ántara

tjurbmunta *geschlossen, verschlossen, regenlos.* ◇ closed, rainless. Ⓛ purpunba

tjurbmunterama *(z.B. mama) die Wunde schießt sich, verheilt.* ◇ wound closes, heals (e.g. mama). Ⓛ purpunáriñi

tjurka *Feigenstrauch (rötliche Schößlinge, dicke lanzenförmige Blätter, roten Früchten) groß wie Stachelbeeren, eßbar (Ficus platypoda).* ◇ fig tree (reddish shoots, thick spear-shaped leaves with edible berry-sized red fruit); *Ficus platypoda* var. *minor* (Latz 1996). Ⓛ witerka, ili

tjurkatjurka *Strauch mit dicken, hellgrünen, lanzenförmigen Blättern, weißen Blüten und roten erbsengroßen Beeren, nicht eßbar.* ◇ bush with thick, light green, spear-shaped leaves, white blossoms and red pea sized berries, not edible. Ⓛ witerkawiterka, iliïli

tjurbiatjurba *Boomerangs mit \\V/// \\V// Linien.* ◇ Boomerangs with \\V/// \\V// lines. Ⓛ warpilikura

tjurunga *die heiligen Lieder, Hölzer und Steine, auch die Aufführungen der heiligen Gebräuche.* ◇ sacred objects, songs and ceremonies. Ⓛ kuntanka

tjurungerama *Tjurunga werden, in Tjurunga verwandelt werden.* ◇ become or change into something at the end of creative activities (see also Strehlow 1908: 77).

tjurunga-retna *heiligen Gesänge.* ◇ sacred songs.

tjutalpa *Vogel specie, Ruf dem der Wachtel ähnlich, (Sphenostoma cristata).* ◇ Bourke's Parrot, *Neopsephotis bourkii* (Pizzey and Knight 2007). Ⓛ tjutalpi, tjituntjitun

tjurtjatjurtja *Beine lupara – Knacken (der Känguruh).* ◇ break legs or thighs (of kangaroo). Ⓛ tjilkirtjilkir

tmaiatuma *prüfen (was der Andere gelernt hat) scherzen?* ◇ test (what the other has learnt), joke?

tmakunama *besiegen (Feind).* ◇ defeat (enemy).

tmakuinama *Stillschweigen auferlegen (den Lebendigen) und den Toten (=Kalk auf das Grab streuen).* ◇ impose silence on (the living and) dead (scatter lime on grave). Ⓛ ápurawonniñi

tmaiatuma *fragen (in der Schule fragt?).* ◇ ask (question at school). Ⓛ aiatapini Ⓓ jekibana

tmakuka, tmakurka, kmakurka *Schnur, lange Schnur, die Frauen um sich schnüren.* ◇ long string that women tie around themselves. Ⓛ wolluwonnu, makutji

tmalabartja *fette Schenkel.* ◇ fat thighs. Ⓛ ilbinkinji

tmakupita *sehr hoch (= tiefer) Haufe (von Schoten), ein sehr große Haufe (von Raupen), eine Menge (Raupen).* ◇ very high (deep) pile (of pods), a very large pile (of caterpillars), a lot (of caterpillars). Ⓛ makungariñi

tmalba *wilde Pfirsichbaum (Santalum acuminatum).* ◇ wild peach or quandong tree; *Santalum acuminatum*. Ⓛ imilbi, mangata

tmalbatmalba *Strauch mit kleinen kirschenartigen Früchten.* ◇ bush with little cherry-like fruit. Ⓛ imilbimilba, tjuturu [Southern dialect]

tmalbambaralenana, tmálbambaralénana *(tmalba = Flamme, baralenana = bartjilelama = scheine) Venus (Morgen oder Abendstern) = Licht-Spender.* ◇ Venus (morning or evening star) = light-giver (see Strehlow 1907: 18–19). Ⓛ intjilpi [Southern dialect], intjilpikujinina, mulati Ⓓ ngamaturukura, ngamaturukuru

tmalkara *sehr weiß, sehr hell (Blitz).* ◇ very white, very bright (lightning). Ⓛ tïtï

tmaltakalta *fertig, beendet.* ◇ ready, finished. Ⓛ unbapalla, pepala

tmaltakalterama *fertig werden, vollenden (Zeitraum).* ◇ finishing, complete (temporal). Ⓛ unbaringañi, pepalaringani

tmaltakaltilama *beendigen.* ◇ finish, to prepare something, to make ready. Ⓛ pepalani

tmaltakaltaïlalajinama *den Genuß des Totem-tieres freigeben.* ◇ release totem animal for consumption. Ⓛ pepalarajani, pepalaraijani

tmaltaramba *süße Saft an den lalba-Sträuchern.* ◇ sweet sap on lalba bushes. Ⓛ amalturumbu

tmakatalama *sich unmäßig freuen, frohlocken.* ◇ be very pleased, be jubilant.

tmarawonka *Lagerpl. der unverheiat. Männer.* ◇ single men's camp. Ⓛ nguratara

tmāna *leise, still (nicht redend), schweigsam.* ◇ quiet (not talking), silent. Ⓛ kanmara, wombata Ⓓ ngaruni?

tmanerama *heranschleichen, spionieren.* ◇ creep up, spy. Ⓛ wombataringañi

tmanatmana *heuchlerisch, schleichend.* ◇ hypocritical, sneaky. Ⓛ wombatawombata

tmarkintja, tmarakintja *Platz (cultus).* ◇ cleared space where ceremonies are performed. Ⓛ amboanta

tmangna *kleines (schlechtes) Feuerholz, Reißig.* ◇ small (bad) firewood, twigs. Ⓛ amila

tmara lukura *Weiber-Camp (der Witwen).* ◇ women's camp (widows). Ⓛ ngura alukuru

tmånjinga *Grashalm.* ◇ grass blade. Ⓛ injirari

tmanjirama *Alpdrücken, im Schlaf stöhnen.* ◇ nightmare, moan in sleep. Ⓛ ngunkupungañi

tmanjirpa *Schlangen (genus).* ◇ snakes. Ⓛ wonjirpi

tmanjiritjilama *erscheinen (Geister), spucken.* ◇ appear (spirits), haunt. Ⓛ ngunkupungañi

tmara ulba *der weiche Lagerplatz.* ◇ comfortable, soft camp. Ⓛ ngura pulpa

tmapala lama *schwimmen (Menschen und Hunde).* ◇ swim (humans and dogs). Ⓛ tarekatiñi

tmara runga *der persönliche Totem Platz.* ◇ personal totem place, conception site. Ⓛ ngura ngainku, ng. woltara

tmara altjira (altjirealtja) *der mütterliche Totem Platz.* ◇ maternal totem place. The first remark on matrifiliation to Aranda country was made by the Lutheran missionary Louis Schulze (1891: 238–39). He recorded the term 'tmara altjira' meaning 'the place where mother of the dead person was born'. Likewise, Carl Strehlow mentioned, as one of his first encounters with connection to country, mother's conception dreaming, called in Aranda 'altjira'. He described the relationship of an individual to mother's dreaming, 'altjira', also called 'garra altjira' or 'deba altjira', and to mother's conception site, called 'tmara altjira or, more precisely, tmara altjirealtja, i.e. the place of the totem associated with me' (Strehlow 1908: 57; 1910b: 2). Altjira is used in this context as meaning mother's conception dreaming. He lists these in his published family trees (Strehlow 1913: Attachments) as 'ara' (kangaroo), 'ilia' (emu), 'jerramba' (honeyant), etc. and mentioned how to ask properly about this particular place: 'unkwanga ntana? i.e. Where is the place of the totem associated with you?' (Strehlow 1908: 58). Ⓛ ngura altjiriwolta

tmara *Lagerplatz.* ◇ camp, home, land, country. Today, Western Aranda people refer to countries that they may claim, usually through their grandparents, and its associated esoteric knowledge, as 'tmara', called 'country' in Aboriginal English and 'estate' in the anthropological literature. Loritja call it 'ngura'. Ⓛ ngura Ⓓ ngura

tmara inkárkara *verlassener Platz.* ◇ abandoned camp. Ⓛ ngura inkírkari

tmara irbonba *verlassener Platz.* ◇ deserted camp. Ⓛ ngura munguna Ⓓ ngura walpa

tmararinja *Bewohner eines Lagerplatzes 'Bürger'; die Endung 'rinja' drückt aus: bewohnend, zu etwas gehörend.* ◇ someone belonging to a place, 'citizen', traditional owner; 'rinja' is a suffix meaning 'belonging to'. Ⓛ ngurakututu, ngurarita

tmarajunta *[Höhlung], Schlafplatz.* ◇ hollow, sleeping place. Ⓛ nguralaiï, nguratōku

tmarankintja *Lagerplatz der unverheirateten Männer.* ◇ single men's camp. Ⓛ ngurankíntji, ngura tauara

tmara kenka *Vaterland, Umgebung, ([unclear] Stammesgebiet).* ◇ fatherland, surroundings, tribal territory. Ⓛ ngura aranka

tmariltja *Bewohner desselben Lagerplatzes.* ◇ inhabitant of the same place, spirit of a place; today these spirits are called pmarakutata (in Carl Strehlow's spelling 'tmarakutata', i.e. tmara (place, country, home) kutata (always). Ⓛ ngurarita Ⓓ ngurala

tmara *Mulde, aus Gummiholz gefertigt.* ◇ bowl (made of gumtree wood). Ⓛ pitila, wilkiri, membu, meka Ⓓ pirra tjapa?

tmarama *fragen.* ◇ to ask. Ⓛ tabini Ⓓ jakalkana, jakalkingana (den ?)

tmaratjua *Gebiet.* ◇ area, region. Ⓛ nguratáti Ⓓ milila

tmaratmara *Käfer, Land oder Wasser Käfer, (genus).* ◇ beetle, land or water beetle. Ⓛ opmaripmari

tmarawonka *Lagerplatz der verheirateten Männer, der verheiratete Mann.* ◇ camp of married men, the married man. Ⓛ nguratara, ngurakambanta

tmariltja *Bewohner desselben Lagerplatzes, Bürger.* ◇ inhabitant of the same place or camp, citizen. Ⓛ ngurarita Ⓓ ngurala

tmararbanana *von einer Stadt zur andern.* ◇ from one place to the other.

tmarkintja, tmarakintja *Platz auf dem Kinder und Weiber.* ◇ cleared (public) place where ceremonies are performed. Ⓛ amboanta

tmaroaroa *alle junge Schlangen, die sich um die alte gewickelt haben, auch die Spuren dieses Schlangenknäuels.* ◇ young snakes who have wound themselves around the old one; tracks of this bundle of snakes. Ⓛ kárbirarbiri

tmata *heuchlerisch, falsch.* ◇ hypocritical, deceitful. Ⓛ talu Ⓓ jeljujelju

tmauulama *in Verwesung oder Fäulnis übergehen.* ◇ decay, rot. Ⓛ tulalárani

tmataka *voller Geschwüre, wunde Stelle, wundgelegen.* ◇ full of abscesses, sore spot, hospital sores. Ⓛ womitara

tmatja *Larve, sehr kleine Raupe, die sich in den Stengeln der terka-Sträucher aufhält.* ◇ grub, very small caterpillar that lives on the stems of terka-bushes. Ⓛ amita

tmatjoïlama *mißhandeln, fortwährend schlagen.* ◇ abuse, hit continuously. Ⓛ wominúrkani

tmatjerilkama *sehr weiß sein (Knochen), bleichen.* ◇ to be very white (bones), bleach. Ⓛ lírbmirani

tmauerkama *zittern, sich schütteln (vor Kälte).* ◇ to tremble, shiver (from cold). Ⓛ árbmárbma ngarañi

tmēba *eben, glatt (Felsenplatte).* ◇ even, smooth (rock plate). Ⓛ walu

tmekaina *kleine Eidechse.* ◇ small lizard. Ⓛ ngurakatikanilba

tmekua *Strauch mit mulgaähnlichen Früchten.* ◇ bush with mulga-like fruit. Ⓛ mintju

tmekua *Larve (weiß) in tmekua Wurzeln.* ◇ grub (white) in tmekua roots. Ⓛ alkunari, mintju

tmeljara *stone curlew (Steinwälzer) mit blaugrau und braunen Federn.* ◇ stone curlew with blue-grey and brown feathers. Ⓛ wilu Ⓓ wiljaru

tmeljalkara *Nasenknochen (Schmuck), Knochen von Adler, itoa und Pelikan von Männern und Jungen getragen.* ◇ nose bone (adornment), bones of eagles, bush turkey and pelicans worn by men and boys. Ⓛ telunku, marapinti

tmeta [Southern dialect], **tmatja** *Larve, sehr kleine Raupe.* ◇ grub, very small caterpillar. Ⓛ amita

tmōra *Baumstamm.* ◇ tree trunk. Ⓛ mutu

tmoara *Zeichen auf dem Rücken.* ◇ sign on back. Ⓛ minburu

tmoara ilkinja *Zeichen auf dem Rücken.* ◇ sign on back. Ⓛ tana minburu

tmorinja *Steinmesser, im Südosten angefertigt (von den Loritja nicht gekannt).* ◇ stone knife, made in the southeast (not known among the Loritja).

tmulpura *Hals, Kehlkopf.* ◇ throat, larynx. Ⓛ leri Ⓓ jerkola

tmultura *trocken, abgeschälte Rinde; die Rinde, die sich von selbst abgeschält hat.* ◇ dry, bark that has peeled off by itself (Strehlow 1910b: 63). Ⓛ lakalaka

tmultatja [Northern dialect], **tmultitja** *Rohr.* ◇ reed, cane. Ⓛ amultatji

tmurunta *abgeschälte (Stamm), ohne Rinde.* ◇ peeled (tree trunk), without bark. Ⓛ mutukuta Ⓓ kulakaru

tmurka [Southern dialect] *cf.* **nguruka** *gestern.* ◇ yesterday. Ⓛ mungatu

tmurkarbuna [Southern dialect] *cf.* ngurukarbuna. ◇ the day before yesterday. Ⓛ mungatukutuba

tmurkakuia [Southern dialect] *ngurukakuia.* ◇ the day before yesterday. Ⓛ mungatumaiu

tmurkalkura [Southern dialect] *cf.* ngurukalkura. ◇ several days ago. Ⓛ mungatunguánba

tnakinjarara *Gläubiger, der Leihende.* ◇ creditor, lender.

tnanjantambala *standhaft.* ◇ firm.

tnanjuntura *standhaft.* ◇ firm.

tnaltjima *treten [?].*

tnabarka *Mist der Känguruhs (zum Feuer-Reiben).* ◇ kangaroo dung (used to rub fire) (Strehlow 1920: 13–14). Ⓛ anunkulu

tnabantalaka *von atna (vagina) und bantalaka (fortwährend gehend) um zu huren. Eine Frau, die mit ihrem Onkel hurt.* ◇ woman who has a forbidden relationship with her uncle. Ⓛ kunnajunkuta (junkuta: *fortwährend gehend*: give continuously)

tnabitjaralenama *rückwärts gehen.* ◇ walk backwards. Ⓛ murunúntunúntu katiñi Ⓓ ngadatikana?

tnabitjeralama *zurückweichen (von Feinden).* ◇ retreat (from enemy).

tnabata *große Laus.* ◇ large louse. Ⓛ putinba

tnabitjerana *weichen (vor den Feinden).* ◇ give way, yield (to enemy).

tnabuta *(atna = vagina, buta = groß) geil, wollüstig (von Frauen).* ◇ horny, voluptuous (women). Ⓛ kunnala Ⓓ palakantji

tnáburùta *kurz, klein (von Steinen).* ◇ short, little (stones). Ⓛ ngatapatti

tnaiangúnjangúnjalama *rückwärts gehen.* ◇ walk backwards. Ⓛ murumurukatiñi Ⓓ ngadatikana

tnaiïnga *hinter (z.B. einem Baum).* ◇ behind (e.g. a tree). Ⓛ mala

tnainama *hüten, behüten, bewahren.* ◇ guard, protect, keep. Ⓛ ngaraljennañi Ⓓ ngamalkana, pariparibana, marapana

tnaininanana *Hirte.* ◇ shepherd. Ⓛ ngaraljennami Ⓓ ngamalkanietja

tnainarinja *Hirte.* ◇ shepherd. Ⓛ ngaraljennami Ⓓ ngamalkanietja

tnainalanama *aufbewahren (jemanden Sachen).* ◇ keep, save (things for somebody). Ⓛ ngaraljenkanáñi Ⓓ kurijinbana, ngulukana

utnánjima *auf einen losfahren (um zu beißen).* ◇ attack (to bite). Ⓛ ngalapatiñi

tnadata [Southern dialect] *Mulgablüten, Akacien-Kätzchen.* ◇ mulga blossoms, acacia catkin. Ⓛ unatjiti

tnalakarelama *groß achten.* ◇ to respect highly.

tnakama *1. glauben, für wahr halten, 2. absondern, austeilen (Geschenke).* ◇ 1. believe (to be true), 2. separate, distribute (gifts). Ⓛ 1. bulkawonniñi, 2. akatatauañi

tnakalama *sich rühmen, sich brüsten, sich selbst vertrauen.* ◇ boast, brag, be confident. Ⓛ bulkawonniñi

tnékanerama *einen abraten, etwas ausreden.* ◇ dissuade someone, talk out of something. Ⓛ minurariñi

(u)tnāka *der (?) Camp dunkel [unclear].* Ⓛ ngurapatipati

tnákerkerama *nicht glauben (eine Botschaft).* ◇ not believe (a message). Ⓛ panpurangani

tnalbitnama *sich aufrecht hinstellen.* ◇ stand up straight. Ⓛ ngarangarañi

tnalama *sich kratzen.* ◇ scratch. Ⓛ tauañi

tnalkintjiuma *austeilen, verteilen (Kleider).* ◇ distribute, hand out (clothes). Ⓛ ilkiwoniñi

tnalbaleala *auf dem Hinterteil sitzend (Menschen), am Boden hinwankend oder am Boden sich hinlegend (niedrige Bäume oder Sträucher und Büsche).* ◇ sit on behind (humans), low lying (trees or bushes). Ⓛ mannapiti

tnakitja *rote Kernfrucht, etwas größer als Kirschen.* ◇ red stone fruit, slightly larger than cherries. Ⓛ kura, peki

tnālba, tnalba *Schwanz (Vogel); Schwanzfedern.* ◇ tail (bird), tail feathers. Ⓛ mannata-aturu

tnalama *von sich treiben.* ◇ drive away. Ⓛ tjingañi

tnalangatnalélama *antreiben zum Weitergehen.* ◇ urge to go on. Ⓛ ngalangalani

tnalanama *aufrecht stehen.* ◇ stand upright. Ⓛ ngaraniñi

tnalapaltarkna *species of night heron (Reiher).* ◇ species of night heron. Ⓛ analapaltarkna

tnalbatnauma *treiben, nötigen zu gehen.* ◇ drive, force to go. Ⓛ wollawollatunañi

tnalkinjiuma *ausbreiten (um etwas zu suchen).* ◇ spread out (to look for something). Ⓛ ilkiwonniñi Ⓓ pirakana, piltana

tnalta *Fußweg, track, (z.B. der Känguruh oder der Ochsen).* ◇ footpath, track (e.g. of kangaroos or bullocks). Ⓛ analti

tnaltja *Exkremente der Raupen.* ◇ excrement of grubs. Ⓛ analtji

tnalbatnanbuma *hüpfen mit in die Höhe geworfenen Knien.* ◇ hop throwing knees up high. Ⓛ wárawárarakátini

tnanopanama *(k. tnama: stehen + nopanama: bleiben) immer nach einiger Entfernung stehen bleiben; nachdem man gegangen ist, stehen bleiben, dann weiter gehen, dann stehen bleiben, u.s.w.; fortwährend, nachdem man einige (Schritte gegangen ist?), stehen bleiben, wieder und wieder stehen bleiben.* ◇ constantly stop and start walking. (A compound of tnama 'stand' and nopanama 'continue'.) Ⓛ mangaralabakabakañi

tnatamatnama *hochaufgerichtet, gebieterisch dastehen.* ◇ stand upright, imperiously. Ⓛ wilalbingarañi

tnaltjama *zertreten, zerstampfen (mit den Füßen).* ◇ tread or stamp (with feet). Ⓛ lurpani Ⓓ nankana, nankanankana

tnaljurbara *night-parrot.* ◇ night parrot. Ⓛ analtjirbiri

tnatjilama *still stehen, warten.* ◇ stop, wait. Ⓛ ngarakatiñi

tnama *aufrechstehen, stehen.* ◇ stand upright, stand. Ⓛ ngarañi Ⓓ terkana

tnátnanama *aufstehen, sich erheben.* ◇ stand up. Ⓛ ngaralatalkañi

tnapitnama *dastehen, in Reihen stehen.* ◇ stand there, stand in rows. Ⓛ ngarangarañi

tnăma *Stock (zum Schlagen), Stecken, Stange.* ◇ stick (to hit with), pole, rod; digging stick. Ⓛ wonna Ⓓ wonna

tnamitoppatoppa *Stock über den Rücken (gelegt).* ◇ stick (placed) over back. Ⓛ tapala

tnatjalbuma *(aus 'tnama: graben, kratzen' und 'albuma: umkehren, heimkehren') nach seiner Rückkehr kratzend stehen oder auf seiner Heimkehr kratzen.* ◇ dig after return or dig during return trip home. Ⓛ ngaranikulbara

tnāma *graben, kratzen.* ◇ dig, scratch, scrape. Ⓛ tauani, wirkani Ⓓ bakuna (*graben*: dig)

tnatjarakalama *tief graben.* ◇ dig deep. Ⓛ tauaraokalingañi

tnatnilauma *scharren, kratzen.* ◇ scrape, scratch. Ⓛ tauatauañi

tnatjalbuma *bei der Heimkehr, kratzen.* ◇ scratch returning home. Ⓛ nauurpungañi

tnamatōra *in einer geraden Linie (kommen).* ◇ (approach) in a straight line. Ⓛ warata ngalajennañi

tnamatnama [Southern dialect] *Strauch.* ◇ shrub, *Canthium* (species). Ⓛ kundikarka

tnaminatuka *gerade, rechtschaffen, gut.* ◇ straight, just, good. Ⓛ pauali

tnapmagunia *bodenlos, Abgrund.* ◇ bottomless, abyss. Ⓓ mariwirri

tnamiwia *nachmittags (3 Uhr).* ◇ in the afternoon (3 o'clock).

tnaminjalkna *Jakobsstab (Sternbild).* ◇ Orion? (star constellation). Ⓛ kaditjina

tnambutaka bauma *umstoßen (einen Mann), zurückstoßen.* ◇ knock over (a man), push back. Ⓛ wilalku untuni

tnāna *Mahlstein, auf dem gemahlen wird.* ◇ grinding stone. Ⓛ tjewa Ⓓ [marda] wati, marda paltiri

tnanakiëkatuma *zerklopfen (mit Steinen).* ◇ to beat (into pieces with stones). Ⓛ tjewakura atuni

tnanbulauma *herabspringen.* ◇ jump down. Ⓛ wararakatiñi

tnanbirkuma *schleichen.* ◇ creep, sneak.

tnanbutjalbuma *hineinspringen.* ◇ jump into. Ⓛ wararakatingu kulbara Ⓓ tampana, tampatampana

tnanbuma *springen, hüpfen, überschreiten, übersteigen, überspringen.* ◇ jump, skip, cross, climb over, jump over. Ⓛ lantarukatiñi, wararakatiñi Ⓓ kulkungana, duldrina (*springen*: jump)

tnanbunama *hinunterspringen.* ◇ jump down. Ⓛ matapulukatiñi [unclear]

tnanbutjikalama *hinunterspringen.* ◇ jump down. Ⓛ wararakatira okalingañi Ⓓ ngarinalu, klukungana

tnanbitninama *hineinspringen (ins Wasser).* ◇ jump into (the water). Ⓛ tapulukatiñi

tnanbulalama *hüpfen (Känguruh).* ◇ skip, hop (kangaroos). Ⓛ matapulukatiñi

tnanbunalanalauma *hineinspringen (mehrere) ins Wasser.* ◇ (a few) jump into the water. Ⓛ matapulukatira wonniñi

tnanbalurulanama *beim Laufen hüpfen (Bluträcher).* ◇ to skip or hop on the move (avenger). Ⓛ wararakatira wonniñi

tnanbatnanbalbuma *(Känguruh) bei der Rückkehr hüpfend laufen.* ◇ to skip returning home (kangaroo). Ⓛ tapultapulkulbañi

tnánoatnánerama *zum Stillstand kommen (Feuer), still stehen.* ◇ to come to a standstill (fire), to stand still, to stop. Ⓛ ngarangarakatini Ⓓ jurakókana

tnanjama *loben, rühmen.* ◇ to praise. Ⓛ bulkawonniñi

tnankua *dicht beieinanderstehend (Männer).* ◇ standing close together (men), crowded. Ⓛ tatutu

tnankua *Blätter an den Zweigspitzen.* ◇ leaves on tips of branches. Ⓛ tatutu

tnankua *Schnüre mit Rechbohnen (Kranz).* ◇ strings with beans (wreath, garland). Ⓛ akaringi

tnankama *vorhersagen.* ◇ predict. Ⓛ wirkañi

jia tnankama *etwas vorherverkündigen.* ◇ predict something. Ⓛ tjiri wirkañi

tnapereuma *jelka-Kuchen machen.* ◇ make jelka cakes. Ⓛ anaparanáñi

tnapatnama *dastehen, stehen bleiben.* ◇ stand there, stop. Ⓛ ngarangarañi

tnapatnapatnama *auf einen Haufen stehen.* ◇ stand together as a mob or group. Ⓛ ngarangarangarañi

tnapara *die jelka-Kuchen (geriebenes und zusammen geballtes jelka).* ◇ jelka cakes (ground and formed into a ball). Ⓛ anapara

tnanterama *Excremente lassen (tjappa).* ◇ to excrete (grub). Ⓛ kunna kuturingañi

tnapuntila *(vulva), (Scheide, vagina).* ◇ vulva, vagina. Ⓛ tuka

tnapma *der Boden, anus, Boden, Grund (Brunnens).* ◇ ground, anus, bottom (of well), floor. Ⓛ manna

tnambinina *(von atna (vagina) und mbinina (fortwährend begierig)), ein Mann, der mit seiner Nichte amba coitus hat.* ◇ man who has forbidden relationship with his niece. Ⓛ kunnatákaba

tnamiwia (tnama, iwia = iwuma) *gegen Abend, 1 Stunde vor Sonnenuntergang.* ◇ towards evening, one hour before sunset. Ⓛ tjirinbirpa

tnaritjalbuma *sich drängen (zu einem), überfallen, hinzuströmen (Volksmasse).* ◇ to crowd, throng (people).

tnata ankarbmálarbmála *der leere Magen.* ◇ empty stomach. Ⓛ wila workulworkula

tnátamatnáta *sich sonnend (z.B. Enten, Vögel).* ◇ sunning (e.g. ducks, birds). Ⓛ wilapurapura

tnāra *Hinterteil des Wildes, die hintere Hälfte des Wildes.* ◇ rear of game, back part of game. Ⓛ karila

tnara *(ehrbar?), mutig, kühn.* ◇ (honourable), courageous, daring.

tnarama *auf den Knien rutschen, kriechen.* ◇ slide on knees, crawl. Ⓛ marañi Ⓓ marakana

tnarakama *kriechen (auf dem Boden).* ◇ crawl. Ⓛ maranáñi

tnaritjerama *erwarten, sich freuen (auf die Ankunft jem.)* ◇ look forward (to someone's arrival). Ⓛ unbaringañi

tnaraparuma *kreisen, Kreise ziehen in der Luft (Adler), rutschen (auf den Knien), hin und her kriechen.* ◇ circle (eagle), slide (on knees), crawl back and forth. Ⓛ maranáni kutara

tnarra *lockere oder lose Gestein, abbröckeln.* ◇ loose rocks, stones, crumbling. Ⓛ mannara

tnaritjinjima *klettern (auf den Berg).* ◇ climb (the mountain). Ⓛ mararakalbañi Ⓓ katina

tnata nturknerama *Totenklage halten.* ◇ mourning. Ⓛ wila alturuñiñi

tnata ulbura *leere Bauch.* ◇ empty stomach. Ⓛ wila jultu

tnata *Bauch, Unterleib.* ◇ belly, abdomen; stomach. Ⓛ wila, julu Ⓓ mandra

tnata erouma *zittern (vor Kälte oder Furcht).* ◇ to shake (from the cold or from fear). Ⓛ wila tjitjitingañi

tnatambuma, tnata wumbuma *(Bauch brennen) wütend sein, zornig sein.* ◇ to be furious, angry, (belly burns). Ⓛ wila kambañi Ⓓ ngarajerkina, ngaradapungana

tnata kunnerama *sich ängstigen (um etwas).* ◇ to be alarmed, frightened, anxious (about something). Ⓛ wilakujaringañi

tnatataláma *jammern, ausgelassen sein (vor Freude).* ◇ to wail, to be joyful. Ⓛ wila wollañi Ⓓ kalu miltjamiltjarina

tnata artjima *sich sonnen (Enten).* ◇ to sun (ducks). Ⓛ wila ngantjiñi

tnatamba *fast leer, flach.* ◇ almost empty, shallow. Ⓛ wilanka

tnatambobula *mitten drin.* ◇ in the middle. Ⓛ wilakara

tnatambalkata *aufgeschlagen (Buch).* ◇ opened (book), open. Ⓛ wilakatukutu, wilapitini

tnatanganjala *unten (am Tisch).* ◇ at the far end (of the table). Ⓛ wilangaiïkuru

tnatala *postp. vor.* ◇ (postposition) before. Ⓛ wilanka

tnataka *postp. vor.* ◇ (postposition) before (a long time ago). Ⓛ wilaku

tnatamba *flach (Wasser), fast leer.* ◇ shallow (water), almost empty. Ⓛ wilanka

tnatapa-irkiljirkilja *der hervortrettende Bauch (bei den kleinen Kindern).* ◇ protruding belly (of little children). Ⓛ wila tútutútu

tnatambalkata *aufgeschlagen (Buch).* ◇ opened (book). Ⓛ wilakatukutu, wilapitini

tnata nturknerama *(Bauch betrübt, zerrissen sein).* ◇ (sad belly, be torn). Ⓛ wila alturuṅiñi

tnatambobula *mitten darinnen.* ◇ in the midst. Ⓛ wilakara

tnatamboba *die Mitte (eines Creek).* ◇ middle (of creek). Ⓛ wilakara

tnatalbatanama (atna-talbatanama) *Exkremente lang hinfallen lassen (itoa) und alle Vögel.* ◇ make droppings (bush turkey as well as all other birds). Ⓛ kunna tunmankula bakabakani

tnatambuma *wütend sein.* ◇ be angry. Ⓛ wilakambañi Ⓓ ngara jerkina

tnatamanáma *in Büscheln zusammen hängen (Feigen).* ◇ hang in bunches (figs). Ⓛ wila ninañi

tnatanga *der untere Baumstamm.* ◇ lower part of tree trunk. Ⓛ wolla

tnatangambea *verheiratete Mann, der Vater ist.* ◇ married man who is a father. Ⓛ wollakambanta

tnatangala *hinter (einem).* ◇ behind (someone). Ⓛ wollanka

tnatangala lama *nachfolgen, hinter einem gehen.* ◇ follow, go behind somebody. Ⓛ wollanka jennañi Ⓓ karipaterina, wapantina, milini palkana

tnatangala ngama *nachtragen.* ◇ carry behind someone. Ⓛ wollanka katini Ⓓ padakijiribana

tnatambalkata indama *auf dem Rücken liegen.* ◇ lie on back. Ⓛ wilakattukutu ngariñi

tnatamindama *auf der Seite liegen, sodaß der Bauch dem Beschauer zugekehrt ist.* ◇ lie on side looking at someone. Ⓛ wilalba ngala ngariñi

tnatanjala; laianga tnatinjala *an, c. abl.; am Meer.* ◇ at (c. abl.); at the sea.

tnatangauma *beistehen (in der Gefahr), anstiften (zu einer Tat), einen warnen (damit er sich vor dem Feinde schützt [unclear]), helfen, erretten, aus dem Wasser herausziehen, retten.* ◇ assist, help (in danger), instigate (to a deed), warn someone (to be aware of the enemy and on guard), help, rescue, pull out of the water, save. Ⓛ tankawokkani

tnatangebía *in einer Reihe (sitzen oder stehen).* ◇ (sit or stand) in a row. Ⓛ taberi

tnatanbuma *umherstreuen (Gummizweig).* ◇ scatter (gumtree twigs). Ⓛ piralanbakani

tnatanganja, tnatanganjala *unten (am Tisch als Zuhörer sitzen).* ◇ at (the table as a listener). Ⓛ wilungaiïnka (ninañi), ngaiïkurunka

tnatankurbma *Schlange (giftig).* ◇ snake (poisonous). Ⓛ wilankurbmu

tnatantja *eine lange mit Garn umwickelte und mit Vogeldaun beklebte Stange.* ◇ long ceremonial pole. Ⓛ anatantji

tnátara *Feuer an dem Fußende.* ◇ fire at feet. Ⓛ nitalku

tnatapanjunta *ein voller Bauch [unclear].* ◇ full belly. Ⓛ wila pokuti

tnatata *Skorpion.* ◇ scorpion; bad spirit being in the form of a tnatata that comes out of the ground at night and stings people up to four times causing their death (Strehlow 1907: 13). Ⓛ wonnatjiti, pirikatuli Ⓓ kandikundi

tnatatalama *jammern, Mitleid haben, ausgelassen sein (vor Freude).* ◇ complain, have pity, frolicsome. Ⓛ wila wollañi

tnatatanama *nicht beschwichtigen können (Streitende).* ◇ not be able to reconcile (opponents). Ⓛ ngambangambanínañi

tnátatăratăra *leere Bauch, sehr hungrig.* ◇ empty belly, very hungry. Ⓛ wila tarutaru

tnatauma *nicht gehorchen, entgegenhandeln, widersprechen.* ◇ not obey, contradict. Ⓛ tanapungañi

tnátjatnátjerama *sich sehr freuen (auf jemanden, auf Kamele).* ◇ look very much forward to (somebody, camels). Ⓛ pantalpantalninañi

tnatjarakalama *sehr tief graben.* ◇ dig very deep. Ⓛ tauaraokalingañi

tnatjatnatja *Vogel (spec.)* ◇ bird species. Ⓛ anatjanatji

tnaltnanama *aufstehen, sich erheben (von den sitzenden Männern).* ◇ stand up, get up (e.g. from the place where the men are sitting). Ⓛ ngaralatalkañi

tnatjilama *treten (zu einem).* ◇ step (towards someone).

tnatnaúma *herabfallen (Frucht von Baum).* ◇ fall down (fruit from tree). Ⓛ patangarañi

tnatjilama *still stehen, warten.* ◇ stand still, wait. Ⓛ ngarakatiñi

tnatnagunama *mit den Krallen umfassen (Adler).* ◇ grab with talons (eagle) (Strehlow 1910b: 38). Ⓛ pirirbini

tnatnilaúma *scharren (Hühner), kratzen.* ◇ scratch (fowls), scrape. Ⓛ tauatauañi

tnatjirkulelama *Angeld geben, anwerben?* ◇ enlist?

tnatoa *Tasche (aus Fellen oder Haaren gemacht).* ◇ bag (made of hides or hair). Ⓛ wapata Ⓓ pailtjita, billi, wandru, pilpanta

tnatoatangatanga *Tasche unter dem Arm tragend.* ◇ carry bag under the arm. Ⓛ wapata katijennañi

tnatulta *(Bauch leer), hungrig, nicht gesättigt.* ◇ (empty belly), hungry, not satisfied. Ⓛ wila jultu

tnauérama *einem Abwesenden Rache androhen, drohen.* ◇ threaten someone who is absent with revenge, threaten. Ⓛ katawonkañi

tnaueria *Strauch.* ◇ shrub. Ⓛ minjina

tnaulajinama *forttreiben.* ◇ drive away.

tnauia *Stock zum Schlagen, Taktstock.* ◇ stick to hit with, baton. Ⓛ tutinba, kunti

tnauuta *Larven (weiß) in tnauuta Wurzeln oder eine Baumart mit giftigen, feigenähnlichen Früchten.* ◇ grub (white) in tnauuta roots or poisonous tree species with fig-like fruit. Ⓛ omarumari

tnauma *wegtreiben.* ◇ chase, drive away. Ⓛ wollatunañi Ⓓ dangana (*fortscheuchen* = to chase away), dikana (*nennen* = to name), narana (*hinausweisen* = to ask someone to leave)

aretna tnauma *nennen.* ◇ to name. Ⓛ ini takani

tnaürba *Stöcke, die die Weiber beim Tanz zusammen schlagen.* ◇ women's clapping sticks used in women's dances. Ⓛ anaúurbi

Tneëra; tnéera *[schön, lieb] göttliche Frauen.* ◇ (beautiful, nice) divine women; female ancestral beings (Strehlow 1907). Ⓛ ineari

tnauma (retna) *nennen.* ◇ to name. Ⓛ takani (ini)

tneëratneëra *liebevoll (zu allen Menschen, Freund und Fremden).* ◇ loving, nice (to everyone, friend and strangers). Ⓛ ulatúngutúngu

tnekanérama *ausreden (etwas), abraten, abhalten (Schlechtes zu tun).* ◇ dissuade, advise against (something), restrain (from doing bad). Ⓛ wilatararingañi, wila kuraringañi

tnekua *conf.* **kamuna** *der Onkel eines Andern.* ◇ uncle of somebody else. Ⓛ kamurura

tnelambara renalitjalbuma *sich alle niederlassen (nach der Rückkehr).* ◇ to sit (or settle) down (i.e. everyone after return). Ⓛ palkilkara ninañi kulbara

tnelanga *Strauch spec. mit roten, fuchsiaartigen Blüten (Eremophila Latrobei).* ◇ shrub species with red blossoms; native fuschia (*Eremophila latrobei*). Ⓛ menjinga, injilingi

tnelbalama *widerstehen.* ◇ resist.

tnelbinélama *sich entschuldigen (wegen Nichtkommens).* ◇ apologise (for not showing up). Ⓛ mekukururingañi

tnéljerama (urbiaka tneljerama) *halten für etwas (z.B. einen Boten).* ◇ regard as (e.g. a messenger). Ⓛ antantani

tnelelta *das abgefallene, vertrocknete Laub oder trockene Zweige.* ◇ fallen, dry leaves or branches. Ⓛ anililti

tnelja *eine rankende Planze.* ◇ vine (plant). Ⓛ anila

tneljiúma *verhören, ausfragen (der Richter den Angeklagten).* ◇ interrogate, question (judge the accused). Ⓛ katurtunañi

tnelupura *Gebüsch.* ◇ undergrowth, thicket. Ⓛ tatajerri

tnĕnama (tnănama) *schalten, schimpfen, beschuldigen, strafen (mit Worten).* ◇ scold, accuse, punish (with words). Ⓛ kujantakañi

tnerenkama *tadeln.* ◇ to fault, to reprove. Ⓛ kujantakañi

tnēnama *ausweiden (Wild).* ◇ to gut (game). Ⓛ wantjiñi, balkañi

tnenba *unausgeweidetes (Wild).* ◇ not gutted (game). Ⓛ kunnakulu

tnenbara *Schwanzfedern (Vogel).* ◇ tail feathers (birds). Ⓛ kalbi

tnānja *Eingang, Öffnung einer Höhle.* ◇ entrance, opening of cave. Ⓛ piti

tnenjurbárana *Eidechse spec.* ◇ lizard species. Ⓛ pitiwaltulba, wonnawirilpa

tnenterinja *aneinanderhängend, aneinandergewachsen (Zellen).* ◇ hang together, grown together (cells). Ⓛ talatitalati

tnenka *Bluträcher.* ◇ avenger. Ⓛ (worbmala) warbmala Ⓓ pinga

tnera *oder* **tnira** *großer Baum [mit pfefferbaumartigem Laub].* ◇ large tree (foliage similar to pepper tree). Ⓛ anjiri

tnánkama (v. atna) *Flatus lassen.* ◇ pass wind. Ⓛ ninjirbmanañi, kunna punmanañi

tninjara *anus.* ◇ anus. Ⓛ kunnata [Southern dialect]

tnērbinama *abschlagen (Bitte), verweigern.* ◇ refuse (request), deny. Ⓛ wiantakañi

tnerenkama *tadeln (Arbeit).* ◇ criticise (work). Ⓛ kujantakañi

tnĕrka *unvermögend, ruhig, still, zurückgezogen, ohnmächtig, nichts machen können, (nicht heiraten können).* ◇ not able, quiet, silent, powerless, cannot do anything, (cannot marry). Ⓛ tami

tnerutjarutja *des Todes schuldig.* ◇ guilty (deserve death). Ⓛ jupajupa

tnerultja [etna = *dicht*, erultja = *Reisig*] *dichtes Gebüsch, dichte trockene Büsche.* ◇ dense thicket, dense dry bushes. Ⓛ malarapuru

tnetnanétnana *Handgelenk.* ◇ wrist. Ⓛ marakunnakunna Ⓓ marapalka

tninjalama *vor einem hinfallen (auf den Boden fallen).* ◇ fall in front of somebody (fall to the ground). Ⓛ ngatapunkani

tnetneúma *verurteilen, Strafe verkündigen.* ◇ sentence, announce punishment. Ⓛ jupa-irbini

tnetura *rote Larve, unter Gummibaumrinde.* ◇ red grub under gumtree bark. Ⓛ anetura

tnimba, tnimbauma *kleine Brote, kleine Brote backen.* ◇ bread loaf, bake small bread loaves. Ⓛ animba, animbani

tnilbitnima *straucheln, taumeln.* ◇ stumble, stagger. Ⓛ patapatangarañi

tnilabakatitja *die Gefallenen im Streit, die Pesttilenz, Erschlagenen (im Kampf), die von der Krankheit dahingerafften (die Seuche).* ◇ the slain in battle or fight, killed by sickness (epidemic). Ⓛ inipalíti

tnima *fallen.* ◇ to fall. Ⓛ patangarañi Ⓓ purina

tnilalama *fallen lassen (etwas von selbst), entfallen (das man trägt).* ◇ to let fall, to fall (something by itself). Ⓛ patangaralatalkañi

tninama *fallen auf einen, zu Fall bringen, sich werfen auf einen, hinwerfen.* ◇ cause to fall, fall on somebody, throw down, (throw oneself onto somebody). Ⓛ mapatangarañi Ⓓ puribana

tnitjikalama *herunterfallen.* ◇ fall down. Ⓛ patangaralaokalingañi Ⓓ kantiterina

tnatnama *abfallen, herabfallen (Frucht vom Baum).* ◇ fall off, fall down (fruit from tree). Ⓛ patangaralatalkañi

tnilauma *abfallen (Frucht vom Baum).* ◇ fall off (fruit from tree). Ⓛ punkaratalkañi

tnilambalturuma *Gefallenes überall umherliegen.* ◇ something that has fallen and is lying around everywhere. Ⓛ ínipàlitiwókkañi

tnipatnima *(duplikation) herabfallen.* ◇ (reduplication) fall off or down. Ⓛ patangaranañi

tnimalkurtja *eine bunte Raupe an den Blättern der Tnima.* ◇ colourful caterpillar on leaves of tnima-bushes. Ⓛ itnimalkurtji

tnima *Strauch mit länglichen Blättern und gelben Blütenkätzchen (Acacia kempeana).* ◇ witchetty bush, *Acacia kempeana.* Ⓛ ilkoara

tnimatja *die Larve, die sich an den Wurzeln der tnima Sträucher aufhält (große, weiße Larve mit roten Querstreifen).* ◇ grub in roots of tnima-bushes (large white grub with red stripes). Ⓛ ilkoara

tnimatnima *Strauch (auf den Hügeln wachsend) mit langen schmalen Blättern und kleinen schwarzen eßbaren Beeren.* ◇ bush (grows on hills) with long narrow leaves and small edible black berries. Ⓛ ilkoarailkoara

tnimamba *Saft der Tnima-Sträucher.* ◇ sap of tnima-bushes. Ⓛ inimami

tninama *zu Fall bringen.* ◇ bring to fall. Ⓛ mapatangarañi

tninja [Eastern dialect] *Mond.* ◇ moon. Ⓛ pira

tninama *warten (Kinder).* ◇ to wait (children). Ⓛ kanjini

tninjarerama *warnen (fortzugehen).* ◇ to warn. Ⓛ mekukurungarañi

tnimirkelja *Tnima-Gebüsch.* ◇ tnima-thicket. Ⓛ ilkowaratata

tninjareralalama *sich trennen (von den andern), die andern zurücklassen.* ◇ to separate (from the others), leave the others behind. Ⓛ ngurtungarala jennañi

tnilbatninama *fortwährend behalten, warten.* ◇ continuously keep, wait. Ⓛ kánjikánjini

tninta *Gras (spec.)* ◇ grass species. Ⓛ aninti

tnitja *eßbare Wurzel (der altjia Pflanze).* ◇ edible roots (of altjia plant). Ⓛ atuju

tnitjenkua *Bündnis, Verspechen [unclear].* ◇ pact, promise. Ⓛ ngalutu

tnitjikalama *herabfallen, herunterfallen.* ◇ fall down. Ⓛ patangaralaokalingañi

tnitjilama, pl. **tninambanama** *niederfallen (aufs Gesicht).* ◇ fall (on face).

tnitjimba *eigenmächtig, mit Gewalt.* ◇ despotic, with force. Ⓛ bakara

tnitjimbala inama *eigenmächtig nehmen, rauben.* ◇ take by force, rob. Ⓛ bakaranka manjiñi Ⓓ watawatali manina

tnoatnoa *reichlich.* ◇ ample.

tnitjirka *native Companion (im Norden).* ◇ native companion (in the north).

tnitjinta *Eidechse spec.* ◇ lizard species. Ⓛ biljanba

tnitnalbánama *langhinfallen (auf den Boden).* ◇ fall (to the ground). Ⓛ bultjulukatiñi

tnitnanama *abfallen, herabfallen (Frucht vom Baum).* ◇ fall off, fall down (fruit from tree). Ⓛ patangaralatalkañi

tnóaroara *sehr viele, Schaar (von Fischen).* ◇ very many, shoal (of fish). Ⓛ antalkariñi

tnoa *viele, circa 30, lang (Predigt oder Gebet) n.* ◇ many, circa 30, long (sermon or prayer). Ⓛ lenku

tnoatnoa *sicher, übermütig (Häuptling).* ◇ confident (chief). Ⓛ anóanoa

tnoatnoa indáma *sicher liegen, sicher schlafen.* ◇ lie, sleep safe. Ⓛ anóanóa ngariñi

tnoala *besonders, insbesonders, insonderheit.* ◇ especially, in particular.

tnoerama *zielen (nach Jemanden) mit (dem Gewehr).* ◇ aim (at someone) with (a gun). Ⓛ wakungarañi

tnoerentjima *herziehen (nach mir z.B.)* ◇ pull (towards me, for example). Ⓛ ngalawakungarañi

tnoantulama *nichts ausrichten, unvermögend sein.* ◇ accomplish nothing, not capable.

tnokulba *Feld, Jelka-Feld.* ◇ field, jelka field. Ⓛ anukulba Ⓓ bukamarru!

tnoaka *am meisten, besonders.* ◇ most of all, especially.

tnoarkara *aufs meiste, höchstens (der Zahl nach).* ◇ not more.

tnolba *unmäßig, üppig.* ◇ immoderate, opulent. Ⓛ bulba

tnolbala ilkuma *fressen.* ◇ devour. Ⓛ bulbanku ngalkuñi Ⓓ mirantjati, murtjana

tnolbutankama *schnell aufbrechen, um weiter zu wandern.* ◇ set out quickly, to continue journey. Ⓛ mannabakalkatiñi

tnolkuma *erschrecken.* ◇ to get a fright, to become scared. Ⓛ ngualankañi Ⓓ ngaruparana

tnolkalélama *trs. einen erschrecken, Schreck einflößen.* ◇ frighten someone (transitive). Ⓛ kukurkutjingani Ⓓ ngaruparibana

tnolkakérama *sich verwundern.* ◇ be astonished. Ⓛ ngualankarbariñi

tnolkinjala rama *erstaunen.* ◇ be amazed. Ⓛ ngualankara nangañi

tnolkinjagata *Wunder, wunderbar.* ◇ miracle, miraculous.

tnuntakatnunta *viereckig.* ◇ square.

tnōnda *Tier; Vieh [unclear].* ◇ animal; cattle. Ⓛ kaki

tnotuparára *Haufe von erlegtem Wild.* ◇ a lot of killed game. Ⓛ nutimurkamurka

tnúnta, tnōnta *schwanger, trächtig.* ◇ pregnant. Ⓛ wilali Ⓓ mandrantju

tnorula *Exkremente der ingunanga-Larven.* ◇ excrement of ingunanga grubs; name of Gosses Bluff. Ⓛ anurulu

tnōta *ungebraten, ganz (Tier).* ◇ not roasted, whole (animal). Ⓛ nuti

tnotulama *schlängelnd weitergehen (die Schlange).* ◇ slither (snake). Ⓛ nutinutiringañi

tn(u)áninja *Gerät.* ◇ tool. Ⓛ julta

tnuåta *Nasenhölzer (von den Mädchen oder Frauen getragen).* ◇ wooden nosepegs (worn by girls or women). Ⓛ unati

tnúkutulbára *grüne Papagei, mit gelben Ring um den Hals (Nachtvogel).* ◇ green parrot, with yellow circle around neck (night bird). Ⓛ anukutulbari

tnunkalelama *singen lassen.* ◇ allow singing.

tnukura *Gras (spec.)* ◇ grass species. Ⓛ wonnukuru

tnulturka *Strauch.* ◇ shrub. Ⓛ tabanmara

tnukutatnama *sich niederknien (zum Trinken).* ◇ kneel down (to drink). Ⓛ murungarañi

tnuma *flechten (Haare), drehen (Schnur).* ◇ plait (hair), twist (string). Ⓛ wakitjinañi

tjankutnuma *Haare flechten.* ◇ plait hair. Ⓛ wakitjinañi

tjimutnuma *Haare flechten.* ◇ plait hair. Ⓛ wakitjipálnañi

tnukutnuraeritjalbuma *mit dem anus sich einen Platz zurechtscharren, sich bequem machen (auf dem Boden).* ◇ make oneself comfortable sitting on the ground. Ⓛ rurarurariugañi

tnumbarélama *klagen (über Schmerzen).* ◇ complain (about pain). Ⓛ urukuliñi

tnungarelinja *eitel, sich etwas einbildend, stolz.* ◇ vain, proud.

tnunbirkuma *Schrei ausstoßen und dann mit einem male ruhig sein, aufschreien.* ◇ cry out and fall silent immediately thereafter. Ⓛ ngokakaniñi

tnunka *Ratten-Känguruh.* ◇ rat kangaroo. Ⓛ malla

tnungarélama *sich brüsten, sich rühmen.* ◇ brag, show off. Ⓛ tananangañi

tnunkalta (tnunka = Ratten-Känguruh, alta = Haar) *Wagen (Sternbild).* ◇ the Big Dipper (star constellation). Ⓛ mallentu

tnunkultjatuma *Zweikampf mit Speeren kämpfen.* ◇ duell fought with spears. Ⓛ pilpilpungañi

tnunta *Ecke, Kante.* ◇ corner, edge. Ⓛ pattipatti Ⓓ burru, tuluru

tnuntajatnunta *eckig, viereckig.* ◇ angular, square. Ⓛ ununtumurkamurka

tnuntilkinja *halbreif (Früchte).* ◇ half-ripe (fruit). Ⓛ urákuráki

tnunmérama *erschlaffen (von der Hitze), erschlaffen, zusammenschrumpfen (Fleisch beim kochen).* ◇ languish (from heat), tire, shrivel up (meat when cooked). Ⓛ tjilunariñi

tnuntanama (tnuntuma) *auf und niedertanzen von Weibern.* ◇ dance (women). Ⓛ makutariñi, akutariñi

utnántanántana *selbsüchtig [unclear].* ◇ selfish. Ⓛ waiangalkunmi Ⓓ muntapata

tnuntuma *auf und abtanzen (Weiber), zu Streit anfeuern.* ◇ dance back and forth (women), instigate a fight. Ⓛ akutariñi

tnurberinja *Gestell, Regal.* ◇ shelf.

tnurbatnurba *scheu, furchtsam.* ◇ timid, fearful, anxious. Ⓛ apúrapúra

tnurinjilama *versprechen (etwas zu geben).* ◇ promise (to give something). Ⓛ tankuñi

tnurbarinja *(z.B. imbara) parallelaufeinander (Linien).* ◇ (e.g. tracks) parallel (lines). Ⓛ warbilinba

tnurunga *Strauch spec. dessen Zweige bei vielen Aufführungen gebraucht werden, Eremophilia longifolia.* ◇ emu bush, *Eremophila longifolia.* Ⓛ tulpura, tulpurba Ⓓ kujamra (*Eremophilia longifolia*)

tnurungatja ntjima *Eier der tnurangatja (große schwarz und gelbe Raupe).* ◇ eggs of a big black and yellow caterpillar. Ⓛ tulpurba ngokuta

tnurungatja *große schwarz und gelbe Raupe, die sich an den tnurunga Büschen aufhält.* ◇ large black and yellow caterpillar that lives on emu bushes. Ⓛ tulpura, tulpurba

tnutukútuka *kleiner Vogel.* ◇ small bird. Ⓛ anútukútuku

tnukutulbara *night-parrot.* ◇ night parrot. Ⓛ murkunba

tōa *dieser.* ◇ this one. Ⓛ toa
nana toa *dieser da.* ◇ this one there. Ⓛ nangata toa
toagata *kleiner schwarzer Vogel, rotbraune Brust, gebogner Schnabel, Pomatostomus rubeculus.* ◇ small black bird with red-brown chest and a bent beak, *Pomatostomus temporalis* (grey-crowned or red-chested babbler) (Pizzey and Knight 2007). Ⓛ tjoakitji
itóalama *übersehen (etwas).* ◇ to oversee, to miss (something). Ⓛ ngálkalariñi Ⓓ wampana
toata *zukünftig.* ◇ in future.
toaparama *einschließen, umzingeln.* ◇ to enclose, to surround. Ⓛ marknatariñi
tolerama *niedrig werden (Berg).* ◇ shrink (mountain).
tóbmatóbmilama *aufhetzen zum Zorn.* ◇ provoke, enrage. Ⓛ mokumokuni Ⓓ popana
tokkulka *ein gerades Dach.* ◇ straight roof.
tokia *Maus.* ◇ mouse. Ⓛ anba Ⓓ nili
tolerama *den festen Boden schlagen, stampfen.* ◇ beat, stamp solid ground. Ⓛ touni
tōla *Lehm, Lehmboden.* ◇ clay, clay ground. Ⓛ akiri
tolera *fester Boden.* ◇ solid ground. Ⓛ (manta) pitjiri
tolakerkuma *umfassen, umklammern.* ◇ clasp, clinch. Ⓛ kapulkuwitini
tolbatakalanama *in den Boden stampfen (etwas).* ◇ stamp into the ground (something). Ⓛ pilupilukatiñi
tolkinja *unstät.* ◇ unsteady, fleeting. Ⓛ katakutara
tolkinja lama *fortwährend umherwandern.* ◇ wander continuously around. Ⓛ katakutara jenañi Ⓓ tadapaterina
tolkiranama *vor (einem) hergehen.* ◇ walk in front of (someone). Ⓛ makatakutaringañi
tolta *sehr müde, matt.* ◇ very tired, feeble. Ⓛ walenku
tonanga *Larve einer fliegenden Ameisenart, nach dem Regen aus den Lehmebenen hervorkommend.* ◇ larvae of flying ant species that comes out of claypans after rain. Ⓛ watunuma
tonkuma *conf.* **tankuma** *schöpfen.* ◇ scoop (e.g. water). Ⓛ urani
tonduritjára *Emukücken (ausgeschlüpfte Emu).* ◇ emu chicks (hatched emu). Ⓛ kúnangámbutara
tōnka *aufrechstehender Kopfschmuck (Cultus), ausgepolstert (lange Hut der Darsteller) gepflastert.* ◇ headdress (ceremonial), decorated, plastered. Ⓛ tapalpa
toppambōba *Zinne, n.* ◇ peak, pinnacle.
toppa (tapa) *Rücken, Gasse (einer Stadt), Straße, Vorhof n., Vorhalle n.* ◇ back, backbone, spine, mountain ridge, lane (in a town), street, courtyard, entrance. Ⓛ tana Ⓓ toko
toppala, pata toppala *oben, z.B. oben auf dem Felsen, auf dem Bergesrücken.* ◇ at the top, e.g. at the top of the rock, of the mountain ridge. Ⓛ tananku, puli tananku
toppa tmoara *die Kreise auf dem Rücken.* ◇ circles on back. Ⓛ tana minburu
toppalákana; *z.B.* **patta toppalankana** *oben; z.B. fliegen.* ◇ above; e.g. fly. Ⓛ tanawonnawonna, puli tanawonnawonna
toppakama *sich umschließen, umgeben, im Kreise umstellen.* ◇ encircle, surround, enclose in a circle. Ⓛ pararintañi
toppanama *sich bücken, sich ducken, sich schnell beugen.* ◇ bend, duck, bend down quickly. Ⓛ bobañi
toppanala njuma *sich bücken, um mit dem Mund trinken.* ◇ bend down to drink with mouth. Ⓛ bobaratjikiñi
topparenama *trs. etwas niederlegen, etwas abladen (Kamele die Ladung).* ◇ (transitive) lay down something, unload something (load of camels). Ⓛ bobatunañi

topparelalama *umkehren [unclear].* ◇ turn back. Ⓛ arurékukátiñi
topparélama *sich rühmen.* ◇ praise (oneself). Ⓛ tananangañi
toppatopparélama *sich fortwährend rühmen.* ◇ continuously praise oneself. Ⓛ tanatananangañi
toppatoppanánama *sich niederbücken.* ◇ bend down. Ⓛ mabobabobarabakañi
toppalélama *trs. umdrehen, einen umkehren machen.* ◇ (transitive) turn around, make someone turn back. Ⓛ aruriljini
topparatoppara *krumm, gebückt.* ◇ bent.
toppaleëlérama *sich umdrehen.* ◇ turn around. Ⓛ tanakuturingañi
toppalealerama *rückwärts gehen.* ◇ go backwards. Ⓛ tanapitinariñi
toppatnánama *brüten (Vogel).* ◇ brood, incubate (birds). Ⓛ bobaljennañi Ⓓ purulkaterina
toppatakálama *einsinken.* ◇ sink in. Ⓛ pilupilukatiñi
topparbarenalitjilama *niederknien zum Angriff.* ◇ kneel down to attack. Ⓛ katuninakatiñi
toppantāta *Rückenschmerzen.* ◇ backache. Ⓛ tana, ā̊ntata
toppatnakama *glauben.* ◇ believe. Ⓛ tanabulkawonniñi
toppata renalama *für einen Andern den Tod erleiden, eintreten für einen Andern (Stellvertretung).* ◇ step in for someone, endure death for someone (substitute). Ⓛ titani
toppatuma *fortwährend schlagen, Rücken zerschlagen (Wild), umhauen, fallen, entwurzeln, vernichten, erschlagen, Einschnitt hauen (in den Baum), fortwährend zusammenschlagen (Stöcke).* ◇ hit constantly, break back (game), cut down, fell, uproot, destroy, kill, cut notch (in tree), hit constantly together (sticks). Ⓛ punkapunkanáñi Ⓓ munkuru ngankana
topperama *umkehren, sich abwenden.* ◇ turn back, turn away. Ⓛ aruringañi Ⓓ karitjina, darpina
topparénama *trs. hinunterbiegen.* ◇ (transitive) bend down.
topperanama *sich abwenden.* ◇ turn away. Ⓛ maruringañi
toppantuma *trs. preisen, rühmen.* ◇ (transitive) praise, glorify.
topperentjima *zuwenden, umkehren und herkommen.* ◇ turn to(wards), turn around and come back. Ⓛ ngalaruringañi, taiïrtninañi
topperalbuma *wieder umkehren.* ◇ turn back again.
topperentjalbuma *bei der Rückkehr sich einem zuwenden.* ◇ turn towards someone on return. Ⓛ ngala arurékula kulbañi
topperentjilama *zurückkehren.* ◇ return. Ⓛ arurékula kulbañi
toppalénba *Rücken des Känguruh.* ◇ back of kangaroo. Ⓛ murbuwaiïlkara
toppalkāra *Streifen längs des Rückens, das Fleisch zu beiden Seiten des Rückens, fleischige Rücken.* ◇ flesh on both sides of back, meaty back. Ⓛ ílara
toppangabunga *Umzäunung.* ◇ enclosure. Ⓛ paratatutatu Ⓓ jerru
toppangabungilama *umzäunen.* ◇ enclose. Ⓛ paratatutatuni
toppangatoppa *Zaun.* ◇ fence. Ⓛ tatutatu
toppangatoppilama *umzäunen.* ◇ to fence in. Ⓛ tatutatuni
toppantanama *herausfließen (Luft [unclear]).* ◇ to flow out (air). Ⓛ tanawákani
topparka *Niere.* ◇ kidney. Ⓛ watatinka, kabulita
toppata *eingedrückt (Nase).* ◇ pressed in (nose). Ⓛ pilta, pita
toppatakalama *einsinken (im Sande).* ◇ sink (into sand). Ⓛ pilupilukatiñi Ⓓ punpina
italbaterama *den Entschluß fassen (zurückzutreten), Rückzug antreten [unclear].* ◇ decide (to retreat). Ⓛ untuunturingañi
toppatoppa *bucklig.* ◇ hunchbacked. Ⓛ tanatana Ⓓ kuldru duruduru

toppatnoa *sehr viele, Haufen [unclear].* ◇ very many, mob. Ⓛ tanaünba

toppatnoerama *sich vermehren.* ◇ multiply. Ⓛ tanaünbaringañi

toppa unkwana *Rückenknochen.* ◇ backbone. Ⓛ tana tarka Ⓓ took wira, took julkuru

topperatoppera *gebückt, bucklig.* ◇ bent, hunchbacked. Ⓛ bóbatubóbatu Ⓓ duruduru (buckling)

toppeatoppa *auf dem Gebirgsrücken.* ◇ on the mountain ridge. Ⓛ luntialuntu

toppinba *alle versammelt, auf einen Haufen.* ◇ all assembled, in a crowd. Ⓛ kutuli

toppinga *hinten.* ◇ behind. Ⓛ parari Ⓓ mileri

toppinjatopperama *herumgehen, im weiten Kreis herumgehen, wider umkehren.* ◇ go around, go around in a wide circle, turn around again. Ⓛ arurékula ngaraníñi

toppintjarenama *den Rücken entlang schneiden.* ◇ cut along the back. Ⓛ purpipungañi

topparbarenalama *sich niederlassen (Vögel).* ◇ settle down (birds). Ⓛ tulturku ninakatiñi

tora *Kamm (des Gebirges, der Sandhügel), Erdwall, Erderhöhung.* ◇ ridge (of mountain range or sandhill). Ⓛ toppunba, toppuna

torindama *(den Finger eines Andern auf eine Stelle legen/drücken).* ◇ (lay/press the finger of somebody on a certain spot).

tōratōra *das Fleisch an den Oberschenkeln.* ◇ flesh on thighs. Ⓛ munturu

tōta *Klopfstein ([unclear] klopfen).* ◇ grinding stone? Ⓛ umbalki

tóterama *grollen (donnern) [unclear].* ◇ rumble (thunder). Ⓛ tūni

tóturatùra *Maulwurf.* ◇ mole. Ⓛ toturuturu, itériteri

tótatóta *kurz.* ◇ short. Ⓛ kalkaturu

tōtja *Unterleib? und (Vesiculae seminales).* ◇ abdomen? and (seminal vesicles). Ⓛ atutu, watuta

toturka *Vater, der Emu Häuptling.* ◇ father, the emu chief. Ⓛ úturúrku

trelka *furchtsam, feige, bange.* ◇ scared, cowardly, anxious. Ⓛ ngula Ⓓ jăpali

trelkilama *furchtsam machen.* ◇ intimidate, make anxious. Ⓛ ngulani Ⓓ japa dangana

trelkalama *fliehen.* ◇ to flee. Ⓛ ngula jennañi

trelta *furchtsam, scheu.* ◇ anxious, fearful. Ⓛ nguluntu Ⓓ japakantji (*furchtsam*: anxious or fearful, *scheu*: shy, timid), japanguru (*furchtlos*: fearless)

trérama *sich fürchten.* ◇ to fear, to be afraid, to be fearful. Ⓛ nguluringañi Ⓓ japali nganana

treranáma *furchtsam aus dem Wege gehen.* ◇ go frightened or fearfully out of the way. Ⓛ manguluringañi

tualtja *eigener, eigener (im Unterschied zu Klassen-Verwandtschaft).* ◇ own (not classificatory kin); Aboriginal kinship systems are classificatory. A classificatory kinship system places all members of a society into kin relationships with each other using a limited range of terms. A core principle of such Australian systems is the equivalence of siblings of the same gender. However, distinctions are often drawn between close consanguineal and affinal relations and those that are more distant geographically or socially, and those that are entirely classificatory (Strehlow 1913). One of the features of this system of kin classification is that the four different grandparents are distinguished. Western Aranda used and still use four different terms for one's grandparents. The terms are 'aranga' for father's father, 'tjimia' for mother's father, 'palla' for father's mother and 'ebmanna' for mother's mother. The grandparental terms are also used to cover one's grandparents' siblings as well as one's grandchildren on a reciprocal basis. The term for one's father's father, aranga, for example, includes father's father's brothers and sisters and son's sons and daughters. Relationships with grandparents are of particular importance to the question of landownership. Carl Strehlow's Loritja kin data records also four grandparental terms (Strehlow 1913: 81–82), but today only two seem to be in use: tjamu for grandfathers (father's father and mother's father) and kami for grandmothers (father's mother and mother's mother). See entries for aranga (father's father), tjimia (mother's father), palla (father's mother) and ebmanna (mother's mother). Ⓛ tutaltji

trērkanama *allen Schmutz wegkehren, reinigen, abwaschen.* ◇ to clean, to wash off. Ⓛ terkalbmanáñi

tualjibuma *den Fuß auf den Boden stellen und ihn schnell ausgleiten lassen – scheuern [unclear].* ◇ put foot down and let it slip quickly, scour, scrub. Ⓛ turbipungañi

tuailarenama *einem nachsehen.* ◇ gaze or look after (someone leaving), watch someone leaving or going away. Ⓛ mirarawonniñi

tuáilanama *einem nach sehen.* ◇ gaze or look after (someone leaving), watch someone leaving or going away. Ⓛ māmírani

tualbinama *hin und her bewegen (Stange).* ◇ move back and forth (pole). Ⓛ punkulapatani

tuákama *biegen, herabbiegen (einen Zweig).* ◇ bend, bend down (a branch). Ⓛ pirpuntanáñi

tuakitjilama *auseinanderbiegen (Zweige).* ◇ bend apart (branches). Ⓛ ngalapirpuntanani

tuakalama *sich bücken, sich verneigen.* ◇ bend, bow. Ⓛ pilukatini

tuanjiraka *ein mythisches Wesen, schwarzer Vogel.* ◇ mythical being, black bird (see Strehlow 1907: 102). Ⓛ maiutu

tuarama *nachsehen (einem).* ◇ look, gaze after (someone). Ⓛ mirani

tuatja *Einschnitt (in Baumrinde), Lücke (Zahnlücke), Raum zwischen den Fingern und Zehen, Raum zwischen 2 Felsen (Schlucht), Tal.* ◇ gap, space between fingers and toes, gap between teeth, space between two rocks, valley. Ⓛ tinki, atiri Ⓓ wipa (*Tal*)

tuatjituatja *lückenhaft, gebuchtet (Blätter), ausgehöhlt (Stein).* ◇ full of gaps, washed out (stone). Ⓛ tinkitinki

tuatjatuatja *langsam, träge.* ◇ slow, lazy. Ⓛ bánbán

tuatjatuatja lama *sehr langsam gehen.* ◇ go very slow. Ⓛ bánbán jennañi

tualitjatuala *krumm (Weg), gewunden (Weg).* ◇ crooked (way), winding (way). Ⓛ wakuntiwakunti

tuéda *ein anderer.* ◇ another one. Ⓛ munu Ⓓ pilki

tuédakata *anders (z.B. machen).* ◇ different (e.g. make). Ⓛ munutara Ⓓ pilkildra

tuédakatuéda *von einander getrennt, zerstreut, einzeln.* ◇ separate from each other, scattered, single. Ⓛ munutumunu

tuja *zugehörig.* ◇ belonging to. Ⓛ tuju

katúja *mir zugehörig (sex-totem, aus dem Tierreich).* ◇ belonging to me (sex-totem, from the animal world). Ⓛ kātuju

unkwangatuja *dem Vogel.* ◇ belonging to the bird. Ⓛ numtubakatuju

tulbatuarama *fortwährend nach dem Weg aussehen.* ◇ look continuously for the path. Ⓛ miramiraniñi

turinja *der Krieg.* ◇ war.

tuederama *verkehrt (gehen).* ◇ go wrong way, get lost. Ⓛ munuringañi

tulunkalunka *voller Geschwüre.* ◇ covered with abscesses or boils. Ⓛ altartji

tuedankama *sich verspechen, Verkehrtes sagen.* ◇ say the wrong thing. Ⓛ munuwonkañi

tuédekeráma *etwas Verkehrtes nehmen, [unclear].* ◇ take the wrong thing. Ⓛ munukuriñi

tuedílama *zu einem unrechten Mann etwas sagen.* ◇ speak to a wrong male kin. Ⓛ munuwottañi

tueljawunawuna *der Speerwerfer.* ◇ spear thrower.

tuedinama *verwechseln, verkehrtes nehmen.* ◇ mistake (verb), take wrong thing. Ⓛ munumanjini

tulba *das Kleine (von Vögeln).* ◇ nestling. Ⓛ kutunba

tuélakama *Genick brechen.* ◇ break neck. Ⓛ nguntintanañi, mulknuntanañi

tuljatulja *schmutzig, schlammig (Wasser).* ◇ dirty, muddy (water). Ⓛ paki

tuelja *der abgeworfene (Speer).* ◇ thrown (spear). Ⓛ tuti

tueljawuma *Speer werfen.* ◇ throw spear. Ⓛ tutiwonniñi Ⓓ dijana

tueljilama *ausholen mit dem Speer.* ◇ take aim with a spear. Ⓛ tutini (totini)

tukulka *eben, wagerecht.* ◇ even, level. Ⓛ tukulku

tuéljilitjilama *den Speer in den Speerwerfer legen.* ◇ lay spear in spear thrower. Ⓛ tutinitalkala

tukulkerama (iltja) *Hand aufhalten.* ◇ hold hand open. Ⓛ tukulkuringañi

tulkurtja *Wachtel.* ◇ quail (bird). Ⓛ ulburumbari

tukuna *dort.* ◇ there. Ⓛ narata

tukura *der Beschnittene, dem Schweigen auferlegt ist.* ◇ the one who has to keep silence. Ⓛ matukuru

tukura *Geschwür, Schwären.* ◇ abscess. Ⓛ bakuru Ⓓ kampa? kududu

tulbatuarama *einen von weitem nachsehen.* ◇ watch from a distance. Ⓛ miramiraniñi

tukuta *Herz.* ◇ heart. Ⓛ kutukutu Ⓓ ngara

tukuta tulinjatulitnama *Herz schlägt.* ◇ heartbeats. Ⓛ kutukutu atuātuni Ⓓ ngara tototungana (*Herz schlagen*: heartbeats)

tulagata *boomerang zum 'Parieren'.* ◇ defence boomerang. Ⓛ tulagata

tulba *das Junge (von Vögeln).* ◇ young one (of birds). Ⓛ kutunba Ⓓ wolka

tuma *schlagen, töten.* ◇ hit, kill. Ⓛ pungañi Ⓓ nandrana

turuma *kämpfen, fechten.* ◇ fight, fence. Ⓛ punkulapungañi Ⓓ tirimalina

tunama *fortwährend schlagen.* ◇ hit continuously. Ⓛ mapungañi

tultatuma *fortwährend schlagen.* ◇ hit continuously. Ⓛ tewalpungañi

turulama *Hände reiben.* ◇ rub hands. Ⓛ ularpungañi

iltarbaka turuma *aneinanderstoßen, Geräusch machen.* ◇ hit against each other, make noise. Ⓛ tirkilta pungañi

tulinjatulitnama *(Herz) schlagen.* ◇ beat (heart). Ⓛ atuātuni

tuna *Stock zum Schlagen.* ◇ hitting stick. Ⓛ tuna

tunama *befehlen.* ◇ command. Ⓛ tjingapungañi, mamutunañi Ⓓ jirijiriban a

tumanérinja *zusammengeklebt (Blätter, Saft).* ◇ glued together (leaves, sap). Ⓛ ngalungalurapunguta

tunatuna *Schläger, Kämpfer.* ◇ fighter. Ⓛ punganmi Ⓓ kaldru?

tulbangaturitjinjima *ganz niedrig über dem Abhang eines Berges auffliegen.* ◇ fly up very low from a mountain slope. Ⓛ punkupunkulakalbañi

tulbangatuma *niedrig am Abhang (eines Berges) hinfliegen.* ◇ fly low along a slope (of a mountain). Ⓛ punkulakálbañi

tunitnanama *befehlen, daß etwas geschieht, Befehl ausgehen lassen.* ◇ command that something happens, order.

intangilúlama *das lange Haar vom Kopf niederhängt.* ◇ long hair that hangs down from head. Ⓛ wonpulukatiñi, ngangurukatiñi

tunkulkna *Nasenschleim der Adler.* ◇ nose mucus of eagle. Ⓛ urkatara

tunbura *Grasart.* ◇ grass species. Ⓛ atunburu

tunga *vielleicht, wahrscheinlich.* ◇ perhaps, probably. Ⓛ atungu Ⓓ kara

túngaláma *für sehr wahrscheinlich halten.* ◇ regard as very probable. Ⓛ wombaputu

tungatungilama *übriglassen (Brot oder Fleisch, weil man satt ist).* ◇ to leave something over, left-over (bread or meat). Ⓛ atungutúnguni

tuñga *Nest des Wallabys (putaia).* ◇ nest of wallaby (putaia). Ⓛ utungu

tunga *Grasart, von der Taschen gemacht wurden.* ◇ grass species from which bags were made to store inkulba. Ⓛ utungu Ⓓ punku?

tungulba *Gummi (an den arganka Bäumen sich findend, ilumbala, iltjantjala).* ◇ gum (sticky substance of arganka trees). Ⓛ atangalbi, ngumu, tao Ⓓ ngulji

túnkunaláma *Mann werden (abgeleitet von atua = Mann).* ◇ become man. Ⓛ paturékulawonnañi

tungurilama *verspechen, ankündigen.* ◇ promise, announce. Ⓛ tankuni

tunjularenalama *herabfallen (Stein vom Gerbirge).* ◇ fall down (stone from mountain). Ⓛ ngungulukatini

tunka *kurz, dick.* ◇ short, thick. Ⓛ tata

turatura [Northern dialect] *kurz, niedrig.* ◇ short, low. Ⓛ tatalitji

tunkara *sperma, Same.* ◇ sperm, seed. Ⓛ watunkuru

tupa *Schlucht, Gebirgstor, Tal (zwischen Sandhügeln).* ◇ gorge, mountain cleft, valley (between sandhills). Ⓛ luntu Ⓓ wipa

turba *Gliedmaßen am Leibe angewachsen, die Brustwarzen.* ◇ extremities on body, nipples. Ⓛ turbu

turkura *Genick, Nacken, Genickknochen.* ◇ nape, neck bone. Ⓛ ngunti Ⓓ wokara

turkura unkwana *Halswirbel.* ◇ neck vertebra. Ⓛ ngunti tarka

turinjilama *hereintreiben (die Ochsen in Yard).* ◇ drive (cattle into yard). Ⓛ ngalakulurninañi

turuma *reiben, ausreiben (Körner).* ◇ rub, husk (seeds). Ⓛ ularpungañi Ⓓ turara ngankana

turulama (iltja) *Hände reiben.* ◇ rub hands. Ⓛ ularpungañi

tururbmintama *über etwas hinweg werfen, es nicht treffen.* ◇ throw over or past something, miss. Ⓛ lurkungariñi

tururbma *die langen Körper (der Larven).* ◇ long bodies (of grubs). Ⓛ lurku

turumba *lange Fett (der Schlangen).* ◇ long fat (of snake). Ⓛ murbulbu

tuta *auch (postp.)* ◇ also (postposition) Ⓛ puruna, tara Ⓓ bakana

tutibuma *kollern (Emu), brüllen (Ochse nach der Kuh), brummen (karakara).* ◇ rumble (emu), bellow (bull for cow), boom (type of trumpet). Ⓛ tukulbmanañi

tutjiatutjilama *in Stücke zerschneiden (Fleisch).* ◇ cut into pieces (meat). Ⓛ pitjilénañi

turura *Stock, bei Darstellung, den Boden gestochen wird.* ◇ stick used at performances to pierce the ground; claping sticks, music sticks. Ⓛ atúruru

tutna *gewiß.* ◇ certain. Ⓛ muntura Ⓓ kantji, mutulu

tútutilama *den Hund hetzen (auf ara oder ilia).* ◇ set a dog on (kangaroo or emu). Ⓛ tututúnañi

tutnilama *beteuern.* ◇ aver, affirm, reassure. Ⓛ munturu wottañi

tútnama *herunterhängen, herunterbiegen (Stiel [unclear]).* ◇ hang down, bend down. Ⓛ jentungarañi

tuturilama *aufstecken, festbinden (Haar).* ◇ tie up (hair). Ⓛ witituruñi

turambatura *dahingleitend (Fuß bei Tanzen).* ◇ glide (foot in dance). Ⓛ turumbaturu

tutja *ein Junges (das schon laufen kann).* ◇ young animal (that can run or hop); joey. Ⓛ atutu

tuwápuwápanáma *aufhalten (damit jemand nicht zurückkommen kann).* ◇ detain, stop, hold up (to prevent someone's return). Ⓛ ángaánganínañi

tútura *(Haarschmuck) wenn das Haar hinten in einem Knoten zusammengebunden und Federn hineingepackt sind (sowohl bei Aranda als Loritja gebäuchlich).* ◇ hair style (customary among Aranda and Loritja): hair bun with feathers. Ⓛ wituturu

tuwapuwapilinoma *aufhaltend vor sich hertreiben (Wolken), auch Ochsen vor sich hertreiben.* ◇ to drive, push along (clouds, cattle). Ⓛ ángaángarabákañi

tutjilama *reißen (der Strom an ein Gebäude).* ◇ tear (river torrent on building).

U

ularambenja *postp. vor (einer Person) z.B. atnanga ularambenja tnama.* ◇ (postposition) in front of (a person), e.g. stand in front of.

ularataka *Vorderteil (Schiffes), Vorzimmer n.* ◇ front part (ship), reception.

ulbanulba *zerklopft (Sämmereien).* ◇ ground (seeds).

ulakara [Northern dialect] *Felsvorsprung.* ◇ rocky outcrop. Ⓛ ulákiri

Uā [Southern dialect] *conf.* **wā** *ja.* ◇ yes. Ⓛ wanku

uliwutiwuta *lange Stirn.* ◇ long forehead. Ⓛ ngala wotjinkuru

ŭla *Stirn.* ◇ forehead, front. Ⓛ ngala

ūla *Beine (die ganzen Beine) [unclear] Bauch.* ◇ legs (the whole leg) belly. Ⓛ ulu

ulaialama *alle miteinander gehen.* ◇ all go together. Ⓛ kuruwápuwápa kátiñi

úluma *Urin lassen (Hunde).* ◇ pass urine (dogs); excrete. Ⓛ intiñi

ulantulantula rama *mit vorgestreckter Stirn sehen.* ◇ to watch with forehead thrust forward (from a hiding spot). Ⓛ ngalakutu ngalakutunku nangañi

ulara *vor, vorn, gegenüber.* ◇ before, in front of, opposite. Ⓛ ngapara

ularakulara *entgegen, sich gegenüber (stehen), vor (einen liegen).* ◇ in opposition, (stand) opposite of each other, (lie) in front of (someone). Ⓛ ngaparkutara, ngáparakungápara

ulara indama *sich gegenüber liegen.* ◇ lie opposite of each other. Ⓛ ngapara ngariñi

ularakularalama *entgegengehen.* ◇ walk towards. Ⓛ ngaparakungapara jenañi Ⓓ mandurina, dankamalina?

uláreráma *sich umsehen.* ◇ look around. Ⓛ ngaparariñi

ulámbulamba [Northern dialect] *Säbler, avocet.* ◇ avocet (bird). Ⓛ ulambulambi Ⓓ muttamutta, muttimutti? ('?' added by CS)

ulanbuma [Northern dialect] *überfließen.* ◇ overflow. Ⓛ wílknáañi

ulanbubanbuma *nachspringen (einem).* ◇ run after (someone). Ⓛ úluwarakátini

ulba *rote Farbe, roter Ocker.* ◇ red colour, red ochre; also used for yellow ochre today. Ⓛ mapana Ⓓ karku maralje

ulbalelama *mit roter Farbe bestreichen.* ◇ paint with red colour. Ⓛ mapananka japani

ulbalúlbala *Morgenrot, farbig (Blumen).* ◇ morning glow (dawn), colourful (flowers). Ⓛ ulbalulbali Ⓓ nguramarana

ulbálerálera *sich gelb färbend (Blätter).* ◇ turn yellow (leaves). Ⓛ wárwár

ulba *weich (geklopfte Erde, Lagerplatz).* ◇ soft (loose ground, camp). Ⓛ pulpa

ulbaia *Creek, Milchstraße.* ◇ creek, Milky Way; river, fine sand. Ⓛ karu Ⓓ kaiari

meȓawara *Milchstraße.* ◇ Milky Way. Ⓛ tukalba

ulbalulbala *Morgenrot, farbig (Blumen).* ◇ morning red, colourful (flower). Ⓛ ulbalulbali

ulbanelbélama *fortwährend schlagen, blutig schlagen.* ◇ beat continuously, beat bloody. Ⓛ pulpainpungañi

ulbanulbatuma *beschädigen, beleidigen.* ◇ damage, insult.

ulberama *weich werden [unclear].* ◇ become soft. Ⓛ pulparingañi

ulbantjima *herausziehen, ausziehen (aus dem Boden).* ◇ pull (out of the ground). Ⓛ wilpiñi, urkuni Ⓓ kulana, kiltarana

ulbantjilalama *herausnehmen 1x (z.B. aus Mulde).* ◇ take out once (e.g. out of a bowl). Ⓛ urkulkatiñi Ⓓ dukarana

ulbantjilinjangama *fortwährend herausnehmen.* ◇ take out continuously. Ⓛ urkurangaraniñi

ulbara *Gipfel [unclear], die Spitze der Pflanze.* ◇ summit, peak, top of plant. Ⓛ walpuru

iltja ulbara *die Finger.* ◇ fingers. Ⓛ mara walpuru

ulbarindama *auf dem Angesicht liegen, das Gesicht in die verschränkten Arme legen.* ◇ lie on face, lay face in folded arms. Ⓛ watungarañi

ulbanulbatuma *schädigen, beschädigen.* ◇ damage.

ulbatjaparra *langes, scharfes Steinmesser.* ◇ long, sharp stone knife. Ⓛ waralitji

ulbaṙinja *Waffe zum Werfen (gewöhnlicher boomerang).* ◇ throwing weapon (ordinary boomerang). Ⓛ kali Ⓓ kirra

ulbaṙinja lupara *kleine boomerang.* ◇ small boomerang. Ⓛ kali tunta

ulbatja *Ring-neck parrot, Papagei mit grünen Flügelfedern, gelben Halsband und Brust, schwarzen Kopf und blauen Wangen, inneren Schwanzfedern grün, die äußern blau (Platycerus xonarius).* ◇ ringneck parrot, Port Lincoln parrot, *Barnadius zonarius* (Pizzey and Knight 2007). Ⓛ batilba

ulbunaláma [Eastern dialect] *pfeifen.* ◇ whistle. Ⓛ winpurangañi

ulbélama *zerklopfen, zermalmen, zerreiben, reiben.* ◇ grind, crush, rub. Ⓛ ulbuni Ⓓ pitana

ulbelama, kanta wuljawulja ulbelama *graben (um etwas).* ◇ dig (for something).

ulbma *eng, schmal.* ◇ tight, narrow. Ⓛ tulu Ⓓ wuldru, nguldru

ulbmerama *cf.* **antjulbmerama** *verdursten, ersticken.* ◇ die of thirst, suffocate. Ⓛ tuluringañi (untu)

ulbmapeatara *zwei eng zusammen stehende (Felsen).* ◇ two (rocks) standing closely beside each other. Ⓛ tulukutara, utukutara

ulbmélalama *ein wenig öffnen (Tür).* ◇ to open a little (door). Ⓛ tuluni

ulbmélama *zusammenbringen, zusammen treiben.* ◇ bring together, drive together. Ⓛ tuluni Ⓓ nguldru ngankana (*zusammen bringen*)

ulbmerama *zusammenhalten (Füße).* ◇ hold together (feet). Ⓛ mulunkuriñi, uburingañi

ulbmara *weiche Erde, Staub.* ◇ soft soil, dust. Ⓛ ulbmuru Ⓓ puturu, ngalara

ulbmaratuma *den Takt schlagen (mit einem Stock die Erde).* ◇ beat time (with a stick on ground). Ⓛ mantatuñi

ulbmarandúlbmara *kleine Habicht spec.* ◇ small hawk species. Ⓛ ulbmurundulbmuru

ulbmaulbma *gedrängt (Haufe).* ◇ crowded. Ⓛ tulutulu

ulbmungulbmungilama *trösten.* ◇ console. Ⓛ kunbukunbuni

ulbmulbulbmelama *etwas verfolgend in die Mitte nehmen.* ◇ surround pursuing. Ⓛ tulutuluni

ulbmunta *Staub, Staubwind.* ◇ dust, dusty wind; flour. Ⓛ ulbmuru Ⓓ puturu (Staub)

ulbmuntabóbuta *Staubsturm.* ◇ dust storm. Ⓛ ulburumúlala Ⓓ winjarina

ulbōlja *welk.* ◇ withered. Ⓛ tjiluna Ⓓ winjarina

ulboljerama *intr. verwelken, verblühen.* ◇ (intransitive) wither, fade. Ⓛ tjilunariñi

ulboljilama *trs. verwelken machen.* ◇ (transitive) make wither. Ⓛ tjilunani

ulboroa *dunkel, schwarz (Kopf und Streifen der tnurungatja Raupe).* ◇ dark, black (head and stripes of tnurungatja caterpillar). Ⓛ ulburukambara

ulbmeritnama (*cf.* **ulbmerama**) *(dicht) zusammenschliessen (Füße) beim Gehen.* ◇ keep (feet) close together when walking (Strehlow 1911: 5). Ⓛ opurikulakulbañi

ulbulatuma *trs. ersticken (vom Rauch).* ◇ (transitive) suffocate (from smoke or from swallowing the wrong way). Ⓛ pulpatuni Ⓓ palimana?

ulbulérelanáma *sich über und über rot beschmieren.* ◇ to completely cover with red colour (reflexive). Ⓛ ulbankarijennañi

ulbulbana *Fledermaus.* ◇ bat. Ⓛ ulbulbuni Ⓓ pintjipindera?, pintjipintjindera

ulbululbula *rötlich gefärbt (Blätter), sich mit roter Farbe beschmieren.* ◇ reddish coloured (leaves), cover yourself with red colour. Ⓛ ulbulúlbulu

ulbululbulérama *sich rötlich färben (Blätter).* ◇ turn reddish (leaves). Ⓛ ulbululbuluṙiñi

ulbunta *Rauch.* ◇ smoke. Ⓛ puju

 For the modern spellings of these words, see the dictionaries and sources in reference list.

ulbuntakelama *räuchern (Novizen), Räucherung.* ◇ to smoke (novices), smoking ceremony. Ⓛ pujurkutunañi

ulbuntununtuna *braune giftige Schlange.* ◇ brown poisonous snake. Ⓛ marumarura

ulbura; tnata ulburu *hohl (Baum), ausgehöhlt (Lagerplatz); leer (Magen).* ◇ hollow (tree, camping place); empty (stomach). Ⓛ ulburu

ulbura, ulbara *weitvoneinandergetrennt (Zehen der Emu).* ◇ far apart (toes of emu). Ⓛ albaranka

ulburtia *Seitenstück (des Wildes).* ◇ flank (of animals). Ⓛ nganbali

ulburkna *Takt (von Weibern schlagen die Hüften).* ◇ time (beaten by women on their hips). Ⓛ ulbantji

ulburknatuma *Hände schlagen (Tanz).* ◇ clap hands (dance). Ⓛ ulbantjiatuñi

ulburkninjatuma *im Takt die Hände auf die Schenkel schlagen (beim Weibertanz).* ◇ beat hands in time on thighs (at women's dance). Ⓛ ulbantjinani

ulburamba *schwarze Saft (honeysuckle-Blumen).* ◇ black juice (honeysuckle flowers). Ⓛ ulburātuni

ulburambirkuma *schwarze Saft auspressen (honeysuckle).* ◇ to squeeze black juice (honeysuckle) out. Ⓛ ulburātuni

ulbura *schwarz, dunkel.* ◇ black, dark. Ⓛ ulburu

ulburulbura *Sau-distel, auch ein kleiner Strauch mit rosenartigen Blättern, hellblaue Blüten; Hibiscus Farragei, Gossypium sturtii.* ◇ small bush with rose-like leaves and light blue blossoms; *Hibiscus farragei*, *Gossypium sturtii* now possibly Radyera farragei (desert rose mallow) (see Latz 1996). Ⓛ ulburulburu

ulburintaînama *schwarz werden (Beeren).* ◇ turn black (berries). Ⓛ ulburuwokkani

ulburulburentánama *(z.B. Katze) im dunkeln herumschleichen.* ◇ (e.g. cat) sneak around in the dark. Ⓛ watuwatungaralabakañi

ulburuwínkima *verdunkeln (der Himmel schwarz werden von Wolken).* ◇ darken (when black clouds cover the sky). Ⓛ úlburukámbaranínañi

ulburarankana *ausgehöhlter Futterplatz.* ◇ hollowed feeding place.

ulbuta *schmutzig, trübe (Wasser oder Eiter).* ◇ dirty, murky, cloudy (water or pus). Ⓛ ulbata Ⓓ murumuru, ngurdi

ulbuterama *schmutzig, trübe werden.* ◇ become dirty, become muddy. Ⓛ ulbataringañi

ulbutilama *schmutzig machen.* ◇ make dirty. Ⓛ ulbatani

ulbutalélama *trüben, schmutzig machen.* ◇ make muddy or dirty. Ⓛ ulbatanáni

ulbutalénama *schmutzig machen (z.B. Wasser, Geräte).* ◇ make dirty (e.g. water, tools). Ⓛ maulbatanáni

ulkuntulkungilama *schwarz und blau schlagen (übertreiben).* ◇ beat black and blue (exaggerate).

ulbutabalankerélama *antreiben zur Arbeit.* ◇ drive to work. Ⓛ parpatanañi

ulentama *auflauern (der Beute), beobachten (Schlange).* ◇ to prey, to lie in wait for (prey), to watch (snake). Ⓛ urakanjini

ulbutía *schnell, fleißig.* ◇ quick, industrious. Ⓛ parpata

ulelelanabanama *trs. zusammenbringen, zuheilen machen.* ◇ (transitive) bring together, heal. Ⓛ purianáni

ulélama [Northern dialect] *zusammenbringen (Ränder von Wunde), zusammenhäufen.* ◇ bring together (edges of wound), pile up. Ⓛ purini

uléra *Garn (aus Menschenhaar).* ◇ thread (of human hair). Ⓛ kunturu

ulérama *sich verbergen.* ◇ conceal, hide. Ⓛ kumbini Ⓓ kutina, ngarurina

ulerapara *große Felsblock, Felsstück.* ◇ large rock. Ⓛ puli manpamanpa

ulia *Anführer.* ◇ leader. Ⓛ tëïra, terba Ⓓ mudlakutja

ulja *Schatten (von Bäumen), Laube?* ◇ shadow (of trees), shade. ('?' added by CS). Ⓛ lunta

ulkuma, *z.B.* **tnata ulkuma** *knurren, z.B. Magen knurrt.* ◇ growl, e.g. stomach growls, rumbles. Ⓛ ulkuni, wila ulkuni

ulka *das Erbrochene, das Ausgespiene.* ◇ vomit, disgorged. Ⓛ ulkapu

ulknalja *Busch (spec.)* ◇ bush species. Ⓛ ulknalji

ulkualala ngama *auf der Schulter tragen.* ◇ carry on shoulder. Ⓛ balkankakatini

ulkualakilama *über die Schulter legen.* ◇ lay over shoulder. Ⓛ balkankañi

ulkuanka *rein, ausgezeichnet, sehr gut, auserlesen, lieblich.* ◇ clean, excellent, very good, exquisite, lovely. Ⓛ ulkanki

ulkábutanama *hinunterwürgen (ein großes Stück Fleisch).* ◇ devour (a large piece of meat). Ⓛ tulkuninañi

uilkulbilkuma *Rauch beißen (in die Augen).* ◇ smoke stings (in the eyes). Ⓛ patapatani

ulkuntulkunga *blau geschlagen.* ◇ beaten up.

ulknaiïta *Bauchfett, das Fett unter d. Nabel.* ◇ belly fat, fat under navel. Ⓛ ngatinba

ulkumba *weich, zerriebene Rinde des Gummibaumes.* ◇ soft, ground gumtree bark. Ⓛ mina, ulkulji Ⓓ jinkapitji?

ulkura *gerade in der Mitte (zwischen zwei Gegenständen).* ◇ exactly in the middle (between two things). Ⓛ ngururmatamata

ulkurtjulkura *grüne Schlamm auf dem Wasser.* ◇ green slime on water. Ⓛ ulkurtjulkuru

ultuma *(Kinn auf dem Handteller) drücken.* ◇ press (chin on palm of hand). Ⓛ palini

ultuitnánama *Kinn in beide Hände stützen.* ◇ to prop up or to rest chin in both hands. Ⓛ palipalini

alkútakákutérama *sich ekeln.* ◇ feel disgust. Ⓛ ulkabulkabariñi Ⓓ kuterina

ultámbiuma *viele Brote machen.* ◇ make many breads. Ⓛ nummawonniñi

ululbulelama *versammeln, zu Hauf bringen.* ◇ assemble, come together. Ⓛ puritjipuritjinañi

ulturtnarenalama *zu Boden stürzen, (vom Schlag getroffen, in die Beine sinken), zusammenbrechen (vom Speer getroffen oder boomerang).* ◇ to fall (to the ground from a blow), collapse (hit by a spear or boomerang). Ⓛ kirbmikatiñi

ultubana *mittleren, in der Mitte (liegend).* ◇ (lie) in the middle. Ⓛ kultuta

ultatjipata *trockner hohler Baum.* ◇ dry hollow tree. Ⓛ jultupilti

ulta *hohl, leer (Gefäß).* ◇ hollow, empty (vessel). Ⓛ jultu

ultakalentjima *sich (Beine) brechen.* ◇ break (legs) (reflexive). Ⓛ ngalakatakatiñi

ulterama *hohl werden.* ◇ to become hollow. Ⓛ julturingañi

ulturtnarenalama *Rücken zerbrechen (Rückgrad), zu Boden stürzen, zusammen brechen.* ◇ break back (backbone), fall to the ground, collapse. Ⓛ tilpurukatiñi, kirbmikatiñi

ulta *Seite, Seitenstück (des Wildes).* ◇ side, flank (of animals). Ⓛ kultu Ⓓ banki

- **útakukúlta** *sehr tief, bis an die Brust (im Wasser), viele im Schatten sitzende [unclear].* ◇ very deep, to the chest (in water), sitting in the shade. Ⓛ kultukutata
- **ultenba (indama)** *auf der Seite (liegend).* ◇ (lie) on one side. Ⓛ kultupiti ngariñi
- **ultabarkabarka** *mit Punkten versehen, gefleckt.* ◇ covered with spots, spotted. Ⓛ kultunintanintan
- **ultabarkabarkilama** *Zeichen einbrennen (auf Zauberhölzern).* ◇ burn marks, designs on something (e.g. pieces of wood). Ⓛ kultunintanintani
- **ultangaléra** *bunt, gefleckt, gestreift.* ◇ colourful, spotted, striped. Ⓛ kultukatiri

ultákalàka ntainama *zu Tode speeren, tödlich treffen.* ◇ spear to death, strike fatally. Ⓛ katawokkañi, kujalpungañi Ⓓ wokaribana

ultakama *brechen, zerbrechen, zermalmen.* ◇ break, crush. Ⓛ katantanañi Ⓓ wokarina

 For the modern spellings of these words, see the dictionaries and sources in reference list.

ultakalama *intrs. zerbrechen.* ◇ break (intransitive). Ⓛ katakatiñi

ultakalakawomma *entzweiwerfen (beim Werfen).* ◇ break (by throwing). Ⓛ katarunkañi

ultáltauma *hinauflegen.* ◇ lay on top (of something). Ⓛ utitunañi

ultitjikama *Leben zerbrechen, Lebensfaden zerreißen.* ◇ break, destroy life. Ⓛ tilburtjingañi

ultambambirkuma *kneten (die Honig Felsblüten ntjuiamba).* ◇ knead (honeysuckle blossoms). Ⓛ ulburuwónniñi Ⓓ pitjambu

ultamba *Honig (von der Honigfliege, inínjira Biene genannt).* ◇ honey from native bee called '(i)nínjira'; native honey, sugarbag. Ⓛ ngalpuru

ultangalera *der schwarze Streifen.* ◇ black stripe. Ⓛ kultukatiri (Kultukatiri was the name of a black and white striped ancestral dog being.)

ultangaléra *bunt, gefleckt, gestreift.* ◇ colourful, spotted, striped. Ⓛ kultukatiri, ulburukwata

ultuma [Northern dialect] *zerdrücken, zermalmen, zertreten.* ◇ crush, stomp. Ⓛ puruni

ultunda *Tropfen (Wasser), Brocken (Erde).* ◇ drop (water), lump (earth). Ⓛ ultuntu, tjilpuntu

ultunta [Southern dialect] *weiße Stein, Art Kalkstein, weiß.* ◇ white limestone. Ⓛ ultuntu

ultunditnima *[Tropfen fallen] tröpfeln.* ◇ drip (drops fall). Ⓛ ultuntúpatangarañi

ultutjérama *mit einem Ruck den Arm ausstrecken.* ◇ stretch arm out with a jerk. Ⓛ tēlbmanáni

ulupaia *lange Maus.* ◇ long mouse. Ⓛ ulkunba

ultunta [Southern dialect] *eine Art Kalkstein.* ◇ limestone. Ⓛ ultuntu

ultútjarama *zerbrechen, (z.B. Speer).* ◇ break (e.g. a spear). Ⓛ telburukatiñi

ultutjarenalama *(intrs.) zerbrechen (in Stücke zerbrechen).* ◇ (intransitive) break (into pieces). Ⓛ telburtjingañi

umba *Urin, Blase.* ◇ urine, bladder. Ⓛ kumbu, manu Ⓓ puratandra (Galle), kipara (Urin)

umbuluma *urinieren.* ◇ urinate. Ⓛ kumburangani Ⓓ kiparana (urinieren)

unángitjunánga *langsam gehend, vorsichtig auftretend.* ◇ walk slowly, tread carefully. Ⓛ kanenku jennañi

unba *stinkend, bitter Galle.* ◇ stink. Ⓛ unbu, maiju

umbaljua ilbmara *erschöpft, kraftlos liegen bleiben, kraftlos und müde.* ◇ exhausted, too weak to move, weak and tired. Ⓛ wolbawolba rarirari

unba ntjainama *stinken.* ◇ stink. Ⓛ unbu pantini

unátala tninama *auf dem Schoß haben (Kinder).* ◇ sit on lap (children). Ⓛ ambunka kanjini

unbintjima *stinken.* ◇ stink. Ⓛ unbu pantini

ultúrbmultúra *weiße Stein, eine Art Kalkstein.* ◇ white limestone. Ⓛ ulturbmu

unbulata *sehr stinkend.* ◇ very smelly. Ⓛ unbuwollata

unba kunna *schlecht riechen (Schweiß).* ◇ bad smelling (sweat). Ⓛ unbukuja

unbaiakunbaia ilama *trotzen, erzürnen.* ◇ defy, enrage. Ⓛ unbaiakunbaiïni

unangarala kalama *sich die Schulter ritzen (bis das Blut fließt, Zeichen der Trauer).* ◇ cut shoulder (until blood flows, sign of mourning). Ⓛ anunuru wirknani

unbulama *nicht mögen, ausschlagen (Gabe), absagen, entsagen.* ◇ to dislike, to reject (gift), renounce. Ⓛ baiïni Ⓓ junkarina (*unzufrieden sein*: be discontented)

unbata *mürrisch.* ◇ surly, sullen. Ⓛ mulara Ⓓ mujarina (*mürrisch sein*: be surly, grumpy), junka (*unzufrieden*: discontent) mikarina

unbarumaruma *weiße Streifen auf der Nase.* ◇ white stripes on nose. Ⓛ mulawiluna

unbaritja *Zeichen auf der Nase.* ◇ marks or designs on nose. Ⓛ wiluna

unbinjerama *vertrocknen (Wasser).* ◇ dry up (water). Ⓛ biltiringañi

unbukebara *wohlrichendes Wasser.* ◇ fragrant water.

unbulata *stinkend.* ◇ stinking, smelly. Ⓛ unbuwollata

úlija *Haufe oder Vorrat (von Samen, die Ameisen sammeln).* ◇ store (of seeds that ants collect). Ⓛ akákuru

unbulunbulélama *stechen, niederstechen (mit dem Speer).* ◇ stab, strike down (with a spear). Ⓛ wakuwakungarañi

unbunba *Spielplatz, Fechtplatz, Handelsplatz.* ◇ playground, fighting ground, trading place. Ⓛ unbunbu

únbuma *wegschicken, wegtreiben.* ◇ send away, drive away. Ⓛ jenbuñi

unda *Clay-pan-water.* ◇ claypan water. Ⓛ wonta

unia *Vorrat (ein Haufe von Speeren, von Kleider), Schatz.* ◇ stores (many spears or clothes), treasure. Ⓛ úni

untjilāka *Genick mit Stacheln besetzt (moloch).* ◇ neck covered with spines (moloch). Ⓛ taltatara

untja *der Nacken, (Schulter oder untja).* ◇ nape, shoulder or neck. Ⓛ pini

  untjala ngama *auf der Schulter tragen (kleine Kinder).* ◇ carry on shoulder (small children). Ⓛ pininka katiñi

  unjikilama *hochheben mit der Schulter.* ◇ lift with shoulder. Ⓛ pinikunañi

  unjikarenama *auf ihren Nacken setzen [unclear].* ◇ lay or position on neck (shoulder). Ⓛ pinikutunañi

unjitja *warm.* ◇ warm. Ⓛ untuna

unjima nama *den Rücken zukehren.* ◇ turn away (from someone). Ⓛ tángamanínañi

uninjuma *duften (angenehm).* ◇ smell (pleasant). Ⓛ pantirknárañi

uninjupinjuma *duplik fortwährend duften.* ◇ reduplication of 'smell'. Ⓛ pantirpantirknárañi

unjuma *brummen (Ochse), brummen (Fliege), summen (Bienen), gurren (Taube).* ◇ grumble (bullocks), buzz (fly), hum (bee), coo (pigeon); whimper (dog). Ⓛ ngunmanañi, ngúnmanañi Ⓓ kaldrintjarina

unkuarindana *Wasservogel (spec.)* ◇ waterbird species. Ⓛ unkarindini

únkulàra *breiter Weg.* ◇ wide path. Ⓛ unkuluru

unkúlinja, inkulinja (= **nturuta**) *Taube.* ◇ pigeon species. Ⓛ eburu

unkulunkulélama *beschädigen, verwunden, Schaden tun.* ◇ damage, wound, harm. Ⓛ unkulunkuluni

unpútupútu *zerschmettert (Arm und Bein gebrochen).* ◇ shattered (broken arm and leg).

unuputuputilama *trs. zerschmettern.* ◇ (transitive) shatter.

unkwala *süß, Zucker.* ◇ sweet, sugar; alcohol. Ⓛ wama, womma

unkwalkara *längerer Weg (circa 2 englische Meilen).* ◇ longish distance (circa 2 miles).

unkwalkna *Nasenschleim, Schnupfen.* ◇ mucus, cold. Ⓛ urkatara Ⓓ mulagildi, kundrukundru

  unkwalkniluma *husten, Schleim auswerfen.* ◇ cough, cough phlegm out. Ⓛ urkataranani, untu kuntulpungañi

unkwaltja *Brocken (Brot), Fetzen (Kleid).* ◇ piece or morsel (of bread), rag (dress). Ⓛ putaputa Ⓓ worduwordu

  unkwaltjerama *zerbröckeln, zerreißen.* ◇ to crumble, to tear. Ⓛ putaputaringañi

  unkwaltjilama *trs. zerbrocken, zerfetzen.* ◇ crumble, tear. Ⓛ putaputani

úrukanáma *warten.* ◇ wait. Ⓛ wonnuninañi

úrukawaí *höre erst [unclear].* ◇ listen first! Ⓛ wonnukulilai

uráma *ob bald (Frage particle).* ◇ if soon (question particle). Ⓛ waiïmba

unkwana *Knochen, Bein.* ◇ bone, leg. Ⓛ tarka Ⓓ mokku

unkwatarperama *einsam werden, auf sich selbst angewiesen [unclear].* ◇ become lonely, be dependent upon oneself. Ⓛ mulururiñi

untja *Genick.* ◇ neck. Ⓛ pini

unma *reif (Frucht), gar (Fleisch), verschmachtet.* ◇ ripe (fruit), cooked (meat), languished. Ⓛ unmi Ⓓ dalku
urarama *auswählen, aussuchen [unclear].* ◇ choose. Ⓛ ekuntanáni
unmerama *reifen.* ◇ ripen. Ⓛ unmiringañi
urailakuraila ndama *ungleich austeilen [unclear].* ◇ distribute unevenly. Ⓛ ekuntarakekuntara jungañi
untatupuntata *tief einsinken (in den Sand).* ◇ sink deep (into sand). Ⓛ tunmirtúnmira
unmerama *verschmachten.* ◇ to dry up, to languish.
untána *gelb.* ◇ yellow. Ⓛ kantawara
untentilalbuma *lauernd (auf Wild), umkehren.* ◇ prey (on game), turn around. Ⓛ mangurira kulbánini
unta *Du.* ◇ you. Ⓛ nuntu Ⓓ jidni, jundru
untenta *du allein.* ◇ you alone. Ⓛ nuntukutu
untjara [Northern dialect] *conf.* **(ntuara)** *blaue Kranich.* ◇ blue crane. Ⓛ untjari
untara *jenseits, postp. c. abl.* ◇ beyond (postposition, with ablative) Ⓛ wirili Ⓓ jerankeri
untuába *Gummirindenstücke.* ◇ gumtree bark pieces. Ⓛ ngántapiri
untárakala *weiter weg.* ◇ further away. Ⓛ wirilikata, tutan
untarakaguia *weiter, jenseits.* ◇ further, beyond. Ⓛ wirilimaiju
untarakua *jenseits.* ◇ beyond. Ⓛ parari
untápma *die beiden Oberschenkel.* ◇ both thighs. Ⓛ palpati
untárunitja *an der andern Seite (z.B. Creek).* ◇ on the other side (e.g. creek). Ⓛ wirilipiti
untárintjirka *ganz hindurch z.B. speeren (wenn der Speer an der anderen Seite wieder herauskommt).* ◇ right through; e.g. to spear (when a spear emerges on the other side of someone or something). Ⓛ wirilipilti
untúra *saftig, der Saft (Raupen), mit dickem Saft, mit Milch gefüllt.* ◇ juicy, juice (caterpillar), with thick juice, filled with milk. Ⓛ unturu
untuarílama *vorbeiwerfen, verfehlen.* ◇ throw past, miss. Ⓛ wirilináni
unúrula rama (inura) *anstarren, starr auf etwas sehen; (lahm).* ◇ stare, stare at something; lame. Ⓛ unturunku nangañi
untjita [Northern dialect] *conf.* **ntjuta** *Kreuzbein.* ◇ sacrum, lower back. Ⓛ titi
unújuna *gebückt, gebeugt.* ◇ bent, stooped. Ⓛ bobatubobatu
unultunulterama *auf einem Haufen stellen, sich versammeln.* ◇ to come together, to assemble. Ⓛ petupetuni
úntuma *conf.* juntama. ◇ search. Ⓛ ngurini
untúma *sich tummeln (Vögel), herumwandern.* ◇ flutter (birds), wander about. Ⓛ jurini
unturuntura *große (Rauch), große (Auge).* ◇ big (smoke), large (eye). Ⓛ teruteru (*Auge*), unturunturu (*Rauch*)
ura *Feuer.* ◇ fire. Ⓛ waru [Western dialect], turata [Southern dialect], pauju [Southern dialect] Ⓓ turu
ura-imbalkna *Brandmal.* ◇ burn (noun).
urakapa *Feuerbrand, Fackel.* ◇ big fire, torch. Ⓛ warutani Ⓓ turumanja
urabarenama *im Rauch ersticken.* ◇ suffocate in smoke.
urapa *Ofen, Feuer in einer Höhlung.* ◇ oven, fire in a hollow. Ⓛ urapi Ⓓ turupiri
uratāra *hellaufloderndes Feuer (Feuerzeichen geben).* ◇ brightly blazing fire (make or give fire signal). Ⓛ waru kurkalba, warukurkala Ⓓ turojapingana
ura-tara etama ◇ light a big fire. Ⓛ waru kurkala kutani
urambuma *Feuer brennen.* ◇ to burn (a fire). Ⓛ warukambañi Ⓓ turu
ura-alknanta *Feuerflamme.* ◇ flame (lit. fire flame). Ⓛ warukala Ⓓ turujaola (*Feuerflamme*)
ura-etama *Feuer anzünden.* ◇ to light a fire. Ⓛ waru kutani Ⓓ turu japina
urána *Mörder.* ◇ murderer. Ⓛ muranu
urabóbuta *Feuerzeichen (Signal).* ◇ fire signal. Ⓛ warutun Ⓓ diakantji

uraia, uraia pitjima *zögernd verziehen, verziehen zum Kommen.* ◇ hesitate, delay to come. Ⓛ waiïmba ngalajennañi

uranburanba *zornig, brennen (vor Zorn).* ◇ angry, burn (with anger). Ⓛ wilawarutara

uráljakurálja *Feuerhitze.* ◇ heat of fire. Ⓛ kámbalkámbala

urándinda *Wasservogel (spec.), schwarzes Wasserhuhn.* ◇ waterbird species, black waterfowl. Ⓛ urandandi Ⓓ marumaru (*Wasserhuhn*)

urápmara *abgebrannte Fläche.* ◇ burnt area. Ⓛ naru, nunma

uráteka *große Feuer, helle Feuerschein.* ◇ big, bright fire. Ⓛ warungana

uralinta *große Feuerflamme.* ◇ big flame. Ⓛ waruteli

uránba *nikotinhaltiges Kraut, das gekaut wird.* ◇ nicotine plant that is chewed.

urangara *Strauch aus dem Speere verfertigt wird.* ◇ bush from which spears are made. Ⓛ warangari

urátna (ura-atna) *der große ziehende Rauch (Rauchwolken).* ◇ clouds of smoke. Ⓛ kúnnarúru Ⓓ turukunna (*Rauchwolke*)

uraiura [Northern dialect] *monatliche Regel (der Frauen).* ◇ monthly period (of women). Ⓛ uraiuri

urálama [Northern dialect] *einsinken (im Sumpf) oder Wasser.* ◇ sink (in mud or water). Ⓛ káralukatiñi Ⓓ punbina

uraljaperuma *untertauchen.* ◇ dive under. Ⓛ tululukatiñi

urara *Echo, Wiederhall, alle zusammen, einstimmig (sprechen oder singen), Konzert.* ◇ echo, reverberation, (speak or sing) all together, concert. Ⓛ marultara Ⓓ kanpu

uráratama *zusammen sprechen oder singen.* ◇ speak or sing together. Ⓛ marultara wonkañi Ⓓ kataana (*Echo machen*)

urara *black-backed Crow-Shrike. Schwarze Kopf und Brust, weiße Hinterkopf, graue Rücken, einzelne weiße Flügelfedern, weiße Schwanzfedern mit schwarzen Rand (Gymnorkina Tibeen).* ◇ shrike species; black head, back and chest, back of head white, grey back, single white wing-feathers, white tail feathers with black edges (*Gymnorhina tibicen*, Australian magpie) (Pizzey and Knight 2007). Ⓛ urári Ⓓ kokula

urartja *kleine Ratte (ohne Beutel).* ◇ small rat (without pouch). Ⓛ arutu

urátjurátja *eine Grasart, auf Bergen wachsend, lange schmale Blätter.* ◇ grass species with long narrow leaves that grows on mountains. Ⓛ uratjuratji

urápurapa *sehr dunkel, sehr finster.* ◇ very dark. Ⓛ mungalmungala

urba *Rückgrad.* ◇ spine, backbone. Ⓛ murbu Ⓓ kuldru, tokowira tokojulkura

uratnitoppa *Schwarm (von flieg. Vögeln).* ◇ flock of flying birds. Ⓛ majuanggariñi

urba unkwana *Rückgrat.* ◇ spine, backbone. Ⓛ murbu tarka Ⓓ kuldru mokku

toppa *das Rückgrat (der Schlangen und Menschen).* ◇ spine, back (of snakes and humans). Ⓛ miti

urbanama *besprengen, bespritzen.* ◇ splash. Ⓛ kurbiñi Ⓓ multibana

urálekurála, uralekerinja *Schlangenlinie.* ◇ snake line. Ⓛ nunkinunki, nunkinunki

urbungalangala *Bergrücken, die Erdwale auf dem alankura-Platz.* ◇ mountain ridge, earth mounds on ceremonial ground. Ⓛ murburiri, tunturuuru

urápara *vom Feuer geschwärzt (Felsen).* ◇ blackened by fire (cliffs). Ⓛ maru

urbarama *auslöschen, auswischen.* ◇ extinguish, wipe out. Ⓛ wapalpinañi Ⓓ kalingana, kalina

urbmultjerama *heftig kämpfen miteinander.* ◇ fight with each other violently. Ⓛ kirbmuntarapungañi

urbia *Bote.* ◇ messenger. Ⓛ wikaru Ⓓ mandra [wapana]?

urbilinjilinja (urba-ilinjiuma) *in einander verschlungen (Äste).* ◇ interlaced, intertwined, interweaved (branches). Ⓛ warbili

urbmalákualákua *mit Narben geschmückt (die Brust der Eingeborenen).* ◇ decorated with scars (chest). Ⓛ worbmatara

urbma *Schote, die an den Schoten befindlichen Erhöhungen, Samenkapsel, Narben, die sich die Eingeborenen über die Brust und an den Armen beibringen.* ◇ pods; decorative scars on chests and arms. Ⓛ worbma

urbmalakua *Zeichen eingeritzt (Stöcke zum Schlagen), mit Narben versehen.* ◇ engraved marks on (hitting sticks), covered with scars. Ⓛ worbmatara

urbmelburbmelba *hin und her schwankend (beim Laufen), wankend, wakelnd.* ◇ sway. Ⓛ urbmelburbmelbi

urbmakana *kl. Steine z. Ritzen der Narben.* ◇ small stones used to scar.

urbmaltjima *zerdrücken, zertreten.* ◇ crush. Ⓛ kirbmuntanáni

urbmaltjalama *intr. in Stücke zerbrechen.* ◇ (intransitive) break into pieces. Ⓛ kirbmuntakatiñi

urbmérama *klopfen (an etwas, mit der Hand oder dem Stock).* ◇ knock (on something with hand or stick). Ⓛ purpurpmanáñi

urbmunjurbmákama *das Innere zerbrechen, mit den Zauberhölzern stechen (nach jemanden).* ◇ destroy the inside, stab (somebody) with a magic stick. Ⓛ multuñi

urbula *schwarz, dunkel.* ◇ black, dark. Ⓛ maru Ⓓ maru

urbánkurbmánka *sehr schnell sich bewegend, sehr beweglich.* ◇ move very quickly, very agile. Ⓛ urbmankurbmanki

urbura *kleiner Vogel (schwarzer Kopf und Flügelfeder, braune Kehle, weißen Rücken und Bauch, black-throated Crow-Shirke (Cracticus nigrigularis) (jackeroo).* ◇ small bird, black head and wings, brown throat, white back and belly; shrike species (*Cracticus nigrogularis*, pied butcherbird) (Pizzey and Knight 2007). Ⓛ kurbaru

uratnitoppa intalabama *in einer langen Reihe (nebeneinander fliegen).* ◇ fly in a long line (beside each other). Ⓛ juangaririerenañi

urknatalinja *faul, verdorben (Frucht).* ◇ rotten (fruit).

uragata *feurig.* ◇ fiery.

urapaua *feurig.* ◇ fiery.

urbutjakalaka *nach circa 3 Wochen.* ◇ circa 3 weeks later. Ⓛ mankurukita

ura taraúlaúla *Feuersäule.* ◇ column of fire.

urbutja *einige, (auch drei oder 4).* ◇ several, some, (also three or four). Ⓛ mankurba Ⓓ palpa

urbutjarbuna *einige andern.* ◇ several others. Ⓛ mankurukutuba

urbutjarpa *einige selbst.* ◇ several. Ⓛ mankurukuta

uréljilalama *zerbrechen (z.B. sich [unclear]).* ◇ break. Ⓛ tuintitalkañi

ureralelama *dampfen (Feuer).* ◇ to steam, to fume (fire).

ureljarenama *untergehen (Welt).* ◇ end (world).

uréljurlja *schlaff, kraftlos, eingeschlafen (Arm).* ◇ limp, slack, listless, powerless, gone to sleep (arm). Ⓛ tulatula

urenama *verschwinden, nicht mehr sehen, sich verstecken.* ◇ disappear, not visible, hide. Ⓛ kumbini, ngalpañi

uréta *blau (abart des roten kangaruh).* ◇ blue (flyer). (Expression for female red kangaroo). Ⓛ urútu

urérama *auslaufen (Wasser), verglimmen (Licht), durchfließen (durch ein Gebirge).* ◇ run dry or flow out (water), fade (light), flow (through a mountain range). Ⓛ waintariñi

uréljilama *Leben abbrechen, Genick umdrehen, den Lebensfaden abschneiden, umbringen.* ◇ end life, wring neck, kill. Ⓛ tuintanáni

uréranama *hindurchgehen (durch Gebirgsspalt), verschwinden (durch Erdhöhle, Tunnel, durch Fenster).* ◇ go, disappear through (cave, tunnel, cliffs, windows). Ⓛ mawaintariñi

urerbinama *hindurchgehen.* ◇ go through.

ureriïlama *durchgraben (Erdwall z.B.)* ◇ dig through (e.g. mound of earth). Ⓛ alkielbinani Ⓓ mirpana

urirbuma *hineinkriechen (in eine Hütte), sich verstecken.* ◇ crawl into (a hut), hide. Ⓛ aritarbani

urerenama *entschwinden.* ◇ slip away, disappear. Ⓛ mawaintarini

uriara *Schutzzaun (Wind-brecher), Einfriedigung.* ◇ windbreak, enclosure. Ⓛ unta, (ju) Ⓓ katu

urkabuma *bereiten, arbeiten.* ◇ prepare, work. Ⓛ palani Ⓓ ngankana, ngankingana

urknerama *sehr weich werden (Fleisch, durch kochen), zu Brei verkochen, zerfallen.* ◇ become very soft (meat, when cooked), stew, fall apart. Ⓛ arknuringañi

urkakuninja *Mastdarm.* ◇ large intestine. Ⓛ urkukuninji

urkia *langer Speer (tjata urkia) aus irkapa (desert oak) oder ititja oder agia verfertigt.* ◇ long spear made from desert oak, ititja or agia. Ⓛ winta

urka *langer Stock (zum Schlagen oder Werfen).* ◇ long stick (for hitting or throwing). Ⓛ kunti

urknerama *flüssig werden, schmelzen (Silber, Metalle).* ◇ melt (silver, metal). Ⓛ arknuringañi

urkna *flüßig, Brei (mana urkna), breiig, Milch (der Frauen), dicke Saft (der Bäume).* ◇ liquid, paste, milk (of women), thick sap (of trees). Ⓛ altji, arknu Ⓓ pandra (*Saft*: juice, *Blut*: blood)

urkāla *weich (Sandhügel).* ◇ soft (sandhills). Ⓛ ṙilbati

urkulta *zickzackförmig, Blitz, gestreift.* ◇ zigzag shaped, lightning, striped. Ⓛ wi͡nba

urkultalawomma *blitzen.* ◇ lightning, flash. Ⓛ wintarunkañi

urkultitnama *blitzen (vorm Einschlagen).* ◇ lightning (before it strikes). Ⓛ winbakañi

urkura *sehr Heiß (ein Feuer), Fieber.* ◇ very hot (fire), fever. Ⓛ ungárañi

urkurélama *heiß machen, wärmen (Sonne).* ◇ make hot, warm (sun). Ⓛ kambalbmanañi

urkna urbula *Tinte (n), aus flüßig/Brei und schwarz.* ◇ ink, derived from 'liquid, paste' and 'black'.

urknúljurknúlja *mit Flüssigkeit oder mit Milch gefüllt (Brust).* ◇ filled with liquid or with milk (breast). Ⓛ urknuljurknulju

urkualarkerama *sich röten (Früchte), reifen.* ◇ turn red (fruit), ripen. Ⓛ urkululuriñi [?]

urkurkinja nama *verehren, dienen (Gott), die Tjurunga Lieder einüben.* ◇ worship, serve (God), practise sacred songs. Ⓛ urkurkinjiriñi

urkunauia (von ura) *der heißeste Monat (Januar).* ◇ hottest month (January). Ⓛ malkarkura

urkwarkérama *verzehren, zerstören (durch Feuer).* ◇ consume, destroy (fire). Ⓛ mululukambañi Ⓓ talpana

urubaruba [Northern dialect] *cf.* **rubaruba** *Wirbelwind, whirlwind.* ◇ whirlwind. Ⓛ unbalara

urubarérama *gären (von Brotteig).* ◇ ferment (bread dough). Ⓛ rārārini

úriakaljíaljía, worrakaljialjia *Pflanze mit großen Blütenköpfen, symbol der Männer und Buben, aljia =altja=zugehörig).* ◇ plant with large blossoms. Ⓛ mulati

úrija, úria *männlich.* ◇ masculine, male. Ⓛ manti

úrukanáma *warten.* ◇ wait. Ⓛ wonnuninañi

urumúruma *Dichtung, Märchen, Fabel.* ◇ fiction, fairytale, fable.

utalja [Southern dialect] *cf.* **urkna** *flüßig.* ◇ liquid (adjective). Ⓛ altji

urtnalamburtnala *Kies, Steingeröll.* ◇ gravel, stone rubble. Ⓛ urkataburkata

úruru úrura lama *urr urr schreiend.* ◇ cry urr urr. Ⓛ tumbirtumbir

ururuerinjarungara *fortwährend urr schreiend.* ◇ cry constantly urr. Ⓛ ngalatumbirbmara

urumitja [Southern dialect] *Wüste.* ◇ desert. Ⓛ urumatji

utárama *nach dem Wege aussehen.* ◇ look for the path. Ⓛ mirani

utulbutarama *fortwährend nach dem Wege aussehen.* ◇ constantly look out for the right way. Ⓛ miramirani

utárináma *dem Hunde ein Wild zeigen.* ◇ direct dog's attention to game. Ⓛ wapini

 For the modern spellings of these words, see the dictionaries and sources in reference list.

uruna *Kirchauff-Ranges.* ◇ Kirchauff Ranges. Ⓛ warana

urtalinja *Schlangenfett.* ◇ snake fat. Ⓛ kumbungari

urúnama *cf.* rúnama. ◇ cause someone's death.

ururérama *der Ruf urr urr (oder turr, turr) ausstoßen.* ◇ cry urr, urr or turr, turr. Ⓛ tumbirbmanañi

ururarunga *den Ruf urr urr schreiend.* ◇ cry urr, urr. Ⓛ tumbirkulurara

urta, patta urta *Hügel, Steinhügel.* ◇ hill, stone hill. Ⓛ urta, puli urta Ⓓ wonpa, mardawonpa

urtanka *hohe Ufer.* ◇ high river bank. Ⓛ nganturtji

urtna *lockere Erde, die Erde in hohlen Bäumen.* ◇ loose earth, earth in hollow trees. Ⓛ urtnu

urtnerama *verrotten.* ◇ rot. Ⓛ urtnuringañi

urtnakalama *einfallen (das Haus, das von Ameisen [unclear]).* ◇ collapse (termite infested? house). Ⓛ pelukatiñi

urturta *Nacht Habicht.* ◇ night hawk. Ⓛ turba

utjinja *die abgeschälte Haut (an verbrannten Stellen).* ◇ peeled-off skin (from burned spots). Ⓛ mokarka

utāla *die aus dem Loch gescharrte Erde, Erdhaufen.* ◇ mound of dirt in front or beside hole. Ⓛ toppalba

utátnera *mit der Seite Eindrücke in den Boden machen.* ◇ to make impressions or tracks with the side of body.

utnea *Schlange, gestreift, cr. 4 Fuß lang mit kleinem Kopf, nicht giftig, spec. = ṙenina.* ◇ snake, striped, circa 4 feet long with small head, not poisonous, renina species. Ⓛ kunnea

utnádata *Blütenkätzchen (der ititja und tnima).* ◇ flower catkin (of ititja and tnima). Ⓛ unatjiti

utnanta *Mulga Scrub.* ◇ mulga scrub or thicket. Ⓛ unatjiti

utnuma *beißen, stechen (mit Zauberknochen), bezaubern.* ◇ bite, stab (with magic bone), point bone, to bone, curse. Ⓛ patañi (*beißen*), multuni (*zaubern*) Ⓓ matana

utnátuma *zerbeißen, zermalmen (Maus, tjappa).* ◇ bite to pieces, crunch (mice, grubs). Ⓛ pulpani

utárelarélala rama *einem (davon gehen), fortwährend nachsehen.* ◇ gaze at or watch continously someone leave and/or go away. Ⓛ miramirara nangañi

utítjutítja *Schlamm (am Grunde der Wasserlöcher).* ◇ mud (on bottom of waterhole). Ⓛ utítutíta

utárelarenáma *einem nachsehen.* ◇ watch someone (go away). Ⓛ mirarijenni

utulútulanáma *kollern, (aufstoßen lassen) Emu.* ◇ rumble (belch) emu. Ⓛ tukulbmanañi

utalérama *sausen machen (Schwirrholz), schwirren lassen.* ◇ make whizz. Ⓛ pulunmanañi

utátuma *in den Mund packen.* ◇ cram into mouth. Ⓛ ngapuñi

utna, rutja *eine grosse Mulde aus ininta Holz.* ◇ big bowl made of bean tree wood. Ⓛ tartu

utitja, ututja *sehr niedrig, sehr kurz.* ◇ very low, very short. Ⓛ tarta, murilja

utnutjikerama *anfangen zu beißen, beißen wollen.* ◇ begin to bite, want to bite. Ⓛ patantakuriñi, patantikitaringañi

utnantanantana *selbstsüchtig.* ◇ selfish, egotistic.

utaïïlarenama *aussehen (nach dem Weg) oder nachsehen (einem davongehenden Freund).* ◇ look (for the path) or watch someone going away (friends). Ⓛ mirara wonniñi

W

wa *ja.* ◇ yes. Ⓛ wanku Ⓓ kau

wabala *ja.* ◇ yes. Ⓛ wanti

wabalélama *seine Zustimmung ausdrücken.* ◇ agree, express consent. Ⓛ wanmanañi Ⓓ kaukangana

wak̇ama *verwahren, in Verwahrung nehmen.* ◇ keep, save (for someone something). Ⓛ oakinani

wakuwaka *Regenwasser im Felsen (oder im Tank), angesammeltes Regenwasser.* ◇ rainwater in a rockhole (or tank). Ⓛ pinangu

wailbiata *die von Weißen eingeführten Blechgefäße (Quartpot).* ◇ tin vessels introduced by white people (quart pot). Ⓛ tabula, ultu

waiïtjuwaia, waiutjuwaia *Waise (Vollwaise).* ◇ orphan. Ⓛ tjitula

wakitja *die Ranke der lankua.* ◇ lankua vine. Ⓛ wakitji

wakuia *ja, wahrlich.* ◇ yes, truly. Ⓛ omanti

ireta, r̔ena *taubstumm.* ◇ deaf and dumb. Ⓛ wāla

walaguta *Witwe.* ◇ widow. Ⓛ walugutu Ⓓ mangawaru

wālama *schwimmen auf dem Wasser (Enten).* ◇ swim on water (ducks). Ⓛ turbiñi

wălama *quellen, hervorquellen (Wasser).* ◇ gush, gush out (water). Ⓛ bôlpungañi

walbunta lama *einen verkehrten Weg gehen, einen andern Weg gehen (sodaß man die Person, der man entgegen geht, nicht erblickt).* ◇ go the wrong way, go a different way (miss the person one has set out to meet). Ⓛ walbuntara jennañi

walbawalba *sehr hungrig, fast verschmachtet, verirrt, die Mühe, Qual, Unruhe.* ◇ very hungry, almost languished, lost. Ⓛ tauiila

walbawalbilama *(sich mühen?), Unruhe machen.* ◇ (to strive?), cause unrest. ('?' added by CS)

walka *Porcupinegras, triodia, mit starken Stacheln.* ◇ porcupine grass, triodia. Ⓛ walki

walja *Zweige, Laubbüschel.* ◇ branches, bunch of leaves.

waltjilama *zerrinnen, flüssig machen (z.B. Fett, Eis).* ◇ melt (e.g. fat, ice). Ⓛ kabilariñi

walukuta *Witwe (= Mannes beraubt).* ◇ widow (robbed of husband). Ⓛ walukuta

waluma [Northern dialect] *ja, vielleicht!* ◇ yes, maybe! Ⓛ waputa

wurinja antálelama *Wind stark wehen.* ◇ wind blows strong. Ⓛ wolbaranáñi

wanama *wehen (Wind).* ◇ blow (wind). Ⓛ wonkañi Ⓓ ngakana

wurinja wanama *Wind wehen.* ◇ wind blows. Ⓛ wolba wonkañi

wángerama *murren, unzufrieden sein.* ◇ grumble, sulk, be a sook, be discontent. Ⓛ ngurkuringañi Ⓓ junkarina?

wantama *ja, genug.* ◇ yes, enough. Ⓛ wantinanga

wantai *ja, gewiß!* ◇ yes, sure! Ⓛ watu!

warrinja *augenblicklich.* ◇ instantaneously.

wapantjilama *herausströmen, (z.B. viele Fledermäuse aus hohlen Ast).* ◇ pour out (e.g. many bats out of a hollow branch). Ⓛ wirkawirkarangáriñi

wăra *nur, bloß.* ◇ only. Ⓛ wiakutu Ⓓ windri

warendama *leihen (einem andern).* ◇ lend (to someone, not give). Ⓛ wiakutujungañi

warinkuta *gewunden, krumm (Creek).* ◇ winding (creek). Ⓛ kalikali

waritja *Hütte.* ◇ hut. Ⓛ minta

wapatuna *eine Laubhütte (in der sich Darsteller niederlassen).* ◇ hut. Ⓛ tulula

warka *Brotkrume.* ◇ bread crumb. Ⓛ lungu

wă̍papàpapà *Jagdruf und Kriegsruf.* ◇ hunting and war cry. Ⓛ wápapàpapà, pă̍papàpapà

warkuntama *Beifall ausdrücken (bei dem Cultus der Eingeborenen) und Aufforderung seine Rolle gut zu spielen.* ◇ applaud, express approval and encourage. Ⓛ wailbmanañi

warpa *Werkzeug zum Glätten der Mulden (Meißel).* ◇ chisel. Ⓛ warpi Ⓓ tula

wataka? *gewiß?* ◇ sure? Ⓛ wankujenku?

wilbawilba *Rute (zum Schlagen).* ◇ rod (for beating).

watinja *frisch, grün, beschmiert (mit Fett).* ◇ fresh, green, coated (with fat). Ⓛ bulpungani Ⓓ tjanka

watinjilama *bestrichen (mit Fett), beschmieren.* ◇ coated (with fat), smear. Ⓛ talpini

watinjalelama *bestrichen.* ◇ coated, covered. Ⓛ talpiranáni

wata *postp. gewiß, sehr, wirklich.* ◇ (postposition) certainly, very, truly. Ⓛ mantu

watoa ankama *ja sagen.* ◇ say yes. Ⓛ watu wonkañi

waulja *Feuerflamme.* ◇ fire flame. Ⓛ warilji

wauulákama *bellen (Hunde).* ◇ bark (dogs). Ⓛ wollalbmanañi Ⓓ wauurkarina

waua *Feuer (von Kindern gebraucht).* ◇ fire (word used by children). Ⓛ wauu

wilia *sehr schnell (laufen).* ◇ very fast (run). Ⓛ wolla

wedawedalama *spionieren.* ◇ to spy. Ⓛ wituwitujennañi

wiarumuruma *Dichter, Märchenerzähler.* ◇ poet, storyteller.

wilka *große Moskito.* ◇ large mosquito, march fly. Ⓛ kunma

wilkawilkilama *der Wind hin und her bewegen (Federn und Zweige).* ◇ wind moves (feathers and branches). Ⓛ kakuntjingani

wilkawilka *hin und her bewegt (vom Winde).* ◇ moved, blown around (by wind). Ⓛ kakunkakun

wilka *weich, biegsam (Binsen).* ◇ soft, flexible (rushes). Ⓛ nali

wilkalama *intrs. hin und her bewegt, biegen (z.B. die Biensen im Winde sich selbst hin und her bewegt).* ◇ (intransitive) sway, bend (e.g. rushes sway in the wind). Ⓛ naliringañi

wilkalelama *trs. biegen, hin und her bewegt.* ◇ (transitive) bend, sway. Ⓛ nalini

wintowinta *lange Schnur.* ◇ long string. Ⓛ kunturu

wenjara *eben (Weg).* ◇ level (way). Ⓛ wenjiri

wetjawetja *Waffe zum Werfen (boomerang).* ◇ throwing weapon (boomerang). Ⓛ wipuwipu Ⓓ kirra

witata *eßbare Knolle spec.* ◇ edible bulb species. Ⓛ mantangaljiri

wintinjintinja *dünn, schlank.* ◇ thin, slim. Ⓛ kábakátjinkátjina

katjutara *Regenbogen.* ◇ rainbow. Ⓛ witutara, tutaringi

wintama *alle hineingehen (z.B. in die Kirche, Haus).* ◇ all go into (e.g. the church, house). Ⓛ taualknáriñi

wôbuta *nur einige, nicht viele.* ◇ only few, not many. Ⓛ tatinba Ⓓ ngalje

wirbiara *die zusammengebundenen (Schwanzenden der aroa).* ◇ tied together (tailends of wallabies). Ⓛ karbikarbi

woia = worra *Junge (in Verwandtschaftsbezeichnung gebraucht).* ◇ boy (word used as part of a kin term). Ⓛ wiï

woia ebmanna, woia ebmannatja *conf.* ebmanna. ◇ sister's daughter's son, daughter's son. Ⓛ wii bakali, wii bakalina

woia tjimia *conf.* tjimia. ◇ grandfather. Ⓛ wii kunarbi

woiamba *conf.* amba. ◇ son or daughter on mother's side, sister's son. Ⓛ wiïukari, wiïkata

woia pallatja, woia pallatja *conf. palla.* Ⓛ wiï apili?, wiï apilli, wiï apilina, wiï apillina

woia aranga *conf.* aranga. ◇ father's father. Ⓛ wii tamuna

woialirra *conf.* alirra. ◇ my son, my daughter. Ⓛ wiïkata, wiïukari

woljitunga *lange (Zehe, z.B. Emu).* ◇ long (toe, e.g. emu). Ⓛ walpuru

wólbmara [wulbmura] *weiche Erde.* ◇ soft soil. Ⓛ wolbmara

wolja *grüne Zweige, Spitzen der Bäume oder Sträucher, Halm (juta).* ◇ green branches, tops of trees or bushes, blades (juta); leafy branches. Ⓛ walpuru

wolkna *Grabeshügel.* ◇ burial mound, grave. Ⓛ tulba, warirki Ⓓ nariwonpa

wolkna inkura *Nische (des Grabes).* ◇ niche (of grave). Ⓛ nulu Ⓓ watimokku (*mit Holz oben*)

woiatakerama *Frau mit Frau huren (lesbische Laster).* ◇ lesbian relationship. Ⓛ nambia pungañi

wolla *Haufe, Menge.* ◇ heap, amount. Ⓛ utulu Ⓓ piriri, ngami (*Schaar*)

wollambarinja *Versammlung.* ◇ assembly, meeting, gathering. Ⓛ útulambára Ⓓ wollara (*Schaar*)

wollerama *sich versammeln.* ◇ assemble, meet, gather. Ⓛ ututuriñi

wollilama *sich versammeln.* ◇ (transitive) assemble, gather. Ⓛ utulutunañi Ⓓ kampana, mapana

wollibuma *trs. sammeln, anhäufen.* ◇ (transitive) gather, accumulate, pile up. Ⓛ utuluni

wollanitjalbuma *zur Versammlung zurückkehren.* ◇ return to meeting. Ⓛ utulurinikulbara

wolla nintilama *auf einen Haufen bringen.* ◇ bring together. Ⓛ utulukutuni

wollawollalama *zusammengehen, in Gemeinschaft gehen.* ◇ walk together, walk in company. Ⓛ utulutulujennañi

wollawollerama *zu Hauf kommen, sich versammeln.* ◇ come together, assemble. Ⓛ ululuturingañi, utulutuleriñi

wollurkuna *Bastard.* ◇ bastard.

wollabanba *Schnur, um den Hals getragen.* ◇ string worn around neck. Ⓛ wollubanbu

wolta *Stock zum Schlagen (vom Norden eingehandelt).* ◇ thick hitting stick (traded from the north). Ⓛ wolta

wollakawollerama *erinnern (sich), gedenken.* ◇ remember. Ⓛ kulilkulilariñi

wollara *eine Holzart aus der eine Art Speer (tjatta wollara) gemacht wird (zum Speeren von Menschen).* ◇ wood species used to make spears to kill people. Ⓛ katji wonna

wollatja *Brüste (der Frauen).* ◇ breasts (of women). Ⓛ ibi Ⓓ ngama

wollitjiwolla *Darmfett.* ◇ intestine fat. Ⓛ wóllabírbmara

wollitjikana *Milchkuh, Euter.* ◇ dairy cow, udder. Ⓛ ibitara

wollurbawolla *viele Haufen.* ◇ many piles. Ⓛ útulumúrkamúrka

womma; imperf: wokka (Vergangenheit), worriraka (plural), wommala *reiben (Feuer), spinnen (irkitja), einschlagen (Blitz).* ◇ rub (fire), spin (yarn), strike (lightning). Ⓛ runkañi (miribana) dakana *oder* dijana

wonga *größere Wasseransammlung (in steinernen Gruben), kleine See, Palm Creek.* ◇ water (in stony ditches), small lake, Palm Creek. Ⓛ juru

wonjama *lecken, saugen, aufsaugen.* ◇ lick, suck, suck up. Ⓛ kuntanañi

wonjalama *sich belecken.* ◇ lick. Ⓛ anturanañi

wonjawonja *langes Gras (spec.)* ◇ long grass species. Ⓛ wonjiwonji

wonjilama *beim kommen werfen.* ◇ to throw at approach. Ⓛ ngalarunkañi

wonjinga *Tante (Vaters Schwester).* ◇ aunt (father's sister). Ⓛ kuntili

wonjurkala *gewunden, sich schlängeln (Wasserlauf).* ◇ winding (watercourse). Ⓛ wakuntiwakunti

wonka *Weib, das nicht verheiratet ist, Jungfer.* ◇ woman who is not married, unmarried girl; teenage girl. Ⓛ okara Ⓓ ngameri

wonkama *schwellen.* ◇ to swell. Ⓛ unkani

wonkara *Ente (kleine Art).* ◇ duck (small species). Ⓛ wonkara Ⓓ taralku

wonkinja *entfernt (vom Lagerplatz).* ◇ distant (from camp). Ⓛ iltji

wonna *Tante (Vaters Schwester), Schwiegermutter (F), Mutters Bruders Frau.* ◇ aunt (father's sister), mother-in-law, mother's brother's wife. Ⓛ kuntili Ⓓ kalari

wonnukua *die Schwiegermutter (eines Andern).* ◇ mother-in-law (of someone else). Ⓛ kuntilira

wonna knara *Vaters ältere Schwester.* ◇ father's older sister. Ⓛ kuntili puntu

wonna larra *Vaters jüngere Schwester.* ◇ father's younger sister. Ⓛ kuntili wonan

wonnatja *meine Tante.* ◇ my aunt. Ⓛ kuntilina

 For the modern spellings of these words, see the dictionaries and sources in reference list.

wonnabaltjila *Zauberstäbe des Ulbaritja-Stammes.* ◇ magic sticks of Ulbaritja tribe. Ⓛ wonnabaltjila

wonnawonnilama *erhalten, versorgen.* ◇ support, look after. Ⓛ wontini

wontja, matja wontja *Erde, heiße Erde.* ◇ earth, hot earth. Ⓛ eba, waru eba

wonta *Strauch (spec.)* ◇ shrub (species). Ⓛ aunta

worka *erlahmt (Flügel), sehr müde, kraftlos.* ◇ weary (wings), very tired, weak. Ⓛ pántalpántala

worba *gebratene Blut.* ◇ cooked blood. Ⓛ mitji

wôra *Dampf, Hauch, Dunst.* ◇ steam, breath, waft, vapour. Ⓛ aüru or aiiru Ⓓ wāru

worbiera *aus gemeinsamer Wurzel hervorgegangene Schößlinge.* ◇ saplings from a common root. Ⓛ wõnkuru

worbilinja *verzweigt, von einem Mittelpunkt ausgehend, Komet; z.B. von einem Stern ausgehende Schweif (Komet), die von einem Baumstumpf hervorsproßenden Schößlinge, die von der Hand sich abzweigenden Finger.* ◇ branched, radiating out from a centre, comet; e.g. trail of comet or shooting star, shoots sprouting from a tree trunk, fingers branching off from the hand (see Strehlow 1907: 25). Ⓛ worralinjiri

workalama *kriechen (kleine Kinder).* ◇ crawl (small children). Ⓛ nalilárani

iworka *dichtes Gebüsch, Gestrüpp.* ◇ dense bush. Ⓛ tata

worbmara *Fledermaus (spec.)* ◇ bat (species). Ⓛ iwirbmini

workaworra *schwach (Weiber).* ◇ weak (women). Ⓛ pantalpantala, nalimba

worra *Knabe.* ◇ boy. Ⓛ ula Ⓓ kanku

wŭra (worra); jingawŭra litjina *adv. postp. bestimmt, sicher; z.B. wirklich, ich bestimmt werde gehen.* ◇ (adverb postposition) certainly; e.g. I will certainly go. Ⓛ ka, ngaiulukā jennañi

worrabakana *die lange Schambedeckung der nördlichen Stämme.* ◇ long pubic covering of northern tribes. Ⓛ maüluru Ⓓ munamunari, ngampapuditji

wórrakalalba *Pflanze, rankende, mit sehr kleinen Blättern.* ◇ vine (plant) with very small leaves. Ⓛ omatupitji

kataratja *Reihe, hintereinander.* ◇ row, behind each other. Ⓛ worrata

worrata lama *im Gänsemarsch gehen.* ◇ walk in single file.

worraworra *ein kleiner auf Steinebenen wachsender Busch mit bläulichen Blättern und lila Blütenköpfen, die als die Köpfe der 'Knaben' angesehen werden. Ptilotus helipteroides und andern.* ◇ small bush with bluish leaves and lilac blossoms that grows on stony plains; *Ptilotus obovatus* and possibly other *Ptilotus* species. Ⓛ tjintatjinta

worrinta *gesund (Holz), sehr stark (Mensch).* ◇ healthy (wood), very strong (human being). Ⓛ kulanba

worrinterama *stark werden.* ◇ grow strong. Ⓛ kulanbariñi

worrupara *Knospen (Gummibaum, honeysuckle, erulanga).* ◇ buds (gumtrees, honeysuckle, erulanga). Ⓛ kuljirtji

worritja, urumitja *Einöde, Wüste.* ◇ wasteland, desert. Ⓛ urumatji Ⓓ pitaru, dara

wortja *eßbare Knolle.* ◇ edible bulb. Ⓛ witita

wotjuailbmara *ganz müde, erschöpft.* ◇ exhausted. Ⓛ pitántaláriñi, tantalarini Ⓓ warriwarrina

wortja *Junge, der für die Einweihungsfeier geschmückt wird.* ◇ boy decorated for 'business' (initiation). Ⓛ walluworitji

wotna *feucht, betaut.* ◇ damp. Ⓛ tōpi

wotnupura *in gerader Linie hintereinander gehen, im Gänsemarsch.* ◇ walk in a straight line behind each other, in single file. Ⓛ wipungarañi

wotta *mehr, wieder.* ◇ more, again. Ⓛ peuku, mara Ⓓ morla

wottamawotta *wieder und wieder; composition: wottalkura mehr. genit: wottakalkura.* ◇ again and again. Ⓛ peukukapeuku

wottajaba *Weg.* ◇ path. Ⓛ iwara

wotjawotja [Southern dialect] *boomerang zum Werfen.* ◇ throwing boomerang. Ⓛ wipuwipu

wottapata *weiter.* ◇ further. Ⓛ peukukaru

wottapata ndama *weiter geben.* ◇ to hand on. Ⓛ peukukaru jungañi

worranta *geschlossen (ilba [Ohr, Gebärmutter oder Nachgeburt]).* ◇ closed. Ⓛ purpunba

wottabangalinama *trs. etwas nach sich ziehen, nach sich schleppen.* ◇ (transitive) pull something behind, drag behind.

wottilbélama *sehr große Begierde haben (nach etwas) z.B. reizen (von der Begierde).* ◇ have great desire (for something), get excited (from desire). Ⓛ taúalngulutariñi

wottilbérama *Ohren spitzen (Hunde, Pferde).* ◇ prick up ears, listen (dogs, horses). Ⓛ wiarururingañi

wulakawulerama *gedenken (an einen).* ◇ think (of somebody).

wulbawollama *untertauchen (im Wasser).* ◇ submerge (in water). Ⓛ turbiturbiñi

wulama *empfinden, fühlen (intr.)* ◇ feel (intransitive). Ⓛ urukúlini

wulinja *Gefühl.* ◇ feeling. Ⓛ urukúlinta

wulbmura *weiche Erde.* ◇ soft soil. Ⓛ wolbmara

wulja *die mit Fett bestrichenen (Männer oder Weiber).* ◇ covered with fat (men or women). Ⓛ aulju

wuljankura *mit Fett bestrichen (Männer oder Frauen).* ◇ covered with fat (men or women), name of a public dance. Ⓛ aulju unkuru

wumbaunga *hellrot, rosa (Früchte).* ◇ light red, pink (fruit).

wuma *hören.* ◇ hear. Ⓛ kuliñi Ⓓ ngarana

wunama *hören.* ◇ hear. Ⓛ makuliñi

wunawuna *Hörer.* ◇ listener. Ⓛ kulinmikulinmi

wupawuma *wieder hören.* ◇ hear again. Ⓛ kuliranañi

wulintitnanama *im Liegen hören.* ◇ to hear while lying (down). Ⓛ kulirangariñi

wumbia *heiß, Heißwind, warm.* ◇ hot, hot wind, warm. Ⓛ aranta Ⓓ kalinguru

wumbierama *heiß werden.* ◇ become hot. Ⓛ arantariñi

wumbuma; ura wumbuma *oder* **urambúma** *brennen; das Feuer brennt.* ◇ to burn; the fire is burning. Ⓛ kambañi, warukambañi Ⓓ jerkina

wungaua *halbreif (Früchte), halbgekocht (Fleisch).* ◇ half ripe (fruit), half cooked (meat). Ⓛ pura

wunjilba *eingefallen (Gesicht), zusammen geschrumpft (Körper).* ◇ hollow (face), shrunken or shriveled (body). Ⓛ kebula Ⓓ ngiringiririna (*faltig sein*: be wrinkly)

wura; nga wura erai! *dort, dorthin; du sieh dorthin.* ◇ there, over there; you, look over there. Ⓛ mai!; nuntu mai nauai!

wurba *flach, nicht tief (Wasser).* ◇ flat, shallow (water). Ⓛ julka

wurawurilama *davonziehen (Rauch).* ◇ float away (smoke). Ⓛ tjingañi

wurinja *Wind.* ◇ wind. Ⓛ wolba Ⓓ watara

wúrupungéreláma *schnell weiter laufen (Känguruh).* ◇ move on swiftly (kangaroo). Ⓛ patanpatantalkañi

wurribaunga *blau (Himmel, helle Blüten).* ◇ blue (sky, light-coloured blossoms). Ⓛ okirokiri

wurinjalaruka *im Winde regnend, (während des Windes Regen fallend), im Winde fließend (Blut).* ◇ raining in the wind, rainy and windy. Ⓛ wolbapuru

Korrektur beendet am 15. Dec. 1909.
Corrections completed on 15 December 1909.

 For the modern spellings of these words, see the dictionaries and sources in reference list.

Select index

This index focuses predominantly on the content of the introductory chapters and not Carl Strehlow's dictionary. However, where an entry does refer to the dictionary the page number is in **bold** type. The content of footnotes is also distinguished by using n. after the page number followed by the number of the footnote (e.g. 1n.1). Images are identified by *italicised* numbers. All other entries in roman type refer to material in the body of the text.

www.ingramcontent.com/pod-product-compliance
Lightning Source LLC
Chambersburg PA
CBHW040243240426
43663CB00045B/2947
* 9 7 8 1 7 6 0 4 6 2 0 6 2 *